LAND AND RESOURCE PLANNING IN THE NATIONAL FORESTS

LAND AND RESOURCE PLANNING IN THE NATIONAL FORESTS

Charles F. Wilkinson

H. Michael Anderson

Foreword by Dr. Arnold W. Bolle

ISLAND PRESS
Washington, D.C. □ *Covelo, California*

About Island Press

Island Press, a nonprofit organization, publishes, markets, and distributes the most advanced thinking on the conservation of our natural resources—books about soil, land, water, forests, wildlife, and hazardous and toxic wastes. These books are practical tools used by public officials, business and industry leaders, natural resource managers, and concerned citizens working to solve both local and global resource problems.

Founded in 1978, Island Press reorganized in 1984 to meet the increasing demand for substantive books on all resource-related issues. Island Press publishes and distributes under its own imprint and offers these services to other nonprofit organizations.

Funding to support Island Press is provided by Mary Reynolds Babcock Foundation, The William H. Donner Foundation, Inc., The Ford Foundation, The George Gund Foundation, The William and Flora Hewlett Foundation, The Joyce Foundation, The Andrew W. Mellon Foundation, Northwest Area Foundation, The J. N. Pew, Jr. Charitable Trust, Rockefeller Brothers Fund, and The Tides Foundation.

For additional information about Island Press publishing services and a catalog of current and forthcoming titles, contact Island Press, P.O. Box 7, Covelo, California 95428.

This volume is an expanded edition of Volume 64 of the *Oregon Law Review,* published by the University of Oregon. The Island Press edition is published by arrangement with the authors and the University of Oregon.

Library of Congress Cataloging-in-Publication Data

```
Wilkinson, Charles F., 1941-
    Land and resource planning in the national forests.

    Includes index.
    1. Forest reserves--Law and legislation--United
States.  I. Anderson, H. Michael.  II. Title.
KF5631.W55  1987        346.7304'675        87-17053
ISBN 0-933280-38-6      347.3064675
```

MANUFACTURED IN THE UNITED STATES OF AMERICA

Summary Table of Contents

Table of Contents

Preface

In 1985 we published what is now this book as a lengthy law review article in Volume 64 of the *Oregon Law Review*. The article, which was issued by the *Law Review* as a special double edition, generated the largest sales of any issue in the history of the *Law Review* and is now out of print. Several people in the field of natural resources policy and law—teachers who wish to use the volume in their classes, Forest Service personnel, lawyers, and others who deal with the national forests—have urged us to republish the article as a book so that it will continue to be available. We are grateful for their support, and, with the help of Island Press and the kind permission of the *Oregon Law Review,* we have been able to reprint the article in this format.

The bulk of this volume, therefore, is the original 373-page article, reproduced here with only a few minor corrections. In addition, we have written a short afterword to bring readers current on developments since 1985. We have also added an index to facilitate use of the material for reference purposes. Finally, we are fortunate to include a foreword by Dr. Arnold Bolle, Dean Emeritus of the University of Montana School of Forestry. Dr. Bolle, who was a major figure in the development of the National Forest Management Act of 1976, discusses our book in his foreword, but also offers his valuable perspectives on the long course of national forest policy. We deeply thank him for his contribution.

Our indebtedness to others in the preparation of this work is heavy and far-reaching. Rick Braun, Kathie Rivers, John Phillipson, Brian Stine, and Tom Phelen spent long and valuable hours during their third years of law school to research portions of the work. Their diligence, attention to detail, and substantive proposals were essential to the project. Bud Sloane, Rolf Anderson, Bob Longcore, Kathy Johnson, Jim Mayo, and Ron Friend from the planning staff of the Willamette National Forest helped us to understand and appreciate the challenges of their profession. The many suggestions of Bob Wolf, Larry Hill, Bill Brizee, Hal Salwasser, Dennis Roth, Larry MacDonnell, Peter Kirby, John

Leshy, and Kaid Benfield improved the work significantly. Doug MacCleery, Jim Giltmier, Tom Hamilton, Mark Reimers, and Bill Burbridge gave us their professional and personal insights into the NFMA and the planning process. Rex Hartgraves supplied us with a complete set of minutes of the meetings of the Committee of Scientists. Dennis LeMaster provided us with the manuscript of his study on national forest legislation, as did John Leshy with his manuscript on hardrock mining. Jeff Jones of the Sawtooth National Recreation Area allowed us an extended interview on mining laws. Mary Jo Guy, with the help of Maxine Lee, Marilyn Martin, and others on the law school's secretarial staff, organized the preparation of the manuscript over a period of two and one-half years. Members of the *Oregon Law Review* staff, working under the supervision of Eveleen Henry, were extraordinarily thorough and creative in their editing. Professor Wilkinson conducted a substantial part of his work on this book at the University of Colorado School of Law, and he extends his thanks to Dean Betsy Levin and the Natural Resources Center of the Colorado Law School. As a general matter we, like many writers on the Forest Service before us, have benefited from the agency's willingness to accord us seemingly unlimited staff time, documents, and ideas.

We dedicate this book to John and Virginia Anderson, who have given us advice and inspiration on this and many another project over the course of four decades.

Charles F. Wilkinson
H. Michael Anderson
April, 1987

Foreword

When Congress enacted the National Forest Management Act of 1976 (the NFMA), those of us who had been involved in putting it together had a sense of accomplishment and satisfaction. This, we believed, would bring about the changes needed for the sound management of our national forests. However, as the succeeding decade has shown, change is never achieved simply by enacting new legislation.

Major alterations in the operation of a federal agency are accomplished only by continuing and unrelenting effort, both within the agency and by concerned citizens' groups. The NFMA will not bring about the new program it embraces unless those who believe that change to be necessary keep working on it until the goal is achieved.

Charles Wilkinson and Michael Anderson have done a masterful job of describing the background and distilling the activities that led to the NFMA. Their clear and detailed account provides us with an understanding of where we are and where we have to go to accomplish the innovations that the law requires. *Land and Resource Planning in the National Forests* is a scholarly book that faithfully sets out the law as Congress intended it and as the courts have interpreted it. Wilkinson and Anderson, to a far greater degree than any other source, have documented "The Law of the National Forests"—not just the law relating to timber, but also that relating to grazing, water, mining, wildlife, recreation, and wilderness. As such, the book's greatest contribution—as an objective, thoroughly researched compendium of the legal principles of forest management—will likely be that it articulates the standards that the Forest Service must obey, thus allowing citizens, Congress, and the courts to hold the agency to those standards. Inevitably, that process will generate change.

And, make no mistake about it, change is badly needed in our national forests. The need in the first place for a law such as the NFMA is troubling to many good citizens. After all, wasn't the

1

Forest Service established to safeguard the national forests? But in the last thirty years, concern has grown that things are not as they should be. Timber production has gotten out of hand. Forests are cut too heavily. Roads are built to excess. Soil is eroding; streams are becoming polluted; wildlife habitat is being destroyed. There has been too much concern with commodity production and not enough concern with that element of quality—the quality of life —that affects every one of us. The rising public unhappiness with this situation has brought about a demand for change. How has this come to be?

The first chief of the Forest Service, Gifford Pinchot, declared in 1905 that the agency would strive to achieve the "greatest good for the greatest number in the long run." For the next fifty years the Forest Service was the custodian of the national forests. During that "Stetson hat" period, forest rangers were held in high esteem, and Americans felt confident that their national forests were protected from fire, insects, disease, and rapacious developers. Wild animals sported happily in the virgin forests, and trout abounded in the cold, clear, sparkling streams.

In the early years of this century, the nation's timber needs were met from private lands, both large industrial lands and smaller private holdings. These are generally the more productive timber-producing lands because they were selected from the public domain first. The national forests, on the other hand, are generally less productive and less accessible lands—often more costly to harvest, more difficult to regenerate, and more subject to soil erosion and water pollution. It was not until the post–World War II housing boom that our national forests became important suppliers of timber for the national market. Then, the rising demand and prices for timber, combined with technological advances in road-building and timber-harvesting equipment, made vast areas of the national forests accessible and profitable for lumber companies. For the first time, timber harvesting became a major activity of the Forest Service.

The sudden demand for national forest timber subverted the "greatest good" policy so that the motto quickly became identified with maximum timber production. Congress agreed that the Forest Service could increase its timber harvesting and road building in return for greater federal revenue. The Forest Service grew in size and power to become the largest agency in the Department of Agriculture, and its growth was tied directly to the item in the budget labeled timber. The appropriations committees of the

House and Senate came to consider the Forest Service primarily as a commodity-producing agency, held in high regard as a source of income for the National Treasury.

Both the internal structure of the agency and its reward system became tied to timber. The concept of multiple use was tilted so that timber harvesting was widely pronounced as beneficial to wildlife, water production, and other uses of the forest. But those other uses were neglected, both in the budget and in the field. Only timber meant money, growth, and power for the agency.

The building boom that started in the mid-1950s continued into the 1960s and peaked in the 1970s. While the concern of the Forest Service had remained focused on timber production and on its own growth and welfare, the rest of the world had changed. The environmental movement of the 1960s and 1970s produced a new ethic and a new set of laws: the National Environmental Policy Act (NEPA), the Wilderness Act, air and water pollution control acts, the Endangered Species Act, and others.

The Forest Service found itself out of step with these changes. It was a shock to many people in the Forest Service suddenly to find themselves the "black hats," the enemies of the environment and the people. Forest Service activities became subject to laws that not only threatened to reduce the timber harvests but also imposed serious limitations on decision-making powers.

During its first fifty years, the Forest Service was deeply concerned with the careful management and conservation of resources for the future. During that period, virtually all of the legislation dealing with forestry and the Forest Service was written by the Forest Service itself, up to and including the Multiple-Use, Sustained-Yield Act of 1960. The modern laws, which were written by others and imposed on the Forest Service, put the agency in a new and uncomfortable relationship with the public and with the committees in Congress that were responsible for Forest Service activities. Members of these committees began to hear from a different audience—citizens and environmental groups who testified to the need for change.

The process started slowly. Initially, local people expressed dissatisfaction with Forest Service activities, often over clearcuts. Their protests to Forest Service officials usually had little effect on policy or activities. So they widened their protests to include letters to the local news media and the congressional delegation. The media became interested, and stories appeared in the newspapers and on television. As the protesters gathered momentum, they caught the attention of Congress. Congressional hearings led to expanding interest and finally to laws specific to the Forest Service: the Resources Planning Act of 1974 (RPA) and the NFMA.

The NFMA combines the basic statutory authority of the Forest Service with the environmental laws of the postwar period. It includes specific requirements, and it treats each of the multiple uses separately and collectively. It requires the sustained yield management of all forest uses. It does not include all the specifics of forest management, but it requires the Forest Service to provide and publish detailed regulations that can be reviewed by the public. Congress, in effect, said to the Forest Service: "Give us a different concept of good forestry, one that gives full respect to recreation, wildlife, and watershed values. You decide what good forestry ought to be within that framework, but state it publicly and get public acceptance, and it will then become the yardstick by which you will be measured."

Individual forest plans required by the NFMA appeared and immediately became the focus of public activity. Public protest and official appeal have surfaced with each plan. Plans are under review, and some have been withdrawn. Forest officials are digging their way out of a mass of public response. Forest planning was conceived as a bottom-up process in which the conditions, hazards, and limitations would be clearly identified. Forest uses, including timber harvesting, were to be based on the capabilities of the land. The process became top-down in the 1980s, partly because of the budget emphasis of the Reagan administration. The interests favoring timber maximization prevailed and increased the timber harvest on forest plans in progress. The higher goals imposed from the RPA budgets were unrealistic and out of step with the goals of the NFMA. The treatment of that relationship in this book is an important clarification and should help to overcome one of the serious obstacles encountered in the planning process.

Nevertheless, progress is being made. Public participation and involvement have been achieved as never before. There has been a considerable increase in general knowledge about forest resources and the consequences of activities. The NFMA stipulates the need for forest planning, and the continuing controversies have intensified the need. Not only has the agency increased its knowledge, but so have the citizens' groups involved. These groups have now become information developers and suppliers, working with universities and other professionals to introduce the best available scientific knowledge into the planning process and to make it available to the public and to Congress as an aid in the decision-making process. We all now have a far better and broader understanding of national forest issues.

The NFMA is an extremely complicated law. Wilkinson and Anderson have done a remarkable job in dealing with this diverse and highly charged issue. The facts are here, treated in the perspective of living history. The multiple uses are given separate and thorough treatment in a clearly understandable, yet authoritative, way. The legislative history underlines the spirit and intent of the law.

To me the most interesting parts of the book are those that evaluate the actions of the Forest Service in response to the law and, in particular, those that show how agency regulations and further instructions to the field can dull the effect of the law. Operations are no longer quite "business as usual," but the Forest Service is still a long way from full implementation of the law. Part of the inertia remains rooted in the appropriations committees of Congress, where pressures can still tilt Forest Service budgets toward commodity production. But forces are mounting for these committees to act more in accordance with the resource committees that produced the NFMA.

The democratic process grinds slowly, but in time, as pressures continue, the will of the public does assert itself. Although some impediments remain, there appears to be strong evidence that success is in the offing for the NFMA. This book is an excellent account of the democratic process in action, and it also gives a revealing report of where we are with this good law. The changes needed include many specifics, but most importantly, they require a change in spirit, a new way for the Forest Service to view its responsibilities, as expressed in Section 2(6) of the NFMA:

> The Forest Service, by virtue of its statutory authority for management of the National Forest System, research, and cooperative programs, and its role as an agency in the Department of Agriculture, has both a responsibility and an opportunity to be a leader in assuring that the Nation maintains a natural resource conservation posture that will meet the requirements of our people in perpetuity . . . .

Wilkinson and Anderson express admiration for the Forest Service as an agency and confidence in its ability to change. I share their confidence because I too recognize the quality of many people in the agency who are fully in sympathy with the NFMA. I believe that they and others to come are capable of making the necessary change. I also believe that this book will help show the way to make that change.

Arnold W. Bolle
Dean Emeritus
University of Montana
School of Forestry

Introduction

The National Forest Management Act[1] (NFMA), which became law on October 22, 1976, is the most adventurous congressional incursion into the on-the-ground activities of the United States Forest Service.[2] There has been an inordinate amount of public, scientific, and administrative activity expended in implementing the Act since its passage nine years ago.[3] Yet the courts have been conspicuously silent, rendering only a few opinions construing the NFMA.[4]

The judicial distance from the NFMA is about to come to an end. In effect, the most important provisions in the Act had no immediate bite. Existing land management plans were given congressional sanction and were allowed to continue in effect.[5] Instead, the NFMA mainly looked well into the future: the Act requires the adoption of Forest Service regulations that, together with the terms of the NFMA, control the land management plans mandated for each national forest.[6] These plans, which the Forest

---

[1] Pub. L. No. 94-588, 90 Stat. 2949 (codified at 16 U.S.C. §§ 1600-1614 (1982) and other scattered sections of 16 U.S.C.).

[2] *See generally* CRISIS IN FEDERAL FOREST LAND MANAGEMENT (D. LeMaster & L. Popovich ed. 1977); 8 ENVTL. L. 239 (1978) (symposium issue on the NFMA).

The Forest Service, the largest bureau in the Department of Agriculture, is responsible for administering 191 million acres of land in the National Forest system. The agency has four primary levels of organization: the national office in Washington, D.C.; 9 regional offices; 155 national forests; and approximately 690 ranger districts. The organizational units are headed, respectively, by the Chief of the Forest Service, regional foresters, forest supervisors, and district rangers. *See generally* G. ROBINSON, THE FOREST SERVICE 26-32 (1975).

[3] The NFMA directed the Forest Service to promulgate regulations implementing the Act within two years. 16 U.S.C. § 1604(g) (1982). The regulations were made effective in September 1979. *See* 36 C.F.R. pt. 219 (1980). The Secretary of Agriculture was directed to appoint a Committee of Scientists to provide scientific and technical advice in developing the regulations. 16 U.S.C. § 1604(h)(1) (1982). The Committee of Scientists held extensive hearings over a period of more than two years. *See generally infra* note 211. The preparation of the land management plans for each individual national forest has received widespread public scrutiny. *See, e.g., infra* note 44.

[4] *See, e.g.,* Texas Comm. on Natural Resources v. Bergland, 573 F.2d 201 (5th Cir.), *cert. denied,* 439 U.S. 966 (1978); Kettle Range Conservation Group v. Bergland, 480 F. Supp. 1199 (E.D. Wash. 1979). *See also* Thomas v. Peterson, 753 F.2d 754 (9th Cir. 1985), discussed in regard to its applicability to the NFMA at *infra* note 868.

[5] 16 U.S.C. § 1604(c) (1982).

[6] Land management plans are required for "units of the National Forest System." 16 U.S.C. § 1604(a) (1982). The Forest Service has interpreted this provision to require forest plans for each national forest or for two or more na-

Service must "attempt to complete" by late 1985,[7] will guide all resource activities on individual forests for up to fifteen years and are the focal point of the NFMA. A handful of the plans have been completed, most of the drafts have been released for public comment, and all of the remaining national forests are undergoing this comprehensive planning process.[8] Many, perhaps most, of the land management plans will be challenged in administrative appeals and litigation.

The NFMA plans are of widespread importance to the nation's land, resources, economy, and society. The national forests affect more people in more ways than any other public land management system. National forests receive 200 million recreation visitor-days per year, more than double the total of any other federal land system, including the national parks.[9] Half of the standing softwood timber in the United States is in the national forests.[10] Each year enough wood is sold to build a million homes.[11] One-quarter of our energy reserves, including vast deposits of low-sulfer coal, are found under national forest lands.[12] Thirty percent of the country's ski lifts, and fifty-four percent of the total vertical transport of all ski lifts, are located in national forests.[13] The Forest Service maintains 93,000 miles of trails, far more than any other state or federal agency,[14] and 310,000 miles of roads—more, it is claimed, than any other jurisdiction in the world.[15] More than

tional forests under the jurisdiction of a single forest supervisor. 36 C.F.R. § 219.4(b)(3) (1984).

[7] The Act requires that the Forest Service "shall attempt to complete [the land management plans] by no later than September 30, 1985." 16 U.S.C. § 1604(c) (1982).

[8] *See Update on Forest Planning Schedules*, FOREST PLANNING, Mar. 1985, at 14.

[9] FOREST SERVICE, U.S. DEP'T OF AGRICULTURE, AN ASSESSMENT OF THE FOREST AND RANGE LAND SITUATION IN THE UNITED STATES 76-78 (1981) [hereinafter cited as 1981 ASSESSMENT].

[10] *Dep't of the Interior and Related Agencies Appropriations for 1985: Hearings before Subcomm. of the Dep't of Interior and Related Agencies of the House Comm. on Appropriations*, 98th Cong., 1st Sess., pt. 2, at 1283 (1984) [hereinafter cited as *1985 Forest Service Budget*].

[11] *Id.*

[12] *Id.*

[13] 1981 ASSESSMENT, *supra* note 9, at 90-93. Most of the famous Rocky Mountain ski resorts operate pursuant to special land use permits issued by the Forest Service. *Id.*

[14] *Id.* at 83.

[15] *1985 Forest Service Budget, supra* note 10, at 1285. The Forest Service estimates that it would cost $10 billion to replace its roads. 1981 ASSESSMENT, *supra* note 9, at 83.

half of all water runoff in the eleven western states originates in headwater streams on national forests.[16] In addition, the national forests contain major stores of hardrock minerals,[17] exceptional wildlife and scenic values,[18] and most of the congressionally designated wilderness in the lower forty-eight states.[19]

Conflicts over resource use, of course, vary by region. Therefore, Forest Service planners face different challenges according to location. Most coal leasing in the national forests occurs in Montana, Wyoming, and Utah.[20] The Overthrust Belt, with its rich but deep oil and gas holdings, runs from northwestern Montana to south central Wyoming then southwest through Colorado down to Arizona.[21] A major competing resource in that region is recreation, which is of great economic value in the Rocky Mountains.[22] In the Pacific Northwest, on the other hand, commercial timber production accounts for about fifty percent of all timber harvested from the entire national forest system.[23] Forest Service officials in that region must plan for proper protection of Pacific salmon and steelhead, which are an extraordinarily valuable commercial and sports resource whose habitat can be devastated by poor timber harvesting practices.[24] Some complicated resource issues affect only a few forests. For example, wolves and grizzly bears need large tracts of wild, undisturbed land, thus posing a challenge to Forest Service planners in areas of Minnesota and the Northern Rocky Mountains, respectively.[25]

Only recently has public land policy squarely recognized the importance of reconciling these diverse and often conflicting inter-

---

[16] *1985 Forest Service Budget, supra* note 10, at 1284. *See also* United States v. New Mexico, 438 U.S. 696, 699 n.3 (1978).

[17] *See infra* note 1279.

[18] *See infra* text accompanying notes 1448-52.

[19] FOREST SERVICE, U.S. DEP'T OF AGRICULTURE, REPORT OF THE FOREST SERVICE, FISCAL YEAR 1981, at 21 (1982) [hereinafter cited as 1981 ANNUAL REPORT].

[20] *1985 Forest Service Budget, supra* note 10, at 1283.

[21] *See generally* PETROLEUM INFORMATION CORP., THE OVERTHRUST BELT—1981 (1981).

[22] *See infra* text accompanying notes 1669-71.

[23] FOREST SERVICE, U.S. DEP'T OF AGRICULTURE, IMPORTANT FACTS ABOUT THE PACIFIC NORTHWEST REGION 1 (1982).

[24] *See generally* Wilkinson & Conner, *The Law of the Pacific Salmon Fishery: Conservation and Allocation of a Transboundary Common Property Resource,* 32 KAN. L. REV. 17 (1983).

[25] *See generally* Craighead & Mitchell, *Grizzly Bear,* in WILD MAMMALS OF NORTH AMERICA 527-41 (J. Chapman & G. Feldhamer ed. 1982); L. MECH, THE WOLF: THE ECOLOGY AND BEHAVIOR OF AN ENDANGERED SPECIES (1981).

ests. Until the 1960s public land law primarily involved the allocation of resources to private commercial interests.[26] During that decade a broader public interest and a fuller recognition of noncommodity resources came to the fore and became firmly enshrined in statutes and case law during the 1970s and 1980s.[27] A requirement of comprehensive land planning has become a central element in Congress's determination to accord equal consideration to all resources and to open public land policy to broader public involvement.[28]

Public land and resource planning is basically a three-stage process.[29] First, the foundation is set by gathering data in order to establish an inventory of commodity and noncommodity resources. The second stage is the creation of an integrated plan, which must be developed with the participation of the public and of professionals in the appropriate disciplines. The plan assesses the inventoried resources, reconciles competing demands for resource allocation, and proposes appropriate actions. Land classification, which prohibits or favors specified uses, is a crucial aspect of this stage. The third stage is the implementation of the plan on a site-specific basis, through such agency activities as contracting for development, providing for construction of roads and other facilities, monitoring performance, and enforcing against infractions. The plan must also include procedures for revision if conditions change.

For many reasons, planning on the public lands is inevitably imprecise. The plans must cover large areas of land and there is usually uncertainty over location of some resources, especially minerals and wildlife. Valuation of some resources, such as recreation and preservation, is difficult. Barriers to development, such

---

[26] The point is made implicitly by the passing references to wildlife, recreation, and preservation in the standard history of public land law. *See* P. GATES, THE HISTORY OF PUBLIC LAND LAW DEVELOPMENT (1968 & photo. reprint 1979).

[27] Wilkinson, *The Field of Public Land Law: Some Connecting Threads and Future Directions*, 1 PUB. LAND L. REV. 1, 4-7 (1980).

[28] Land use planning is also a centerpiece of Bureau of Land Management responsibilities under the Federal Land Policy and Management Act of 1976, signed into law by President Ford on the same day as the NFMA. *See* 43 U.S.C. §§ 1701-1782 (1976).

[29] *See, e.g.*, FOREST SERVICE, U.S. DEP'T OF AGRICULTURE, PRINCIPLES OF LAND AND RESOURCE MANAGEMENT PLANNING 5-6 (1982) [hereinafter cited as PRINCIPLES OF PLANNING], which contains a detailed description of the Forest Service planning process. *See also* Cortner & Schweitzer, *Institutional Limits and Legal Implications of Quantitative Models in Forest Planning*, 13 ENVTL. L. 493 (1983). *See generally* K. DAVIS, LAND USE (1976).

as fragile soil conditions, may not be apparent until the implementation stage of the plan. Changing demands for various resources and the occurrence of natural phenomena such as insect infestation, droughts, and forest fires, add to the difficulty. For these and other reasons, planning on the federal lands has properly been called "an inexact art."[30]

All of the major public land agencies now engage in land and resource planning. The National Park Service and the United States Fish and Wildlife Service face somewhat less difficult questions because their dominant-use statutes do not require them to consider the full range of commercial development.[31] The two multiple-use agencies, the Forest Service and the Bureau of Land Management, both have explicit congressional guidelines governing land and resource planning.[32]

The Forest Service planning statutes are the most extensive of any federal land agency. The statutes require planning on several tiers, although the national forests are the basic functional unit at which plans are made and carried out. The Forest and Rangeland Renewable Resources Planning Act of 1974[33] (RPA) requires several procedures at the national level: an Assessment, which includes an inventory of all resources, every ten years; a Program, proposing resource goals, every five years; and a Statement of Policy, to be used in framing budget requests, also every five years.[34] Long-range plans, called Regional Guides, are also made by each of nine Forest Service regions for activities within each region.[35]

---

[30] Coggins & Evans, *Multiple Use, Sustained Yield Planning on the Public Lands*, 53 U. Colo. L. Rev. 411, 413 (1982).

[31] *See* 16 U.S.C. § 1 (1982) (National Parks) and 16 U.S.C. § 668(dd) (1982) (National Wildlife Refuges). Planning in the national parks is quite elaborate, and a Service Center has been established in Denver to support planning activities in the park system. *See* Nat'l Park Service, U.S. Dep't of the Interior, Denver Service Center Operations Manual (July 1984); Nat'l Park Service, U.S. Dep't of the Interior, Planning Process Guidelines (Sept. 1982). On planning in the National Parks and National Wildlife Refuges, see generally Coggins & Evans, *supra* note 30, at 415-16.

[32] Planning in the Bureau of Land Management is analyzed in Coggins, *The Law of Public Rangeland Management IV: FLPMA, PRIA, and the Multiple Use Mandate*, 14 Envtl. L. 1, 78-109 (1983).

[33] Forest and Rangeland Renewable Resources Planning Act of 1974, 16 U.S.C. §§ 1600-1610 (1976), *as amended by* the National Forest Management Act of 1976, Pub. L. No. 94-588, 90 Stat. 2949.

[34] The RPA process is described in more detail *infra* in text accompanying notes 185-89.

[35] 36 C.F.R. § 219.4(b)(2) (1984).

At the national forest level, land management plans (alluded to in the RPA[36] but elaborated upon in the NFMA[37]) guide activities for ten to fifteen years and make projections for up to fifty years.[38] These individual forest plans are the engines that drive the management process. Finally, the forest plans are implemented, usually at the ranger district or national forest level, by permits, contracts, and other instruments; examples are timber contracts, camping permits, grazing leases, rights-of-way, and special land use permits. Mineral leases for national forest lands are issued by the Department of the Interior, but the Forest Service is heavily involved in the planning process and the Department of the Interior usually follows its recommendations.[39] Similarly, under the General Mining Law of 1872, the Department of the Interior adjudicates issues relating to mining claims and patents, but the Forest Service has independent regulatory authority over hardrock mining; even on issues solely within the jurisdiction of the Department of the Interior, the views of the Forest Service are given great weight.[40]

While the NFMA is the principal statute guiding Forest Service planning, the scope of this Article is much broader. The law governing land and resource planning on the national forests derives from many sources and has evolved over several decades. Accordingly, the first section traces the history of planning in the Forest Service and sets the premises for the adoption of the NFMA.

The second section analyzes three legal issues that permeate planning for each of the resources: the nature of Forest Service management authority, the scope of judicial review, and the relationship between the national and local levels of forest planning. The last is crucial to the mechanics of the planning process: does the national office of the Forest Service set goals for the national forests or does the Forest Service's tradition of decentralization control, with planning being done mainly on-the-ground and with

---

[36] 16 U.S.C. § 1604(a) (1982).

[37] The NFMA's planning provisions are mainly found in 16 U.S.C. § 1604(g) (1982).

[38] The forest plans typically cover a fifty year period. The effective life of the plans, however, cannot be longer than fifteen years, the time period in which they must be revised. *Id.* § 1604(f)(5). The fifty year projections are made to provide additional information to the public and to mesh with the RPA planning "horizon" of fifty years. *Id.* § 1602.

[39] *See infra* text accompanying notes 1384-96.

[40] *See infra* text accompanying notes 1367-83.

national goals reflecting decisions made at the national forest level?

The remaining seven sections analyze the law of planning as it affects each resource that the Forest Service manages. Two opposing thrusts are reflected in the legislative history of the NFMA. First, many provisions in the NFMA are rigorously drafted. The statute, due to the tumultuous times in which it was passed, breaks from the historical pattern of delegating near-unfettered authority to the Forest Service. Thus the NFMA channels agency action on a number of fronts, especially in the area of timber harvesting, by setting judicially enforceable standards.[41] Second, and very much to the contrary, an array of issues is not addressed explicitly by Congress in the NFMA but is within the agency's traditional, broad grant of authority to "regulate . . . occupancy and use"[42] within the national forests on a multiple-use, sustained-yield basis.[43] As a result, on many issues the Forest Service retains its ability to create new concepts and strategies to meet changing demands.

Sections III and IV treat grazing and timber, the two earliest areas of Forest Service planning. Forest Service management of grazing is of special importance because aggressive administrative regulation of grazing during the early twentieth century established broad Forest Service authority to protect national forest land and resources. The timber section is the longest section in the article because timber received the most extensive treatment by Congress in the NFMA.

Section V analyzes water resource planning. Conservation and enhancement of timber and water resources were the primary purposes for creating the national forests. Although Congress has lodged primary authority over water quality in other federal agencies and has deferred to state law in regard to the acquisition of water rights, we conclude that the Forest Service possesses delegated authority to manage the water resource on national forests in several respects, including the power to set minimum stream flows administratively.

Section VI examines Forest Service planning as it relates to mineral production, a major commercial use of national forests.

---

[41] *See infra* section II(B).

[42] 16 U.S.C. § 551 (1982), discussed *infra* in section II (A)(1).

[43] *See* Multiple-Use Sustained-Yield Act of 1960, 16 U.S.C. §§ 528-531 (1982), discussed *infra* in section II (A)(3).

Congress has given the Department of the Interior significant authority over mineral development on the national forests, but several statutory and regulatory provisions grant extensive authority to the Forest Service. Perhaps surprisingly, the Forest Service may make more decisions regarding mining in the national forests than does the Department of the Interior.

The final three sections analyze the law as it relates to wildlife, recreation, and wilderness planning in the national forests. Each of these resources is perceived as being "new" to national forest policy. In a general sense the perception is accurate—historically the primary focus has been on timber, water, and grazing, as opposed to these "non-economic" resources. However, the Forest Service has a long and considerably proud record of managing these nonconsumptive resources. That record provides a fitting backdrop for modern statutes that require equal consideration for wildlife, recreation, and preservation during the planning process.

Modern Forest Service planning has been controversial. Some of our colleagues have argued that the process is too technical and expensive and that planning drains human resources away from actual on-the-ground management.[44] We respect those concerns and it may be that, as a policy matter, the next generation of forest plans should be somewhat simplified. Nevertheless, during our years of work on this project, we have come to appreciate the essential wisdom of the NFMA planning process. It creates valuable inventories, offers the potential of engaging the public and diverse disciplines, and holds out the promise of creating ordered and principled decisionmaking. Granted, these benefits will accrue over time, not instantly, and they will come at some cost, but we believe that the basic goals and process of the NFMA will prove out. Ultimately, we expect that some of the methodology and other particulars of national forest planning will likely be altered in upcoming years but that the essence of current law is likely to survive for the foreseeable future. It is to that body of law—not truly new but rather an extension of historic Forest Service practices—to which we will now turn.

---

[44] *See, e.g.*, Fairfax, *RPA and the Forest Service*, in A CITIZEN'S GUIDE TO THE RESOURCES PLANNING ACT AND FOREST SERVICE PLANNING 210 (1980); Behan, *RPA/NFMA - Time to Punt*, 79 J. FORESTRY 806 (1981).

I

THE HISTORY OF LAND AND RESOURCE PLANNING IN THE NATIONAL FORESTS

The Forest Service has always considered planning to be necessary for good management. For seventy-five years the agency developed and implemented plans with virtually no congressional direction other than the broad mandate of its legislative charter, directing the Secretary of Agriculture to "regulate [the] occupancy and use" of the national forests to "preserve [them] from destruction."[45] This section provides an overview of the evolution of Forest Service planning, extending from the ideas of Gifford Pinchot, the first Chief of the Forest Service, to the current National Forest Management Act (NFMA) planning regulations. The section begins with information on the origins of the national forests and the Forest Service. Next it examines the development of timber and range planning during the Pinchot era, followed by recreation and wilderness planning during the 1920s and 1930s. Then it discusses land use planning in the 1960s and 1970s, when Congress began to assert its constitutional prerogatives. The section concludes with a summary of the Forest and Rangeland Renewable Resources Planning Act of 1974 (Resources Planning Act or RPA) and a preliminary look at the NFMA and NFMA planning regulations.

A. *Origins of the National Forests (1876-1907)*

The origins of the national forests and the Forest Service trace back to 1876, exactly one century before passage of the NFMA. At that time, Congress took two modest steps toward eventual protection and administration of the public forest lands. First, Representative Greenbury L. Fort of Illinois introduced a bill "for the preservation of the forests of the national domain adjacent to the sources of navigable rivers and other streams of the United States."[46] Although the Fort bill did not receive serious attention, it marked the first time that Congress considered legislation to establish national forest reserves. Second, Congress appropriated two thousand dollars for the Commissioner of Agriculture to employ "some man of approved attainments" to prepare a wide-

---

[45] 16 U.S.C. § 551 (1982), discussed *infra* in section II(A)(1).
[46] H.R. 2075, 44th Cong., 1st Sess., 4 CONG. REC. 1070 (1876).

ranging report on forestry matters.[47] The four forestry reports that followed helped to shape federal forest policy, including the central concept that public timber could be sold to private parties while land title remained in the United States.[48] Furthermore, a Division of Forestry, later to become the Forest Service, grew out of the reports.[49] In 1886 the Division of Forestry was confirmed by an act of Congress[50] and came under the direction of Bernhard Fernow, the first professional forester in the federal government.[51]

---

[47] Act of Aug. 15, 1876, ch. 287, 19 Stat. 143, 167. The appropriation was inspired by the American Association for the Advancement of Science's (AAAS) recommendation to President Grant to create a forestry commission. The recommendation originated from an AAAS committee appointed to direct legislative attention to "the importance of promoting the cultivation of timber and the preservation of forests." S. DANA, FOREST AND RANGE POLICY 80-81 (1956). One member of the AAAS committee was Dr. Franklin B. Hough, who was later appointed to prepare the report commissioned by Congress. *Id.* at 81.

[48] Hough's first report in 1877 included a favorable analysis of the Canadian government's system of selling trees while retaining title to the land. J. ISE, THE UNITED STATES FOREST POLICY 110 (1920). A year later the Commissioner of the General Land Office, James A. Williamson, recommended to Secretary of the Interior Carl Schurz that "[t]he soil should not be sold with the timber where the land is not fit for cultivation." *Id.* Secretary Schurz, in turn, proposed legislation to withdraw all public timber lands from sale. S. 609, 45th Cong., 2nd Sess., 7 CONG. REC. 605 (1878). President Rutherford B. Hayes endorsed Schurz's bill in his annual message to Congress in 1879. The bill, Hayes stated, would enable

> the Government to sell timber from the public lands without conveying the fee, where such lands are principally valuable for the timber thereon, such sales to be regulated as to conform to domestic wants and business requirements, while at the same time guarding against a sweeping destruction of the forests.

President's Third Annual Message (Dec. 1, 1879), *reprinted in* VII J. RICHARDSON, A COMPILATION OF THE MESSAGES AND PAPERS OF THE PRESIDENTS, 1789-1897, at 578 (1898).

[49] The Commissioner of Agriculture administratively established the Division of Forestry in 1881 and appointed Hough as Chief of the Division. H. STEEN, THE U.S. FOREST SERVICE 17 (1976).

[50] Act of Jan. 30, 1886, ch. 575, 24 Stat. 103.

[51] Prior to Fernow's appointment in 1886, the Division of Forestry was headed by Dr. Nathaniel H. Egleston, who replaced Hough as Chief in 1883. Although Gifford Pinchot described Egleston's tenure as "three years of innocuous desuetude," G. PINCHOT, BREAKING NEW GROUND 135 (1947), Egleston strongly advocated protection of public timber lands. In 1883 Egleston reported to the Commissioner of Agriculture:

> [N]othing seems clearer than that the Government should take care of its own property and use it for the general welfare. And to day [sic] it has no property so valuable as its forests. Its mines, its forts, its ships, the coined money in its vaults, taken together, are hardly comparable to them. These might all be lost without essential or permanent injury to the nation, while

Fernow spearheaded efforts by the administration to convince Congress to set aside forest reserves.[52]

The forest reserve proposals were prompted by fears that excessive logging was damaging watersheds and depleting future timber supplies. In 1877, for instance, Secretary of the Interior Carl Schurz warned of timber shortages and various impacts on lowland watercourses if Congress did not protect forest land adequately:

> The rapidity with which this country is being stripped of its forests must alarm every thinking man. It has been estimated by good authority that, if we go on at the present rate, the supply of timber in the United States will, in less than twenty years, fall considerably short of our home necessities. How disastrously the destruction of the forests of a country affects the regularity of the water supply in its rivers necessary for navigation, increases the frequency of freshets and inundations, dries up springs, and transforms fertile agricultural districts into barren wastes, is a matter of universal experience the world over. It is the highest time that we should turn our earnest attention to this subject, which so seriously concerns our national prosperity.[53]

At the urging of Fernow and others,[54] Congress provided for withdrawal of forest lands from the public domain in the Creative

---

the loss of the forests would threaten desolation and national decay and destruction. [1883 ANNUAL] REPORT OF THE CHIEF OF THE DIVISION OF FORESTRY, H.R. EXEC. DOC. NO. 109, 47th Cong., 2d Sess. 455 (1883).

[52] Fernow became particularly alarmed at the condition of the public forest lands during a trip to the Rocky Mountains in 1887. In the same year Fernow drafted a forest reserve bill that would have withdrawn public timber lands from entry and required classification of the withdrawn lands for agricultural, forest, and preservation uses. S. DANA, *supra* note 47, at 99. Fernow collaborated on the bill—which was introduced by Senator Hale of Maine—with Edward A. Bowers, a lawyer in the General Land Office. *Id.* at 98-99. Bowers had written the first detailed plan for management of the proposed forest reserves. Bowers's plan called for the reserves to be administered by a Forestry Bureau with authority to issue timber cutting licenses. S. DANA & S. FAIRFAX, FOREST AND RANGE POLICY 55 (2d ed. 1980).

[53] ANNUAL REPORT OF THE SECRETARY OF THE INTERIOR, H.R. EXEC. DOC. NO. 1, 45th Cong., 2d Sess., pt. 5, at XVI (1877).

[54] Congressional approval to create the reserves followed memorials from the American Forestry Association and the American Association for the Advancement of Science. S. DANA, *supra* note 47, at 100. The AAAS's action came after a speech by Fernow in 1889. *Id.* Representing the American Forestry Association's law committee, Fernow, Egleston, and Bowers met with President Benjamin Harrison and Secretary of the Interior John Noble in 1889 to urge protection of public forest lands. H. STEEN, *supra* note 49, at 26.

Act of 1891.[55] Section 24 of the Act[56] gave the President authority to "set apart and reserve . . . public lands wholly or in part covered with timber or undergrowth . . . as public reservations."[57] The 1891 Act simply allowed forest land to be set aside; it failed to call for any affirmative regulatory program. In order to provide protective management authority and direction for the forest reserves, Congress passed the Organic Administration Act of 1897.[58] The Act stated that forest reserves were to be established only to secure favorable water flow conditions and to furnish a continuous timber supply.[59]

The forest reserves were first administered by the General Land Office in the Department of the Interior. In 1905 Congress transferred virtually all administrative responsibilities over the reserves to the Department of Agriculture,[60] where Gifford Pinchot was in charge of the Division of Forestry. The Division was renamed the Forest Service shortly after the passage of the Transfer Act,[61] and in 1907 the forest reserves were designated national forests.[62]

---

[55] Act of Mar. 3, 1891, ch. 561, 26 Stat. 1095, 1103, *repealed by* 90 Stat. 2792 (1976).

[56] Section 24 was added in the conference committee, probably at the insistence of Secretary of the Interior Noble. *See* H. STEEN, *supra* note 49, at 26-27. Since neither the House bill nor the Senate bill made any reference to the forest reserves, legislative history of section 24 is almost nonexistent.

[57] Section 24 of the Creative Act provides:

> That the President of the United States may, from time to time, set apart and reserve, in any State or Territory having public land bearing forests, in any part of the public lands wholly or in part covered with timber or undergrowth, whether of commercial value or not, as public reservations, and the President shall, by public proclamation, declare the establishment of such reservations and the limits thereof.

Act of Mar. 3, 1891, ch. 561, § 24, 26 Stat. 1103, *repealed by* 90 Stat. 2792 (1976). President Harrison quickly exercised his new authority; on March 30, 1891, he established the Yellowstone Park Forest Reserve. During the next two years Harrison set aside 14 additional reserves in the West with a total area of 13 million acres. *See* S. DANA, *supra* note 47, at 102.

[58] Act of June 4, 1897, ch. 2, 30 Stat. 34, (codified as amended at 16 U.S.C. §§ 473-482, 551 (1982)). The passage of the 1897 Act, still a primary source of Forest Service authority, is discussed *infra* in text accompanying notes 235-59.

[59] 16 U.S.C. § 475 (1982).

[60] Transfer Act of Feb. 1, 1905, ch. 288, § 1, 33 Stat. 628 (codified at 16 U.S.C. § 472 (1982)).

[61] Act of Mar. 3, 1905, ch. 1405, 33 Stat. 872.

[62] Act of Mar. 4, 1907, ch. 2907, 34 Stat. 1256, 1269.

B. The Origins of Planning (1897-1910)

Within four months of becoming Chief of the Division of Forestry in 1898,[63] Pinchot committed the agency to an ambitious planning effort. Although he would have no federal lands under his jurisdiction for another seven years, Pinchot offered to prepare "working plans," virtually free of charge, for owners of private timber lands.[64] These early timber management plans were based on Pinchot's experience in previous work managing the Biltmore Forest on the Vanderbilt estate in North Carolina.[65] To meet the steady flow of requests,[66] the Division added a Section of Working Plans in 1899.[67]

Later that year Secretary of the Interior Ethan Hitchcock requested "a suggested working plan for the harvesting of timber in each of the existing [forest] reserves."[68] Pinchot began this massive project with a study of the Black Hills Forest Reserve in

---

[63] Pinchot took office on July 1, 1898. H. STEEN, *supra* note 49, at 53.

[64] [The purpose of the offer] was to provide a series of practical examples of improved treatment of private timber forest lands. . . . The harvest of the timber crop on these private timber lands is commonly accompanied, under the usual methods of lumbering, by the destruction of the forest . . . . It is to prevent these public and private losses that the Division offers its assistance.

DIVISION OF FORESTRY, U.S. DEP'T OF AGRICULTURE, PRACTICAL ASSISTANCE TO FARMERS, LUMBERMEN, AND OTHERS IN HANDLING FOREST LANDS 1-4 (Circular No. 21) (1898).

[65] Pinchot recalled:

I agreed to make working plans for the management of Biltmore Forest
. . . .

Here was my chance. Biltmore could be made to prove . . . that trees could be cut and the forest preserved at one and the same time. . . .

Biltmore Forest became the beginning of practical Forestry in America. It was the first piece of woodland in the United States to be put under a regular system of forest management whose object was to pay the owner while improving the forest.

G. PINCHOT, *supra* note 51 at 49-50.

[66] In the first year, the division received 123 applications for working plans to cover over 1.5 million acres of private land. S. DANA, *supra* note 47, at 120.

[67] Pinchot appointed Henry Graves as superintendent of the section. [1899 ANNUAL] REPORT OF THE CHIEF OF THE DIVISION OF FORESTRY, H.R. DOC. NO. 6, 56th Cong., 1st Sess. 110 (1899). Graves succeeded Pinchot as Chief in 1910 and served until 1920. H. STEEN, *supra* note 49, at 104, 143.

[68] S. DANA, *supra* note 47, at 122. Pinchot arranged the request through an associate in the General Land Office. *Id.* Pinchot viewed the request for working plans as a means to gain control over the reserves. "If we could not get the whole loaf of forest administration, we were anxious to take half a loaf. . . . It was all water on the wheel of the transfer." G. PINCHOT, *supra* note 51, at 173.

South Dakota.[69] The Black Hills working plan "included a thorough study of . . . local questions of lumbering, grazing, and fire, and of those conditions generally which must determine the best management of the reserve."[70] By 1903 the agency had begun field examinations on twenty million acres of the forest reserves.[71]

After passage of the Transfer Act of 1905,[72] Pinchot required working plans for all timber sales.[73] As sales increased rapidly,[74]

---

[69] Pinchot selected the Black Hills Reserve because its timber "was more in demand than that of all the others put together." G. PINCHOT, *supra* note 51, at 173. The first timber sale on any forest reserve occurred on the Black Hills Reserve soon after passage of the 1897 Act. The federal government subsequently sued the purchaser, Homestead Mining Company, for stealing timber. *Id.* at 174-75.

[70] REPORT OF THE CHIEF OF THE DIVISION OF FORESTRY, H.R. DOC. NO. 6, 57th Cong., 1st Sess. 329 (1901) [hereinafter cited as 1901 ANNUAL REPORT OF THE CHIEF]. Pinchot hailed the Black Hills working plan as the "first step toward conservative lumbering on the national forest reserves." [1900 ANNUAL] REPORT OF THE CHIEF OF THE DIVISION OF FORESTRY, H.R. DOC. NO. 6, 56th Cong., 1st Sess. 104 (1900). Following is Pinchot's description of the preparation of a typical working plan:

A thorough examination of the tract is made both from the forester's and from the lumberman's points of view. Sample acres are selected through the forest, generally in successive strips, and the stand of merchantable and immature trees upon them is counted and measured. From these measurements is calculated the stand on the whole tract. The rate of growth is determined from the stem analysis of sample trees. Studies are made of reproduction, of the danger from fire, from grazing, and from insect attack, and of the best means of preventing such injuries. Market and transportation facilities are carefully investigated, and a map showing the character and distribution of the forest and the stand of timbers is prepared.

When the needed data have been collected they are worked up into the plan, which takes into account the special needs or purpose of the owner, as, for instance, to secure permanent supplies of mining timbers, to maintain a game preserve, or to protect a watershed. The recommendations embraced in the plan enable him to derive from the forest the fullest and most permanent revenue which is consistent with his special requirements.

FOREST SERVICE, U.S. DEP'T OF AGRICULTURE, THE FOREST SERVICE: WHAT IT IS AND HOW IT DEALS WITH FOREST PROBLEMS 9 (Circular No. 36) (1905). *See also* FOREST SERVICE, U.S. DEP'T OF AGRICULTURE, A WORKING PLAN FOR FOREST LANDS IN CENTRAL ALABAMA (Bulletin No. 68) (1905).

[71] [1903 ANNUAL] REPORT OF THE FORESTER, BUREAU OF FORESTRY, U.S. DEP'T OF AGRICULTURE, H.R. DOC. NO. 6, 58th Cong., 2d Sess. 531 (1903).

[72] *See supra* note 60.

[73] "To permit the use of the standing timber and at the same time to maintain the full productive power of the forest for the future, working plans were needed wherever cutting was to take place . . . . The practice of forestry . . . has now definitely begun on the National reserves." FOREST SERVICE, U.S. DEP'T OF AGRICULTURE, [1905 ANNUAL] REPORT OF THE FORESTER, H.R. DOC. NO. 6, 59th Cong., 1st Sess. 209 (1905).

[74] *See supra* text accompanying note 270.

the plans ensured that no part of the reserves would be overcut.[75] Although the agency discontinued work plans for private landowners when Pinchot left in 1909,[76] planning had become firmly installed in the Forest Service's management of the national forests.

Range management required a system different from the working plans for timber management. The timber of most forest reserves was not programmed for harvest because demand could be met by private forests and because access to remote federal timberlands was so difficult. In contrast, the rangelands were already overcrowded with sheep and cattle by the turn of the century. Overgrazing during this period was causing unacceptable damage to watersheds and forest cover.[77]

Forest Service range planning began in 1900, when Pinchot took part in a three-week inspection of sheep grazing in the Southwest.[78] The next year Pinchot directed his Section on Special Investigations to study the effects of grazing on twelve forest reserves, at the request of Secretary of the Interior Ethan Hitchcock.[79] Hitchcock adopted Pinchot's recommendation to restrict sheep grazing to areas where it would not damage water-

---

[75] Pinchot reported in 1908: "To avoid overcutting, the approximate annual yield of each forest has been computed. Sales are regulated in the light of this yearly increment and prospective local needs." FOREST SERVICE, U.S. DEP'T OF AGRICULTURE, 1908 ANNUAL REPORT OF THE FORESTER 423 (1909) [hereinafter cited as 1908 ANNUAL REPORT OF THE CHIEF]. President Theodore Roosevelt was imbued with Pinchot's concern over potential timber shortages caused by overcutting. In 1903 Roosevelt stated, "The United States is exhausting its forest supplies far more rapidly than they are being produced. The situation is grave . . . ." Roosevelt, *Forestry and Foresters*, in BUREAU OF FORESTRY, U.S. DEP'T OF AGRICULTURE, FORESTRY AND THE LUMBER SUPPLY 6 (Circular No. 25) (1903).

[76] H. STEEN, *supra* note 49, at 55.

[77] *See infra* text accompanying notes 495-97.

[78] *See* G. PINCHOT, *supra* note 51, at 177-81. Pinchot found that "overgrazing by sheep does destroy the forest" because the sheep eat and trample seedlings. *Id.* at 179. He also found that "[o]vergrazing loosens the soil so that heavy rains sweep it from the hillsides where it belongs into the streams where it does not belong . . . ." *Id.* He concluded, "John Muir called them hoofed locusts, and he was right." *Id. See also infra* note 497 and accompanying text. Early grazing policy is discussed in more detail *infra* in section III(A).

[79] Pinchot reported that the studies would develop "a workable system of proposed regulations, whose enforcement would sustain equally the welfare of the forest, of the uses of water, and of the grazing interests." 1901 ANNUAL REPORT OF THE CHIEF, *supra* note 70, at 332.

sheds.[80] Hitchcock also decided to limit the amount of all livestock grazing on the forest reserves by establishing a permit system.[81]

After the transfer of the forest reserves to the Department of Agriculture in 1905, Pinchot continued Hitchcock's grazing policies and divided the national forests into grazing districts.[82] He instructed that "[w]hen required for the protection of camping places, lakes and streams, roads and trails, etc., or of areas which are to be reforested, stock will be excluded from specified areas for such period of time as is necessary."[83] Forest supervisors were responsible for protecting their forests from overgrazing:

> At the end of each season the supervisors will go over the grazing grounds without delay and examine the effect of grazing on the reserve. He will make a full report to the Forester, with recommendations as to the number of stock to be allowed the following year, the division of the range into districts, and the areas to be opened or closed to grazing.[84]

Thus, planning for timber and range began for different reasons and reflected different priorities. Timber planning sought, first, to facilitate use (i.e., cutting) of the trees and, second, to ensure reforestation after cutting. Range planning sought, first, to protect the range resource from overuse and, second, to facilitate use (i.e., grazing) of the forage. Then, as now, emphasis was placed on the water resource; a paramount objective of both timber and grazing planning was to protect watersheds by preserving the forest cover and preventing soil erosion and compaction.

Two traditions of planning—utilitarian and protective—developed from the early timber and range plans. Both traditions evolved naturally from Pinchot's belief that wise use and preservation of all the forest resources were compatible.[85] He relied on careful planning to implement his conservationist philosophy.

---

[80] Hitchcock reported, "I have adopted the policy of permitting sheep to graze in that portion of certain reserves where it is shown, after careful examination, that such grazing is in no way injurious to or preventive of the conservation of the water supply." ANNUAL REPORT OF THE SECRETARY OF THE INTERIOR, H.R. DOC. NO. 5, 57th Cong., 1st Sess., at LXXI (1901).

[81] S. DANA, *supra* note 47, at 115-16.

[82] FOREST SERVICE, U.S. DEP'T OF AGRICULTURE, THE USE BOOK 80 (1906 ed.) [hereinafter cited as 1906 USE BOOK].

[83] *Id.* By 1929, over four million acres had been closed to grazing "in the interest of game, timber, watershed, and recreational protection." FOREST SERVICE, U.S. DEP'T OF AGRICULTURE, [1930 ANNUAL] REPORT OF THE CHIEF 37 (1930).

[84] 1906 USE BOOK, *supra* note 82, at 80.

[85] *See infra* note 269.

Pinchot required planners to prepare detailed inventories,[86] monitor the condition of the reserves,[87] determine sustainable use levels,[88] and exclude use from specific areas where necessary to protect the watershed and other resources.[89] These four features were the hallmarks of Pinchot's conservation planning. They became a fundamental part of Forest Service policy and in the 1970s received Congress's imprimatur in the NFMA.

C. Conservation Planning (1910-1960)

The Forest Service continued to emphasize planning after Pinchot left the agency. Resource planning became a regular activity of local Forest Service officials.[90] In addition to timber and range resource planning, district rangers and forest supervisors developed work plans to guide daily activities[91] and financial plans to

---

[86] *See supra* note 70.

[87] *See supra* text accompanying note 84.

[88] *See supra* text accompanying note 75.

[89] *See supra* note 83.

[90] The key local officials in the Forest Service are the district ranger and the forest supervisor. The ranger is primarily responsible for administering the routine work of forest management assigned to his district. The supervisor is responsible for most planning functions of his national forest and oversees the work of the ranger districts. Rangers generally reside in small communities near their districts, while the supervisors live typically in the principal city close to their national forests. *See* G. Robinson, *supra* note 2, at 31. *See generally* H. Kaufman, The Forest Ranger (1960).

[91] Planning became a means for district rangers to budget their work efficiently and ensure consistency with agency policy:

Day by day the ranger must decide which of the numerous things clamoring for his time shall be done next . . . .

The main priorities and objectives, necessarily broad and simple as they are set up by the [Chief] forester, become more detailed down the line of organization which spreads out to 817 ranger districts. The translation of priorities and objectives into work on the ground is done through plans. . . .

Work plans lay out, in the form of job lists, the specific things to be done by a forest officer . . . . [This system] requires only the most brief and simple records and is flexible enough to be readily modified as new demands are created by forest fires, unexpected sales of timber, or other unforeseeable calls on time.

Forest Service, U.S. Dep't of Agriculture, Report of the Chief 15 (1925) [hereinafter cited as 1925 Annual Report of the Chief].

request annual funding.[92] Fire control plans were also prepared as needed.[93]

Resource planning emphasized traditional range and timber management[94] because range and timber were the focus of activity in virtually all national forests. Timber sale receipts and grazing fees constituted the great majority of the agency's revenue,[95] and congressional appropriations for timber and grazing generally exceeded funding for other resources.[96]

By the 1920s the Forest Service had begun to prepare detailed timber management plans for timber-producing national forests.[97]

---

[92] Financial planning required the district ranger to estimate personnel, equipment, and other needs for the coming year. The forest supervisor then submitted the estimates to the regional forester as budget requests. The regional forester revised the requests and forwarded them to the Chief's office. After receiving "allotments" from the Chief, the regional forester revised the requests again, and returned them to the forest supervisor. "These [became] the financial working plan which the forest supervisor [was] authorized and required to carry out during the year." *Id.* at 15. *See generally* G. ROBINSON, *supra* note 2, at 43-44. The Forest Service's current budget planning system is similar to the described system.

[93] 1925 ANNUAL REPORT OF THE CHIEF, *supra* note 91, at 15-16.

[94] "Resource plans outline the methods to be followed in managing timber, range, recreational opportunities, etc., by suitable area units." *Id.* at 15.

[95] Timber and grazing receipts usually accounted for more than 90% of annual revenue during this era. In 1925, for instance, timber sale receipts were $2.9 million, grazing fees were $1.7 million, and all other receipts were $0.3 million. *Id.* at 12. In 1930 timber and grazing receipts were $6.3 million, compared to $0.4 million for all other receipts. 1930 ANNUAL REPORT OF THE CHIEF, *supra* note 83, at ·79. Receipts for these two major resources remained relatively high even during the depths of the Depression; in 1936, for example, timber and grazing brought in $3.6 million. FOREST SERVICE, U.S. DEP'T OF AGRICULTURE, REPORT OF THE CHIEF 60 (1936) [hereinafter cited as 1936 ANNUAL REPORT OF THE CHIEF]. By 1955 timber receipts had risen to $73.2 million, grazing receipts were $3 million, and other receipts were $1.5 million. FOREST SERVICE, U.S. DEP'T OF AGRICULTURE, [1955 ANNUAL] REPORT OF THE CHIEF 14 (1955).

[96] During the 1920s expenditures for administration of grazing and timber were generally eight times the amount expended for recreation and wildlife. In 1925, for instance, timber and grazing administration received $1.43 million while recreation and wildlife expenditures were only $0.16 million. 1925 ANNUAL REPORT OF THE CHIEF, *supra* note 91, at 11. During the 1930s, however, funding for the noncommodity resources increased. In 1936, for example, timber and grazing received $1.9 million, while recreation and wildlife received $1.3 million. 1936 ANNUAL REPORT OF THE CHIEF, *supra* note 95, at 57. By 1955 timber and range resource management received $12.3 million, while recreation and wildlife habitat received $2.7 million. FOREST SERVICE, U.S. DEP'T OF AGRICULTURE, FOREST SERVICE BUDGET ESTIMATES, 1955-59, *reprinted in* 106 CONG. REC. 12,081 (1960).

[97] The timber management plans examined prospective sale areas in considerable detail:

The plans determined the amount of timber that could be harvested from "working circles," areas large enough to support local forest-based industries.[98] Most of the forage-producing forests were divided into individual grazing allotments, and range management plans were written in cooperation with allottees.[99] These

They give definite answers to such questions as what shall be the area unit from which a "continuous supply of timber" is to be obtained; how much timber can be cut from that area annually or by decades and still have the growth on the whole unit replace the amount cut; what conditions must govern the cutting in order to obtain the best crops of timber for future cutting; what bodies of overripe or deteriorating timber need cutting promptly; how the greatest aid can be given to local industrial and community stability through the provision of employment in woods work and of raw material for the manufacture of forest products; and, finally, what definite areas of timber are to be offered for sale during the next 10 or 20 years.

FOREST SERVICE, U.S. DEP'T OF AGRICULTURE, 1928 ANNUAL REPORT OF THE CHIEF 29 (1928) [hereinafter cited as 1928 ANNUAL REPORT OF THE CHIEF]. Due to the low demand for timber prior to World War II, the Forest Service was able to plan timber sales conservatively. *See infra* text accompanying notes 690-705. In addition to the detailed timber management plans, the agency also developed "statements of policy which define the markets to be served, the policy for the sale of the timber, and the general silvicultural methods to be followed in its cutting." FOREST SERVICE, U.S. DEP'T OF AGRICULTURE, A NATIONAL PLAN FOR AMERICAN FORESTRY, S. DOC. NO. 12, 73rd Cong., 1st Sess. 580 (1933 & photo. reprint 1979). By 1932, 21% of the national forest timber was covered by timber management plans and another 61% by statements of policy. *Id.* at 581.

[98] By 1961 timber management plans directed activity in 380 working circles. FOREST SERVICE, U.S. DEP'T OF AGRICULTURE, REPORT OF THE CHIEF 12 (1961) [hereinafter cited as 1961 ANNUAL REPORT OF THE CHIEF].

[99] 1928 ANNUAL REPORT OF THE CHIEF, *supra* note 97, at 35. The plans consisted of maps with detailed instructions:

They analyze the grazing and related problems of each range unit, set up the management objectives, and specify the manner of use called for to attain the desired objective. They determine the class and numbers of stock that the range can carry, the grazing season, and the distribution necessary to utilize the forage evenly. . . . They incorporate the knowledge obtained by research regarding the stage of development at which the plants on each range may be safely grazed, the measures necessary to allow depleted ranges to recuperate, the best methods of developing water, the best salting practices, successful means of eradicating poisonous plants, the control of livestock diseases and of range-destroying rodents, and like matters.

FOREST SERVICE, U.S. DEP'T OF AGRICULTURE, [1929 ANNUAL] REPORT OF THE CHIEF 37 (1929) [hereinafter cited as 1929 ANNUAL REPORT OF THE CHIEF]. By 1929, 70% of approximately 7,000 total allotments were covered by range management plans. *Id.* Grazing allotments numbered 11,300 by 1961. 1961 ANNUAL REPORT OF THE CHIEF, *supra* note 98, at 17.

two systems of resource planning, working circles and grazing allotments, continued basically unchanged into the 1960s.[100]

Watershed protection also received major emphasis in resource planning. The Weeks Act of 1911,[101] which provided for land acquisition for eastern national forests, evidenced Congress's concern for watersheds. Pinchot's successor, Henry Graves, recognized watershed protection as the greatest value of the western national forests. Plans for road construction, logging, and grazing were subordinated to the overriding concern for protecting municipal water supplies.[102]

Following World War I, the Forest Service began to plan for recreational resources.[103] In 1921 the Forest Service Manual stated, "No plan of national forest administration would be complete which did not conserve and make [recreation resources] fully available for public use."[104] That year Aldo Leopold, an assistant forester in the southwest region, boldly proposed setting aside a vast area of wilderness in the Gila National Forest in New Mexico.[105] Although planning that excluded any economic use was antithetical to Pinchot's policies, Leopold's innovative proposal for administrative wilderness was adopted in 1924 and followed in other parts of the country.[106]

During the 1930s recreation and wilderness planning expanded, largely through the efforts of Robert Marshall. While Marshall was chief of the Division of Recreation, the Forest Service enlarged the wilderness system to fourteen million acres by 1939.[107] Marshall's U-Regulations, which established guidelines for wilderness management planning, later became the model for the Wilderness Act of 1964.[108] The Forest Service also directed plan-

---

[100] In 1972 the Forest Service abandoned working circle planning and began to write timber management plans for each national forest. G. ROBINSON, *supra* note 2, at 62.

[101] 16 U.S.C. §§ 480, 500, 515-519, 521-522, 563 (1982), discussed *infra* in text accompanying notes 1050-51.

[102] *See infra* text accompanying notes 1055-66.

[103] *See infra* text accompanying notes 1680-1714.

[104] Kneipp, *Recreational Use of the National Forests*, 28 J. FORESTRY 618, 620 (1930).

[105] *See infra* text accompanying notes 1811-15.

[106] *See infra* text accompanying notes 1816-17.

[107] *See infra* text accompanying note 1831.

[108] *See infra* text accompanying notes 1832-34.

ners to preserve land for scientific, archaeological, and other noncommodity resources.[109]

While Forest Service planning largely occurred at the local forest and district levels, this era also saw early efforts toward comprehensive national planning. In 1920 Senator Arthur Capper of Kansas sponsored a resolution directing the Forest Service to study "the alleged depletion of the forest resources of the United States."[110] Eight years later, Congress required the Secretary of Agriculture to maintain "a comprehensive survey of the present and prospective requirements for timber and other forest products in the United States."[111] In 1933, in response to a resolution introduced by Senator Royal S. Copeland of New York,[112] the Forest Service prepared a 1650-page National Plan for American Forestry.[113] The report recommended extensive public regulation and acquisition of private forest land.[114] Congress, however, did

---

[109] *See infra* note 1702.

[110] S. Res. 311, 66th Cong., 2d Sess. (1920). The Forest Service instigated the Capper Report in part to prompt Congress to appropriate more funds for the agency. *See* H. STEEN, *supra* note 49, at 182.

[111] McSweeney-McNary Forest Research Act of 1928, ch. 678, 45 Stat. 699, *repealed by* Forest and Rangeland Renewable Resources Research Act of 1978, 16 U.S.C. § 1647(a) (1982).

[112] The resolution requested the Secretary of Agriculture "to advise the Senate as soon as practicable whether, in his opinion, the Government should undertake to aid the States in the utilization for forestation purposes of those areas of land in the United States suitable for forestation only." S. Res. 175, 72nd Cong., 1st Sess. (1932), *reprinted in* FOREST SERVICE, U.S. DEP'T OF AGRICULTURE, A NATIONAL PLAN FOR AMERICAN FORESTRY, S. DOC. NO. 12, 73rd Cong., 1st Sess. 81 (1933 & photo. reprint 1979) [hereinafter cited as COPELAND REPORT]. The Forest Service initiated the resolution. *See* Wolf, *Past Planning Experience in the United States*, in FORESTS IN DEMAND 64 (C. Hewett & T. Hamilton ed. 1982) [hereinafter cited as FORESTS IN DEMAND].

[113] *See* COPELAND REPORT, *supra* note 112.

[114] In the letter of transmittal accompanying the Copeland Report, Secretary of Agriculture Henry Wallace stated that "practically all of the major problems of American forestry center in, or have grown out of, private ownership." *Id.* at v. The report recommended federal or state purchase of 244 million acres of private forest land, including 134 million acres to be added to the national forest system. *Id.* at ix. Ferdinand A. Silcox, Chief of the Forest Service from 1933 to 1939, actively supported the Copeland Report's recommendations through a "Three-Point Program." The program called for (1) increased public ownership of forests, (2) cooperation with private owners, and (3) public regulation to protect against "ruthless exploitation" by private owners. FOREST SERVICE, U.S. DEP'T OF AGRICULTURE, REPORT OF THE CHIEF 2 (1937) [hereinafter cited as 1937 ANNUAL REPORT OF THE CHIEF].

not provide funds to implement fully the recommendations,[115] and the Forest Service abandoned the plan after World War II.[116]

Prior to the 1950s, the Forest Service planner's job was relatively uncomplicated because management of range, timber, and noncommodity resources did not often interfere with each other. Even where grazing and timber uses occurred in the same area, they rarely conflicted.[117] Thus, local range and timber planners did not have to accommodate each others' needs. Further, setting aside lands for wilderness or other recreational purposes was relatively uncontroversial because the pressure for reconciling other national forest uses was not yet acute.

During the 1950s this harmonious planning framework began to break down because of the increased demand for timber and all other resources. Between 1950 and 1959, the annual timber harvest on national forest lands increased from 3.5 billion board feet[118] to 8.3 billion board feet.[119] During the same period, annual

---

[115] *See* P. GATES, *supra* note 26, at 600.

[116] The Forest Service continued to follow the multiple use concepts contained in the Copeland Report. The report states, for instance, that "timber, . . . watershed protection control, recreation, wild-life production, and forage [are] treated as multiple uses, several or all of which usually apply in varying degree to the same tract." COPELAND REPORT, *supra* note 112, at 83. In 1936 Forest Service Chief Silcox elaborated on the multiple use concept in the context of land use planning:

[T]he national forests are put, and must be put, to a multiplicity of uses. Often these uses conflict. Sometimes the conflict can be harmonized, sometimes one use must give way. Making the forests of greatest possible public service would be wholly impossible without careful planning to govern land use. Economic as well as physical factors are of primary importance. Uncorrelated growth of the local and commercial structure supported by forest use has set up many conflicts of interest in the resources, and many attendant strains, demanding equitable adjustment. Yet that eleventh part of the United States which comprises the national forests now presents an advanced example of systematically planned and balanced use, worked out on the basis of promoting the permanent public welfare.

1936 ANNUAL REPORT OF THE CHIEF, *supra* note 95, at 2.

[117] In the Umpqua National Forest in western Oregon, for example, agency planners have found that "[d]omestic livestock grazing is quite compatible with the primary timber use. Forage is made available by timber harvest opening up areas. Grazing can be used as a tool. For example, sheep are sometimes used to reduce brush competition in regeneration plantation areas." FOREST SERVICE, U.S. DEP'T OF AGRICULTURE, PACIFIC NORTHWEST REGION, FINAL ENVIRONMENTAL STATEMENT, UMPQUA NATIONAL FOREST LAND MANAGEMENT PLAN 36 (1978) [hereinafter cited as UMPQUA NAT'L FOREST LMP].

[118] FOREST SERVICE, U.S. DEP'T OF AGRICULTURE, REPORT OF THE CHIEF 38 (1950) [hereinafter cited as 1950 ANNUAL REPORT OF THE CHIEF].

[119] FOREST SERVICE, U.S. DEP'T OF AGRICULTURE, REPORT OF THE CHIEF 14 (1959) [hereinafter cited as 1959 ANNUAL REPORT OF THE CHIEF].

recreational visits to the national forests increased from 26 million[120] to 81.5 million.[121]

Forest Service planners responded to the increasing demands by attempting to coordinate resource planning. After preparing an inventory of resources, local managers developed composite plans that identified recreation and special management areas, watercourses, transportation routes, and other characteristics.[122] The content of these early land use plans varied from forest to forest, since the agency did not attempt to apply uniform standards.[123] Planning decisions during this transition period were based on the intuitive judgments of forest supervisors and district rangers concerning the best use for each part of the forest.[124]

D. *Environmental and Multiple-Use Planning (1960-1974)*

Passage of the Multiple-Use Sustained-Yield [MUSY] Act of 1960[125] marked the beginning of a new and unsettled era of Forest Service planning. During the late 1950s, the agency was under increasing pressure to change its management policies. Lumber interests sought further increases in the allowable rate of timber cutting[126] while preservation interests urged legislation to prohibit the agency from harvesting or developing the remaining wilderness in the national forests.[127] The agency responded to these pressures for "overuse" and "single use" by proposing legislation mandating multiple-use.[128] The MUSY Act placed outdoor

---

[120] 1950 ANNUAL REPORT OF THE CHIEF, *supra* note 118, at 43.

[121] 1959 ANNUAL REPORT OF THE CHIEF, *supra* note 119, at 9.

[122] *See* 44 Fed. Reg. 53,935 (1979).

[123] *See* Wilson, *Land Management Planning Processes of the Forest Service,* 8 ENVTL. L. 461, 467 (1978).

[124] *Id.*

[125] 16 U.S.C. §§ 528-531 (1982).

[126] McArdle, *Why We Needed the Multiple Use Bill,* 76 AM. FORESTS 10, 59 (1970).

[127] *See infra* text accompanying notes 1839-52.

[128] Chief Richard McArdle reported in 1960:
With the ever-growing value of National Forest resources and their increased use and accessibility, the pressures for single use of large areas are increasing tremendously. This statutory recognition of multiple use and sustained yield management will help materially to prevent possible future overuse of one resource or impairment of land productivity resulting from economic pressure or pressures of single-interest groups.
FOREST SERVICE, U.S. DEP'T OF AGRICULTURE, REPORT OF THE CHIEF 19 (1960) [hereinafter cited as 1960 ANNUAL REPORT OF THE CHIEF]. *See also* H.R. REP. NO. 1551, 86th Cong., 2d Sess. 7, *reprinted in* 1960 U.S. CODE CONG.

recreation, range, wildlife, and fish on equal statutory footing with timber and watershed uses.[129] However, the Act only required the agency to give equal "consideration" to all resources,[130] not to administer them equally.[131] Accordingly, the Forest Service chose, in effect, to implement the Act by increasing its consideration of recreation, wildlife, and watershed through planning.[132]

& AD. NEWS (USCCAN) 2377, 2380 (executive communication on the MUSY bill from the Department of Agriculture).

[129] 16 U.S.C. § 528 (1982) states: "It is the policy of Congress that the national forests are established and shall be administered for outdoor recreation, range, timber, watershed, and wildlife and fish purposes." A House Committee Report introducing the Act stated, "It is also clear that the Secretary of Agriculture shall administer the national forests for all of their renewable natural resources, and none of these resources is given a statutory priority over the others." H.R. REP. NO. 1551, 86th Cong., 2d Sess. 4, *reprinted in* 1960 USCCAN at 2380. On the politics of listing the multiple uses in alphabetical order, *see* Crafts, *Saga of a Law, Part I*, 76 AM. FORESTS 13, 18-19, 52 (1970).

[130] 16 U.S.C. § 531(a)(1982). The House Committee Report stated that "all of these resources in general are entitled to equal consideration, but in particular or localized areas relative values of the various resources will be recognized." H.R. REP. NO. 1551, 86th Cong., 2d Sess. 3, *reprinted in* 1960 USCCAN at 2379. The committee report simply reiterated the Department of Agriculture's executive communication on the bill. *Id.* at 7, *reprinted in* 1960 USCCAN at 2382. In Sierra Club v. Hardin, 325 F. Supp. 99 (D. Alaska 1971), *vacated and remanded sub nom.* Sierra Club v. Butz, 3 ENVTL. L. REP. (ENVTL. L. INST.) 20,292 (9th Cir. 1973), the court concluded that evidence of "some" consideration would satisfy the MUSY Act's requirements. *Id.* at 123 n.48. The Court of Appeals for the Ninth Circuit vacated the lower court decision, stating that " 'due consideration' to us requires that the values in question be informedly and rationally taken into balance. The requirement can hardly be satisfied by a showing of knowledge of the consequences and a decision to ignore them." Sierra Club v. Butz, 3 ENVTL. L. REP. at 20,293. *See also* National Wildlife Federation v. Forest Service, 592 F. Supp. 931, 938 (D. Or. 1984), *appeal docketed*, No. 84-4274 (9th Cir., Oct. 29, 1984).

[131] *See, e.g.*, Perkins v. Bergland, 608 F.2d 803 (9th Cir. 1979), where the court stated that the MUSY Act "can hardly be considered concrete limits upon agency discretion." *Id.* at 806.

[132] Professor Coggins has argued that the "due consideration" section of the MUSY Act:

> [R]equires the manager to go through a certain rough thought process, with at least two major steps, before any "on-the-ground" decisions are possible. The usual label for such thinking is "planning." To consider relative values, one must know what values or resources are available for allocation or protection on the area in question. In science, this "fact-finding" function is known as the inventory phase. Following this semi-objective exercise . . . the manager must consider overall mixes of production. This is the essence of management planning, and planning is the essence of effective management.

Coggins, *Of Succotash Syndromes and Vacuous Platitudes: The Meaning of "Multiple Use, Sustained Yield" For Public Land Management*, 53 U. COLO. L.

The expansion of planning after passage of the MUSY Act took two forms. First, the agency began to write separate functional resource plans for wildlife, recreation, and other resources.[133] Second, the Forest Service began to experiment with zoning of land uses.[134] The two types of planning are the parents of the integrated land and resource planning required by the NFMA.

In 1961 the Forest Service initiated a two-stage planning process to divide the national forests into management zones.[135] In the first stage each of the nine regions wrote a Multiple-Use Planning Guide. The regional guides provided designations,[136] general definitions,[137] and broad management guidelines[138] for several land zones. The second stage required each district ranger to prepare a District Multiple-Use Management Plan. The district

---

REV. 229, 259 (1981). *See also* National Wildlife Federation v. Forest Service, 592 F. Supp. at 938-39.

[133] *See infra* text accompanying notes 1531-44 and 1731-34.

[134] The agency had begun zoning areas of the national forest for preservation in the 1920s. *See infra* text accompanying notes 1811-27.

[135] The procedure was developed at a Multiple-Use Work Conference in April, 1961. The Forest Service issued Multiple-Use planning handbooks and manuals that summer. 1961 ANNUAL REPORT OF THE CHIEF, *supra* note 98, at 11.

[136] Every regional guide included a Water Influence Zone, a Travel Influence Zone, and a Special Zone for formally designated wilderness, scenic, and geologic areas. Other zones varied from region to region. Wilson, *supra* note 123, at 468.

[137] For example, the Pacific Northwest Region defined one high-elevation zone as follows:

The Alpine Resource Association extends from near timberline to the crest of the mountains. Much of this area is above 5,000 feet. It contains high-elevation lakes, open alpine meadows, glaciers, and outstanding scenery. Soils are fragile and precipitation, mostly snow, is heavy. Access generally is by trail and public use is correspondingly light. Most of the existing and potential winter sports recreational areas and classified wilderness areas are located in this Association.

FOREST SERVICE, U.S. DEP'T OF AGRICULTURE, MANAGEMENT OBJECTIVES AND POLICIES FOR THE HIGH MOUNTAIN AREAS OF NATIONAL FORESTS OF THE PACIFIC NORTHWEST REGION 5 (1962).

[138] Management objectives [for the Alpine Resource Association] emphasize retention of natural conditions, particularly in classified Wilderness Areas, but recognize the need to provide for other types of recreational experience which can best be met in this resource Association. Management to produce optimum yields of water, fish, wildlife, and forage for domestic livestick including saddle and pack stock are concurrent objectives.

Id.

plan classified all land in the district into zones,[139] and suggested how to coordinate various resource uses in each zone.

These plans were the Forest Service's first systematic attempt to resolve problems of conflicting use. The district plans helped local land managers decide where logging and other activities could take place. However, the plans suffered from chronically poor inventory data concerning soil stability, wildlife habitats, and other site-specific conditions.[140] Consequently, district rangers were reluctant to establish management guidelines that were any more concrete than those stated in regional guides.[141]

The Wilderness Act of 1964[142] prompted an increase in wilderness planning. In addition to the newly mandated protection of areas designated by Congress in the 1964 Act, the Forest Service

---

[139] Some district plans further classified the land into subzones, or "management units," to show grazing allotments, unstable soils, and other areas of special significance. Heyman & Twiss, *Environmental Management of the Public Lands*, 58 Cal. L. Rev. 1364, 1383 (1970).

[140] A Forest Service study commissioned by Chief John McGuire suggested greater integration of multiple use and timber management planning.

> The principal factor undermining timber inventory data has been the incompleteness of past multiple use plans. The areas to receive special management that would reduce or eliminate timber yield possibilities have not all been identified and mapped. . . . Only after really meaningful multiple use plans are prepared will it be possible to accurately classify land for timber management planning.

Forest Service, U.S. Dep't of Agriculture, Stratification of Forest Land for Timber Management Planning on the Western National Forests 8 (1971).

[141] Carl Wilson, former planning director for the Pacific Northwest Region, identified two weaknesses with the multiple-use plans. First, they did not attempt to identify the optimum combination of uses for each district. Second, they implied that every acre of the forest was suitable for many, if not all, uses. Wilson, *supra* note 123, at 469.

District rangers sometimes were able to consider specific areas in detail. For instance, one district plan identified a potential landslide area located within a zone that allowed timber harvesting. The plan stated these management guidelines for the landslide area:

> (1) The preservation of soil and water values will be emphasized on this management unit.
> (2) Road construction will not be permitted on or immediately adjacent to the slide areas.
> (3) Neither timber harvest nor other intensive use will be permitted in the management unit until a detailed study, conducted by soils specialists, provides the administration with an evaluation of proposed management practices.

Heyman & Twiss, *supra* note 139, at 1391 (quoting Forest Service, U.S. Dep't of Agriculture, Forest Service Handbook, Multiple Use Management Guide, Pacific Northwest Region).

[142] 16 U.S.C. §§ 1131-1136 (1982).

voluntarily initiated an inventory of its remaining roadless areas. During the early 1970s the agency conducted a Roadless Area Review and Evaluation (RARE) to identify areas suitable for wilderness designation. Roadless area planning came under intense public and judicial scrutiny during the 1970s.[143]

In response to litigation over RARE and criticism of multiple-use planning, the Forest Service launched a new round of land use planning in 1973. By then Congress had enacted several environmental laws pertaining to the national forests.[144] The most important of these for planning was the National Environmental Policy Act of 1969 (NEPA).[145]

NEPA had several important effects on Forest Service planning. First, participation by other government agencies and the public increased substantially. Second, roadless area planning assumed greater significance because an environmental impact statement (EIS) was required before any roadless area could be developed.[146] Third, NEPA's mandate to protect the environment encouraged the Forest Service to apply environmental planning requirements to regulate mining.[147] Fourth, and perhaps most important, NEPA's requirements spurred the Forest Service to develop vastly more complete resource inventories. The agency assigned soil scientists, wildlife biologists, hydrologists, and other specialists to assemble and analyze basic information.[148]

In 1973, local land use or "unit" plans replaced the multiple-use plans and became the Forest Service's principal means of complying with NEPA's EIS requirements.[149] A major objective

---

[143] *See infra* text accompanying notes 1863-93.

[144] *See infra* text accompanying notes 322-28.

[145] Pub. L. No. 91-190, 83 Stat. 852 (1970) (codified as amended at 42 U.S.C. §§ 4321-4370 (1982).

[146] *See infra* text accompanying notes 1867-68.

[147] *See infra* text accompanying notes 1353-55.

[148] For example, the Umpqua National Forest prepared a detailed Soil Resource Inventory in conjunction with the Land Management Plan. The inventory identified approximately 250 soil types on detailed maps of the entire national forest. The planning team grouped the soil types into Resource Analysis Units, estimating site productivity, erosion potential, and reforestation capacity. Umpqua Nat'l Forest LMP, *supra* note 117, at 175-98 (1978).

[149] In 1972 the Forest Service agreed to prepare an EIS for each roadless area in the national forests. *See infra* text accompanying note 1869. The agency began to undertake this task through the Unit Plans. Dissatisfaction with this procedure led the Department of Agriculture to initiate a nationwide Roadless Area Review and Evaluation (RARE II) in 1977. Some Unit Plans, nevertheless, included roadless area analyses and allocations. *See* California v. Bergland, 483

of unit planning was to ensure greater consistency between national and local land use priorities.[150] To accomplish this objective, the Forest Service established a hierarchy of planning. Based on broad policy direction from the Chief, each regional forester prepared Planning Area Guides for geographical subdivisions of the region.[151] Area Guides, in turn, provided the general direction for Forest Land Use Plans for each national forest.[152] The Area Guides advised forest planners of the area's relative ability to achieve national objectives for various resources.[153] Finally, the Forest Plans guided the preparation of local Unit Plans within each national forest.[154] The Unit Plans, which did not follow ranger district lines, usually encompassed a large drainage or several small watersheds. Their size ranged from fifty thousand acres to several hundred thousand acres.[155]

Notwithstanding the changes caused by NEPA, the basic purpose of the Unit Plans was still to classify the national forests into land use zones. The Unit Plans generally contained a wider variety of zones and more detailed management guidelines than the previous multiple use plans. Some plans, for instance, precisely defined streamside buffer zones, where timber management was prohibited or modified. Soil characteristics and wildlife habitats became increasingly important criteria for establishing zones and guidelines.[156]

F. Supp. 465 (E.D. Cal. 1980), *aff'd sub nom.* California v. Block, 690 F.2d 753 (9th Cir. 1982).

[150] FOREST SERVICE, U.S. DEP'T OF AGRICULTURE, FOREST SERVICE MANUAL § 8213 (1973).

[151] *Id.* § 8220.

[152] *Id.*

[153] *Id.* § 8222.2.

[154] *Id.* § 8220.

[155] Wilson, *supra* note 123, at 471.

[156] The Unit Plan for the Umpqua National Forest is an illustrative case. The plan contained over 20 separate zones, or "land allocations," including eight watershed zones, four recreation zones, and two wildlife habitat zones. UMPQUA NAT'L FOREST LMP, *supra* note 117, at 36-41. The plan allocated the majority of the land to a general forest zone, which emphasized timber management. *Id.* at 42, table 8. The Umpqua Plan also designated four different streamside zones, based on the size of the stream, and management direction for one of those zones required "a buffer strip one-half chain [33 feet] wide on each side of the stream with no programmed timber yield and an additional strip one and one-half chains wide with a rotation age of 200 years." *Id.* at 39. The Umpqua Plan also included a critical soils zone, based on information contained in the Soil Resource Inventory, *see generally supra* note 148; this zone designation was an attempt to identify "those lands which possess a high risk of mass soil movement that threatens to damage fish habitat and other resource values." *Id.* The critical soils

There were also several national planning efforts during this era. Indeed, the immediate predecessors of the national planning required by the Resources Planning Act of 1974[157] were plans that the Forest Service developed on its own initiative. In 1959 the Department of Agriculture proposed to Congress a Program for the National Forests.[158] Nicknamed "Operation Multiple-Use" by the Forest Service,[159] the Program set short- and long-term objectives for resource development.[160] Congress's budgetary reaction to the Forest Service's ambitious Program was restrained. The House Agriculture Committee endorsed the 1959 Program,[161] but Congress largely ignored it soon afterwards.[162] The failure of Operation Multiple-Use convinced some top agency officials that national planning could not succeed without statutory reform.[163] As a result the Forest Service actively supported RPA legislation in the early 1970s.[164]

---

zone included some lands "not suitable for most management activities" where "no programmed timber yields are assumed." *Id.* at 40.

[157] 16 U.S.C. §§ 1601-1613 (1982). *See generally infra* notes 173-92 and accompanying text.

[158] 105 CONG. REC. 5126 (1959).

[159] 1959 ANNUAL REPORT OF THE CHIEF, *supra* note 119, at 2. Forest Service Chief Richard McArdle expressed great optimism about the impact of Operation Multiple-Use. He wrote to Secretary of Agriculture Ezra Taft Benson, "You sent to Congress the Program for the National Forests. I believe this will be looked upon in the years ahead as a turning point in the management of these public lands." *Id.* at iii.

[160] Timber resource goals, for instance, were to sell 11 billion board feet within 10 to 15 years and 21.1 billion board feet by year 2000. FOREST SERVICE, U.S. DEP'T OF AGRICULTURE, PROGRAM FOR NAT'L FORESTS, 86th Cong. 1st Sess., 105 CONG. REC. 5126, 5128 (1959). Short-term wildlife goals included 7000 miles of fishing stream improvements. *Id.* at 5129. Overall, the Program proposed to double the intensity of resource management. 1959 ANNUAL REPORT OF THE CHIEF, *supra* note 119, at 2.

[161] Crafts, *supra* note 129, at 16.

[162] D. LEMASTER, DECADE OF CHANGE: THE REMAKING OF FOREST SERVICE STATUTORY AUTHORITY DURING THE 1970's, at 73 (1984). The Forest Service "dusted off" Operation Multiple-Use in 1961 for President John Kennedy to propose to Congress. Crafts, *supra* note 129, at 16. By 1963, however, the Forest Service acknowledged that the new Development Program for the National Forests was lagging behind its goals. FOREST SERVICE, U.S. DEP'T OF AGRICULTURE, REPORT OF THE CHIEF 4 (1963) [hereinafter cited as 1963 ANNUAL REPORT OF THE CHIEF].

[163] D. LEMASTER, *supra* note 162, at 73.

[164] *Id.* at 72. After retiring from his position as Chief of the Forest Service in 1962, Richard McArdle continued to urge Congress to increase appropriations for the Forest Service. 1961 ANNUAL REPORT OF THE CHIEF, *supra* note 98, at iii. *See infra* note 176.

In the early 1970s the Forest Service developed another national long-range plan, the Environmental Program for the Future.[165] The plan included a comparison of resource outputs anticipated under low, moderate, and high levels of funding for a ten-year period.[166] The plan apparently was intended to be a guide for local and regional planners, as well as a basis for long-term funding increases.[167] Much of the RPA was based on the planning concepts used in the Environmental Program for the Future.[168]

E. *Congressionally Mandated Planning (1974-Present)*

Historically, Congress seldom intruded into Forest Service resource planning or management. To be sure, Congress had required various studies over the years; indeed, the 1876 Appropriations Act that ultimately spawned the Forest Service was a directive to study the nation's supply of timber and other resources.[169] There were other early examples of congressional planning mandates,[170] but these legislative directives were sporadic and did not set positive law. For all practical purposes, before 1974 the Forest Service conducted its land and resource

---

[165] Forest Service, U.S. Dep't of Agriculture, Environmental Program for the Future (1974).

[166] *Id.* at ch. VI.

[167] The Environmental Program for the Future will be one of the key products of a unified Forest Service planning process that has been evolving over the past 3 years . . . . After thorough review, discussion, and appropriate revision, a national plan will be developed to serve as a guide for the development of other plans to meet regional and local objectives. *Id.* at I-3-4. The hierarchical unit planning system is discussed *supra* at text accompanying notes 149-55. The significance of hierarchical or top-down planning is discussed *infra* in section II(C)(2).

[168] *See* McGuire, *The RPA—Something for Everyone,* in Forests in Demand, *supra* note 112, at 147. The RPA was enacted just two months after the draft of the Environmental Program for the Future was issued. *Id.* at 149.

[169] *See supra* text accompanying notes 47-48. Portions of the 1876 Act and the RPA are remarkably similar. The 1876 provision called for a study "with the view of ascertaining the annual amount of consumption, importation, and exportation of timber and other forest-products, the probable supply of future wants, and the measures . . . for the . . . restoration or planting of forests." Act of Aug. 15, 1876, ch. 287, 19 Stat. 167. The RPA Assessment requires "an analysis of present and anticipated uses, demand for, and supply of the renewable resources, with consideration of the international resource situation, and an emphasis of pertinent supply and demand and price relationship trends." 16 U.S.C. § 1601(a)(1) (1982). The RPA also set a target date for "restoration" of cutover national forest land. *Id.* § 1607.

[170] *See supra* text accompanying notes 110-16.

planning solely under the sweeping terms of the 1897 Organic Act.[171]

The two main statutes of the mid-1970s changed much of this. The Resource Planning Act of 1974, although providing in general terms for interdisciplinary, integrated local planning,[172] is mainly concerned with national planning. The National Forest Management Act of 1976, on the other hand, deals specifically and comprehensively with local planning and sets limitations that directly affect timber harvesting. The following subsections provide an overview of those two landmark statutes, and much of the remainder of the Article interprets their specific provisions.

1. The Resources Planning Act of 1974

Senator Hubert Humphrey of Minnesota introduced the first RPA bill, S. 2296, on July 31, 1973.[173] The bill reflected many features of the Forest Service's previous national plans. Similar to the Forest Service's earlier programs, S. 2296's primary purpose was to improve funding to achieve "long- and short-term goals for national forest use."[174] By putting the goals into a "Statement of Policy" adopted by Congress, Humphrey hoped to ensure consistently higher appropriations to meet the goals.[175] Congressional in-

---

[171] 16 U.S.C. § 551 (1982), discussed *infra* in section II (A)(1).

[172] Section 6 of the RPA provides in its entirety:

(a) As a part of the Program provided for by section 1602 of this title, the Secretary of Agriculture shall develop, maintain, and, as appropriate, revise land and resource management plans for units of the National Forest System, coordinated with the land and resource management planning processes of State and local governments and other Federal agencies.

(b) In the development and maintenance of land management plans for use on units of the National Forest System, the Secretary shall use a systematic interdisciplinary approach to achieve integrated consideration of physical, biological, economic, and other sciences.

16 U.S.C. § 1604 (1982).

[173] S. 2296, 93d Cong., 1st Sess., 119 CONG. REC. 26,797 (1973), *reprinted in* SENATE COMM. ON AGRICULTURE, NUTRITION, AND FORESTRY, 96TH CONG., 1ST SESS., COMPILATION OF THE FOREST AND RANGELAND RENEWABLE RESOURCES ACT OF 1974, at 20-24 (Comm. Print 1979) [hereinafter cited as RPA COMPILATION].

[174] *Id., reprinted in* RPA COMPILATION, *supra* note 173, at 20 (remarks of Sen. Humphrey). The original version of S. 2296 required the Secretary of Agriculture to recommend to Congress every 10 years a "natural resources physical budget." S. 2296, 93rd Cong., 1st Sess. § 105(b), 119 CONG. REC. 26,797, 26,798 (1973), *reprinted in* RPA COMPILATION, *supra* note 173, at 22.

[175] Senator Humphrey criticized the "shortsighted" Forest Service budget proposed by the Nixon administration. He declared, "To correct this deplorable condition, we must reform the budget process. One-eyed bookkeepers must be gotten

volvement in the goal-setting, Humphrey believed, would solve the problems that were fatal to the Forest Service's 1959 Program.[176] The Senate passed a revised version of S. 2296 in 1974 with three main elements. First, the bill required the Forest Service to prepare an assessment of the nation's public and private resources every ten years.[177] Second, every five years the Secretary of Agriculture was directed to give the President a Program proposing long-term resource goals.[178] Third, Congress was to adopt a non-binding Statement of Policy[179] to guide the President's annual

---

out of the Nation's forests." 119 CONG. REC. 26,797 (1973), *reprinted in* RPA COMPILATION, *supra* note 173, at 20. *See generally* Wolf, *The Goals of the Authors of the RPA,* in FORESTS IN DEMAND, *supra* note 112, at 137.

[176] Former Chief McArdle's advice to Humphrey was "one of the important determinants in deciding on the approach" of the RPA bill. 120 CONG. REC. 26,554 (1974), *reprinted in* RPA COMPILATION, *supra* note 173, at 209 (remarks of Senator Humphrey). Humphrey continued,

> Dr. McArdle pointed out that the 1960 [MUSY Act] was a clear success as a basic policy tool, but a major omission was the lack of a procedure to assure that the President and Congress could secure the timely enactment of program goals.
>
> Also missing was a vehicle for keeping before policymakers an agenda to realize the program's goals.
>
> This is the bill's purpose.

Id. See also Wolf, *Architects and Architecture,* in THE RPA PROCESS: MOVING ALONG THE LEARNING CURVE 5, 7-10 (G. Stairs & T. Hamilton ed. 1982).

[177] S. 2296, 93rd Cong., 2d Sess. § 3, 120 CONG. REC. 3826 (1974), *reprinted in* RPA COMPILATION, *supra* note 173, at 123. The Assessment is similar to previous inventories that Congress has asked the Forest Service to conduct. *See supra* text accompanying notes 110-16.

[178] S. 2296, 93rd Cong., 2d Sess. § 4, 120 CONG. REC. 3826-27 (1974), *reprinted in* RPA COMPILATION, *supra* note 173, at 123. The RPA Program is similar to the program proposed by the Forest Service in 1959. *See supra* text accompanying notes 158-160.

[179] In response to objections raised by the administration, S. REP. NO. 686, 93rd Cong., 2d Sess. 27 (1974), *reprinted in* RPA COMPILATION, *supra* note 173, at 83, the Senate committee report clarified the non-binding nature of the Statement of Policy:

> The Department of Agriculture recommended a change in language so that the President would only have to "consider" the Program in framing budgets, rather than using it as a "guide." The argument is made that the term "guide" restricts the flexibility of the President.
>
> This it certainly does not do.
>
> What the legislation does is make it clear that this Program is a "guide"; thus it is one of several possibilities. The President takes into account fiscal issues, the national defense and general welfare as other "guides" in formulating overall budget policy. He is required under this language simply to consider the Program as the guide in setting resource conservation criteria.

Id. at 14, *reprinted in* RPA COMPILATION, *supra,* at 70.

budget requests for the Forest Service.[180] If a budget request was for an amount less than that required to achieve the Statement of Policy goals, the President would be required to explain the reasons for the low request.[181]

The House bill, H.R. 15,283, closely resembled S. 2296. There was, however, one significant difference. H.R. 15,283 required the President, rather than Congress, to formulate the Statement of Policy.[182] The President's policy statement would go into effect unless Congress modified or amended it or if either the Senate or House adopted a resolution disapproving the statement.[183] This is the version of the Statement of Policy provision that was accepted by the conference committee.[184]

In summary, the RPA requires the Forest Service periodically to prepare three planning documents:

(1) every ten years an Assessment describing the renewable resources of all the nation's forest and range lands;[185]

(2) every five years a Program proposing long-range objectives, with a planning horizon of at least forty-five years, for all Forest Service activities;[186]

(3) an Annual Report evaluating Forest Service activities in comparison with the objectives proposed in the Program.[187]

In addition, the RPA requires the President to submit two documents:

---

[180] S. 2296, 93rd Cong., 2d Sess. § 8, 120 CONG. REC. 3827 (1974), *reprinted in* RPA COMPILATION, *supra* note 173, at 124.

[181] S. 2296, 93rd Cong., 2d Sess. § 8(e), 120 CONG. REC. 3826 (1974), *reprinted in* RPA COMPILATION, *supra* note 173, at 89. After the conference committee had agreed on the final version of the RPA, Senator Humphrey stated, "The Congress may agree with the changes proposed [in the President's budget], but to suggest that the President can change policy without advising the Congress flies in the face of sound policy direction." 120 CONG. REC. 26,555 (1974), *reprinted in* RPA COMPILATION, *supra*, at 210.

[182] H.R. 15,283, 93rd Cong., 2d Sess. § 7(a), 120 CONG. REC. 21,870-71 (1974), *reprinted in* RPA COMPILATION, *supra* note 173, at 178.

[183] The House bill stated that "the President shall, subject to other actions of the Congress, carry out programs already established by law in accordance with such Statement of Policy." H.R. 15,283, 93rd Cong., 2d Sess. § 7(a), 120 CONG. REC. 21,871 (1974), *reprinted in* RPA COMPILATION, *supra* note 173, at 178.

[184] S. REP. NO. 1069, 93rd Cong., 2d Sess. 9 (Joint Explanatory Statement of the Conference Comm.) (1974), *reprinted in* RPA COMPILATION, *supra* note 173, at 202.

[185] 16 U.S.C. § 1601(a) (1982).

[186] *Id.* § 1602.

[187] *Id.* § 1606(c).

(1) every five years a Statement of Policy to be used in framing budget requests for Forest Service activities;[188]

(2) an explanation accompanying each budget that does not request funds necessary to achieve the objectives of the Statement of Policy.[189]

Despite the expectations of Senator Humphrey and others, the RPA has not fundamentally altered the Forest Service budgetary process. Budget proposals and appropriations almost immediately fell behind the amounts recommended in the 1975 Program.[190] The economic recession of the early 1980s resulted in similar problems for the 1980 Program.[191] The RPA, however, has had an important impact on the way the Forest Service has structured the planning process required by the NFMA.[192]

2. *The National Forest Management Act of 1976*

The RPA was a long-range planning statute enacted in a relatively calm, almost ivory-tower setting in comparison with the profound social, environmental, economic, political, and legal turbulence that surrounded the passage of the NFMA just two years later. The 1976 Act amounted to a bitterly-contested referendum on Forest Service timber harvesting practices.

---

[188] *Id.* § 1606(a).

[189] *Id.* § 1606(b). For descriptions of the RPA, see generally National Wildlife Federation v. United States, 626 F.2d 917, 919-20 (D.C. Cir. 1980); Coggins & Evans, *supra* note 30, at 432-40 (1982); Note, *The National Forest Service and the Forest and Rangeland Renewable Resources Planning Act of 1974*, 15 NAT. RES. J. 603 (1975).

[190] *See* National Wildlife Federation v. United States, 626 F.2d at 920-21 (plaintiffs challenge of President Carter's failure to comply with 16 U.S.C. § 1606(b) (1982), which requires an explanation accompany any budget request for an amount less than that necessary to satisfy the Statement of Policy).

[191] The 1980 RPA Program projected appropriations of $1.5 billion by 1985. In 1984, however, the Forest Service estimated that only $1 billion would be appropriated. *See 1985 Forest Service Budget, supra* note 10, at 1282. Between 1979 and 1982 timber harvesting from national forests fell from 10.4 to 6.7 billion board feet. *Id.* at 1325. Much of the unharvested timber had been purchased at high prices and could not be economically harvested. In 1984 the Forest Service estimated that 200-400 million board feet would need to be resold annually until the wood products market had fully recovered. *Id. See also* North Side Lumber Co. v. Block, 753 F.2d 1482 (9th Cir. 1985); Federal Timber Contract Payment Modification Act, Pub. L. No. 98-478, 98 Stat. 2213, 16 U.S.C. § 618 (Supp. II 1984).

[192] *See infra* accompanying text notes 408-21.

During the 1960s the Forest Service had continued to increase timber sales[193] and also had expanded the use of clearcutting.[194] These practices generated severe criticism in West Virginia, Montana, and other parts of the country.[195] Critics of the Forest Service called for remedial action by Congress.[196] The agency's legal authority to clearcut also was challenged in court. On August 21, 1975, the Court of Appeals for the Fourth Circuit ruled in the famous *Monongahela* case that the 1897 Organic Act effectively prohibited clearcutting in the national forests.[197] The Forest

---

[193] Timber sales increased from 9.4 billion board feet in 1959, 1959 ANNUAL REPORT OF THE CHIEF, *supra* note 119, at 14, to 13.4 billion board feet in 1970, FOREST SERVICE, U.S. DEP'T OF AGRICULTURE, 1970-71 ANNUAL REPORT OF THE CHIEF 20 (1972) [hereinafter cited as 1970-71 ANNUAL REPORT OF THE CHIEF].

[194] *See* SUBCOMM. ON PUBLIC LANDS OF THE SENATE COMM. ON INTERIOR AND INSULAR AFFAIRS, 92ND CONG., 2D SESS., CLEARCUTTING ON FEDERAL TIMBERLANDS 3-4 (Comm. Print 1972) [hereinafter cited as CHURCH SUBCOMMITTEE REPORT], *reprinted in* FOREST AND RANGELAND MANAGEMENT: JOINT HEARINGS BEFORE THE SUBCOMM. ON ENVIRONMENT, SOIL CONSERVATION, AND FORESTRY OF THE SENATE COMM. ON AGRICULTURE AND FORESTRY AND THE SUBCOMM. ON THE ENVIRONMENT AND LAND RESOURCES OF THE SENATE COMM. ON INTERIOR AND INSULAR AFFAIRS, 94th. Cong., 2d Sess. 953-54 (Comm. Print 1976) [hereinafter cited as SENATE NFMA HEARINGS].

[195] *See* ENVTL. POLICY DIVISION, CONG. RESEARCH SERVICE, LIBRARY OF CONGRESS, 92ND CONG., 2D SESS., AN ANALYSIS OF FORESTRY ISSUES IN THE FIRST SESSION OF THE 92ND CONGRESS 3-8 (Comm. Print 1972). Robert Wolf, an influential staff advisor on the NFMA, has observed:

> It would be comforting to think that the fervor raised over clearcutting was simply an attempt by a few environmentalists to lock all forest land into wilderness; but the concern that existed had a base among solid citizens, people who felt that what happens on public land is public business. Neither a slaughterhouse worker who daily stood up to his knees in blood from beef carcasses nor a surgeon who daily was up to his wrists in blood at the operating table could accept clearcutting as a wound that in a few years would be healed with a new forest. Because it occurred on public forest, they believed they had every right to say, "Stop!"

Wolf, *supra* note 176, at 6.

[196] For instance, in April 1971, Senator Gale McGee of Wyoming introduced legislation that would have barred clearcutting on federal timberlands for two years. *See* S. 1592, 92d Cong., 1st Sess., 117 CONG. REC. 10,908-10 (1971).

[197] West Virginia Div. of the Izaak Walton League of America, Inc. v. Butz, 522 F.2d 945 (4th Cir. 1975). The Court of Appeals for the Fourth Circuit upheld an injunction against clearcutting in the Monongahela National Forest in West Virginia. Pursuant to the 1897 Organic Act, the Forest Service was authorized to sell "dead, matured, or large growth of trees" that had been "marked and designated" before sale. The court reviewed the Act's legislative history and held that trees must be physiologically (not just economically) mature to meet the first requirement and that a blaze must be struck on each individual tree to meet the second. *Id.* at 949. The court criticized, and refused to follow, the reasoning in Sierra Club v. Hardin, 325 F. Supp. 99 (D. Alaska 1971), *vacated and*

Service and timber interests sought congressional relief to correct the offending language in the 1897 Act.[198]

There was general agreement in Congress that Forest Service timber practices required substantial revision.[199] Legislative attention focused on two bills: S. 2926, sponsored by Senator Jennings Randolph of West Virginia,[200] and S. 3091, sponsored by Senator Humphrey.[201] The Randolph bill was a comprehensive reform measure that prescribed numerous specific standards for timber management.[202] The Humphrey bill simply amended the 1897 Act to permit clearcutting and amended the RPA to require additional regulation of timber cutting through local Forest Service plans.[203] The Forest Service opposed the Randolph bill and supported the Humphrey bill.[204]

The Senate passed the Humphrey bill after making extensive revisions, most of which were based on the Randolph bill.[205] The House then approved a generally less restrictive bill.[206] The conference committee agreed on a compromise bill after three days of negotiation.[207] President Gerald Ford signed the NFMA into law on October 22, 1976.[208]

---

remanded sub nom. Sierra Club v. Butz, 3 ENVTL. L. REP. (ENVTL. L. INST.) 20,292 (9th Cir. 1973), holding that the individual designation of trees for harvesting would be too "onerous" on the Forest Service. The court's reasoning in the *Monongahela* case was promptly adopted in Zieske v. Butz, 406 F. Supp. 258 (D. Alaska 1975).

[198] *See Senate NFMA Hearings, supra* note 194, passim.

[199] *See infra* text accompanying notes 362-78.

[200] S. 2926, 94th Cong., 2d Sess., 122 CONG. REC. 2216-18 (1976), *reprinted in* SENATE NFMA HEARINGS, *supra* note 194, at 2-10.

[201] S. 3091, 94th Cong., 2d Sess., 122 CONG. REC. 5620-21 (1976), *reprinted in* SENATE NFMA HEARINGS, *supra* note 194, at 10-12.

[202] For instance, the bill prohibited clearcuts larger than 25 acres, or closer than 1000 feet apart within 10 years. S. 2926, 94th Cong., 2d Sess. § 7(c)(2)(B), 122 CONG. REC. 2217 (1976), *reprinted in* SENATE NFMA HEARINGS, *supra* note 194, at 5.

[203] S. 3091, 94th Cong., 2d Sess., §§ 3, 4, 122 CONG. REC. 5620 (1976), *reprinted in* SENATE NFMA HEARINGS, *supra* note 194, at 11-12.

[204] SENATE NFMA HEARINGS, *supra* note 194, at 1055, 1063 (statement of John McGuire, Chief of the Forest Service).

[205] *Compare* the initial version of S. 3091, *supra* note 201, *with* the final version of S. 3091, 94th Cong., 2d Sess., 122 CONG. REC. 27,651-54 (1976), *reprinted in* RPA COMPILATION, *supra* note 173, at 491-97.

[206] H.R. 15069, 94th Cong., 2d Sess., 122 CONG. REC. 31,062-65 (1976), *reprinted in* RPA COMPILATION, *supra* note 173, at 725-29.

[207] 122 CONG. REC. 33,834-35 (1976), *reprinted in* RPA COMPILATION, *supra* note 173, at 768-69 (remarks of Sen. Humphrey).

[208] 12 Weekly Comp. of Pres. Doc. 1564 (Oct. 22, 1976), *reprinted in* RPA COMPILATION, *supra* note 173, at 789.

The NFMA, the specific provisions of which will be analyzed throughout this Article, greatly expanded the RPA's terse directive[209] to prepare local land and resource management plans. This was accomplished by requiring the Secretary of Agriculture to promulgate regulations for Forest Service planning, modeled on guidelines stated in the Act.[210] A Committee of Scientists, appointed by the Secretary of Agriculture, was to provide advice on the regulations.[211] The NFMA also required all contracts, permits, and other legal instruments allowing use of a national forest to conform to that forest's management plan.[212] The NFMA imposed numerous limitations on timber harvesting, including a ceiling on the amount of timber to be sold each year.[213] Finally, the Act required the Forest Service to "attempt" to complete the new plans by the end of fiscal year 1985.[214] Until the new plans were completed, the Forest Service could continue to operate under pre-NFMA management plans.[215]

After eighteen meetings of the Committee of Scientists, the Department of Agriculture adopted final planning regulations on September 17, 1979.[216] Less than three years later, the Depart-

---

[209] *See* 16 U.S.C. § 1604(a) (1982).

[210] *Id.* § 1604(g).

[211] *Id.* § 1604(h).

The Secretary of Agriculture enlisted the National Academy of Sciences . . . to help him select the members of the committee . . . . The members of the committee [were]: Thaddeus Box, Utah State University; R. Rodney Foil, Mississippi Agricultural and Forestry Experiment Station; Ronald W. Stark, University of Idaho: Dennis E. Teeguarden, University of California, Berkeley; William L. Webb, previously State University of New York, Syracuse; and the chairman, Arthur W. Cooper, North Carolina State University . . . . At its first meeting in May 1977, [Assistant Secretary of Agriculture] Dr. M. Rupert Cutler [instructed the committee to examine] all parts of section 6 of NFMA as the National Academy of Sciences had proposed when it recommended that "[t]he committee deliberations should embrace all parts of secion 6 of the Act." Dr. Cutler also stressed the need for public participation in the development of the regulations. The committee expanded its own role slightly to include an assessment as to how well the proposed regulations meet the intent of Congress as expressed in NFMA, as suggested in the legislative history of the act.

43 Fed. Reg. 39,057 (1978).

[212] *Id.* § 1604(i).

[213] *Id.* § 1611. *See infra* section IV(c).

[214] 16 U.S.C. § 1604(c) (1982).

[215] *Id.*

[216] 44 Fed. Reg. 53,928 (1979). The Committee of Scientists published an extensive technical review of the draft regulations. *See infra* note 864.

ment proposed several changes in the regulations.[217] On September 30, 1982, the Department promulgated the revised rules, after reconvening the Committee of Scientists to obtain its advice.[218]

The 1982 NFMA regulations cover five major areas of the planning process. First, the regulations describe the content and role of "regional guides," a level of planning not mentioned in the RPA or NFMA.[219] Second, they establish a ten-step process to develop local plans.[220] Third, they explain how to determine where and how much timber can be harvested.[221] Fourth, they state planning requirements for each resource.[222] Fifth, they state "minimum specific management requirements" for timber harvesting and other activities.[223]

After enactment of the NFMA the Forest Service gradually changed its planning procedures to accommodate the requirements of the new law. Interdisciplinary teams were assigned to prepare management plans for each forest.[224] By the early 1980s local planners began to issue draft plans for public and interagency review. Although some plans were completed prior to 1985, most have been delayed by additional directions from the Department of Agriculture.[225]

---

[217] 47 Fed. Reg. 7,678 (1982).

[218] National Forest System Land and Resource Management Planning, 36 C.F.R. pt. 219 (1984).

[219] 36 C.F.R. §§ 219.4(b)(2), 219.9 (1984).

[220] 36 C.F.R. § 219.12 (1984).

[221] *Id.* §§ 219.14, 219.16 (1984). *See infra* section IV(D).

[222] Requirements are stated for wilderness, fish and wildlife, grazing, recreation, minerals, water, and soil. 36 C.F.R. §§ 219.18-.25 (1984).

[223] *Id.* § 219.27.

[224] For example, the Willamette National Forest appointed a 10-person core planning team. The planning team included resource specialists and specialists in economics, social science, and computers. Interview with Rolf Anderson, Director of Planning and Programming, Willamette Nat'l Forest, in Eugene, Or. (Oct. 6, 1983).

[225] There were two primary reasons for the delays. First, in response to the Ninth Circuit Court of Appeals's decision to invalidate the RARE II EIS, the Department of Agriculture on February 1, 1983, directed the Forest Service to reevaluate most roadless areas through the NFMA planning process. *See infra* text accompanying notes 1888-91. Second, the Department on January 19, 1983, directed the Forest Service to undertake additional "trade-off analysis" in local planning. Letter from John B. Crowell, Jr., Assistant Secretary for Natural Resources and Environment, U.S. Dep't of Agriculture, to R. Max Peterson, Chief, Forest Service, 6 (Jan. 19, 1983) (on file at Oregon Law Review office). The Department's directions caused some regions to predict "significant delays" in completion of local plans. Letter from Jeff M. Sirmon, Regional Forester, Pa-

To summarize, the Forest Service has a long tradition of land and resource planning. Early plans focused on developing the timber resource and protecting rangelands. Recreation and wilderness planning became important elements in national forest management soon after World War I. As timber demand increased following World War II, the Forest Service attempted to resolve multiple-use conflicts through a land zoning system. Following enactment of NEPA in 1969, planners sought better inventory data and public involvement. Finally, during the 1970s Congress established elaborate national and local planning structures for the national forests. The NFMA and its implementing regulations required the Forest Service to follow a range of legal standards in developing local forest plans and to manage the national forests in accordance with the plans.

cific Northwest Region, Forest Service, to Forest Supervisors (Mar. 18, 1983) (on file at Oregon Law Review office).

II

THE LEGAL CONTEXT FOR PLANNING

This section examines three fundamental issues in Forest Service planning: the nature and extent of Forest Service and state regulatory authority, the proper standard of judicial review for planning decisions, and the degree to which local Forest Service planning must conform to national resource planning allocations. The applicable legal principles frame the relationships among Congress, the Forest Service, and the states; between the courts and the Forest Service; and between local and national offices within the Forest Service. The law set out here thus establishes many of the planning premises for each of the resources, which this Article considers after discussing this foundational material.

A.   *Forest Service Regulatory Authority*

1.   *Passage of the Organic Act of 1897*

When Congress passed the 1891 Creative Act,[226] it included no specific authority for management of the reserves or any provision for mining, grazing, or other use. Secretary of the Interior John Noble interpreted Congress's silence on these matters as showing an intent to withdraw the reserves from all forms of economic utilization.[227] In the Agriculture Department, the Chief of the Division of Forestry, Bernhard Fernow, read the statute very differently from Noble in at least two major respects. First, Fernow favored a liberal interpretation of the amount of authority and discretion delegated by the 1891 Act.[228] Second, he viewed the

---

[226] Act of Mar. 3, 1891, ch. 561, 26 Stat. 1095, 1103, *repealed by* the Federal Land Policy and Management Act of 1976, Pub. L. No. 94-579, § 704(a), 90 Stat. 2743, 2792. *See supra* notes 54-57 and accompanying text.

[227] *See* S. DANA, *supra* note 47, at 102. Secretary Noble viewed the new reserves as quasi-park areas and urged Congress to provide statutory authority and appropriations to preserve them. H. STEEN, *supra* note 49, at 28. Noble reported to Congress, "[I]t is to be considered also that these parks will preserve the fauna, fish and flora of our country, and become resorts for the people seeking instruction and recreation." [1891 ANNUAL] REPORT OF THE SECRETARY OF THE INTERIOR, H.R. EXEC. DOC. NO. 1, pt. 5, 52d Cong., 1st Sess. 15 (1891). *See also* Fairfax & Tarlock, *No Water for the Woods: A Critical Analysis of* United States v. New Mexico, 15 IDAHO L. REV. 509, 543-44 (1979).

[228] In his 1891 report to the Secretary of Agriculture, Fernow stated, "[I]t is to be hoped that the broadest construction will be given to the section relating to reservations without delay and that full use be made of the authority conferred

reserves from a utilitarian perspective, placing special emphasis on maintaining stable water flows and providing long-term timber supplies for local communities.[229] Fernow recognized the legitimacy of the "aesthetic" purposes for the reserves, but he considered them to be "secondary" to water flow and timber supply.[230] Taking issue with Noble's interpretation, Fernow sought to distinguish the role of the forest reserves from that of the national parks.[231] Although Fernow believed that the reserves could be managed for economic benefits without adversely affecting "aesthetics" or wildlife,[232] he emphasized the overriding need to ensure the future productivity of the land, particularly in regard to timber management.[233]

---

therein. This authority is given unconditionally . . . ." REPORT OF THE CHIEF OF THE DIVISION OF FORESTRY, H.R. EXEC. DOC. No. 1, pt. 6, 52d Cong., 1st Sess. 224 (1891).

[229] Fernow stated in his 1891 Report that the purposes of the reserves are left unexplained by the law. There can hardly be any doubt, however, as to what objects and considerations should be kept in view in reserving such lands and withdrawing them from private occupancy. These are first and foremost of economic importance, not only for the present but more specially for the future prosperity of the people residing near such reservations, namely, first, to assure a continuous forest cover of the soil on mountain slopes and crests for the purpose of preserving or equalizing waterflow in the streams which are to serve for purposes of irrigation, and to prevent formation of torrents and soil washing; second, to assure a continuous supply of wood material from the timbered areas by cutting judiciously and with a view to reproduction.
Id.

[230] *Id.*

[231] Since there have arisen misconceptions . . . it may, perhaps, be proper to emphasize the fact that the multiplication of national parks in remote and picturesque regions was not the intent of the law, but it was specially designed to prevent the great annual conflagrations, to prevent useless destruction of public property, to provide benefit and revenue from the sale of forest products as needed for fuel and lumber by residents of the locality, and altogether to administer this valuable and much-endangered resource for present and future benefit. These, I take it, are the objects of the proposed reservations.
Id.

[232] Forest management, such as contemplated, does not destroy natural beauty, does not decrease but gives opportunity to increase the game, and tends to promote the greatest development of the country, giving regular and steady employment, furnishing continuous supplies, and making each acre do its full duty in whatever direction it can produce most.
Id. at 224-25.

[233] Two considerations must always be kept in view in [timber] management, namely, the needs of the consumer and the condition, present and prospective, of the reserve. The former should never be satisfied to the det-

Thus, the Division of Forestry proposed a multiple-use and sustained yield policy for managing the reserves, with special emphasis on water flow and timber supply, as early as 1891—fourteen years before the agency obtained administrative jurisdiction over the forest reserves. In the absence of any statutory authority the Division relied on its own extraordinarily broad interpretation of the 1891 Act to justify this policy.[234]

Soon after passage of the 1891 Act, Congress came under pressure to delegate additional management authority over the forest reserves.[235] The principal sponsor of legislation was Representative Thomas R. McRae of Arkansas, Chairman of the House Committee on Public Lands.[236] In 1893 McRae introduced H.R. 119,[237] which generally reflected Fernow's utilitarian policies.[238]

Section 3 of McRae's bill was to be the source of the Forest Service's broad organic authority. It authorized the Secretary of the Interior to "make such rules and regulations and establish such service as will insure the objects of such reservations."[239] Section 3 also specifically authorized the Secretary "to utilize the timber of commercial value" through sale to the highest bidder.[240]

---

riment of the latter, but all reasonable wants should be satisfied as far as possible. *Id.* at 229.

[234] Fairfax and Tarlock have argued persuasively that Noble's interpretation of the Act was, in fact, correct and that Noble and President Harrison properly rejected Fernow's "partisan priorities." Fairfax & Tarlock, *supra* note 227, at 541-44.

[235] J. Ise, *supra* note 48, at 121. President Cleveland, for instance, initially declined to set aside additional reservations on the ground that they received no more protection than public domain land. *Id.* at 120.

[236] *Id.* at 122; *see also* H. Steen, *supra* note 49, at 29.

[237] 53rd Cong., 1st Sess., 25 Cong. Rec. 2371 (1893).

[238] Fernow commonly referred to H.R. 119 as "our administration bill." *See* A. Rodgers, Bernhard Eduard Fernow 206 (1968). The report of the House Committee on Public Lands on H.R. 119 reiterated Fernow's view that the forest reserves were for different purposes than national parks. "These reservations are not in the nature of parks set aside for nonuse, but they are established solely for economic reasons." H.R. Rep. No. 78, 53rd Cong., 1st Sess., 25 Cong. Rec. 2372 (1893). Steen states that McRae credited Fernow "for convincing him that forestry meant use of forests, not reservation from use." H. Steen, *supra* note 49, at 29. During debate on H.R. 119, McRae said that forests "cannot be preserved if you leave the ripe trees to decay and die, and the young trees to dwarf for want of room to grow. There is a certain amount of cutting necessary in these forests to make them thrive and prosper." 25 Cong. Rec. 2433 (1893).

[239] H.R. 119, 53rd Cong., 1st Sess. § 3, 25 Cong. Rec. 2371 (1893).

[240] *Id.* Under then-existing authority, the Secretary of the Interior could issue permits only for free use of timber. *See id.* at 2373-74. McRae argued that the federal government should obtain some revenue for use of its timber. *Id.* at 2374.

The McRae bill received support from the new Secretary of the Interior, Hoke Smith,[241] as well as Fernow.[242] Many western congressmen, however, objected that the bill was antithetical to the purposes of the forest reserves.[243] In particular, they opposed giving the Secretary of the Interior authority to sell timber.[244] Otherwise, the broad grant of authority provided by section 3 of the McRae bill aroused little controversy.

The following year McRae agreed to revise H.R. 119 in response to amendments proposed by Representative Hermann of Oregon and others.[245] The revised bill retained broad regulatory powers in section 3 but deleted the nearly unlimited authority "to utilize the timber of commercial value."[246] Instead, section 3 al-

---

[241] *Id.* at 2372. Secretary Smith endorsed the favorable comments on the bill submitted by Acting Commissioner of the General Land Office, Edward A. Bowers, who had collaborated with Fernow in proposing legislation to create the forest reserves. *See supra* note 52. Bowers's letter on H.R. 119 stated:

Prompt and effective legislation on this subject can not be too strongly urged. Forest reservations have been made which are such only in name . . . . Information comes almost daily showing continued trespassing and depredating within the reserves, committed by lumbermen, prospectors, sheep-herders, and others, and forest fires, caused by the careless and vicious, resulting in irreparable damage, especially those started by sheepherders in the mountain districts in the fall to create new pasturage for the following season.

25 CONG. REC. 2373 (1893).

[242] *See* H. STEEN, *supra* note 49, at 29.

[243] Representative Simpson of Kansas, for example, objected to the excessive power delegated to "allow the Secretary of the Interior to sell timber on the lands in these reservations which have been set aside for the special purpose of holding the moisture." 25 CONG. REC. 2432 (1893). Similarly, Congressman Pickler of South Dakota commented that "this bill . . . puts it in the power of the Secretary of the Interior to sell this timber, to cut it off, to denude the land entirely . . . and so the very object of the law, which is the setting apart and protection of these timber reservations, will be defeated." *Id.* at 2431.

[244] Representative Hermann of Oregon called H.R. 119 "[a] bill to denude the public forest reservations." *Id.* Representative Doolittle of Washington declared, "You might just as well turn a dozen wolves into a corral filled with sheep and expect the wolves to protect the sheep as to expect your timber to be protected if you permit the lumbermen to go upon the reservations at all." *Id.* at 2432.

[245] Upon introduction of his revised H.R. 119, Congressman McRae stated, "These amendments represent the views of those gentlemen [Congressmen Hermann, Coffeen, and Hartman], who had theretofore opposed the bill, and are embodied now, as it was then proposed to embody them, by amendments in the bill. They are satisfied and I agree to their amendments." 27 CONG. REC. 364 (1894). Representative Hermann's amendment to §5 of H.R. 119 opened the forest reserves to mining. *See infra* text accompanying note 248.

[246] 25 CONG. REC. 2391 (1893). The author of the amendment, Representative Coffeen of Wyoming, explained that

lowed the Secretary to sell only "carefully designat[ed]" "dead or matured timber," "for the sole purpose of preserving the living and growing timber."[247] In addition, the House mandated that miners "shall have access" to prospect and work their claims on the forest reserves.[248]

The McRae bill, as it emerged from the House at the end of 1894, would have divided the authority of the Secretary of the Interior. Authority to sell timber and prohibit mining was narrowly limited, but for all other purposes the Secretary received very broad power to manage the land and resources of the reserves. The Senate version of H.R. 119, sponsored by Senator Teller of Colorado, further accentuated the dual character of the Secretary's authority. Section 3 of the Teller bill placed an additional limit on timber sale authority by requiring salable trees to be "marked."[249] On the other hand, section 3 of the bill gave the

---

the loose and general provisions in that bill for the sale of the living and commercial timber on these lands have now all been eliminated; and . . . the only provision for sale embraced in this bill is a provision for selling dead and matured timber; and such timber can only be sold for the purpose of preserving living and growing timber.

27 CONG. REC. 367 (1894).

[247] 27 CONG. REC. 86 (1894). The author of the amendment, Representative Hermann remarked,

I myself should prefer that no clause should be retained in the bill permitting the cutting of a single thousand feet of either dead or matured timber. But it was represented to us that it is absolutely necessary that the dead timber should be eliminated from the forest, and so much of the mature timber as might conflict with the proper development of that which remains; and therefore we have so guarded the bill that only that part of the mature timber shall be touched, under restrictions to be imposed by the Secretary of the Interior, as may conflict with the preservation of the balance of the forests.

Id. at 366. The legislative history of this section is discussed further in West Virginia Div. of the Izaak Walton League of Am., Inc. v. Butz, 522 F.2d 945 (4th Cir. 1975).

[248] 27 CONG. REC. 364 (1894). This provision to open the reserves to mining was later supplemented to require miners to "comply with the rules and regulations covering such forest reservations." 30 CONG. REC. 900 (1897). *See infra* notes 1302-03.

[249] 27 CONG. REC. 2780 (1895). The Court of Appeals for the Fourth Circuit in the *Monongahela* decision, *see generally supra* note 197, stated that the marking requirement was added by Congress "to quiet the critics who were concerned that the loggers would cut whatever timber they wanted and continue to denude the forest." *Izaak Walton League v. Butz*, 522 F.2d at 952. The Senate bill also would have reduced the Secretary's power to forbid public access or livestock grazing on forest reserves. 27 CONG. REC. 2780 (1895).

Secretary additional authority to regulate "use" of the reserves.[250] Teller also added a new section to H.R. 119 that recognized concurrent state "civil and criminal jurisdiction over persons within such reservations"[251] and permitted appropriation of water for irrigation and domestic use under state law.[252] Teller's bill passed the Senate without discussion, but the conference committee failed to agree on a compromise between the Teller and McRae bills.[253]

In 1897 Congress enacted the terse statute that governed Forest Service activities until the mid-1970s and continues to be the starting point for analysis of Forest Service regulatory authority. This "Organic Act" was a newly revised version of H.R. 119, sponsored by Senator Richard F. Pettigrew of South Dakota, as an amendment to a Sundry Civil Appropriations bill.[254] Like the

---

[250] 27 CONG. REC. 2779 (1895). Although the Teller bill passed the Senate without comment on the addition of "use" to § 3, the contemporaneous significance of the term is fairly clear. In the context of forest reserve management, "use" meant economic development of the resources, including timber cutting. An 1894 resolution of the American Forestry Association, AFA for instance, praised the original McRae bill as "a law providing not only for the care and protection, but also for the rational *use*, of the timber and other resources in the forest reservations." 27 CONG. REC. 366 (1894) (emphasis added). The AFA resolution stated further, "This association emphatically denies that it advocates in the policy of forest reservations the unintelligent exclusion from *use* of large territories and of the resources contained therein." *Id.* (emphasis added). It was probably unnecessary to add "use" to § 3 of the McRae bill, since regulation of use could be implied from the committee report, which directs the Secretary to "prescribe the manner and methods" in which the resources of the reserves "shall be used." H.R. REP. NO. 78, 53rd Cong., 1st Sess., 25 CONG. REC. 2372 (1893).

[251] 27 CONG. REC. 2780 (1895).

[252] *Id. See infra* text accompanying notes 1097-98.

[253] H. STEEN, *supra* note 49, at 30. In 1896 the House passed a further revision of H.R. 119. The 1896 bill would have required the Secretary to "make such rules and regulations and . . . establish such service as shall be required . . . to preserve the timber and other natural resources, and such natural wonders and curiosities and game as may be therein, from injury, waste, fire, spoliation, or other destruction." 28 CONG. REC. 6410 (1896). The bill passed the House with little comment, but the Senate took no action. *See* J. ISE, *supra* note 48, at 128.

[254] Act of June 4, 1897, ch. 2, 30 Stat. 34-36 (codified as amended at 16 U.S.C. §§ 473-482, 551 (1982)). The legislation passed in the aftermath of the "Washington's Birthday reserves," President Cleveland's controversial creation in early 1897 of 13 new reserves, totaling more than 21 million acres. The 1897 Act temporarily restored the reserves to the public domain. Senator Pettigrew introduced the amendment at the urging of Charles Walcott, director of the U.S. Geologic Survey, who modeled the amendment on H.R. 119. For historical accounts of the events leading up to passage of the 1897 Act, see generally J. ISE,

earlier bills, it granted broad general agency authority but placed limits on timber sales.

First, and most important, Congress delegated broad regulatory power over virtually all forms of use in the forest reserves and authorized rulemaking to implement the substantive powers:

> The Secretary of the Interior shall make provisions for the protection against destruction by fire and depredations upon the public forests and forest reservations . . . and he may make such rules and regulations and establish such service as will insure the objects of such reservations, namely, to regulate their occupancy and use and to preserve the forests thereon from destruction . . . . [255]

This provision is now codified, in slightly revised form, in 16 U.S.C. § 551. Second, the Act retained the principal features of the limitations on timber sale authority first proposed by Congressman Hermann.[256] Third, Congress permitted water on the reserves to be used for "domestic, mining, milling, or irrigation purposes," under state or federal regulation.[257] Similarly, the law permitted mining activity on the reserves under federal regulation.[258] Finally, the Act contained a modified provision for concurrent state and federal jurisdiction "over persons within such reservations."[259]

2. Judicial Construction of the 1897 Organic Act

The Department of the Interior wasted no time in asserting its new authority to manage "use" of the forest reserves.[260] Less than a month after President McKinley signed the 1897 Act, Interior moved decisively to close off the reserves to sheep grazing.[261] The following year the United States Attorney General rendered an opinion upholding the Secretary of the Interior's authority under 16 U.S.C. § 551 to enforce the grazing regulations by criminal

---

supra note 48, at 128-41; H. STEEN, *supra* note 49, at 30-36; Huffman, *A History of Forest Policy in the United States*, 8 ENVTL. L. 239, 258-64 (1978).

[255] Ch. 2, 30 Stat. 35 (current version at 16 U.S.C. § 551 (1982)).

[256] Act of June 4, 1897, ch. 2, 30 Stat. 35, 16 U.S.C. § 476, *repealed by* the National Forest Management Act of 1976, Pub. L. No. 94-588, 13, 90 Stat. 2949, 2958.

[257] Ch. 2, 30 Stat. 36 (1897) (current version at 16 U.S.C. § 481 (1982)).

[258] Ch. 2, 30 Stat. 36 (1897) (current version at 16 U.S.C. § 478 (1982)).

[259] Ch. 2, 30 Stat. 36 (1897) (current version at 16 U.S.C. § 480 (1982)).

[260] The reserves remained under the jurisdiction of the Interior Department until 1905, when they were transferred to the Department of Agriculture. *See infra* note 268.

[261] *See infra* text accompanying notes 500-01.

prosecution.[262] The Attorney General concluded that through the 1897 Act "the control of the occupancy and use of these reservations is handed over to the Secretary for the purpose of preserving the forests thereon."[263]

In 1898, leadership of the Division of Forestry in the Agriculture Department passed from Fernow to Gifford Pinchot.[264] With Pinchot as the new Division Chief and Theodore Roosevelt as President, the executive branch instituted an aggressive forest management policy.[265] Soon after taking office, for instance, Roosevelt sought an Attorney General's opinion on executive authority to establish wildlife sanctuaries on the forest reserves. Undaunted by the Attorney General's opinion that the 1897 Act did not provide that authority,[266] Roosevelt asked Congress repeatedly, though unsuccessfully, for additional authority.[267]

With the transfer of the forest reserves from Interior to the Department of Agriculture in 1905,[268] Pinchot was able to direct

---

[262] 22 Op. Att'y Gen. 266 (1898). After six years of lobbying by the Department of the Interior, Congress in 1905 authorized federal officials to arrest, without process, violators of forest reserve regulations. Act of Mar. 3, 1905, ch. 1405, 33 Stat. 873 (codified as amended at 16 U.S.C. § 559 (1982)). Dana states, "This act constituted the first authorization for a civil officer to make an arrest without a court warrant." S. DANA, *supra* note 47, at 115.

[263] 22 Op. Att'y Gen. 266, 268 (1898). Subsequent court challenges to grazing regulations are discussed *infra* at text accompanying notes 515-42.

[264] Prior to his appointment as Chief, Pinchot served on a Forest Commission appointed by the National Academy of Sciences in 1896 to prepare a study on forest reserves for the Secretary of the Interior. *See generally* S. DANA, *supra* note 47, at 103-04; H. STEEN, *supra* note 49, at 30-33.

[265] Roosevelt expanded the forest reserves system from 46.4 million acres in 1901 to 194.5 million acres in 1909. P. GATES, *supra* note 26, at 580. Ise has observed:

> Not only did Roosevelt and Pinchot enforce the laws vigorously, but they often did things which no law required—went beyond the mandatory provisions of the law, where it was necessary to protect the public interests. They did not hang back, after the fashion of ordinary government bureaus, and wait for Congress to give specific orders; but vigorously took the initiative whenever conditions demanded action.

J. ISE, *supra* note 48, at 175.

[266] 23 Op. Att'y Gen. 589 (1901). *See infra* text accompanying notes 1476-81.

[267] *See infra* text accompanying notes 1482-91.

[268] The Transfer Act of 1905, 33 Stat. 628, *amended by* 16 U.S.C. § 472 (1982), gave the Department of Agriculture executive power over the forest reserves, except that administration of the mining laws remained with the Department of the Interior. The Transfer Act resulted from Pinchot's persistent efforts to wrest control of the reserves from Division R of the General Land Office in Interior. *See generally* H. STEEN, *supra* note 49, at 60-61, 71-74. Later

management of the reserves toward the utilitarian objectives he shared with Fernow.[269] Timber sales increased by nearly 1000 percent during Pinchot's first two years as Chief.[270] Notwithstanding the 1897 Act's prescriptions to sell only "dead, matured, or large growth of trees,"[271] Pinchot instructed his foresters that "[g]reen timber may be sold except where its removal makes a second crop doubtful, reduces the timber supply below the point of safety, or injures the streams."[272]

---

that year, the Bureau of Forestry was renamed the Forest Service. *Id.* at 74. "Forest reserves" became "national forests" in the Agricultural Appropriations Act of Mar. 4, 1907, 34 Stat. 1269.

[269] On Fernow's views, see *supra* notes 228-33. Pinchot set forth his general policy in the famous "Pinchot Letter" of February 1, 1905, signed by the Secretary of Agriculture.

In the administration of the forest reserves it must be clearly borne in mind that all land is to be devoted to its most productive use for the permanent good of the whole people, and not for the temporary benefit of individuals or companies. All the resources of forest reserves are for *use*, and this use must be brought about in a thoroughly prompt and business-like manner, under such restrictions only as will insure the permanence of these resources. The vital importance of forest reserves to the great industries of the Western States will be largely increased in the near future by the continued steady advance in settlement and development. The permanence of the resources of the reserves is therefore indispensable to continued prosperity, and the policy of this Department for their protection and use will invariably be guided by this fact, always bearing in mind that the *conservative use* of these resources in no way conflicts with their permanent value.

You will see to it that the water, wood, and forage of the reserves are conserved and wisely used for the benefit of the home builder first of all, upon whom depends the best permanent use of lands and resources alike. The continued prosperity of the agricultural, lumbering, mining, and livestock interests is directly dependent upon a permanent and accessible supply of water, wood, and forage, as well as upon the present and future use of these resources under businesslike regulations, enforced with promptness, effectiveness, and common sense. In the management of each reserve local questions will be decided upon local grounds; the dominant industry will be considered first, but with as little restriction to minor industries as may be possible; sudden changes in industrial conditions will be avoided by gradual adjustment after due notice, and where conflicting interests must be reconciled the question will always be decided from the standpoint of the greatest good of the greatest number in the long run.

1906 USE BOOK, *supra* note 82, at 16-17 (emphasis in original).

[270] Sales increased from 113 million board feet in 1905 to 1.044 billion board feet in 1907. 1908 ANNUAL REPORT OF THE CHIEF, *supra* note 75, at 409, 421.

[271] Ch. 2, 30 Stat. 35, 16 U.S.C. § 476 (repealed 1976).

[272] 1906 USE BOOK, *supra* note 82, at 35. Pinchot further directed that:
All timber on forest reserves which can be cut safely and for which there is actual need is for sale. Applications to purchase are invited . . . . The prime object of the forest reserves is use. While the forest and its depen-

Pinchot also took an expansive view of his authority to regulate grazing,[273] but he approached the matter with greater caution. Beginning in 1900 the Department of the Interior had unsuccessfully lobbied Congress to authorize sale of grazing permits.[274] Pinchot and Secretary of Agriculture James Wilson decided to try to establish the authority to sell permits under the 1897 Organic Act.[275] The Forest Service's legal officer, George Woodruff, composed a letter for Wilson to submit to Attorney General W.H. Moody,[276] asking for an opinion on a related but uncontroversial permit fee question.[277] Pinchot convinced President Roosevelt to advise Moody of the administration's support for grazing fees.[278] The Attorney General issued an opinion that construed 16 U.S.C. § 551 liberally[279] and concluded that the 1897 Act authorized "reasonable" permit fees.[280] The 1905 opinion laid the groundwork for the Supreme Court's landmark *Grimaud* ruling in 1911 that firmly established the Forest Service's broad regulatory authority.[281]

---

dent interests must be made permanent and safe by preventing overcutting or injury to young growth, every resonable effort will be made to satisfy legitimate demands.
Id. at 35-36.

[273] In his autobiography Pinchot said, "I hate a sheep, and the smell of a sheep." G. PINCHOT, *supra* note 51, at 270.

[274] J. ISE, *supra* note 48, at 172. Pinchot attempted to attach a grazing fee clause to a bill transferring administration of the forest reserves from Interior to the Department of Agriculture. *See* G. PINCHOT, *supra* note 51, at 271.

[275] J. ISE, *supra* note 48, at 172.

[276] G. PINCHOT, *supra* note 51, at 271.

[277] Wilson's letter raised the fee issue in the remote context of a permit application for a fish processing plant on a forest reserve in Alaska. *See* 25 Op. Att'y Gen. 470 (1905).

[278] G. PINCHOT, *supra* note 51, at 272.

[279] The Attorney General reasoned that since the 1897 Act "contains nothing inconsistent with the making of a reasonable charge on account of the use of the reserves," the Secretary had adequate authority to impose a fee. 25 Op. Att'y Gen. 470, 473 (1905). The Attorney General thus established a presumption that Forest Service regulations are authorized by the 1897 Act.

[280] Wilson phrased his question: "Have I legal authority to require a reasonable compensation or rental for such permit or lease within the forest reserve?" Attorney General Moody stated in response:
I have to advise you that, in my opinion, you are authorized to make a reasonable charge in connection with the use and occupation of these forest reserves, whenever, in your judgment, such a course seems consistent with insuring the objects of the reservation and the protection of the forests thereon from destruction.
Id.

[281] United States v. Grimaud, 220 U.S. 506 (1911).

Judicial interpretation of the scope of agency authority under the 1897 Act developed in a series of challenges to the grazing regulations. The lower courts split on the issue of whether 16 U.S.C. § 551 unconstitutionally delegated legislative power to the Secretary of Agriculture.[282] The courts that upheld the constitutionality of the delegation also concluded that the regulations did not exceed the scope of authority delegated by Congress.[283] This early litigation involved test cases in the most modern sense: under Pinchot's guidance the Forest Service pressed charges only where the government's equities were strong and where the judges were thought to be sympathetic to the agency's regulatory efforts.[284]

Finally, in *United States v. Grimaud*,[285] the Supreme Court resolved the conflicting lower court decisions on the constitutional issue in favor of the government. The Court also addressed the scope of authority issue:

> It was argued that, even if the Secretary could establish regulations under which a permit was required, there was nothing in the act to indicate that Congress had intended or authorized him to charge for the privilege of grazing sheep on the reserve. . . .
> The Secretary of Agriculture could not make rules and regulations for any and every purpose. As to those here involved, they all relate to matters clearly indicated and authorized by Congress. The subjects as to which the Secretary can regulate are defined. The lands are set apart as a forest reserve. He is required to make provision to protect them from depredations and from harmful uses. He is authorized "to regulate the occupancy and use and to preserve the forests from destruction."[286]

The Court decided that the agency's authority under the 1897 Act was broad enough to encompass the grazing fees. The fees could be justified as a means "to meet the expenses of management," as well as to "protect the young growth, and native grasses, from destruction" by preventing excessive grazing.[287]

Though the Court's discussion is brief and its conclusions are open-ended, *Grimaud* remains the Court's major statement on the

---

[282] *Id.* at 515.

[283] *See, e.g.*, United States v. Domingo, 152 F. 566, 567 (D. Idaho 1907); United States v. Shannon, 151 F. 863, 869 (D. Mont. 1907).

[284] H. STEEN, *supra* note 49, at 88. Steen accurately described these efforts as a "sophisticated legal program." *Id.* at 89. *See also* S. DANA, *supra* note 47, at 146-47.

[285] 220 U.S. 506 (1911). Justice Lamar, the author of the opinion, was formerly Secretary of the Interior.

[286] *Id.* at 521-22 (citation omitted).

[287] *Id.* at 522.

Forest Service's scope of authority.[288] Coming almost two years after Pinchot had left the Forest Service,[289] *Grimaud* was a fitting epilogue to the Pinchot era. The landmark decision is directly traceable to Pinchot's tenacious campaign to give the Forest Service maximum authority over the national forests.[290]

Lower court decisions since *Grimaud* have consistently upheld assertions of Forest Service regulatory power. The agency has withstood challenges to its permitting procedures, a basic element of the agency's authority by which it regulates various uses of the national forests.[291] Applications of the permit system to such disparate ventures as saloons,[292] ski instruction schools,[293] and microwave relay facilities[294] have been sustained under the auspices of the Organic Act. The Forest Service's "dual permit" system, commonly used for the more than 200 ski areas on national forests, presented even more difficult questions but it too has been upheld. A 1915 statute[295] expressly allows the Forest Service to issue land use permits, but the provision is limited to an area of eighty acres and a term of thirty years. For most ski areas, the Forest Service issues two permits, one under the 1915 Act for eighty acres and a

---

[288] The only other Supreme Court decision to consider the scope of authority issue is Hunt v. United States, 278 U.S. 96 (1928). The Court stated, in dicta, that the direction to kill and remove deer from a national forest, in contravention of state law, "was within the authority conferred upon [the Secretary of Agriculture] by act of Congress." *Id.* at 100. United States v. New Mexico, 438 U.S. 696 (1978), analyzed the 1897 Act in depth, holding that Congress did not intend to reserve water flows for wildlife and recreation. *New Mexico*, however, dealt only with the purposes for establishing forest reserves, not the scope of administrative authority to administer the reserves. *See infra* text accompanying note 1216. *See also infra* text accompanying notes 319-21.

[289] Pinchot was dismissed by President Taft on January 9, 1910, after Pinchot had accused Secretary of the Interior Richard Ballinger of concealing fraudulent mining claims in Alaska. *See generally* S. DANA, *supra* note 47, at 166-70; H. STEEN, *supra* note 49, at 100-02. Pinchot's departure put the Forest Service in a position of defending, rather than expanding, its policies and lands for several years. *See generally id.* at 105-22, 148-68.

[290] *See supra* H. STEEN, note 49, at 89. *See also infra* note 542.

[291] The Forest Service adopted a rudimentary permitting requirement in the 1905 Use Book. *See, e.g.*, United States v. Rizzinelli, 182 F. 675, 677 (D. Idaho 1910). The current regulations fall under the category of special use permits. *See* 36 C.F.R. §§ 251.50-.64 (1984). The regulations exempt timber harvesting, mining, and grazing, all of which are covered elsewhere, but otherwise cover a wide range of commercial operations. *See id.* § 251.53.

[292] United States v. Rizzinelli, 182 F. 675 (D. Idaho 1910).

[293] Sabin v. Butz, 515 F.2d 1061 (10th Cir. 1975).

[294] Mountain States Tel. & Tel. Co. v. United States, 499 F.2d 611 (Ct. Cl. 1974).

[295] 16 U.S.C. § 497 (1982).

second for a larger area under the general terms of the 1897 Organic Act. Over objections of Hopi and Navajo Indians who protested a proposed ski area on the San Francisco Peaks, one of their sacred areas, the Court of Appeals for the District of Columbia held that the 1915 Act was not a limit on Forest Service authority and that the agency could supplement the statute by resorting to the authority to "regulate . . . occupancy and use" in the 1897 Act.[296]

Numerous other applications of the Organic Act have been approved. The Court of Appeals for the Ninth Circuit allowed the imposition of a fine for operating a motorized vehicle in contravention of Forest Service regulations in an administratively designated primitive area.[297] The Court of Appeals for the Eighth Circuit upheld a game management program calling for the impoundment of stray razorback hogs.[298] In recent and bitterly-contested litigation, the Forest Service's asserted authority to regulate hardrock mining in national forests was affirmed on the basis of the 1897 Organic Act.[299] Another line of recent cases has allowed Forest Service regulation of private activities on nonfederal lands within the exterior boundaries of national forests.[300] Thus the

---

[296] Wilson v. Block, 708 F.2d 735, 756-60 (D.C. Cir.), *cert. denied,* _ U.S. _, 104 S. Ct. 371 (1983). A similar result had been reached in Sierra Club v. Hickel, 433 F.2d 24, 34-35 (9th Cir. 1970), *aff'd on other grounds sub nom.* Sierra Club v. Morton, 405 U.S. 727 (1972). In Wilderness Society v. Morton, 479 F.2d 842 (D.C. Cir.) (en banc), *cert. denied,* 411 U.S. 917 (1973), the Court of Appeals for the District of Columbia had struck down the Bureau of Land Management's issuance of special land use permits to supplement § 28 of the Mineral Lands Leasing Act of 1920, which required all construction work for the Alaska pipeline to keep within a 54-foot right-of-way. In *Wilson,* the court distinguished *Wilderness Society* on the ground that § 28 was an exclusive grant of authority to the BLM in regard to pipeline easements while the 1915 Act, 16 U.S.C. § 497 (1982), was not exclusive and could be supplemented by the Forest Service pursuant to the 1897 Organic Act. 708 F.2d at 759-60.

[297] McMichael v. United States, 355 F.2d 283 (9th Cir. 1965).

[298] Jones v. Freeman, 400 F.2d 383 (8th Cir. 1968). In *Jones* the court considered the "close and difficult question" of whether the Forest Service exceeded its regulatory authority by impounding razorback hogs foraging in the Ozark National Forest. *Id.* at 387.

[299] United States v. Weiss, 642 F.2d 296 (9th Cir. 1981). *See also, e.g.,* United States v. Goldfield Deep Mines Co. of Nevada, 644 F.2d 1307 (9th Cir. 1981), *cert. denied,* 455 U.S. 907 (1982); United States v. Langley, 587 F.Supp. 1258 (E.D. Cal. 1984).

[300] *See* United States v. Arbo, 691 F.2d 862 (9th Cir. 1982); United States v. Lindsey, 595 F.2d 5 (9th Cir. 1979). National Park Service authority to regulate activities on inholding has also been sustained. *See* United States v. Richard, 636 F.2d 236 (8th Cir. 1980); United States v. Brown, 552 F.2d 817 (8th Cir. 1977).

charter to regulate "use" in the forests is extraordinarily broad and will support Forest Service regulations and management, coupled with fines and penalties, unless some specific statute limits Forest Service powers.[301]

During the early 1950s a question arose as to the Forest Service's authority to manage roadless areas in the national forests for purely recreational purposes. In *United States v. Perko*,[302] a federal district court in Minnesota upheld the Forest Service's authority, but only on the basis of a statute mandating protection of that particular roadless area. The court intimated that the 1897 Act, by itself, did not delegate the power claimed by the Forest Service.[303] Whatever doubts *Perko* created about the scope of the agency's authority, however, were quickly dispelled through pas-

---

[301] The Organic Act allows the imposition of $500 in fines and six months imprisonment for each violation of the regulations adopted pursuant to the Act. *See* 16 U.S.C. § 551 (1982); United States v. Grimaud, 220 U.S. 506 (1911).

Only once has a court found a Forest Service regulation to be *ultra vires* of the 1897 Act. In United States v. Minchew, 10 F. Supp. 906 (S.D. Fla. 1935), a Florida district court summarily concluded that a regulation prohibiting dogs from running loose in a national forest "has no reference whatever to the purpose for which the power to make regulations is committed to the Secretary." *Id.* at 908. In United States v. Reeves, 39 F. Supp. 580 (W.D. Ark. 1941), however, an Arkansas district court chose not to follow *Minchew*. In upholding the same dog control regulation, the Arkansas court stated:

> The statute authorizes the Secretary of Agriculture in the management of the forests to issue rules "to regulate their occupancy and use." As long as such rules and regulations tend to protect the lands and faithfully preserve the interest of the people of the whole country in the lands, the courts should enforce such rules and regulations.

Id. at 583, *quoted in* United States v. Hymans, 463 F.2d 615 (10th Cir. 1972) (upholding authority to forbid nude bathing).

[302] 108 F. Supp. 315 (D. Minn. 1952), *aff'd* 204 F.2d 446 (8th Cir.), *cert. denied*, 346 U.S. 832 (1953).

[303] The court stated:

> Perhaps the most difficult question pertains to the authority of the Secretary of Agriculture in establishing Roadless Areas in this Forest Reserve. Such regulations were directed primarily to the preservation of this region for its unique recreational facilities. The purpose of establishing a Forest Reserve under the statute is to conserve the timber and water flowage within its boundaries for the citizens of the United States. Section 475, Title 16 U.S.C.A. The use of the forest for recreational purposes is incidental to this main purpose. It is urged, therefore, that any regulation by the Secretary which is directed to any purpose other than conservation of the timber and water resources is outside the purposes for which the national forests are established and hence unenforcible [sic].

Id. at 322.

sage of the Multiple-Use Sustained-Yield (MUSY) Act of 1960.[304]

3.   The Multiple-Use Sustained-Yield Act of 1960

In addition to the troublesome *Perko* decision, the 1950s brought other challenges to the Forest Service's management authority and policies.[305] Wilderness advocates, timber companies, and other users of the national forests pressured the agency and Congress to protect their respective interests.[306]

In 1956 Senator Hubert Humphrey introduced the first national forest wilderness[307] and multiple-use bills.[308] After some hesitation by the Forest Service, Chief Richard McArdle decided to support multiple-use legislation.[309] Accordingly, on February 5, 1960, the Department of Agriculture formally proposed the Forest Service's own multiple-use bill to Congress.[310]

---

[304] 16 U.S.C. §§ 528-531 (1982).

[305] Prior to the 1950s, the Forest Service's authority and management policies remained relatively stable and uncontroversial:

[F]or 55 years the Forest Service administered nearly 20 million acres of forests, rivers, mountains, and ranges with little legislative guidance, not much interest from the public and, frequently, tremendous pressures from exploiters of range, timber, and mineral resources. The Forest Service acted both as protector and as arbitrator. Pride in work, pride in the land, dedication to duty, and a tradition of keeping a distance from special interests lent credence to the characterization of the Forest Service as a "priesthood." Although not without fault, better stewardship during this period would have been hard to find.

Flamm, *Evolution of National Forest Management: The Statutory Stimulus* in CRISIS IN FEDERAL FOREST LAND MANAGEMENT, *supra* note 2, at 49.

[306] *See generally* S. DANA & S. FAIRFAX, *supra* note 52, at 179-201; H. STEEN, *supra* note 49, at 278-304.

[307] S. 4013, 84th Cong., 2d Sess. (1956).

[308] S. 3615, 84th Cong., 2d Sess. (1956). The bill would have created citizen advisory councils to recommend policy to the Secretary of Agriculture. In addition, it listed range, timber, water, minerals, wildlife, and recreation as resources to be protected.

[309] Assistant Chief of the Forest Service Edward Crafts called this the "most critical decision" of McArdle's administration. H. STEEN, *supra* note 49, at 304-05. McArdle made his decision in spite of fears among his staff that the bill could jeopardize the agency's authority if Congress failed to enact the bill. Once McArdle decided to support the bill, however, members of the agency gave their unanimous support. *Id.*

[310] *National Forests - Multiple Use and Sustained Yield: Hearings on H.R. 10,572 Before the Subcomm. on Forests of the House Comm. on Agriculture,* 86th Cong., 2d Sess. 1-4 (1960) (letter with draft bill from Acting Secretary E.L. Peterson) [hereinafter cited as *Hearings on H.R. 10,572*]. The administration's bill stated, in full:

The Forest Service bill, while not proposed as an amendment to the 1897 Act, clearly sought to confirm, if not to expand, the scope of the agency's regulatory authority under 16 U.S.C. § 551.[311] Nevertheless, during testimony on the bill, McArdle asserted confidently that the agency already had the authority to manage for recreation, range, and wildlife purposes. He declared, "The national forests have been administered for many years under the dual conservation policies of multiple use and sustained yield. There is no question as to the Department's authority to so manage the national forests, and the recommendation that this bill be enacted should not be so construed."[312] Congress generally

---

Be it enacted by the Senate and House of Representatives of the United States of America in Congress assembled, That it is the policy of the Congress that the national forests are established and shall be administered for outdoor recreation, range, timber, watershed, and wildlife and fish purposes. Nothing herein shall be construed to affect the authority of the Secretary of the Interior provided by law with respect to mineral resources.

Sec. 2. The Secretary of Agriculture is authorized and directed to develop and administer the renewable surface resources of the national forest for multiple use and sustained yield of the several products and services obtained therefrom. In the administration of the national forests due consideration shall be given to the relative values of the various resources in particular areas.

Sec. 3. In the effectuation of this Act the Secretary of Agriculture is authorized to cooperate with interested State and local governmental agencies and others in the development and management of the national forests.

Id. at 1.

[311] The first section of the Forest Service bill proposed to expand the section of the 1897 Act concerning purposes for establishment (16 U.S.C. § 475) by adding recreational, grazing, and wildlife purposes. This section was later amended, at the request of the timber interests, to state that the three new purposes were "supplemental to, but not in derogation of," the timber and water purposes of the 1897 Act. 16 U.S.C. § 528 (1982). *See* Note & Comment, *Natural Resources — National Forests — The Multiple Use - Sustained Yield Act of 1960*, 41 Or. L. Rev. 49, 53-55 (1961). Similarly, section 2 of the bill "authorized and directed" the Secretary "to develop and administer" the five resources named in the first section. Section 2, then, eliminated the possibility that the agency's administrative authority could be limited to fulfilling the purposes of water flow and timber supply. *See infra* text accompanying notes 317-19.

[312] *Hearings on H.R. 10,572, supra* note 310, at 36. Dana and Fairfax have explained the ambivalent posture the Forest Service had to maintain:

The Forest Service position in pressing the legislation was quite awkward. On the one hand, they had to convince Congress that the need for legislation was real and haste was necessary in passing the act. On the other hand, they were required to assert that the proposed legislation was nothing new; the agency had all the authority required to practice multiple use management of the forests and had been doing so for over fifty years.

accepted McArdle's claim that the bill would not affect the amount of authority over the national forests that Congress had already delegated to the executive branch.[313] With the support of virtually all national forest user groups,[314] as well as the administration,[315] Congress quickly approved a revised version of the Forest Service bill.[316]

Notwithstanding the Forest Service's official position, the MUSY Act has fortified the agency's defense against legal challenges to its regulatory authority. *McMichael v. United States*[317] illustrates the Act's effect on judicial review. In *McMichael* the Court of Appeals for the Ninth Circuit upheld the agency's authority under 16 U.S.C. § 551 to prohibit use of motorized vehicles in an administratively designated "primitive area."[318] The court concluded that in the MUSY Act Congress had "expressly manifested its approval" of the Forest Service's policy to regulate the national forests for recreational purposes.[319] The same result

---

Clearly, the agency did not want to be left, if their legislative initiative failed, with the implication that they had no authority to provide recreation facilities on the National Forests.
S. DANA & S. FAIRFAX, *supra* note 52, at 201.

[313] During floor debate on the bill, Representative Harold Cooley, Chairman of the House Committee on Agriculture, stated, "The law does not give the Secretary of Agriculture any new authority." 106 CONG. REC. 11,707 (1960). Later, Cooley said, "This bill simply tries to clarify the administrative responsibilities of the Secretary of Agriculture . . . . I do not think that we make any basic change at all." *Id.* at 11,711. Senator James Eastland, Chairman of the Senate Committee on Agriculture and Forestry, explained during the Senate floor debate, "The bill requires no change from existing policy and gives the Secretary no new authority." *Id.* at 12,078.

[314] *See generally, Hearings on H.R. 10,572, supra* note 310.

[315] *See* Letter from Richard E. McArdle to Hon. James O. Eastland (June 2, 1960), *reprinted in* 106 CONG. REC. 12,078 (1960) (expressing Forest Service's approval of MUSY bill).

[316] The enacted version included recognition of concurrent state jurisdiction over wildlife, specific authorization to establish wilderness areas, reiteration of the purposes stated in the 1897 Act for establishing forest reserves, and definitions of "multiple use" and "sustained yield." *See* 16 U.S.C. §§ 528-531 (1982).

[317] 355 F.2d 283 (9th Cir. 1965).

[318] *McMichael* was similar to United States v. Perko, 108 F.Supp. 315 (D. Minn. 1952), *aff'd* 204 F.2d 446 (8th Cir.), *cert. denied*, 346 U.S. 832 (1953), except that the primitive area in *McMichael* had no special congressional recognition. Thus, *McMichael* directly confronted the "question" raised in *Perko. See supra* note 303.

[319] The court of appeals stated:
The consistent administrative interpretation of section 551 . . . has been that while recreational considerations alone will not support the establishment of a national forest, they are appropriate subjects for regulation. Congress has tacitly shown its approval of this interpretation by appropri-

should logically flow from the broad terms of 16 U.S.C. § 551 as construed in *United States v. Grimaud*[320] and other cases,[321] but passage of the MUSY Act made the judicial task much easier.

4. The Modern Legislation

During the 1960s Congress began to restrict the Forest Service's authority through environmental legislation. The Wilderness Act of 1964[322] limited the types of management that could occur in wilderness areas. The Endangered Species Act of 1973[323] precluded activities that could adversely affect the habitats of threatened and endangered wildlife. The Wild and Scenic Rivers Act of 1968[324] required protective management of certain river corridors. The National Trails System Act of 1968[325] restricted management activities in the areas through which national scenic trails pass. Each of these laws limited the Forest Service's authority to alter the environment of specific areas.

After 1968 Congress enacted broader environmental safeguards for the national forests. The National Environmental Policy Act of 1969[326] (NEPA) required the Forest Service to analyze environmental effects prior to undertaking any major federal action. NEPA, for example, caused the Forest Service to stop development activity in all national forest roadless areas.[327] The Federal Water Pollution Control Act of 1972[328] placed general limits on activity that would violate water quality standards on national forest watercourses. The Alaska National Interest Lands Conservation Act of 1980[329] has been construed to require the Forest Service to allow reasonable access to private lands located in wilderness study lands in all national forests, not just those in

---

ating the sums required for its effectuation. Further Congress has expressly manifested its approval by actually adopting and furthering administrative policy in [the Multiple-Use Sustained-Yield Act].
McMichael, 355 F.2d at 285. The court did not examine the legislative history in the MUSY Act that sought to ensure the validity of primitive-type areas.

[320] 220 U.S. 506 (1911), discussed *supra* in text accompanying notes 285-87.

[321] *See, e.g.*, Hunt v. United States, 278 U.S. 96 (1928), and *supra* notes 292-300.

[322] 16 U.S.C. §§ 1131-1136 (1982), discussed *infra* section IX.

[323] 16 U.S.C. §§ 1531-1543 (1982), discussed *infra* notes 1548-50.

[324] 16 U.S.C. §§ 1271-1287 (1982), discussed *infra* section VIII (C).

[325] 16 U.S.C. §§ 1241-1249 (1982).

[326] 42 U.S.C. §§ 4321-4370 (1982).

[327] *See infra* text accompanying notes 1863-93.

[328] 33 U.S.C. §§ 1251-1376 (1982), discussed *infra* section V(B)(1).

[329] 16 U.S.C. §§ 3101-3233 (1982).

Alaska.[330] The NFMA's numerous procedural requirements and limitations on timber harvesting apply to all forested land managed by the Forest Service.

In some respects Congress has expanded the Forest Service's authority to regulate use and occupancy. The NFMA repealed the provision of the 1897 Organic Act that effectively had precluded even-aged timber management, thus allowing the Forest Service to engage in a broader range of silvicultural activities.[331] The Federal Land Policy and Management Act of 1976[332] (FLPMA), signed into law the same day as the NFMA, deals mainly with the Bureau of Land Management (BLM), but it has several provisions dealing with the Forest Service. For example, certain sections of FLPMA govern acquisition of land,[333] exchanges of land,[334] and grazing within the national forests.[335] FLPMA may also have expanded Forest Service authority to regulate use of water[336] and wildlife resources.[337]

FLPMA also dealt with the crucial issue of regulation of access to national forest lands. Road construction and other means of entry are of central concern to economic interests who must have legally assured, economical routes of access to their operations. On the other hand, roads must be carefully planned and constructed because they often have greater environmental impact on water and soils than the mining, timber, or other commercial operations to which they provide access. FLPMA responded to a patchwork quilt of existing statutes[338] by repealing most existing

---

[330] Montana Wilderness Ass'n v. United States Forest Service, 655 F.2d 951 (9th Cir. 1981), *cert. denied*, 455 U.S. 989 (1982) (construing access provision of Alaska National Interest Lands Conservation Act, 16 U.S.C. § 3210 (1982)).

[331] National Forest Management Act of 1976, Pub. L. No. 94-588, 13, 90 Stat. 2949, 2958.

[332] 43 U.S.C. §§ 1701-1784 (1982).

[333] *Id.* § 1715.

[334] *Id.* § 1716.

[335] *Id.* §§ 1751-1753. *See also* Public Rangelands Improvement Act of 1978, 43 U.S.C. §§ 1901-1908 (1982). On grazing in the national forests, see generally *infra* section III.

[336] *See infra* text accompanying notes 1242-52.

[337] *See infra* text accompanying notes 1642-44.

[338] Several of these laws are discussed in Biddle, *Access Rights over Public Lands Granted by the 1866 Mining Law and Recent Regulations*, 18 ROCKY MTN. MIN. L. INST. 415 (1973); Due, *Access over Public Lands*, 17 ROCKY MTN. MIN. L. INST. 171 (1971). The Public Land Law Review Commission recommended comprehensive reform. PUBLIC LAND LAW REVIEW COMM'N, ONE-THIRD OF THE NATION'S LAND 219 (1976).

access provisions,[339] protecting existing access routes by a grandfather clause,[340] and granting to the Forest Service and BLM comprehensive authority over issues relating to access.[341] Under FLPMA, the Forest Service has broad discretion to grant, condition, or deny access based on a number of factors, including economic efficiency, good engineering practices, and the need to minimize adverse environmental impacts.[342]

The more modern statutes cover several specific subject areas, but the Organic Act of 1897 continues to hold a special place in the law of the Forest Service. Congress has never amended the agency's basic grant of authority to regulate occupancy and use in 16 U.S.C. § 551. That expansive charter remains the starting

---

[339] Some 30 statutes relating to rights-of-way were repealed in part or in their entirety. Pub. L. No. 94-579, § 706(a), 90 Stat. 2743, 2793 (1976).

[340] Pub. L. No. 94-579, § 701(a), 90 Stat. 2743, 2786 (1976); *see* Legislative Note, 43 U.S.C. § 1701 (1985). In some cases this can mean that administration of a right-of-way under a repealed statute will remain with the BLM, even though the access route crosses Forest Service lands. City and County of Denver v. Bergland, 695 F.2d 465, 475-76 (10th Cir. 1982).

[341] 43 U.S.C. §§ 1761-1771 (1982).

[342] *Id.* §§ 1763, 1765. Congress intended that the Forest Service have "broad authority" to implement the FLPMA right-of-way provisions. H. R. REP. NO. 94-1163, at 22 (1976). Environmental concerns are mentioned repeatedly and expansively in the statute. *See, e.g.,* 43 U.S.C. § 1765(a) (1982) (terms and conditions in each right-of-way shall "minimize damage to scenic and esthetic values and fish and wildlife habitat and otherwise protect the environment"). *See also* S. REP. NO. 94-583, at 72. Current Forest Service regulations treat access questions under the umbrella of special use permits. 36 C.F.R. §§ 251.50-.64 (1984). Grounds for denial are set out at 36 C.F.R. § 251.54(h) (1984). The general regulations on "prohibitions" also apply to rights-of-way. 36 C.F.R. pt. 361 (1984). Separate provisions cover access by hardrock miners, whose "rights of ingress and egress" are expressly recognized by FLPMA. 43 U.S.C. § 1732(b) (1982). The Forest Service regulations dealing with hardrock mining are found at 36 C.F.R. pt. 228 (1984). They provide that miners are "entitled to access," 36 C.F.R. § 228.12 (1984); the introductory text to the regulations, first proposed in 1974, stated that access would not be "unreasonably restricted." 39 Fed. Reg. 31,317 (1974). For a current treatment of access to mineral interests, see Martz, Love & Kaiser, *Access to Mineral Interests by Right, Permit, Condemnation, or Purchase,* 28 ROCKY MTN. MIN. L. INST. 1075 (1983). On Forest Service activities in regard to hardrock mining, see generally *infra* section VI. As already mentioned, see *supra* note 330, owners of land within national forests are guaranteed "reasonable" access by the Alaska National Interest Lands Conservation Act of 1980, 16 U.S.C. § 3210 (1982). To date, the Forest Service has not adopted regulations specifically implementing § 3210. In some instances, stringent state regulations designed to protect the environment may limit access to commercial operations within the national forests. Gulf Oil Corp. v. Wyoming Oil & Gas Conservation Comm'n, 693 P.2d 227 (Wyo. 1985).

point for analysis when Forest Service regulatory authority is challenged.

5. The Role of State Law

Until recently, the relative powers of the United States and the states over the public lands remained in some doubt.[343] Then, in 1976, the Supreme Court rendered its leading decision in *Kleppe v. New Mexico*,[344] an expansive opinion acknowledging a nearly unlimited congressional authority to preempt, or override, state law on the federal lands under the Property Clause.[345] There was ample precedent for *Kleppe*,[346] but the decision was the Court's first extended and definitive treatment of the issue.

Congress can delegate to a land management agency the authority to preempt state law. The agency can then override state laws by specific actions, typically in the form of administrative regulations, that implement the general provisions in the statute.[347] As the Supreme Court has put it, "agency regulations im-

---

[343] *See generally* Engdahl, *State and Federal Power Over Federal Property*, 18 ARIZ. L. REV. 283 (1976).

[344] 426 U.S. 529 (1976).

[345] U.S. Const. art. IV, § 3, cl.2 ("The Congress shall have Power to dispose of and make all needful Rules and Regulations respecting the Territory or other Property belonging to the United States . . . "). The Court quoted older cases to the effect that federal power on the public lands is "complete" and "without limitations." 426 U.S. at 539, 540-41. The opinion is probably better understood, however, as requiring a rational relationship between the federal action and the development or preservation of federal land and resources. *See* Wilkinson, *supra* note 27, at 11-15. Federal power extends to private inholdings, and probably nearby private lands beyond the exterior boundaries of the national forests, if there is a rational basis for the regulation. *See, e.g.*, Minnesota v. Block, 660 F.2d 1240 (8th Cir. 1981), *cert. denied*, 455 U.S. 1007 (1982); United States v. Hell's Canyon Guide Services, Inc., 660 F.2d 735 (9th Cir. 1981); Gaetke, *The Boundary Waters Canoe Act of 1978: Regulating Nonfederal Property Under the Property Clause*, 60 OR. L. REV. 157 (1981). On various aspects of federal and state authority on the public lands, see Coggins & Ward, *The Law of Wildlife Management on the Federal Public Lands*, 60 OR. L. REV. 59 (1981); Note, *State and Local Control of Energy Development on Federal Lands*, 32 STAN. L. REV. 373 (1980).

A very small number of Forest Service parcels are under exclusive jurisdiction. For materials on the special rules dealing with federal enclaves, see G. COGGINS & C. WILKINSON, FEDERAL PUBLIC LAND AND RESOURCES LAW 144-60 (1981).

[346] *See, e.g.*, Hunt v. United States, 278 U.S. 96 (1928); Utah Power & Light Co. v. United States, 243 U.S. 389 (1917); Camfield v. United States, 167 U.S. 518 (1897).

[347] *See, e.g.*, United States v. Brown, 552 F.2d 817, 821 (8th Cir.), *cert. denied*, 431 U.S. 949 (1977) (Park Service regulation prohibiting hunting within national parks preempts state hunting laws).

plementing federal statutes have been held to preempt state law under the supremacy clause."[348] The Forest Service, of course, has as its principal source of authority 16 U.S.C. § 551, perhaps the most expansive charter of any federal land agency. As a result, the courts have upheld Forest Service administrative actions, not expressly set out in any statute, that have overridden state livestock fencing laws,[349] hunting laws,[350] normal rules of contract construction,[351] and a state law requiring a permit for hard-rock mining.[352]

The existence of an extensive federal power to preempt state laws, however, does not reflect the actual importance of state law within the national forests. Congress and the Forest Service may have authority to act but, until they do, state regulatory powers apply.[353] Federal statutes recognize that state law governs within the national forest in the first instance.[354] State laws often apply, for example, in the following subject matter areas: taxation;[355]

---

[348] Chrysler Corp. v. Brown, 441 U.S. 281, 295-319 (1979).

[349] Light v. United States, 220 U.S. 523 (1911).

[350] Hunt v. United States, 278 U.S. 96 (1928).

[351] Hi-Ridge Lumber Co. v. United States, 443 F.2d 452 (9th Cir. 1971).

[352] Granite Rock Co. v. California Coastal Comm'n, 768 F.2d 1077 (9th Cir. 1985).

[353] Kleppe v. New Mexico, 426 U.S. 529, 543 (1976) ("The Federal Government does not assert exclusive jurisdiction over the public lands in New Mexico, and the State is free to enforce its criminal and civil laws on those lands."); McKelvey v. United States, 260 U.S. 353, 359 (1922) ("It also is settled that the States may prescribe police regulations applicable to public land areas, so long as the regulations are not arbitrary or inconsistent with applicable congressional enactments."); Omaechevarria v. Idaho, 246 U.S. 343, 346 (1918) ("The police power of the State extends over the federal public domain, at least when there is no legislation by Congress on the subject.").

[354] *See* 16 U.S.C. § 480 (1982):

The jurisdiction, both civil and criminal, over persons within national forests shall not be affected or changed by reason of their existence, except so far as the punishment of offenses against the United States therein is concerned; the intent and meaning of this provision being that the State wherein any such national forest is situated shall not, by reason of the establishment thereof, lose its jurisdiction, nor the inhabitants thereof their rights and privileges as citizens, or be absolved from their duties as citizens of the State.

See also 16 U.S.C. § 551a (1982).

[355] *See, e.g.,* United States v. County of Fresno, 429 U.S. 452 (1977), upholding a county tax levied on the possessory interests of Forest Service employees in government-owned housing and recognizing broad state authority to tax private activities within the national forests. *See also* Commonwealth Edison Co. v. Montana, 453 U.S. 609 (1981). The intergovernmental immunities doctrine, however, prohibits direct taxation of federal property and discriminatory taxes

regulation of hunting and fishing;[356] the diversion of water and the setting of minimum stream flows;[357] and regulation of hardrock mining activities.[358] Although generalities can be somewhat treacherous, the statutes and traditional policies in the field create a framework in which the states exercise broad authority within the national forests in regard to wildlife and water; somewhat less power in regard to hardrock mining; and comparatively little power over mineral leasing, grazing, recreation, and timber operations. These prerogatives of the states increasingly have been employed to provide for environmental regulation more stringent than that required by federal land management agencies.[359]

Facets of management within the national forests, then, are effectively carried on as a partnership with the states. The NFMA reflects this, and requires consultation and coordination with state

---

directed at those dealing with federal entities. *See County of Fresno,* 429 U.S. at 460-64; Van Brocklin v. Tennessee, 117 U.S. 151 (1886).

[356] Baldwin v. Montana Fish & Game Comm'n, 436 U.S. 371 (1978). *See generally infra* section VII (D).

[357] *See infra* text accompanying notes 1086-89.

[358] State ex rel. Andrus v. Click, 97 Idaho 791, 554 P.2d 969 (1976); State ex rel. Cox v. Hibbard, 31 Or. App. 269, 570 P.2d 1190 (1977). In two other cases, courts recognized state power to impose reasonable regulations on hardrock mining on federal lands but struck down county land use provisions flatly prohibiting hardrock mining on the areas of public lands in question. Brubaker v. Board of County Comm'rs of El Paso County, 652 P.2d 1050 (Colo. 1982); Elliott v. Oregon Int'l Mining Co., 60 Or. App. 474, 654 P.2d 663 (1982). Granite Rock Co. v. California Coastal Comm'n, 768 F.2d 1077 (9th Cir. 1985), held invalid a state permitting scheme as applied to a miner working under an operating plan approved by the Forest Service. The court acknowledged that a state "may enact environmental regulations in addition to those established by federal agencies," but that an independent state permitting process "would undermine the Forest Service's own permitting authority and thus is preempted." *Id.* at 1083.

The federal mineral leasing statutes, regulations, and lease provisions are more comprehensive than is the case with hardrock mining, with the result that there is generally less room for state law to operate. *See generally* Ventura County v. Gulf Oil Corp., 601 F.2d 1080 (9th Cir. 1979), *aff'd,* 445 U.S. 947 (1980). State provisions relating to federal mineral leasing, however, have been approved in Texas Oil & Gas Corp. v. Phillips Petroleum Co., 277 F. Supp. 366 (W.D. Okla. 1967), *aff'd per curiam,* 406 F.2d 1303 (10th Cir.), *cert. denied,* 396 U.S. 829 (1969) (upholding state forced pooling provisions) and *Wyoming Oil & Gas Conservation Comm'n,* 693 P.2d 227 (Wyo. 1985) (upholding state-imposed restrictions, to provide environmental protection, on access to drilling operations within national forest).

[359] *See, e.g.,* the authorities cited *supra* in note 358.

and local governments.[360] The states properly consider themselves important factors in the Forest Service planning process.[361]

B. Judicial Review of Forest Service Planning Under the NFMA

After passing the 1897 Organic Act, Congress generally left national forest management policy to the judgment of the agency. The MUSY Act continued the tradition of congressional deference, adding only the limitation that the agency give due consideration to all resources. The NFMA left intact the agency's authority to regulate most uses within the national forests. Nevertheless, the 1976 Act fundamentally altered the traditional relationship between Congress, the courts, and the Forest Service by adding procedural requirements for planning and by imposing substantive restrictions on timber harvest in the national forests.

Senators Humphrey and Randolph—the two principal sponsors of NFMA legislation—exemplified the change in Congress' attitude toward the Forest Service. Both senators had actively supported the MUSY Act in 1960.[362] Humphrey had generously praised the Forest Service as a dedicated, conscientious, established agency.[363] Except for concern over wilderness areas, Humphrey and his congressional colleagues had few misgivings about entrusting national forest management to the agency's professional judgment.

By 1976 the mood of Congress had shifted dramatically in the wake of the clearcutting controversy. Upon introducing his bill, Humphrey observed that the MUSY Act had not succeeded and that a "fundamental reform" was needed.[364] Humphrey stated: "We have had 15 years since the 1960 Multiple Use and Sustained Yield Act was passed. Much has happened, and as we look at what has transpired, the need for improvement is evident."[365]

---

[360] *See, e.g.*, 16 U.S.C. §§ 1604(a), 1612 (1982). *See also, e.g.*, Intergovernmental Cooperation Act, 42 U.S.C. §§ 4231-4233 (1982).

[361] *See, e.g.*, C. RICHMOND, STATE PARTICIPATION IN FEDERAL LAND PLANNING (1983).

[362] *See* 122 CONG. REC. 5619 (1976) (remarks of Sen. Humphrey).

[363] 106 CONG. REC. 12,083-84 (1960). Humphrey stated, "I know of no service in the Government which has more dedicated people or a group of more conscientious or better trained public servants who are more willing to make the necessary sacrifices in order to have a good program." *Id.* at 12,084.

[364] 122 CONG. REC. 5618-19 (1976).

[365] *Id.* at 5619.

He identified the central problem as the predominance of timber production over protection of other resources. Humphrey declared:

The days have ended when the forest may be viewed only as trees and trees viewed only as timber. The soil and the water, the grasses and the shrubs, the fish and the wildlife, and the beauty that is the forest must become integral parts of resource managers' thinking and actions.[366]

During the Senate hearings Humphrey observed that the Forest Service's record had brought into question the extent to which the agency could be trusted to guard and manage public resources.[367] He proposed that the NFMA legislation be shaped to prevent the Forest Service from "turning the national forests into tree production programs which override other values."[368]

Senator Randolph and other members of Congress shared Humphrey's views. Randolph's bill included a finding that the Forest Service had "utilized on the national forests of the United States management practices—such as excessive clearcutting—which are unduly harmful to the environment and to uses of the national forest other than timber production."[369] Similarly, Senator Floyd K. Haskell of Colorado, chairman of the Senate Subcommittee on the Environment and Land Resources, stated that protection of nontimber resources "must be assigned as great a priority in any forest management policy as the production of timber."[370] Haskell favored legislation establishing a basic policy framework and recognizing that "the era of full delegation of land management decisionmaking authority to Federal agencies is over."[371]

Congressional opinion differed over the degree of specificity that the management guidelines should contain. Senator Humphrey advocated broad policy guidelines that would give agency managers flexibility to make decisions based on professional expertise and local conditions.[372] Senator Randolph, on the other hand, pro-

---

[366] *Id.*

[367] SENATE NFMA HEARINGS, *supra* note 194, at 260.

[368] *Id.* at 262.

[369] S. 2926, 94th Cong., 2d Sess. 2(a)(2) (1976), *reprinted in* SENATE NFMA HEARINGS, *supra* note 194, at 2.

[370] SENATE NFMA HEARINGS, *supra* note 194, at 1054.

[371] *Id.* at 1055. Haskell's subcommittee was also working on comprehensive legislation to guide management of lands administered by the Bureau of Land Management. *See* S. REP. No. 583, 94th Cong., 1st Sess. (1975).

[372] Humphrey testified, "This is a complex and scientific profession. We need to provide effective guidance, both in law and regulation, but allow enough flexi-

posed specific timber management standards and procedures.[373] The Senate settled on a compromise between flexibility and specificity. At the conclusion of the Senate joint committee mark-up sessions, Senator Lee Metcalf of Montana, acting chairman of the Interior and Insular Affairs Committee, commented that the Humphrey and Randolph bills had been "shuffled together."[374]

A similar shuffling process occurred in the House. While the House bill omitted some of the Senate provisions, the bill contained several specific requirements. Representative John Melcher of Montana, acting chairman of the House Subcommittee on Forests, stated that the House bill "directs that the Forest Service must protect watersheds, . . . must protect streams, must protect wildlife habitat, and must preserve esthetic values in planning all of the timber sales in any of the units of the national forest."[375] Reforestation was another area where both the House and Senate chose to give instructions.[376] On the other hand, Congress declined to write prescriptions on issues such as the size of clearcuts and the use of pesticides.

The remarks of key legislators suggest that the NFMA amounted to a new organic act for the Forest Service. For example, Representative Thomas S. Foley of Washington, chairman of the House Agriculture Committee, stated that the NFMA established "the strongest environmental and silvicultural controls ever imposed by any legislation dealing with the national forests."[377]

---

bility so that the professional foresters can do the job, rather than lawyers and judges." SENATE NFMA HEARINGS, *supra* note 194, at 262.

[373] S. 2926, 94th Cong., 2d Sess. § 2(b) (1976), *reprinted in* SENATE NFMA HEARINGS, *supra* note 194, at 3. Randolph had engaged in a decade-long skirmish with the Forest Service over clearcutting practices on the Monongahela National Forest in West Virginia. *See infra* text accompanying notes 722-24.

[374] *Senate Comm. on Agriculture and Forestry and Senate Comm. on Interior and Insular Affairs, Transcript of Proceedings, S. 3091 As Amended*, May 4, 1976, at 118, located in Senate Comm. on Agriculture and Forestry files, Washington, D.C. [hereinafter cited as *[date] Transcript of Senate Mark-up*]. Senator Humphrey, acknowledging that many features of the Randolph bill had been incorporated into the Senate bill, said that the bill "has the flexibility and yet provides guidelines to the Forest Service." *Id.* at 116-17.

[375] 122 CONG. REC. 30,526 (1976), *reprinted in* RPA COMPILATION, *supra* note 173, at 662.

[376] 16 U.S.C. § 1604(g)(3)(E)(ii) (1982).

[377] 122 CONG. REC. 34,227 (1976), *reprinted in* RPA COMPILATION, *supra* note 173, at 782.

Similarly, Senator Henry M. Jackson of Washington, Chairman of the Senate Interior and Insular Affairs Committee, said that the NFMA provided "the most comprehensive set of policy guidelines for management of our national forests

Although the significance of the NFMA with respect to Forest Service authority should not be overstated, there is no doubt that the NFMA's central purpose was to reform national forest timber management policies. In regard to timber management, the NFMA "put new responsibilities on the Forest Service, heavier than they have ever had in the past."[378] The NFMA does not, however, alter the agency's broad multiple-use management authority over nontimber resources.

By abandoning its traditionally deferential role in national forest management, Congress also implicitly redefined the role of the courts. For most of its lifetime, the Forest Service was largely immune from judicial oversight. For example, between 1911 and 1972 the agency was in the Supreme Court on just two occasions.[379] Forest Service decisions were considered protected by an aura of virtual unreviewability and the few court challenges were routinely dismissed.

The classic example of deferential review is the 1971 district court opinion in *Sierra Club v. Hardin*.[380] The Forest Service had approved a plan to liquidate as soon as possible the old-growth timber on about ninety-five percent of the commercial forest land in the Tongass National Forest in southeast Alaska. The court rejected the Sierra Club's argument that the agency was violating the MUSY Act by administering the Tongass National Forest predominantly for timber production:

> While the material undoubtedly shows the overwhelming commitment of the Tongass National Forest to timber harvest objectives in

which Congress has ever adopted." 122 CONG. REC. 33,837 (1976), *reprinted in* RPA COMPILATION, *supra* note 173, at 773.

[378] *May 4, 1976, Transcript of Senate Mark-up, supra* note 374, at 117 (remarks of Sen. Humphrey).

[379] *See* United States v. Grimaud, 220 U.S. 506 (1911); Light v. United States, 220 U.S. 523 (1911); Utah Power & Light Co. v. United States, 243 U.S. 389 (1917); Hunt v. United States, 278 U.S. 96 (1928); Sierra Club v. Morton, 405 U.S. 727 (1972). We are aware of no injunction being sustained against any Forest Service activity until Parker v. United States, 309 F.Supp. 593 (D. Colo. 1970), *aff'd*, 448 F.2d 793 (10th Cir. 1971).

[380] 325 F. Supp. 99 (D. Alaska 1971), *rev'd sub nom.* Sierra Club v. Butz, 3 ENVTL. L. REP. (ENVTL. L. INST.) 20,292 (9th Cir. 1973). *See also* Kisner v. Butz, 350 F. Supp. 310, 324-25 (N.D.W. Va. 1972); Dorothy Thomas Found., Inc. v. Hardin, 317 F. Supp. 1072 (W.D.N.C. 1970). The cases are analyzed in depth in Coggins, *supra* note 132, at 243-67. *See also* Comment, *The Conservationists and the Public Lands: Administrative and Judicial Remedies Relating to the Use and Disposition of the Public Lands Administered by the Department of the Interior*, 68 MICH. L. REV. 1200 (1970).

preference to other multiple use values, Congress has given no indication as to the weight to be assigned each value and it must be assumed that the decision as to the proper mix of uses within any particular area is left to the sound discretion and expertise of the Forest Service.[381]

The *Monongahela* decision by the Court of Appeals for the Fourth Circuit in 1975[382] stands in stark contrast to the earlier multiple-use cases. The injunction against clearcutting on the Monongahela National Forest in West Virginia was based on a strict interpretation of the timber sale provision of the 1897 Organic Act. The court made a detailed analysis of the statutory language, reviewing the background and legislative history of the Act in order to determine the purposes of Congress.

The traditional deference to Forest Service decisions has changed due both to the passage of modern statutes and a changing perception of the role of the judiciary in public law disputes. NEPA has been employed to provide judicial oversight of Forest Service activities. Because of inadequate environmental analysis by the agency, courts have delayed timber sales,[383] road developments,[384] herbicide spraying,[385] and other planned activities. The Endangered Species Act has also been employed to require reconsideration of development projects.[386] In these cases the courts have generally applied a "hard look" standard of review.[387]

---

[381] *Id.* at 123. For a leading article arguing that the MUSY Act in fact provides judicially enforceable standards, *see* Coggins, *supra* note 132. The reasoning was followed in dictum in National Wildlife Federation v. United States Forest Service, 592 F. Supp. 931, 938 (D. Or. 1984), *appeal docketed*, No. 84-4274 (9th Cir., Oct. 29, 1984) ("The standards in the MUSY are broad but they exist. The MUSY is not entirely discretionary.").

[382] West Virginia Div. of the Izaak Walton League of Am. v. Butz, 522 F.2d 945 (4th Cir. 1975).

[383] *E.g.*, California v. Block, 690 F.2d 753 (9th Cir. 1982).

[384] Northwest Indian Cemetery Protective Ass'n v. Peterson, 764 F.2d 581 (9th Cir. 1985); Thomas v. Peterson, 753 F.2d 754 (9th Cir. 1985); Foundation for North Am. Wild Sheep v. United States, 681 F.2d 1172 (9th Cir. 1982); Earth First v. Block, 569 F. Supp. 415 (D. Or. 1983).

[385] *E.g.*, Merrell v. Block, 747 F.2d 1240 (9th Cir. 1984).

[386] *See* Thomas v. Peterson, 753 F.2d 754 (9th Cir. 1985).

[387] The "hard look" standard of judicial review was first articulated by Judge Leventhal. *See, e.g.*, Pikes Peak Broadcasting Co. v. FCC, 422 F.2d 827 (D.C. Cir. 1972). The leading Supreme Court opinion on strict review is Citizens to Preserve Overton Park v. Volpe, 401 U.S. 402 (1971). The Court has employed the "hard look" doctrine with somewhat less vigor in recent cases, see Baltimore Gas & Electric Co. v. Natural Resources Defense Council, 462 U.S. 87, 97-100 (1983); Kleppe v. Sierra Club, 427 U.S. 390, 410 n.21 (1976), but there is no doubt that modern federal judicial review remains substantially more rigorous

The NFMA will require courts to scrutinize forest plans, and activities based on those plans, on both procedural and substantive grounds. The 1976 Act contains several substantive guidelines that are markedly more specific than the broad multiple-use language at issue in *Hardin*, although less absolute than the Organic Act provision in *Monongahela*. In addition, the NFMA requires forest plans to be developed in accordance with NEPA's procedural requirements.[388] The Forest Service has correctly stated the controlling law in advising its planners that reviewing courts are likely to conduct a "searching inquiry" into the procedural adequacy of forest plans and to require "full, fair, and bona fide compliance" with the NFMA.[389] Once the plans become final and are determined to be valid, they themselves become law. Much like zoning requirements or administrative regulations, the plans are controlling and judicially enforceable until properly revised.[390]

---

than before *Overton Park* in 1971. *See generally* J. BONINE & T. MCGARITY, THE LAW OF ENVIRONMENTAL PROTECTION 132-36 (1984), and the authorities cited therein.

[388] 16 U.S.C. § 1604(g)(1) (1982).

[389] PRINCIPLES OF PLANNING, *supra* note 29 at 148 set out the following analysis:

For the planning document (and accompanying final EIS), the underlying premise for judicial review will probably be 5 USC Section 706(2)(D). At least the Ninth Circuit Court of Appeals has specifically named this as the proper scope of review for an EIS under NEPA (*Lathan v. Brinegar*, 506 F.2d 677 (9th Cir. 1974)). The actual review used by the Ninth Circuit and the majority of other courts under 5 USC 706(2)(D) to determine whether or not an EIS satisfies NEPA's procedural compliance, has been one of "reasonable compliance" (sometimes referred to as Rule of Reason) or to the "fullest extent possible." These two tests are representative of the range of review used by most courts under 5 USC 706(2)(D). Review under either of these tests provides for a searching inquiry into the facts, data, and other information supporting procedural compliance in preparing a document. Application of these tests of review to planning documents indicates that the plan must show full, fair, and bona fide compliance with NFMA and 36 CFR 219. What full, fair, and bona fide compliance will mean to each reviewing court will ultimately be fashioned to meet the needs of the particular case in which the tests are applied. The courts will have to fix precise measures of compliance to the needs of a particular case (*American Timber Co. v. Berglund*, 473 F. Supp. 310 (D. Mont., 1979)). NEPA cases indicate that the precise measure of compliance in the majority of courts will be guided by the test of "reasonable compliance" rather than "to the fullest extent possible." Some courts may not use either test but adopt the "arbitrary and capricious" standard to test the adequacy of a regional or Forest plan. This standard may be cited by a minority of courts, however.

Id.

[390] *See* 16 U.S.C. § 1604(i) (1982):

A useful example of pre-NFMA forest planning litigation is *American Timber Co. v. Berglund.*[391] In that case a group of sawmill owners challenged the Flathead National Forest timber management plan EIS that proposed a substantial reduction in the quantity of timber to be sold. The reduction resulted from alteration of the suitable land base, the timber harvest conversion period, and projections of future timber yields. Although these and other issues involved complex economic and silvicultural questions, the court analyzed each issue and determined that the EIS was adequate in some respects and not in others.

American Timber is instructive because it involves forest management issues that are likely to arise in challenges to NFMA plans. Since the Flathead plan was not developed under NFMA guidelines, the court did not examine the plan for compliance with the Act. Nevertheless, the court made a probing, methodical review, applying a standard of review that fit the facts of the case.[392]

As much of this Article will demonstrate, review of NFMA planning decisions will call for judicial analysis of complex statutory provisions and even more complex factual situations. General formulations of principles of judicial review are notoriously slippery—they almost always seem to dissolve into the specific facts, law, expertise, and equities of the case at bar. But if the NFMA stands for anything it is that the mystique is gone from federal timber law. The courts have been called in to measure agency performance against new statutory provisions of considerable specificity—and that basic fact of principled judicial oversight and enforcement has had, and will continue to have, a pronounced influence on the nature of Forest Service decisionmaking.

Resource plans and permits, contracts, and other instruments for the use and occupancy of National Forest System lands shall be consistent with the land management plans. Those resource plans and permits, contracts, and other such instruments currently in existence shall be revised as soon as practicable to be made consistent with such plans. When land management plans are revised, resource plans and permits, contracts, and other instruments, when necessary, shall be revised as soon as practicable. Any revision in present or future permits, contracts, and other instruments made pursuant to this section shall be subject to valid existing rights.
Id.

[391] 473 F. Supp. 310 (D. Mont. 1979).

[392] For helpful opinions involving judicial review of BLM planning, see *American Motorcyclist Ass'n v. Watt,* 534 F. Supp. 923 (C.D. Cal. 1981), *aff'd,* 714 F.2d 962 (9th Cir. 1983); *American Motorcyclist Ass'n v. Watt,* 543 F. Supp. 789 (C.D. Cal. 1982).

C. The Relationship Between Local and National Planning

Before examining the requirements of the NFMA and the regulations, it is necessary to understand the relationship between local and national planning. Although the relationship between the national and field offices remains clouded due to vague directions by Congress, this section attempts to clarify the applicable law.

1. Background of the Controversy

Uneasiness over the respective roles of local and national planning began with the advent of land use planning in the 1960s. Frequently the objectives of land use planning—ensuring resource protection and multiple use management—conflicted with efforts to increase resource outputs. Furthermore, land use planning required basic changes in traditional resource management planning assumptions.

Prior to the 1960s forest planners assumed that virtually all commercial forest land was available for timber sales.[393] Based on the amount of available commercial land, local planners calculated the "allowable cut" for individual national forests.[394] The national forests would, in turn, schedule timber sales based on the allowable cut. The Forest Service simply aggregated the allowable cuts of the local forests to determine the national allowable cut.[395] The national office only disseminated general policy direction and congressional appropriations.

Unlike pre-1960s timber planning, modern land use planning did not assume that timber production was an appropriate use of all available commercial forest land. Some land use zones prohibited any timber cutting, while other zones required less than full production.[396] As a result, national forests began to classify more commercial land as unavailable for full timber production, to reduce their allowable cuts, and to schedule fewer timber sales.[397]

---

[393] *See infra* text accompanying notes 633-37.

[394] Under the new NFMA regulations, nonproductive land is not automatically excluded from the allowable cut. *See infra* section IV(D).

[395] G. ROBINSON, *supra* note 2, at 65.

[396] Timber land use classifications are discussed further *infra* text accompanying notes 766-83.

[397] Timber sales dropped from 12.2 billion board feet (bbf) in 1963, to 11.7 bbf in 1964, and to 11.4 in 1966. [1966 ANNUAL] REPORT OF THE CHIEF 13 (1960) [hereinafter cited as 1966 ANNUAL REPORT OF THE CHIEF]. Between 1966 and 1971 the national allowable cut rose by less than 0.5 bbf. REPORT OF

As the Forest Service reduced timber sales on some national forests, the timber industry began to complain about the loss of land available for timber production.[398] The industry criticized the Forest Service for allowing local planning officials to sacrifice national lumber and housing priorities in order to placate local concerns.[399] Partly in response to this criticism, the Forest Service instituted the more hierarchical unit planning system.[400] Regional offices issued approximate targets for timber production in order to provide additional guidance to local planners. Nevertheless, local planners continued to reduce the amount of land available for full timber production on many national forests.[401]

2. The Issue and Why It Is Important

The basic local-national planning issue is whether Congress intended local forest plans to meet the resource output goals of the RPA Program. There are three general theories on the question. The "top-down" theory maintains that Congress did not intend to allow parochial priorities of local plans to frustrate achievement of national needs.[402] The "bottom-up" theory, on the other hand, ar-

THE PRESIDENT'S ADVISORY PANEL ON TIMBER AND THE ENVIRONMENT 161 (1973). Timber management plans prepared in the early 1970s often called for sizeable reductions in allowable cut. *Id.* at 162-63.

[398] During hearings on the NFMA, for instance, the National Forest Products Association (NFPA) testified:

As part of the Forest Service land use planning process, large blocks of land are classified into land use zones which severely restrict timber management activities. This is often done without any real evidence that timber related activities are, in fact, incompatible with other management objectives.

Forest Management Practices: Hearings Before the Subcommittee on Forests of the House Committee on Agriculture, 94th Cong., 2d Sess. 445 (1976) [hereinafter cited as *House NFMA Hearings*].

[399] The NFPA testified: "In making major land use decisions, field units are responding primarily to local pressures, without guidance on how national policy and goals should be translated into local resource decisions. Local decisions often are made to eliminate or reduce controversy. Local land use decisions once made are difficult to change." *Id.* at 442. Later the NFPA reiterated, "The lack of national goals for the National Forests allows local pressures to influence output decisions to a much greater extent than national priorities." *Id.* at 445.

[400] *See supra* text accompanying notes 149-55.

[401] For example, the Umpqua National Forest in 1978 reduced its allowable cut by 17.2 million board feet as a result of unit planning. UMPQUA NAT'L FOREST LMP, *supra* note 117, at 69.

[402] For instance, the National Forest Products Association advised the Committee of Scientists, "Section 6(g)(3) of the NFMA requires that National Forest land management plans be developed to achieve the goals of the RPA Pro-

gues that the NFMA wrote into law the Forest Service's tradition of decentralized control over local land use decisions. A third theory—which most closely characterizes the Forest Service's current position—is that the RPA and NFMA call for an "iterative" exchange of information from local plans and direction from national plans.[403]

The local-national question is important because the answer will determine the location of decisionmaking authority within the Forest Service. Traditionally, the agency has followed Pinchot's directive that local decisions are to be made on local grounds.[404] Decisions on budget allocations, policy direction, and regulations have always originated in the Chief's office.[405] However, the agency has left management planning decisions about such issues as timber sales, range allotments, and recreation zoning to the local ranger districts and national forests.[406]

---

gram." NATIONAL FOREST PROD. ASS'N, RELATIONSHIP OF PLANNING LEVELS, *reprinted in Committee of Scientists, [Unpublished] Minutes of Meeting, Oct. 9, 1978.* [Hereinafter all references to Minutes of the Committee of Scientists will be cited as *Committee of Scientists, Minutes of* [date]. These are on file with the Land Management Planning Office, Forest Service, U.S. Dep't of Agriculture, Washington, D.C.] The NFPA suggested that the NFMA regulations should "force a change in the existing National Forest planning structure, which is still basically bottom up." *Id.* Similarly, the Society of American Foresters' Task Force on RPA Implementation has interpreted § 6(g)(3) as requiring top-down planning.

> Regardless of the iterations, feedback loops, or other procedures enabling a "bottom up" rather than "top down" approach to Program development, once the Program is established at the national level the nationally defined goals become controlling. Section 6(g)(3) requires that land management plans (now termed forest plans) be developed "to achieve the goals of the Program."

SOCIETY OF AMERICAN FORESTERS, THE RPA PROCESS — 1980, at 10 (1981). The report continues:

> For the purpose of this RPA evaluation, we will assume the centralized model is required by the legislation although this review recognizes the difficulty of attempting centralized management of a geographically and politically decentralized land resource which has a long tradition of decentralized management.

Id. at 11.

[403] The NFMA regulations state: "The planning process is essentially iterative in that the information from the forest level flows up to the national level where in turn information in the RPA Program flows back to the forest level." 36 C.F.R. § 219.4(a) (1984).

[404] *See supra* note 269.

[405] *See supra* notes 52, 165-68.

[406] *See supra* text accompanying notes 63-109.

A top-down approach would change the agency's traditional planning and decisionmaking processes. Local planners would receive binding targets or quotas for various resources. These targets would control local officials' decisions on matters traditionally left to their discretion. For example, a high RPA target for dispersed or wilderness recreation on a national forest would require the local planners to zone land accordingly, even if they agreed that the land was better suited for nonrecreational uses. On the other hand, a high timber production target would require enough land to be zoned to meet that target. As former Assistant Secretary of Agriculture John Crowell observed, "The [RPA] process has great potential for vastly increasing outputs from the national forest system . . . ."[407]

3.ˎ The Forest Service's Interpretation

The Forest Service's current position is essentially an uneasy compromise between the top-down and bottom-up theories. The NFMA regulations create a hierarchical structure designed to meet both national and local needs. At the top of the hierarchy is the President's Statement of Policy,[408] which establishes broad

---

[407] In 1977 John B. Crowell—who in 1981 became an Assistant Secretary for Conservation, Research, and Education in the Department of Agriculture —wrote the following to the Committee of Scientists:
> Never to be lost sight of is the overriding requirement that the land management plans for each national forest are the blueprints by which each national forest will meet its portion of the national goals prescribed by the overall Program.
>
> For a number of years now, the Forest Service has been engaged in developing land management plans for each national forest. Unfortunately, none of these plans have been developed with any direction or guidance concerning the volume of outputs they are expected to achieve over both short and long-term for the many amenities provided by the national forests. In summary, the planning process has been taking place from the bottom upward. RPA reverses that process and calls for the planning to take place in a logical progression down to application on the ground with clear direction for each unit of the national forest system to contribute a share of outputs toward the national goals prescribed by the Program. *The prescribed process has great potential for vastly increasing outputs from the national forest system*, reducing the unit costs of such outputs, and assuring a combination of outputs which better serve the national interest.

Letter from John B. Crowell, Jr., Chairman, Forest Industries Task Group on Implementation of Forestry Legislation, to Dr. Arthur W. Cooper, Chairman, Committee of Scientists (July 18, 1977) (emphasis added), *reprinted in Committee of Scientists, Minutes of July 27-28, 1977.*

[408] For a discussion of the Statement of Policy and the RPA, *see supra* text accompanying notes 175-90.

policy goals for funding and managing the national forests.[409] The
Statement goals are based on the Department of Agriculture's
RPA Program goals and objectives. The Forest Service's national
office distributes the Program objectives among the nine Forest
Service regions.[410] Each region then divides its share of the
Program objectives among the various national forests.[411] Finally,
each national forest develops a draft forest plan in which at least
one alternative must incorporate the forest's share of its regional
RPA objectives.[412]

The Forest Service does not consider the RPA Program objectives to be legally binding on the local forest plans. If the selected
alternative does not meet the forest's share of the RPA objectives,
the NFMA regulations provide for negotiation and adjustment of
the objectives.[413] The capability information in the selected forest
plan will be incorporated into the next revision of the RPA
Program.[414] However, if there is a dramatic difference between

---

[409] In the Analysis of Public Comment accompanying the 1982 revised
NFMA regulations, the agency states: "There should be no misunderstanding
. . . of the preeminent role of the President's Statement or [sic] Policy and the
RPA Program upon which the statement is based. That role is firmly established
by the Renewable Resources Planning Act." 47 Fed. Reg. 43,026, 43,028
(1982). The Forest Service is somewhat uncertain, however, about the legal effect of congressional actions permitted by section 8(a) of the RPA. 16 U.S.C. §
1606(a) (1982). If Congress adopts or revises a President's Statement by enacting it as a statute or as an appropriation act, the statement becomes "law." Interview with Clarence W. Brizee, Ass't Gen. Counsel, Natural Resources Div.,
Office of Gen. Counsel, U.S. Dep't of Agriculture, in Washington, D.C. (June
23, 1983). If Congress's response is in the form of a committee report, the Forest
Service would attempt to "glean" congressional intent. *Id.* The Forest Service is
also uncertain whether congressional inaction would mean that Congress had
"adopted" the Statement or merely "acquiesced" and whether it would make
any practical difference. Interview with Mark A. Reimers, Director of Legislative Affairs, Forest Service, U.S. Dep't of Agriculture, in Washington, D.C.
(June 21, 1983). Finally, the effect of either the Senate or the House adopting a
resolution of disapproval is uncertain. One possibility is that the President would
have to submit a different Statement of Policy. Interview with Clarence W.
Brizee, *supra.* The issue is clouded, however, by the Supreme Court's ruling that
"one-house vetoes" of executive action are unconstitutional. Immigration and
Naturalization Service v. Chadha, 462 U.S. 919 (1983). If the RPA's resolution
of disapproval is construed as a one-house veto, then presumably it would have
no effect on the President's Statement of Policy.
[410] 36 C.F.R. § 219.4(b)(1)(ii) (1984).
[411] *Id.* § 219.4(b)(2).
[412] *Id.* § 219.4(b)(3).
[413] *Id.*
[414] Interview with Thomas E. Hamilton, Director, Resources Program &
Assessment Staff, Forest Service, U.S. Dep't of Agriculture, in Washington,
D.C. (Jan. 31, 1985). In the Analysis of Public Comment section preceding the

local forest plans and RPA objectives, then the Forest Service—as a matter of policy—might attempt to revise local plans to reduce the disparity.[415]

The Forest Service regards the regional foresters as mediators between local NFMA plans and the RPA Program.[416] Under the 1982 planning regulations the regional foresters are responsible for approving local forest plans.[417] The regional forester has the discretion to shift a portion of a forest's tentative RPA objective to another forest[418] or to request a reduction in the region's objective.[419] Such a regional reduction, however, would require approval by the Chief.[420] The NFMA regulations do not specifically address the issue of whether the Chief can or must grant a regional forester's request for an adjustment in RPA objectives. However, the 1982 regulations indicate that national planning goals are only tentatively selected and, thus, can be revised by the Chief.[421]

4. Congressional Intent

Although Congress enacted the NFMA as an amendment to the RPA, the Forest Service has found that they "do not fit like a plug in a socket."[422] The RPA and NFMA deal with two different levels and traditions of Forest Service planning. The RPA is a

---

1982 NFMA regulations, the agency stated: "The analysis of [the 1985 RPA Program] . . . is to be based in part on data generated in the forest planning process . . . . This process is an iterative one, both during each round of planning, and between rounds. In this manner each Forest's capabilities and needs are reflected in the National RPA program." 47 Fed. Reg. 43,026, 43,028 (1982). Similarly, the regulations specify that "local supply capabilities . . . will be considered" by the Chief while assigning resource goals to each region. 36 C.F.R. § 219.4(b)(1)(ii) (1984).

[415] Interview with Thomas E. Hamilton, *supra* note 414. The NFMA regulations provide that local plans "may be revised . . . when changes in RPA policies, goals, or objectives would have a significant effect on forest level programs." *Id.* § 219.10(g). See also *1985 Forest Service Budget, supra* note 10, at 1502. ("The approved 1985 RPA Program may necessitate revision or amendment to the Regional Guides and Forest Plans.")

[416] Interview with Thomas E. Hamilton, Director of Resources Program & Assessment, Forest Service, U.S. Dep't of Agriculture, in Washington, D.C. (June 17, 1983).

[417] 36 C.F.R. § 219.4(b)(3) (1984).

[418] Interview with Thomas E. Hamilton, *supra* note 416.

[419] 36 C.F.R. § 219.4(b)(2) (1984).

[420] *Id.*

[421] *Id.*

[422] Interview with Clarence W. Brizee, *supra* note 409.

national planning law that mentions local planning only in passing. In enacting the NFMA Congress did not consider in detail exactly how local and national levels of planning would fit together.[423] Understandably, attempts by the Forest Service to merge the two laws into a coherent planning process have resulted in confusion and dissension in the agency.[424]

---

[423] Interview with Mark A. Reimers, *supra* note 409.

[424] Some of the problems stemming from the RPA-NFMA planning process are expressed in the following letters from two forest supervisors to the regional forester for the Pacific Northwest region. The supervisors both strongly objected to the regional forester's selection of a regional guide that differed from the local forest plans. The supervisor of the Wallowa-Whitman National Forest in Oregon wrote:

> I am concerned with the failure of the RPA Regional Preferred Alternative to acknowledge the Wallowa-Whitman National Forest Plan Preferred Alternative. The Forest Preferred Alternative has a substantially higher commodity emphasis than the current situation, yet is one for which we can provide strong supporting rationale and can probably gain a reasonable level of public support. It, as you have observed, was not without controversy, but appeared to balance the concerns equitably between those well-entrenched battle lines.
>
> Forest Plan Alternative A, the most commodity oriented alternative generated by the Wallowa-Whitman, is instead selected for the Regional Preferred Alternative (RPA Alternative L). This alternative meets only minimum management requirements for wildlife and other resources, and substantially reduces visual quality objectives across the entire Forest. Selecting it for the Regional Preferred dismisses concerns for elk cover and diversity of recreation experience which were identified as major issues in our public involvement process. Alternative A is selected not only for the Regional Preferred Alternative, but is also selected for the Regional high nonmarket alternative. This is puzzling to say the least. It further appears, given the mix of alternatives selected, that no rational combination exists which will satisfy the Regional timber target. The RPA process would appear to consider this the most significant target. I do not believe that was the intent of Congress in the linking of the RPA and National Forest Management Act processes. The process envisioned by the Forest Service is one of two-way communication of information, not only a top-down assignment of targets, but a bottom-up assimilation of data which would support such decisions. It appears this is not the case.
>
> We are a Forest noted for its ammenity [sic] values as well as timber. In numerous public meetings within the past year and extending back through the completion of all our unit plans, we have assured our public that we will hear all sides and propose a course which reflects a reasonable balance between the issues and concerns expressed. The selection of Alternative L for the Wallowa-Whitman will appear so illogical to our publics it will make a mockery of our issue identification and public involvement process. I want to make sure this is recognized when the Forest RPA targets are assigned through the Regional Guide.

Letter from Jerry G. Allen, Forest Supervisor, Wallowa-Whitman Nat'l Forest, to Regional Forester (Aug. 30, 1983) (on file at Oregon Law Review office).

(a) The RPA

The relationship between local and national planning was not an issue in the RPA. The RPA's primary purpose was to enhance the Forest Service's ability to obtain long-term appropriations.[425] The Act was designed to give the agency budgetary leverage against both the administration and Congress. The RPA Statement of Policy did not "open the doors to the treasury,"[426] but it did provide a standard for measuring the adequacy of alternative budget proposals to meet long-term goals. Nevertheless, the RPA seems to address the local-national planning issue at one point.

Section 8(a) of the RPA provides that "the President shall, subject to other actions of the Congress, carry out programs already established by law in accordance with [the] Statement of Policy or any subsequent amendment or modification thereof approved

---

The forest supervisor of the Okanogan National Forest in Washington expressed similar concerns.

The Regional Alternatives, including the Regional Preferred, have been received recently. Of major concern is a lack of consistency between the RPA program and Forest Planning decisions.

As an example, the Okanogan National Forest developed a preferred alternative through the forest planning process. My Planning Team, Staff, Rangers and I made site-specific evaluations and detailed issue resolutions - evaluations and resolutions not possible in the budget planning process. Not only was the Okanogan's preferred alternative not selected for the RPA program but it wasn't part of any of the RPA alternatives. This negates the planning effort including especially public involvement.

Given the efforts and decisions made in forest planning, it seems worse than unproductive to ignore such recently made decisions. This is especially true in this case because the RPA assessment is based on less information than forest planning.

I suggest that in RPA, all forests deal with static land allocations and only deal with different investment levels as variables. In that way, the worst that can happen is still implementable. The major contention here is whether we are planning through the RPA budget process or the forest planning process.

Letter from William D. McLaughlin, Forest Supervisor, Okanogan Nat'l Forest, to Regional Forester (June 17, 1983) (on file at Oregon Law Review office).

See generally Behan, *supra* note 44; O'Toole, *Forest Planning in Crisis*, 4 FOREST PLANNING 16 (1983). Former Chief John McGuire has modest expectations for successful merger of local and national planning. He hopes that "the relationship between program planning and land management planning will have [been] worked out" within the next 50 years. McGuire, *The RPA — Something For Everyone*, in FORESTS IN DEMAND *supra* note 112, at 151.

[425] *See supra* text accompanying notes 180-90.

[426] Wolf, *The Goals of the Authors of the RPA*, in FORESTS IN DEMAND, *supra* note 112, at 142.

by the Congress . . . ."[427] The mandatory direction to "carry out" the Statement of Policy suggests that Congress intended to impose a top-down planning system on the Forest Service. The House committee report lends some support to this interpretation by stating that "[t]he intent of the legislation is to establish more Congressional control over the management activities and appropriations of the National Forest System lands."[428]

Although section 8(a) has not been interpreted by any court, the Department of Agriculture's Office of General Counsel in April 1982 issued two opinions construing this language. The first opinion, responding to a question concerning the RPA's one-House veto provision, stated: "It is clear from RPA § 8 that the Statement of Policy is no more than a mechanism by which Congress evaluates budget requests for Forest Service activities."[429] The opinion further noted that the RPA's direction to carry out programs in accordance with the Statement of Policy only limited agency discretion to "alter levels of funding actually allocated to such programs."[430] In other words, the Forest Service was required to follow Congress's annual appropriations, but not the Statement of Policy.

The second opinion further undercut the significance of the Statement of Policy for local planning.[431] The Forest Service asked whether section 8 required local forest plans to meet the forty-one million acre wilderness target of the 1980 revised Statement of Policy. The reply distinguished between a wilderness shortfall caused by changing national direction and a shortfall resulting from cumulative recommendations of individual forest plans. A change in national direction probably would require con-

---

[427] 16 U.S.C. § 1606(a) (1982).

[428] H.R. REP. No. 1163, 93rd Cong., 2d Sess. 1 (1974).

[429] Memorandum from Clarence W. Brizee, Ass't Gen. Counsel, Natural Resources Div., Office of Gen. Counsel, U.S. Dep't of Agriculture, to R. Max Peterson, Chief, Forest Service (Apr. 8, 1982) (on file at Oregon Law Review office). "The Statement of Policy mechanism is consistent with 31 U.S.C. § 11 (1976), which provides that the President's annual budget request to Congress should be accompanied by detailed supporting background information." *Id.* The opinion concluded that the Statement of Policy was readily distinguishable from agency rulemaking and, therefore, not covered by constitutional protection from a one-House veto. *Id.*

[430] *Id.*

[431] Memorandum from Clarence W. Brizee, Ass't Gen. Counsel, Natural Resources Div., Office of Gen. Counsel, U.S. Dep't of Agriculture, to Thomas E. Hamilton, Director, Resources Program & Assessment, Forest Service, U.S. Dep't of Agriculture (Apr. 29, 1982) (on file at Oregon Law Review office).

gressional approval.[432] On the other hand, cumulative local planning decisions would require at most only that the agency inform Congress of the shortfall.[433] The opinion concluded, "[E]ven under the most expansive interpretation of the effect which the Statement of Policy has on ongoing Forest Service programs, an individual forest plan recommendation for designated wilderness acreage which falls short of delivering its assigned portion of the national wilderness target does not violate the RPA."[434]

Thus, the Office of General Counsel has narrowly construed the significance of section 8(a). This interpretation is well-supported by both the legislative history of the RPA and by the historical background of national planning. If the RPA by itself does not require top-down planning, the question remains whether the NFMA imposes or permits such an approach.

(b) The NFMA

Congress addressed the issue of top-down planning for timber management early in the development of the NFMA. Section 15(g) of Senator Randolph's bill, S. 2926, explicitly prohibited

---

[432] The Office of General Counsel stated that its April 8 interpretation of section 8(a) "may be too narrow when applied to changes in policy regarding wilderness recommendations to Congress." *Id.*

[433] At some point it may become evident, from a review of numerous individual forest plan recommendations, that the national wilderness target in the Statement of Policy will not be met if Congress follows those recommendations. At this point, Section 8 of RPA appears to obligate the Executive Branch to inform Congress of this trend, and the reasons therefor, either as part of the annual budget request or in the annual progress report.

Id.

[434] *Id.* The opinion also concluded the the NFMA planning regulations did not require local plans to conform to the RPA:

[T]he forest supervisor is not prohibited from recommending, nor is the Regional Forester obligated to disapprove, an alternative which recommends less acreage for wilderness designation than the assigned share of the RPA wilderness target (36 CFR § 219.5(i)). Criteria for choice of an alternative for adoption as a forest plan may be based on numerous legal, economic, ecological, technical, and public issue considerations in addition to national and regional RPA policies and objectives (36 CFR § 219.5(c)). If a forest's assigned share of RPA wilderness targets cannot be met in accordance with other constraints and objectives considered in the forest planning process, readjustment of the assigned share of the target is provided for (36 CFR § 219.4(b)(3)).

Id.

top-down planning of timber harvest levels.[435] The bill sought to ensure that local agency professionals would not simply rationalize timber management decisions already made by their superiors.[436] The original Humphrey bill, S. 3091, made only general reference to the relationship between local and national planning. Section 3 of the Humphrey bill left the local-national planning question to the discretion of the Secretary óf Agriculture.[437] By proposing the legislation as amendments to the RPA Senator Humphrey apparently intended to improve funding for management activities proposed by the local plans.[438]

The two bills were considered jointly by the Senate committees on Agriculture and Forestry and on Interior and Insular

---

[435] Neither the Secretary nor any other officer of the United States shall set or cause to be set the amount of timber to be harvested from any national forest except as arrived at through the process of preparing a multiple use-sustained yield plan. No quotas, target figures or numbers of a similar nature shall be communicated by the Secretary or any other officer of the United States to those designated to prepare a plan which would cause or encourage them to derive a harvest figure related thereto. S. 2926, 94th Cong., 2d Sess. § 15(g), 122 CONG. REC. 2218 (1976), *reprinted in* SENATE NFMA HEARINGS, *supra* note 194, at 8.

[436] The main drafter of the Randolph bill, James Moorman of the Sierra Club Legal Defense Fund, testified during the Senate hearings:
One of our goals in the drafting of S. 2926 was to place timber management goals more squarely with the professional than it has been. We sought to free the professional, frankly, from high-level bureaucratic control and industry pressure, and we have incorporated a number of techniques in this bill to specifically bring about that end . . . . [S]ection 15 provides [the local planning teams] are not to be given, specifically not to be given by management, any quota or target figure which they are to meet in drafting the plan which they are to rationalize, but they are to determine the amount to be cut by examining the resource base.
SENATE NFMA HEARINGS, *supra* note 194, at 42-43.

[437] S. 3091 directed the Secretary to promulgate regulations "[s]pecifying the type or types of plans that will be prepared and specifying the relationship of those plans to the [RPA] program." S. 3091, 94th Cong., 2d Sess. § 3, 122 CONG. REC. 5620 (1976), *reprinted in* SENATE NFMA HEARINGS, *supra* note 194, at 11. The provision was included in the bill approved by the Senate, S. 3091, 94th Cong., 2d Sess. § 5, 122 CONG. REC. 27,651 (1976), *reprinted in* RPA COMPILATION, *supra* note 173, at 503, but deleted by the conference committee. S. REP. No. 1335, 94th Cong., 2d Sess. 26-27 (1976), *reprinted in* 1976 U.S. CODE CONG. & AD. NEWS 6721, 6728-29, and RPA COMPILATION, *supra* note 173, at 754-55.

[438] During the Senate hearings Humphrey commented on the significance of relating S. 3091 to the RPA. He stated, "[S. 3091] ties together the multiple-use plan, with the specific resource plans that flow from it, and the contracts and permits that flow from the resource plans. It ties this to the budget process through the Renewable Resources Planning Act of 1974." SENATE NFMA HEARINGS, *supra* note 194, at 260 (emphasis added).

Affairs.[439] Prior to mark-up, the Agriculture and Forestry Committee staff revised the Humphrey bill but made no change relating to local-national planning issues.[440] Senator Metcalf, acting chairman of the Committee on Interior and Insular Affairs, offered several amendments to S. 3091,[441] including one virtually identical to the first sentence of section 15(g) of the Randolph bill.[442] During the first day of mark-up the committees directed that S. 3091 be merged with the amendments proposed by Metcalf and by industry and labor groups.[443] The new revision of S. 3091 included an abbreviated version of Metcalf's bottom-up timber planning amendment. The new bill required Forest Service planning regulations to "provide that the amount of timber to be harvested from any National Forest System lands shall be deter-

---

[439] The Committee on Interior and Insular Affairs had jurisdiction over forest reserves created from the public domain. The Committee on Agriculture and Forestry had jurisdiction over forestry in general and over national forests not created from the public domain. S. REP. NO. 905, 94th Cong., 2d Sess. 3 (1976), *reprinted in* RPA COMPILATION, *supra* note 173, at 397.

[440] *See Comm. on Agriculture and Forestry and Committee on Interior and Insular Affairs, Comparison of S. 3091, as Amended, With Proposed Amendments By Sen. Metcalf*, 94th Cong., 2d Sess. (1976) [hereinafter cited as *Comparison of S. 3091*], *reprinted in* D. LEMASTER, *supra* note 162.

[441] In his opening remarks at the first mark-up session, Senator Metcalf explained:

There are a lot of amendments here that are labeled "Metcalf amendments." Some of them are mine, some of them are amendments that other members of the Interior Committee have submitted to me and asked to have considered during the course of this discussion, and we have submitted them all together, so this series of amendments are really Senate Interior Committee amendments.

Apr. 27, 1976, Transcript of Senate Mark-up, supra note 374, at 3.

[442] The amendment stated:

Neither the Secretary of Agriculture nor any other officer of the United States shall establish or cause to be established the amount of timber to be harvested from any Forest Service region, national forest, or any national forest district or unit except as determined through the process of preparing a land management plan and resource plan.

Comparison of S. 3091, supra note 440, 3(g), *reprinted in* D. LEMASTER, *supra* note 162, at 286. *See also supra* note 403.

[443] While temporarily chairing the mark-up session, Humphrey stated, "Might I suggest, in light of what seems to be a desire to bring about some amalgamation, that we ask our respective staffs, because we can't finish this bill today anyway, to try to pull these together and see what we can do?" *Apr. 27, 1976, Transcript of Senate Mark-up, supra* note 374, at 48. In response to Senator Metcalf's request to have his amendments considered by the staffs, Humphrey replied, "Obviously that would have to be a major part of the staff consideration." *Id.* at 50.

mined only through the process of preparing land management plans."[444]

Senator Mark Hatfield of Oregon proposed to add "developed to achieve the goals of the program" to the end of the Metcalf provision.[445] The committees adopted Hatfield's amendment without further discussion, but when S. 3091 emerged from mark-up, Hatfield's amendment had been placed in a more general planning context,[446] while Metcalf's provision remained intact.[447]

Like the Senate, the House did not consider the local-national planning issue at length. Attention focused on H.R. 13,236, sponsored by Jerry Litton of Missouri, chairman of the Subcommittee on Forests of the Committee on Agriculture.[448] The Litton bill did not contain either provision of the Senate bill concerning local-

---

[444] *Apr. 29, 1976, Transcript of Senate Mark-up, supra* note 374, at 57. *See also* S. 3091, 94th Cong., 2d Sess. § 5, 122 CONG. REC. 27,651 (1976), *reprinted in* RPA COMPILATION, *supra* note 173, at 505-06.

[445] *Apr. 29, 1976, Transcript of Senate Mark-up, supra* note 374, at 57. Hatfield explained briefly that the purpose of his amendment was to make "more explicit" the tie between the RPA and S. 3091. *Id.*

[446] The Committee had authorized Forest Service Chief John McGuire and staff advisor Robert Wolf to insert Hatfield's amendment where they thought it "more appropriate." *Id.* at 58. Wolf and McGuire had moved Hatfield's amendment to an introductory part of the same subsection. The bill now read:

(d) the regulations shall include . . .

(6) specifying guidelines for land management plans *developed to achieve the goals of the Program* which . . .

(H)(i) provide that the amount of timber to be harvested from any National Forest System lands shall be determined only through the process of preparing land management plans.

S. 3091, 94th Cong., 2d Sess. § 5, 122 CONG. REC. 27,651 (1976), *reprinted in* RPA COMPILATION, *supra* note 173, at 504-05 (emphasis added).

[447] Although the Hatfield and Metcalf provisions were located in the same subsection of the bill, the report of the Committee on Agriculture and Forestry indicates that the Senate did not consider them to be contradictory. The report states:

The Committee developed a number of provisions designed to insure that appropriate lands are included in the land base and reasonable harvest levels are established as part of the land management planning process. *S. 3091 assures that harvest levels are based on management plans and not set by arbitrary determination.*

S. REP. NO. 893, 94th Cong., 2d Sess. 37 (1976), *reprinted in* RPA COMPILATION, *supra* note 173, at 317 (emphasis added). The report contains no further discussion of the relationship between local and national planning.

[448] H.R. 13,236, 94th Cong., 2d Sess. (1976), *reprinted in* HOUSE COMM. ON AGRICULTURE, 94TH CONG., 2D SESS., BUSINESS MEETINGS ON NATIONAL FOREST MANAGEMENT ACT OF 1976, at 455-61 (Comm. Print 1976) [hereinafter cited as TRANSCRIPT OF HOUSE MARK-UP]. Rep. Litton introduced H.R. 13236 on April 13, 1976, 122 CONG. REC. 10,843 (1976), following three days of hearings by the Subcommittee on Forests of the Committee on Agriculture.

national planning. Instead, the bill required the Secretary of Agriculture to assure that local plans determine, among other things, "harvesting levels."[449] The meaning of the provision was clarified during the subcommittee mark-up.

Representative James Weaver of Oregon proposed to add the Senate bill's requirement that harvest levels be determined only through local planning.[450] Special Counsel for the Committee on Agriculture, John Kramer, stated that "in effect" Weaver's amendment had "already been adopted by this subcommittee."[451] He stated further, "If the subcommittee will draw its attention back to section (E)(ii), the requirement is imposed that the unit plan be developed and that each unit plan contain a harvest level."[452] Representative Weaver then queried Chief McGuire, "As counsel says, are these provisions the same?" McGuire responded, "I think they would work out the same."[453]

The foregoing legislative history indicates that the House Subcommittee on Forests and Chief McGuire generally agreed on the meaning of section (e)(2) of the Litton bill. They interpreted the provision to be equivalent in effect to the Senate's requirement for bottom-up timber management planning. Section (e)(2) remained unchanged in the bill that passed the House.[454]

The bill adopted by the Conference Committee included section (e)(2) of the Litton bill and the Hatfield amendment but not the revised Metcalf provision.[455] The report contains no explanation of

---

[449] H.R. 13,236, 94th Cong., 2d Sess. § 2(c)(2) (1976), *reprinted in* TRANSCRIPT OF HOUSE MARK-UP, *supra* note 448, at 456.

[450] TRANSCRIPT OF HOUSE MARK-UP, *supra* note 448, at 76; *see also id.* at 68.

[451] *Id.* at 78.

[452] *Id.* Kramer asked the committee: "Do you want to have a duplicate requirement?" *Id.* at 79.

[453] *Id.* at 80. Weaver then stated, "If this is the same language as that which we have already adopted, Mr. Chairman, I ask unanimous consent to withdraw my motion." *Id.* Weaver's motion was approved. *Id.* at 81.

[454] H.R. 15069, 94th Cong., 2d Sess. § 6, 122 CONG. REC. 31063 (1976), *reprinted in* RPA COMPILATION, *supra* note 173, at 726. The report of the Committee on Agriculture did not discuss local-national planning, except to state that "*subsection (e) requires that the Secretary assure that plans for units of the National Forest System determine* forest management systems, *harvesting levels*, and procedures, and the availability of lands and their suitability for management." H. R. REP. NO. 1478, pt. 1, 94th Cong., 2d Sess. 19 (1976), *reprinted in* RPA COMPILATION, *supra* note 173, at 594 (emphasis added).

[455] S. REP. NO. 1335, 94th Cong., 2d Sess. 24-27, 122 CONG. REC. 34,056-57 (1976), *reprinted in* RPA COMPILATION, *supra* note 173, at 752-55.

the conferees' intentions in regard to local-national planning.[456] In light of the discussion in the House mark-up, however, the deletion of the Metcalf provision does not appear to be significant.[457]

In sum, the RPA and NFMA do not require the Forest Service to follow a top-down system of planning. On the contrary, with respect to the timber resource the legislative history of the NFMA indicates that Congress intended harvest levels to be determined by local plans—from the bottom-up rather than from the top-down. As for resources other than timber, there simply is no clear direction from Congress on how to relate the RPA Program to local forest plans. Perhaps the best that can be said for the non-timber resources is that Congress expects there to be some connection between the goals of the national program and local planning. How this is supposed to work in practice—that is, the determination of the guidelines to attain this connection—is left to the discretion of the Forest Service.[458]

---

[456] The Joint Explanatory Statement simply restates § (e)(2) of the House bill, id. at 24, 122 CONG. REC. 34,056 (1976), reprinted in RPA COMPILATION, supra note 173, at 752, but makes no reference to the Hatfield amendment. Id. at 26, 122 CONG. REC. 34,057 (1976), reprinted in RPA COMPILATION, supra note 173, at 754.

[457] Seven of the ten House conferees were present during the mark-up discussion of section (e)(2). Compare TRANSCRIPT OF HOUSE MARK-UP, supra note 448, at 63, with S. REP. NO. 1335, supra note 455, at 17, 122 CONG. REC. 34,055 (1976), reprinted in RPA COMPILATION, supra note 173, at 746 (Representatives Melcher, Weaver, Vigorito, Krebs, Brown, Symms, and Johnson present at both sessions). If the House conferees sought to delete the Metcalf provision, presumably they would have deleted it on the ground that it was duplicative of section (e)(2) in the House version.

[458] Cf. S. REP. NO. 893, 94th Cong., 2d Sess. 35 (1976) reprinted in RPA COMPILATION, supra note 173, at 315. ("The Secretary . . . will describe the type of plans that will be prepared and the relationship of those plans to the Renewable Resource Program.") The Senate committee report simply paraphrased a section of the Senate bill that was omitted by the conference committee. See S. 3091, 94th Cong., 2d Sess. § 5(d)(2) (1976), reprinted in RPA COMPILATION, supra note 173, at 375; S. REP. NO. 1335, 94th Cong., 2d Sess. 26-27 (1976) (conference report), reprinted in RPA COMPILATION, supra note 173, at 754-55.

III

RANGE

More land in the national forests is used for grazing domestic stock than for any other economic use.[459] The national forests contain more open rangeland than many realize: fifty million acres, which represents nearly one-third of the entire system.[460] The Forest Service also permits grazing on a roughly equal amount of forested land, so that domestic cattle, sheep, horses, and goats use a total of approximately 102 million acres of national forest lands.[461]

The amount of acres devoted in whole or in part to domestic livestock, however, tends to overstate the importance of commercial grazing on Forest Service lands. First, domestic grazing in the system is light in many areas and is usually seasonal due to the comparatively high elevation of the national forests.[462] Second, commercial grazing must be limited to permit sufficient forage for substantial populations of wildlife such as antelope, elk, deer, bighorn sheep, and moose.[463] Third, in a few regions the Forest Service must accommodate the needs of wild horses and burros.[464] Finally, good range management practices must be employed to limit the number of animal unit months (AUMs) in order to protect watercourses and the ground itself from the omnipresent danger of erosion caused by overgrazing.[465]

The economic returns from grazing on national forest lands are not great. Grazing fees have always been below the market

---

[459] PUBLIC LAND LAW REVIEW COMM'N, *supra* note 338, at 105.

[460] 1981 ASSESSMENT, *supra* note 9, at 156-57.

[461] *1985 Forest Service Budget, supra* note 10, at 1347. Although the term "rangeland" often refers only to open and nonforested grasslands, for our purposes range is any open or forested land that can provide forage for wild or domestic animals.

[462] PUBLIC LAND LAW REVIEW COMM'N, *supra* note 338, at 108-12.

[463] Inventories of wild animals are far less precise than counts of domestic stock, but there is no doubt that the use of grazing lands by wildlife is high. *See generally* Swanson, *Wildlife on the Public Lands* in WILDLIFE IN AMERICA 428 (1978).

[464] Wild horses and burros are far more prevalent on Bureau of Land Management (BLM) lands, apparently because of the higher elevations and steeper terrain of Forest Service lands. 1981 ASSESSMENT, *supra* note 9, at 166. The most recent estimate puts 1700 wild horses and burros in the national forests. *1985 Forest Service Budget, supra* note 10, at 1350. These animals must be managed in accordance with the Wild, Free-Roaming Horses and Burros Act of 1971, 16 U.S.C. §§ 1331-1340 (1982), discussed *infra* note 601.

[465] *See generally supra* note 78.

value[466] and Forest Service expenditures for grazing exceed revenues.[467] Receipts from recreation user fees are more than triple all of the receipts from grazing activities.[468] Total grazing receipts, of course, are dwarfed by the revenues generated by timber sales.[469]

It is useful to draw general comparisions between grazing administered by the Forest Service and by the Bureau of Land Management (BLM), which is popularly regarded as the federal grazing agency. The BLM permits 4.3 million animals[470] to graze on an area seventy percent larger than the Forest Service grazing lands[471] and receives about $14.6 million in fees annually.[472] The Forest Service, on the other hand, permits about 3.3 million domestic animals[473] to graze on the national forests for an annual return of approximately $8 million.[474] National forest rangelands are in substantially better condition than BLM lands[475] because the Forest Service instituted a regulatory program three decades

---

[466] *See generally* SECRETARY, U.S. DEP'T OF THE INTERIOR & SECRETARY, U.S. DEP'T OF AGRICULTURE, STUDY OF FEES FOR LIVESTOCK ON FEDERAL LANDS (1977) [hereinafter cited as FEDERAL GRAZING FEES STUDY]; Coggins, *The Law of Public Rangeland Management IV: FLPMA, PRIA, and the Multiple Use Mandate*, 14 ENVTL. L. 1 (1983).

[467] In its most recent report, the Forest Service estimated revenues of $10 million for fiscal year 1985, and requested $25 million for its grazing program. *1985 Forest Service Budget, supra* note 10, at 1346-47. The Service recognized the disparity between receipts and expenditures but stated that a direct comparison "does not take into consideration benefits such as wildlife habitat, soil and water quality, watershed protection, and additional forage for non-game species resulting from range management activities." *Id.* at 1347.

[468] Grazing receipts in 1983 were $8.1 million while recreation fees (primarily from campground user fees and leases of ski areas) totaled $27.7 million. *Id.* at 1192.

[469] Timber receipts in 1983 totaled $388.6 million. *Id.*

[470] *Dep't of the Interior and Related Agencies Appropriations for 1985: Hearings before Subcomm. of the Dep't of Interior and Related Agencies of the House Committee on Appropriations*, pt. 2, 98th Cong., 1st Sess., 101 (1985) [hereinafter cited as *1985 BLM Budget*].

[471] Grazing occurs on 170 million acres of BLM land, *id.*, and on 101.8 million acres of Forest Service land. 1981 ASSESSMENT, *supra* note 9, at 165.

[472] *1985 BLM Budget, supra* note 470, at 16.

[473] *1985 Forest Service Budget, supra* note 10, at 1347.

[474] *Id.* at 1192.

[475] The two agencies compute their range condition statistics differently so that direct comparisons are somewhat difficult to make, 1981 ASSESSMENT, *supra* note 9, at 158 n.12, but there is general agreement as to the superior condition of the Forest Service range. *See, e.g.*, W. VOIGHT, PUBLIC GRAZING LANDS: USE AND MISUSE BY INDUSTRY AND GOVERNMENT 309-25 (1976); Coggins, *The Law of Public Rangeland Management II: The Commons and the Taylor Act*, 13 ENVTL. L. 1, 39 (1982).

earlier than the BLM.[476] Range resource planning was a center-piece of the Pinchot administration and the policy area where Forest Service regulatory authority was most strenuously exercised.[477]

Today grazing issues concerning the national forests are not in the forefront because the early comprehensive planning by the Forest Service has resulted in a status quo that is generally acceptable to most of the competing interest groups. We focus first on range resource management, not because of its contemporary importance in national forest management, but because planning came first to grazing and because the history of the competing interests on national forest rangeland illustrates the benefits that can accrue as a result of careful, long-term planning.

A. Evolution of Policy

1. Unregulated Grazing (1846-1891)

Until the end of the nineteenth century, federal grazing policy was one of benign neglect. The government's primary objective was to transfer ownership of the public domain in small parcels to farmers under the homesteading and preemption laws.[478] Since government ownership was envisioned as temporary, neither Congress nor the Department of the Interior bothered to regulate the use of the public range during the interim. Furthermore, range was not viewed as a particularly valuable or potentially scarce resource. Thus, the federal government allowed anyone to graze animals on public lands free of charge or regulation. As the Supreme Court observed in 1890, "Everybody used the open unenclosed country, which produced nutritious grasses, as a public common on which their horses, cattle, hogs and sheep could run and graze."[479]

This great common pool resource was misused during that period, however, and modern policy is directed largely toward resuscitating the public rangelands from extreme overgrazing by generations past. Millions of cattle and sheep descended on the

---

[476] Voight quotes a BLM official who succinctly described the situation on the BLM range: "[B]asically the problems we are faced with today result from historical situations: too early use, too heavy use, and too long use." W. VOIGHT, *supra* note 475, at 309.

[477] *See infra* notes 500-10 and accompanying text.

[478] *See generally* G. COGGINS & C. WILKINSON, *supra* note 345, at 65-74.

[479] Buford v. Houtz, 133 U.S. 320, 327-28 (1890).

previously uncrowded rangelands following the Civil War.[480] High beef prices, the spread of railroads, and discovery of gold in the Rocky Mountains motivated grazers to expand into the remote regions of the West.[481] Numerous conflicts arose, pitting sheep grazers against cattle grazers, grazers against farmers, and large grazing corporations against small owners and rustlers. The overcrowding and intense competition quickly resulted in severe depletion of forage.

As was the case with western mining and water law, local custom stepped in to provide rules to govern use of the western range. Cattle were customarily allowed to roam at will and western courts endorsed this practice, which was contrary to common law trespass principles, by exempting owners of livestock from trespass damages.[482] Western legislatures also passed "fence laws," providing farmers with a cause of action against trespassing grazers only

---

[480] *See* R. ATHEARN, HIGH COUNTRY EMPIRE (1960); P. FOSS, POLITICS AND GRASS (1960); T. WATKINS & C. WATSON, THE LAND NO ONE KNOWS (1975); FOREST SERVICE, U.S. DEP'T OF AGRICULTURE, THE WESTERN RANGE, S. DOC. NO. 199, 74th Cong., 2d Sess. 121 (1936) [hereinafter cited as THE WESTERN RANGE]. Western livestock grazing was first established around 1700 at Jesuit missions located in Texas, New Mexico, and Arizona. Missions in California had over 800,000 livestock by 1834. *Id.* at 120.

[481] THE WESTERN RANGE, *supra* note 480, at 121.

[482] *See, e.g.,* Morris v. Fraker, 5 Colo. 425 (1880), where the Colorado Supreme Court denied trespass damages to a farmer whose grain and potato crops were trampled by the defendant's cattle. The court acknowledged that the Colorado Legislature had formally adopted the common law of England, which included a rule that "[e]very one was bound to keep his beasts within his own close, and if they went upon the grounds of others, the owners were liable in damages." *Id.* at 427. Nevertheless, the court concluded that this common law rule did not apply in Colorado.

> It must be apparent . . . to any person at all familiar with the character of the country, its soil and climate, and with the material interests and industrial pursuits of the people, that such a rule of law is wholly unsuited and inapplicable to the present condition of the State and its citizens.
>
> . . . .
>
> These commons and the numerous parks in the mountains furnish excellent grass for horses, cattle and other animals, and stock raising, in consequence, has become one of the leading industries of the State. . . . This industry would be seriously crippled by the adoption of a rule requiring each owner to keep his stock within his own close. It would be impracticable, as well as impossible, for the several owners of these animals to provide and inclose suitable pasture lands for their herds. Nor is there any necessity for such a rule. The commons are now owned principally by the State and by the general government, and if the grasses which grow thereon are not depastured, they will waste and decay.

Id. at 428-29.

if the landowners had erected legally adequate fences around their property.[483]

An elaborate system of quasi-property rights developed for use of the public range. The Supreme Court in *Buford v. Houtz*[484] held that ranchers had an "implied license" from the United States to use the public domain, subject to entry by homesteaders.[485] Through custom, grazers established so-called "range rights" to public domain located adjacent to their homesteads.[486] Some states went so far as to levy property taxes on ranchers' possessory rights to adjacent federal land.[487]

By the early 1880s the General Land Office (GLO) in the Department of the Interior began to express concern over the growth of unlawful property interests on federal range land.

---

[483] For example, in 1872 Montana adopted a statute requiring fences to be at least four and one-half feet high and

> constructed of four or more strong poles or rails, the lower pole or rail to be not more than two feet from the ground . . . . Any portion of an enclosure bordering on any stream more than four feet deep, swamp, bluff, ditch, or wall, which shall be as difficult for stock to pass as the fence described in this section, may be used as a lawful fence.

MONT. REV. STAT., 5th Div. § 612 (1879).

[484] 133 U.S. 320 (1890).

[485] We are of [sic] opinion that there is an implied license, growing out of the custom of nearly a hundred years, that the public lands of the United States, especially those in which the native grasses are adapted to the growth and fattening of domestic animals, shall be free to the people who seek to use them where they are left open and unenclosed, and no act of government forbids this use. For many years past a very large proportion of the beef which has been used by the people of the United States is the meat of cattle thus raised upon the public lands without charge, without let or hindrance or obstruction. The government of the United States, in all its branches, has known of this use, has never forbidden it, nor taken any steps to arrest it.

Id. at 326.

[486] *See* Scott, *The Range Cattle Industry: Its Effect on Western Land Law*, 28 MONT. L. REV. 155, 162-63 (1967). Range rights were transferrable through sale of the cattle that typically grazed on a certain tract. *Id.* at 163. Although range rights created no property interest as against the United States and courts generally saw them as being based only on "moral recognition," some courts did ascribe possessory rights to prior settlers on public range to oust later entrants. *See, e.g.,* Healy v. Smith, 14 Wyo. 263, 83 P. 583 (1905). *See also* Atherton v. Fowler, 96 U.S. 513 (1877); Nickals v. Winn, 17 Nev. 188, 30 P. 435 (1882). State legislatures provided first-in-time ranchers with prescriptive rights against newcomers by making it a crime to drive stock from their accustomed range. *See, e.g.,* N.M. COMP. LAWS § 60 (1884).

[487] *See* U.S. DEP'T OF THE INTERIOR, ANNUAL REPORT, H.R. EXEC. DOC. NO. 1, pt. 5, 47th Cong., 2d Sess. 13 (1882) [hereinafter cited as 1882 INTERIOR REPORT].

Commissioner N.C. McFarland was particularly concerned about fences built by large cattle companies and wealthy individual cattle raisers.[488] In 1882 McFarland reported that "[i]t is manifest that some decisive action on the part of the Federal Government is necessary for the maintenance of the supremacy of the laws and to preserve the integrity of the public domain."[489] The Department of the Interior in 1883 issued a notice to grazers that fencing of the public domain was illegal and "against the right of others who desire to settle or graze their cattle on the inclosed tracts."[490] By 1884 over four million acres were unlawfully fenced.[491] The next year Congress responded to the Interior Department's requests for legislation by passing the Unlawful Inclosures Act "to prevent unlawful occupancy of the public lands" by "force, threats, intimidation, or by any fencing or inclosing."[492] The Act was intended to reinforce the homesteading laws by ensuring access to the public domain by settlers. However, the law was more significant as the first intrusion of federal authority into an area previously governed by local custom and state law.[493]

---

[488] U.S. DEP'T OF THE INTERIOR, ANNUAL REPORT, H.R. EXEC. DOC. NO. 1, pt. 5, 48th Cong., 1st Sess. 210 (1883) [hereinafter cited as 1883 INTERIOR REPORT].

[489] 1882 INTERIOR REPORT, *supra* note 487, at 13. The report continued:
It is undoubtedly true that the vast plains and mountain ranges west of the Mississippi River must be relied upon for an important proportion of the sheep and cattle husbandry required by the necessities of national consumption, but it does not therefore follow that this industry should be the subject of individual or corporate monopoly . . . .
The unimpeded progress of settlement will in due time bring the whole of the territory of the United States within the compass of private ownership. Meanwhile the unappropriated public lands suitable for grazing herds of cattle should be equally free to the enterprise of all citizens unembarrassed by attempts at exclusive occupation.
Id.

[490] 1883 INTERIOR REPORT, *supra* note 488, at 30.

[491] U.S. DEP'T OF THE INTERIOR, ANNUAL REPORT, H.R. EXEC. DOC. NO. 1, 48th Cong., 2d Sess. 17 (1884).

[492] Act of Feb. 25, 1885, ch. 149, 23 Stat. 321.

[493] A challenge to the constitutionality of the Inclosures Act resulted in a leading Supreme Court decision on the extent of congressional power over federal property. In Camfield v. United States, 167 U.S. 518 (1897), the owners of alternate sections of land in Colorado had effectively enclosed 20,000 acres of public lands by building fences entirely on their own land. The Court decided that Congress had constitutional power to remove the fence in order to protect federal land:
The general Government doubtless has a power over its own property analogous to the police power of the several States, and the extent to which it may go in the exercise of such power is measured by the exigencies of the

2. Establishment of Authority (1891-1911)

Passage of the Forest Reserves Act of 1891[494] marked a break in federal range policy. The government continued to pay scant attention to the public domain lands but the creation of forest reserves, some of which included rangeland, generated a new attitude toward the reserved lands. The result was a twenty-year period of intense controversy over grazing policy on national forests.

Initially, the government's concerns focused on the destructive impact of sheep grazing.[495] Drastic government action to control sheep grazing was presaged in a scathing report by Gifford Pinchot and other members of a committee appointed by the National Academy of Sciences in 1896. The committee reported that "[n]omadic sheep husbandry has already seriously damaged" the newly-created and proposed forest reserves.[496] Invoking John Muir's description of sheep as "hoofed locusts," the committee accused sheep, among other things, of causing early-summer floods, reducing late-summer irrigation supply, and trampling and eating

---

particular case . . . . While we do not undertake to say that Congress has the unlimited power to legislate against nuisances within a State, which it would have within a Territory, we do not think the admission of a Territory as a State deprives it of the power of legislating for the protection of the public lands, though it may thereby involve the exercise of what is ordinarily known as the police power, so long as such power is directed solely to its own protection. A different rule would place the public domain of the United States completely at the mercy of state legislation. *Id.* at 525-26. In recent times *Camfield* has been cited as authority for federal regulation of private lands adjacent to public lands. *See, e.g.,* United States v. Brown, 552 F.2d 817, 822 (8th Cir. 1977). *But see* Leo Sheep Co. v. United States, 440 U.S. 668, 684-86 (1979) (*Camfield* does not support government's claim to easement over private land).

[494] Act of Mar. 3, 1891, ch. 561, § 24, 26 Stat. 1095, 1103 *repealed by* Federal Land Policy and Management Act of 1976, Pub. L. No. 94-579, § 704(a), 90 Stat. 2743, 2792, discussed *supra* text accompanying at notes 54-57.

[495] During the late 1880s the western sheep population quickly grew from a comparatively small number to veritable hordes. *See* THE WESTERN RANGE, *supra* note 480, at 125. The increasing numbers of sheep created conflict with cattle ranchers, who sometimes resorted to scattering flocks of sheep or driving them over precipices. *Id.* Farmers blamed sheep for damaging watersheds and causing shortages of irrigation water. *See, e.g.,* WATERSHED OF THE RAINIER FOREST RESERVE, WASHINGTON, S. DOC. NO. 403, 57th Cong., 1st Sess. 1, 2, 5, 14, 15 (1902). Furthermore, in 1893 the GLO alerted Congress to reports that sheep grazers were intentionally setting fire to "the mountain districts in the fall to create new pasturage for the following season." 25 CONG. REC. 2373 (1893) (letter from Edw. A. Bowers, Acting Comm'r, General Land Office, U.S. Dep't. of the Interior (Sept. 25, 1893)).

[496] REPORT OF THE NATIONAL ACADEMY OF SCIENCES, S. DOC. NO. 57, 55th Cong., 2d Sess. 45 (1898).

tree seedlings as well as grass and shrubs.[497] The committee concluded that sheep grazers had come to believe that they had "acquired vested rights in the public forests"; thus, "their trespass can only be checked by the employment of vigorous measures."[498]

Notwithstanding the committee's concerns about sheep grazing, Congress did not mention grazing in the 1897 Organic Act.[499] However, asserting the general statutory authority to regulate occupancy and use,[500] the Department of the Interior invoked the 1897 Act to impose severe limitations on grazing in the forest reserves. On June 30, 1897—less than one month after the Organic Act was signed—the General Land Office issued regulations prohibiting all sheep grazing on forest reserves outside of Oregon and Washington.[501]

---

[497]Feeding as they travel from the valleys at the foot of the mountains to the upper alpine meadows, they carry desolation with them. Every blade of grass, the tender, growing shoots of shrubs, and seedling trees are eaten to the ground. The feet of these "hoofed locusts," crossing and recrossing the faces of steep slopes, tread out the plants sheep do not relish and, loosening the forest floor, produce conditions favorable to floods. Their destruction of the undergrowth of the forest and of the sod of alpine meadows hastens the melting of snow in spring and quickens evaporation.

The pasturage of sheep in mountain forests thus increases the floods of early summer, which carry away rapidly the water that under natural conditions would not reach the rivers until late in the season, when it is most needed for irrigation, and by destroying the seedling trees, on which the permanency of forests depends, prevents natural forest reproduction, and therefore ultimately destroys the forests themselves.
Id.

[498] *Id.* at 46. The committee reported no evidence of government efforts to protect the forest reserves from overgrazing, "except in the north end of the Cascade Reserve, in Oregon, where in August [the committee] found a single agent of the Interior Department actively and successfully engaged in scattering several large flocks of sheep that had been devastating this reservation for several weeks." *Id.* at 43.

[499] The Act simply allowed "any person" to enter the forest reserves "for all proper and lawful purposes," providing those "persons comply with the rules and regulations covering such forest reservations." Ch. 2, 30 Stat. 36 (1897). A predecessor bill introduced in 1895 provided, "[N]othing herein shall be construed to exclude the settlers . . . from pasturing their cattle on the said reservations . . . *Provided*, That they comply with the statutes covering such forest reservations." H.R. 119, § 3, 53d Cong., 3d Sess., 27 CONG. REC. 2780 (1895).

[500] The Act authorized the Secretary of the Interior to "make such rules and regulations and establish such service as will insure the objects of such reservations, namely, to regulate their occupancy and use and to preserve the forests thereon from destruction." 16 U.S.C. § 551 (1982). *See generally supra* section II(A)(1).

[501] *See* ANNUAL REPORT OF THE SECRETARY OF THE INTERIOR, H.R. DOC. No. 5, 55th Cong., 2d Sess. CXI (1897). The agency explained that "sheep-grazing has been found injurious to the forest cover, and, therefore, of serious

The prohibition raised a storm of protest among the sheep grazers.[502] The GLO responded in 1899 by agreeing to consider applications to graze sheep on ten forest reserves.[503] Meanwhile, local superintendents in the GLO were instructed to undertake detailed studies of sheep grazing conditions on all forest reserves.[504] In 1900 Gifford Pinchot, then Chief of the Division of Forestry, made a three-week inspection of range lands in the southwest.[505] Pinchot subsequently directed the Section on Special Investigations, within the Division of Forestry, to study the effects of grazing on twelve forest reserves.[506] Thus by the turn of the century

---

consequence in regions where the rainfall is limited." *Id.* In Oregon and Washington sheep grazers were required to apply to the GLO for permission to graze. "Permission will be refused or revoked," the agency reported, "whenever it shall appear that sheep are pastured on parts of the reserves specially liable to injury, or upon . . . well-known places of public resort or reservoir supply." *Id.*

The following year the GLO reported that "the Government needs to take the matter of nomadic sheep ranging vigorously in hand. To such an extent has this business of ranging sheep in public forests been carried that in some localities the forest growth on great areas is in danger of extermination." ANNUAL REPORT OF THE COMM'R OF THE GENERAL LAND OFFICE, H.R. DOC. No. 5, 55th Cong., 3rd Sess. 88 (1898) [1898 GLO REPORT].

[502] *See* S. DANA, *supra* note 47, at 115.

[503] ANNUAL REPORT OF THE COMM'R OF THE GENERAL LAND OFFICE, H.R. DOC. No. 5, 56th Cong., 1st Sess. 108 (1899) [hereinafter cited as 1899 GLO REPORT].

[504] The GLO superintendents were to report on

[t]he probable number of sheep and number of flocks that seek the different reservations; duration of the grazing season; character and location of the grazing lands; extent and general course of ranging; nature of the trees, undergrowth, and vegetation in general in the reserves, and effect of sheep grazing on same; the damage done, if any; the methods pursued by the herders, and whether they are in the habit of setting out fires to increase the pasturage of the next season; whether grazing tends to increase or to lessen the damage by fires; relation of grazing to the water supply—whether the water supply is either lessened or seriously polluted thereby; importance of the sheep industry in those regions . . . . If pasturage should be permitted, state whether there are any particular portions of the reserves specially liable to injury, and from which it would be advisable to exclude sheep; and if so, suggest limits of such closed areas; whether advisable to grant the grazing privilege to sheep owners without charge therefor in return for the protection of the reserves from forest fires, overgrazing, or other evils; or whether advisable, in connection with requiring such protection, to make a charge per acre for the privilege of grazing; and if so, what would be a reasonable charge per acre in the several localities.

You will confer freely with sheep owners and others interested in the subject and endeavor to obtain their cordial cooperation.

1898 GLO REPORT, *supra* note 501, at 99-100.

[505] *See* G. PINCHOT, *supra* note 51, at 177-80.

[506] 1901 ANNUAL REPORT OF THE CHIEF, *supra* note 70, at 332.

federal grazing policy had become a subject of intense controversy and intensive study on national forest reserve range land.

In late 1901 and early 1902, well before the transfer of the forest reserves to the Department of Agriculture in 1905, the Department of the Interior made several decisions that formed the basis for national forest grazing policy in the twentieth century. The agency implemented the first two decisions on December 23, 1901, by amending the grazing regulations. The amendment partially lifted the ban on sheep grazing and established an annual permit system for all livestock.[507] On January 8, 1902, the GLO issued a circular establishing an order of preference for permit applicants.[508] In February 1902 Interior decided to allow associations of sheep owners to recommend the allotment of grazing permits.[509] In return, it became "the duty of the qualified associations to see that all the rules and regulations and the terms of the applications and permits were fully complied with."[510]

By 1903 the grazing permit system was forcing reductions in the numbers of livestock on the forest reserves.[511] Sheep and cattle owners competed fiercely for permission to continue grazing.[512] Many grazers who did not succeed in obtaining permits simply

---

[507] ANNUAL REPORT OF THE COMM'R OF THE GENERAL LAND OFFICE, H.R. DOC. NO. 5, 57th Cong., 2d Sess. 331 (1902).

[508] The preference order was:
   1. Stock of residents within the reserve.
   2. Stock of persons who own permanent stock ranches within the reserve, but who reside outside of the reserve.
   3. Stock of persons living in the immediate vicinity of the reserve, called neighboring stock.
   4. Stock of outsiders who have some equitable claim.
Id. at 332.

[509] *Id.* at 332-33.

[510] *Id.* at 333. Associations were recognized in Arizona, Oregon, Utah, and Washington. *Id.* However, the arrangement resulted in an excessive sheep population during the summer of 1902, and in October the agency decided to eliminate the association's supervision and allotment responsibilities. *See* ANNUAL REPORT OF THE COMM'R OF THE GENERAL LAND OFFICE, H.R. DOC. NO. 5, 58th Cong., 2d Sess. 322 (1903) [hereinafter cited as 1903 GLO REPORT].

[511] On eight forest reserves open to sheep grazing, the authorized sheep grazing dropped from 1,400,000 head in 1901 to 877,000 head in 1903. *See* 1903 GLO REPORT, *supra* note 510, at 324.

[512] The GLO reported in 1903, "[A]s soon as the departmental order fixing the number to be allowed in the reserve is issued, the struggle between owners of sheep and between the cattlemen and the sheepmen begins, this Office being flooded with petitions and letters urging the rights and equities of either the one or the other." *Id.* at 323.

ignored the regulations.[513] Although in some instances the GLO was able to obtain injunctions against unauthorized grazing, the agency was seriously hampered by the refusal of courts to impose criminal sanctions for violations.[514]

In *Dastervignes v. United States*,[515] the Court of Appeals for the Ninth Circuit upheld the constitutionality of the injunctive remedy for grazing violations.[516] Since injunctions were a less efficient enforcement mechanism than criminal sanctions,[517] the Department of the Interior requested Congress to declare unper-

---

[513] In 1903 the GLO reported:
The grazing question is the most perplexing one with which this office has to deal in connection with forest-reserve administration. Those persons who have been in the habit of ranging their stock upon lands included within a forest reservation are insistent upon continuing the practice after the reserve is established, some of them going to the extent of openly defying all rules and orders from the Department prohibiting grazing therein.
Id. at 322.

[514] In 1898 the Attorney General had advised the agency that sheep grazers who violated the regulations could be criminally prosecuted. *See* 22 Op. Att'y Gen. 266 (1898). However, in 1900 a federal district court in southern California dismissed a criminal prosecution for violating the grazing regulations. United States v. Blasingame, 116 F. 654 (S.D. Cal. 1900). The court held that the 1897 Organic Act had unconstitutionally delegated legislative power to the Secretary of the Interior, insofar as it authorized the Secretary to declare any violation of the regulations to be a criminal offense. *Id.* This ruling was followed by courts in northern California, Arizona, Utah, and Washington. *See* 1903 GLO REPORT, *supra* note 510, at 324.

[515] 122 F. 30 (9th Cir. 1903).

[516] The court found particularly persuasive an affidavit alleging
that the devouring and destruction of the vegetation, grasses, undergrowth, young and growing trees and seedlings . . . leaves the earth bare and liable to disastrous washings out by the rains, leaving no soil or earth, but bare rock, which renders the growth of vegetation, grasses, undergrowth, young and growing trees and seedlings, extremely difficult, and in many cases impossible, all to the irreparable damage and injury of said Stanislaus forest reserve, and the purposes for which said forest reserve were created.
Id. at 33. The court agreed that injunctive relief was proper because sheep were causing irreparable damage to the Stanislaus Forest Reserve.

[517] A United States attorney for southern California described the logistical problems of enforcing an injunction against trespassing sheep grazers in the Sierra Forest Reserve:
In order to reach the defendants to serve papers on them the marshal would be obliged to travel a very great distance . . . either going by way of Sacramento, Cal., and Reno, Nev., thence to Independence, a distance of 619 miles, or by way of Mohave and to Independence by stage, a distance of about 400 miles from Fresno . . . .
1903 GLO REPORT, *supra* note 510, at 325.

mitted grazing on forest reserves to be a criminal offense.[518] Congress ignored the agency's request.[519]

By 1905, when the Forest Service took charge of the forest reserves,[520] grazing policy had become "far and away the bitterest issue of the time."[521] Despite the refusal by Congress and the courts to allow criminal prosecution for violating the grazing regulations, Pinchot continued to press for their enforcement. The first attempt was denied—again on constitutional grounds—in 1906.[522] Later that year, the agency chose to prosecute a sheep grazing violation in the Stanislaus Forest Reserve—the same reserve that was at issue in *Dastervignes*. This time the district court upheld the constitutionality of the regulations.[523] Two other criminal prosecutions for unauthorized sheep grazing were upheld in 1907, thereby bolstering the legal authority of the Forest Service to enforce its permit system.[524]

In 1906 Pinchot further stoked the fire of controversy by imposing fees for grazing permits. The GLO had considered charging a sheep grazing fee as early as 1898,[525] but concluded that the agency lacked authority.[526] Congress did not respond to the GLO's requests for authorizing legislation.[527] Undaunted, Pinchot began by obtaining a favorable opinion on the general issue of fees from the Attorney General in 1905.[528] Then, relying on the broad authority of the 1897 Organic Act, the Forest Service included a fee requirement in the 1906 edition of The Use Book.[529] The minimum seasonal charge was fixed at a modest five to eight cents per head of sheep and twenty to thirty-five cents per head of cattle

---

[518] *Id.*

[519] *See* S. DANA, *supra* note 47, at 116.

[520] *See supra* notes 60-62 and accompanying text.

[521] G. PINCHOT, *supra* note 51, at 265.

[522] *See* United States v. Matthews, 146 F. 306 (E.D. Wash. 1906).

[523] *See* United States v. Deguirro, 152 F. 568 (N.D. Cal. 1906).

[524] *See* United States v. Domingo, 152 F. 566 (D. Idaho 1907); United States v. Bale, 156 F. 687 (D.S.D. 1907).

[525] *See supra* note 504.

[526] After reporting that local GLO superintendents were recommending sheep-grazing fees, the Commissioner stated: "It is not thought that there is any authority in existing law . . . to exact payment for sheep-grazing privileges." 1899 GLO REPORT, *supra* note 503, at 108.

[527] *See* J. ISE, *supra* note 48, at 172.

[528] *See supra* text accompanying notes 276-80.

[529] 1906 USE BOOK. *supra* note 82, at 77-79.

and horses.[530] Rangers were informed that prices would "be gradually advanced as the market conditions, transportation facilities, and demand for reserve range warrant it, but the grazing fee charged will in all cases be reasonable."[531] Western legislators reacted furiously to the imposition of grazing fees and called on President Theodore Roosevelt to reverse Pinchot's decision.[532] However, President Roosevelt was an enthusiastic supporter of grazing fees and declined to intervene.[533]

Pinchot succeeded in easing the grazers' hostility to the fee system by recognizing grazing advisory boards in 1906. Livestock associations were invited to appoint advisory boards to confer with Forest Service officials regarding maximum numbers and distribution of stock to be allowed on forest lands.[534] Pinchot reported that the advisory board policy had produced "[a] marked improvement in sentiment among stockmen."[535] Still, many grazers continued to defy the regulations. The number of grazing trespass cases increased from 183 in 1907 to 358 in 1909.[536]

The question of the Forest Service's authority to regulate grazing and to charge grazing fees was settled by two test cases decided by the Supreme Court in May 1911. Both were resolved in favor of the Forest Service. In *United States v. Grimaud*,[537] the Court upheld the constitutionality of the regulations, including the power to assess fines for violations. In *Light v. United States*,[538] the Court held that while state laws required landowners to erect fences in order to claim damages for trespass by animals, the federal government was not required to erect fences to establish such

---

[530] *Id.* at 77. In the first year the Forest Service collected $514,000 in grazing fees. *See* 1906 ANNUAL REPORT OF THE CHIEF, H.R. DOC. NO. 6, 59th Cong., 2d Sess. 278 (1907) [hereinafter cited as 1906 ANNUAL REPORT OF THE CHIEF].

[531] 1906 USE BOOK, *supra* note 82, at 77.

[532] G. PINCHOT, *supra* note 51, at 272.

[533] *Id.*

[534] *See* 1906 ANNUAL REPORT OF THE CHIEF, *supra* note 530, at 280 (1907).

[535] *Id.*

[536] *See* 1907 ANNUAL REPORT OF THE CHIEF, *reprinted in* ANNUAL REPORT OF THE [U.S.] DEP'T OF AGRICULTURE 372 (1908); 1909 ANNUAL REPORT OF THE CHIEF, *reprinted in* ANNUAL REPORT OF THE [U.S.] DEP'T OF AGRICULTURE 391 (1910).

[537] 220 U.S. 506 (1911), discussed *supra* in text accompanying notes 285-90.

[538] 220 U.S. 523 (1911). The case was brought against Fred Light, of Snowmass, Colorado, for grazing his stock in the Holy Cross Forest Reserve without a permit. The case was a cause celebré in Colorado, and Light received financial support not only from local stock growers' associations but also from an appropriation from the Colorado legislature. *See, e.g.,* L. SHOEMAKER, SAGA OF A FOREST RANGER 128-30 (1958).

damages claims.[539] The Court also stated that grazers could claim
no vested right to use the public lands,[540] thereby dispelling the
notion that grazers on national forests continued to have the implied license recognized by the Court twenty years earlier in
Buford v. Houtz.[541] Thus, the legal foundation for regulating
grazing in the national forests was finally in place.[542]

3. Stabilizing Range Conditions and Policies (1911-1978)

The Supreme Court rulings in *Grimaud* and *Light* ended a
twenty-year debate over grazing policy on the national forests.
The Forest Service felt that its grazing policies had been vindi-
cated, both by the Supreme Court's decisions and by improved
range conditions. Chief Henry S. Graves reported in 1912:

> Seven years of actual range administration has convincingly
> demonstrated the correctness of the fundamental principles upon
> which it is based by tangible and striking results. A maximum of
> forage production and a maximum of benefit to the stock industry
> and to the meat-eating public are combined with protection of
> other forest interests and with healthy community development.
> Overgrazing has been stopped, range productiveness raised, losses
> from predatory animals, poisonous plants, and contagious diseases
> of stock lessened, inaccessible range opened to use, and each class
> of stock assigned to the kind of range best adapted to it.[543]

---

[539] *Id.* at 536-37.

[540] *Id.* at 535.

[541] 133 U.S. 320, 326 (1890). See *supra* note 479.

[542] While *Grimaud* and *Light* were pending in the federal courts, Pinchot took
the issue to the public. In a sophisticated exposition, he argued for broad Forest
Service authority under the "occupancy and use" provision of the 1897 Organic
Act, citing McCulloch v. Maryland, 17 U.S. (4 Wheat.) 159 (1819) and other
authorities. G. PINCHOT, THE FIGHT FOR CONSERVATION 56-78 (1910). One of
his conclusions was this:

> When action is needed for the public good there are two opposite points of
> view regarding the duty of an administrative officer in enforcing the law.
> One point of view asks, "Is there any express and specific law authorizing
> or directing such action?" and, having thus sought and found none, noth-
> ing is done. The other asks, "Is there any justification in law for doing this
> desirable thing?" and, having thus sought and found a legal justification,
> what the public good demands is done. I hold it to be the first duty of a
> public officer to obey the law. But I hold it to be his second duty, and a
> close second, to do everything the law will let him do for the public good,
> and not merely what the law compels or directs him to do.

Id. at 57-58.

[543] 1912 ANNUAL REPORT OF THE CHIEF, *reprinted in* ANNUAL REPORT OF
THE U.S. DEP'T OF AGRICULTURE 515 (1913).

Indeed, the grazing system developed for the national forests early this century has proved to be remarkably successful and durable.

In 1906 Pinchot expressed the basic policy objective of Forest Service range planning: "[W]henever a reserve is being injured by too much stock . . . the number will be reduced until the damage is stopped."[544] To determine whether range was being overgrazed Pinchot divided the land into districts (later called allotments) and instructed his rangers to inspect the land after each grazing season.[545] Based on this inspection, the rangers estimated the grazing capacity of each district and recommended the number of stock to be allowed to graze during the following year.[546] In addition, grazing was excluded altogether where "required for the protection of camping places, lakes and streams, roads and trails, etc."[547] The Forest Service implemented reductions in stock through adjustments in the number of annual permits issued.[548]

The Forest Service was forced temporarily to adjust its range management policies during World War I; high demand for meat caused the agency to allow over one million additional head of livestock to graze on national forest lands.[549] When the excess livestock were removed in 1923, considerable damage to the range was found to have occurred, necessitating further reductions.[550] During this post-World War I period the Forest Service began to prepare range management plans for each grazing allotment. The plans, which were developed cooperatively with the allottees, established the grazing capacity of each allotment.[551] If an allottee's grazing use exceeded the capacity of the allotment, the permit was modified to reduce the number of livestock or the length of the grazing season.[552] The permit modification was usually

---

[544] 1906 USE BOOK, *supra* note 82, at 72.

[545] *Id.* at 80. See *supra* text accompanying notes 82-84.

[546] 1906 USE BOOK, *supra* note 82, at 80-81.

[547] *Id.* at 80.

[548] *Id.* at 72.

[549] *See* THE WESTERN RANGE, *supra* note 480, at 130.

[550] *Id.*

[551] *See* 1928 ANNUAL REPORT OF THE CHIEF, *supra* note 97, at 34-35.

[552] 1925 ANNUAL REPORT OF THE CHIEF, *supra* note 91, at 32. To counter the allottees' objections to the post-war reductions, the Forest Service in 1925 began to issue 10 year permits to "all qualified applicants where safe carrying capacities have been arrived at." *Id.* at 33.

effected at the time the permit was transferred through inheritance or sale of the allottee's ranch property and livestock.[553]

The Forest Service pursued its range protection and permit reduction policies resolutely, cutting livestock grazing use by more than fifty percent between the end of World War I and the end of World War II.[554] Concurrently, big-game wildlife use more than tripled.[555]

The reductions in permitted livestock use generated intense hostility among stockmen and strong political opposition in the West. In 1947 the National Livestock Association requested congressional action to curtail the Forest Service's authority. The Association alleged that:

> [t]he subterfuge of range protection has been resorted to in making cuts on transfers of permits from fathers to sons and in many cases to the detriment of veterans of the recent World War; and . . . the present Forest Service, self-made, self-interpreted, and self-executed type of bureaucratic administration is the most vicious type of dictatorship in a democratic government, a detriment to our form of government in causing widespread dissatisfaction among forest permittees.[556]

---

[553] The use of "transfer adjustments" was originally adopted in cooperation with stockmen on the theory that where reductions were necessary it would be preferable "to make them on the fellow that is going out of business than on the man that is staying in business." *Forest Service Policy: Hearings Before the Subcomm. on Public Lands of the House Comm. on Public Lands*, 80th Cong., 1st Sess. 20 (1947) (testimony of C.M. Granger, Asst. Chief of the Forest Service) [hereinafter cited as *Hearings on Grazing Policy*]. However, ranchers later argued that the transfer adjustment policy lowered the sale value of their property, since purchasers customarily paid an extra premium to the permit-holder, amounting to several hundred dollars per head of cattle. A leading study has stated that the value of grazing permits is "capitalized into the value of the ranch." P. Foss, *supra* note 480, at 197. The agency revised its policy in 1953 to allow reduction at any time, rather than only at transfer. *See* Forest Service, U.S. Dep't of Agriculture, Report of the Chief 12, 17 (1953) [hereinafter cited as 1953 Annual Report of the Chief].

[554] 1953 Annual Report of the Chief, *supra* note 553, at 4.

[555] *Id.*

[556] 93 Cong. Rec. 1328 (1947). The Association recommended transferring the administration of range land from the Forest Service to the Grazing Service in the Department of Interior. *Id.* During this period Bernard DeVoto, writing his famous articles for the "Easy Chair" column in Harper's magazine, defended the Forest Service against the attacks of ranchers and other economic interests. Several of these columns are collected in B. DeVoto, The Easy Chair (1955).

Western state legislatures also denounced Forest Service grazing policy.[557]

The Committee on Public Lands of the House of Representatives responded to the widespread complaints by conducting investigatory hearings on Forest Service range management policies.[558] The committee made six recommendations, including a three-year moratorium on livestock permit reductions.[559] The Secretary of Agriculture accepted all of the committee's recommendations, except for the three-year moratorium.[560] Chief Lyle F. Watts reported in 1948: "This would have meant postponement of action badly needed to stop serious deterioration of certain watershed and range lands and start them on the road to recovery."[561]

Congress declined to overrule the Forest Service's refusal to retreat from its range protection policies. Instead of the strong remedial legislation favored by some stock interests, Congress enacted the Granger-Thye Act of 1950.[562] The Act simply provided statutory recognition of livestock advisory boards[563] and authorized the Forest Service to grant grazing permits for up to ten-year terms[564]—both existing agency policies. Although the Granger-Thye Act did not satisfy the ranchers' demands for reform, it

---

[557] A memorial passed by the Colorado Legislature accused the Forest Service of "dictatorially exercising legislative and judicial functions in regard to grazing on the national forests, instead of limiting itself to the administration of the forests." Colo. S.J. Mem. 2, 36th Leg., 1947 Colo. Sess. Laws 990, *reprinted in Hearings on Grazing Policy, supra* note 553, at 5. A similar resolution by the Wyoming legislature complained that the agency had disregarded the advice of "experience-seasoned, capable, and patriotic advisory board members" and had adopted grazing policies that were "vacillating, unreasonable, and dangerously restrictive." Wyo. S.J. Res. 1, 29th Leg., 1947 Wyo. Sess. Laws 253, *reprinted in Hearings on Grazing Policy, supra* note 553, at 6.

[558] *See Hearings on Grazing Policy, supra* note 553.

[559] *See* FOREST SERVICE, U.S. DEP'T OF AGRICULTURE, REPORT OF THE CHIEF 26 (1948) [hereinafter cited as 1948 ANNUAL REPORT OF THE CHIEF].

[560] The other recommendations concerned written agreements, hearing rights, cooperative range improvements, consideration of local economic conditions, and advisory appeal boards. *Id.* The Forest Service felt that "[a]cceptance of these proposals was in large measure confirmation of policies already long in effect." *Id.*

[561] *Id.*

[562] Act of Apr. 24, 1950, ch. 97, 64 Stat. 82 (codified as amended at 16 U.S.C. § 490 et seq. (1982)).

[563] 16 U.S.C. § 580k (1982).

[564] Act of Apr. 24, 1950, ch. 97, 64 Stat. 88 (codified as amended at 16 U.S.C. § 580l (1982)).

remained Congress's last word on national forest grazing until the 1970s.[565]

B. Modern Legislation and Planning

Several statutes enacted in the 1970s provide general guidance for Forest Service range planning. The principal statutes are the Federal Land Policy and Management Act of 1976[566] (FLPMA), the National Forest Management Act of 1976[567] (NFMA), and the Public Rangelands Improvement Act of 1978[568] (PRIA). Congress also has adopted specific management guidelines covering grazing in national forest wilderness areas.[569]

1. The Federal Land Policy and Management Act of 1976

Although FLPMA was enacted primarily to regulate the public lands administered by the Bureau of Land Management (BLM), the range management section of FLPMA applies to the national forest lands as well. FLPMA provides for regulation of grazing on the national forests through allotment management plans (AMPs). Section 402(d) of FLPMA states: "[A]ll permits and leases for domestic livestock grazing . . . may incorporate an allotment management plan developed by the Secretary concerned."[570] Although the language of the statute is discretion-

---

[565] Congress classified range as an administrative purpose of the national forests in the Multiple-Use Sustained-Yield Act of 1960. 16 U.S.C. § 528 (1982). Since the Act essentially codified the agency's traditional multiple-use policies, Congress required no more of the agency in range management than it had done in the past. By 1960 the number of livestock on the national forests had declined to 3.6 million. 1960 ANNUAL REPORT OF THE CHIEF, *supra* note 128, at 22. In 1970, 3.2 million livestock were permitted, but total use was 7.3 million animal unit months (AUMs)—nearly the same level as in 1949. 1970-71 ANNUAL REPORT OF THE CHIEF, *supra* note 193, at 84; 1953 ANNUAL REPORT OF THE CHIEF, *supra* note 553, at 4.

[566] 43 U.S.C §§ 1701-1784 (1982).

[567] 16 U.S.C. §§ 1600-1614 (1982).

[568] 43 U.S.C. §§ 1901-1908 (1982).

[569] *See infra* text accompanying notes 1916-27.

[570] 43 U.S.C. § 1752(d) (1982).

ary,[571] the Forest Service's regulations make development of AMPs mandatory for each allotment.[572]

FLPMA contains general guidelines for the Forest Service to follow in developing the AMPs. The Act requires planners to consult with the allottees, to plan for range improvements, and to prescribe how livestock operations will be conducted.[573] The House Committee Report states: "The plan could be as simple or as complex as circumstances warrant. The scope of detail included in it would be a matter in the discretion of the Secretary concerned."[574]

FLPMA gives the Forest Service broad discretion to modify the numbers of livestock grazing and set limits on seasonal use of grazing lands. Grazing permits and leases are subject to cancellation, suspension, or modification, in whole or in part.[575] In addition, agency planners are authorized to reexamine the condition of the range at any time and to adjust grazing to the extent

---

[571] The House bill required AMPs to contain provisions for the administration of grazing permits and leases. *See* H.R. 13,777, 94th Cong., 2d Sess. § 47 (1976), *reprinted in* SENATE COMM. ON ENERGY AND NATURAL RESOURCES, 95 CONG., 2ND SESS., LEGISLATIVE HISTORY OF THE FEDERAL LAND POLICY AND MANAGEMENT ACT OF 1976, at 371 (Comm. Print 1978) [hereinafter cited as FLPMA LEGISLATIVE HISTORY]. The AMPs subsequently were made discretionary by the conference committee. *See* H.R. REP. No. 1724, 94th Cong., 2d Sess. 63 (1976) (conference report), *reprinted in* FLPMA LEGISLATIVE HISTORY, *supra*, at 933.

[572] 36 C.F.R. § 222.2(b) (1984). AMPs are discussed in Coggins, *supra* note 32, at 121-22.

[573] The AMP is defined as follows:

An "allotment management plan" means a document prepared in consultation with the lessees or permittees involved, which applies to livestock operations on the public lands or on lands within National Forests in the eleven contiguous Western States and which:

(1) prescribes the manner in, and extent to, which livestock operations will be conducted in order to meet the multiple-use, sustained-yield, economic and other needs and objectives as determined for the lands by the Secretary concerned; and

(2) describes the type, location, ownership, and general specifications for the range improvements to be installed and maintained on the lands to meet the livestock grazing and other objectives of land management; and

(3) contains such other provisions relating to livestock grazing and other objectives found by the Secretary concerned to be consistent with the provisions of this Act and other applicable law.

43 U.S.C. § 1702(k) (1982).

[574] H.R. REP. No. 1163, 94th Cong., 2d Sess. 13, *reprinted in* 1976 U.S. CODE CONG. & AD. NEWS (USCCAN) 6175, 6187.

[575] 43 U.S.C. § 1752(a) (1982).

necessary.[576] As a general principle, the current allottee must receive preference on permit renewals; however, FLPMA specifically allows withdrawal of any land from grazing use through NFMA planning.[577] If an allotment is devoted to a public use other than grazing, the allottee's permit will not be renewed and the allottee is entitled to compensation only for the value of any permanent improvements on the withdrawn land.[578]

2. The National Forest Management Act of 1976

Although range management was not an issue during the NFMA debates, the Act has important implications for range planning. Section 6(i) of the NFMA states: "Resource plans and permits . . . shall be consistent with the land management plans . . . . When land management plans are revised, resource plans and permits . . ., when necessary, shall be revised as soon as practicable."[579] This means that the NFMA's land management plans govern both the AMPs required by FLPMA and the individual grazing permits. Therefore, the guidelines contained in the NFMA regulations are key elements in range planning.

The grazing section of the NFMA regulations combines traditional planning policy with recent statutory requirements. For instance, one regulation requires planners to identify lands suitable for grazing and browsing, determine their present and future condition, and plan "appropriate action" to restore lands that are in

---

[576] *Id.* § 1752(e). *See* Perkins v. Bergland, 608 F.2d 803 (9th Cir. 1979). Congress later provided that any reduction of AUMs that exceeds 10% of the former permit shall be suspended during any administrative appeal. The administrative appeal must be completed within two years. Pub. L. No. 96-126, 93 Stat. 954, 956 (1979). *See* Valdez v. Applegate, 616 F.2d 570 (10th Cir. 1980).

[577] The allottee has preference only "[s]o long as . . . the lands for which the permit or lease is issued remain available for domestic livestock grazing in accordance with land use plans prepared pursuant to . . . [§ 6 of the Rangelands and Renewable Resources Planning Act]." 43 U.S.C. § 1752(c) (1982).

[578] *Id.* § 1752(g). No permit may be cancelled under the public use provision without two years' notice, except in case of emergency. *Id.* Several earlier cases held that grazing permits were privileges and did not confer any vested rights. *See, e.g.*, United States v. Fuller, 409 U.S. 488 (1973). This point of law was not modified by FLPMA. 43 U.S.C. § 1752(h) (1982). The House Committee Report emphasized that the legislation "would not change the fact that grazing use of the public and national forest lands is a privilege and not a right." H.R. REP. No. 1163, 94th Cong., 2d Sess. 12, *reprinted in* 1976 USCCAN 6175, 6186.

[579] 16 U.S.C. § 1604(i) (1982).

"less than satisfactory condition."[580] This regulation basically re-states the central purpose of Forest Service range planning since the Pinchot era—to manage livestock grazing so as to prevent or repair resource damage.[581] On the other hand, the same regulation speaks of "providing habitat for management indicator species."[582] The management indicator species (MIS) regulation adds a new dimension to range planning. The concept was devised by the Committee of Scientists in the late 1970s to implement the NFMA's wildlife protection requirements.[583] The Committee de-cided to cross-reference wildlife protection provisions with the range regulations after agreeing that grazing was not the only purpose of range management.[584]

The NFMA wildlife protection regulations direct planners to set objectives in the forest plans for maintaining or improving MIS habitats.[585] For instance, a national forest might select elk as an MIS and set a twenty percent increase in elk habitat as the planning objective. If competition with livestock for forage were the principal factor limiting increases in the elk population, a re-duction in livestock grazing would be required. The reduction would be accomplished by revising the AMPs and the grazing per-mits on the national forest.

3. The Public Rangelands Improvement Act of 1978

PRIA[586] contains several significant planning provisions. First, the Act, conspicuously using the word "shall," establishes a na-tional policy of improving soil quality, wildlife habitat, watershed, plant communities, and other elements of range condition.[587]

---

[580] 36 C.F.R. § 219.20(a) (1984). The most recent estimate is that 30% of Forest Service rangelands are in less than satisfactory condition. *1985 Forest Service Budget, supra* note 10, at 1347.

[581] *See supra* text accompanying note 544.

[582] 36 C.F.R. § 219.20 (1984).

[583] *See infra* text accompanying notes 1597-1617.

[584] *See Committee of Scientists, Minutes of Nov. 1-2, 1978, supra* note 402, at 15.

[585] 36 C.F.R. § 219.19(a) (1984).

[586] 43 U.S.C.]§ 19]01-1908 (1982) and scattered sections of FLPMA, 43 U.S.C. §§ 1701-1784 (1982).

[587] The declaration of policy is made in 43 U.S.C. § 1901(a), (b)(2) (1982). The policy is mandated to be carried out in § 1903(b), which the leading legal study of BLM rangelands has called "the most important provision in all of the range management statutes." Coggins, *supra* note 32, at 115-17. Section 1903 may not, however, apply to the Forest Service. Although several provisions of PRIA do apply to the Secretary of Agriculture, PRIA's definitions specify that

Second, PRIA amended FLPMA's grazing provisions to emphasize that AMPs must be developed with input from the allottees, advisory boards, and state agencies.[588] Third, AMPs must be "tailored to the specific range conditions" and must be reviewed periodically to determine whether they have been "effective in improving the range condition."[589] Finally, Congress directed the Forest Service to initiate experimental stewardship programs,[590] a provision with potentially far-reaching effects on range planning. The purpose of range stewardship programs is to provide incentives for grazing allottees to improve the condition of the range[591] by reducing grazing fees, which have been a source of controversy since the Forest Service first imposed them in 1905.[592] Stewardship planning offers allottees the opportunity to spend up to one-half of their grazing fees on range improvements such as fences, stockponds, and stocktrails.[593] The program is intended to benefit both the ranchers, by reducing grazing fees, and the Forest

---

"Secretary" means the Secretary of the Interior unless otherwise designated. 43 U.S.C. § 1902(h) (1982). Section 1903(b) begins with "the Secretary." *Id.* § 1901(b)(2). On the other hand, the policy declarations in § 1901 refer to "public rangelands", which are defined to include Forest Service, as well as BLM, lands. *Id.* § 1902(a).

[588] 43 U.S.C. § 1752(d) (1982). This provision expressly applies to Forest Service as well as BLM lands.

[589] *Id.* Professor Coggins comments:

These words are pregnant with implications for the direction of public rangeland management. Ranchers and managers will ignore this strong language only at their peril. The secretarial duties imposed, while permitting some administrative leeway, offer outsiders an avenue to challenge specific decisions and general policies. The duties are both mandatory and reviewable for consistency with the overall improvement standard.

Coggins, supra note 32, at 121-27.

[590] 43 U.S.C. § 1908(a) (1982).

[591] The stewardship program is aimed primarily at areas of mixed ownership and jurisdiction. *See* S. REP. NO. 1237, 95th Cong., 2d Sess. 12, *reprinted in* 1978 USCCAN at 4069, 4076. Modeled after a successful cooperative program in Grant County, Oregon, stewardship planning is supervised by a steering committee of representatives from the Forest Service, BLM, state agencies, livestock producers, and landowners. *Id.* at 13, *reprinted in* 1978 USCCAN at 4077. The BLM sought to implement § 1908(a) by means of "Cooperative Management Agreements" but a district court struck down the program as not congressionally authorized on the ground that it was a permanent system that unlawfully abdicated the BLM's duty to prescribe the number of livestock that may be grazed on the federal lands. *See* Natural Resources Defense Council v. Hodel, ____ F. Supp. ____ (E.D. Cal. 1985).

[592] *See generally* FEDERAL GRAZING FEES STUDY, *supra* note 466; Pankey Land & Cattle Co. v. Hardin, 427 F.2d 43 (10th Cir. 1970).

[593] 43 U.S.C. § 1908(a)(2) (1982).

Service, by improving range conditions without additional appropriations. Finally, PRIA requires the Forest Service to report to Congress on the results of the experiment by the end of 1985.[594]

4. Authority to Protect Rangeland

There is little case law bearing directly on Forest Service grazing decisions.[595] In part this is due to the relative paucity of statutory law: the Forest Service continues to enjoy the generally untrammeled regulatory authority sketched out in *United States v. Grimaud*[596] more than seventy years ago. Nevertheless, although there is nothing equivalent to the far-reaching restraints placed on timber harvesting by the NFMA,[597] there is plainly law to apply to grazing on the national forests. Both FLPMA and PRIA address the key issue of stock permit reductions on overgrazed land by providing the authority to reduce permits and to prescribe general limits for the Forest Service's exercise of that power.[598] Procedurally, the Forest Service must comply with NEPA,[599] FLPMA,[600] and the general planning process in the NFMA. Wild

---

[594] *Id.* § 1908(b).

[595] *See generally* Coggins, Evans & Lindberg-Johnson, *The Law of Public Rangeland Management I: The Extent and Distribution of Federal Power*, 12 ENVTL. L. 537, 602-21 (1982) (addressing judicial review of BLM grazing decisions).

[596] 220 U.S. 506 (1911). *See generally supra* section II(A)(1).

[597] *See generally infra* section II(B).

[598] *See supra* text accompanying notes 570-78, 586-89.

[599] 42 U.S.C. §§ 4321-4370 (1982). Major litigation resulted in a ruling that the BLM's national Programmatic Environmental Impact Statement for its grazing program was insufficiently site-specific. Natural Resources Defense Council (NRDC) v. Morton, 388 F. Supp. 829 (D.D.C. 1974), *aff'd per curiam*, 527 F.2d 1386 (D.C. Cir.), *cert. denied*, 427 U.S. 913 (1976). The court gave the BLM flexibility regarding the geographic level at which EIS's must be prepared, and the BLM ultimately decided to do 212 site-specific EIS's pursuant to a court-ordered schedule. *See* Natural Resources Defense Council v. Andrus, 448 F. Supp. 802, 804 (D.D.C. 1978). The BLM expects to complete over 8000 AMPs. *NRDC v. Morton*, 388 F. Supp. at 832.

The same reasoning presumably applies to the Forest Service's grazing program. By analogy, the EIS for each NFMA forest plan will have to assess "the specific environmental effects of the [grazing] permits issued, and to be issued," for that national forest. *Id.* at 841.

[600] The Forest Service currently conducts site-specific analyses of the range environment as the basis for the content of each AMP required by FLFMA. *See* FOREST SERVICE MANUAL § 2214.11 (1984). The district ranger is responsible for conducting the analysis and documenting the results in an *Analysis of the Management Situation—Summary Report. Id.* § 2214.04c. The Summary Report discusses the historical and present use of the range, the ecological condition and grazing capacity, and alternatives for meeting the objectives of the national

horses and burros on national forest lands must be managed in accordance with the Wild Free-Roaming Horses and Burros Act.[601] In addition, the Forest Service must comply with the NFMA's substantive "diversity" requirement, and the implementing regulations that protect wildlife on rangelands through the device of management indicator species.[602] Thus the public rangeland is no longer just for domestic stock.

Three modern cases directly consider the scope of judicial review of substantive federal agency decisions involving grazing on public lands. *Valdez v. Applegate*[603] is inconclusive but suggests that very little deference should be given to agency decisions on

---

forest's NFMA plan. *Id.* § 2213.21. Although the Summary Report is not equivalent to a NEPA document, the Forest Service Manual suggests that planners should incorporate by reference the Summary Report's descriptions and analysis of alternatives for actions that require NEPA documentation. *Id.* § 2213.3. The range analysis procedure is set out in considerable detail in §§ 2213-2213.19c of the Forest Service Manual.

[601] 16 U.S.C. §§ 1331-1340 (1982). *See generally* M. BEAN, THE EVOLUTION OF NATIONAL WILDLIFE LAW 154-66 (1983). The Chief of the Forest Service is responsible for establishing wild horse and burro territories. 36 C.F.R. § 222.21(a)(3) (1984). A management plan must be developed for each territory. *Id.* § 222.21(a)(4). The plans follow the same outlines as regular AMPs but must also comply with specific provisions in the Forest Service Manual including means of capture and removal and other matters specifically related to wild horse and burro management. FOREST SERVICE MANUAL § 2264.1 (1984). In addition, herd unit plans may be developed for wild horses and burros that range as one band. *Id.* §§ 2260.5, 2264.1. In special situations, the Chief may designate Horse and Burro Ranges, *id.* § 2263.3, where management is devoted principally to the herd's welfare. *Id.* § 2260.4. Ordinarily, though, management of each territory is coordinated with existing livestock and wildlife use and is directed at maintaining a biologically sound population. *Id.* at § 2264.11a. In cases where wild horse and burro territory overlaps with a livestock grazing allotment, separate management plans are prepared and "closely coordinated." *Id.* at § 2214.1.

The agency recognizes its responsibility to protect wild horses and burros that migrate or stray onto private lands. *Id.* at § 2264.2. However, the Manual does not authorize Forest Service personnel to enter private land to inspect or protect the animals. *Id.* Instead, Forest Service personnel are directed to initiate "appropriate administrative and/or criminal and civil judicial procedures" when necessary. *Id.* As noted, the numbers of wild horses and burros in the national forests are relatively low. *See supra* note 464.

[602] *See supra* text accompanying notes 579-85, 1597-1617.

[603] 616 F.2d 570 (10th Cir. 1980). Plaintiffs challenged a BLM order reducing local grazing permits. The district judge refused to issue a preliminary injunction, finding that plaintiffs failed to show the likelihood of irreparable harm. The Court of Appeals for the Tenth Circuit reversed, halting the pending BLM stock reductions, and remanded. The remand order, however, did not provide any substantive standards to guide the lower court in finally determining whether to enjoin the permit reductions. *Id.* at 572.

stock reductions. *Hinsdale Livestock Co. v. United States*[604] is unlikely to be followed because it virtually disregards BLM stock reduction decisions and effectively looks to the plaintiff ranchers as the primary experts on whether stock reductions are necessary.[605] Whether animal units months are increased or decreased, agency expertise should be given primary weight.[606]

The leading case on judical review of livestock grazing reductions is *Perkins v. Bergland*.[607] In the early 1970s the forest supervisor of the Prescott National Forest in Arizona reduced by one-half the number of cattle allowed on the Perkins's permits,[608] based on a finding that the allotments had been damaged by overgrazing.[609] The Court of Appeals for the Ninth Circuit first rejected the argument that the reductions amounted to a revocation, stating that "[h]owever drastic an effect on their livelihood the reductions here may have had, the permits were not revoked."[610]

The court then rejected the government's position that under FLPMA the Forest Service's discretion to determine grazing capacity was so broad as to be unreviewable.[611] The court based this conclusion primarily on FLPMA's policy statement that "judicial review of public land adjudication decisions be provided by law."[612] The judicial role, however, is very limited. In order for a court to set aside a decision to reduce grazing permits for conservation purposes, the plaintiffs must prove that the agency's

---

[604] 501 F. Supp. 773 (D. Mont. 1980).

[605] The district judge briefly reviewed the administrative record allegedly supporting emergency stock reductions based upon a drought, and found that "these reasons do not create an emergency" within the meaning of 43 U.S.C. § 1752(a) (1982), allowing emergency reductions without notice. 501 F. Supp. at 776. The court then found that the "plaintiffs have been ranching their entire adult lives, were raised ranching, and . . . have had . . . [extensive] experience in conducting ranching operations" on public lands. *Id.* at 777. The court resolved the evidentiary conflict by expressly adopting "[t]he opinion of plaintiffs . . . that the range resources will not be severely damaged" if their stock were allowed to graze the remainder of the season. *Id.*

[606] *See, e.g.*, 5 U.S.C. § 706 (1982) (Administrative Procedure Act).

[607] 608 F.2d 803 (9th Cir. 1979).

[608] *Id.* at 803-04.

[609] *Id.* at 804.

[610] *Id.*

[611] *Id.* at 805-06. The lower court had ruled against the Perkins on the ground that the agency's decisions were "committed to agency discretion by law" under the Administrative Procedure Act (5 U.S.C. § 701(a)(2) (1982)). *Id.* at 804.

[612] 43 U.S.C. § 1701(a)(6) (1982).

methods for calculating carrying capacity were "irrational."⁶¹³
The court noted that "a contesting party must show that there is
virtually no evidence in the record to support the agency's methodology in gathering and evaluating the data."⁶¹⁴

Thus the scope of future judicial review is likely to be determined by the administrative record in individual cases. If Forest
Service officials adequately document their decisions on stock reductions and increases, the decisions are likely to be upheld. The
same is true with policy decisions based on management indicator
species. The fact is that Congress has not been offended by traditional Forest Service grazing policy; consequently, rigorous legislative standards have not been imposed.

---

⁶¹³ 608 F.2d at 807. The standard of review is based on the court's authority
under the Administrative Procedure Act to set aside agency action that is found
to be arbitrary and capricious. 5 U.S.C. § 706(2)(A) (1982). *See also* Borrego v.
United States, 577 F.Supp. 408 (D.N.M. 1983).
⁶¹⁴ 608 F.2d at 807, n.12.

IV

TIMBER

Timber planning is at the center of many of the controversies that Congress addressed in the NFMA and sought to resolve through local forest planning. Historically, the principal occupation of the Forest Service has been to plan for timber conservation and production. Prior to World War II, the Forest Service emphasized fire suppression and trail access to preserve the timber resource. However, with the depletion of private forests and the post-war demand for housing, timber sale planning and road access became the dominant activity on many national forests.

Relatively heavy cutting and lack of reforestation on private lands have left the national forests today with a disproportionate share of the nation's timber. This is particularly true in the West, where many national forests were set aside from the public domain and many areas remain roadless. More than half of the nation's inventory of softwood sawtimber is located in national forests,[615] although they constitute less than twenty percent of the nation's commercial timberland.[616] As a résult, the national forests are an important source of wood products: nearly one-third of the nation's softwood timber supply comes from the national forests.[617] On the other hand, remote location, high elevation, low productivity, and other factors make many national forest timberlands economically less attractive for wood production than better-situated private lands.

The majority of Forest Service receipts and expenditures are attributable to timber production. Gross revenues from national forest timber sales are substantial.[618] However, the net income to the federal government is diminished by expenditures through the return of twenty-five percent of the receipts to local governments;[619] through appropriations for timber sale administration,

---

[615] *1985 Forest Service Budget, supra* note 10, at 1283.

[616] 1981 ASSESSMENT, *supra* note 9, at 228.

[617] *1985 Forest Service Budget, supra* note 10, at 1283. The other major sources of commercial timber production from federal lands are the former "Oregon and California" railroad lands, now administered by the BLM. *See generally* BUREAU OF GOVTL. RESEARCH & SERV., UNIV. OF OREGON, THE O & C LANDS (1981).

[618] For example, national forest timber receipts for fiscal year 1981 were $947 million, which constituted 83% of all commercial timber receipts. 1981 ANNUAL REPORT, *supra* note 19, at 2 (1982).

[619] *Id.*

intensive management, reforestation, and other costs;[620] and through subtraction of road access costs from the purchase price of timber sales.[621] In many national forests the expenditures far exceed the receipts.[622]

The national forests differ greatly in the condition of their timber and productive capacity of their land. For instance, little old-growth timber[623] remains on the southern and eastern national forests, but growth rates in those young, vigorous stands are relatively high.[624] Conversely, the northern Rocky Mountain and West Coast forests often contain large volumes of timber, but these mature stands produce little growth; in addition, the second-growth[625] may regenerate slowly due to steep slopes and poor soils. This diversity of forest types and of other resources is one factor that led the Forest Service to pursue a decentralized system of management and planning.[626] It is also one reason why Congress decided to rely on the agency's local planning system to implement the guidelines of the NFMA.[627]

---

[620] *See* Wilkinson, *The Forest Service: A Call For a Return to First Principles*, 5 PUB. LAND L. REV. 1, 18 n.92 (1984).

[621] For an explanation of the "purchaser credit" system for financing timber access roads and its relationship to appropriated road funds, see S. REP. NO. 686, 93d Cong., 2d Sess. 18-21 (1974), *reprinted in* RPA COMPILATION, *supra* note 173, at 74-77.

[622] *See, e.g.*, U.S. GEN. ACCOUNTING OFFICE, CONGRESS NEEDS BETTER INFORMATION ON FOREST SERVICE'S BELOW-COST TIMBER SALES 9-11 (1984).

[623] Foresters generally refer to timber as either "old-growth" or "second-growth." A stand of old-growth timber consists of trees that are mostly over 200 years old. *See generally* Juday, *Old Growth Forests: A Necessary Element of Multiple Use and Sustained Yield National Forest Management*, 8 ENVTL. L. 497 (1978). Second-growth is the stand of young trees that replaces the old-growth timber after harvesting. Old-growth and second-growth are sometimes referred to as "natural" and "managed" stands, respectively. *E.g.*, S. REP. NO. 893, 94th Cong., 2d Sess. 78-83, 1976, *reprinted in* RPA COMPILATION, *supra* note 173, at 357-62.

[624] *See* 1981 ASSESSMENT, *supra* note 9, at 231-35.

[625] *See supra* note 623.

[626] If timber and forage could be produced in a factory, it would not be necessary to depend so largely on the judgment, personal skill and managing ability of the . . . forest supervisors [and] district rangers . . . . But 158,000,000 acres are under management throughout the country and present the most variable conditions of climate, soil, and human use. A decentralized form of organization with wide latitude in dealing with local conditions on the ground is essential.

1925 ANNUAL REPORT OF THE CHIEF, *supra* note 91, at 15.

[627] *See* S. REP. NO. 893, 94th Cong., 2d Sess. 26, *reprinted in* 1976 U.S. CODE CONG. & AD. NEWS 6662, 6685.

Until the late 1970s, Forest Service timber planners operated with little statutory or regulatory direction. The 1897 Organic Act strictly limited the Forest Service's authority to sell timber, but neither national nor local agency planners observed those limitations.[628] The Multiple-Use Sustained-Yield Act of 1960 generally deferred to the agency's timber management policies.[629] The Department of Agriculture's regulations for timber management planning during the 1960s and early 1970s occupied barely one column of the Code of Federal Regulations.[630] The principal source of official direction for local timber planners was the Forest Service Manual.[631] The NFMA converted many of the Manual's timber planning guidelines and procedures into statutory and regulatory requirements.[632]

---

[628] *See* West Virginia Div. of the Izaak Walton League of Am., Inc. v. Butz, 522 F.2d 945 (4th Cir. 1975).

[629] *See supra* text accompanying notes 379-81.

[630] The timber planning regulations stated in their entirety:
Management plans for national forest timber resources shall be prepared and revised, as needed, for working circles or other practicable units of national forest. Such plans shall:
(1) Be designed to aid in providing a continuous supply of national forest timber for the use and necessities of the citizens of the United States.
(2) Be based on the principle of sustained yield, with due consideration to the condition of the area and the timber stands covered by the plan.
(3) Provide, so far as is feasible, an even flow of national forest timber in order to facilitate the stabilization of communities and of opportunities for employment.
(4) Provide for coordination of timber production and harvesting with other uses of national forest land in accordance with the principles of multiple use management.
(5) Establish the allowable cutting rate which is the maximum amount of timber which may be cut from the national forest lands within the unit by years or other periods.
(6) Be approved by the Chief, Forest Service, unless authority for such approval shall be delegated to subordinates by the Chief.
36 C.F.R. § 221.3(a) (1984).

[631] The Forest Service Manual, which was originally issued by Gifford Pinchot as The Use Book, is a detailed and lengthy set of loose-leaf volumes located in each Forest Service office. The Manual traditionally has been the principal source of direction and guidance for Forest Service managers and planners. *See generally* G. ROBINSON, *supra* note 2, at 38. While the Manual does not have the same legal effect as formal regulations adopted pursuant to the Administrative Procedure Act, some courts have treated the Manual as binding on the Forest Service, see National Forest Preservation Group v. Butz, 343 F. Supp. 696, 703 (D. Mont. 1972), or as a limitation on the agency's discretion to implement statutory law, see Parker v. United States, 448 F.2d 793, 797 (10th Cir. 1972). *See also* Morton v. Mancari, 417 U.S. 535 (1974).

[632] *See* Wolf, *supra* note 176, at 17, 22.

This section first introduces the basic concepts in modern federal timber planning. It then reviews the historical development of timber harvest planning in the Forest Service. Special attention is directed to the crucial years of 1966 to 1976, the time of intense controversy preceding the passage of the NFMA; the so-called Church guidelines, issued by a Senate Interior subcommittee in 1972, figure prominently during that era. Finally, the section examines the existing law governing timber harvesting in the national forests.

A. Issues in Modern Forest Service Timber Planning

Ever since the Pinchot era, Forest Service planners have considered three elements in formulating timber management plans. First, the planners determine what land is suitable for timber management. This is the inventory of land that can be considered for harvest. Second, they calculate the amount of timber that can be sold from the suitable land base. Third, they determine the appropriate methods to harvest and regenerate the timber. The NFMA and its implementing regulations deal with each element in considerable detail. We begin by introducing some of the basic concepts and terminology of timber planning.

1. Suitability

The suitability requirements of the NFMA and its regulations derive from two sources. One source is the congressional response to public controversy over Forest Service timber management practices in the late 1960s and early 1970s. The second source is the traditional agency policies for classifying land in timber management plans. The latter source evolved over the years from common sense standards developed by local timber planners.

Prior to the NFMA, a basic aspect of timber management planning was to determine the amount of commercial and noncommercial forest land within the planning area.[633] Commercial forest land consisted of all land that met three criteria. First, if at least ten percent of the land was covered with trees, it was considered forest land.[634] Second, if the land could grow twenty cubic feet of

---

[633] Timber planning areas were called "working circles." *See* G. ROBINSON, *supra* note 2, at 62. The Forest Service has generally replaced working circles with national forests as the planning unit for timber management. *Id.*

[634] The tree cover had to consist of "utilizable" species, but the range of species was very broad. Interview with Bud Sloan, Interdisciplinary Team Leader,

wood per acre annually, it was considered "capable" (or productive) forest land.[635] Third, if the soil, terrain, or location would make logging operations too costly for the timber sale purchaser to earn a profit or too damaging to the other forest resources, the land was considered unsuitable due to "inoperability."[636] Land that was nonforest, not capable, or inoperable was classified as noncommercial and removed from the land base used to determine the allowable cut.

The Forest Service also excluded land from the allowable cut base if it was not "available" for timber production due to congressional or administrative action, such as wilderness or wilderness study designation.[637] The Forest Service sold timber and collected inventory data only on the available commercial land.

The timber planners' traditional three-step system to assess suitability according to the commercial/noncommercial classification began to break down in the 1960s. As the amount of timber harvesting increased, it became more important to determine accurately the size and location of the commercial land base.[638] This

---

Willamette Nat'l Forest, in Eugene, Or. (Dec. 6, 1983). The forest land definition has remained essentially unchanged. 36 C.F.R. § 219.3 (1984).

[635] The "capable" category was changed to "productive" in 1972, see REPORT OF PRESIDENT'S ADVISORY PANEL ON TIMBER AND THE ENVIRONMENT 183 (1973) [hereinafter cited as ADVISORY PANEL REPORT], quoting FOREST SERVICE MANUAL § 2413.13, and then changed back to "capable" in 1979. 36 C.F.R. § 219.12(b) (1982). The 1982 NFMA regulations dropped the capable/ productive category completely. *See* 47 Fed. Reg. 43,033 (1982).

[636] Interview with Bud Sloan, *supra* note 634. Characteristically, land considered inoperable would contain cliffs with scattered areas of timber and nonforest land. *Id.* In 1972 the agency began to consider only "permanently inoperable" land as noncommercial. *See* ADVISORY PANEL REPORT, *supra* note 635, at 183, quoting FOREST SERVICE MANUAL § 2413.13. Neither the 1979 nor 1982 NFMA regulations directly address the suitability of inoperable or inaccessible land. Under the current regulations this type of land could presumably be considered as either technologically unsuitable, 36 C.F.R. § 219.14(a)(2) (1984), or economically unsuitable. *Id.* § 219.14(c)(3).

[637] In 1972 the Forest Service divided the unavailable land into two subclasses: deferred and reserved. Reserved was officially withdrawn from timber production by statute, administrative regulation, or land-use plan. *See* ADVISORY PANEL REPORT, *supra* note 635, at 183. Deferred land, such as a wilderness study area, was land currently considered or proposed for withdrawal. *Id.*

[638] FOREST SERVICE, U.S. DEP'T OF AGRICULTURE, STRATIFICATION OF FOREST LAND FOR TIMBER MANAGEMENT PLANNING ON THE WESTERN NATIONAL FORESTS 1 (1971) [hereinafter cited as STRATIFICATION STUDY]. The size of the commercial land base was important because it directly affected the annual allowable cut. One commentator stated, "The most important factor resulting in reduced allowable cuts under revised timber management plans is the reduction in land base available for full timber yields due to multiple use and

question was especially critical on land with difficult terrain and other economic and environmental problems.[639]

In addition, the timber classification system often conflicted directly with the land use planning system that the Forest Service adopted during the 1960s.[640] While the land use plans generally did not withdraw commercial land from timber production,[641] they directed local planners to protect scenery, water quality, and other values within designated land use zones.[642] Since it was usually necessary that at least some trees remain uncut in order to protect those values, timber sales within the zones would normally yield less timber than anticipated by the timber management plans. Separate planning for nontimber resources created similar conflicts.[643] As will be seen below, the NFMA has several provisions that focus on the initial question of what land is suitable for harvesting.

2. Harvest Level

The Forest Service has always placed a ceiling on each national forest's annual timber sales from the suitable land base in order to insure a perpetual sustained yield of timber. This ceiling is called the harvest level, the annual allowable cut, or the allowable sale quantity (ASQ). Planners have used a variety of formulas, computer programs, and assumptions to determine the ASQ on

---

environmental constraints which are being reflected primarily through classification of the land into categories." Newport, *The Availability of Timber Resources From the National Forests and Other Federal Lands*, in ADVISORY PANEL REPORT, *supra* note 635, at 169.

[639] *See* STRATIFICATION STUDY, *supra* note 638, at 6.

[640] For a discussion of early Forest Service land use plans, see *supra* text accompanying notes 125-41.

[641] Rather than withdraw land from production, multiple-use plans would provide "coordinating requirements" for management of the resources within a zone. *See supra* text accompanying notes 135-41. Timber management plans only considered land to be unavailable if it had been officially withdrawn from timber production. Since the multiple-use zones remained officially available, timber planners had no grounds for classifying the zone as noncommercial land. Therefore, prior to the 1970s the timber management plans assumed that commercial land within restrictive multiple-use zones would produce as much timber as any other commercial land. Interview with Bud Sloane, *supra* note 634.

[642] *See supra* text accompanying notes 135-39.

[643] For instance, wildlife resource plans often designated areas of commercial timberland as elk winter range. Since wildlife habitat protection was not considered a reason to classify land as noncommercial, timber planners could not reduce the anticipated timber yield from the winter range area. Interview with Bud Sloan, *supra* note 634.

different types of forest.[644] The two primary factors used to calculate the ASQ are the volume of timber[645] and the rotation period anticipated between future harvests.[646]

In a hypothetical national forest that has been fully managed on an even-aged basis, the ASQ would be calculated by dividing the total volume of the forest by the average rotation period. For example, an even-aged forest with 100 million board feet (mmbf) and a rotation age of 100 years would have an ASQ of 1 mmbf:

$$ASQ = volume/rotation$$
$$ASQ = 100 \text{ mmbf}/100 \text{ years}$$
$$ASQ = 1 \text{ mmbf}$$

---

[644] During the early 1900s the Forest Service generally used a simple volume/rotation formula to calculate the allowable cut. The Von Mandel formula was Y = 2 G/r; where Y = annual yield (i.e. ASQ); G = growing stock volume; and r = rotation age. *See* Parry, Vaux & Dennis, *Changing Conceptions of Sustained-Yield Policy on the National Forests*, 81 J. FORESTRY 150, 151 (1983). The formula originated in Europe, where timber stands consisted of relatively young and intensively managed trees. On these managed forests roughly the same amount of timber volume grew back each year to replace the amount harvested. The situation on the American forests was just the opposite: the forests consisted of wild, slow-growing, old-growth stands. The American forests had much larger volumes but smaller growth rates than the European forests. Therefore, using the Von Mandel formula would have caused harvest levels to far exceed growth rates. Conversely, equating ASQ with actual growth rates would have permitted only nominal harvest levels for centuries on some mature stands. As a result, the Forest Service adopted other formulas that provided for orderly liquidation of the old-growth on an even-flow, sustained-yield basis. The most popular formula of the mid-1900s was first proposed by E.J. Hanzlick in 1922. The Hanzlick formula was Y = I + Vm/r; where I = annual growth of immature timber, and Vm = volume of mature timber. *See* Hanzlick, *Determination of the Annual Cut on a Sustained Basis for Virgin American Forests*, 20 J. FORESTRY 611 (1922).

[645] Volume of timber is the estimated quantity of wood that can be processed and marketed. Traditionally, timber volume has been measured in terms of "board feet." One board foot equals a piece of timber 12 inches square and one inch thick. ADVISORY PANEL REPORT, *supra* note 635, at 538. Timber volume can also be measured in terms of "cubic feet," in which case a greater proportion of the tree is assumed to be commercially usable. The relationship of board feet to cubic feet is relative to the age of the tree. For example, one cubic foot of old-growth Douglas fir equals approximately five board feet. With smaller Douglas fir trees in a second-growth forest, one cubic foot equals about 3.5 board feet. UMPQUA NAT'L FOREST LMP, *supra* note 117, at 167. Accordingly, using cubic feet instead of board feet to measure a forest containing at least some second-growth will produce relatively greater estimates of volume.

[646] Rotation period is defined as "[t]he planned number of years between the formation of a forest crop and its final cutting at a specified stage of maturity." ADVISORY PANEL REPORT, *supra* note 635, at 540.

It is important to note that the ASQ will increase if either the volume increases or the rotation period decreases:

$$ASQ = 200 \text{ mmbf}/100 \text{ years}$$
$$ASQ = 2 \text{ mmbf}$$

or

$$ASQ = 100 \text{ mmbf}/50 \text{ years}$$
$$ASQ = 2 \text{ mmbf}$$

Volume and rotation period are determined in part by three factors: the definition of sustained yield on old-growth forests, the definition of rotation period, and the estimates of future volume and rotation period. The NFMA provides direction to the Forest Service on each of these factors.

(a) Nondeclining Even Flow (NDEF)

Determining the ASQ on old-growth forests posed a dilemma to the Forest Service and to Congress. Due to their stands of large trees typically hundreds of years old, old-growth forests generally contain greater volumes of timber now than they will when converted into managed forests of second-growth. In order to prevent the harvest level from declining after this conversion period, planners do not consider the current volume of old-growth. Instead, they base their calculations on the amount of timber expected to be produced from the managed, second-growth stands that replace the old-growth.[647] This policy is called non-declining even flow (NDEF).

Critics of NDEF argue that it effectively erases a potential "bonus" of timber volume that could be harvested from old-growth forests without reducing the eventual, post-conversion harvest level, or long-term sustained yield capacity (LTSYC).[648] Others maintain that NDEF enhances multiple-use values by allowing a

---

[647] At present the Forest Service uses a formula that is similar to the Von Mandel formula discussed in *supra* note 644. The formula is LTSY = V/r; where LTSY = long-term sustained yield and V = volume of intermediate and final harvests of future managed stands. LTSY will equal ASQ on forests with large amounts of old-growth. The Forest Service refers to this situation as an old-growth "surplus" forest. The ASQ of a forest with mostly immature timber will be lower than the forest's LTSY level until the timber matures. This is called an old-growth "deficit" forest. *See* U.S. Dep't of Agriculture, *A Primer on Non-Declining Yield and Departures*, WESTERN WILDLANDS, Winter 1983, at 2.

[648] *See* MacCleery, *Non-Declining Yield and Community Stability: The False Connection*, WESTERN WILDLANDS, Winter 1983, at 4-5. *See generally* G. COGGINS & C. WILKINSON, *supra* note 345, at 532-33.

more gradual transition from natural to managed forest conditions.[649] Nevertheless, the NFMA requires the Forest Service to follow NDEF policy, with some exceptions.[650]

(b) Culmination of Mean Annual Increment (CMAI)

The NFMA's definition of the minimum rotation period (the planned number of years between stocking of new trees and harvesting) is called "culmination of mean annual increment" (CMAI).[651] CMAI is the age at which the rate of growth among a stand of young trees peaks and after which annual growth remains level or declines. CMAI is a traditional silvicultural definition designed to maximize the volume yield from a given area.[652] For most tree species, CMAI will occur after 80 to 100 years of growth.[653] Use of the CMAI standard promotes conservative timber harvesting because most stands can be harvested economically well before reaching CMAI.

The NFMA requires that stands must generally have reached CMAI before they are harvested.[654] The Forest Service has interpreted "generally" to mean within ninety-five percent of CMAI.[655] Since growth rates of some tree species, such as Douglas fir, tend to remain near CMAI for long periods of time, the agency's interpretation could permit rotation ages to be significantly less than CMAI.[656]

(c) Earned Harvest Effect (EHE)

Since ASQ is determined by future rather than current timber volumes, timber planners must attempt to estimate future growth rates and stand conditions. Future growth rates can be increased substantially above natural rates through intensive management

---

[649] *See infra* note 904.

[650] *See infra* text accompanying notes 898-932.

[651] 16 U.S.C. § 1604(m) (1982).

[652] *See generally* G. ROBINSON, *supra* note 2, at 96-97.

[653] *See* THE WILDERNESS SOCIETY, SIERRA CLUB, NATIONAL AUDUBON SOCIETY, NATURAL RESOURCES DEFENSE COUNCIL & NATIONAL WILDLIFE FEDERATION, NATIONAL FOREST PLANNING 59 (1983) [hereinafter cited as NATIONAL FOREST PLANNING].

[654] *See infra* text accompanying notes 933-46.

[655] FOREST SERVICE MANUAL § 2413.21 (1984).

[656] The graph below illustrates how setting the rotation period at 95% of CMAI could shorten the rotation from 100 to 75 years.

practices such as restocking, thinning, and brush control.[657] Intensive management can increase future volume over a period of time by accelerating the growth rate of trees. For example, thinning a stand of trees may increase available sunlight and reduce competition, thereby augmenting the growth rate of the remaining trees. Increasing the ASQ by projection of accelerated growth rates, termed the "allowable cut effect"[658] or "earned harvest effect" (EHE), is conditionally allowed by the NFMA.[659]

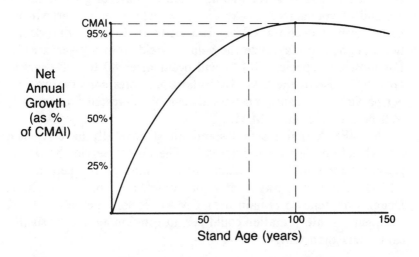

The difference between rotation periods set at CMAI and 95% of CMAI can vary significantly, based on the tree species and management prescriptions used in a given area. However, the effect on the ASQ will always be the same: harvesting an area at 95% of CMAI will produce 5% less volume than harvesting at full CMAI. One advantage of harvesting at 95% of CMAI can be to increase the present net value of timber by shortening the period of time required for the government to recover its costs of managing the timber. Interview with Jim Mayo, Timber Planner, Willamette Nat'l Forest, in Eugene, Or., (Jan. 10, 1985).

[657] Some timber management plans in the 1970s correlated specific management practices with potential increases in harvest levels. For example, the Umpqua National Forest's plan estimated that the annual harvest level could potentially be increased from 258.5 mmbf to 399.1 mmbf through precommercial thinning. FOREST SERVICE, U.S. DEP'T OF AGRICULTURE, FINAL ENVIRONMENTAL STATEMENT, TIMBER RESOURCE PLAN FOR THE UMPQUA NATIONAL FOREST 34-35 (1978) [hereinafter cited as UMPQUA NAT'L FOREST TIMBER PLAN].

[658] *See generally* Schweitzer, Sassaman & Schallau, *Allowable Cut Effect*, 70 J. FORESTRY 415 (1972); Teeguarden, *The Allowable Cut Effect: A Comment*, 71 J. FORESTRY 224 (1973).

[659] *See infra* text accompanying notes 947-57.

On old-growth forests EHE partially offsets the conservative influence of NDEF, since intensive management raises the anticipated harvest level of the post-conversion forest. The Forest Service can set the current ASQ of old-growth at the same level as the expected future ASQ of second-growth, thereby recovering some of the "bonus" lost through NDEF.[660] However, basing a current ASQ on projections of the effects of intensive management on different parts of a forest can be risky business because the projected increases in growth exist only on paper.[661] Drought, insect infestation, and other natural occurrences can reduce growth rates significantly. In some cases the anticipated EHE may be based as much on speculation as fact.[662] The use of phenoxy herbicides and other chemicals may play a role in the

---

[660] The existence of a reserve of merchantable timber is necessary to apply EHE. *See* Schweitzer, Sassaman & Schallau, *supra* note 658, at 415. Such a reserve will always exist in national forests with large amounts of old-growth timber. One critic has charged that EHE "is no more than a pseudo-scientific way to get at more old-growth timber. Perhaps old-growth liquidation is the real goal of intensive management, rather than increased conifer growth for the future." J. NEWTON, AN ECONOMIC ANALYSIS OF HERBICIDE USE FOR INTENSIVE FOREST MANAGEMENT, PT. II: CRITICAL ASSESSMENT OF ARGUMENTS AND DATA SUPPORTING HERBICIDE USE 48 (1979).

[661] The validity of the projected increases in future growth attributable to EHE depends on the accuracy of the yield tables used to make the projections. Timber planners use "empirical" yield tables to calculate the existing volume of old-growth timber and "managed" yield tables to predict the future volume of second-growth stands. *See* J. NEWTON, *supra* note 660, at 45. While the empirical yield tables are based on data taken from actual field plots, managed yield tables rely primarily on research findings and personal experience. *Id.* at 43-47. *See generally* O'Toole, *Taking Stock in Future Yields*, FOREST PLANNING, Apr. 1983, at 16.

A recent administrative appeal of the NFMA plan for the Santa Fe National Forest in New Mexico questioned the accuracy of the yield tables used to calculate harvest levels. The appellants alleged that timber planners had significantly overestimated future growth rates of both old-growth and second-growth stands. *See* O'Toole, *Reviewing the Santa Fe*, FOREST PLANNING, Jan.-Feb. 1984, at 15, 16-18. The Forest Service subsequently withdrew the plan due to "economic problems." *See id.* at 19.

[662] In 1978 the Government Accounting Office (GAO) reported that some national forest planners had dramatically overestimated EHE in their timber management assessments. The GAO found that the Forest Service had overestimated the EHE of precommercial thinning of young ponderosa pine stands in the Deschutes National Forest in Oregon by over 250%. U.S. GEN. ACCOUNTING OFFICE, TIMBER HARVEST LEVELS FOR NATIONAL FORESTS—HOW GOOD ARE THEY? REPORT TO THE CONGRESS BY THE COMPTROLLER GENERAL OF THE UNITED STATES 18-19 (1978) [hereinafter cited as GAO TIMBER HARVEST REPORT]. The GAO also found that timber planners for the Gifford Pinchot National Forest in Washington had overestimated the EHE of thinning and planting by 100%. *Id.* at 19-20.

projection of EHE but not be usable for intensive management.[663] Also troublesome is the fact that EHE is premised on Congress's presumed willingness to appropriate sufficient funds for long-term intensive management.[664]

3. Harvesting Practices

Much of the controversy preceding the NFMA concerned on-the-ground timber harvesting methods—particularly clearcutting. The NFMA contains several guidelines that limit the use of clearcutting and other forms of "even-aged" management.

The Forest Service manages stands of suitable timber land on either an even-aged or uneven-aged basis.[665] Even-aged

---

[663] In the Northwest herbicides are commonly sprayed over stands of young conifers to reduce the amount of competing brush. Herbicide spraying has been highly controversial and the subject of numerous lawsuits. *See* Save Our Ecosystems v. Watt, 13 ENVTL. L. REP. (ENVTL. L. INST.) 20,887 (D. Or. 1983), *aff'd sub nom* Save Our Ecosystems v. Clark, 747 F.2d 1240 (9th Cir. 1984); Merrell v. Block, 14 ENVTL. L. REP. (ENVTL. L. INST.) 20,225 (D. Or. 1983), *aff'd*, 747 F.2d 1240 (9th Cir. 1984); Oregon Envtl. Council v. Kunzman, 714 F.2d 901 (9th Cir. 1983); Southern Oregon Citizens Against Toxic Sprays (SOCATS) v. Watt, 13 ENVTL. L. REP. (ENVTL. L. INST.) 20,174 (D. Or. 1982), *aff'd sub nom.* SOCATS v. Clark, 720 F.2d 1475 (9th Cir. 1983); Alaska Survival v. Weeks, 12 ENVTL. L. REP. (ENVTL. L. INST.) 20,949 (D. Alaska 1982); Southern Oregon Citizens Against Toxic Sprays v. Andrus, 9 ENVTL. L. REP. (ENVTL. L. INST.) 20,715 (D. Or. 1979); Citizens Against Toxic Sprays v. Bergland, 428 F. Supp. 908 (D. Or. 1977); People for Envtl. Progress v. Leisz, 373 F. Supp. 589 (C.D. Cal. 1974). Currently, the Forest Service's entire herbicide spraying program has been enjoined until the agency investigates the health effects of using herbicides in the areas to be sprayed. Merrell v. Block, 747 F.2d at 1250. In the meantime, the Forest Service must rely on more expensive mechanical and manual methods of brush control.

Although chemicals are also used to eradicate insects and disease, alternative methods are available. The NFMA regulations require use of "integrated pest management" techniques, such as "natural controls, harvesting, use of resistant species, maintenance of diversity, removal of damaged trees, and judicious use of pesticides." 36 C.F.R. § 219.27(a)(3) (1984).

[664] A second-growth stand may require several treatments at different stages of development. For example, brush control in the first decade after harvest may be followed by precommercial thinning during the third decade. Timber planners assume that Congress will appropriate funds for those treatments when the time arrives to apply them. The General Accounting Office has questioned whether this assumption is permitted under the NFMA. "It is not clear whether the Congress intended that the expected timber growth increases from performing management practices in future decades should be used as a basis for justifying increases in harvest levels and timber sales in the current decade." GAO TIMBER HARVEST REPORT, *supra* note 662, at 21.

[665] The foregoing discussion of harvest methods is based on Forest Service testimony contained in *"Clear-cutting" Practices on National Timberlands:*

management means that stands are harvested by clearcutting, shelterwood cutting, or seed-tree cutting. A clearcut removes all merchantable trees from a unit of forest land at one time. A shelterwood cut removes most of the timber volume from the unit while leaving designated trees to provide seed, shelter, and shade for regeneration. After the new stand is established by natural seeding or planting, a final harvest removes the remaining trees. A seed-tree cut is similar to a shelterwood cut, except that only enough trees are left after the first cut to reseed the unit. The phrase "even-aged" is used because each of these cutting methods results in a new stand of trees approximately equal in age and size.

Uneven-aged management means that designated trees within stands are harvested by selective cutting. The selection method generally removes only specified trees, either singly or in small groups. The trees may be selected because they are either mature, poorly spaced, or silviculturally undesirable. Periodic selective cutting results in a diverse stand with varying ages and sizes of trees.

Selective cutting is considered to be generally inappropriate for commercial management of shade-intolerant tree species such as Douglas fir and lodgepole pine. Because these species need direct sunlight in the first two decades for optimum growth, units are typically clearcut so that the newly-stocked trees will have ample light. Clearcutting is also favored silviculturally for stands with large-scale insect infestations, fire damage, or disease infection.

Of course, clearcutting is typically unsightly and, if not carried out properly, can cause serious erosion. On the other hand, selective cutting generally requires multiple entries and more roading, which can have a greater long-term impact on the soil, wildlife, and ecosystem of an area than clearcutting. Further, any form of timber harvesting has the potential of causing unacceptable levels of disturbance to watercourses and wildlife populations under certain circumstances. As will be seen, the NFMA speaks with considerable specificity to the issue of harvesting practices.

Hearings Before the Subcomm. on Public Lands of the Senate Comm. on Interior and Insular Affairs, 92d Cong., 1st Sess. 920 (1971) (statement of Edward P. Cliff, Chief, Forest Service, U.S. Dep't. of Agriculture) [hereinafter cited as *Senate Hearings on Clearcutting*]. *See also* G. ROBINSON, *supra* note 2, at 68.

B. Evolution of Policy

1. The Early Years (19th Century-1905)

During most of the nineteenth century the federal government pursued an incongruous timber policy. On the one hand, the government virtually gave away millions of acres of federal timberland to private interests. On the other hand, timber cutting on land that remained in federal ownership was strictly illegal. The General Land Office (GLO) in the Department of the Interior was responsible for administering this anomalous set of laws. The Commissioner of the GLO in 1897 summarized nineteenth century federal timber policy on public domain lands as follows:

> The course adopted at the outset in respect to timber on public lands . . . was that of a severely restrictive policy, the provisions of the act of 1817, as expanded in 1831, being the most severely stringent and restrictive that could possibly have been enacted, the public being thereby prohibited from procuring timber from any public lands for use in any manner whatever other than for the use of the Navy of the United States.[666]

The Act of March 2, 1831, provided for "the punishment of offenses committed in cutting, destroying, or removing live oak and other timber or trees reserved for naval purposes."[667] In 1850 the Supreme Court, in *United States v. Briggs*,[668] interpreted "other timber" to mean all timber located on the public domain. Thereafter, the GLO was legally entrusted with the formidable task of policing the entire public domain to apprehend timber trespassers.

1850 also marked the beginning of massive land grants to railroads. The GLO Commissioner in 1897 commented that the first railroad land grant

> can best be described as opening the floodgates; after which the generosity of Congress in this direction was for more than twenty years a rising tide, which was not long in becoming an overrunning flood that swept from the Gulf States to the lakes, and thence rap-

---

[666] GENERAL LAND OFFICE, U.S. DEP'T OF INTERIOR, ANNUAL REPORT, H.R. DOC. NO. 5, 55th Cong., 2d Sess. 71 (1897) [hereinafter cited as 1897 GLO REPORT]. *See generally* S. DANA & S. FAIRFAX, *supra* note 52, at 35-38; P. GATES, *supra* note 26, at 531-61.

[667] Act of Mar. 2, 1831, ch. 66, 4 Stat. 472. The Act expanded the scope of the Act of Mar. 1, 1817, ch. 22, 3 Stat. 347, which prohibited cutting live oak and red cedar from public land.

[668] 50 U.S. (9 How.) 351, 354 (1850).

idly onward to the Pacific, making grants of public lands, with the timber thereon, in princely munificence.[669]

Homesteading and preemption laws allowed commercial operators and speculators to obtain vast tracts of timberland at minimal cost.[670] The munificent attitude of Congress deterred the GLO's efforts to enforce the prohibition on cutting timber from public lands.[671] In response to charges that the GLO's timber agents were harassing settlers, the agency adopted a policy in 1852 of prosecuting only commercial timber operators.[672] In 1855, the GLO fired its timber agents and began to follow a more permissive enforcement policy toward commercial trespassers.[673] The customary procedure was to allow trespassers to keep the timber after paying "a reasonable stumpage according to the market value of the timber cut."[674] In effect, the GLO began to sell federal timber at market rates, often by prior agreement with local officials.[675] In 1862 the Secretary of the Interior, responding to objections from a local district attorney, defended the practice of "settling" with trespassers:

> The subject is one of interest, and not free from embarrassment. I do not concur with the district attorney in the opinion that no settlement is to be made with trespassers. It appears to me that the main object proper to be kept in view, should be to make the timber produce to the Government the price of the land.[676]

---

[669] 1897 GLO REPORT, *supra* note 666, at 72.

[670] *See* P. GATES, *supra* note 26, at 535-36. The GLO reported in 1876: Settlement upon these lands under the homestead and pre-emption laws is only a pretense, which enables the destruction of the value of the land by cutting off the timber, and when that is done the homestead or pre-emption is abandoned. In all the pine region of Lake Superior and the Upper Mississippi, where vast areas have been settled under the pretense of agriculture under the homestead and pre-emption laws, scarcely a vestige of agriculture appears. The same is true on the Pacific coast and in the mountain regions of Colorado, Utah, Montana, and Idaho. GENERAL LAND OFFICE, U.S. DEP'T OF INTERIOR, ANNUAL REPORT, H.R. EXEC. DOC. NO. 1, pt. 5, 44th Cong., 2d Sess. 8 (1876) [hereinafter cited as 1876 GLO REPORT].

[671] *See* P. GATES, *supra* note 26, at 538-39.

[672] *Id.* at 539.

[673] *Id.* at 542-44.

[674] GENERAL LAND OFFICE, U.S. DEP'T OF INTERIOR, ANNUAL REPORT, H.R. EXEC. DOC. NO. 1, pt. 5, 45th Cong., 2d Sess. 18 (1877) [hereinafter cited as 1877 GLO REPORT].

[675] *Id.* at 19.

[676] *Id.* at 18.

During the 1870s public sentiment began to develop in opposition to the widespread destruction of forests. The first bill to establish forest reserves was introduced in Congress in 1876.[677] GLO Commissioner James A. Williamson lamented "the wicked and wanton waste of the timber on the public lands" and warned that "[a] national calamity is being rapidly and surely brought upon the country by the useless destruction of the forests."[678] He advocated drastic changes in current laws that were "granting a license to destroy millions of acres of pine forests of almost incalculable value, which should be preserved as a nation's heritage."[679] Despite congressional authorization for the "domestic" use of federal timber,[680] Williamson and Secretary of the Interior Carl Schurz supported forest reserve legislation and began to enforce the timber laws more vigorously.[681]

Passage of the General Revision Act of 1891[682] marked a major turning point in the evolution of federal timber policy. Rather than encouraging the transfer of public timberland to private ownership, section 24 of the Act provided for reservation of the land.[683] Congress approved the forest reserve section largely in response to requests by Secretary of the Interior John Noble and Chief of the Division of Forestry Bernhard Fernow.[684] As discussed earlier, Noble and Fernow held different views on the proper management of timber and other resources.[685] Noble preferred park-like management, while Fernow favored selling timber to "assure a continuous supply of wood material from the timbered areas."[686]

The 1897 Organic Act[687] struck a balance between preservation and use of forest reserve timber. The Act recognized timber

---

[677] *See supra* text accompanying note 46.

[678] 1876 GLO REPORT, *supra* note 670, at 7.

[679] *Id.* at 9.

[680] Act of June 3, 1878, ch. 150, 20 Stat. 88 (mineral lands); Act of June 15, 1880, ch. 227, 21 Stat. 237.

[681] Williamson ordered a halt to settling with trespassers after finding that the total revenue from settlements after 20 years was "little more, if any, than the value of timber on five thousand acres of good pine land." 1877 GLO REPORT, *supra* note 674, at 20.

[682] Ch. 561, 26 Stat. 1095.

[683] 16 U.S.C. § 471 (1982).

[684] *See supra* text accompanying notes 54-56.

[685] *See supra* text accompanying notes 227-33.

[686] *See supra* note 229.

[687] Act of June 4, 1897, ch. 2, 30 Stat. 11, 35-36.

production as a major purpose of the reserves.[688] On the other hand, Congress, against the wishes of Fernow and Representative Thomas R. McRae, declined to delegate broad authority over timber management.[689] Instead, the Act specified strict guidelines to "preserv[e] the living and growing timber."[690] Thus, by the end of the nineteenth century, Congress finally resolved the conflicting policy influences that had prevailed up to that time. Congress did not significantly modify the 1897 Act's timber policy until it passed the National Forest Management Act of 1976.

2. The Custodial Years (1905-1941)

Early Forest Service timber policy was based on the precepts of conservative use and scientific forestry advocated by Gifford Pinchot. Reforestation, watershed protection, and sustained-yield were the hallmarks of Pinchot's policy. He summarized these elements in his instructions to local rangers in 1906: "Green timber may be sold except where its removal would make a second crop doubtful, reduce the timber supply below the point of safety, or injure the streams."[691] Pinchot instructed his foresters to undertake a two-step examination of timber stands being considered for sale. The first step was to determine whether the land was suitable for harvesting, based on reforestation potential, watershed protection, and relative utility. Pinchot stated:

The most vital question concerning the removal of any living timber is whether it can be spared. To decide this question the approving officer must know whether another growth of timber will replace the one removed or whether the land will become waste, whether the water supply will suffer, and whether the timber is more urgently needed for some other purpose. One of the foremost points to be studied is the reproduction of the forest under various conditions. Wherever possible a stand of young, thrifty trees should be left to form the basis for a second crop. Good reproduction and in mixed forests reproduction of the more valuable species must be assured before a sale can be recommended . . . . The growth on similar areas which have been logged affords the best guide in this study.[692]

---

[688] 16 U.S.C. § 475 (1982).
[689] *See supra* text accompanying notes 239-47.
[690] Act of June 4, 1897, ch. 2, 30 Stat. 11, 35, (repealed by 16 U.S.C. § 476 (1976)). *See* West Virginia Div. of the Izaak Walton League of Am., Inc. v. Butz, 522 F.2d 945, 952 (4th Cir. 1975).
[691] 1906 Use Book, *supra* note 82, at 35.
[692] *Id.* at 43.

The second step was to determine the optimal method or system of harvest. Pinchot cautioned his foresters not to maximize immediate monetary returns at the expense of assuring reforestation and watershed protection:

> If the timber may be cut safely, then the best method of cutting must be decided; whether all the trees below a certain diameter should be left to form the next crop or only selected seed trees of the valuable species; whether the surrounding timber will furnish enough and the right kind of seed; or, in other words, what system will be surest to bring about satisfactory reproduction. The object of a sale is not solely to realize the greatest possible money return from the forest. The improvement and future value of the stand both for forest cover and for the production of timber must always be considered. In many cases the need of preserving an unbroken forest cover for the protection of watersheds will influence the method of cutting recommended.[693]

Another important element of Pinchot's policy was to convert the wild, old-growth stands to scientifically managed second-growth. Pinchot reported in 1908 that

> [f]ull utilization of the productive power of the Forests . . . does not take place until after the land has been cut over in accordance with the rules of scientific forestry. The transformation from a wild to a cultivated forest must be brought about by the ax. Hence the importance of substituting, as fast as practicable, actual use for the mere hoarding of timber.[694]

Pinchot was careful, however, to limit timber sales to the sustained-yield level.[695] Thus, a third step for timber planners was to calculate the annual allowable cut on the basis of approximate annual growth.[696]

The three-step procedure devised by Pinchot became firmly ingrained in Forest Service timber planning. Half a century later, the three factors involved in the Pinchot formula, where to cut, the method of cutting, and the annual amount of cutting allowable, would become the center of great controversy. For now, it is

---

[693] *Id.*

[694] 1908 ANNUAL REPORT OF THE CHIEF, *supra* note 75, at 15.

[695] For a discussion of the various definitions of sustained-yield, see Behan, *Political Popularity and Conceptual Nonsense: The Strange Case of Sustained Yield Forestry*, 8 ENVTL. L. 309 (1978). The Multiple-Use Sustained-Yield Act of 1960 defines sustained-yield as "the achievement and maintenance in perpetuity of a high-level annual or regular periodic output of the various renewable resources of the national forests without impairment of the productivity of the land." 16 U.S.C. § 531(b) (1982).

[696] *See supra* note 644.

worth noting that Pinchot's criteria are strikingly similar to the guidelines enacted in the NFMA.

Pinchot's dream of rapidly transforming the wild forests into cultivated stands was frustrated by chronically low timber prices.[697] The Forest Service adopted a policy of selling timber primarily to local mills and communities.[698] The policy was designed, in part, to avoid competing with private timber owners on national markets and thereby further reducing prices.[699] Economic considerations also became more important in examining timber stands for prospective sale. Foresters began to weigh the costs of removing timber against the expected value of the timber. Sales were permitted only where they would "warrant the investment required for constructing a railroad or other means of transportation into comparatively inaccessible regions."[700]

Following the Pinchot era, and until the beginning of World War II, Forest Service timber policy remained remarkably stable. The agency played a largely custodial role, emphasizing fire control and watershed protection in its management of national forest timber. Annual harvests rarely exceeded 1.5 billion board feet (bbf) and averaged about 1 bbf.[701] Approximately 125,000 acres were cut each year—less than one-fifth of one percent of the 75 million acres of the national forests' commercial timberland.[702] By comparison, private timber production generally removed more than 50 bbf from 10 million acres annually during this time.[703]

One notable change occurred in the early 1920s, when timber planners began to discard Pinchot's cut-equals-growth formula for calculating the allowable cut on old-growth forests. Instead, planners adopted the more flexible Hanzlick formula, which permitted the rate of harvest to exceed rate of growth in the slow-growing

---

[697] *See* Parry, Vaux & Dennis, *supra* note 644, at 151.

[698] *Id.* In his final annual report, Pinchot acknowledged that large-scale harvesting of national forest timber was undesirable, at least on the short-term. He stated, "Timber, which brings relatively little now, because it is relatively little needed, but for which there will be a strong demand shortly, neither can nor should be sold too freely." 1908 ANNUAL REPORT OF THE CHIEF, *supra* note 75, at 17.

[699] *See* Popovich, *Harvest Schedules — The Road to Regulation*, 74 J. FORESTRY 695 (1976).

[700] FOREST SERVICE, U.S. DEP'T OF AGRICULTURE, THE USE BOOK 32 (1915 ed.) [hereinafter cited as 1915 USE BOOK].

[701] *See* 1929 ANNUAL REPORT OF THE CHIEF, *supra* note 99, at 30.

[702] *See* COPELAND REPORT, *supra* note 112, at 2.

[703] *Id.* at 13, 24.

old-growth forests.[704] However, the shift away from Pinchot's traditional sustained-yield policy had little practical effect prior to the 1950s. As Professor Behan has observed, allowable cut levels in timber management plans

> were essentially academic. They were plans for the management of timber resources that nobody wanted, as long as the private, commercial, and industrial forests of the country continued to supply sufficient old-growth timber at a lower cost. The federal land harvests never approached a growth constraint called for by the plans because they were scarcely needed at all.[705]

3. The Production Years (1942-1966)

The events following the outbreak of World War II commenced a new era in Forest Service timber policy. The emphasis shifted from protection to production and remained that way for many years after the war. The production era began abruptly in 1942, when wood was classified as a critical war material and supplies of construction lumber were frozen for immediate war use.[706] Demand for lumber was estimated to be 6 bbf in excess of expected production.[707] At the same time, harvest on private lands was decreasing due to labor shortages and other factors.[708] The crisis atmosphere was evident in the agency's 1942 annual report:

> The nation's forests are being called upon for a tremendous output of materials essential to the war effort. Billions of feet of lumber are needed to house the expanding American armed forces and the growing army of workers in war industries. Wood and wood derivatives are needed for ships, wharves, airplanes, gunstocks, explosives, and a host of other war materials and facilities. Some 8 billion board feet of lumber is the estimated 1942 requirement for boxing and crating war materials, agricultural products, and essential civilian goods. Orders for Army beds will call for from 30 to 40 million feet of hardwoods this year. A million feet a day will be needed for Army truck bodies.[709]

---

[704] *See* Hanzlick, *supra* note 644, at 611; *see generally* Parry, Vaux & Dennis, *supra* note 644, at 151-52.

[705] Behan, *supra* note 695, at 314-15.

[706] *See* FOREST SERVICE, U.S. DEP'T OF AGRICULTURE, ANNUAL REPORT OF THE CHIEF 3 (1942) [hereinafter cited as 1942 ANNUAL REPORT OF THE CHIEF].

[707] *Id.* at 1.

[708] *Id.* at 3-4.

[709] *Id.* at 3.

To meet the increased demand, the Forest Service more than doubled timber production from national forests.[710]

After the war, demand for timber continued to increase, but for a different reason—the need for new housing to satisfy the postwar economic surge. Many of the prime private lands had been logged over during the war years; the supply from these lands was inadequate in some regions. Chief Lyle F. Watts reported in 1946 that "[a]s private timber gives out, many communities and industries are becoming more and more dependent on national-forest timber."[711] Lumber and stumpage prices rose sharply, allowing the Forest Service to sell some species that had never been considered merchantable.[712] Timber sale receipts tripled between 1946 and 1950 and tripled again by 1956.[713]

Road construction for timber access also began to increase in 1946, when the Federal Housing Expediter supplied $12.9 million for road construction to provide more lumber for veterans' housing.[714] Chief Watts declared access road construction to be the Forest Service's "first priority."[715] Complaining that the national forests were "woefully deficient" in access roads,[716] the agency persistently and successfully argued for greater appropriations to build roads. In 1952 Chief Richard E. McArdle reported:

> Roads in the western forests are . . . the key to attaining full timber harvest and net growth in the national forests. Millions of acres of wild forest land must await an adequate road system before they will return their full worth in forest products and in growing capacity. As these acres now stand, undeveloped, a large part of their

---

[710] *Compare* FOREST SERVICE, U.S. DEP'T OF AGRICULTURE, ANNUAL REPORT OF THE CHIEF 12 (1944) [hereinafter cited as 1944 ANNUAL REPORT OF THE CHIEF] (3.3 bbf) *with* FOREST SERVICE, U.S. DEP'T OF AGRICULTURE, [1941] ANNUAL REPORT OF THE CHIEF 34 (1941) (1.5 bbf).

[711] FOREST SERVICE, U.S. DEP'T OF AGRICULTURE, ANNUAL REPORT OF THE CHIEF 18 (1946) [hereinafter cited as 1946 ANNUAL REPORT OF THE CHIEF].

[712] FOREST SERVICE, U.S. DEP'T OF AGRICULTURE, ANNUAL REPORT OF THE CHIEF 26 (1947) [hereinafter cited as 1947 ANNUAL REPORT OF THE CHIEF].

[713] *Compare* 1946 ANNUAL REPORT OF THE CHIEF, *supra* note 711, at 42 ($10.5 million) *with* 1950 ANNUAL REPORT OF THE CHIEF, *supra* note 118, at 69 ($29.4 million) *and* FOREST SERVICE, U.S. DEP'T OF AGRICULTURE, ANNUAL REPORT OF THE CHIEF 3 (1956) [hereinafter cited as 1956 ANNUAL REPORT OF THE CHIEF] ($107 million).

[714] 1947 ANNUAL REPORT OF THE CHIEF, *supra* note 712, at 26.

[715] 1946 ANNUAL REPORT OF THE CHIEF, *supra* note 711, at 20.

[716] FOREST SERVICE, U.S. DEP'T OF AGRICULTURE, ANNUAL REPORT OF THE CHIEF 51 (1951) [hereinafter cited as 1951 ANNUAL REPORT OF THE CHIEF].

growing capacity is continually being wasted by fire, insects, diseases, and wind.[717]

During Chief McArdle's ten-year administration, timber production doubled from 4.4 bbf to 9 bbf by 1962.[718] Thereafter, timber production continued to increase, reaching an all-time high of 12.1 bbf in 1966.[719] In total, approximately twice as much national forest timber was cut during the sixteen years between 1950 and 1966 as had been cut during the previous forty-five years. The Court of Appeals for the Fourth Circuit accurately summarized the shift in policy during this era:

> For nearly half a century following its creation in 1905, the National Forest System provided only a fraction of the national timber supply with almost ninety-five per cent coming from privately owned forests. During this period the Forest Service regarded itself as a custodian and protector of the forests rather than a prime producer, and consistent with this role the Service faithfully carried out the provisions of the Organic Act with respect to selective timber cutting. In 1940, however, with private timber reserves badly depleted, World War II created an enormous demand for lumber and this was followed by the post-war building boom. As a result the posture of the Forest Service quickly changed from custodian to a production agency.[720]

4. The Church Guidelines and the Prelude to the NFMA (1967-1976)

By the late 1960s the Forest Service's production-oriented timber policy began to receive unprecedented criticism from sources both inside and outside the agency. Public opposition to the agency's timber harvesting practices resulted in Senate investigations and recommended guidelines by the Public Lands Subcommittee, chaired by Senator Frank Church of Idaho. At the same time, the agency decided to overhaul much of its timber planning system to reduce concern over environmental protection and overcutting. These congressional and administrative actions,

---

[717] FOREST SERVICE, U.S. DEP'T OF AGRICULTURE, ANNUAL REPORT OF THE CHIEF 22 (1952) [hereinafter cited as 1952 ANNUAL REPORT OF THE CHIEF].

[718] *Compare id.* at 19 *with* FOREST SERVICE, U.S. DEP'T OF AGRICULTURE, ANNUAL REPORT OF THE CHIEF 13 (1962) [hereinafter cited as 1962 ANNUAL REPORT OF THE CHIEF].

[719] *See* 1966 ANNUAL REPORT OF THE CHIEF, *supra* note 397, at 12.

[720] Izaak Walton League v. Butz, 522 F.2d at 954-55.

taken to resolve the controversies of the early 1970s, laid the foundation for the NFMA.

(a) Suitability and Timber Harvesting Practices

National controversy over Forest Service timber management practices began in the late 1960s.[721] In 1967 and 1970 the West Virginia legislature adopted two resolutions to investigate timber harvesting practices on the Monongahela National Forest.[722] The second resolution expressed "extreme concern" that clearcutting could cause "erosion, flooding and other major catastrophes."[723] United States Senator Jennings Randolph of West Virginia requested a moratorium on clearcutting in his state's national forests.[724]

Similarly, public outcry in Montana prompted Senator Lee Metcalf in 1968 to commission a study of the Bitterroot National Forest by Professor Arnold Bolle and other faculty members of the University of Montana.[725] The faculty's report, A University View of the Forest Service (hereinafter the Bolle Report), concluded, "Multiple use management, in fact, does not exist as the governing principle on the Bitterroot National Forest . . . ."[726] The report criticized the Forest Service's "overriding concern for

---

[721] The starting point of the controversy can be traced to 1964, when the Forest Service began clearcutting on the Monongahela National Forest in West Virginia and elsewhere in the eastern national forests. CHURCH SUBCOMMITTEE REPORT, *supra* note 194, *reprinted in* SENATE NFMA HEARINGS, *supra* note 194, at 953. Before that time, the Forest Service harvested hardwoods on eastern national forests by partial cutting. *Id.*

[722] The resolution in 1967 established a study committee and charged that "[t]he great national beauty and game habitat of West Virginia is being depleted" by national forest management practices. W. Va. H. Con. Res. 47, 58th Leg., 1st Sess. (1967). The resolution in 1970 established a similar study commission and requested the Secretary of Agriculture to suspend all clearcutting in the state pending completion of the study. W. Va. H. Con. Res. 26, 59th Leg., 2d Sess. (1970).

[723] W. Va. H. Con. Res. 26, 59th Leg., 2d Sess. (1970).

[724] *Senate Hearings on Clearcutting, supra* note 665, at 13.

[725] Metcalf observed, "The Bitterroot is a typical mountain timbered valley and the results of such a study might well be extended to recommendations national in scope." Letter from Senator Metcalf to Dr. Arnold Bolle (Dec. 2, 1969), *reprinted in* S. DOC. No. 115, 91st Cong., 2d Sess. v (1970) [hereinafter cited as BOLLE REPORT].

[726] BOLLE REPORT, *supra* note 725, at 13.

sawtimber production"[727] and the "economic irrationality" of some aspects of the agency's timber management policies.[728]

The Forest Service responded to the rising tide of controversy by appointing agency task forces in 1969 to study the Monongahela and Bitterroot National Forests.[729] The agency appointed a third task force in 1970 to study four national forests in Wyoming.[730] On March 26, 1971, Chief Edward Cliff issued an official report on the agency's timber management practices.[731]

---

[727] *Id.* at 14.

[728] *Id.* at 21. The Bolle Report recommended less intensive management of low quality timber land:

> We see a need to reclassify timber land on an economic basis instead of on a physical, cellulose-quantitative basis. Land which is economic to manage for timber crops will return a decent rate of interest on capital invested. On this land, timber harvesting as a step in timber *management* is rational. But land which supports timber that is economical *only to cut* is not capable of earning a satisfactory return, in which case the harvest is tantamount to a mining operation.

Id. at 24 (emphasis in original).

[729] The Bitterroot report concluded that the Forest Service had exceeded its allowable cut. FOREST SERVICE, U.S. DEP'T OF AGRICULTURE, MANAGEMENT PRACTICES ON THE BITTERROOT NATIONAL FOREST 64 (1970) [hereinafter cited as BITTERROOT REPORT]. The report recommended greater control over timber management through land-use planning. *Id.* at 10-11. The Monongahela report was also highly critical of Forest Service timber management practices. *See* CHURCH SUBCOMMITTEE REPORT, *supra* note 194, at 4, *reprinted in* SENATE NFMA HEARINGS, *supra* note 194, at 954.

[730] The Wyoming study found that "[e]ach of the Forests has allowed logging in areas that would have been better left uncut; each has allowed some cutting with apparent disregard for other values and other resources; and each has experienced some regeneration failure." FOREST SERVICE, U.S. DEP'T OF AGRICULTURE, FOREST MANAGEMENT IN WYOMING 7 (1971), *reprinted in Senate Hearings on Clearcutting, supra* note 665, at 1127. Like the Forest Service report on the Bitterroot, the Wyoming report emphasized the need for greater control over timber management through land-use planning:

> During the 1960's, when timber harvest was accelerated, inadequate multiple use plans, together with incomplete assessment of key values as judged today, resulted in a variety of unacceptable management actions. The Forests are making progress in multiple use planning, and some of the plans are well conceived. Nevertheless, we do not believe that even current plans give proper weight to values other than timber production.

Id. at 16, *reprinted in Senate Hearings on Clearcutting, supra* note 665, at 1136.

[731] FOREST SERVICE, U.S. DEP'T OF AGRICULTURE, NATIONAL FOREST MANAGEMENT IN A QUALITY ENVIRONMENT: TIMBER PRODUCTIVITY i-ii (1971), *reprinted in Senate Hearings on Clearcutting, supra* note 665, at 423-24. The report was prepared by the directors of the Forest Service's timber, watershed, and timber research management divisions and by officials in the wildlife and recreation divisions. *Id.*

The 1971 report, entitled National Forest Management in a Quality Environment—Timber Productivity, foreshadowed important changes in Forest Service timber policies and planning. The agency identified thirty timber-related problems, based in part on the Monongahela and Bitterroot studies.[732] The report suggested that land be withdrawn from timber production where reforestation could not be assured within five years after logging[733] and where "unacceptable" environmental impacts could not be avoided by any "practical alternative."[734] The report also announced that the agency was developing new timber planning procedures.[735]

On April 15, 1971, less than two weeks after the Forest Service released its 1971 report, the Church Subcommittee held the first of three investigative hearings on the agency's timber management practices. Most of the witnesses, including Senator Randolph, were critical of clearcutting and other Forest Service

---

[732] *Id.* at 6-60.

[733] *Id.* at 34, *reprinted in Senate Hearings on Clearcutting, supra* note 665, at 460. The explanatory comment stated:

In some areas, soil and site conditions are marginal for assured reestablishment of commercial trees of any kind within an acceptable time. Areas of very shallow soil on dry sites in the ponderosa pine type are one example. Several other timber types occurring at the elevational margins of Western forest zones have this constraint. *Problem areas of this kind should be identified and removed from the allowable-cut base in developing timber-management plans.* Existing timber-sale contracts in such areas must be honored, but new contracts should not be made. Consequences of this policy could be significant enough to jeopardize industrial and community interests. If so, it will be necessary to advise the interested parties well in advance of any significant curtailments.

Id. (emphasis added).

[734] *Id.* at 31, *reprinted in Senate Hearings on Clearcutting, supra* note 665, at 457. The explanatory comment stated, "In some National Forest situations, specific environmental considerations determine that clearcutting is clearly unacceptable. If there is no practical alternative system, the timber in such areas should not be harvested and *the area should be withdrawn from the resource base* used in allowable cut calculations." *Id.* (emphasis added).

[735] The report stated:

This work is intended to provide each resource manager with the information he needs before deciding which areas are suitable and available for timber production. It will help determine which lands should be included in the calculation of the allowable cut. These new procedures should help to fit timber management more tightly into multiple-use plans, reduce the adverse environmental impacts of timber harvesting, and increase the reliability of estimates of future timber production.

Id. at 42, *reprinted in Senate Hearings on Clearcutting, supra* note 665, at 468.

timber policies.[736] Senator Gale McGee of Wyoming, for instance, called clearcutting "a shocking desecration that has to be seen to be believed" and charged that clearcutting was damaging streams and forest productivity.[737] Two weeks after the first hearing, McGee introduced a bill to ban clearcutting for two years while a congressional commission conducted a study.[738]

Chief Cliff, appearing before the Church Subcommittee, testified that he had decided to adopt the policy and procedural changes contained in the agency's timber report.[739] Cliff specified the major changes the agency intended to make:

> We will identify those areas where timber will not be harvested because there is no suitable alternative to clearcutting and environmental impacts make clearcutting unacceptable.
>
> We will identify areas where cuts will be discontinued or deferred because there is not assurance of adequate regeneration.
>
> We will develop and apply a system to identify areas that will be excluded from the allowable cut base because they cannot be harvested within acceptable environmental quality standards by using foreseeable technology . . . .[740]

The subcommittee questioned Cliff about an issue that the Forest Service had not explicitly addressed in its report—timber management of economically marginal land. Senators Church and Metcalf were particularly concerned about the use of expensive reforestation techniques like those used on the Bitterroot National

---

[736] Three other United States senators and one United States representative submitted statements but did not testify in person. Only Senator Paul Fannin of Arizona defended the Forest Service's timber management practices. *Senate Hearings on Clearcutting, supra* note 665, at 228-29.

[737] *Id.* at 3. Recalling a field trip to the Bridger National Forest, McGee stated that

[t]he consequences [of clearcutting] were visibly in evidence, runoffs producing erosion, clouded streams that once were sparklingly clear, whole mountainsides laid bare. And some of those mountainsides, I may add, according to the Forest Service personnel with me, had been replanted two and three times in the last 10 or so years, and still no reforestation.

Id.

[738] S. 1592, 92d Cong., 1st Sess. (1971). In introducing the bill, McGee remarked that some clearcuts on the Bridger National Forest "looked as if a squadron of B-52's had ravaged the pristine beauty of the Wind River Mountains." 117 CONG. REC. 10,909 (1971). A similar bill was introduced in the House by Representative Teno Roncalio of Wyoming on May 18, 1971. *Id.* at 15,660.

[739] *Senate Hearings on Clearcutting, supra* note 665, at 911.

[740] *Id.*

Forest.[741] The Bolle Report had focused on the "economic irrationality" of commercial timber production on the Bitterroot.[742] Senator Metcalf—the initiator of the Bolle Report—thought that the study of economic issues was the most important part of the report.[743] Citing figures from the Bolle Report, Senator Church characterized the Forest Service's timber practices on the Bitterroot as "an enormous subsidy."[744] Chief Cliff replied that he considered reforestation of cutover land to be the agency's duty.[745] Metcalf then stated that lands requiring public subsidies for adequate reforestion should never be harvested in the first place.[746]

Shortly after the first hearing, Senator Metcalf introduced a bill that contained several planning requirements and timber management guidelines similar to provisions of the NFMA.[747] Metcalf's

---

[741] *Id.* at 833-35. The Forest Service was using a reforestation technique on the Bitterroot and other national forests called "terracing." In order to prepare a clearcut for tree planting, a bulldozer would excavate parallel rows into the hillside. *See* BITTERROOT REPORT, *supra* note 729, at 32. Terracing followed by machine planting proved to be the most successful method of reforestation on the Bitterroot. *Id.* at 34. The Forest Service's study of the Bitterroot, however, recommended that, due to erosion, terracing should not be used on slopes steeper than 30%. *Id.* at 40.

[742] BOLLE REPORT, *supra* note 725, at 21. The committee argued that the Forest Service's reforestation practices were a poor long-term investment of federal funds. Because of the slow growth rates on much of the Bitterroot, the eventual return to the government from sale of the next timber stand (120 years hence) would be far less than the return from government bonds making 5% annual interest. *Id.* at 22. The committee suggested that the Forest Service should rely on natural regeneration methods or else "postpone all cutting to some indefinite future date." *Id.* at 23.

[743] *Senate Hearings on Clearcutting, supra* note 665, at 185-86.

[744] *Id.* at 833. Church calculated from the Bolle Report that the government could only expect a 1½% return from its investment in reforesting parts of the Bitterroot. *Id.* at 834. He stated that, based on the rate of return, "the Bitterroot forest is being managed in such a way that the government is going to suffer a considerable loss because we are now paying 4 and 5 percent for our borrowed money." *Id.*

[745] Cliff did not contest the figures used by Church and the Bolle committee; rather, he argued that federal subsidy of timber production might be necessary to meet the nation's resource needs. *Id.*

[746] *Id.* at 835. Metcalf also stated:

These forests are tremendously important for watersheds, as you suggested, for game, for recreation, all of these things are so important that it looks to me as if you should reevaluate and look to your forest resources and say, "Well, some of these should not even be harvested at all . . . ."

Id.

[747] S. 1734, 92d Cong., 1st Sess. (1971), *reprinted in* MANAGEMENT PRACTICES ON PUBLIC LANDS: HEARINGS BEFORE THE SUBCOMM. ON PUBLIC LANDS OF THE SENATE COMM. ON INTERIOR AND INSULAR AFFAIRS, 92d Cong., 2d Sess. 40 (Comm. Print 1972) [hereinafter cited as SENATE HEARINGS ON

bill prohibited timber harvesting where it would "impair multiple-use values relating to water quality, recreation, range and forage, watershed, wildlife and plant life."[748] The bill also required the Forest Service to prepare "timber harvesting and land management plans"[749] and to consider four factors before clearcutting:

(i) the effect of clear cutting on all other resource values and the environment;
(ii) the compatibility of clear cutting with the maintenance and enhancement of long-term productivity of the forest lands and the integrity of the environment;
(iii) the practicability of reforestation and other work to restore forest lands which are clear cut; and
(iv) all feasible and prudent alternatives to clear cutting.[750]

The Forest Service testified in opposition to Metcalf's bill. On March 10, 1972, Associate Chief John F. McGuire[751] told the Church Subcommittee that the restrictions on timber harvesting in the Metcalf bill were "unnecessary and undesirable in light of actions we are taking to improve the overall quality of National Forest timber management activities."[752] McGuire stated that the Forest Service had already begun to classify and withdraw areas from timber production,[753] as Chief Cliff had promised the subcommittee in May of 1971.

In addition to public and congressional criticism, the Forest Service also had to contend with pressure from within the executive branch. The Council on Environmental Quality (CEQ) in

---

MANAGEMENT PRACTICES]. Another member of the Senate Public Lands Subcommittee, Senator Mark O. Hatfield of Oregon, introduced a bill to create an advisory board and a management fund for the Forest Service, but the bill did not address the agency's management authority. *See* S. 350, 92d Cong., 1st Sess. (1971), *reprinted in id.* at 2. In introducing his bill, Hatfield hoped to increase timber production "without destruction of our forests—without the destruction of our environment." 117 CONG. REC. 727 (1971).

[748] S. 1734, 92d Cong., 1st Sess. § 210 (1971), *reprinted in* SENATE HEARINGS ON MANAGEMENT PRACTICES, *supra* note 747, at 39-40.

[749] *Id.* § 202(a).

[750] *Id.* § 202(c)(2), *reprinted in* SENATE HEARINGS ON MANAGEMENT PRACTICES, *supra* note 747, at 41-42.

[751] McGuire became Chief of the Forest Service less than two months later, on April 29, 1972. 78 AM. FORESTS at 39 (1972).

[752] SENATE HEARINGS ON MANAGEMENT PRACTICES, *supra* note 747, at 59.

[753] *Id.* at 62. The Department of Agriculture's official comments on Metcalf's bill reinforced McGuire's statements: "The Forest Service is already taking steps to limit clearcutting, consistent with the ecological requirements of the tree species being grown. Specific steps are described in the recent Forest Service publication, National Forest Management in a Quality Environment." *Id.* at 53.

1971 contracted with five forestry schools to investigate clearcutting on national forests.[754] In January 1972 the CEQ considered recommending the issuance of a Presidential Executive Order to regulate timber harvesting.[755] The draft order contained guidelines to prohibit clearcutting where severe erosion, lack of prompt reforestation, or harm to scenic, recreational or wildlife values would occur.[756] The draft order also required the Forest Service to identify and protect "fragile areas."[757] In mid-January 1972 the

---

[754] 118 CONG. REC. 6228 (1972) (remarks of Sen. Hatfield). Members of Congress and others had requested CEQ to undertake the investigation. *Id.* None of the forestry school reports recommended a complete ban on clearcutting. *Id.* at 6229. Four out of five recommended zoning and classification of forest land. *Id.* The report on the Rocky Mountain states commented on soil erosion, reforestation, and economic problems:

> In some cases we have clearcut very steep and very sensitive slopes right up to timberline and have harvests of disaster with respect to erosion and soil movement. Often such areas have also proved to be utter failures insofar as regeneration is concerned. Many of these areas should have been left uncut or at best only cut selectively.
> Further, in an effort to achieve artificial regeneration some areas have been heavily terraced and replanted (often unsuccessfully). In the opinion of some of the public the areas are definite eyesores, they detract from other uses, and have resulted in inordinate costs.

Id.

[755] The Forest Service opposed the CEQ's proposed order. *See Agricultural, Environmental and Consumer Protection Appropriations for Fiscal Year 1973: Hearings Before a Subcomm. of the Senate Comm. on Appropriations,* pt. 1, 92d Cong., 2d Sess. 39-42 (1972) (testimony of Earl Butz, Secretary of Agriculture) [hereinafter cited as *1972 Appropriation Hearings*].

[756] The draft order required the Secretary of Agriculture to issue guidelines to limit clearcutting, including the following:

> (2) There will be no clear-cutting in areas of outstanding scenic beauty, nor in areas where clear-cutting would adversely affect existing or projected intensive recreational use or critical wildlife habitat.
> (3) Clear-cutting will not be used on sites where slope, elevation, and soil type, considered together, indicate severe erosion may result.
> (4) No area will be clear-cut unless there is assurance that the area can be regenerated promptly.

PRESIDENT'S COUNCIL ON ENVIRONMENTAL QUALITY, ENVIRONMENTAL GUIDELINES FOR TIMBER HARVESTING ON THE PUBLIC LANDS 2-3 [hereinafter cited as CEQ TIMBER GUIDELINES], *reprinted in 1972 Appropriations Hearings, supra* note 755, at 47-48.

[757] The draft order required the Secretary of Agriculture to

> [i]dentify within 18 months fragile areas that are unable to withstand timber harvesting or other intensive uses without significant environmental or resource damage. Once identified, these areas shall be protected, to the extent permitted by law, until methods are developed that will permit use without significant damage.

CEQ TIMBER GUIDELINES, *supra* note 756, at 7, *reprinted in 1972 Appropriations Hearings, supra* note 755, at 52.

CEQ withdrew the proposed order at the request of Secretary of Agriculture Earl Butz.[758]

On March 29, 1972, the Church Subcommittee issued its influential report on Forest Service timber practices. The concluding section of the report, entitled Harvesting Guidelines, dealt with "two major problem areas relating to the selection and conduct of timber harvesting operations on Federal forest lands."[759] One problem area was the excessive use of clearcutting and inadequate administration of timber sales. The other area related to the broader question of where timber harvesting should be permitted. The subcommittee identified four classes of land where timber harvesting should not occur: highly scenic land, land with fragile soils, land with low reforestation potential, and land where reforestation or environmentally acceptable harvesting would be uneconomical. In the subcommittee's words:

> [C]ertain areas have been selected for cutting which should not have been subjected to any activity relating to timber harvesting for any of a number of reasons. These were areas of special scenic values, fragile soils, or other limiting physiographic conditions, areas where adequate regeneration could not be assured, and areas where the costs of special measures to avoid environmental damage or assure regeneration were so high that the activity was imprudent and relatively uneconomic.[760]

In order to protect the four classes of land, the Church Subcommittee proposed far-reaching timber harvesting guidelines for the Forest Service. The so-called "Church guidelines" provided in part:

> Clear-cutting should not be used as a cutting method on federal land areas where:
> a. Soil, slope, or other watershed conditions are fragile and subject to major injury.
> b. There is no assurance that the area can be adequately restocked within five years after harvest.
> c. Aesthetic values outweigh other considerations . . . .

---

[758] *See 1972 Appropriations Hearings, supra* note 755, at 39. The decision to withdraw the proposed order resulted, in part, from an intensive lobbying effort by timber industry executives. *See id.* Secretary Butz feared that, since the Executive Order would have the force of law, the order would have resulted in lawsuits to stop timber sales. He commented, "It takes an occasional nut to get an injunction in an occasional court where there is an occasional nut for a judge." *Id.* at 53.

[759] CHURCH SUBCOMMITTEE REPORT, *supra* note 194, at 6, *reprinted in* SENATE NFMA HEARINGS, *supra* note 194, at 958.

[760] *Id.*

Clear-cutting should be used only where:

a. It is determined to be silviculturally essential to accomplish the relevant forest management objectives.

b. The size of clear-cut blocks, patches or strips are kept at the minimum necessary to accomplish silvicultural and other multiple-use forest management objectives.

c. A multidisciplinary review has first been made of the potential environmental, biological, aesthetic, engineering and economic impacts on each sale area.

d. Clear-cut blocks, patches or strips are, in all cases, shaped and blended as much as possible with the natural terrain.[761]

The Church guidelines also directed the Forest Service to adjust their timber harvest levels "to assure that the lands on which they are based are available and suitable for timber production under these guidelines."[762]

The Church Subcommittee's report stated that the guidelines were intended to "strengthen and supplement" the Forest Service's "ongoing actions" to improve timber management practices.[763] It seems likely that the subcommittee was referring to three agency actions that were finalized in 1972 and 1973.

In the first of these actions, the Forest Service issued a report entitled Action Plan for National Forests in a Quality Environment.[764] The Action Plan, which was released on June 14, 1972, reiterated the thirty problems and solutions outlined in the Timber Report that Chief Cliff had presented to the Church Subcommittee in 1971.[765]

Second, the agency instituted a new system of timber land classification intended to implement the policy changes contained in the Action Plan.[766] The system was based on a Forest Service report issued in October 1971 entitled Stratification of Forest Land for Timber Management Planning on the Western National Forests (hereinafter the Stratification Study).[767] The agency

---

[761] *Id.* at 9, *reprinted in* SENATE NFMA HEARINGS, *supra* note 194, at 959.

[762] *Id.*

[763] *Id.* at 8.

[764] *See* D. BARNEY, THE LAST STAND 54-56 (1972).

[765] *See supra* text accompanying notes 732-40.

[766] The agency implemented the new system by revising the timber management planning section of the Forest Service Manual. *See* ADVISORY PANEL REPORT, *supra* note 635, at 169. As planners updated their ten-year timber management plans, they reclassified their commercial land base according to the new system.

[767] STRATIFICATION STUDY, *supra* note 638. The study was directed by the agency's Intermountain Forest and Range Experiment Station and involved personnel from all six western regions. *Id.* at 2. The agency examined six national

found that many timber management plans contained inflated estimates of the amount of land available and suitable for timber production.[768] The Stratification Study concluded that "a simple commercial-noncommercial division of forest land is too general and not adequate to meet National Forest planning needs . . . ."[769] As an alternative to the traditional approach, the report called for the establishment of a system that would divide commercial land into subclasses. The proposed system included a "marginal utility at present" subclass for land with erosion, reforestation, and economic problems.[770]

The new classification system—implemented through an amendment to the Forest Service Manual in May 1972—estab-

---

forests—the Lolo in Montana, Arapaho in Colorado, Coconino in Arizona, Boise in Idaho, Klamath in Oregon, and the Gifford Pinchot in Washington. *Id.*

[768] The study disclosed that, although 4.2 million acres were classified as commercial forest land,

this timber growing base is reduced to 3.2 million acres when careful account is taken of soil-slope conditions, land productivity, and land use. In other words, the area suitable and available for growing tree crops on these six national forests is 22 percent less than had been previously estimated.

Id. at 4. Land withdrawn through multiple-use planning was the single greatest factor in the discrepancy. *Id.* at 5. However, areas with unstable soil and areas producing less than 20 cubic feet per acre per year accounted for about 40% of the error. *Id.* In addition to the 22% reduction in commercial land, the study found that 13% of the remaining commercial land "is either economically or technologically unavailable at present." *Id.* at 6. Land was economically unavailable because "high development costs or low product values may in some cases preclude utilization in the foreseeable future." *Id.* The technologically infeasible land posed "a more serious problem. Some of the timber . . . is growing on steep slopes that are unstable and should not be logged using conventional systems." *Id.*

[769] *Id.* at 24.

[770] The report read in part:

To avoid the possibility of overcutting, certain areas of the timber growing base are not included in the calculation of current cutting budgets because the current utility of these areas is shadowed by limitations or restrictions. These "marginal" areas include the following:

Areas where there is low probability of the timber being utilized in the immediate future because of excessive development costs or low timber-product values.

Unstable land areas that cannot be logged using present methods without damaging the environment but which may be utilized for timber once a logging system is developed that will not damage the environment.

Merchantable stands on sites where reforestation following logging would be extremely difficult or expensive because of adverse site and/or habitat conditions.

Extensive unstocked areas for which money for planting or seeding is not likely to be available in the near future.

Id. at 11.

lished subclasses, or components, of commercial forest land.[771] The "special" component, for instance, included land zoned in multiple-use or unit plans to protect water, aesthetics, and other resources.[772] Timber production from land in the special component could range from zero to 100 percent yield.[773]

The "marginal" component corresponded to the "marginal utility at present" subclass proposed in the Stratification Study. Marginal land was characterized by "excessive development cost, low-product values, or resource protection constraints."[774] This component also included land that had been cutover and had not regenerated.[775] The marginal component did not specifically include land with standing timber where reforestation was not likely

---

[771] *See* ADVISORY PANEL REPORT, *supra* note 635, at 169-89. The Forest Service's Timber Management Division first prepared a tentative subclassification scheme in 1967. *See* STRATIFICATION STUDY, *supra* note 638, at 6. By 1972 most national forests had made some attempt to adjust their timber plans to recognize variations within the commercial land class. *Id.*

[772] *See* ADVISORY PANEL REPORT, *supra* note 635, at 185, quoting FOREST SERVICE MANUAL § 2412.15. The Manual defined the special component as
  commercial forest land area that is recognized in the multiple-use plan as needing specially designed treatment of the timber resource to achieve landscape or other key resource objectives. Areas where timber management activities are informally delayed pending multiple use planning studies and management decisions, travel and water influence zones, peripheral portions of developed sites, and classified recreation areas . . . where timber harvest is a secondary or minor management objective should be included in this classification.
Id. Multiple-use planning is described at *supra* text accompanying notes 135-41.

[773] The Manual stated, "Areas identified as special will be included in this component whether or not there is a reduction in yield or no harvest at all expected in the 10-year-land period." ADVISORY PANEL REPORT, *supra* note 635, at 185, quoting FOREST SERVICE MANUAL § 2412.15. A 1973 study of eight national forests found a 29% average reduction of timber production from land in the special component. *Id.* at 169.

[774] *Id.* at 185, quoting FOREST SERVICE MANUAL § 2412.15. The terms "excessive development cost" and "low product values" were also used to define the marginal land class in the 1971 Stratification Study. *See supra* note 638.

[775] The Forest Service Manual defined this land as "the backlog of nonstocked areas that would otherwise be classed as standard, but are in need of reforestation that cannot be accomplished with Knutson-Vanderberg Act funds." ADVISORY PANEL REPORT, *supra* note 635, at 185, quoting FOREST SERVICE MANUAL § 2412.15. The Knutson-Vandenburg Act of 1930, 16 U.S.C. §§ 576-576b (1982), authorizes the Secretary of Agriculture to require purchasers of national forest timber to pay for reforestation costs. 16 U.S.C. § 576b (1982). Ordinarily, "K-V" funds must be spent within 10 years after the purchaser finishes removing the timber. Interview with Bud Sloan, *supra* note 634. Otherwise, local personnel must either use appropriated funds or request special extension. *Id.* In practice, the agency made little effort to reforest land if K-V funds were no longer available. Thus, the 1972 manual provision simply recognized that cut-

to occur.[776] Nevertheless, some national forests began to classify commercial land as marginal if reforestation appeared unlikely.[777] Very little timber harvesting occurred on land in the marginal component.[778] By 1977 Forest Service planners had classified over one-third of all commercial forest land as marginal or special.[779]

The Forest Service's third action following the Church report was to revise its land-use planning system.[780] The new system required timber planners to follow the land-use allocations of the local unit plans.[781] Thus, areas delineated as recreation, streamside, critical soils, and other zones in the unit plans were also classified as special or marginal components in the timber management plans.[782] Land-use planners, in turn, were required to

over land for which K-V funds were unavailable was no longer being managed on a commercial basis.

[776] The omission of prospectively unreforestable land from the marginal component reflected the Forest Service's ambivalent policy toward reforestation problems. Traditionally, the agency assumed that trees growing on commercial land could grow back after cutting. *Cf. House NFMA Hearings, supra* note 398, at 228-29 (statement of Chief McGuire that he had "trouble conceiving" of trees not growing back after harvesting). By 1972, however, five million acres of national forest land was in need of reforestation, partly as a result of clearcutting. *See Senate Hearings on Clearcutting, supra* note 665, at 832. In 1971 the agency officially recognized prospective reforestation failures as a problem and recommended withdrawing land from timber production as one solution. *See supra* note 733.

[777] The Pacific Northwest Region, for example, directed local planners to include within the marginal component "[f]orest types or ecotypes where experience has indicated that satisfactory restocking will not occur after regeneration cutting by techniques currently available." FOREST SERVICE MANUAL § 2412.15, (R-6 Supp. No. 184, March 1973).

[778] A 1973 study of eight national forests found a 77% reduction of timber production from forest land in the marginal component. ADVISORY PANEL REPORT, *supra* note 635, at 169.

[779] FOREST SERVICE MANUAL § 2411.11 (Interim Directive No. 82, Feb. 2, 1983). For a detailed breakdown of the timber land stratification on national forests as of 1982, *see* Miller, *Genetic Diversity and National Forest Tree Improvement Programs*, in NATURAL DIVERSITY IN FOREST ECOSYSTEMS: PROCEEDINGS OF THE WORKSHOP, NOV. 29-DEC. 1, 1982, at 105, 115-16 (1984) [hereinafter cited as NATURAL DIVERSITY IN FOREST ECOSYSTEMS].

[780] *See supra* text accompanying notes 135-55.

[781] *See* FOREST SERVICE MANUAL § 8213 (1973).

[782] *See* ADVISORY PANEL REPORT, *supra* note 635, at 169. For instance, the Umpqua National Forest Land Management Plan included a "critical soils" land allocation for "those lands which possess a high risk of mass soil movement that threatens to damage fish habitat and other resource values." UMPQUA NAT'L FOREST LMP, *supra* note 117, at 39. The planners identified the lands based on the Umpqua National Forest's Soil Resource Inventory Handbook. *Id.* at 40. The plan divided the critical soils allocation into three classes. First, where road construction was the anticipated cause of erosion, "road density as well as

observe the timber production objectives determined at the regional and national levels of the agency.[783]

(b) Harvest Levels

A second general area of controversy in the late 1960s and early 1970s concerned the amount of timber being harvested from the national forests. As timber sales began to reach the current allowable cut ceiling, the Forest Service came under attack from both environmentalists and the timber industry. The agency was accused of both overcutting and undercutting the national forests.

The controversy over harvest levels focused on the definition and implementation of the Forest Service's traditional sustained-yield policy. The Forest Service in the 1920s had begun to take a more liberal approach toward calculating the allowable cut for old-growth forests.[784] In the 1950s the Forest Service officially recognized three ways to interpret sustained-yield: (1) plan for equal harvest rates, (2) vary the harvest rate depending on the particular stand of timber, and (3) plan to harvest the old-growth as soon as possible.[785] The flexible policy allowed planners to raise allowable cut levels sharply due to improved market conditions and road access. The MUSY Act,[786] along with subsequent agency regulations[787] requiring an "even flow" of harvests, reflected the Forest Service's belief that its selected allowable cut levels could be sustained indefinitely.

The agency's belief was shattered by its Douglas-Fir Supply Study in 1969. The study revealed that current harvest levels on

---

harvest scheduling and harvest unit size will be more restrictive, but full timber yield is assumed." *Id.* Second, where removing more than 50% of the vegetation from an area would cause erosion, "the maximum clearcut size will be five acres and the maximum shelterwood unit size will be 10 acres." *Id.* Third, where removing *less* than 50% of the vegetation would cause erosion, "the lands are not suitable for most management activities and no programmed timber yields are assumed." *Id.* The Umpqua National Forest's Timber Resource Plan subsequently classified the critical soils land as either special or marginal. UMPQUA NAT'L FOREST TIMBER PLAN, *supra* note 657, at 26.

[783] *See* Advisory Panel Report, *supra* note 635, at 169. *See also* FOREST SERVICE MANUAL § 8220 (1973).

[784] *See supra* note 644.

[785] *See* Parry, Vaux & Dennis, *supra* note 644, at 153.

[786] 16 U.S.C. § 531 (1982).

[787] 36 C.F.R. § 221.3(a)(3) (1984). Also, in 1963 the actual sale volume exceeded the allowable cut for the first time. *See* FOREST SERVICE, U.S. DEP'T OF AGRICULTURE, ANNUAL REPORT OF THE CHIEF 6 (1965) [hereinafter 1965 ANNUAL REPORT OF THE CHIEF].

West Coast national forests could not be sustained once the old growth was harvested.[788] The agency explained:

> The reason for this ultimate decline is that, during the first rotation, cutting is confined to old-age, high-volume stands. Some of these took centuries to grow. Large volumes are "stored on the stump." After old-growth conversion at the end of the first rotation, stands are allowed to grow only to rotation age, and hence produce much less sawtimber.[789]

In 1973 the Forest Service responded to the Douglas-Fir Supply Study by abandoning the flexible Hanzlik formula[790] and establishing the more rigorous nondeclining even-flow policy (NDEF).[791] Timber planners were directed "to assure that [harvest] levels achieved can be maintained" after the old-growth conversion period.[792] The timber industry strongly objected to NDEF, arguing that the policy was unjustifiably wasteful of old-growth timber.[793]

---

[788] FOREST SERVICE, U.S. DEP'T OF AGRICULTURE, DOUGLAS-FIR SUPPLY STUDY v, 14 (1969). The agency studied 7.3 million acres of national forest land in western Washington, western Oregon, and northwest California. *Id.* at v. About 2.9 bbf were being harvested annually from the area. *Id.* The study projected timber harvests for the next 12 decades, based on four alternative levels of management. *Id.* The agency concluded that harvests would decline after 100 years by approximately 45%. *Id.* at 14.

[789] *Id.*

[790] *See supra* note 644.

[791] *See supra* text accompanying notes 647-50.

[792] Parry, Vaux & Dennis, *supra* note 644, at 154, quoting Forest Service Emergency Directive 16.

[793] Chief Cliff described the reasons for the industry's demands in testimony at a congressional hearing in 1969:
> We in the Department of Agriculture are deeply concerned over the rising prices of softwood forest products. These price increases are having a serious impact on the American consumer.
>
> . . . .
>
> In January 1969, prices of softwood lumber were more than 40 percent higher than in mid-1967. Prices of softwood plywood were more than 100 percent higher. Softwood lumber and plywood prices have climbed much more rapidly than the prices of all commodities as measured by the wholesale price index.
>
> . . . .
>
> There have been many suggestions that the Forest Service increase allowable cuts on the national forests to meet the problems of timber supplies and prices. For example, some are demanding that allowable cuts be increased 10 to 15 percent arbitrarily to meet the "emergency."

Problems in Lumber Pricing and Production: Hearings Before the Subcomm. on Housing and Urban Affairs of the Senate Comm. on Banking and Currency, 91st Cong., 1st Sess. 584-86 (1969) [hereinafter cited as *Hearings on Lumber Problems*].

The Forest Service largely offset potential NDEF-caused reductions in harvest levels by increasing reforestation, thinning, and other intensive management practices. In 1968 Chief Cliff told a congressional subcommittee, "In all forest regions supplies of timber could be substantially increased . . . through an annual program of investing funds to intensify management."[794] Raising the allowable cut in anticipation of future increases in timber volume was known as the "allowable cut effect" (now called "earned harvest effect" or EHE).[795]

Initially, the agency was reluctant to increase the allowable cut based on EHE unless intensive management was funded by Congress and actually completed.[796] A less cautious approach, Cliff stated in 1968, could "sell the public short on the national forests."[797] By the early 1970s the Forest Service began to apply

---

One report prepared for the Oregon legislature recommended that the Forest Service more than double the allowable cuts on some national forest lands. W. RICKARD, THE ACTION FOREST, *reprinted in* TIMBER MANAGEMENT POLICIES: HEARINGS BEFORE THE SUBCOMM. ON RETAILING, DISTRIBUTION, AND MARKETING PRACTICES OF THE SENATE SELECT COMM. ON SMALL BUSINESS, 90th Cong., 2d Sess. 413 (Comm. Print 1968) [hereinafter cited as HEARINGS ON TIMBER MANAGEMENT POLICIES]. The National Forest Products Association endorsed the Rickard Report's "frontal attack" on Forest Service allowable cut policies. *Id.* at 531.

[794] HEARINGS ON TIMBER MANAGEMENT POLICIES, *supra* note 793, at 240-41. Cliff said that the Douglas-Fir Supply Study and other studies showed that "allowable cuts could—in time—be increased about two-thirds by intensifying timber culture on the more productive portions of national forest commercial timberlands." *Id.* at 242. The following year Cliff testified:

When we plant trees, reforest some of the deforested areas, or when we do the stand improvement work which will result in increased growth, we can immediately start counting that increased growth into our allowable cuts and crank it into allowable cut calculations. So if we make current investments in stand improvements and reforestation and other intensive management measures, we can start getting a payoff immediately.

Hearings on Lumber Problems, supra note 793, at 605-06.

[795] EHE is described *supra* in text accompanying notes 657-64.

[796] Cliff stated that "[t]he allowable cut on the national forests should be increased, we feel, only when we earn the right to do so by performing these forest management practices." HEARINGS ON TIMBER MANAGEMENT POLICIES, *supra* note 793, at 242.

[797] *Id.* at 256. Actually, the Forest Service had traditionally increased harvest levels based on the assumption that all cutover areas would be restocked. The agency felt justified in this assumption because funding for reforestation was automatically available from timber sale receipts. *See supra* note 775. However, other intensive management practices had to be funded through annual congressional appropriations. Because of the uncertainty of these appropriations, the agency would not use EHE until after work which required appropriated money was actually completed on the ground. R. Worthington, Some Current Issues

EHE based on anticipated funding and performance.[798] However, the agency discouraged planners from relying on "the effects of intensive activities that, at this time, remain speculative or with unquantified benefit over large portions of the country such as genetics, fertilization, and irrigation."[799] Similarly, the Church Subcommittee recommended the following guideline to the Forest Service:

> Increases in allowable harvests based on intensified management practices such as reforestation, thinning, tree improvement and the like should be made only upon demonstration that such practices justify increased allowable harvests, and there is assurance that such practices are satisfactorily funded for continuation to completion.
> If planned intensive measures are inadequately funded and thus cannot be accomplished on schedule, allowable harvests should be reduced accordingly . . . .[800]

Thus, by 1976 the Forest Service had settled on an uneasy compromise premised on a two-part sustained-yield policy aimed at preserving the status quo. NDEF perpetuated the agency's traditional even-flow principles, while EHE prevented existing harvest levels from dropping dramatically.

C. Limitations on Timber Harvesting

The Forest Service's efforts to respond to public criticism in the early 1970s did not end the controversy. A 1974 Forest Service report, for instance, revealed that only one-third of the cutover land in the Rocky Mountain national forests was successfully regenerating.[801] The report characterized the reforestation failures as "galloping desolation."[802] Meanwhile, in 1973 a group of West

---

Concerning Allowable Timber Harvesting Calculations 6 (1974) (unpublished report on file at Oregon Law Review office).

[798] The agency first ventured into EHE based on anticipated funding on the Gifford Pinchot National Forest in Washington. The forest was allowed to raise its allowable cut based on a commitment by the Chief of the Forest Service to fund the intensive management annually for a ten-year period from congressional appropriations. *Id.*

[799] ADVISORY PANEL REPORT, *supra* note 635, at 186, quoting FOREST SERVICE MANUAL § 2415.14 (1972).

[800] CHURCH SUBCOMMITTEE REPORT, *supra* note 194, at 9, *reprinted in* SENATE NFMA HEARINGS, *supra* note 194, at 959.

[801] FOREST SERVICE, U.S. DEP'T OF AGRICULTURE, THE ROCKY MOUNTAIN TIMBER SITUATION 1970, at 25-26 (Research Bulletin INT-10) (1974).

[802] *Id.* at 26. Senator Randolph cited the report as evidence that "timber has been cut from lands that will not regenerate." 122 CONG. REC. 2222 (1976).

Virginia environmentalists had succeeded in enjoining timber sales in the Monongahela National Forest on the ground that clearcutting violated the 1897 Organic Act. Affirmation of the *Monongahela* ruling by the Fourth Circuit Court of Appeals[803] precipitated prompt congressional action.

The NFMA was enacted in 1976 to resolve both the immediate impact of the *Monongahela* decision and the underlying controversies over timber policy. The Act addresses virtually all major aspects of timber planning, including physical and economic suitability, ecological diversity, harvest levels, and harvesting methods. This section discusses existing law in each of these areas.

1. The Current Relevance of the Church Guidelines

Several of the major sections in the NFMA, including the physical suitability and harvesting method provisions, are essentially the Church guidelines, with significant additions from Senator Randolph's bill.[804] One commentator on the NFMA has claimed that the legislative history is of "limited worth" and "not much help" in interpreting the Act's suitability and harvesting provisions.[805] Our review of the legislative history directs us to a different conclusion, especially in light of apparent Congressional intent, as discussed in the remainder of this subsection, that the Church guidelines be used to analyze the legislative history of the NFMA.

The NFMA's suitability and harvesting provisions were agreed upon during the Senate mark-up. Senator Humphrey's bill contained broad guidelines, while the standards in the Randolph bill were specific.[806] During the first day of mark-up, Senator Metcalf,

---

[803] West Virginia Div. of the Izaak Walton League of Am., Inc. v. Butz, 522 F.2d 945 (4th Cir. 1975), discussed *supra* in note 197.

[804] *See, e.g., infra* text accompanying notes 826-29.

[805] Stoel, *The National Forest Management Act*, 8 ENVTL L. 549, 554 (1978).

[806] Randolph's bill required the Secretary of Agriculture to promulgate "standards for determining those areas of the national forests from which timber may be sold." S. 2926, 94th Cong., 2d Sess. § 4(a), *reprinted in* SENATE NFMA HEARINGS, *supra* note 194, at 3. The suitability standards were to insure that timber sales from national forest lands are made only from—

(1) lands which are stable and do not exceed the maximum degree of slope appropriate for each soil type on which roads may be constructed or timber cut;

(2) lands on which the timber does not consist solely of patches and stringers;

acting as chairman of the Interior and Insular Affairs Committee, proposed strict requirements[807] similar to those in Randolph's bill.[808] Metcalf stated that the Interior Committee's proposed amendment "says you have to do some specific things, but which

---

(3) lands which, within five years after being timbered, will regenerate the growth of trees naturally or will do so with a modest reforestation investment;

(4) lands which are capable of regenerating a commercial stand of timber;

(5) lands sufficiently distant from streambanks, shorelines, and wetlands to avoid disturbance of streams, other bodies of water, and wetlands; and

(6) lands on which timber cutting will not substantially impair important nontimber resources.

Id. at 4(b), *reprinted in* SENATE NFMA HEARINGS, *supra* note 194, at 4. The bill also required "minimum reforestation requirements for national forest lands that are hot, dry, wet, frost prone, at high elevations, or characterized by thin soils, or that for other reasons have a low probability of regeneration." *Id.* § 4(c).

The main drafter of the Randolph bill was James Moorman, then a staff member of the Sierra Club Legal Defense Fund and later Assistant Attorney General for Lands and Natural Resources. Moorman testified that the purpose of section 4's standards was to prohibit logging on "inappropriate lands." SENATE NFMA HEARINGS, *supra* note 194, at 516. Moorman explained:

One of the most difficult problems is that of "timber mining," or the cutting of trees from inappropriate lands where the costs are too high or the likelihood of regeneration is uncertain. This problem occurs, for example, when timber is cut from lands of high elevation, arid lands, lands with an excess of moisture, or from poor or erosible soils.

Id. at 516-17.

[807] Michael Harvey, Deputy Chief Counsel of the Senate Committee on Interior and Insular Affairs, explained that these requirements, in the form of an amendment, consisted of two modified Church guidelines and four modified guidelines from the Randolph bill, *April 27, 1976, Transcript of Senate Markup, supra* note 374. The amendment, in part, required the Forest Service to insure that timber sales will be executed only for lands—

(aa) which do not possess fragile soil, slope or other watershed conditions or wildlife habitat which would be subject to significant injury from timber cutting;

(bb) which are capable of regenerating a commercial stand of timber;

(cc) which, within five years after timber harvest, will regenerate the growth of trees naturally or with a modest reforestation investment;

(dd) which are sufficiently distant from wetlands, streambanks, and shorelines to avoid significant disturbance of wetlands, streams, lakes, and other bodies of water, or upon which measures, such as provision of blowdown-resistant buffer strips are to be taken to insure the avoidance of such disturbance . . . .

Comparison of S. 3091, supra note 440, Senator Metcalf's Amendments, § 3(d)(5)(C)(v), *reprinted in* D. LeMASTER, *supra* note 162, at 201-03.

[808] S. 2926, § 4(b)(1), (3), (4), and (5), *reprinted in* SENATE NFMA HEARINGS, *supra* note 194, at 4.

the Forest Service hasn't done."[809] Several senators voiced a preference for the original Church guidelines.[810] Senator Mark Hatfield of Oregon, for instance, argued that the Church guidelines would provide a more authoritative legislative history "than just creating them out of chrome promises here at this table."[811] Senator Humphrey agreed: "I think it is necessary to get the benefit of the hearings that were held in '71 . . . . They give legislative background and legislative history, so in case there is a court case you have something to go on."[812] The committees then decided to merge the provisions in Senator Metcalf's amendment with the Church guidelines.[813] The House, which adopted a

---

[809] *April 27, 1976, Transcript of Senate Mark-up, supra* note 374, at 74.

[810] Senator McClure and Chief McGuire both objected specifically to prohibiting timber sales where land would be subject to "significant" injury. *Id.* at 67-68. McClure commented that the Church guidelines had only prohibited "major" injury and that "the difference between 'significant' and 'major' is a major difference." *Id.* at 68. Chief McGuire concurred with McClure:

The main problem here is [the] interpretation of the word "significant." . . . We would say that in our interpretation, of course, we are doing this sort of thing now . . . . Nevertheless I can see where there might be some future challenges over in the court for what some of these words mean.

Id. at 68-69. McClure also objected that the amendment's reforestation requirement "greatly changes the thrust of the recommendation" in the Church subcommittee report. *Id.* at 68.

[811] *Id.* at 70. Hatfield's comment occurred during the following exchange with Metcalf, who was also a member of the Church subcommittee in 1972:

SENATOR HATFIELD. I would like to make one observation and that is the Subcommittee of Public Lands have held hearings and have established a rather significant record and therefore even though they may be subject to interpretation by courts, *we would certainly have far more of a base upon which to move using the language directly from that report* than creating new language now where we have not had such hearings and have not had such discussions and input of citizens and of various groups. I would like to feel that perhaps the Metcalf amendments, if they could more closely follow the language of those reports made in the subcommittee, we might be on a stronger foundation now that we are initiating this broader language.

SENATOR METCALF. What do you want to put in there, you and Senator McClure?

SENATOR HATFIELD. Well, we have already had examples like "significant" and I think in the subcommittee we used the word "major" and we discussed that at some length and *the record will show what we intended,* and therefore I think we have more substantive records to base some of these clarifications or new descriptions upon than *just creating them out of chrome promises here at this table* or with staff after recent hearings on two bills.

Id. (emphasis added).

[812] *Id.* at 72-73.

[813] *See supra* text accompanying note 443.

similar version of the Church guidelines,[814] generally acceded to
the Senate language in the conference committee.[815] The Senate
and House committee reports and floor debates are replete with
references to the Church subcommittee report and hearings.[816]

Based on this record, it seems clear that Congress intended to
incorporate the legislative history of the Church guidelines in order to provide a basis for statutory interpretation of the NFMA
provisions, especially in regard to suitability and harvesting practices. Thus, the starting point for interpretation should be a comparison of the NFMA and the Church guidelines. Identical provisions can be interpreted through reference to the Church
subcommittee report and the lengthy hearing record. Differences
between the two sets of guidelines should be analyzed to determine Congress's purpose in choosing the different language.

The Church guidelines remain pertinent for purposes other than
construing the NFMA. Many of the Act's provisions went into
effect immediately, including some of the provisions relating to

---

[814] *See* H.R. 15,069, 94th Cong., 2d Sess. § 6(f)(4)-(5) (1976), *reprinted in*
RPA COMPILATION, *supra* note 173, at 562-64. The Church guidelines were not
a point of controversy in the House mark-up. For instance, Representative
Melcher commented that the guidelines "have quite a little credibility where I
come from." TRANSCRIPT OF HOUSE MARK-UP, *supra* note 448, at 46. Similarly,
Representative Symms stated, "If we want to pass this bill, . . . the Church
guidelines are one of the things with which I think our friends from urban districts with environmental concerns maybe feel more comfortable." *Id.* at 74. The
subcommittee voted to approve the guidelines after a brief discussion. *Id.* at 56-
58.

[815] *See* S. REP. NO. 1335, 94th Cong., 2d Sess. 30 (Conf. Report), *reprinted in*
1976 U.S. CODE CONG. & AD. NEWS (USCCAN) 6721, 6732, *and in* RPA
COMPILATION, *supra* note 173, at 758.

[816] *See* S. REP. NO. 893, 94th Cong., 2d Sess. 36, 39, *reprinted in* 1976 USC-
CAN 6662, 6695, 6698, *and in* RPA COMPILATION, *supra* note 173, at 316, 319;
S. REP. NO. 905, 94th Cong., 2d Sess. 3, 15, *reprinted in* 1976 USCCAN 6718,
6720, *and in* RPA COMPILATION, *supra*, at 397, 407; H.R. REP. NO. 1478, pt. 1,
94th Cong., 2d Sess. 30 (1976), *reprinted in* RPA COMPILATION, *supra*, at 605;
122 CONG. REC. 27,618 (1976) (remarks of Sen. Hatfield), *reprinted in* RPA
COMPILATION, *supra*, at 433; *id.* at 27,621 (remarks of Sen. Metcalf), *reprinted
in* RPA COMPILATION, *supra*, at 438; *id.* at 27,619, 27,624 (remarks of Sen.
McClure), *reprinted in* RPA COMPILATION, *supra*, at 435, 444; *id.* at 27,624
(remarks of Sen. Humphrey), *reprinted in* RPA COMPILATION, *supra*, at 444-45;
id. at 27,646 (remarks of Sen. Talmadge), *reprinted in* RPA COMPILATION,
supra, at 483; *id.* at 27,648 (remarks of Sen. Haskell), *reprinted in* RPA
COMPILATION, *supra*, at 487; *id.* at 31,047 (remarks of Rep. Melcher), *reprinted
in* RPA COMPILATION, *supra*, at 698; *id.* (remarks of Rep. Symms), *reprinted in*
RPA COMPILATION, *supra*, at 697.

harvest levels.[817] Section 6 of the NFMA, on the other hand, sets requirements that must be complied with in land management plans; examples are the provisions on physical and economic suitability,[818] EHE,[819] and harvesting practices.[820] Since few final plans have been released, the NFMA per se does not yet apply to these issues. Congress, however, indicated that the Church guidelines, where applicable, should be adhered to during the hiatus.[821] Three courts have concluded that the Church guidelines control harvesting practices until the plans are released.[822] Thus, the Church guidelines should be consulted on some issues for those forests where the Forest Service has not completed management plans pursuant to the NFMA.

2. Suitability

(a) Physical Suitability

The suitability guidelines set out in section 6(g)(3)(E) are some of the strongest medicine that Congress prescribed in the NFMA. They require the Forest Service to

> insure that timber will be harvested from National Forest System lands only where—
> (i) soil, slope, or other watershed conditions will not be irreversibly damaged;
> (ii) there is assurance that such lands can be adequately restocked within five years after harvest;
> (iii) protection is provided for streams, streambanks, shorelines, lakes, wetlands, and other bodies of water from detrimental changes in water temperatures, blockages of water courses, and

---

[817] *E.g.*, 16 U.S.C. § 1611 (1982), discussed *infra* in text accompanying notes 896-932.

[818] *Id.* § 1604(g)(3)(E), § 1604(k), discussed *infra* in text accompanying notes 823-72.

[819] *Id.* § 1604(g)(3)(D), discussed *infra* in text accompanying notes 947-57.

[820] *Id.* § 1604(g)(3)(E), (F), discussed *infra* in text accompanying notes 823-31.

[821] S. Rep. No. 1335, 94th Cong., 2d Sess. 24, *reprinted in* 1976 USCCAN 6721, 6726, *and in* RPA Compilation, *supra* note 173, at 752. The diversity and CMAI provisions are contained in § 6 but are not in the Church guidelines; therefore, they are probably not legally enforceable in the interim.

[822] National Wildlife Federation v. United States Forest Service, 592 F. Supp. 931 (D. Or. 1984), *appeal docketed*, No. 84-4274 (9th Cir., Oct. 29, 1984); California v. Block, 690 F.2d 753, 775 (9th Cir. 1982); Texas Comm. on Natural Resources v. Bergland, 573 F.2d 201, 209-10 (5th Cir.), *cert. denied*, 439 U.S. 966 (1978).

deposits of sediment, where harvests are likely to seriously and adversely affect water conditions or fish habitat.[823]

The first two subsections—on soil erosion and reforestation—came directly from the Church guidelines. However, the NFMA provisions differ from the Church guidelines in two important respects.

First, Congress broadened the scope of harvesting activities to which the guidelines apply. While the Church guidelines only limited the use of clearcutting, the NFMA applies to all timber harvesting activity. Land that does not meet these standards must be classified as unsuitable for timber production.[824] Presumably, the NFMA proscription extends to road construction necessarily undertaken in conjunction with timber harvesting.[825] For example, the agency could not consider land to be suitable for harvesting if the only feasible way to reach the timber were to build a road across unstable land where slope conditions would be irreversibly damaged.

Second, section 6(g)(3)(E)(iii) of the NFMA goes beyond the Church guidelines by "preclud[ing] timber harvesting from areas where . . . harvesting cannot be accomplished without serious and adverse damage to water condition or fish habitat," unless "protection can be afforded."[826] The provision originated in the Randolph bill[827] and was incorporated into the Senate bill when the committees merged the Metcalf amendment with the Humphrey bill. It expands on the soil erosion guideline by requiring protection from "detrimental changes," such as thermal pollution caused by removing trees from streambanks. The amount of protection required for fish habitat will necessarily vary according to the sensitivity of the resident fish. For instance, the standard for a salmon, steelhead, or trout fishery will be higher than for

---

[823] 16 U.S.C. § 1604(g)(3)(E)(i)-(iii) (1982).

[824] *See id.* § 1604(k); *see also* S. REP. NO. 905, 94th Cong., 2d Sess. 2, *reprinted in* 1976 USCCAN 6718, 6719, *and in* RPA COMPILATION, *supra* note 173, at 396.

[825] The Church Subcommittee report, for instance, indicates that the guidelines apply "to any activity relating to timber harvesting." *See* CHURCH SUBCOMMITTEE REPORT, *supra* note 194, at 8, *reprinted in* SENATE NFMA HEARINGS, *supra* note 194, at 958.

[826] S. REP. NO. 893, 94th Cong., 2d Sess. 39, *reprinted in* 1976 USCCAN 6662, 6698, *and in* RPA COMPILATION, *supra* note 173, at 319.

[827] *Compare* 16 U.S.C. § 1604(g)(3)(E)(iii) (1982) *with* S. 2926, 94th Cong., 2d Sess. §§ 4(b)(5), 14(a), *reprinted in* SENATE NFMA HEARINGS, *supra* note 194, at 4, 7-8.

most other types of fish habitat.[828] The Senate Agriculture Committee's discussion of section 6(g)(3)(E)(iii) stressed that activities affecting "significant fish and wildlife habitat must be very carefully planned and monitored to assure that habitat values are recognized and properly protected."[829]

In sum, a fair reading of the NFMA's physical suitability guidelines places a high standard of care on Forest Service planners. These provisions impose safeguards that trace back to the origins of the Forest Service's "conservative use" policy.[830] They require the agency to provide empirical guarantees that timber harvesting will not damage soils, water conditions, and fish habitats. The five-year reforestation deadline is equally straightforward and specific. Together they give firm statutory direction to exclude timber production from environmentally sensitive portions of the national forests.

The suitability guidelines have special applicability to plans for timber harvesting and logging road construction in previously roadless areas. Typically, these are lands where harvesting has not yet taken place due to their steeper slopes, thinner and less stable soils, and shorter growing seasons.[831] Further, because of the remoteness of roadless areas, less factual data on soils and reforestation potential is likely to be available. Planners must carefully inventory and evaluate these areas to "insure" their suitability before allowing timber harvesting to occur.

---

[828] *See generally* OREGON DEP'T OF FISH & WILDLIFE, COMPREHENSIVE PLAN FOR PRODUCTION AND MANAGEMENT OF OREGON'S ANADROMOUS SALMON AND TROUT pt. I (1982) (decline of anadromous fisheries tied to loss and degredation of habitat caused by various human activities, including logging, sedimention, and road construction). *See also generally* Northwest Indian Cemetery Protective Ass'n v. Peterson, 565 F. Supp. 586, 605 (N.D. Cal. 1983), *aff'd*, 764 F.2d 581 (9th Cir. 1985) (increase in sediment reducing survival rate of anadromous fish eggs laid in spawning gravel would constitute an unreasonable effect on a beneficial use); National Wildlife Federation v. Forest Service, 592 F. Supp. at 943 (worst case analysis should reflect damage to anadromous fish habitat caused by landslides).

[829] S. REP. No. 893, 94th Cong., 2d Sess. 39, *reprinted in* 1976 USCCAN 6662, 6698, *and in* RPA COMPILATION, *supra* note 173, at 319.

[830] *See supra* text accompanying notes 691-705.

[831] *See generally* NATIONAL RARE II SYMPOSIUM PROCEEDINGS: PROFESSIONAL PERSPECTIVES ON RARE II DECISIONMAKING FOR THE WESTERN UNITED STATES (Univ. of Montana 1978).

(b) Economic Suitability

While the NFMA is primarily concerned with environmental safeguards, the Act also requires economically sound timber management. Section 6(k) provides:

> In developing land management plans pursuant to this [Act], the Secretary shall identify lands within the management area which are not suited for timber production, considering physical, economic, and other pertinent factors to the extent feasible, as determined by the Secretary, and shall assure that, except for salvage sales or sales necessitated to protect other multiple-use values, no timber harvesting shall occur on such lands for a period of 10 years. Lands once identified as unsuitable for timber production shall continue to be treated for reforestation purposes, particularly with regard to the protection of other multiple-use values. The Secretary shall review his decision to classify these lands as not suited for timber production at least every 10 years and shall return these lands to timber production whenever he determines that conditions have changed so that they have become suitable for timber production.[832]

The section was the product of a long and often confused debate over whether to allow timber management on economically marginal lands.

During the early 1970s, uneconomical timber management practices were a major concern of the Bolle Report and the Church Subcommittee.[833] The 1972 subcommittee report indicates that the Church guidelines were intended to eliminate timber harvesting activity in areas "where the costs of special measures to avoid environmental damage or assure regeneration were so high that the activity was imprudent and relatively uneconomic."[834] The Forest Service subsequently included a marginal component in its timber planning system. Land was classified as marginal and generally withdrawn from timber production due to "excessive development cost, low-product values, or resource protection constraints."[835] By the end of 1976, the Forest Service had classified almost one-quarter of its commercial forest land as marginal.[836]

---

[832] 16 U.S.C. § 1604(k) (1982).

[833] *See supra* text accompanying notes 725-46.

[834] *See supra* text accompanying note 760.

[835] *See supra* text accompanying note 774.

[836] 19.2 million acres out of 89.0 million acres of commercial timberland were classified as marginal. FOREST SERVICE MANUAL § 2411.11 (Interim Directive No. 82, Feb. 2, 1983).

Economic suitability was not specifically addressed by either the Humphrey or Randolph bills. The issue was first raised during the Senate hearings by Dr. Marion Clawson, a leading economist at Resources for the Future and professor at the University of California.[837] Clawson generally favored eliminating timber management on economically marginal areas and investing more money in intensive management on land where it was economically advantageous in terms of revenue exceeding cost.[838] He specifically opposed managing timber on land capable of growing less than fifty cubic feet of wood fiber per acre per year—known as site V land.[839] The traditional Forest Service dividing line for

---

[837] Clawson had recently published an article on the economics of national forest management. Clawson, *The National Forests*, 191 SCIENCE 762 (1976), *reprinted in* SENATE NFMA HEARINGS, *supra* note 194, at 780-89. In the article Clawson analyzed the receipts and expenditures for timber management for each of the national forests and regions. *Id.* at 765-66, *reprinted in Senate NFMA Hearings*, *supra* note 194, at 786-88. The analysis showed a wide disparity in profitability among the forests and regions, leading Clawson to conclude that

> expenditures for timber management are being made in regions, on forests, and on sites where timber values are so low that areas should be abandoned for timber growing purposes. Other outputs of these forests may be worth managing, and existing stands of trees may be valuable for this purpose, but the growing of more timber is not economically sound.

Id. at 765, *reprinted in* SENATE NFMA HEARINGS, *supra* note 194, at 785, *and in* 122 CONG. REC. 27,631 (1976).

[838] Clawson explained to the committees:

> By intensified management I mean timber management on the better timber sites, and leaving aside those sites where for conservation reasons, as well as environmental and economic reasons, you would not practice such forestry.
>
> On the better sites there would be prompt replanting of the site after harvest in order to reduce the time of regeneration, which is estimated to average 7 years with natural regeneration, and for good timber practice it can be cut in a year; replanted with carefully selected stock; replanted at optimum densities, thinning of stands at proper ages, at first to obtain proper spacing, but later to salvage substantial amounts of wood.

SENATE NFMA HEARINGS, *supra* note 194, at 275. He also stated, "[W]e could set aside very substantial areas of the national forests exclusively for other uses and either practice no timber harvest or practice it at long intervals or very rarely." *Id.* at 276.

[839] *Id.* at 279. Commercial timber land (all available forest land capable of growing at least 20 cubic feet of timber per acre per year, *see supra* text accompanying notes 633-37) has traditionally been divided into five site classes, I-V. Site class V land, providing growth between 20 to 50 cubic feet, is the least productive classification. Clawson explained that the site V lands are located primarily in the western national forests,

> where either the soils are thin or because they are a higher elevation, the weather, the climate is not so good, where there may be a pretty good

commercial suitability has been twenty cubic feet.[840]

During the Senate mark-up, Senator Metcalf and Senator Dale Bumpers of Arkansas offered an amendment that precluded timber production in areas where management costs were expected to exceed returns from future timber sales.[841] Bumpers explained that the amendment was inspired by Clawson's testimony and was intended to prevent "raping and pillaging" of site V land.[842] Chief McGuire suggested that the amendment should take into account nonmonetary returns, such as wildlife habitat improvement.[843] After lengthy discussion,[844] the committees agreed on a cost-benefit test that was apparently intended to permit consideration of McGuire's concern.[845]

---

stand of timber now, but if you cut it, the regeneration is slow and uncertain and the growth is slow and the dangers of erosion of getting it out are great and the costs of getting it out are high. I would say let those trees stand. Let them stand as a reserve if we should ever need them for some desperate national emergency.
Id. at 280.

[840] *See supra* text accompanying note 635.

[841] The amendment required the Forest Service to
identify the suitability of lands for timber production on the basis of the total monetary costs for managing for such production and the prospective monetary returns from future timber sales: Provided, That those lands shall not be managed for timber production on which the total monetary costs of managing for such production generally exceed the prospective monetary returns on future timber sales therefrom.
April 27, 1976, Transcript of Senate Mark-up, supra note 374, at 77.

[842] *Id.* at 77-78.

[843] McGuire explained, "Frequently we may make a timber sale primarily for wildlife reasons, and if we were limited in that, we would have to do that wildlife improvement solely with appropriated funds . . . ." *Id.* at 78-79.

[844] The committee staffs revised Senator Bumpers's marginal land provision after the first day of mark-up. *April 29, 1976, Transcript of Senate Mark-up, supra* note 374, at 30-31.
During the second day of mark-up Senator McClure offered an amendment giving the agency greater flexibility to manage timber on marginal lands. *See id.* at 29. McClure, Hatfield, and Chief McGuire argued that Bumpers' provision could prohibit the Forest Service from cutting trees for purposes of wildlife enhancement, infestation control, and other nontimber purposes. *See id.* at 29-35. Hatfield also objected to establishing a cost-benefit requirement for timber production because "you could end up with fewer forests." *Id.* at 38-39. Talmadge replied to Hatfield, "Mark, only an idiot forester would plant trees on land that he knows would not grow trees adequately." *Id.* at 39. The committee narrowly rejected McClure's amendment. *Id.* at 40-43.

[845] *See* S. 3091, 94th Cong., 2d Sess. § 5(d)(6)(H)(iii), 122 CONG. REC. 27,651 (1976), *reprinted in* RPA COMPILATION, *supra note* 173, at 378. An exemption for nontimber costs was added during the third day of mark-up, while Senator Bumpers was absent. The committee staff and Forest Service had drafted the exemption, which appeared to satisfy McGuire's desire to be able to

The House bill did not contain a marginal lands provision. Most members of the Subcommittee on Forests wanted to address the issue, but they could not agree on satisfactory language.[846] Similarly, some members of the House Committee on Agriculture preferred to "leave it up to the conference [committee] to decide the guidelines to be used."[847] Other committee members objected to the loss of timber supply that might result from the Senate's cost-benefit test.[848] The committee, however, agreed to an amendment requiring the agency to provide information on costs and benefits of its timber management.[849]

---

sell timber on marginal lands for wildlife and other purposes. *See May 3, 1976, Transcript of Senate Mark-up, supra* note 374, at 79-83.

During the fourth and final day of mark-up Bumpers asked for an explanation of the exemption. *May 4, 1976, Transcript of Senate Mark-up, supra* note 374, at 113. McGuire explained, "[W]e do not intend to manage the submarginal lands for timber production, but, on the other hand, we may want to do some [timber] harvesting for wildlife, water, or other reasons." *Id.* at 114. Bumpers said that he was "not at all satisfied with this language," but did not attempt to change it. *Id. See also* 122 CONG. REC. 27,631-32 (1976) (remarks of Sen. Bumpers), *reprinted in* RPA COMPILATION, *supra* note 173, at 457-58; S. REP. No. 893, 94th Cong., 2d Sess. 37-38, *reprinted in* 1976 USCCAN 6662, 6696-97, *and in* RPA COMPILATION, *supra* note 173, at 317-18.

[846] Four of the seven subcommittee members made suggestions. One of the members, Representative Ray Thornton of Arkansas, stated, "[M]y efforts to shed light upon the area of confusion seem to have led, perhaps, to more haziness than light . . . ." TRANSCRIPT OF HOUSE MARK-UP, *supra* note 448, at 131. Much of the confusion centered on distinguishing timber production from other management goals. During questioning of R. Max Peterson, Deputy Chief of the Forest Service, Representative Weaver commented, "What you are really saying, I think Mr. Peterson, is that you do not know what the words management goal mean in this context . . . ." *Id.* at 129. Peterson replied, "I think that is correct." *Id.* Chief McGuire, however, clarified the agency's position that "we should not be spending the taxpayers' dollars where we are not getting sufficient return for that expenditure." *Id.* at 121.

[847] *Id.* at 281 (remarks of Rep. Thornton). Representative Melcher urged the committee not to adopt the Senate provision on marginal lands because it would leave "no room for conference." *Id.* Melcher quoted remarks made by Senator Humphrey during the Senate floor debate that the conference committee would more precisely define the meaning of the provision. *Id.* Melcher concluded, "If we are going to follow his recommendation, we better leave it out of the House bill so there can be a conference on that point . . . ." *Id.*

[848] *See id.* at 276-81. *See also* H.R. REP. NO. 1478, pt. 1, 94th Cong., 2d Sess. 36, *reprinted in* RPA COMPILATION, *supra* note 173, at 611.

[849] TRANSCRIPT OF HOUSE MARK-UP, *supra* note 448, at 355-57. The sponsor of the amendment, Representative Brown, explained, "It is basically intended to determine that the Government is getting back what it invests in forest management processes . . . . I think it is clear that we do not have the information that we need to have for making policy decisions." *Id.* at 356. During the House floor debate Representative Brown offered an amendment that included a marginal

In the conference committee the House offered the language in section 6(k) as a substitute for the marginal land provision in the Senate bill.[850] Bumpers reportedly studied the House language overnight and concluded that it would accomplish what he had first proposed in the Senate mark-up.[851] The following day, Bumpers and the other Senate conferees accepted the House language without further discussion.[852] The conferees also adopted

---

lands provision. 122 CONG. REC. 31,045-46 (1976), *reprinted in* RPA COMPILATION, *supra* note 173, at 694-95. The House rejected the amendment. *Id.* at 31,050, *reprinted in* RPA COMPILATION, *supra* note 173, at 703.

[850] Section 6(k) was proposed by Representative Thomas Foley, Chairman of the House Committee on Agriculture. Interview with Robert E. Wolf, Ass't Chief, Environment & Natural Resources Policy Div., Congressional Research Service, Library of Congress, in Washington, D.C. (June 22, 1983).

[851] Robert E. Wolf, a key advisor to the Senate on the NFMA, has provided the following first-hand account of the conference committee's action on § 6(k). Senator Metcalf assigned to Senator Bumpers the responsibility of acting as chairman of the Interior and Insular Affairs Committee during the conference. Metcalf let it be known that if the bill came out of conference without sustained-yield and marginal lands provisions, he would filibuster it. Industry was lobbying for the House not to agree. Clearly, agreement was going to occur, but how? The House offered the § 6(k) substitute late one afternoon, and Bumpers asked the conferees to postpone action until the next morning. He called Wolf to his office, where they reviewed the House proposal. Bumpers read it as banning timber sales except for salvage sales. His staff and Wolf agreed. Wolf expected the industry and the Forest Service to offer numerous objections. After they discussed possible changes, Bumpers decided he would accept the House proposal "as is." Wolf advised Bumpers to call Senator Talmadge—who led the Senate conferees and presided as chairman of the conference committee—to advise him that the House proposal was acceptable and that Bumpers would move to adopt it the first thing in the morning. Wolf pointed out that if Bumpers kept his statement short, Talmadge would likely gavel it through at once and move to the next issue. Bumpers contacted Talmadge at once. Wolf later talked to Talmadge, who told Wolf of Bumpers's call. Talmadge told Wolf that he thought the language in the House proposal would stop marginal sales. Letter from Robert E. Wolf to the authors (Dec. 11, 1984).

[852] Senate advisor Robert E. Wolf recalls that when the conferees reconvened the next morning, Senator Talmadge recognized Senator Bumpers to speak on the marginal lands issue. Bumpers made a brief statement that he wanted to cooperate and thought that the language proposed by the House would put timber sales on a solid economic footing while permitting evaluation of areas taken out of the allowable cut land base every 10 years. Bumpers then moved for adoption. Talmadge said, "The Senate recedes"—which meant that the Senate conferees accepted the House language—and said, "The next item is . . . ." Wolf recalls that the House conferees and the industry were flabbergasted, but they could do nothing. After another section of the bill had been disposed of, Representative Symms sought to add "to the extent feasible," and Talmadge agreed for the Senate. *Id.*

Dennis LeMaster wrote the following account of the conferees' decision to adopt § 6(k):

the House provision requiring information on costs and benefits of timber management.[853]

The formal legislative history of section 6(k) does little to elucidate the conferees' intent. The conference committee report states that the section modifies the marginal lands provision of the Senate bill, but it does not suggest any standards or examples of economic suitability.[854] Representative Thomas Foley of Washington, who led the House conferees and proposed section 6(k),[855] simply remarked that the House and Senate had a "difference of opinion" over the marginal lands issue, without explaining how the difference was resolved.[856] However, Foley implied that the House had been unwilling to accept the Senate's "economic test," which he thought would have been difficult to administer and "would have barred [timber harvesting] in great portions of the national forests."[857] Representative Symms, the only other conferee who discussed section 6(k) and an opponent of the Senate provision, stated that the conference committee "agreed that it would be unwise to impose rigid and inflexible economic or other constraints

---

The marginal-lands issue was resolved in the final hours of the last meeting of the conferees. Congressman Foley was able to break the deadlock on the issue by establishing the intent of the Senate sponsors of the marginal-lands provision: to stop timber harvesting on national forest lands not suited for growing timber. It was not their intent, as might be inferred from a literal reading of section 5(d)(6)(H)(iii) of the Senate version of S. 3091, to eliminate timber production as a management objective on lands where such production is inefficient as determined by an economic test. The difference is significant. The established intent was narrower than the inferred intent.

D. LeMaster, *supra* note 162, at 77.

[853] S. Rep. No. 1335, 94th Cong., 2d Sess. 28-29, *reprinted in* 1976 USCCAN 6721, 6730-31, *and in* RPA Compilation, *supra* note 173, at 756-57.

[854] *Id.* at 8, *reprinted in* RPA Compilation, *supra* note 173, at 737. The conference report stated:

The Conferees expect the Secretary to give appropriate consideration to such things as advances in logging techniques, improved genetic stock, or improved knowledge about the relationship between the resource components of the general land area. While this list is by no means exhaustive, the Conferees intend the Secretary to review and keep abreast of all developments in the field of forestry and its related sciences and to refer to these developments as necessary in making the determination required by this section.

Id. at 28-29, *reprinted in* 1976 USCCAN 6721, 6730-31, *and in* RPA Compilation, *supra* note 173, at 756-57.

[855] *See supra* note 850.

[856] 122 Cong. Rec. 34,227 (1976), *reprinted in* RPA Compilation, *supra* note 173, at 782.

[857] *Id.*

to be applied to all national forest lands."[858] Similarly, Senator Randolph, who was not a conferee, declared that the Senate's provision had been rendered "virtually meaningless" by the action of the committee.[859] On the other hand, some members of Congress thought that the conference committee had retained the thrust of the Senate provision.[860] Two key congressional advisors on the NFMA have observed that the conferees simply "agreed not to agree" on the marginal lands issue[861] and hoped that their own understanding of what was intended would ultimately prevail.[862]

The Committee of Scientists[863] analyzed section 6(k) in detail and concluded that Congress failed to give clear direction regarding the use of economic criteria.[864] The Committee said that Congress avoided prescribing a specific formula and that the cost-benefit test was only one of a variety of criteria that could be applied.[865] However, the Committee also determined that the legislative history "implied Congressional concern that timber harvesting is generally not to take place when, by some rules of reason, public benefits are less than production costs."[866] The Committee did not attempt to define any "rule of reason" for economic suitability.

While no court has ruled on the meaning of section 6(k), a decision by the Court of Appeals for the Ninth Circuit suggests that judges may be reluctant to prohibit unprofitable timber sales. In *Thomas v. Peterson*,[867] plaintiffs sought to bar construction of a logging road, relying in part on a section of the Rangeland and

---

[858] 122 CONG. REC. 34,228 (1976) (remarks of Rep. Symms), *reprinted in* RPA COMPILATION, *supra* note 173, at 783.

[859] *Id.* at 33,838 (remarks of Sen. Randolph), *reprinted in* RPA COMPILATION, *supra* note 173, at 774.

[860] *See* 122 CONG. REC. 33,958 (1976) (remarks of Sen. Nelson) ("The conference report retains the Senate's prohibition on managing an area for timber production on marginal lands if the cost of management exceeds the sale price of the timber that is proposed to be harvested."); *cf. id.* at 34,231 (remarks of Rep. Baucus) (NFMA limits "use of environmentally fragile or commercially unproductive land for timber.").

[861] Interview with James Giltmier, former staff member, Senate Comm. on Agriculture and Forestry, in Washington, D.C. (June 17, 1983).

[862] Letter from Robert E. Wolf, *supra* note 851.

[863] *See supra* note 211 and accompanying text.

[864] *Final Report of the Committee of Scientists*, 44 Fed. Reg. 26,599, 26,607 (1979) [hereinafter cited as *Comm. of Scientists Final Report*]. For a discussion of the Committee of Scientists, see *supra* text accompanying note 211.

[865] *Id.*

[866] *Id.; see also id.* at 26,629-30.

[867] 753 F.2d 754 (9th Cir. 1985).

Renewable Resources Planning Act of 1974 (RPA) that directs the Forest Service to carry forward its transportation system "on an economical . . . basis."[868] Plaintiffs argued that a logging road is not economical within the meaning of the statute if the road cost exceeds the value of the timber it accesses. The court rejected the plaintiffs' reading of the RPA, saying, "We must assume that if Congress had wanted to include such a specific requirement it would have done so."[869] Rather, the opinion accepted the Forest Service's interpretation that " 'economical' . . . permit[s] consideration of benefits other than timber access, such as motorized recreation, firewood gathering, and access to the area by local residents."[870] Although section 6(k) comes from a different statute with an entirely different legislative history, it may well be that courts will construe the NFMA's "economic" suitability provisions to allow broad Forest Service discretion, as was the case with the RPA's "economical" roads provision at issue in *Thomas v. Peterson.*

In sum, section 6(k) creates enforceable standards but does not establish the strict economic guidelines that Bumpers originally intended.[871] Thus, section 6(k) probably does not exclude all site V lands from timber production and does not prohibit all below-cost timber sales. On the other hand, the NFMA clearly reinforces the concern of uneconomical timber management first expressed by the Bolle Report and the Church Subcommittee in the early 1970s. Congress apparently was attempting to address the problem of unprofitable timber management, not by outlawing all below-cost sales, but by requiring the Forest Service to tighten up, in a serious way, its existing system of classifying marginal lands.

It is important to recognize that section 6(k) is related to section 6(g)(3)(E) and other sections of the NFMA that deal with suitability. Thus, section 6(k) should be interpreted in conjunction

---

[868] 16 U.S.C. § 1608(a) (1982). The court erroneously refers to this provision as part of the National Forest Management Act of 1976. *See* 753 F.2d at 761, 762. Unlike the economic suitability provision of the NFMA, the provision enacted in the 1974 RPA has virtually no legislative history from which to determine congressional intent.

[869] 753 F.2d at 761.

[870] *Id.* at 762. "An agency's interpretation of the statute that it is charged with administering is entitled to substantial deference and will be upheld unless unreasonable." *Id.* (citations omitted).

[871] For a contrary view see Stoel, *supra* note 805, at 563-65 ("the central thrust of § 6(k) is to prohibit commercial timber production on lands where predicted economic returns are less than predicted costs.") *Id.* at 565.

with the NFMA's other suitability provisions, as well as the Act's overall purpose of requiring environmentally sensitive forest·management on a reasonably cost-efficient basis. At the minimum, section 6(k) requires economic feasibility to be a factor in determining whether land is suitable. For example, land probably may not be classified as suitable if irreversible soil damage can be avoided only by helicopter logging, unless the value of the timber is reasonably commensurate with the government's production and investment costs. The Committee of Scientists probably has put it best by concluding that section 6(k) allows administrative flexibility but that the Forest Service is constrained by a "rule of reason" when uneconomical sales are involved.[872]

3. Diversity of Plant and Animal Communities

The diversity section of the NFMA is considered by some to be one of the Act's most perplexing provisions.[873] Section 6(g)(3)(B) requires the agency to

> provide for diversity of plant and animal communities based on the suitability and capability of the specific land area in order to meet overall multiple-use objectives, and within the multiple-use objectives of a land management plan adopted pursuant to this section, provide, where appropriate, to the degree practicable, for steps to be taken to preserve the diversity of tree species similar to that existing in the region controlled by the plan.[874]

The provision derives from a decision by the conference committee to join the different diversity provisions of the Senate and House

---

[872] *See supra* text accompanying note 866. For the Forest Service regulations and a recent ruling by the Chief of the Forest Service on economic suitability, see *infra* notes 985-94.

[873] *E.g., Comm. of Scientists Final Report, supra* note 864, at 26,608.

[874] 16 U.S.C. § 1604(g)(3)(B) (1982). Chief R. Max Peterson made the following comment on this part of the NFMA:

> If one thought emerges from reading this diversity paragraph over and over again, it is that it is not very specific, and therefore leaves much room for judgment. The law does not provide very detailed direction on diversity; certainly, it contains no definition of diversity, nor an indication of how much diversity is required . . . . [I]t does not say that whatever diversity is there now must be kept. With proper justification, and to meet multiple use objectives, diversity could be altered or even reduced.

Peterson, *Diversity Requirements in the National Forest Management Act*, in NATURAL DIVERSITY IN FOREST ECOSYSTEMS, 21, 22, 26 (1984).

bills.[875] The first part of the section, ending with "overall multiple use objectives," comes from the Senate bill, and the remainder is from the House bill.

The Senate language represents a merger of objectives sought by Senators Humphrey, Randolph, and Bumpers. In the Senate mark-up, the committees first considered a revised draft of the Humphrey bill which directed the agency to "provide for plant and animal communities based on the suitability and capability of the specific land area."[876] This language mirrored Humphrey's earlier testimony that he wanted the Forest Service to select harvesting methods "that are adapted to the site in establishing a healthy plant and animal community."[877] Humphrey's general purpose was to elevate wildlife and ecological values in relation to timber by prohibiting the Forest Service from "turning the national forests into tree production programs which override other values."[878]

Senators Bumpers and Metcalf proposed an amendment requiring the agency to "insure the use of such systems of silviculture which maintain the diversity of forest types and species found naturally in each national forest."[879] The amendment was based on a section of the Randolph bill aimed at preserving natural forest ecosystems.[880] Senator James McClure of Idaho objected that the language could "eliminate the alternative to get a productive forest" on some cutover lands in the West.[881] Metcalf replied that Bumpers's chief concern was to "continue to maintain the hardwood forests and not cut them off and just go to southern pine or something of that sort."[882] Metcalf indicated that the provision could be changed to "apply only east of the 100th meridian."[883] Bumpers stated that he offered the amendment because

---

[875] S. REP. No. 1335, 94th Cong., 2d Sess. 26-27 (Conf. Report), *reprinted in* 1976 USCCAN 6721, 6728-6729, *and in* RPA COMPILATION, *supra* note 173, at 754-55.

[876] *See Comparison of S. 3091, supra* note 440, § 3(d)(5)(B) (S. 3091 as amended), *reprinted in* D. LeMASTER, *supra* note 162, at 198.

[877] SENATE NFMA HEARINGS, *supra* note 194, at 261.

[878] *Id.* at 262. *See supra* text accompanying notes 362-68.

[879] *See Comparison of S. 3091, supra* note 440, § 3(d)(5)(C)(iii) (Senator Metcalf's amendments), *reprinted in* D. LeMASTER, *supra* note 162, at 201.

[880] *See infra* text accompanying note 1561.

[881] *April 27, 1976, Transcript of Senate Mark-up, supra* note 374, at 51.

[882] *Id.* at 51-52.

[883] *Id.* at 52. Metcalf told McClure, "As you and Senator Hatfield and the rest of us know, we have forests, the douglas fir and ponderosa pine and so forth, that don't have the problems that Senator Bumpers has with the dogwood." *Id.*

"[i]n the past ten years about 35,000 acres in the forest in my State have been converted from [hardwood] two [sic] pines and I am concerned about the conversion."[884] The committees approved the Humphrey language with the understanding that it would be "meshed by the staff with the [diversity] language."[885]

The staff combined the Humphrey and Bumpers provisions by adding the words "diversity" and "in order to meet overall multiple use objectives" to the bill. Bumpers clarified the meaning of these terms in his separate comments to the report of the Interior and Insular Affairs Committee.[886] Bumpers explained that the language was intended to discourage, rather than forbid, forest type conversions.[887] He said that the pine forests in Arkansas did not "support the quantity nor the diversity of wildlife sustained by" hardwood forests.[888] In addition, he cited a "general aesthetic loss," particularly in the loss of the "impressive fall colors display of the hardwoods so important to our tourist industry."[889] Finally, Bumpers emphasized that the "great demand on [the eastern national forests] for their water, wildlife, aesthetic, and recreational values in addition to their timber resources" evidenced the need for a broadly-based timber management policy.[890]

Senator Bumpers's remarks indicate that forest conversions are not allowed for the sole purpose of increasing timber production. The agency must be able to justify the conversion in terms of the "overall," nontimber resource objectives.[891] If wildlife, aesthetics, and other resources will benefit, then the conversion may occur.[892]

See also S. REP. No. 905, 94th Cong., 2d Sess. 1-2, *reprinted in* 1976 USCCAN 6718, 6718-19, *and in* RPA COMPILATION, *supra* note 173, at 395-96. ("diversity . . . is a particular concern in eastern hardwood forests").

[884] *April 27, 1976, Transcript of Senate Mark-up, supra* note 374, at 54. *See also Senate NFMA Hearings, supra* note 194, at 296-97.

[885] *April 27, 1976, Transcript of Mark-up, supra* note 374, at 57.

[886] S. REP. No. 905, 94th Cong., 2d Sess. 11-12, *reprinted in* RPA COMPILATION, *supra* note 173, at 403-04.

[887] *Id.*

[888] *Id.* at 11, *reprinted in* RPA COMPILATION, *supra* note 173, at 403.

[889] *Id.*

[890] *Id.* at 12, *reprinted in* RPA COMPILATION, *supra* note 173, at 404.

[891] Bumpers also raised the conflict he perceived between conversions and multiple-use policy during the Senate hearings. He told Chief McGuire, "[Y]ou can only do [conversions] for one purpose in the long run; that is for timber production. It is not compatible with multiple use; is it?" SENATE NFMA HEARINGS, *supra* note 194, at 296.

[892] The example cited by both Bumpers and Representative Steven Symms of Idaho is cut-over land in the East and South that had grown back in non-native and undesirable vegetation. S. REP. No. 905, 94th Cong., 2d Sess. 11, *reprinted*

The House diversity provision was more straightforward than the Senate's. Representative Ray Thornton of Arkansas proposed the amendment during the mark-up by the House Subcommittee on Forests.[893] Chief McGuire approved of the language and explained that "this means that we would try to keep all of the different kinds of species that are there at the time of harvest in the area controlled by the plan . . . . [W]e would not go toward a completely uniform forest of a single species."[894] The House committee report simply states that the provision was intended to prevent monoculture in the national forests.[895]

To summarize, section 6(g)(3)(B) has three complementary meanings in the context of timber planning. First, it is a general mandate to bring timber production into balance with wildlife and ecological values. Second, it limits the use of forest conversions to cases where the conversion can be justified by its benefit to non-timber resources. Third, it prohibits monoculture. These three elements, when taken together, require the Forest Service to look at the forest as an ecological whole and to ensure that, over time, the forest is not converted into a "tree farm."

4. Harvest Levels

The NFMA contains three sections that govern the amount of timber that the Forest Service can sell. Two sections originated in the Randolph bill and one came from the Church guidelines. By far the most controversial provision was based on the nondeclining even-flow (NDEF) policy adopted by the Forest Service in 1973.[896] Sections on the earned harvest effect (EHE) and rotation age were less controversial but still significantly affected this portion of the Act. Together, as Senator Metcalf put it, they "make a package" of guidelines for determining the allowable sale quantity.[897]

---

in RPA COMPILATION, *supra* note 173, at 403; 122 CONG. REC. 34,229 (1976) (remarks of Rep. Symms), *reprinted in* RPA COMPILATION, *supra* note 173, at 785.

[893] TRANSCRIPT OF HOUSE MARK-UP, *supra* note 448, at 191.

[894] *Id.* at 192.

[895] H.R. REP. NO. 1478, pt. 1, 94th Cong., 2d Sess. 31, *reprinted in* RPA COMPILATION, *supra* note 173, at 606.

[896] *See supra* text accompanying notes 791-92.

[897] *See* 122 CONG. REC. 33,839 (1976) (remarks of Sen. Metcalf), *reprinted in* RPA COMPILATION, *supra* note 173, at 776.

(a) NDEF and Departures

Section 11(a) of the NFMA requires the Forest Service to adhere to the general rule of NDEF unless departures are needed to meet "overall multiple-use objectives":

> The Secretary of Agriculture shall limit the sale of timber from each national forest to a quantity equal to or less than a quantity which can be removed from such forest annually in perpetuity on a sustained-yield basis: *Provided,* That, in order to meet overall multiple-use objectives, the Secretary may establish an allowable sale quantity for any decade which departs from the projected long-term average sale quantity that would otherwise be established: *Provided further,* That any such planned departure must be consistent with the multiple-use management objectives of the land management plan.[898]

Section 11(b) provides an additional exception to NDEF in cases of damaged or imminently threatened timber:

> Nothing in subsection (a) of this section shall prohibit the Secretary from salvage or sanitation harvesting of timber stands which are substantially damaged by fire, windthrow, or other catastrophe, or which are in imminent danger from insect or disease attack. The Secretary may either substitute such timber for timber that would otherwise be sold under the plan or, if not feasible, sell such timber over and above the plan volume.[899]

The Randolph bill contained an NDEF provision similar to the enacted version.[900] Senator Metcalf offered NDEF language from the Randolph bill as an amendment during the Senate mark-up. Metcalf charged that the Forest Service had "wiped out the whole [Bitterroot] National Forest without any sustained yield operation."[901] The next day the Forest Service requested authority to

---

[898] 16 U.S.C. § 1611(a) (1982) (emphasis in original). Most of the NFMA requirements become enforceable only upon the adoption of the plans developed pursuant to § 6 of the Act, 16 U.S.C. § 1604 (1982). The provisions governing NDEF, however, were not included in § 6, and apparently went into effect immediately upon the passage of the NFMA.

[899] *Id.* § 1611(b).

[900] *See* S. 2926, 94th Cong., 2d Sess. § 5, *reprinted in* SENATE NFMA HEARINGS, *supra* note 194, at 4.

[901] *May 3, 1976, Transcript of Senate Mark-up supra* note 374, at 87. Metcalf was probably overstating the situation in regard to the Bitterroot. The Bolle Committee reported that an error in Forest Service calculation had resulted in an overcut of ponderosa pine for several years. *See* BOLLE REPORT, *supra* note 725, at 16. The Forest Service found only a "slight overcut" of less than 3% during the previous four years. *See* BITTERROOT REPORT, *supra* note 729, at 64. The study team acknowledged, "Because of the imponderables and

depart from NDEF by five percent over a decade.[902] Metcalf objected to the request, and the committees adopted Metcalf's amendment without revision.[903] The Senate Agriculture Committee's report stated that the intent of the provision was to prevent rapid liquidation of old-growth at the expense of other public values and resources. It read in part:

> The rapid, widespread cutting of currently mature trees may well be an advisable practice on privately-held lands where the basic management objective is maximizing short-term economic returns. The Committee believes, however, that such practices are incompatible with the management of the National Forests, where decisions must be based on the numerous public values of the forest, in addition to economic returns . . . . This approach also provides the best assurance that the other forest resources will not be subjected to sudden potentially adverse changes or disruptions.[904]

---

unknowns involved, the calculation of allowable cut is not and cannot be an exact science." *Id.*

[902] *May 4, 1976, Transcript of Senate Mark-up, supra* note 374, at 27. Chief McGuire explained that the agency considered Metcalf's language to be "just a little too tight. We think that we ought to have 5% latitude and our studies to date show that in the long run there may be some multiple-use benefits for allowing some more rapid . . . liquidation to the extent of 5% of the even flow level." *Id.* at 28.

The agency also proposed to include language—identical to an existing timber planning regulation—providing for "an even flow of National Forest timber in order to facilitate the stabilization of communities and of opportunities for employment." *Id.* at 27. *Compare* 36 C.F.R. § 221.3(a) (1984). The committees did not discuss this latter proposal during the mark-up sessions.

[903] Metcalf stated, "I hate to again retreat from a position where I have already fallen back into quite a retreat from the rigidity I offered yesterday." *Id.* at 29. Metcalf remained adamant even after Senators Bumpers and Randolph expressed willingness to accept the Forest Service's request. Senator Randolph, for instance, called the Forest Service proposal "a reasonable approach." *Id.* at 31.

[904] S. REP. NO. 893, 94th Cong., 2d Sess. 27, *reprinted in* 1976 USCCAN 6662, 6686, *and in* RPA COMPILATION, *supra* note 173, at 307. The Forest Service supported NDEF, citing the positive effect of NDEF on community stability and environmental protection:

> [N]ondeclining even-flow tends to support income flows and community stability, and minimizes chances of community disruption caused by significant reduction or acceleration in timber harvest. Some supporters contend harvest schedules on an even-flow basis are also more environmentally acceptable, because an even-flow of timber output also provides assurance that the other forest resources will not be subjected to sudden potentially adverse changes or disruption. Thus, it is more consistent with the multiple-use and sustained-yield concepts.

Letter from John R. McGuire, Chief, Forest Service, to Hon. Hubert H. Humphrey (Aug. 24, 1976), 122 CONG. REC. 27,613 (1976), *reprinted in* RPA COMPILATION, *supra* note 173, at 424.

In the House, an NDEF amendment proposed by Representative Weaver was rejected twice during the mark-up sessions.[905] Objections to NDEF focused on its potential effect on the Rocky Mountain forests, where much of the timber was said to be damaged by disease and insects.[906] House members also objected to eliminating the Forest Service's discretion in applying sustained-yield to set allowable harvest levels.[907] Chief McGuire advised the Agriculture Committee that "we do have, as I understand it, some discretion to alter [NDEF] policy from time to time as long as we do not depart generally from the sustained-yield concept."[908]

The conference committee's resolution of the NDEF issue is one of the most controversial and ambiguous parts of the NFMA's legislative history.[909] Early in the conference, Senator Hatfield offered language allowing the agency to depart from NDEF based on three factors—local economic stability, coordination with state and local governments, and mortality losses.[910] The conferees did not adopt Hatfield's proposal and remained deadlocked until the final hours of the conference.[911] The conferees revised the Senate language to allow the Forest Service to depart from NDEF "in

---

[905] *See* TRANSCRIPT OF HOUSE MARK-UP, *supra* note 448, at 170-78, 335-42.

[906] *See* H.R. REP. NO. 1478, pt. 1, 94th Cong., 2d Sess. 38, *reprinted in* RPA COMPILATION, *supra* note 173, at 612-13.

[907] *Id.* at 37, *reprinted in* RPA COMPILATION, *supra* note 173, at 612.

[908] *Id.* at 38, *reprinted in* RPA COMPILATION, *supra* note 173, at 613.

[909] A member of the Senate Agriculture Committee's staff during passage of the NFMA observed that "nobody knows what the language means." Interview with James Giltmier, *supra* note 861.

[910] Memorandum from Robert E. Wolf to Senator Herman E. Talmadge, Sept. 24, 1976, on file at Congressional Research Service, Library of Congress, Washington, D.C. *See also* 122 CONG. REC. 33,836-37 (1976) (remarks of Sen. Hatfield), *reprinted in* RPA COMPILATION, *supra* note 173, at 772.

[911] LeMaster gives the following account of the conference committee's action on the NDEF issue:

> The most difficult problem was the . . . nondeclining even-flow provision. Senator Hatfield attempted to break the deadlock by offering an amendment that would relax the Senate provision. But the deadlock remained firm. Finally, [Representative] Foley made an impassioned plea to advocates of a strict nondeclining even-flow policy. He pointed out that unless more flexibility was given to the Forest Service, enormous political objections would reduce the possibility of transferring allowable cut reductions from one forest to another as a result of a wilderness designation. This argument led to a modification of the Senate provision to make it more flexible.

D. LeMASTER, *supra* note 162, at 77-78. *See also* McGuire, *National Forest Policy and the 94th Congress,* 74 J. FORESTRY 800, 802 (1976).

order to meet overall multiple-use objectives."[912] The conference report elaborated on the departure provision:

> This section gives the Secretary discretion to vary the allowable sale quantity where he determines that so doing would meet multiple use management objectives and would be consistent with the basic directives of the Multiple-Use Sustained-Yield Act of 1960. The Conferees understand that the Secretary may choose to exercise this discretion for a number of reasons, including, but not limited to, such things as the desirability of improving the age-class distribution on a forest to facilitate future sustained yield management, or the desirability of reducing high mortality losses.[913]

Individual conferees expressed somewhat different opinions on the circumstances under which departures would be permitted. Representative Weaver, for instance, stated that Chief McGuire had assured the conferees that the enacted language "would prevent the rapid liquidation of the old growth."[914] Representative Symms said the conferees agreed to give the agency "reasonable flexibility" to depart from NDEF.[915] Senator Hatfield insisted that the conferees had agreed to allow departures based on community stability and other factors contained in the language he had proposed during the conference.[916] Senator Metcalf stated

---

[912] 16 U.S.C. § 1611(a) (1982).

[913] S. REP. NO. 1335, 94th Cong., 2d Sess. 33, *reprinted in* 1976 USCCAN 6721, 6735, *and in* RPA COMPILATION, *supra* note 173, at 761.

[914] 122 CONG. REC. 34,229 (1976) (remarks of Rep. Weaver), *reprinted in* RPA COMPILATION, *supra* note 173, at 786.

[915] *Id.* at 34,228 (remarks of Rep. Symms), *reprinted in* RPA COMPILATION, *supra* note 173, at 783.

[916] Hatfield left the conference committee early, believing that "there was full agreement to the compromise language" he had proposed to be included in the conference report. *Id.* at 33,836 (remarks of Sen. Hatfield), *reprinted in* RPA COMPILATION, *supra* note 173, at 772. In Hatfield's absence, though, the conferees decided not to include Hatfield's language. *Id.* (remarks of Sen. Humphrey). Staff advisor Robert Wolf explained the reasons for the conferees' action:

> Senator Humphrey raised the point that in citing examples he would have included that the authority did not include raising sales levels where the private timber had been overcut or logs were exported. It was one of several suggestions for examples that were under discussion at that time. Chairman Foley said that he would recommend that no examples that dealt with the proviso dropped from [Hatfield's] amendment be cited as examples and that the statement cites examples such as improving age class distribution. Chairman Talmadge agreed and the conferees were in agreement that one or two examples be cited merely as illustrative.

Letter from Robert E. Wolf to Sen. Hatfield (Oct. 1, 1976) (on file at Oregon Law Review office). During final drafting of the conference report by staff members, a third example was proposed, allowing departure "to ameliorate the consequences of a significant change in the commercial forest land base resulting from

that the departure language provided "a reasonable but circum-
scribed amount of flexibility" and that the conferees only intended
departures in "unusual situations."[917]

The Office of General Counsel (OGC) in the Department of
Agriculture issued an opinion on the departure issue in late 1977.
Chief McGuire asked OGC about "the meaning of overall multiple-use objectives . . . . Are departures to meet social or economic objectives permissible? For instance, maintenance of com-

---

legislative action or significant reductions in inventory resulting from catastrophic losses of timber." *Id.* The staff decided not to include the example after
Wolf objected that it did not comport with the conferees' instructions. *Id.*

In a colloquy with Senator Humphrey on the conference report, Hatfield asserted that "the decision had been made by the conference committee" to include
his language in the report and that "it was in the wrap-up time when the staff
moved in and took advantage of this whole situation." 122 CONG. REC. 33,837
(1976) (remarks of Sen. Hatfield), *reprinted in* RPA COMPILATION, *supra* note
173, at 772. Senator Humphrey replied:

> That is not the case at all, because the Senator from Minnesota along with
> Chairman Foley of the House Agriculture Committee moved that in the
> report, we should make it clear that this matter was not to be cited as a
> special example of the kinds of considerations that the Secretary was to
> take into account. The Secretary has wide flexibility. We can establish
> here, in this colloquy, that in that flexibility, one of the points that he
> should take into consideration is the economic impact upon a community.

Id. (remarks of Sen. Humphrey).

[917] Metcalf discussed the departure section in considerable depth:

> [T]here was concern that the language we had adopted in the Senate
> might be somewhat more restrictive than was intended. Frankly I was con-
> cerned that in some limited cases, despite the flexibility that we had in-
> cluded, we had not provided for unusual situations that congressional pol-
> icy should give latitude to cover.
>
>   . . . .
>
> It is true that we have stands with a low rate of growth, as well as stands
> with a high mortality rate, that could benefit from careful silviculturally
> sound cutting of the trees in danger of loss through death and old age. It is
> true that for a future high sustained yield that respects multiple-use val-
> ues, the various stands that compose the management unit must be ar-
> ranged in a manageable order.
>
>   . . . .
>
> [The departure provision] constitutes a reasonable but circumscribed
> amount of flexibility. It is limited by the basic goal. It will be circum-
> scribed by the realities on each national forest.
>
>   . . . .
>
> [W]hen one gets down to specific national forests, a case might be made
> with all the facts on display, that would justify a short-term increase. But
> this would only make sense if the basic sale program and the additional
> volume were made up of the proper quantities of the species that needed to
> be cut.

Id. at 33,839 (remarks of Sen. Metcalf), *reprinted in* RPA COMPILATION, *supra*
note 173, at 776-77.

munity stability."[918] OGC replied that "[n]either [the] NFMA
nor its legislative history provides much helpful insight into the
meaning of the phrase 'overall multiple-use objectives.' "[919] Nevertheless, OGC offered the following interpretation: "In our opinion, [overall] multiple-use objectives . . . are those established for
the entire National Forest System. Our conclusion is based, in
part, on the use of the word 'overall,' which indicates that
Congress meant objectives for multiple uses from a national aspect . . . ."[920] OGC also arrived at its conclusion by contrasting
"overall" multiple-use objectives with a later reference in the
same section to multiple-use objectives of the local forest plan.[921]
In addition, OGC found some support in other provisions of the
RPA that refer to setting national goals and objectives.[922] OGC
concluded that social and economic objectives, such as community
stability, do not constitute multiple-use objectives but may be relevant to a decision whether to depart from NDEF.[923]

Curiously, the OGC opinion makes no reference to the existence
of the identical phrase, "in order to meet overall multiple-use
objectives," in section 6(g)(3)(B)—the diversity section.[924] As discussed earlier, the phrase was added, along with the term "diversity," when the Senate committees agreed to mesh Senator Bumpers's amendment with Senator Humphrey's plant and animal
community language.[925] There is no indication in the legislative
history of the diversity section that the phrase was intended to
refer to nationwide objectives. Rather, Bumpers was attempting to
limit the use of forest conversions by requiring the agency to
justify them in terms of enhancing nontimber resources.[926] By using the same words to define the circumstances in which depar-

[918] Memorandum from Richard L. Fowler, Director, Natural Resources Div.,
Office of Gen. Counsel, U.S. Dep't of Agriculture, to John R. McGuire, Chief,
Forest Service 7 (Dec. 9, 1977) (on file at Oregon Law Review office).
[919] *Id.* at 9.
[920] *Id.* at 10.
[921] "[T]he specific reference to a plan covering a distinct land area implies
that Congress had a larger land base in mind when referring to 'overall multiple-
use objectives.' " *Id.*
[922] *Id.*
[923] *Id.* at 12.
[924] 16 U.S.C. § 1604(g)(3)(B) (1982).
[925] *See supra* text accompanying notes 873-95.
[926] *See supra* text accompanying notes 886-92. During the Senate mark-up,
Bumpers stated that he had proposed the diversity language "with the intention
of placing the burden on the Secretary" to justify conversions. *May 4, 1976,
Transcript of Senate Mark-up, supra* note 374, at 84.

tures would be permitted, Congress apparently intended to impose a similar burden of justification on the agency.[927]

Thus, NFMA section 11(a) seems to permit exceptions to NDEF in the form of "multiple-use" departures in a narrow set of circumstances. The two situations mentioned in the conference committee report—improving age-class distribution and reducing high mortality losses—are uncommon.[928] Departure for community stability receives no more than tenuous support in the

---

[927] Senator Metcalf, for instance, stated that departures "would have to be justified under the 1960 act terms." 122 CONG. REC. 33,839 (1976) (remarks of Sen. Metcalf), *reprinted in* RPA COMPILATION, *supra* note 173, at 777. Furthermore, Representative Wampler, a conferee, expressed an interpretation of "overall multiple-use objectives" that was similar to Bumpers's interpretation. In his floor remarks on the conference report, Wampler used the phrase to explain the circumstances under which the Forest Service could harvest trees before they reach maturity under the CMAI standard. He stated, "I believe it was clear that the conferees intended that stands of trees should generally not be harvested until they have attained [CMAI] . . . . The committee also recognized that exceptions to this general goal might also be necessary in managing some forest stands *to achieve overall multiple-use objective.*" 122 CONG. REC. 34,230 (1976) (remarks of Rep. Wampler) (emphasis added), *reprinted in* RPA COMPILATION, *supra* note 173, at 788. The provision to which Wampler referred establishes CMAI as the general rule but allows "exceptions to these standards for the harvest of particular species of trees in management units after consideration has been given to the multiple uses of the forest including, but not limited to, recreation, wildlife habitat, and range . . . ." 16 U.S.C. § 1604(m)(2) (1982). Thus, Wampler apparently understood "overall multiple-use objectives" to mean recreation and other nontimber objectives.

[928] During congressional consideration of the harvesting level issue, the Forest Service specifically addressed the questions of age-class distribution and high mortality loss. The agency's comments were in response to a timber industry representative's article that criticized the Forest Service's NDEF policy as wasteful. First, regarding the age-class distribution issue, the agency stated, "If the Forest Service were to accelerate harvest of the old growth, then . . . the uneven age classes would complicate reaching higher future sustained yields for timber. In short, the adoption of [a departure] policy would delay attaining the benefits of a high level output on a sustained basis." Letter from John R. McGuire, *supra* note 904, *reprinted in* RPA COMPILATION, *supra* note 173, at 424-25. Second, in reference to high mortality losses, the Forest Service stated, "Much of the potential loss is mitigated through programs to increase mortality harvest, increases in intermediate harvests, . . . and priority scheduling of harvest cuts in the older high risk stands." *Id.* at 27,612, *reprinted in* RPA COMPILATION, *supra* note 173, at 424.

Thus, Congress apparently understood that departures from NDEF would only be necessary to improve age-class distribution and reduce high mortality losses if other management policies and techniques could not accomplish the desired results. One example might be managing mature stands of lodgepole pine that are threatened by epidemic levels of mountain pine beetles. The Forest Service explained to Congress that strict application of NDEF under these circumstances "would make major losses to insects and fire rather certain in many parts of the

legislative history and should be allowed only in extraordinary cases.[929] The NFMA does not allow departures in order to liquidate old-growth stands more rapidly or to increase timber production.[930]

On the other hand, section 11(b) provides somewhat more flexibility to depart from NDEF in order to salvage damaged or imminently threatened timber. The agency may sell above the NDEF level only if it is "not feasible" to substitute the damaged timber for other timber scheduled for sale.[931] For example, if damaged material resulting from a catastrophic fire or infestation constituted most of a national forest's total sale volume, local mills might be unable to obtain adequate amounts of sound timber, unless the national forest departed from NDEF.[932] In any event,

---

West." Letter from John R. McGuire, Chief, Forest Service, to Hon. Lee Metcalf, 122 CONG. REC. 27,324 (1976). *See also infra* note 1013.

[929] The Forest Service advised Congress that "nondeclining even-flow tends to support income flows and community stability, and minimizes chances of community disruption caused by significant reduction or acceleration in timber harvest." Letter from John R. McGuire, *supra* note 904, *reprinted in* RPA COMPILATION, *supra* note 173, at 424. *See also* Letter from John R. McGuire, Chief, Forest Service, to Hon. Henry M. Jackson, 122 CONG. REC. 27,322 (1976) ("The strict even flow policy avoids any eventual decline in the flow of timber from the National Forests and thus contributes to community stability."); *but see id.* ("It would also be desirable to permit minor fluctuations, less than 5 percent, to moderate effects of large reduction in National Forest timber supply. This would reduce local impacts on employment and permit a phasing-in period.") *See also infra* text accompanying note 1016. For discussions of departures and community stability, see generally WESTERN WILDLANDS, Winter 1983.

[930] For instance, the Forest Service's following justification for a proposed departure in the Klamath National Forest in California probably is inadequate:

The general purpose of departure from nondeclining even flow timber yield for this alternative is to increase growth rates, improve the age and size class distribution and increase timber production from the currently designated capable, available and suitable timber producing lands by approximately 15-20 percent; meet the RPA output and activity projections for the next 2 decades; and prevent adverse impacts on the economic stability of the dependent communities.

FOREST SERVICE, U.S. DEP'T OF AGRICULTURE, KLAMATH NATIONAL FOREST, DRAFT ENVIRONMENTAL IMPACT STATEMENT 30 (1983). The improvement in age-class distribution sought by the departure is aimed at "currently mature or overmature" timber, which constitutes 75% of the national forest. *Id.* at 31.

[931] 16 U.S.C § 1611(b) (1982).

[932] This appears to be the case on the Deschutes National Forest in Oregon, where local mills may not be able to substitute a large volume of beetle-threatened lodgepole pine for the more valuable ponderosa pine. *See* FOREST SERVICE, U.S. DEP'T OF AGRICULTURE, DRAFT ENVIRONMENTAL IMPACT STATEMENT FOR DESCHUTES NATIONAL FOREST LAND AND RESOURCE MANAGEMENT PLAN 168 (1982).

at the time the forest plan is revised, the impacts of the catastrophe and the departure must be included in calculating the new harvest levels.

(b) Rotation Age and CMAI

Section 6(m) directs the Forest Service to allow stands of trees to reach maturity before harvest. The provision is important because it defines the rotation period for timber planners to use in calculating allowable harvest levels.[933] The provision requires the agency to "insure that, prior to harvest, stands of trees throughout the National Forest System shall generally have reached the culmination of mean annual increment of growth (calculated on the basis of cubic measurement or other methods of calculation at the discretion of the Secretary)."[934] The section allows exceptions for damaged or imminently threatened timber stands of particular tree species.[935]

The culmination of mean annual increment (CMAI) provision originated in the Randolph bill.[936] The bill used the CMAI standard to define the age at which trees could ordinarily be cut.[937] During the mark-up, Senator Randolph offered an amend-

---

[933] *See supra* text accompanying notes 644-56.

[934] 16 U.S.C. § 1604(m)(1) (1982).

[935] The remainder of § 6(m) states:
Provided, That these standards shall not preclude the use of sound silvicultural practices, such as thinning or other stand improvement measures: *Provided further*, That these standards shall not preclude the Secretary from salvage or sanitation harvesting of timber stands which are substantially damaged by fire, windthrow or other catastrophe, or which are in imminent danger from insect or disease attack; and
(2) exceptions to these standards for the harvest of particular species of trees in management units after consideration has been given to the multiple uses of the forest including, but not limted to, recreation, wildlife habitat, and range and after completion of public participation processes utilizing the procedures of subsection (d) of this section.
Id. § 1604(m) (emphasis in original).

[936] James Moorman, a spokesman for the Randolph bill, argued that
the American people do not want its [sic] National Forests to be short rotation forests, in essence monoculture pulp farms, uniform in species and aspects, marked by trees in even rows, silent of insect, animal, and bird life, lacking in bushes, berries, nuts and flowers, old snags, nests and all non-pulp features of the natural woodlands.
It may be that the "tree farms" have their place, but, by and large, that place is not the National Forest.
SENATE NFMA HEARINGS, *supra* note 194, at 515.

[937] *See* S. 2926, 94th Cong., 2d Sess. §§ 3(3), 8(a), (b) (1976), *reprinted in* SENATE NFMA HEARINGS, *supra* note 194, at 3, 5. Moorman testified that "the

ment to allow harvesting, based on CMAI, only of mature trees.[938] Chief McGuire objected to the amendment because "it would force us to manage individual trees rather than stands . . . . We might wind up taking out [trees] that are mature and then trying to figure out what to do with what is left."[939] The Senate committee voted to reject Randolph's amendment.[940]

The CMAI standard was subsequently proposed by Representative George Brown of California and adopted during the House subcommittee mark-up. Brown explained that the CMAI language restated the definition of maturity currently used by the Forest Service.[941] Brown's amendment specified that the standard applied to "stands" of trees, thereby satisfying the Forest Service's objections to Randolph's proposal.[942] Chief McGuire stated that the amendment would "direct us to put our effort on growing the larger trees for final harvest . . . . We would not be cutting back on our rotation lengths to where we are just growing continuing crops of small pulpwood-size trees."[943]

The House Committee on Agriculture adopted two amendments to the CMAI section which give the agency discretion to choose between methods of calculating rotation periods. First, planners could measure CMAI in either cubic feet or board feet.[944] CMAI is attained in fewer years under cubic foot rule since it measures the entire volume of the tree rather than just the volume that can be converted to lumber. Second, planners could calculate growth

---

definition of maturity was consciously drafted by us to set the point of maturity at approximately the place where the Forest Service now sets it. That is, at the culmination of mean annual increment." *Id.* at 42; *see also id.* at 517.

[938] *May 4, 1976, Transcript of Senate Mark-up, supra* note 374, at 77-78.

[939] *Id.* at 79.

[940] *Id.* at 82.

[941] *Transcript of House Mark-up, supra* note 448, at 194.

[942] Brown stated that he had "drafted this in such a fashion as to leave considerable leeway for variation from this standard." *Id.* at 193.

[943] *Id.* at 197.

[944] Representative David R. Bowen of Mississippi first offered an amendment requiring CMAI to be calculated on the basis of cubic measurement. *Id.* at 264. Bowen feared that courts might interpret the existing language to require board foot measure, which would necessitate reductions in the current allowable cut. *Id.* at 264-65. Representative Brown stated that it was "ridiculous" to put "an additional specific limitation on the Forest Service in the event that they might want to use board feet or cubic meters or any other method of measuring." *Id.* at 266. The committee subsequently adopted an alternative suggested by Representative Berkley Bedell of Iowa which allowed CMAI to "be calculated on the basis of cubic measurement or other methods of calculation at the discretion of the Forest Service." *Id.* at 271.

rates based on either net or gross growth.[945] Calculating rotation with net growth generally results in higher estimates of future harvest levels.[946] The conference committee accepted the House's CMAI provision without change.

(c) Intensive Management and EHE

The NFMA requires the agency to justify any increase in harvest levels claimed through the earned harvest effect (EHE).[947] Section 6(g)(3)(D) allows the Forest Service to

> permit increases in harvest levels based on intensified management practices, such as reforestation, thinning, and tree improvement if (i) such practices justify increasing the harvests in accordance with the Multiple-Use Sustained-Yield Act of 1960, and (ii) such harvest levels are decreased at the end of each planning period if such practices cannot be successfully implemented or funds are not received to permit such practices to continue substantially as planned.[948]

Neither the Humphrey nor the Randolph bill addressed the EHE issue. The Senate adopted an EHE provision during mark-up,[949] using language that originally appeared in the Church guidelines.[950] The committee report specified that EHE increases in harvest levels "should be continued only if planned practices are carried out on schedule and field monitoring indicates they are

---

[945] Representative Brown offered an amendment to delete the word "net" from the phrase "culmination of mean annual increment of net growth." *Id.* at 273. He stated, "I would prefer to leave to the Forest Service the discretion of whether to use net yield tables or gross yield tables in making their calculations with regard to allowable cut, rotation and so on." *Id.* at 274.

[946] *See id.* at 274 (comments by Rep. Brown).

[947] For an explanation of EHE, see *supra* text accompanying notes 657-64.

[948] 16 U.S.C. § 1604(g)(3)(D) (1982).

[949] *See supra* text accompanying note 800. The Senate provision required "that increases in allowable harvests based on intensified management practices such as reforestation, thinnings, or tree improvement, shall be made only upon demonstration that such practices justify increased allowable harvests, and that the outputs projected are being secured." S. 3091, 94th Cong., 2d Sess. § 5(d)(6)(H)(iv), 122 CONG. REC. 27,651 (1976), *reprinted in* RPA COMPILATION, *supra* note 173, at 506. The only discussion of the EHE provision came in the context of an amendment by Senator Jesse Helms of North Carolina. Helms was concerned that the Senate provision would be "inviting litigation down the road" as a result of uncertainty over the meaning of the terms "demonstration" and "secure." *April 29, 1976, Transcript of Senate Mark-up, supra* note 374, at 48. The committees took no action on Helms's amendment. *Id.* at 49.

[950] *See* CHURCH SUBCOMMITTEE REPORT, *supra* note 194, at 9, *reprinted in* SENATE NFMA HEARINGS, *supra* note 194, at 959.

producing the estimated growth response."[951] Chief McGuire advised the Senate that the agency would only use EHE if yield increases were supported by research or other evidence and adequate funding could be reasonably expected.[952]

The House adopted an EHE section similar to the Senate's. During the subcommittee mark-up, Representative Weaver of Oregon proposed the Senate language as a substitute for the Litton bill's EHE language.[953] The subcommittee rejected Weaver's amendment because it saw no practical difference between the two versions.[954] However, it added language requiring the agency to reduce harvest levels if intensive management practices "cannot be successfully implemented."[955] The House committee report explained that the modifying language reflected

> the Subcommittee's intent that intensified harvesting would be cut back 'at the end of each planning period' if the level of cutting were based on management practices such as reforestation which were not being implemented within the planning period or funds had not been received substantially as planned for such practices.[956]

---

[951] S. REP. No. 893, 94th Cong., 2d Sess. 38, *reprinted in* 1976 USCCAN 6662, 6697, *and in* RPA COMPILATION, *supra* note 173, at 318. The report further emphasized the need for monitoring of EHE:

The Committee bill is designed to insure that increases in harvest rates are instituted only when a sound basis exists for projecting future yields and when control and monitoring procedures are incorporated in the management plan to insure that practices are carried out on schedule and that they produce the anticipated results.

Id.

[952] Letter from John McGuire, Chief, Forest Service, to Sen. Lee Metcalf, July 27, 1976, 122 CONG. REC. 27,608-09 (1976), *reprinted in* RPA COMPILATION, *supra* note 173, at 416-17.

[953] Weaver felt that the term "demonstrate" in the Senate version was critical to ensure that harvest levels would not be indiscriminately increased. Special Committee Counsel John Kramer stated that " 'demonstrate' is not a public demonstration . . . . I think it is to the satisfaction of the Forest Service, primarily." TRANSCRIPT OF HOUSE MARK-UP, *supra* note 448, at 70.

[954] Representative Melcher stated, "We are talking about two comparable sections, neither of which varies one from the other very much. If we accept either one, we are not deviating very much from either side." *Id.* at 73. Staff counsel Kramer agreed: "As Mr. Melcher said, it is six of one and half dozen of the other. It is not going to change their practice either way." *Id.* at 74.

[955] Representative John Krebs of California offered the amendment to address Weaver's concerns. Krebs stated, "This gets away from the demonstration. By the same token, it would also call for decrease in the harvest if these practices cannot be carried out." *Id.*

[956] H.R. REP. No. 1478, 94th Cong., 2d Sess. 31, *reprinted in* RPA COMPILATION, *supra* note 173, at 606. Representative Weaver had cited reforestation as

The conference committee adopted the House version and included a statement in its committee report similar to the House report.[957]

5. *Harvesting Practices*

Congress resolved the controversy over clearcutting by enacting an expanded version of the Church guidelines. Section 6(g)(3)(F) directs the agency to

> insure that clearcutting, seed tree cutting, shelterwood cutting, and other cuts designed to regenerate an evenaged stand of timber will be used as a cutting method on National Forest System lands only where—
> (i) for clearcutting, it is determined to be the optimum method, and for other such cuts it is determined to be appropriate, to meet the objectives and requirements of the relevant land management plan;
> (ii) . . . potential environmental, biological, esthetic, engineering, and economic impacts on each advertised sale area have been assessed . . . ;
> (iii) cut blocks, patches, or strips are shaped and blended to the extent practicable with the natural terrain;
> (iv) there are established . . . maximum size limits for areas to be cut in one harvest operation . . . ;
> (v) such cuts are carried out in a manner consistent with the protection of soil, watershed, fish, wildlife, recreation, and esthetic resources, and the regeneration of the timber resource.[958]

The guidelines were modified primarily through amendments offered by Senator Randolph during the Senate mark-up. At Randolph's request, the scope of the guidelines was enlarged to include shelterwood and seed tree cutting methods, in addition to clearcutting.[959] Randolph also gained approval of guideline (v),

---

an example of his concern for misuse of EHE: "[I]n my congressional district I can tell you that the funds are there, in many instances, but the trees are not growing. We have restocked six, seven, and eight times in some areas." TRANSCRIPT OF HOUSE MARK-UP, *supra* note 448, at 71.

[957] S. REP. No. 1335, 94th Cong., 2d Sess. 29, *reprinted in* 1976 USCCAN 6721, 6731, *and in* RPA COMPILATION, *supra* note 173, at 757.

[958] 16 U.S.C. § 1604(g)(3)(F) (1982).

[959] The committees approved Randolph's amendment after Chief McGuire commented that "broadening the Church guidelines to apply to different kinds of cutting . . . is very good." *May 4, 1976, Transcript of Senate Mark-up, supra* note 374, at 70-71.

which requires protection of esthetic and other noncommodity resources.[960]

Guideline (i) was the primary focus of controversy in the Senate mark-up. The Church guidelines permitted clearcutting only if it was determined to be "silviculturally essential."[961] Senator Herman Talmadge, chairman of the Senate Committee on Agriculture and Forestry, proposed to substitute "desirable" for "essential."[962] Senator McClure suggested that the term "silviculturally" be removed.[963] Randolph and Bumpers objected because "desirable" would allow too much flexibility.[964] Apparently, the compromise language—"optimum method"—was designed to broaden the scope of the Church guidelines by looking beyond silvicultural concerns and directing that other factors, such as aesthetics and wildlife, must be considered.[965] For instance, clearcut-

---

[960] *See id.* at 69-71. The language was taken directly from Randolph's bill. *See* S. 2926, 94th Cong., 2d Sess. § 7(c)(2)(D) (1976), *reprinted in* SENATE NFMA HEARINGS, *supra* note 194, at 5.

[961] CHURCH SUBCOMMITTEE REPORT, *supra* note 194, at 9, *reprinted in* SENATE NFMA HEARINGS, *supra* note 194, at 959.

[962] Talmadge stated, "I thought maybe 'essential' is too strong a term. We could substitute the word 'desirable' and have somewhat the same effect, but not as restrictive." *April 29, 1976, Transcript of Senate Mark-up, supra* note 374, at 4.

[963] McClure explained that "the relevant land management plan may also call for game habitat improvement, in which clearcutting can be a tool, and maybe that is a desirable practice from a management standpoint, as well as from a silvicultural standpoint." *Id.* at 3-4.

[964] Randolph argued that " 'essential' . . . is a word that locks something in, and I think in this context it needs to be locked in." *Id.* at 14. Bumpers said that "the word 'desirable' . . . almost leaves this to the whimsy of somebody." *Id.* at 16. Chief McGuire stated, "It seems to me that whatever words you put in here are not going to change what we are now doing. We are going to meet the objective of the plan, whatever it takes." *Id.* at 19.

[965] The Senate Agriculture and Forestry Committee report states, "The term 'optimum method' means it must be the most favorable or conducive to reaching the specified goals of the management plan. This is, therefore, a broader concept than 'silviculturally essential' or 'desirable'—terms considered and rejected by the Committee." S. REP. NO. 893, 94th Cong., 2d Sess. 39, *reprinted in* 1976 USCCAN 6662, 6698, *and in* RPA COMPILATION, *supra* note 173, at 319. The report's use of the term was probably based on Senator McClure's suggestion that the word "desirable" would give the Forest Service "a broader mandate for the management than just what is best from [a] silvicultural standpoint." *April 29, 1976, Transcript of Senate Mark-up, supra* note 374, at 17. Since this was the only part of the Church guidelines on which Talmadge and Bumpers disagreed during the mark-up, this change was probably what they had in mind when Bumpers commented later that the Church guidelines had been "weakened," S. REP. NO. 905, 94th Cong., 2d Sess. 15, *reprinted in* RPA COMPILATION, *supra* note 173, at 407, and Talmadge stated that the guidelines

ting could be used for non-silvicultural purposes, such as wildlife habitat improvement. On the other hand, selective cutting might be "optimum" for recreation management in certain areas. The conference committee amended guideline (i) to allow shelterwood and seed-tree cutting wherever "appropriate."[966]

D. Current Timber Planning Regulations

The NFMA regulations address timber planning primarily in three sections—suitability, management requirements, and sale scheduling. The three sections generally correspond to the NFMA's provisions on physical and economic suitability, diversity and harvesting methods, and harvest levels.

1. Suitability

The Committee of Scientists found suitability to be a "very difficult problem" in drafting the regulations.[967] The Forest Service had rejected an early Committee proposal that would have classified land as unsuitable based on several environmental factors and a strict cost-benefit economic test.[968] Instead, the agency adopted

---

had been "cleaned . . . up a bit to make them even less restrictive." 122 CONG. REC. 27,646 (1976) (remarks of Sen. Talmadge), *reprinted in* RPA COMPILA-TION, *supra*, at 483.

[966] S. REP. NO. 1335, 94th Cong., 2d Sess. 30 (Conf. Report), *reprinted in* 1976 USCCAN 6721, 6732, *and in* RPA COMPILATION, *supra* note 173, at 758.

[967] *Supplementary Final Report of the Committee of Scientists*, 44 Fed. Reg. 53,972 (1979) [hereinafter cited as *Comm. of Scientists Supplementary Report*].

[968] The committee's proposal, which was initially accepted by the Forest Service, classified land unsuitable if timber harvesting would:

    (1) result in serious environmental damage due to accelerated erosion, deposition, or lost [sic] of productivity;

    (2) impair achievement of multiple use objectives established for the Forest Plan;

    (3) adversely affect streams, streambanks, shorelines, lakes, and wetland areas through changes in water temperature, blockage of water courses, and deposit of seidment [sic];

    (4) have a serious adverse effect on important esthetic values for an extended period of time;

    (5) [not assure reforestation within five years, *inter alia*];

    (6) provide anticipated direct benefits from growing and harvesting timber that are less than the anticipated direct costs to the government, including interest on capital investments required by timber production activities

    . . . .

Forest Service Proposed Rule, Apr. 11, 1978, § 219.8(e)(4)(i)(A), *reprinted in Committee of Scientists, Minutes of Apr. 17-18, 1978, supra* note 402.

a two-part classification system that combines the NFMA guidelines with traditional suitability criteria.

(a) Unsuitable Land

36 C.F.R. § 219.14(a) directs agency planners to classify lands as not suited for timber production if they fall into any of four categories:
(1) nonforest;
(2) irreversible soil or watershed damage;
(3) no assurance of reforestation within five years; or
(4) legislatively or administratively withdrawn.[969]

The first and fourth criteria are traditional Forest Service methods for identifying noncommercial forest land.[970] Administratively withdrawn lands include research natural areas, special interest areas, and other formally classified areas, but not land previously withdrawn through local land-use planning.

The second criterion, concerning soil and watershed protection, essentially restates section 6(g)(3)(E)(i) of the NFMA.[971] However, the regulations only require land to be classified as unsuitable where "technology is not available" to insure that no irreversible damage will occur.[972] Planners on at least one national forest—the San Juan in Colorado—have interpreted the regulations so narrowly that no land was classified unsuitable on this basis. The San Juan plan states:

---

[969] The regulations state:
During the analysis of the management situation, data on all National Forest System lands within the planning area shall be reviewed, and those lands within any one of the categories described in paragraphs (a)(1) through (4) of this section shall be identified as not suited for timber production—
(1) The land is not forest land as defined in § 219.3.
(2) Technology is not available to ensure timber production from the land without irreversible resource damage to soils productivity, or watershed conditions.
(3) There is not reasonable assurance that such lands can be adequately restocked as provided in § 219.27(c)(3).
(4) The land has been withdrawn from timber production by an Act of Congress, the Secretary of Agriculture or the Chief of the Forest Service.
36 C.F.R. § 219.14(a) (1984).
[970] *See supra* text accompanying notes 633-37.
[971] *See supra* text accompanying note 823.
[972] 36 C.F.R. § 219.14(a)(2) (1984).

Availability of technology is judged on whether technology is currently developed and available for use. This is not an economic test, and the technology does not necessarily have to be available in the local area. The conclusion is that technology is available to harvest timber from all areas of the Forest while adequately protecting the soil and water resource.[973]

The third criterion, dealing with reforestation within five years, is based on section 6(g)(3)(E)(ii) of the NFMA.[974] The regulations rephrase the Act by requiring "that the technology and knowledge exists [sic] to adequately restock the lands within 5 years after final harvest."[975] Again, this language has been interpreted narrowly by some agency planners.[976] On the Grand Mesa, Uncompahgre, and Gunnison National Forests in Colorado, for instance, planners classified none of their nearly three million acres as unsuitable due to potentially inadequate reforestation.[977] Furthermore, the five-year requirement is timed from the "final" harvest, which implies that reforestation can be delayed so long as some trees remain uncut. The regulations apparently allow considerable latitude on the reforestation deadline when even-aged harvesting methods other than clearcutting are used.[978]

(b) Tentatively Unsuitable Land

36 C.F.R. § 219.14(c) imposes a further screening procedure based on three criteria. Lands that are (1) proposed in the forest plan for exclusively nontimber use; (2) incompatible with manage-

---

[973] FOREST SERVICE, U.S. DEP'T OF AGRICULTURE, SAN JUAN NATIONAL FOREST LAND AND RESOURCE MANAGEMENT PLAN, FINAL ENVIRONMENTAL IMPACT STATEMENT app. K-2 (1983).

[974] *See supra* text accompanying note 823.

[975] 36 C.F.R. § 219.27(c)(3) (1984).

[976] *See* Coon, *When Will the Trees Be "Free to Grow"?*, FOREST PLANNING, Oct. 1984, at 11.

[977] FOREST SERVICE, U.S. DEP'T OF AGRICULTURE, GRAND MESA, UNCOMPAHGRE, AND GUNNISON NATIONAL FORESTS LAND AND RESOURCE MANAGEMENT PLAN app. F-3 (1983) [hereinafter cited as GRAND MESA, UNCOMPAHGRE, AND GUNNISON LMP]. The plan allows the agency to exceed the NFMA's five-year reforestation requirement "[w]hen other resource objectives dictate a different period." *Id.* at III-48.

[978] The regulations state, "Five years after final harvest means 5 years after clearcutting, 5 years after final overstory removal in shelterwood cutting, 5 years after the seed-tree removal cut in seed tree cutting, or 5 years after selection cutting." 36 C.F.R. § 219.27(c)(3) (1984). This language could be construed to allow the removal of all but a few trees from an area that will not regenerate within 5 years. So long as the overstory or seed trees were left uncut, the area could remain unstocked for an indefinite period.

ment objectives other than timber production; or (3) not cost-efficient for timber production are to be identified as "tentatively" unsuitable,[979] implying that they may be reclassified as suitable at the discretion of the agency.[980]

The first criterion encompasses areas recommended for wilderness or administratively designated by local planners as roadless recreation, backcountry, and similar nontimber production zones.[981] The second criterion excludes timber production where necessary to protect streamsides, watersheds, forest diversity, wildlife habitat, scenery, and other resources.[982] Although the regulations imply that these two suitability criteria are discretionary, in some instances they may be mandatory. For instance, steep and fragile land located in the watershed of a sensitive fishery may be legally unsuitable for timber production.[983] Similarly, areas of a

---

[979] The regulations provide:

Lands shall be tentatively identified as not appropriate for timber production to meet objectives of the alternative being considered if—

(1) Based upon a consideration of multiple-use objectives for the alternative, the land is proposed for resource uses that preclude timber production, such as wilderness;

(2) Other management objectives for the alternative limit timber production activities to the point where management requirements set forth in § 219.27 cannot be met; or

(3) The lands are not cost-efficient, over the planning horizon, in meeting forest objectives, which include timber production.

36 C.F.R. § 219.14(c) (1984).

[980] Unlike lands classified as unsuitable under 36 C.F.R. § 219.14(a), the amount of tentatively unsuitable land may vary substantially from alternative to alternative. Indeed, in one alternative of the draft 1985 RPA Program, the Forest Service proposed to reclassify literally all of the tentatively unsuitable land to suitable status. *See* FOREST SERVICE, U.S. DEP'T OF AGRICULTURE, DRAFT ENVIRONMENTAL IMPACT STATEMENT FOR 1985 RESOURCES PLANNING ACT PROGRAM 2-48 (1984).

[981] The Forest Service has classifed lands for recreational and preservation purposes since the 1920s. *See infra* text accompanying notes 1687-99, and 1811-24.

[982] The regulations require planners to match the characteristics of all potentially suitable land against the lengthy requirements set out in 36 C.F.R. § 219.27 (1984).

[983] *See supra* text accompanying notes 826-29. The regulations require planners to give "[s]pecial attention" to riparian areas, which are strips of land bordering streams and lakes. 36 C.F.R. § 219.27(e) (1984). Apparently, the agency has incorporated the NFMA's fish habitat and water quality guideline into the "special" component of the commercial forest land classification system adopted in 1972. For a discussion of the special component, *see supra* text accompanying notes 771-73.

forest may be unsuitable because they provide habitat for wildlife that cannot tolerate roads or logging activity.[984]

The third criterion concerns the difficult and controversial issue of economic suitability.[985] 36 C.F.R. § 219.14(b) requires planners to conduct an elaborate economic analysis to determine the costs and benefits of timber management.[986] The purpose of the analysis is not to exclude lands that are unprofitable to manage. Instead, planners must "consider" the cost-benefit analysis in developing plan alternatives.[987]

---

[984] *See infra* section VII.

[985] Economic suitability was analyzed at length by the Committee of Scientists. *See Comm. of Scientists Final Report, supra* note 864, at 26,629-37, discussed *supra* text accompanying notes 863-72; *see also Comm. of Scientists Supplementary Report, supra* note 967, at 53,972-73. Environmental groups advocated a strict "financial" test, while timber industry groups favored the "efficiency" test subsequently adopted by the agency. *See* 43 Fed. Reg. 39,057-59 (1978).

[986] The regulations state:

For the purpose of analysis, the planning area shall be stratified into categories of land with similar management costs and returns. The stratification should consider appropriate factors that influence the costs and returns such as physical and biological conditions of the site and transportation requirements. This analysis shall identify the management intensity for timber production for each category of land which results in the largest excess of discounted benefits less discounted costs and shall compare the direct costs of growing and harvesting trees, including capital expenditures required for timber production, to the anticipated receipts to the government . . . .

(1) Direct benefits are expressed as expected gross receipts to the government. Such receipts shall be based upon expected stumpage prices and payments-in-kind from timber harvest considering future supply and demand situation for timber and upon timber production goals of the regional guide.

(2) Direct costs include the anticipated investments, maintenance, operating, management, and planning costs attributable to timber production activities, including mitigation measures necessitated by the impacts of timber production.

(3) In addition to long-term yield, the financial analysis must consider costs and returns of managing the existing timber inventory.

36 C.F.R. § 219.14(b) (1984).

[987] *Id.* § 219.14(c). The Department of Agriculture has insisted that forest plans fully consider and discuss "the economic implications of continuing and increasing a timber sales program where costs substantially exceed revenues." U.S. Dep't of Agriculture, Review of Administrative Decision by the Chief of the Forest Service Related to the Forest Plans and EISs for the San Juan National Forest and the Grand Mesa, Uncompahgre, and Gunnison National Forest 11 (July 31, 1985) [hereinafter cited as USDA Decision]. For example, the plans must consider "whether it is possible to achieve the non-timber benefits more cost effectively through a management program of a different nature," such as using prescribed fire instead of timber harvesting to maintain a healthy forest.

Initially, all physically suitable land is assumed to be economically suitable. Land may be classified as economically unsuitable only when the specified harvest level does not require all physically suitable land to be called into production. In other words, "lands that are uneconomic for producing timber on the basis of timber values and costs alone, can nonetheless be identified as suitable for timber production if the timber goals for a national forest are set at a sufficiently high level to cause this result."[988] If some land is not needed to meet the harvest level, the most unprofitable lands are selected as economically unsuitable.[989]

It is important to understand a basic difference between economic and physical suitability as they are treated in the regulations. The amount of physically unsuitable land determines the land base upon which harvest levels are subsequently calculated. On the other hand, the amount of economically unsuitable lands is determined by harvest levels that have already been assigned. Thus, economic suitability has no practical effect on the land base used to calculate harvest levels.

The original 1979 regulations used the traditional twenty cubic foot growth standard as a determining factor to identify unsuitable lands.[990] The Committee of Scientists grudgingly accepted the standard because "it removes from consideration . . . those lands that are plainly unable to produce commercial timber."[991] In 1982 the Committee persuaded the agency to eliminate the cubic foot standard in favor of a site-specific test[992] based on "a proper eco-

---

Id. at 8. In addition, the plans must explain why increasing "submarginal timber sales" will not "result in potentially greater instability." *Id.* at 9.

[988] USDA Decision, *supra* note 987, at 11.

[989] "Where lands are surplus to meeting the Forest objective for the entire RPA planning horizon (50 years), then the least efficient of these lands required to meet Forest objectives would be tentatively classed as not suited for timber production." PRINCIPLES OF PLANNING, *supra* note 29, at 76.

[990] The 1979 regulations directed the agency to establish minimum growth standards through regional planning. *See* 36 C.F.R. § 219.12(b)(1)(ii) (superseded 1982). All of the regional plans selected the traditional 20 cubic-foot standard. *See* FOREST SERVICE AND PANEL OF CONSULTANTS, SUMMARY REPORT ON PROPOSED REVISION OF NFMA REGULATIONS attachment B, at 3 (June 30-July 2, 1982) (on file at Forest Service Land Management Planning office, Washington, D.C.).

[991] 44 Fed. Reg. 26,632 (1979). The Committee's initial report is quoted in *supra* note 968.

[992] *See* 47 Fed. Reg. 43,033 (1982).

nomic analysis [to] identify those lands whose biological productivity is too low for commercial use."[993]

Apparently, the Committee's intent was to compel planners to apply the analysis required by 36 C.F.R. § 219.14(b) in order to identify economically unsuitable lands.[994] However, omitting the twenty cubic foot test has left planners with virtually no guidance except for the non-determinative economic efficiency test. As a result, some lands classified as noncommercial or marginal in pre-NFMA timber resource plans could be classified as suitable in the new plans. This result would appear to run directly contrary to the remedial intent of Congress in enacting section 6(k) of the NFMA.

(c) Summary

The suitability provisions of the 1982 regulations appear to be less restrictive than the requirements of the NFMA in at least four respects. First, the regulations limit the scope of the soil erosion and reforestation guidelines by requiring only theoretical assurance. Second, the five-year reforestation requirement is applied only to clearcutting. Third, the regulations treat certain mandatory suitability criteria—in particular, protection of water quality and fish habitat—as discretionary. Fourth, the regulations provide no standard or "rule of reason"[995] for planners to identify economically unsuitable lands.

2. Diversity

The Committee of Scientists believed that the NFMA regulations "should go beyond a narrow and limited restatement of the language of the [NFMA] to assure that the Forest Service shall

---

[993] Letter from Arthur W. Cooper, Chairman, Comm. of Scientists, to R. Max Peterson, Chief, Forest Service 8 (July 26, 1982) (quoting 44 Fed. Reg. 26,632 (1979)) (on file at Forest Service Land Management Planning office, Washington, D.C.).

[994] In its Final Report on the 1979 regulations the Committee stated that the proposed procedure does not lay down a specific formula for making a comprehensive benefit-cost test to determine suitability for timber, but it does clearly require a type of benefit-cost analysis with the implicit objective of classifying lands as suitable for timber use if (other things equal) direct costs are less than direct benefits, or if net benefits from timber use, including complementary benefits and opportunity costs, are positive. *Comm. of Scientists Final Report, supra* note 864, at 26,635.

[995] *See supra* text accompanying notes 863-72.

indeed 'provide for' diversity by maintaining and preserving existing variety."[996] The Committee wanted planners to "consider diversity a major concern" and to provide "detailed justification" for any significant reductions in diversity.[997] The regulations reflect the Committee's concerns by giving particularly strong direction to planners in the area of diversity.

36 C.F.R. § 219.27(g) generally requires planners to "preserve and enhance the diversity of plant and animal communities . . . so that it is at least as great as that which would be expected in a natural forest."[998] Reductions in diversity—such as forest type conversions—are permitted only where needed to meet overall multiple-use objectives and must be justified by an elaborate analysis of potential consequences.[999]

In sum, the NFMA regulations require Forest Service planners to deal with diversity on a comprehensive basis, rather than limiting their focus to the issue of forest conversion and monoculture. Planners must ensure that the essential ecological components of each national forest are adequately protected.[1000] For instance, the old-growth forest ecosystem in the Pacific Northwest is a distinct plant community that is rapidly diminishing in size.[1001] The Forest Service is attempting to plan for old-growth forests and other eco-

---

[996] *Comm. of Scientists Final Report, supra* note 864, at 26,609 (1979).

[997] *Id.*

[998] 36 C.F.R. § 219.27(g) (1984).

[999] *Id.* The regulations also require planners to consider diversity throughout the planning process and to assess the effects of proposed management practices on diversity. *Id.* § 219.26.

[1000] The regulations emphasize that planners must recognize national forests as ecosystems and consider the interrelationships of environmental factors within those ecosystems. 36 C.F.R. § 219.1(b)(3) (1984).

[1001] *See* FOREST SERVICE, U.S. DEP'T OF AGRICULTURE, ECOLOGICAL CHARACTERISTICS OF OLD-GROWTH DOUGLAS-FIR FORESTS (1981). Jerry Franklin, a Forest Service ecologist, has identified four key structural features of old-growth forests: large live trees, large snags (i.e., standing dead trees), large down logs on land, and large down logs on streams. Franklin, *Comments on Natural Diversity*, in NATURAL DIVERSITY IN FOREST ECOSYSTEMS, *supra* note 779, at 31, 33. Franklin concluded that:

abundant snags and down logs are characteristic of natural forests of all ages. They are important features and cannot be eliminated without numerous ecological consequences. A challenge in forestry is learning to provide structural and, hence, ecological diversity. We must learn to appreciate snags and down logs, to manage dead wood as cleverly as we do live. You could describe it as "managing for decadence."

Id. at 34.

systems by identifying and protecting wildlife species with special habitat requirements.[1002]

3. Harvest Levels and Departures

36 C.F.R. § 219.16(a) provides planners with guidance in determining the harvest level, or allowable sale quantity (ASQ).[1003] The section draws together the NFMA's provisions covering nondeclining even flow (NDEF),[1004] intensive management,[1005] and rotation periods.[1006] By far the most controversial part of this section concerns the conditions under which departures from NDEF are allowed.

The regulations direct consideration of departure alternatives for four purposes:

(1)   to achieve the goals of the RPA Program, when necessary;

(2)   to reduce high mortality losses or to improve forest age-class distribution;

(3)   to prevent serious local economic and community instability;

[1002] Interview with Douglas MacCleery, Deputy Ass't Sec'ty for Natural Resources & Environment, U.S. Dep't of Agriculture, in Washington, D.C. (June 14, 1983). For a discussion of the diversity requirement in the context of the Forest Service's wildlife planning system, *see infra* section VII.

[1003] The basic method of calculating the ASQ is discussed *supra* text accompanying notes 644-46. The regulations require planners to include a "sale schedule" with each alternative. 36 C.F.R. § 219.16 (1984). The sale schedule of the selected alternative becomes the ASQ for the planning period. *Id.* § 219.16(b).

[1004] The regulations provide that "the planned sale for any future decade shall be equal to, or greater than, the planned sale for the preceding decade, provided that the planned sale is not greater than the long-term sustained-yield capacity consistent with the management objectives of the alternative." *Id.* § 219.16(a)(1). The significance of NDEF is discussed *supra* at text accompanying notes 647-50.

[1005] The regulations direct planners to "assume intensities of management . . . consistent with the goals, assumptions, and requirements contained in, or used in, the preparation of the current RPA Program and regional guide." 36 C.F.R. § 219.16(a)(2)(i) (1984). The importance of intensive management practices in calculating the ASQ is discussed *supra* at text accompanying notes 657-61.

[1006] The regulations require planners to "assure that all even-aged stands scheduled to be harvested during the planning period will generally have reached the culmination of mean annual increment of growth . . . based on expected growth . . . and on forest type and quality." 36 C.F.R. § 219.16(a)(2)(iii) (1984). The relationship between CMAI, rotation periods, and ASQ is discussed *supra* at text accompanying notes 651-64.

(4) to improve attainment of overall multiple-use objectives.[1007]

The first purpose—achieving RPA goals—apparently is based on the Office of General Counsel's opinion that in the NFMA "overall multiple use objectives" refers to the national planning objectives contained in the RPA Program.[1008] As discussed earlier, this interpretation is not supported by the legislative history. Rather, the intent of Congress was to limit the use of departures to circumstances in which multiple uses other than timber production alone would benefit.[1009] Furthermore, the NFMA requires timber harvest levels to be set through local planning, not by national goals.[1010] Therefore, a departure from NDEF to achieve RPA timber goals would violate the NFMA.

The second purpose simply reiterates the two examples stated in the conference committee report.[1011] The issue, then, is not whether this two-part purpose is allowed by the NFMA, but how liberally the agency may apply these examples. Arguably, more rapid liquidation of virtually any old-growth forest would reduce mortality or improve age-class distribution. However, such a broad reading would contradict the basic purpose of the NDEF provision.[1012] A better, more conservative interpretation would limit the use of departures to special situations where adherence to NDEF would seriously interfere with sound multiple-use management.[1013] These situations should be thoroughly documented and explained in the forest plan.

[1007] 36 C.F.R. § 219.16(a)(3) (1984).

[1008] *See supra* text accompanying notes 918-23.

[1009] *See supra* text accompanying notes 924-27.

[1010] *See supra* text accompanying notes 435-58.

[1011] *See supra* text accompanying notes 913, 928.

[1012] *See supra* text accompanying note 904.

[1013] Robert E. Wolf, Senate staff advisor during preparation of the NFMA conference committee report, has elaborated on the instances in which departures may be appropriate to improve age-class distribution or to reduce mortality losses:

> In the case of a Forest with a large area in trees of poor quality and utility the departure might be one that diminishes current sales levels, while removing and replacing these areas with a more productive forest. In another situation the existing forest may have very heavy mortality losses covering a large area that can be identified and represents a virtually universal stand condition for that area. Even after devising a transportation system to blanket this area and concentrating sales there, the total harvest for the decade of trees that would fail to survive the decade may be above the long term average sale quantity. An accelerated harvest for the decade directed

The third purpose—preserving community stability—raises difficulties. The legislative history of the NFMA offers scant support for this purpose.[1014] Furthermore, community stability is not a "multiple use" recognized by the NFMA, the RPA, or the MUSY Act.[1015] Even assuming community stability to be a permissible ground for departure, documenting the justification may prove difficult. For example, in the Douglas-fir region of the Pacific Northwest—where the pressures to depart are greatest—sawtimber supplies from private lands are expected to decline steadily for at least the next fifty years.[1016] In that case, departures from NDEF would provide only short-term stability and would be followed by a more precipitous decline in supply, because private lands could not pick up the slack. Long-term community stability would therefore be seriously jeopardized.[1017]

The fourth purpose—to attain overall multiple-use objectives—basically reiterates the language of the NFMA.[1018] Again,

---

solely at this material might be the only way to capture losses that are certain unless this alternative is adopted.
Memorandum from Robert E. Wolf, Ass't Chief, Environment & Natural Resources Policy Div., Congressional Research Service, Library of Congress, to Hon. James Weaver, Chairman, Subcomm. on Forestry, House Comm. on Agriculture 50 (Dec. 11, 1978) (on file at Oregon Law Review office). *See also supra* notes 917, 928.

[1014] *See supra* notes 916, 929.

[1015] The only statute explicitly linking the national forests to community stability was the Sustained-Yield Forest Management Act of 1944, 58 Stat. 132, as amended; 16 U.S.C. § 583-583i (1982). The Sustained-Yield Act authorized the Secretary of Agriculture to establish cooperative sustained-yield units of private and federal land "[i]n order to promote the stability of forest industries, of employment, of communities, and of taxable forest wealth, through continuous supplies of timber." 16 U.S.C § 583 (1982). Only one private-federal unit—the Shelton Unit in Washington—was ever established under the Act. *See* Schallau, *Departures from What?*, WESTERN WILDLANDS, Winter 1983, at 8. The management plan for the Shelton Unit included a harvest schedule that allowed national forest land within the unit to be harvested much faster than the sustained-yield level. *Id.* at 9. Presumably, the depleted private lands will have regenerated sufficiently by the end of the century to compensate for the inevitable drop in the harvest from the national forest part of the unit. *Id.* at 9-10.

[1016] FOREST SERVICE, U.S. DEP'T OF AGRICULTURE, ANALYSIS OF THE TIMBER SITUATION IN THE UNITED STATES 1952-2030, at 478 (1982). The sawtimber inventory on private industry lands is expected to decline from 124 bbf to 39 bbf by 2030, while the national forest inventory will drop from 270 bbf to 168 bbf. *Id.*

[1017] For an analysis of the potential impact of departures on specific communities, see FOREST SERVICE, U.S. DEP'T OF AGRICULTURE, CONSIDERING DEPARTURE FROM CURRENT TIMBER HARVEST POLICIES: CASE STUDIES OF FOUR COMMUNITIES IN THE PACIFIC NORTHWEST 306 (1983).

[1018] 16 U.S.C. § 1611(a) (1982). *See supra* text accompanying notes 924-27.

the circumstances under which this purpose may be invoked are limited by the basic purpose of NDEF. To fall under this provision, planners will be required to demonstrate that a departure will enhance the agency's ability to provide fish and wildlife habitat, recreational opportunities, visual quality, and soil and watershed protection.

4. Harvesting Practices

Recognizing that "[t]he NFMA is legislation born in controversy over harvesting methods,"[1019] the Committee of Scientists paid particular attention to questions of size and location of harvest units, as well as to choice of harvesting methods. At the same time, the Committee endeavored to make the regulations "pragmatic and scientific, rather than narrowly legal."[1020] The Committee decided that many of the considerations used to plan harvesting methods were "wholly local in their applicability."[1021] Accordingly, the regulations often rely on regional planning guides to furnish more detailed guidelines.

36 C.F.R. § 219.27(b) states general guidelines for selecting harvesting methods. Clearcutting and other even-aged methods are allowed when they are "best suited to multiple-use goals," based on aesthetic, environmental, and other factors.[1022] The regulations attempt to define a middle ground for economic factors. Planners must consider economics as a factor, but economics cannot be the primary basis for choosing a particular method.[1023] At the same time, the method must be "practical" from the standpoint of economics.[1024]

36 C.F.R. § 219.27(d) provides direction for setting limits on size and dispersion of harvest units. The regulations generally establish 40 acres as the maximum size of harvest units, with 60, 80, and 100 acres permitted in parts of the Northwest, Southeast, and Alaska, respectively.[1025] However, the Forest Service may establish larger or smaller size limits in the regional guides, and

---

[1019] *Comm. of Scientists Final Report, supra* note 864, at 26,623.

[1020] *Id.*

[1021] *Id.* at 26,624.

[1022] 36 C.F.R. § 219.27(b)(1) (1984). The Committee decided not to distinguish between clearcutting and other even-aged harvesting methods. *See Comm. of Scientists Final Report, supra* note 864, at 26,624.

[1023] 36 C.F.R. § 219.27(b)(3) (1984).

[1024] *Id.* § 219.27(b)(7).

[1025] *Id.* § 219.27(d)(2).

even the regional limits can be exceeded in case of catastrophe or for individual timber sales.[1026] Standards for dispersion—the distance required between harvest units—are found primarily in the regional guides.[1027] The regulations require only that the new growth in a unit be "established" before an adjoining area can be harvested.[1028]

[1026] *Id.* § 219.27(d)(2)(ii), (iii).
[1027] *Id.* § 219.27(d)(1).
[1028] *Id.*

V

WATER

The headwaters of most rivers in the western states are located in national forests, with the result that more than half of the annual runoff in the American West originates on Forest Service lands.[1029] Relatively little water, however, is consumed within the national forests. Although some mining and ranching operations use water within national forest boundaries, virtually all of the cities, industrial plants, and irrigated farmlands requiring large quantities of water are located in low-elevation areas outside of the forests. Nevertheless, downstream users, including many western municipalities, rely on the national forest watersheds for a dependable flow of clean water from streams originating on federal lands. In addition, some operations on low-lying lands utilize diversion points within the forests and gravity-flow transportation systems for their water supplies. Further, deep canyons within the national forests are often coveted sites for reservoirs.

There also is a steadily growing recognition of the nonconsumptive uses of water within the national forests. Wildlife and fish, including trout and anadromous salmon and steelhead, require clean, cool water in quantities sufficient for their habitat needs. Rivers, streams, and lakes within the national forests are major recreational and aesthetic resources.

Water resource issues are critical to national forest management decisions because most natural resources development affects water quality or quantity. Mining and most forms of power production are water-intensive. Mining, timber harvesting, and stock grazing can cause substantial movement of soils into watercourses. Road construction, which is necessary for most projects within the national forests, particularly aggravates erosion.

This section examines two issues: water quality and water quantity. Although the two are often related, the law and policy related to each has developed differently.

[1029] *See supra* note 16 and accompanying text. *See generally* 1981 ASSESSMENT, *supra* note 9, at 287-316.

A. Evolution of Policy

1. Watershed Protection

Watershed protection was a principal theme of the nineteenth century forest preservation movement.[1030] Early western settlers held two beliefs about the interaction of forests and water. First, many influential persons of the time, including George Perkins Marsh and Franklin B. Hough, believed that forests actually caused rainfall.[1031] Second, massive periodic flooding on the western plains led to calls for watershed management to prevent erosion.[1032]

This concern for watershed protection was expressed in congressional action in 1873, when Congress passed the Timber Culture Act.[1033] The Act allowed prospective settlers to plant trees as a substitute for the residence requirement of the Homestead Act of 1862.[1034] In 1875 Commissioner Williamson of the General Land Office reported to Congress on the beneficial effects of a vegetative canopy in preventing destructive flooding:

> The mountain streams, whose steady flow is important, [for mining and agriculture] . . . are fed by the melting snows. The steadiness of the flow of these streams . . . is in great measure due to the fact that over large areas of the higher levels the rapid melting of the winter's accumulation is prevented by the dense shade of the

---

[1030] Two leading commentators have observed:

Water has been at the heart of national concern about forest destruction from the very beginning of the conservation and preservation movement. Fear of timber famine was a factor, aesthetic and scenic preservation was a factor, but water was the center of it. . . . The belief that forests cause rain is frequently encountered in the literature and public debates of the day. Preservation of forest cover was, thus, tantamount in the minds of many to assuring an adequate water supply for western development . . . . Eastern activists might have been bent on scenery or forest management, but for every Westerner opposed to the forest protection movement, there were thirsty Westerners, many with thirsty livestock, who believed, at some level of analytic sophistication, that water grew on trees.

S. DANA & S. FAIRFAX, *supra* note 52, at 41.

[1031] *See* H. STEEN, *supra* note 49, at 123.

[1032] *See* W. GREELEY, FOREST POLICY 7 (1953).

[1033] Act of Mar. 3, 1873, ch. 277, 17 Stat. 605, *amended by* Act of June 14, 1878, ch. 190, 20 Stat. 113. The Timber Culture Act was repealed by the Act of Mar. 3, 1891, ch. 561, 26 Stat. 1095 (current version at 43 U.S.C. § 1181 (1982)).

[1034] Act of May 20, 1862, ch. 75, 12 Stat. 392 (codified at 43 U.S.C. §§ 161-302, repealed 1976).

forests. This removed, destructive floods in the season of returning warmth, to be followed later by scarcity, become the rule.[1035]

One year later, Representative Fort introduced "a bill . . . for the preservation of the forests of the national domain adjacent to the sources of the navigable rivers and other streams of the United States."[1036] The proposal failed, but from that time until presidential withdrawal of the forest reserves was authorized by the Creative Act of 1891,[1037] at least one similar bill was introduced in each congressional session.[1038] Meanwhile, scientists continued to extoll the moderating influence of forests on water flows.[1039]

The legislative history of the 1897 Organic Act[1040] indicates that many congressmen considered watershed protection to be the paramount, if not exclusive, purpose of establishing forest reserves.[1041] Indeed, in 1894 the House of Representatives had

---

[1035] ANNUAL REPORT OF THE COMM'R OF THE GENERAL LAND OFFICE, H.R. EXEC. DOC. NO. 1, pt 5, 44th Cong., 1st Sess. 11 (1875) [hereinafter cited as 1875 GLO REPORT].

[1036] H.R. 2075, 44th Cong., 1st Sess., 4 CONG. REC. 1070 (1876).

[1037] 16 U.S.C § 481 (1982).

[1038] *See* J. ISE, *supra* note 48, at 112-14.

[1039] A team of scientists, including Gifford Pinchot, was appointed by the National Academy of Sciences in 1896 to study the forest reserves. *See id.* at 128-29. The scientists reported that:

> Whether a grand climatic change in Europe be in progress or not, it would seem that the observed facts [decrease in annual run-off] can be more simply explained by the well-established change in regimen often following the destruction of forests, especially in mountain regions. The more rapid melting of snow and the reduced obstructions to surface drainage hurry the water forward and increase the number and sometimes the extreme height of the spring freshets, leaving a less volume to be absorbed by the ground and gradually returned through springs and brooks during the low-water season. Destructive floods are thus rendered more frequent, and summer droughts more to be dreaded.

REPORT OF THE NATIONAL ACADEMY OF SCIENCES, *supra* note 496, at 32.

[1040] 16 U.S.C. § 475 (1982), discussed *infra* Section II(A)(1).

[1041] For instance, Representative Bell of Colorado stated during a floor debate on proposed forest reserve legislation: "We understood it in [Colorado] when those reservations were put upon us that they were declared for the purpose of preserving the snow and thereby conserving the water supply of the streams." 25 CONG. REC. 2434 (1893). Similarly, Representative Simpson of Kansas stated, "I call attention to the fact that these reservations have been set aside for the purpose of holding the moisture and maintaining the water supply in the interest of agriculture . . . ." *Id.* at 2432. Representative Pickler of South Dakota said he was "especially interested in the preservation of these forests, owing to the influence they have on rainfall and water supply." 27 CONG. REC. 114 (1894). *See also* 30 CONG. REC. 982 (1897) (remarks of Rep. Shafroth of Colorado); *id.* at 985-86 (remarks of Rep. Bell); *id.* at 1399 (remarks of Rep. Loud of California).

passed a predecessor bill providing that the sole purpose of establishing forest reserves was to secure favorable water flow conditions.[1042] The 1897 Organic Act as enacted, however, treated timber production as co-equal with watershed protection.[1043]

Watershed management continued to receive emphasis in the early 1900s, due in part to President Theodore Roosevelt's personal concern about water conservation.[1044] Roosevelt's administration championed improvement of navigability,[1045] construction of reclamation projects,[1046] and withdrawal of potential hydroelectric sites from entry under the homesteading acts.[1047] Congress created the National Waterways Commission in 1909.[1048] The Commission's final report in 1912 advocated preservation of forests for their positive effect on precipitation, runoff, and erosion.[1049]

The Weeks Act of 1911[1050] was a milestone, providing for the purchase of forested, cutover, or denuded lands within the head-

---

[1042] H.R. 119, 53d Cong., 3d Sess., 27 CONG. REC. 364 (1894); *see* J. ISE, *supra* note 48, at 126-27.

[1043] The Act states: "No national forest shall be established, except to improve and protect the forest within the boundaries or for the purpose of securing favorable conditions of water flows, and to furnish a continuous supply of timber for the use and necessities of citizens of the United States." 16 U.S.C. § 475 (1982).

[1044] *See* S. DANA & S. FAIRFAX, *supra* note 52, at 75. Roosevelt expressed his advocacy for watershed management and conservation: "The man who would so handle his forest as to cause erosion and injure stream flow must be not only educated, but he must be controlled." Report of the National Conservation Commission of 1909, at 4.

[1045] Act of June 13, 1902, ch. 1079, § 3, 32 Stat. 331 (codified at 43 U.S.C. § 541 (1982)).

[1046] In 1902 Congress passed the Reclamation Act of June 17, 1902, ch. 1093, 32 Stat. 388 (current version as amended at 43 U.S.C. §§ 371-600 (1982)). This major piece of legislation was intended to further the westward expansion by providing low cost water for irrigation. Under the Act, the United States has constructed, owned, and operated water storage facilities and distributed water to irrigators throughout the arid West. *See generally* 2 WATERS AND WATER RIGHTS §§ 110-125 (R. Clark ed. 1967); Taylor, *California Water Project: Law and Politics*, 5 ECOLOGY L.Q. 1 (1975).

[1047] *See* § 3 of the Reclamation Act, ch. 1093, § 3, 32 Stat. 388-89 (codified as amended at 43 U.S.C. § 416 (1982)).

[1048] For a discussion of the history of the National Waterways Commission, *see* J. ISE, *supra* note 48, at 151.

[1049] *See* S. DANA & S. FAIRFAX, *supra* note 52, at 77.

[1050] Act of Mar. 1, 1911, ch. 186, 36 Stat. 962 (codified at 16 U.S.C. §§ 513-519 (1982)) (§§ 13, 14 repealed in 1976).

waters of navigable streams.[1051] This Act was a clear indicator that public land policy was moving away from disposition toward reservation and acquisition. The McSweeney-McNary Act of 1928[1052] authorized research at regional forest experiment stations to "determine, demonstrate, and promulgate the best methods of . . . maintaining favorable conditions of water flow and the prevention of erosion."[1053] Similarly, the Flood Control Act of 1936[1054] required a stepped-up survey of flood control techniques on national forests.

At the agency level, Forest Service policy prior to the 1940s was also highly protective of watershed resources. Early on, Gifford Pinchot instructed his foresters not to remove timber if it would cause stream damage.[1055] In 1918 Pinchot's successor, Henry Graves, wrote:

> Undoubtedly the greatest value of the mountain ranges of the West, most of which are within the National Forests, lies in their influence upon the regularity of the water supply . . . . The vegetative covering has a very decided influence on runoff. For this reason Congress made the preservation of conditions favorable to stream flow one of the principal objects in the establishment and administration of the National Forests.[1056]

District rangers were required to report to their supervisors any citizen requests for protective measures concerning the watersheds. They were also directed to use their special permit authority to impose corrective measures if a watershed were jeopardized: "It is the duty of every forest officer before granting a permit for any use of the National Forests to consider its effect upon the water supply, and when necessary to incorporate in the permit or

---

[1051] Congress initially limited Weeks Act purchase authority to headwaters of navigable streams based on the belief that congressional power was restricted to regulation of navigable waterways. *See* Young v. Anderson, 160 F.2d 225 (D.C. Cir.), *cert. denied*, 331 U.S. 824 (1947). The Clarke-McNary Act of 1924, ch. 348, 43 Stat. 653 (codified at 16 U.S.C. § 471, repealed 1976), extended the purposes for which land could be acquired to include lands valuable for timber production as well as for watershed protection.

[1052] Act of May 22, 1928, ch. 678, 45 Stat. 699, 16 U.S.C. § 581 (repealed by Pub. L. No. 95-307, § 8(a), 92 Stat. 356 (1978)).

[1053] *Id.*

[1054] Ch. 688, 49 Stat. 1570 (codified at 33 U.S.C. § 701a (1982)).

[1055] *See supra* text accompanying note 691.

[1056] FOREST SERVICE, U.S. DEP'T OF AGRICULTURE, THE USE BOOK 27 (1918).

contract stipulations which will afford protection from possible injury."[1057]

Massive flooding of the lower reaches of the Mississippi River in 1927 aroused additional support for the Forest Service's protective policy. That year Chief William Greeley wrote: "Forests can not prevent floods, but can reduce them. They retard the melting of snow. They retard surface run-off both directly and through the greater porosity of the underlying soil which they maintain. They retard erosion and reduce the silt burden of streams."[1058] Greeley called protection of municipal water supplies the "paramount consideration" in any decision to allow timber cutting, grazing, or recreational use.[1059] Several years later the Forest Service conducted erosion investigations to gauge the effect of vegetative cover on flooding. Finding vegetation beneficial, the agency launched special efforts to maintain tree cover on land with steep slopes.[1060]

After World War II the Forest Service's traditional protective watershed policy came under increased attack as pressures developed to produce more timber products and to devote more water to consumptive uses.[1061] Initially, the agency defended its traditional policy. For instance, in 1947 Chief Lyle F. Watts stated that "[t]he watershed services of national-forest lands at the sources of western rivers transcend all other values attached to these lands."[1062] He particularly criticized the notion that timber harvesting could increase water yield.[1063] Watts also stressed the

---

[1057] *Id.*

[1058] FOREST SERVICE, U.S. DEP'T OF AGRICULTURE, ANNUAL REPORT OF THE CHIEF 2 (1927) [hereinafter cited as 1927 ANNUAL REPORT OF THE CHIEF].

[1059] *Id.* at 12.

[1060] "Protection by some form of vegetation is necessary, and the best interests of all would be served if slopes of more than 25 per cent gradient were kept in timber and protected from fire and overgrazing . . . ." FOREST SERVICE, U.S. DEP'T OF AGRICULTURE, ANNUAL REPORT OF THE CHIEF 67 (1931) [hereinafter cited as 1931 ANNUAL REPORT OF THE CHIEF].

[1061] *See infra* notes 1066-69 and accompanying text.

[1062] 1947 ANNUAL REPORT OF THE CHIEF, *supra* note 712, at 9.

[1063] Watts observed:

In parts of the West where water is scarce, some people have had the idea that removal of vegetative cover on the watersheds would be desirable, because a bare watershed, like a tin roof, would produce more water to fill the irrigation reservoirs. Bare watersheds certainly would produce quicker surface runoff—but the soil would be unprotected against erosion; the runoff would carry damaging sediments; mud as well as water would pour into the reservoirs. Any improvements or developments in the drainage area would be subject to damage by flash floods. The economic value of the

need to avoid the inevitable damage to watersheds resulting from excessive timber harvesting, road construction, and grazing.[1064] Watts was optimistic about the agency's ability to protect watersheds through careful management and improved technology,[1065] and his conservative approach was generally supported by congressional efforts to promote sound watershed management.[1066]

The post-war increase in timber harvesting posed a threat of new magnitude to national forest watersheds. As timber operators began to use bulldozers and other heavy logging equipment, the impact of timber harvesting on watersheds became more acute.[1067]

---

watershed lands for grazing or timber production would be destroyed. Also, much farm land in the West is irrigated by water pumped from wells. The water in those wells comes largely from mountain watersheds where vegetative cover promotes absorption of water into the ground. The more water that runs off the surface, the less there is available for replenishing underground supplies, and the greater the likelihood of wells going dry.
Id. at 7.

[1064] *Id.* at 8.

[1065] Watts wrote in 1948:
Watershed protection therefore must be tied in with all timber management, grazing management, recreation, road construction, and other activities on the national forests. In some localities, it is the paramount consideration. Where critical watershed values are involved, other uses must be restricted to the extent necessary to protect those watershed values. Usually, however, regulated timber harvesting and grazing use can be carried on without serious impairment of watersheds. Research is developing techniques by which timber cutting can be better coordinated with watershed protection; in some cases it can actually be made to improve watershed conditions.
1948 ANNUAL REPORT OF THE CHIEF, *supra* note 559, at 14.

[1066] *See, e.g.,* Anderson-Mansfield Reforestation and Revegetation Act of 1949, ch. 674, 63 Stat. 762:
Whereas these national-forest lands comprise the principal source of water supply for domestic, irrigation, and industrial purposes for thousands of communities, farms, and industries, and good forest and other vegetative cover is essential for watershed protection.

. . . .

[I]t is the declared policy of the Congress to accelerate and provide a continuing basis for the needed reforestation and revegetation of national-forest lands.
See also Watershed Protection and Flood Prevention Act of 1954, 16 U.S.C. §§ 1001-1009 (1982) (instituting a program of federal and state cooperation in watershed improvement, soil and water conservation programs and the like in order to combat "[e]rosion, floodwater, and sediment damages in the watersheds of the rivers and streams of the United States . . . [that] constitute a menace to the national welfare." *Id.* § 1001).

[1067] Problems of runoff and erosion caused by logging roads and skid trails have become worse in recent years, especially in the East, because of

The Forest Service attempted to reduce impacts through protective specifications in timber sale contracts,[1068] but the conflict between timber production and watershed protection remained a persistent source of controversy.[1069]

Accelerated demand for water for consumptive uses during the mid-1950s prompted the Forest Service to adjust its watershed policy to increase stream flow for downstream uses. In 1957 Chief Richard McArdle announced that "management of these public lands has always included protection of water quality. Now, with the growing need, more attention is being directed toward increasing water yield."[1070] Chief McArdle referred to water as "one of the most valuable crops supplied by the national forests."[1071] The Forest Service appeared to endorse the idea that timber harvesting in the upper watersheds increased stream yields, providing more abundant downstream runoff.[1072]

The Multiple-Use Sustained-Yield (MUSY) Act of 1960[1073] broadened the designated purposes of national forest management[1074] but did not affect the Forest Service's watershed management direction.[1075] After passage of the MUSY Act the Forest Service established streamside buffer zones through land-use plan-

---

increased use of tractors and bulldozers in logging operations. In earlier times, most of the log skidding in the East was done with animals, with only moderate disturbance of the forest soil. Now, with heavy mechanical equipment, the job of laying out skid roads that will not develop into gullies is more difficult.

1952 ANNUAL REPORT OF THE CHIEF, *supra* note 717, at 26.

[1068] *Id.*

[1069] *See infra* text accompanying notes 1165-66.

[1070] FOREST SERVICE, U.S. DEP'T OF AGRICULTURE, [1957] ANNUAL REPORT OF THE CHIEF 12 (1957).

[1071] 1956 ANNUAL REPORT OF THE CHIEF, *supra* note 713, at 3.

[1072] In the dry Southwest, removal of phreatophytes, shrubs that consume large quantities of water, was studied to increase stream yield. FOREST SERVICE, U.S. DEP'T OF AGRICULTURE, [1958 ANNUAL] REPORT OF THE CHIEF 10-11 (1958). For high elevation climates, Chief McArdle reported that "dense stands of coniferous forests . . . [caused some] 10 to 35 percent of the precipitation caught in the tree crowns" to be lost to evaporation. Intensive cutting, removing virtually all merchantable timber, was shown to increase the depth of high mountain snow packs by 28%. 1959 ANNUAL REPORT OF THE CHIEF, *supra* note 119, at 8.

[1073] 16 U.S.C. §§ 528-531 (1982), discussed *infra* Section II(A)(3).

[1074] These purposes remained as stated in the 1897 Organic Act, 16 U.S.C. § 475 (1982), until the changes in the MUSY Act.

[1075] The MUSY Act's purposes were "supplemental to, but not in derogation of, the purposes for which national forests were established." 16 U.S.C. § 528 (1982).

ning[1076] and also explored using chemicals in watershed management. Defoliants were used to reduce the evapotranspiration of streamside foliage;[1077] other chemicals were used to increase soil stability and prevent erosion on bare slopes.[1078]

During the late 1960s and the 1970s Congress enacted five pieces of environmental legislation that directly affect water resource management. The National Environmental Policy Act of 1969[1079] (NEPA) has been invoked to enjoin, and require further study of, timber harvesting and road construction that would damage water quality and fish habitat.[1080] The purposes of the Wild and Scenic Rivers Act of 1968[1081] and the Wilderness Act of 1964[1082] include the enhancement of water quality and water quantity.

Two of these modern laws relate specifically to water pollution in the national forests: the Clean Water Act,[1083] comprehensive water pollution legislation that greatly expanded nineteenth century federal regulation of refuse discharges into navigable waters,[1084] and the National Forest Management Act.[1085] Both impose substantive and procedural limitations on national forest management activities adversely affecting water quality. These statutes complement and expand the directive of the 1897 Organic Act to protect watersheds. All of these recent statutes are examined in detail later in this Article.

[1076] *See supra* text accompanying note 156.

[1077] 1963 ANNUAL REPORT OF THE CHIEF, *supra* note 162, at 23-24.

[1078] The chemical hexadecanol was applied to both exposed soil and snow pack to suppress chemically the evaporation rate. The reduction in evaporation "ranged from 13 to 90 percent." *Id.* at 23. In 1971 Chief Edward Cliff reported, "[t]o date, water yield improvement practices have been applied on over 165,000 acres and similar opportunities exist on an additional 12.5 million acres within the national forests." 1970-71 ANNUAL REPORT OF THE CHIEF, *supra* note 193, at 19.

[1079] 42 U.S.C. §§ 4321-4370 (1982).

[1080] *See, e.g.*, Northwest Indian Cemetery Protective Ass'n v. Peterson, 764 F.2d 581 (9th Cir. 1985); National Wildlife Federation v. United States Forest Service, 592 F. Supp. 931 (D. Or. 1984), *appeal docketed*, No. 84-4274 (9th Cir., Oct. 29, 1984).

[1081] 16 U.S.C. §§ 1271-1287 (1982), discussed *infra* section V(E)..

[1082] 16 U.S.C. §§ 1133-1136 (1982), discussed *infra* section IX.

[1083] 33 U.S.C. §§ 1251-1376 (1982), discussed *infra* section V(B)(1).

[1084] Act of Mar. 3, 1899, ch. 425, 30 Stat. 1121. *See generally* Comment, *The Refuse Act of 1899: Its Scope and Role in Control of Water Pollution*, 1 ECOLOGY L.Q. 173 (1971).

[1085] 16 U.S.C. §§ 1601-1613 (1982), discussed in regard to water pollution, *infra* in text accompanying notes 1165-82.

2. Regulation of Water Use

Juxtaposed against the federal government's efforts to protect water quality is a tradition of federal deference to the states in allocating rights to consume specific quantities of water.[1086] Most water rights disputes have arisen in the West, beyond the 100th meridian, where water is generally scarce. Accordingly, this analysis is directed primarily to the western states.

From the days of the early non-Indian settlement of the West, water law has been based on the "first in time, first in right" prior appropriation system that grew out of the mining practices of the nineteenth century.[1087] Under the prior appropriation doctrine, the first person to divert water from a stream and apply it to a "beneficial use" acquires a vested right to that particular quantity of water. A senior user's right is superior to the right of all later, or junior, appropriators. Beneficial uses traditionally included only commercial or consumptive uses such as agriculture, mining, stockwatering, domestic, and industrial uses.[1088] The idea that recreational or aesthetic purposes are beneficial uses of water is a relatively recent development.[1089] There is no requirement that an appropriator own the riparian land bordering the point of diversion. Nor is it necessary that an appropriator own the land over

---

[1086] *See generally* California v. United States, 438 U.S. 645 (1978). On federal activity in water law and policy, see Kelley, *Staging a Comeback—Section 8 of the Reclamation Act*, 18 U.C.D. L. Rev. 97, 117-18, 123-24, 171-81, 190-95 (1984).

[1087] The leading case is Irwin v. Phillips, 5 Cal. 140 (1855), in which the California Supreme Court endorsed the custom of "first in time, first in right" practiced by the miners in the gold country. The doctrine is summarized in Ranquist, *The* Winters *Doctrine and How It Grew: Federal Reservation of Rights to the Use of Water*, 1975 B.Y.U. L. Rev. 639. The standard treatises are WATERS AND WATER RIGHTS, *supra* note 1046, and W. HUTCHINS, WATER RIGHTS LAWS IN THE NINETEEN WESTERN STATES (1971).

The common law riparian doctrine, which calls for an equitable sharing of water among the landowners bordering on a watercourse, has had limited application in the West. Among the eleven western states, the riparian doctrine coexisted with the prior appropriation doctrine in California, Oregon, and Washington. Statutory reforms in Oregon and Washington, however, now require that any new uses must be established under prior appropriation law. *See, e.g.*, II W. HUTCHINS, *supra*, at 1-144. California is limiting unused riparian rights by administrative adjudications. In re Waters of Long Valley Creek System, 25 Cal. 3d 339, 599 P.2d 656, 158 Cal. Rptr. 350 (1979).

[1088] *See generally* I W. HUTCHINS, *supra* note 1087, at 9-19.

[1089] *See generally* Tarlock, *Appropriation for Instream Flow Maintenance: A Progress Report on "New" Public Western Water Rights*, 1978 UTAH L. REV. 211.

which water is transported from the diversion to its ultimate use. Because of the importance of water to development in the American West, the prior appropriation doctrine has become deeply embedded in the region's law, economics, and societies.

During the latter half of the nineteenth century, Congress formally sanctioned the private appropriation, pursuant to state law, of waters flowing on the public lands in the West. The Mining Act of 1866[1090] protected any water user under the prior appropriation doctrine against a competing claim by the United States. An 1870 statute provided that future land patents issued by the United States would be subject to preexisting water rights.[1091] Finally, the Desert Lands Act of 1877[1092] was construed by the Supreme Court to leave to the states the right to allocate water, including water on public lands, according to any system chosen by the state.[1093]

Despite Congress's general deference to state water law, several statutes relating to the Forest Service bear upon the use of water resources in national forests.

As discussed previously, the Creative Act of 1891[1094] withdrew forest reserves from all forms of use.[1095] To satisfy the objections of miners and local residents who desired access to forest reserve resources, Congress enacted specific provisions in the 1897

[1090] Act of July 26, 1866, ch. 262, 14 Stat. 253 (giving recognition to "appropriations of water on the public lands of the United States . . . and rights of way in connection therewith, provided that appropriations conformed to principles established by customs of local communities, State or Territorial laws, and decisions of courts").

[1091] Act of July 9, 1870, ch. 235, § 17, 16 Stat. 217, 218 (codified at 30 U.S.C. § 52 (1982)) (partially repealed in 1976).

[1092] Desert Lands Act of 1877, ch. 107, 19 Stat. 377 (codified as amended at 43 U.S.C. § 321 (1982)).

[1093] *See* California-Oregon Power Co. v. Beaver Portland Cement Co., 295 U.S. 142 (1935). The Court concluded that as of the passage of the Desert Lands Act in 1877, "if not before," state water law governed in determining the water rights of federal patentees on non-navigable watercourses. *Id.* at 163-64. The Court also found that the Desert Lands Act "effected a severance of all waters upon the public domain, not theretofore appropriated, from the land itself." *Id.* at 158. The Court had earlier recognized the superior right of Congress to preempt state water law, so that the general rule of state allocation of water announced in *California-Oregon* was subject to express congressional action to the contrary. *See* Winters v. United States, 207 U.S. 564 (1908), and *infra* section V(C)(1).

[1094] Act of Mar. 3, 1891, ch. 561, 26 Stat. 1095, 1103, *repealed by* 90 Stat. 2792 (1976).

[1095] *See supra* text accompanying note 227.

Organic Act[1096] relating to use of water. The first specific reference to water use appeared in a bill sponsored by Senator Henry M. Teller in 1895.[1097] Teller's bill provided for exclusive state jurisdiction over the use of national forest water for domestic and irrigation purposes, stating: "Nothing herein shall be construed to prohibit the use of any and all water on such reservations for domestic use or for the purpose of irrigation under the laws of the State wherein such forest reserves are situated."[1098] A House bill with similar language was introduced the following year.[1099] Nevertheless, the provision adopted by Congress in 1897 inserted a measure of federal jurisdiction, stating: "All waters on such reservations may be used for domestic, mining, milling, or irrigation purposes, under the laws of the State wherein such forest reservations are situated, *or under the laws of the United States and the rules and regulations established thereunder.*"[1100]

Thus, in 1897, Congress apparently intended to establish concurrent state and federal regulatory authority over water in the national forests. Congress thereby distinguished forest reserves from public domain lands, which were covered by the 1866 Act,[1101] in regard to water use. As explained in an opinion by Attorney General Charles Bonaparte in 1906:

> It is true that the Congress and the courts have recognized a right to appropriate water on the public lands under State laws or local customs, but lands within the forest reserves are not covered by general statutes referring to the public lands; and the right to use water on such reserves can be secured, it would seem, only under the provisions of the [1897 Organic Act] . . . and of other legislation specifically referring to the reserves.[1102]

[1096] *See supra* section II(A)(1).

[1097] H.R. 119, 53d Cong., 3d Sess. § 5, 27 CONG. REC. 2779, 2780 (1895).

[1098] *Id.*

[1099] H.R. 119, 54th Cong., 1st Sess. § 7, 28 CONG. REC. 6410 (1896).

[1100] Act of June 4, 1897, ch. 2, 30 Stat. 31, 36 (current version at 16 U.S.C. § 481 (1982)) (emphasis added).

[1101] *See supra* note 1090.

[1102] 26 Op. Att'y Gen. 421, 426 (1906). In the context of ruling on federal reserved rights in the national forests, the Supreme Court has held that 16 U.S.C. § 481 (1982) does not allocate water to certain private users, such as ranchers within the forests, outside of state law. United States v. New Mexico, 438 U.S. 696, 717 n.24 (1978).

The Forest Service chose not to exercise fully this authority granted by the 1897 Act.[1103] Indeed, one year after Bonaparte's opinion, Gifford Pinchot disclaimed any infringement on state water law: "The creation of a National Forest has no effect whatever on the laws which govern the appropriation of water. This is a matter governed entirely by State and Territorial laws."[1104]

Notwithstanding Pinchot's disclaimer, the Forest Service historically has exercised some authority over national forest water use as exemplified in the following four situations. First, the Forest Service issues special use permits for water-related uses of national forest lands. Although permit authority was generally authorized by the 1897 Organic Act, the Act of February 15, 1901,[1105] explicitly authorized issuing special use permits for constructing water works. The Secretary of the Interior was empowered to permit rights-of-way on the national forests "for canals, ditches, pipes and pipelines, flumes, tunnels, or other water conduits," provided the permits were "not incompatible with the public interest."[1106] Right-of-way permits were authorized for a wide variety of water-dependent uses.[1107]

The Transfer Act of 1905[1108] redistributed most of the authority for administering the national forests to the Department of Agriculture. However, the Secretary of the Interior retained authority to permit rights-of-way for "dams, reservoirs, water plants, ditches, flumes, pipes, tunnels, and canals, within and across the forest reserves . . . for municipal or mining purposes, and for the purposes of the milling and reduction of ores."[1109] Until 1976 the Department of the Interior retained this authority as an incident

---

[1103] There is no indication that the Department of the Interior exercised any power under § 481 prior to the transfer of the forest reserves to the Department of Agriculture.

[1104] FOREST SERVICE, U.S. DEP'T OF AGRICULTURE, THE USE OF THE NATIONAL FORESTS 13 (1907) [hereinafter cited as 1907 USE BOOK].

[1105] Act of Feb. 15, 1901, ch. 372, 31 Stat. 790 (repealed 1976). Current authority is found in the Federal Land Policy and Management Act of 1976 (FLPMA), 43 U.S.C. § 1761(a) (1982), discussed *infra* in text accompanying notes 1242-52.

[1106] 31 Stat. at 791.

[1107] Permitted waterworks could be constructed "to promote irrigation or mining or quarrying, or the manufacturing or cutting of timer or lumber, or the supplying of water for domestic, public or any other beneficial uses." *Id.*

[1108] Act of Feb. 1, 1905, ch. 288, 33 Stat. 628.

[1109] *Id.*

of its continuing jurisdiction over mining claims located on national forests lands.[1110]

Thus, the Transfer Act split jurisdiction over water-related uses of forest lands between Interior and Agriculture. Generally, Interior was empowered to issue permits for uses that involved granting rights-of-way, but the Forest Service issued permits for water works and development on national forests "when no easement in the land occupied is required."[1111] In 1976, the Federal Land Policy and Management Act (FLPMA) consolidated all permitting authority regarding the national forests in the Forest Service except for the administration of permits issued by Interior prior to 1976.[1112] Permitting authority remains an important aspect of Forest Service water policy.[1113]

The second area over which the Forest Service has exercised some authority is the use of water for administrative purposes, such as domestic use by ranger stations. Initially, the Forest Service neither notified the state of this use nor formally complied with state water laws. Rangers simply diverted the water and re-

---

[1110] In 1976 the authority to issue and manage rights-of-way across national forests was finally consolidated in the Department of Agriculture under § 501(a) of FLPMA, 43 U.S.C. § 1761(a) (1982). *See* City and County of Denver v. Bergland, 695 F.2d 465, 475 (10th Cir. 1982). The Department of the Interior retains management authority over permits issued up to 1976. *Id.* at 476.

[1111] 1906 USE BOOK, *supra* note 82, at 28. Pinchot divided permit authority between Class I permits, which gave "permission to occupy or use lands, resources, or products of a forest reserve which occupation and use is temporary . . . and which . . . will in no wise affect the fee or cloud the title of the United States," and Class II permits, "the granting of which amounts to an easement running with the land." *Id.* at 27. Class I permits were then granted by the Secretary of Agriculture, while Class II permits were granted by the Secretary of the Interior. *Id.* Class I permits were needed for "canals, ditches, flumes, pipelines, tunnels, dams, tanks and reservoirs, within the forest reserves, when no easement in the land occupied is required." *Id.* at 28. Class II permits were needed for "rights of way to use water for municipal or mining purposes and rights of way for irrigation purposes." *Id.*

The Forest Service held broad discretion to grant or revoke permits. A money charge was levied on permits based on the value of the use to the permittee. A distinction was made between commercial and noncommercial uses. Occupancy of the land did not grant anything to the permittee beyond the rights contained in the permit. While the granting of the permit for conveyance of water did not amount to granting of a water right per se, the Forest Service suggested that such rights were not granted exclusively by the states. Pinchot instructed, "[p]ermits granted under these regulations are only for the improvements necessary to store or conduct water and do not carry any right to the water itself, the appropriation of which is subject to Federal, State or Territorial law." *Id.* at 68.

[1112] *See supra* note 1110.

[1113] *See infra* text accompanying notes 1242-52.

corded the origin and amount used.[1114] More recently, however, the Service's policy has been to defer to state water law.[1115]

The third area over which the Forest Service has exerted regulatory authority concerns water used to generate electricity. Prior to the passage of the Federal Power Act[1116] in 1920, which established the Federal Power Commission (now the Federal Energy Regulatory Commission), the Forest Service had authority to grant or deny permits for water power projects in the national forests.[1117] After 1920, the Federal Power Commission held authority to issue licenses, although the Forest Service asserted the right to impose conditions on projects constructed in the national forests.[1118] The Forest Service investigated and evaluated applications for the Federal Power Commission when permittees attempted to locate in the national forests.[1119] Nevertheless, the

---

[1114] FOREST SERVICE, U.S. DEP'T OF AGRICULTURE, THE USE BOOK 53 (1908 ed.) [hereinafter cited as 1908 USE BOOK].

[1115] In 1936 the Forest Service changed its policy, declaring that "rights to the use of water for National Forest purposes will be obtained in accordance with state law." United States v. New Mexico, 438 U.S. 696, 703 n.7 (1978), quoting the Forest Service Manual. Later, the Forest Service took a middle ground, deferring to state law as a matter of policy and comity. *Id.* Current policy is set out in FOREST SERVICE MANUAL § 2541.51 (1984).

[1116] The Federal Water Power Act of June 10, 1920, ch. 285, 41 Stat. 1077 (current version at 16 U.S.C. §§ 791a-828c (1982)).

[1117] Secretarial authority to grant or deny permits was based upon the Act of February 15, 1901, discussed *supra* at notes 1105-07 and accompanying text, authorizing the Secretary to permit dam construction on the forest reserves. The Act of March 4, 1911, ch. 238, 36 Stat. 1235, 1253, authorized the Secretary to grant easements for power transmission and telephone and telegraph lines. Diligence in construction was necessary, *id.* at 1254, and a fixed fee based on each net electrical horsepower per year was levied on permittees. The two statutes are analyzed in the 1915 Use Book. *See* 1915 USE BOOK, *supra* note 700, at 123-27.

[1118] *See* 16 U.S.C. § 797(e) (1982); FOREST SERVICE, U.S. DEP'T. OF AGRICULTURE, [1921] ANNUAL REPORT OF THE CHIEF 29-31 (1921). *Cf.* Federal Power Comm'n v. Oregon, 349 U.S. 435 (1955) (limitations on state authority under the Federal Power Act). *See also,* 1928 ANNUAL REPORT OF THE CHIEF, *supra* note 97, at 41-42, stating:

The Federal water power act gives the commission authority to make requirements in the interest of public safety or the proper development of the power resources of the Government's lands. This authority is exercised on the national forests through the Forest Service.

[1119] Pursuant to a cooperative arrangement between the Departments of War, Agriculture, and the Interior, the Forest Service inspected operations of plants on Forest Service lands and aided the Federal Power Commission in evaluating permittees. *See, e.g.,* 1931 ANNUAL REPORT OF THE CHIEF, *supra* note 1060, at 51. During the 1920s the majority of permits issued by the Federal Power Commission were for sites on Forest Service lands. *Id. See also* 1927 ANNUAL REPORT OF THE CHIEF, *supra* note 1058, at 35. By 1936, 77% of the applications

Forest Service was often hamstrung in its efforts to control the impact of dams for power purposes. Dam construction in the national forests sometimes destroyed Forest Service facilities and resources, particularly roads necessary for timber protection and production.[1120] In addition, by 1959 nearly 2.8 million acres of national forest land had been withdrawn by the United States Geological Survey or the Federal Power Commission for protection as potential dam sites.[1121] Finally, a 1984 decision established the Forest Service's right to play a major role in federal dam siting by attaching conditions to permits issued by the Federal Energy Regulatory Commission.[1122]

Fourth, the Forest Service has made some effort to prevent excessive appropriation of water from national forest watercourses. Overappropriation became particularly acute following World War II, when intensive use of water for irrigation and hydroelectric power generation began to degrade the fish habitat and recreation.[1123] In 1966 the agency initiated a six-year study to determine the long-term water needs of the western national forests

---

filed with the Federal Power Commission involved use of national forest lands. 1936 ANNUAL REPORT OF THE CHIEF, *supra* note 95, at 32.

[1120] In 1951 Chief Watts reported:

The value of the water resources of the national forests thus becomes more apparent each year. Although all this construction for water development is being done by other agencies, the Forest Service is faced with a growing problem of keeping up its transportation system, administrative work centers and improvements, recreation, fire-control, and other facilities that are impaired by the new water developments. Some of the new large reservoirs in the national forests are submerging thousands of acres of what were formerly timber-producing lands. Submergence of roads is complicating the fire protection and timber harvesting on other thousands of acres. Provision is needed for effective restoration of national-forest services so impaired.

1951 ANNUAL REPORT OF THE CHIEF, *supra* note 716, at 46. The next year Chief McArdle reported:

During the year more than 50 dams were built on national-forest lands by irrigation farmers, power companies, and Federal agencies (Bureau of Reclamation and Corps of Engineers). The many proposals for multiple-purpose water developments in mountainous headwater areas, where the national forests lie, bring new problems of insuring proper consideration for forest resources such as timber, recreation, wildlife, and grazing in the areas involved.

1952 ANNUAL REPORT OF THE CHIEF, *supra* note 717, at 34-35.

[1121] 1959 ANNUAL REPORT OF THE CHIEF, *supra* note 119, at 17-18.

[1122] *See* Escondido Mutual Water Co. v. La Jolla, Rincon, San Pasqual, Pauma, and Pala Bands of Mission Indians, 104 S. Ct. 1260 (1984), and *infra* text accompanying notes 1253-62.

[1123] In 1950 Chief Clapp reported:

"for such uses as recreation, timber production, municipal needs and administration."[1124] In the 1970s, the Forest Service attempted, in the main unsuccessfully, to control overappropriation by claiming reserved water rights for fish, wildlife, recreation, and aesthetic purposes.[1125]

Historically, then, Forest Service water policy has moved in fits and starts. The primary purposes of setting aside national forests for watershed protection has always been well accepted. The authority to manage the water resource within the forests, however, has been clouded by ambiguous statutes and practices. One major result has been various institutional conflicts among the Forest Service, other federal agencies, and the states. The following subsections treat the current law on the regulation of water pollution and water quantity.

B. Water Pollution

1. The Clean Water Act

The Clean Water Act[1126] is one of the most important pieces of environmental legislation of the 1970s in regard to its impact on federal forest and range management.[1127] The Act delegates regulatory authority primarily to the states and to the Environmental Protection Agency (EPA) and the Army Corps of Engineers (Corps), rather than to the Forest Service. Nevertheless, three

---

Use of water from the national forests increases at an accelerating rate. Hydroelectric power in particular is being developed in many forests to meet mounting needs. Where domestic water-supply requirements, irrigation needs, fishing, recreation, or other uses are competing for the same stream flow, conflicts may develop. The Forest Service, as administrator of the lands that are the source of the water, must plan for the greatest benefit to the greatest number. Studies to establish priorities are necessarily a part of this work. Overappropriation of some stream flow in the West is requiring attention to water rights.

1950 ANNUAL REPORT OF THE CHIEF, *supra* note 118, at 50.

[1124] FOREST SERVICE, U.S. DEP'T OF AGRICULTURE, [1972] ANNUAL REPORT OF THE CHIEF 20 (1972); *see also* 1966 ANNUAL REPORT OF THE CHIEF, *supra* note 397, at 14.

[1125] *See* United States v. New Mexico, 438 U.S. 696 (1978), discussed *infra* at notes 1191-97 and accompanying text.

[1126] 33 U.S.C. §§ 1251-1376 (1982). The Federal Water Pollution Act was originally passed in 1948. There were numerous amendments between 1948 and 1977; in 1977 it was renamed the Clean Water Act. *See generally* W. RODGERS, HANDBOOK ON ENVIRONMENTAL LAW 354-61 (1977), 187-205 (1984 Supp.).

[1127] S. DANA & S. FAIRFAX, *supra* note 52, at 246.

aspects of the Act bear directly on the national forests and call for Forest Service involvement.[1128]

First, the National Pollutant Discharge Elimination System (NPDES) in section 402 of the Act[1129] requires a permit for the discharge of a pollutant from a point source into the waters of the United States. These terms are broadly defined. "Discharge of a pollutant" encompasses mining wastes and soil erosion from activities such as timber harvesting, roadbuilding, and grazing.[1130] A "point source" is "any discernible, confined and discrete conveyance including but not limited to any pipe, ditch, channel, tunnel, conduit."[1131] Initially, in 1973, the EPA adopted regulations exempting all silvicultural operations from the NPDES permit requirements,[1132] but this blanket exemption was held invalid in *Natural Resources Defense Council, Inc. v. Costle*.[1133] The current EPA regulations require NPDES permits for discharges from rock crushing, gravel washing, log sorting, or log storage facilities.[1134] However, most logging activities such as timber harvesting, surface drainage, and road construction are largely exempted from section 402 NPDES point source permits and are regulated less stringently as nonpoint sources.[1135] Finally, "waters of the United States" reaches far beyond the traditional "navigable waters" standard to include virtually all watercourses in the country.[1136] NPDES permits are issued either by the EPA or, more commonly, by those states that have taken over the administration of the NPDES program within their borders.[1137]

[1128] For a discussion of the manner in which the Clean Water Act applies to the national forests, see II C. BRUBANY, B. KRAMER, F. SKILLERN & J. MERTES, FOREST SERVICE, U.S. DEP'T OF AGRICULTURE, FEDERAL STATUTES AFFECTING THE LAND MANAGEMENT PLANNING FUNCTIONS OF THE FOREST SERVICE 43-53 (1982) [hereinafter cited as II BRUBANY].

[1129] 33 U.S.C. § 1342 (1982).

[1130] *Id.* § 1362(6), and (12).

[1131] *Id.* § 1362(14). "Return flows from irrigated agriculture" are expressly exempted from the point source requirement. *Id.*

[1132] 40 C.F.R. § 125.4(j) (1975).

[1133] 564 F.2d 573 (D.C. Cir. 1977).

[1134] 40 C.F.R. 122.27(b) (1984).

[1135] *Id.* See *infra* text accompanying notes 1142-49.

[1136] 33 U.S.C. § 1362(7) (1982), *construed in* Minnehaha Creek Watershed Dist. v. Hoffman, 597 F.2d 617 (8th Cir. 1979); United States v. Phelps Dodge Corp., 391 F. Supp. 1181 (D. Ariz. 1975); United States v. Holland, 373 F. Supp. 665 (M.D. Fla. 1974).

[1137] *See* 33 U.S.C. § 1342(b) (1982).

Thus, national forests users who discharge pollutants from a point source must comply with section 402. Quantitative effluent limitations have been set by EPA regulations for certain silvicultural activities.[1138] It is not always necessary for users with point source discharges to obtain separate permits for each operation; if operations are substantially similar, the user can apply for a general permit.[1139] The Clean Water Act requires all Forest Service licensees or permittees who discharge pollutants from point sources to provide a certificate that the requirements of the NPDES program have been met.[1140] In addition, Congress has waived federal sovereign immunity for federal agencies for the NPDES permitting process so that the Forest Service itself must obtain an NPDES permit from the state when the agency discharges pollutants from point sources.[1141]

The second relevant provision of the Clean Water Act relates to nonpoint sources of pollution. As suggested above, regulation of nonpoint sources is particularly important in national forests because the EPA excludes major categories of forest activities from point source regulation. Soil erosion sediments, pesticides, petrochemicals, and wood waste pollution caused by road building and timber harvesting are not categorized as point source pollution because such runoff is diffuse and does not emanate from a "discernible, confined, and discrete conveyance."[1142] Close questions have also been raised as to whether specific mining activities constitute point or nonpoint sources.[1143]

[1138] *See* 40 C.F.R. §§ 436.20-.22 (1984) (rock crushing and gravel washing); *id.* § 429.110-16 (log washing). The regulations are summarized in II BRUBANY, *supra* note 1128, at 45-46.

[1139] 40 C.F.R. § 122.48 (1984).

[1140] 33 U.S.C. § 1341(a) (1982).

[1141] The Supreme Court construed the 1972 amendments to the Clean Water Act to mean that federal facilities were required to comply with state substantive requirements, such as effluent limitations, but that federal facilities were not required to obtain permits from the states. Environmental Protection Agency v. State Water Resources Control Bd., 426 U.S. 200 (1976). In 1977, Congress amended the Act to require that federal agencies comply with "any [NPDES] requirement," "substantive or procedural." 33 U.S.C. § 1323(a) (1982).

[1142] 33 U.S.C. § 1362(14) (1982). For a suggestion that many timber harvesting activities treated as nonpoint sources are in fact subject to point source regulation, *see* J. BONINE & T. McGARITY, *supra* note 387, at 434-35 (1984).

[1143] *See, e.g.,* Sierra Club v. Abston Constr. Co., 620 F.2d 41 (5th Cir. 1980) (runoff from spoil piles through discernible ditches created by erosion held to be point sources); United States v. Earth Sciences, Inc., 599 F.2d 368 (10th Cir. 1979) (overflow of mine water wastes from gold leaching operation held to be point source).

Section 208 of the Act[1144] is the only provision regulating nonpoint sources of pollution. States are required to prepare area-wide water quality management plans.[1145] Methods of controlling nonpoint pollution are called "best management practices" (BMPs)[1146] and may include (for silvicultural nonpoint pollution) riparian zones where harvesting is prohibited and restrictions on soil types and slope gradients where harvesting may occur. Although the states have authority to regulate nonpoint source pollution on public lands,[1147] that authority has been exercised sparingly, usually by entering into "memoranda of understanding" with federal land management agencies, which simply lodge general responsibility for nonpoint pollution control within the federal agencies.[1148] With section 208 planning moving slowly in most states, the control of nonpoint source pollution remains a major obstacle to achieving the Clean Water Act's goal of "fishable and swimmable" water, originally mandated for 1983.[1149]

[1144] 33 U.S.C. § 1288 (1982).

[1145] *See generally* 40 C.F.R. § 35.1521 (1984).

[1146] The EPA regulations define best management practices [BMPs] as follows:

> BMPs are those methods, measures, or practices to prevent or reduce water pollution and include but are not limited to structural and nonstructural controls, and operation and maintenance procedures. BMPs can be applied before, during, and after pollution-producing activities to reduce or eliminate the introduction of pollutants into receiving waters. Economic, institutional, and technical factors shall be considered in developing BMPs.

40 C.F.R. § 35.1521-(4)(c)(1) (1984).

[1147] The Clean Water Act explicitly permits the states to enact more stringent regulations, 33 U.S.C. § 1370 (1982); thus, federal preemption is waived. Northwest Indian Cemetery Protective Ass'n v. Peterson, 764 F.2d 581, 588-89 (9th Cir. 1985). *See also* Comment, *Regulation of Nonpoint Sources of Water Pollution in Oregon Under Section 208 of The Federal Water Pollution Control Act*, 60 OR. L. REV. 184 (1981). On state authority within the national forests, *see generally infra* text accompanying notes 343-61.

[1148] An example of the memoranda of understanding is discussed in Comment, *supra* note 1147, at 189.

[1149] 33 U.S.C. § 1251(a)(2) (1982). Section 1251(a)(2) states the congressional policy that "whenever attainable, an interim goal of water quality which provides for the protection and propagation of fish, shellfish, and wildlife and provides for recreation in and on the water be achieved by July 1983." On the implementation of § 208, see F. ANDERSON, D. MANDELKER & A. TARLOCK, ENVIRONMENTAL PROTECTION: LAW AND POLICY 362-64 (1984); J. BONINE & T. MCGARITY, *supra* note 387, at 436-38; Thaler, *Solutions for Water Pollution in Our Forests*, FOREST PLANNING, Jan.-Feb. 1984, at 20; Wilkins, *The Implementation of Water Pollution Control Measures—Section 208 of the Water Pollution Control Act Amendments*, 15 LAND & WATER L. REV. 479 (1980).

Finally, the third provision of the Act that directly affects water quality is section 404, which provides for federal regulation of dredge and fill activities.[1150] Under the Rivers and Harbors Act of 1899,[1151] the Corps had exclusive authority over dredge and fill activities. In 1972 the Clean Water Act amendments provided for a greatly expanded regulatory program.[1152] Coverage was extended to all waters of the United States.[1153] The Corps continues to issue dredge and fill permits under section 404,[1154] but the EPA has the authority to set permit guidelines,[1155] to veto any individual permit,[1156] and to authorize states to take over substantial portions of the program.[1157]

In 1977, section 404 was amended to exclude certain minor operations.[1158] Several of the exemptions apply to the national forests. "Normal" silvicultural activities involving earthmoving, presumably including routine stream crossings, are exempted.[1159] In addition, the construction and maintenance of temporary mining and logging roads are not subject to section 404 provided they are constructed in accordance with best management practices.[1160] As with the NPDES system,[1161] the EPA can grant general permits.[1162] In addition to the authority that states may obtain under section 404 itself, states retain independent authority to enforce more stringent local dredge and fill laws on public lands.[1163]

[1150] 33 U.S.C. § 1344 (1982).

[1151] Act of Mar. 3, 1899, ch. 425, 30 Stat. 1121. *See generally* Comment, *supra* note 1084.

[1152] On the interaction of § 404 and the Refuse Act of 1899, see Comment, *Discharging New Wine Into Old Wineskins: The Metamorphosis of the Rivers and Harbors Act of 1899*, 33 U. PITT. L. REV. 483 (1972).

[1153] *See supra* note 1136.

[1154] 33 C.F.R. pt. 325 (1984).

[1155] 33 U.S.C. § 1344(b) (1982).

[1156] *Id.* § 1344(c).

[1157] *Id.* § 1344(h) (authority to enable states to administer the program, except for permits relating to waters within the classic definition of navigability); *id.* § 1344(g)(1)).

[1158] Clean Water Act of 1977, Pub. L. No. 95-217, § 67, 91 Stat. 1600 (codified at 33 U.S.C. §§ 1251-1376 (1982)).

[1159] 33 U.S.C. § 1344(f)(1) (1982). Although exempt from § 404, these activities are still subject to regulation under § 208 as nonpoint sources. *See supra* notes 1144-49 and accompanying text.

[1160] 33 U.S.C. § 1344(f)(1)(E) (1982).

[1161] *See supra* text accompanying notes 1129-41.

[1162] 33 U.S.C. § 1344(e) (1982).

[1163] *Id.* § 1370 (states allowed to impose more stringent regulations). *See generally* State ex rel. Cox v. Hibbard, 31 Or. App. 269, 570 P.2d 1190 (1977), and *supra* text accompanying notes 343-61.

The Forest Service has a relatively limited role under the Clean Water Act. The primary actors are the EPA, the Corps, and the states that have assumed responsibilities pursuant to the Act. The Forest Service is left mainly with the secondary, although potentially important, job of applying its expertise and prestige to persuade the primary governmental agencies to adopt programs that will adequately protect water resources in the national forests. In any event, the lack of explicit authority under the Clean Water Act in no way limits the Forest Service's specific responsibilities for water resources in the National Forest Management Act.[1164]

2. The National Forest Management Act of 1976

The controversy over the effects of timber harvesting on water quality provided a major impetus for adoption of the Church guidelines[1165] and the National Forest Management Act (NFMA).[1166] As a result, some of the NFMA's most prescriptive provisions concern water quality. The Act prohibits timber harvesting unless the Forest Service can ensure that "soil, slope, or other watershed conditions will not be irreversibly damaged."[1167] More specifically, the agency must ensure that "protection is provided for streams, streambanks, shorelines, lakes, wetlands, and

---

[1164] *See infra* section V(B)(2)

[1165] *See supra* text accompanying notes 721-83. Water quality was addressed several times during the Church subcommittee hearings. *See, e.g., Senate Hearings on Clearcutting, supra* note 665, at 290 (testimony by a conservationist that logging and road construction caused a national forest stream in Oregon to be "running thick enough to plow, causing a very heavy silting of the North Umpqua salmon and steelhead spawning beds"); *id.* at 308-09, 313 (testimony by the director of the EPA Water Quality Office that clearcutting generally causes stream sedimentation to increase 7000 times and stream temperatures to increase by 14° F); *id.* at 623, 624 (testimony by a civil engineering professor that the "frequency of landslides is some 250 times greater in road rights-of-way as opposed to virgin undisturbed timber" in the Willamette National Forest); *id.* at 843-47 (testimony by Forest Service Chief Edward Cliff responding to previous testimony concerning water quality).

[1166] 16 U.S.C. §§ 1600-1614 (1982). Water quality was discussed several times during the NFMA hearings and floor debates. *See, e.g.,* SENATE NFMA HEARINGS, *supra* note 194, at 356 (Sen. Randolph's testimony that "following a clearcut . . . in the Monongahela National Forest . . . the Cranberry River ran muddy. Not for 1 day, not for 1 week, it ran muddy, very muddy for 7 weeks"); *House NFMA Hearings, supra* note 398, at 249-50 (testimony of Forest Service Chief John McGuire).

[1167] 16 U.S.C. § 1604(g)(3)(E)(i) (1982). The language is based on a Church guideline. *See supra* text accompanying note 761.

other bodies of water from detrimental changes in water temperatures, blockages of water courses, and deposits of sediment, where harvests are likely to seriously and adversely affect water conditions or fish habitat."[1168] Furthermore, clearcutting is allowed only where "such cuts are carried out in a manner consistent with the protection of soil, watershed, fish, wildlife, recreation, esthetic resources."[1169]

Taken together, the NFMA water quality provisions require strong measures to protect water resources and fish habitats from detrimental impacts of timber harvesting and road construction. The NFMA's mandate echoes the emphasis on watershed protection consistently expressed by Congress and the Forest Service prior to World War II.[1170]

Recognizing that the NFMA "expresses strong concern about protecting streams and lakes,"[1171] the Committee of Scientists addressed water quality at several places in the NFMA regulations. First, the regulations require planners to compile information necessary to identify and evaluate potentially hazardous watershed conditions, such as unstable soils.[1172] Second, soil and water resource management must follow instructions contained in official agency technical handbooks to avoid or mitigate damage at specific sites.[1173] Third, planners must give "special attention" to riparian areas, strips of land "approximately 100 feet from the edges of all perennial streams, lakes, and other bodies of water."[1174]

The Committee of Scientists considered riparian areas to be "an extremely important fraction of the forest area" because they provide highly productive timber and range land, critical wildlife habitat, water-oriented recreation, and potential road corridors.[1175] While the regulations do not specifically prohibit any activity in riparian areas, the Committee hoped to "assure intensive planning" and "provide further safeguards for protection of soil and water at the critical meeting zone of the two resources."[1176]

[1168] 16 U.S.C. § 1604(g)(3)(E)(iii) (1982). For a discussion of the legislative history of this section of the NFMA, see *supra* text accompanying notes 826-29.
[1169] 16 U.S.C. § 1604(g)(3)(F)(v) (1982).
[1170] *See supra* text accompanying notes 1055-60.
[1171] *Comm. of Scientists Final Report, supra* note 864, at 26,626.
[1172] *See* 36 C.F.R. § 219.23(e) (1984).
[1173] *Id.* § 219.27(f).
[1174] *Id.* § 219.27(e).
[1175] *Comm. of Scientists Final Report, supra* note 864, at 26,599.
[1176] *Id.* at 26,653.

Another provision with potentially far-reaching implications for water quality planning is the requirement that national forest fish habitats be managed to maintain viable populations of all existing native vertebrate species.[1177] For example, for western national forests that have declining populations of salmon and other anadromous fish, the provision strongly suggests that the Forest Service has a duty under NFMA to protect viable populations of this valuable fish resource. Nevertheless, a former Regional Forester of the Pacific Northwest Region, which includes many of the nation's major salmon streams, concluded that the Clean Water Act sets the only applicable standards.[1178] Some forest plans for other regions, however, have set viable populations for fish.[1179]

Curiously, the regulations provide only limited guidance for implementing the NFMA's requirement that plans ensure protection from timber harvesting that will "seriously and adversely affect water conditions or fish habitat."[1180] The only reference in the regulations to the statutory requirement is in the context of riparian area management.[1181] However, the language of the NFMA does not appear to apply only to riparian areas; timber harvesting on erosive slopes outside riparian areas can also have serious adverse effects on water quality and fish resources.

In order to implement the NFMA's requirements, the Forest Service should establish specific water quality standards in the forest plans. At a minimum, the water quality standards should include maximum temperature and sediment levels. If timber

---

[1177] 36 C.F.R. § 219.19 (1984). The origin and meaning of this provision are discussed *infra* at text accompanying notes 1587-96.

[1178] *See* Memorandum on Viable Fish Populations from Regional Forester Worthington, Region VI, Forest Service (Dec. 1, 1981). The memorandum stated:

> We do not believe that we need to establish minimum viable population levels for anadromous fish as it is reasonable to assume that water quality law, which we are directed to follow, establishes a level of aquatic resources management that will maintain the Region's fisheries habitat at a level capable of sustaining or exceeding minimum viable populations for the various species of anadromous fish.

(Copy on file at Oregon Law Review office.)

[1179] *See, e.g.,* FOREST SERVICE, U.S. DEP'T OF AGRICULTURE, PROPOSED LAND AND RESOURCE MANAGEMENT PLAN, HURON-MANISTEE NATIONAL FORESTS IV-93 (1985) (one brook trout per 100 square meters in tributaries not used for spawning, and three trout per 100 square meters in tributaries used for spawning).

[1180] 16 U.S.C. § 1604(g)(3)(E)(iii) (1982). For a discussion of the legislative history of this provision, *see supra* text accompanying notes 826-29.

[1181] 36 C.F.R. § 219.27(e) (1984).

cannot be harvested in an area without exceeding the water quality standards—due to steep slopes, unstable soils, or other factors—the forest plan should identify the area as unsuitable for timber production.

Unfortunately, confusion and misconceptions about the NFMA's applicability to national forest water quality issues seem to be pervasive. The Forest Service Manual's cursory provisions on water quality[1182] may result from a perceived lack of agency authority over water quality. But the NFMA water quality provisions, which are subsequent to and more specific than section 208 of the Clean Water Act of 1972, plainly supplement the Clean Water Act requirements for national forest lands.

C. Water Quantity Regulation and Maintenance

1. Congressionally Reserved Water Rights

The reserved rights, or *Winters*, doctrine, derives from the Supreme Court's leading decision in *Winters v. United States*.[1183] In *Winters* the Court held that the United States, as trustee for the Indian tribes occupying the Fort Belknap Indian Reservation in Montana, had, by the creation of the reservation, impliedly reserved a sufficient quantity of water to fulfill the purposes of the reservation.[1184] In essence, *Winters* superimposed a judicially implied federal water right on state prior appropriation water law. The *Winters* right is inchoate and does not require either a diversion or an application of the water to a beneficial use—the hallmarks of prior appropriation law.[1185] Importantly, the priority date of a reserved water right is no later than the date that the reservation was created, notwithstanding any subsequent uses of

---

[1182] *See* FOREST SERVICE MANUAL §§ 2526, 2542 (1984).

[1183] 207 U.S. 564 (1908). The earliest suggestion of the doctrine came in United States v. Rio Grande Dam and Irrigation Co., 174 U.S. 690 (1899), where the Supreme Court stated in dictum that "[a] state cannot by its legislation destroy the right of the United States, as the owner of lands bordering on a stream, to the continued flow of its waters; so far at least as may be necessary for the beneficial uses of the government property." *Id.* at 703.

[1184] In *Winters*, the Court construed the agreement establishing the reservation in favor of the tribe, *id.* at 576, and found that the reservation had been established for the purposes of hunting, grazing, and developing the "arts of civilization," *id.* at 576. Thus, the purposes of the reservation included a sufficient quantity of water for an irrigation system and to meet domestic needs.

[1185] *See supra* notes 1087-89 and accompanying text.

water that may have developed under state law without actual notice of the reserved rights.[1186]

Nearly six decades passed after *Winters* until the Court, in 1963, expressly stated that the reserved rights doctrine applies to federal, as well as Indian, lands.[1187] In *Arizona v. California,* as part of a final decree dividing Colorado River waters among competing states in the Southwest, the Supreme Court ruled that "the principle underlying the reservation of water rights for Indian Reservations . . . [is] equally applicable to other federal establishments such as National Recreation Areas and National Forests."[1188]

In 1976 the Supreme Court applied the reserved rights doctrine to land set aside as a national monument in *Cappaert v. United States.*[1189] However, the Court qualified the doctrine by limiting the reserved right to "only that amount of water necessary to fulfill the purpose of the reservation, no more."[1190]

The capstone in the development of federal reserved water rights is *United States v. New Mexico,*[1191] a 1978 decision that significantly narrowed judicially recognized federal reserved rights on Forest Service lands. In 1966 New Mexico initiated a general stream adjudication on the Rio Mimbres. In 1970 the United

---

[1186] The priority dates of Indian reserved rights may in some cases predate the establishment of the reservation. In one instance, an Indian reservation created by treaty was held to have an aboriginal priority date due to the tribe's aboriginal possession of the land. *See* United States v. Adair, 723 F.2d 1394 (1983), *cert. denied,* 104 S. Ct. 3536 (1984). However, forest reserves are created by statute or executive order, without any preexisting rights analogous to tribal possession, so that priority dates are the date of reservation. *See infra* note 1225.

[1187] Although the reserved rights doctrine was not actually extended to federal lands until Arizona v. California, 373 U.S. 546, 599 (1963), this extension was suggested in dictum by the Court in Federal Power Comm'n v. Oregon, 349 U.S. 435, 444 (1955).

[1188] 373 U.S. at 601. Rights to reserved water were recognized for Lake Mead National Recreation Area, Havasu Lake National Wildlife Refuge, Imperial National Wildlife Refuge, and the Gila National Forest.

[1189] 426 U.S. 128 (1976). Chief Justice Burger wrote, "[W]hen the Federal Government withdraws its land from the public domain and reserves it for a federal purpose, the Government, by implication, reserves appurtenant water then unappropriated to the extent needed to accomplish the purpose of the reservation. In so doing the United States acquires a reserved right in unappropriated water which vests on the date of the reservation and is superior to the rights of future appropriators." *Id.* at 138.

[1190] *Id.* at 141.

[1191] 438 U.S. 696 (1978).

States was joined as a party[1192] in order to determine the extent of federal reserved water rights in the Gila National Forest.[1193] The New Mexico Supreme Court denied the Forest Service's claim of reserved water rights for stock watering, and for aesthetic, environmental, recreation, and fish habitat purposes.[1194] The United States Supreme Court, in a five-four decision, held that Congress in passing the 1897 Organic Act had not impliedly reserved water for the diverse purposes the United States later claimed. Justice Rehnquist, writing for the majority, concluded that water was reserved only to accomplish the original purposes of the forest reservation. Thus, water was reserved only to secure "favorable conditions of water flows" and "to furnish a continuous supply of timber."[1195] The Court refused to find a third, more general, purpose implied in the statutory language, "to improve and protect the forest."[1196] In effect, the Court announced a rule of strict construction against the assertion of federal reserved rights.[1197]

[1192] The McCarran Amendment, 43 U.S.C. § 666(a) (1982), authorizes joinder of the United States in general stream adjudications in state courts by waiving federal sovereign immunity when federal water rights are at issue. The statute covers assertions of federal reserved rights. United States v. District Ct. in and for the County of Eagle, 401 U.S. 520 (1971).

[1193] One might surmise that overriding policy considerations caused the Forest Service to choose the Gila National Forest as a test case to determine the breadth of the reserved rights doctrine. The Gila is unique in at least two respects. First, it is the area out of which America's first wilderness area was carved in 1924. *See infra* text accompanying notes 1811-17. Second, the Gila National Forest was specifically designated in the 1963 decree in *Arizona v. California*, as a national forest for which water had been reserved, 373 U.S. at 601. Despite these speculations, we discovered the real, and more basic, reason for litigating reserved rights in the Gila National Forest: "I don't know what it's like where you come from, but there just isn't very much water down here. We were trying to claim as much water as we could." Telephone conversation with Adrian Pedron, Office of Gen. Counsel, Forest Service, Albuquerque, N. M. (Oct. 13, 1983).

[1194] Mimbres Valley Irrigation Co. v. Salopek, 90 N.M. 410, 564 P.2d 615 (1977), *aff'd sub nom.*, United States v. New Mexico, 438 U.S. 696 (1978).

[1195] 438 U.S. at 718.

[1196] *Id.* at 711. The Organic Act statutory language appears in 16 U.S.C. § 475 (1982).

[1197] The opinion is criticized in Fairfax & Tarlock, *supra* note 227. The Court also found that the Multiple-Use Sustained-Yield Act of 1960, 16 U.S.C. §§ 528-531 (1982), although broadening the purposes of the national forests, did not expand the United States's reserved rights. 438 U.S. at 713. The purposes listed in the 1960 MUSY Act were deemed "secondary" to the purposes for which water had been reserved in 1897. *Id.* at 714-15. Reservation of water under the MUSY Act was never directly at issue in the case. The dissent stated: "Although the Court purports to hold that passage of the 1960 Act did not have the effect of reserving any additional water in then-existing forests . . . this

The Forest Service has continued to assert reserved water rights for the two purposes recognized in *New Mexico*: watershed protection and timber production.[1198] The Forest Service Manual sets out several types of water needs that fit within the purposes of the 1897 Act.[1199] One group of uses deals with water needed for the administration of the forests in connection with the two primary purposes of the Act.[1200] Reserved rights for administration include water for domestic use at ranger stations and other facilities; for fire protection; for road construction; for irrigation of tree nurseries; for stockwatering and pasture irrigation for Forest Service stock; and for domestic use by permittees.[1201] A consent decree filed in one action recognizes all of these uses under the reserved rights doctrine.[1202] In addition to the reserved rights for administration, the Forest Service claims instream flows for channel maintenance, that is, a sufficient water flow each spring to flush debris out of the stream channel for "the purposes of securing favorable conditions of water flows and protecting against the loss of productive timber lands adjacent to the stream channels."[1203] Forest Service arguments for reserved rights for channel

---

portion of its opinion appears to be dicta." *Id.* at 719 n.1 (Powell, J., dissenting). The Colorado Supreme Court later held that the 1960 Act did not reserve water rights. United States v. City and County of Denver, 656 P.2d 1, 24-27 (1982).

[1198] Two recent decisions have ruled on reserved water rights for the national forests. In United States v. Alpine Land & Reservoir Co., 697 F.2d 851 (9th Cir.), *cert denied*, 104 S. Ct. 193 (1983), the court denied the United States's claim for an instream flow to protect the banks of the Carson River's tributaries within the Toiyabe National Forest from erosion. The court held the proof insufficient and noted that, in any event, a declaration that the Carson River was overappropriated would prevent future appropriations and therefore would have the same result as granting the United States a future reserved right for instream flows. *Id.* at 858-59. In United States v. City and County of Denver, 656 P.2d at 21-27, the court reversed the lower court's decree subordinating national forest reserved rights to all past and future private appropriations, but denied Forest Service arguments, substantially similar to those raised in United States v. New Mexico, 438 U.S. 696 (1978), for an expansive reserved right. For a decision on reserved rights in wilderness areas, see *infra* note 1212.

[1199] *See* FOREST SERVICE MANUAL § 2541.1 (1984).

[1200] *Id.* § 2541.1(a)-(f).

[1201] *Id.* § 2541.1(f). This includes use by permitted logging camps, insect control, and work centers.

[1202] In the Matter of the Application of the United States of America for Water Rights in the Arkansas River, etc. Findings of Fact, Conclusions of Law and Decree, Nos. 82CW59 and 82CW73 (Colo. Dist. Ct., Water Div. #2, Apr. 25, 1984).

[1203] FOREST SERVICE MANUAL § 2541.1(g) (1984). "This includes the volume and timing of flows required for adequate sediment transport, maintenance of streambank stability, and proper management of riparian vegetation." *Id.*

maintenance, which would include substantial instream flows during the spring, have not yet been conclusively litigated.[1204]

Federal reserved water rights in areas designated under the National Wilderness Preservation System[1205] and the National Wild and Scenic Rivers System [1206] are determined by the formula in *Cappaert*[1207] and *United States v. New Mexico*.[1208] The analysis, however, yields different results because the preservation purposes for wild and scenic rivers and wilderness areas are much broader, and more clearly stated, than the purposes of the 1897 Act. Wild and scenic rivers are designated because they "possess outstandingly remarkable scenic, recreational, geologic, fish and wildlife, historic, cultural, or other similar values."[1209] Thus, the Act expressly provides for instream flows by requiring that rivers in the system "shall be preserved in free-flowing condition, and . . . they and their immediate environments shall be protected for the benefit and enjoyment of present and future generations."[1210] A wilderness area in the NWPS is "an area of undeveloped Federal land retaining its primeval character and influence, without permanent improvements or human habitation, which is protected and managed so as to preserve its natural conditions."[1211]

Only two pronouncements have recognized federal reserved rights for these preservation systems. A perfunctory district court opinion stated that "wilderness areas have been withdrawn from the public domain; therefore the United States has reserved water rights which are unperfected at this time."[1212] An opinion by the

---

[1204] In two instances, similar Forest Service arguments were rejected because the records were weak. *See* United States v. City and County of Denver, 656 P.2d at 22 n.35; United States v. Alpine Land & Reservoir Co., 697 F.2d at 859, discussed *supra* in note 1198. Reserved rights for channel maintenance will soon be submitted to water courts in Colorado based upon extensive quantitative field work and legal briefing. Interview with John Hill, Attorney, U.S. Dep't of Justice, in Boulder, Colo. (June 6, 1984).

[1205] 16 U.S.C. §§ 1271-1287 (1982). *See infra* section IX.

[1206] 16 U.S.C. §§ 1131-1136 (1982). *See infra* text at notes 1263-78.

[1207] 426 U.S. 128 (1976).

[1208] 438 U.S. 696 (1978).

[1209] 16 U.S.C. § 1271 (1982).

[1210] *Id.*

[1211] *Id.* § 1311(c).

[1212] Sierra Club v. Block, 615 F. Supp. 44 (D. Colo. 1984). In this preliminary ruling, the court refused to determine the extent or nature of the reserved rights because the issue was pending, and could be decided, in the state water court. The federal court then ordered the United States to produce the administrative record so the court would have a sufficient basis for ruling on the plaintiff's re-

Solicitor of the Department of the Interior[1213] presented a more extended analysis. The Solicitor concluded that federal reserved rights existed to fulfill the conservation, recreation, aesthetic, and scientific purposes of congressionally designated wilderness areas and Wild and Scenic Rivers.[1214] Determining the specific quantity of reserved water for instream purposes in any individual area, however, is a complicated matter that must be left to detailed field work.[1215]

2. Congressionally Delegated Authority to Control Water Quantity

The reserved rights doctrine is one method of federal control over water consumption on federal lands, including national forests. Congress, by reserving water, preempts water allocation under state law to the extent that a certain quantity of water is necessary to achieve the purposes of the reservation. A different approach is the congressional delegation of the authority to protect the purposes for which land is administered by federal agencies. Congress has the power both to control water use on the public lands without deferring to state law[1216] and to delegate such power to federal land management agencies.[1217] The inquiry is

---

quest for an order that the United States had acted arbitrarily in not perfecting its rights in the state proceeding. *Id.* As this Article was about to go to press, the court issued a much more expansive opinion upholding federal reserved water rights in wilderness areas. Sierra Club v. Block, No. 84-K-2 (D. Colo. Nov. 25, 1985). Water development interests have announced that they intend to appeal the ruling.

[1213] 86 Interior Dec. 553 (1979). This opinion was later supplemented on other issues, *infra* note 1218, but the analyses discussed here remain undisturbed.

[1214] *Id.* at 607-09 (wild and scenic rivers), 609-10 (wilderness areas). Each Act contains an ambiguous provision that the Act is neither "an express or implied claim or denial on the part of the Federal Government as to exemption from State water laws." 16 U.S.C. § 1284(b) (1982); *id.* § 1133(d)(6). In light of the clearly stated purposes of the Acts, *see infra* text accompanying notes 1209-11, the Solicitor reasoned that "the provision is intended to continue the application of then-existing principles of federal-state relations in water law, which includes the reserved water rights doctrine." 86 Interior Dec. at 610.

[1215] *See, e.g.,* 86 Interior Dec. at 609.

[1216] Justice Rehnquist stated in *United States v. New Mexico*: "The question posed in this case—what quantity of water, if any, the United States reserved out of the Rio Mimbres when it set aside the Gila National Forest in 1899—is a question of implied intent and not power." 438 U.S. at 698. On congressional authority to preempt state law, see generally *infra* section II(A)(5).

[1217] The courts have long recognized the power of Congress in public land law, as in other fields, to delegate authority to administrative agencies "to fill up the details." *See, e.g.,* United States v. Grimaud, 220 U.S. 506 (1911). On Forest

whether Congress in fact has made such a delegation as part of the organic authority of a particular agency. This subsection discusses two different types of administrative power over water that could be delegated to the Forest Service: (1) the authority to set instream flows for nonconsumptive uses; and (2) the authority to deny or condition access to developers seeking to establish new diversions of water within the national forests.

(a) Authority to Set Instream Flows

The issue of whether federal land management agencies can set instream flows for nonconsumptive purposes such as recreation and wildlife preservation has generated considerable commentary in federal administrative opinions[1218] and in legal literature.[1219]

Service delegated authority under the Organic Act of 1897, see *infra* section II(A)(2).

[1218] A series of four legal interpretations has been rendered, three by successive Interior Solicitors and one by the Office of Legal Counsel of the Department of Justice. First, Solicitor Leo Krulitz concluded that the BLM possessed delegated authority under FLPMA to set instream flows for fish and wildlife purposes and scenic values. 86 Interior Dec. 553, 612-15 (1979). The opinion stated: "[t]he management programs mandated in . . . [FLMPA] require the appropriation of water by the United States in order to assure the success of the programs and carry out the objectives established by Congress." *Id.* at 612. Solicitor Clyde Martz then issued a supplemental opinion explaining that Congress had power to delegate such authority but that it had not done so in FLPMA. 88 Interior Dec. 253 (1981). Solicitor William Coldiron then issued yet another opinion, denying the existence of such delegated authority altogether. This opinion stated:

As to FLPMA, it is clear . . . that FLPMA authorizes a wide range of land management activities that require the use of water. . . . However, FLPMA does not authorize or otherwise mandate the Department to appropriate or otherwise utilize water outside state recognized beneficial use concepts for the broad general purposes outlined as management objectives in the Act.

Id. at 257. 88 Interior Dec. 1055, 1064-65 (1981). Finally, Assistant Attorney General Carol Dinkins of the Department of Justice issued a memorandum concluding that Congress may preempt state law by delegating authority to land management agencies, but that "the federal constitutional authority to preempt state water law must be clearly and specifically expressed; if it is not, the traditional deference to State water law should be presumed." U.S. Dept. of Justice, Office of Legal Counsel, Federal "Non-Reserved" Water Rights (June 16, 1982) [hereinafter cited as Justice Dep't Memorandum] (on file at Oregon Law Review office).

[1219] *See, e.g.,* Shurts, *FLPMA, Fish and Wildlife, and Federal Water Rights,* 15 ENVTL. L. 115 (1985); Trelease, *Uneasy Federalism—State Water Laws and National Water Uses,* 55 WASH. L. REV. 751 (1980); Note, *Federal Non-Reserved Water Rights: Fact or Fiction,* 22 NAT. RES. J. 423 (1982); Note, *Federal Non-Reserved Water Rights,* 48 U. CHI. L. REV. 758 (1981); Note, *Federal*

Although the phrase "non-reserved" rights has been used to describe such administrative authority,[1220] the term is singularly unhelpful: by phrasing the concept in the negative, the term "non-reserved" rights lacks content. Most water rights are "non-reserved." Water rights established by the Supreme Court in equitable apportionment cases[1221] or by the Secretary of the Interior pursuant to the power of congressional apportionment[1222] are "non-reserved" rights, as are water rights established under state law.

The Forest Service's power to set instream flows is better described—and understood—simply as a congressional delegation of authority over water resources within the agency's jurisdiction. There is no connection with the reserved rights doctrine except that the ultimate source of authority is lodged in Congress.

It is useful to compare the reserved rights claimed by the federal government in *United States v. New Mexico*[1223] with the rights asserted under the Forest Service's delegated power. In *New Mexico*, the Forest Service argued for a far-flung system of minimum stream flows that would apply to every watercourse within all national forests.[1224] Importantly, the Forest Service claimed a priority dating back to 1897, when the Organic Act was passed, or to the date that a forest was subsequently added to the system.[1225] Many saw this result as unfair because users with later priority dates had no actual notice of the federal reserved rights. If the federal position in *New Mexico* had been accepted, water users in or above national forests with priority dates in the late nineteenth or early twentieth century would have become subordinated to senior federal rights that were not announced until

---

Acquisition of Non-Reserved Water Rights After New Mexico, 31 STAN. L. REV. 885 (1979).

[1220] *See, e.g.,* 88 Interior Dec. 1055, 1056 (1981).

[1221] *See, e.g.,* Nebraska v. Wyoming, 325 U.S. 589 (1945).

[1222] *See* Arizona v. California, 373 U.S. 546 (1963).

[1223] 438 U.S. 696 (1978), discussed *supra* in notes 1191-97 and accompanying text.

[1224] The United States in *New Mexico* based its argument for instream flows on the 1897 Organic Act, 16 U.S.C. § 475 (1982), an umbrella statute that applies to all national forests. 438 U.S. at 696.

[1225] The priority date for forests created prior to the Organic Act would be 1897, while seniority for forests established subsequent to the Act would be the date of proclamation. The Gila National Forest, for example, was proclaimed in 1899. *Id.* at 698.

1978.[1226] Such rights would not technically be retroactive, because Congress would have reserved them in 1897; further, federal officials could have accounted for possible inequities by not asserting reserved rights in individual cases. Nevertheless, many westerners perceived such sleeping federal rights as retroactive and unjust.[1227]

There are indications that the reserving of instream flows for recreation and wildlife was indeed consistent with Congress's purposes in passing the 1897 Organic Act.[1228] However, the extraordinary geographic reach and perceived retroactive nature of the rights were undoubtedly factors that contributed to the Court's decision in *New Mexico* to restrict the Forest Service to comparatively limited congressionally reserved rights.[1229]

In contrast, instream flows set pursuant to delegated administrative authority are conceptually different and the actual impacts are much more modest. Instream flows established by delegated authority are site-specific and prospective. The Forest Service, managing water much like any other resource pursuant to the agency's broad authority, would take action on a particular stream only when its planning process showed a need to protect that resource.[1230] If the stream flow were dangerously low, the agency would proceed according to administrative rules. It would give notice to the public, including the state water agency, that it is considering the establishment of a minimum instream flow of a specific quantity of water at specific times of the year for the particular stream. Importantly, the priority date would be the date of the public notice. The agency would take action only after public hearings. Thus, no existing rights would be affected by these prospective rights and all potential future users would be given notice.

[1226] Only water users within, or upstream from, a national forest would be affected by a recognition of reserved instream flows. Downstream users could fully appropriate the waters of the stream.

[1227] *See, e.g.,* Trelease, *supra* note 1219, at 752-58. "If the government were to take the water for use on the reserved land, it would have the better right, though not the first use, and the first user could lose his water." *Id.* at 757.

[1228] *See* Fairfax & Tarlock, *supra* note 227, at 533-54.

[1229] *See supra* text accompanying notes 1191-97.

[1230] The NFMA regulations require forest planners to provide for "[g]eneral estimates of current water uses, both consumptive and non-consumptive, including instream flow requirements with the area of land covered by the forest plan." 36 C.F.R. § 219.23(a) (1984).

Delegated administrative authority to set instream flows is a logical and essential aspect of the Forest Service's organic authority to manage its lands on a multiple-use basis. Several western states lack instream flow programs, while others are moving slowly to establish instream flows.[1231] The Forest Service, however, has an independent statutory mandate to manage the wildlife and recreation resources on all national forest lands.[1232]

The notion that Congress has delegated authority to the Forest Service to make site-specific, future-looking decisions follows from the case law. Although Congress has traditionally deferred to state water law,[1233] Congress also has delegated to the Forest Service expansive management authority over diverse activities under the 1897 Organic Act's mandate to regulate "occupancy and use" in the national forests.[1234] As early as 1911, the Court recognized delegated administrative authority that allowed the Forest Service to override state fencing laws.[1235] Fencing laws, like state water laws, are deeply engrained in the West. Yet the agency's power to regulate was found in the "occupancy and use" directive. More recently, delegated administrative authority has permitted federal regulation of wildlife, a traditional prerogative of the states.[1236] Forest Service regulatory authority also was confirmed in the controversial domain of hardrock mining, another area with strong traditions of local control.[1237] Forest Service delegated authority over water resources is fortified by the highly specific provision in the 1897 Organic Act that "waters within the boundaries of national forests may be used . . . under the laws of

---

[1231] *See, e.g.*, CAL. WATER CODE § 1243 (West 1984); COLO. REV. STAT. § 37-92-102(3) (1983); IDAHO CODE § 67-4301 (1984); MONT. CODE ANN. § 89-866(2) (1977); OR. REV. STAT. §§ 537.170(3)(a), 543.225(3)(a) (1983). *See generally* Fairfax & Tarlock, *supra* note 227; Tarlock, *Recent Developments in the Recognition of Instream Uses in Western Water Law*, 1975 UTAH L. REV. 871; Tarlock, *supra* note 1089; UTAH WATER RESEARCH LABORATORY, UTAH STATE UNIV., ADAPTING APPROPRIATION WATER LAW TO ACCOMODATE EQUITABLE CONSIDERATION OF INSTREAM FLOW USES (1983).

[1232] *See, e.g.*, 16 U.S.C. §§ 481, 551, 559, 1600(6) (1982); 42 U.S.C. § 4332(1) (1982).

[1233] *See supra* text accompanying notes 1090-93.

[1234] *See supra* section II(A).

[1235] Light v. United States, 220 U.S. 523 (1911).

[1236] *See, e.g.*, Kleppe v. New Mexico, 426 U.S. 529 (1976); United States v. Brown, 552 F.2d 817 (8th Cir.), *cert. denied*, 431 U.S. 949 (1977) (preemption of state hunting law by valid administrative regulation).

[1237] United States v. Weiss, 642 F.2d 296 (9th Cir. 1981), discussed *infra* in text accompanying notes 1361-62.

the State or under the laws of the United States and the rules and regulations established thereunder."[1238]

Ultimately, the question is whether the congressionally defined management purposes for the national forests are broad enough to encompass the kinds of control over water discussed here. Whatever the law may be with regard to the Bureau of Land Management,[1239] it is certain that the Forest Service's organic statutes define a considerably broader scope of agency authority. The most extensive administrative opinion on the subject, issued in 1981 by the Department of Justice,[1240] acknowledged Congress's authority to preempt state law by delegating authority over water matters to federal agencies and recognized that the question boils down to the construction of each land management agency's statutory authorization:

> Federal water rights may be asserted without regard to state law [through] specific congressional directives that override inconsistent state law, and the establishment of primary purposes for the management of federal lands . . . that would be frustrated by the application of state law.[1241]

The issue is not free from uncertainty, but a principled analysis supports the conclusion that the Forest Service possesses delegated authority to set instream flows on designated watercourses.

(b) Authority to Condition or Deny Access

Regardless of the Forest Service's delegated authority to set instream flows, there is no question that the agency has the power to deny or condition access to developers seeking to divert water within the national forests. The right-of-way provisions of FLPMA[1242] grant discretionary authority to allow water

---

[1238] 16 U.S.C. § 481 (1982), discussed *supra* in text accompanying notes 1094-1104. The Court has found that statute does not grant authority to allocate water rights to private parties, see *supra* note 1102, but no opinion has cast doubt on the statute's plain meaning to provide for administrative regulatory authority over water use within the forests.

[1239] *See supra* notes 1218-19.

[1240] Justice Dep't Memorandum, *supra* note 1218.

[1241] *Id.* at 76.

[1242] *See* 43 U.S.C. §§ 1761-1771 (1982). The regulations on special use permits are set out at 36 C.F.R. §§ 251.50-.64 (1984). The Forest Service Manual provisions on special use permits for water developments are at FOREST SERVICE MANUAL § 2541.6 (1984). Stop orders may be issued against persons engaging in construction without authorization. 36 C.F.R. § 251.61 (1984). The FLPMA provisions replaced existing authority, which divided responsibility between the

works.[1243] If a diversion is permitted, the Forest Service has a duty to impose conditions that will protect the environment.[1244]

Regulating water diversions in this manner does not protect a watercourse as fully as would setting an instream flow. Diversions jeopardizing the streamflow level still can be made upstream from the national forests or on private holdings within the forests; these diversions would be outside of the permitting process. Nevertheless, the Forest Service's authority to deny or condition future water diversions on national forests gives the agency considerable potential for protecting water resources.

A recent example of the Forest Service's ability to achieve instream flows through the permitting process was provided by the agency's grant of conditional easements over national forest lands

---

Forest Service and the Department of the Interior. *See supra* text accompanying notes 1108-13. Forest Service authority under the FLPMA is discussed in City and County of Denver v. Bergland, 517 F. Supp. 155, 178-80 (D. Colo. 1981), *modified on other grounds*, 695 F.2d 465 (10th Cir. 1982).

[1243] *See* 43 U.S.C. § 1761(a) (1982) (Secretary of Agriculture authorized to grant rights of way for water development and transportation systems).

[1244] 43 U.S.C. § 1765 (1982) requires that each special use authorization "shall contain":

(a) terms and conditions which will (i) carry out the purposes of this Act and rules and regulations issued thereunder; (ii) minimize damage to scenic and esthetic values and fish and wildlife habitat and otherwise protect the environment; (iii) require compliance with applicable air and water quality standards established by or pursuant to applicable Federal or State law; and (iv) require compliance with State standards for public health and safety, environmental protection, and siting, construction, operation, and maintenance of or for rights of way for similar purposes if those standards are more stringent than applicable Federal standards; and

(b) such terms and conditions as the Secretary concerned deems necessary to (i) protect Federal property and economic interests; (ii) manage efficiently the lands which are subject to the right-of-way or adjacent thereto and protect the other lawful users of the lands adjacent to or traversed by such right-of-way; (iii) protect lives and property; (iv) protect the interests of individuals living in the general area traversed by the right-of-way who rely on the fish, wildlife, and other biotic resources of the area for subsistence purposes; (v) require location of the right-of-way along a route that will cause least damage to the environment, taking into consideration feasibility and other relevant factors; and (vi) otherwise protect the public interest. . . ."

In wilderness areas, authorization for water development must be granted by the President. 16 U.S.C. § 1133(d)(4) (1982). Of course, Congress can include special authorization for water projects in legislation, as it did in the Holy Cross Wilderness Area in Colorado. Colorado Wilderness Act § 102(a)(5), 94 Stat. 3266 (1980).

in Colorado for the Homestake II project.[1245] Homestake II contemplated transporting water from the western slope of the Rockies to two eastern slope cities. The Forest Service, acting as lead agency in preparing the Homestake II environmental impact statement (EIS), required:

> [T]hat environmental maintenance flows be provided in all streams affected by diversions. This means that a set amount of water [will] be provided at all times to protect fisheries, maintain channel stability, and enhance visual resources . . . . The bypass flow mechanism will be nonadjustable and one that is permanently and unalterably fixed.[1246]

Moreover, the Forest Service required mitigation of stream "dry-up" caused by Phase I of the same project. The Forest Service declared: "Prior to the start of construction on Phase II, the mitigation of impacts resulting from Phase I must be initiated. . . . A major mitigation action will be provision of instream flows."[1247] The Homestake II EIS acknowledged that water rights for the project were properly under the jurisdiction of the state of Colorado.[1248] Nevertheless, the Forest Service concluded that "[t]he request of the Cities to use the National Forest land without the conditions and stipulations of the easement would violate FLPMA and the request would be denied."[1249] The final project authorization required the cities to protect environmental, fish, and wildlife values during and after construction;[1250] required instream flow bypasses to correct Phase I impacts;[1251] and established "FLPMA flows" (minimum streamflows imposed as condi-

---

[1245] FOREST SERVICE, U.S. DEP'T OF AGRICULTURE, RECORD OF DECISION FOR HOMESTAKE PHASE II PROJECT (1983) [hereinafter cited as HOMESTAKE II RECORD OF DECISION], FINAL ENVIRONMENTAL IMPACT STATEMENT (1983) [hereinafter cited as HOMESTAKE II EIS] (on file at Oregon Law Review office).

[1246] HOMESTAKE II RECORD OF DECISION, *supra* note 1245, at 3-4.

[1247] *Id.* at 4.

[1248] *Id.* at 6. The Forest Service's position in Colorado is that instream flows required by the permitting process do not restrict private acquisition of water under state law; they merely condition entry into the national forests in order to protect environmental amenities. "The Forest Service can't stop you from getting all the water you want under state law, but it can make you get it elsewhere." Telephone conversation with Mike Gippert, Deputy Regional Attorney, Office of Gen. Counsel, U.S. Dep't of Agriculture (Feb. 2, 1984).

[1249] HOMESTAKE II EIS, *supra* note 1245, at 9.

[1250] "The Grantee shall protect the scenic aesthetic values and the fish and wildlife habitat values of the area under this easement, and the adjacent land, as far as possible, during construction, operation, and maintenance of the improvements." HOMESTAKE II RECORD OF DECISION, *supra* note 1245, exhibit 4, at 6.

[1251] *Id.* at 8.

tions under the FLPMA permitting authority) on all project-affected streams.[1252]

D. Water Power Projects

The Forest Service has reacted with some uncertainty concerning the extent of its authority to regulate hydroelectric facilities within national forests.[1253] The regulatory competitor for authority over dam siting and operation is not the states but another federal agency, the Federal Energy Regulatory Commission (FERC), formerly the Federal Power Commission. FERC has claimed sole discretion over dam siting, including dams that will be located on national forest lands.[1254] The Federal Power Act of 1920, however, delegates concurrent authority to land management agencies to impose "such conditions as the Secretary of the department under whose supervision such reservation falls shall deem necessary for the adequate protection and utilization of such reservations."[1255]

The problem of hydroelectric dam siting has become particularly acute since enactment of the Public Utility Regulatory and Power Act of 1978[1256] (PURPA), which requires utilities to purchase power from private renewable energy sources on an avoided cost basis.[1257] Since the Act provides a guaranteed market for energy producers, hundreds of private developers sought preliminary permits for hydroelectric facility construction in the West. The "dam rush" has generated concern over the adverse effects on commercial and game fish that spawn in the same national forest streams proposed as dam sites.[1258] In 1984 the Forest

---

[1252] *Id.* at 8-9.

[1253] *See generally supra* notes 1116-21 and accompanying text.

[1254] *Id.*

[1255] 16 U.S.C. § 797(e) (1982).

[1256] *Id.* § 824a.

[1257] *Id.* § 824a-3(b).

[1258] The Chairman of FERC has written:

The debate over hydro proposals is not inexorably between energy and the environment. In fact, hydro projects can substantially enhance trout fisheries if properly managed. Examples are numerous: the Delaware River system in New York and Pennsylvania, the White and Little Red Rivers in Arkansas, the Taylor River in Colorado, and the Missouri River in Montana, among many others. There may, indeed, be cases where conservationists would like to promote hydro projects . . . . In other cases, mitigating license conditions result in both energy increments and relatively benign environmental consequences. Always the question centers on the facts of the case.

Service estimated "that in the next decade, 3,000 hydroelectric projects will be proposed for licensing on [national forest] lands."[1259]

The Supreme Court recently resolved the issue in favor of the Forest Service and other land management agencies. In *Escondido Mutual Water Company v. La Jolla, Rincon, San Pasqual, Pauma, and Pala Bands of Mission Indians*,[1260] the Court strictly construed the language in 16 U.S.C. § 797(e) that licenses "shall be subject" to conditions deemed necessary by the affected agency: "[W]hile Congress intended that the Commission would have exclusive authority to issue all licenses, it wanted the individual Secretaries to continue to play the major role in determining what conditions would be included in the license in order to protect the resources under their respective jurisdiction."[1261] The conditions imposed by the Secretary must be reasonable and supported by the record.[1262]

In sum, the Forest Service appears to have ample authority to condition dam licenses granted by FERC in order to protect fish, wildlife, and recreation.

Letter from Mike Butler, in Fly Fisherman 17, 20 (Dec. 1983). The conservation chairman of the Northern California Council of the Federation of Fly Fishers responded:

> Here in northern California, small hydro projects are—next to major water development projects—the one significant threat to our fisheries in general and our anandromous fisheries in particular.
>
> Applications have been filed for more than 700 projects (over 40 in the Trinity River watershed alone) and 44 projects are ongoing. Without tax benefits and rate-payer subsidies, small hydro projects can not be economical. By way of illustration, the maximum output of the 700-plus plants would be less than that of one average power plant.
>
> The council is filing objections to certain specific projects and has convinced the Department of Fish and Game to take a closer look at the possible consequences of these projects. Fisherfolk in other parts of the nation should also get involved—bemoaning the loss of a fishery after the fact does no good.

Letter from S. T. Reynolds, in Fly Fisherman 22 (March 1984).

[1259] Letter from J.B. Hilmon, Acting Deputy Chief, Forest Service, to Christopher Meyer (Feb. 14, 1984), *reprinted in* Brief of Amici Curiae National Wildlife Federation at B-5 app., Escondido Mut. Water Co. v. La Jolla, Rincon, San Pasqual, Pauma, and Palla [sic] Bands of Mission Indians, 104 S. Ct. 2105 (1984) (available on Lexis, Genfed library, Briefs file).

[1260] 104 S. Ct. 2105 (1984).

[1261] *Id.* at 2111.

[1262] *Id.* at 2112.

E. The Wild and Scenic Rivers Act

The Wild and Scenic Rivers Act of 1968[1263] was Congress's first effort to provide specific protection for national forest waterways. The legislation was patterned after laws adopted by various western states that had dedicated portions of rivers to "free flowing" status.[1264] The Act recognizes three designations of protected rivers: (1) wild rivers are "essentially primitive and . . . unpolluted [representing] vestiges of primitive America";[1265] (2) scenic rivers are "largely undeveloped, but accessible in places by roads";[1266] and (3) recreational rivers are "readily accessible" and "may have some development" including impoundments or diversions.[1267] Dams are prohibited "on or directly affecting" any river designated under the Act.[1268]

All federal lands within the boundaries of any designated river are withdrawn from "entry, sale, or other disposition,"[1269] but mining is treated specially. Subject to existing rights, minerals situated within one-quarter mile of the bank of any wild, but not scenic or recreational, river are withdrawn from mineral leasing and location;[1270] mining near scenic and recreational rivers may continue but only subject to regulation designed to "provide safeguards against pollution . . . and unnecessary impairment of the scenery."[1271] Surface coal mining is prohibited on all wild, scenic, and recreational rivers by the Surface Mining Control and Reclamation Act of 1977.[1272]

Administration of designated rivers remains in the agency that had jurisdiction over the land before designation. Management authority is stated in general terms for all three classes of rivers.

[1263] 16 U.S.C. §§ 1271-1287 (1982). *See generally* Fairfax, Andrews & Buchsbaum, *Federalism and the Wild and Scenic Rivers Act: Now You See It, Now You Don't,* 59 WASH. L. REV. 417 (1984); Tarlock & Tippy, *The Wild and Scenic Rivers Act of 1968,* 55 CORNELL L. REV. 707 (1970).

[1264] The first state program was formulated in Oregon, when a 1915 statute withdrew from appropriation streams forming scenic waterfalls. OR. REV. STAT. § 538.200 (1983). The list of designated streams has been expanded. *See id.* ch. 538. *See also* IDAHO CODE §§ 67-4301 to -4312 (1984).

[1265] 16 U.S.C. § 1273(b)(1) (1982).

[1266] *Id.* § 1273(b)(2).

[1267] *Id.* § 1273(b)(3).

[1268] *Id.* § 1278(a).

[1269] *Id.* § 1279(a). Detailed descriptions of boundaries are established by the agency administering the land surrounding the designated river. *Id.* § 1274(b).

[1270] *Id.* § 1280(a)(iii).

[1271] *Id.* § 1280(a) (1982).

[1272] 30 U.S.C. § 1272(e)(1) (1982).

They "shall be administered in such manner as to protect and enhance the values which caused . . . [the river] to be included in said system."[1273]

Pollution is expressly addressed in the Act. It requires: "Particular attention shall be given to scheduled timber harvesting, road construction, and similar activities which might be contrary to the purposes" of the Act.[1274] The Forest Service must cooperate with state water pollution control agencies to ensure the elimination of pollution from the rivers.[1275] In spite of these broad statutory goals and directives to build a structured administrative program, the Forest Service's regulations are perfunctory.[1276]

The Wild and Scenic Rivers Act requires the Secretary of Agriculture to study whether additional rivers should be added to the system.[1277] The Forest Service is presently engaged in such a study, which will likely have important ramifications for many forests.[1278]

[1273] 16 U.S.C. § 1281(a) (1982).

[1274] *Id.* § 1283(a).

[1275] *Id.* § 1283(a).

[1276] *See* 36 C.F.R. pt. 297 (1984).

[1277] 16 U.S.C. § 1276(d) (1982).

[1278] That study is discussed in the section on recreation. *See infra* section VIII.

VI

MINERALS

The national forests contain a significant portion of the nation's store of minerals,[1279] but regulation of mineral development is not an activity traditionally associated with the Forest Service. Over time a number of factors, unique to the mineral resource, have inhibited effective and comprehensive management of the mineral resource within the forests. Most notable is the extraordinary character of the General Mining Law of 1872[1280] (1872 Act or Hardrock Act), which dominates the acquisition of metalliferous minerals in national forests. This century-old statute allows entry, exploration, and mining as a matter of self-initiation; no permit is required for hardrock mining. Accordingly, the Forest Service's authority over miners historically has been weaker than over any other user group.

The Forest Service shares control over mineral policy with the Department of the Interior, through the Bureau of Land Management (BLM). The BLM has authority through the Hardrock Act and the Mineral Leasing Act of 1920[1281] to issue hardrock patents and mineral leases. Thus in mining law and policy, as with the regulation of water quality, a degree of management authority within the national forests is vested in a federal agency other than the Forest Service. This overlapping jurisdiction has been a second obstacle to effective mineral management by the Forest Service.

[1279] The primary mineral-producing areas are:
the National Forests of the Rocky Mountains, the Basin and Range Province, the Cascade-Sierra Nevada Ranges, the Alaska Coast Range, and the States of Missouri, Minnesota, and Wisconsin. Less known but apparently good mineral potential exists in the southern and eastern National Forests.

Geologically, the National Forest system lands contain some of the most favorable host rocks for mineral deposits. Approximately 6.5 million acres are known to be underlain by coal. Approximately 45 million acres or one-quarter of the National Forest System lands have potential for oil and gas, while 300,000 acres have oil shale potential. Another 300,000 acres have known phosphate potential. A large proportion of the most promising areas for geothermal development occur in the National Forests of the Pacific Coast and Great Basin States.

FOREST SERVICE, U.S. DEP'T OF AGRICULTURE, MINING IN NATIONAL FORESTS 1 (1979) [hereinafter cited as MINING IN NATIONAL FORESTS].

[1280] 30 U.S.C. §§ 22-54 (1982).

[1281] *Id.* §§ 181-287.

The 1872 Act has also created a land use problem of far-reaching proportions. At the ill-defined moment when a miner makes a "discovery" of a valuable hardrock mineral, the miner acquires an unpatented mining claim, a property right that entitles the miner not only to the minerals in the deposit but also to "exclusive use and possession" of twenty acres of land overlying the find.[1282] The national forests are blanketed with hundreds of thousands of such claims, many of which are of doubtful validity.[1283] Weeding the bad claims from the good is an inordinately time-consuming task for federal land managers.

In spite of these obstacles, over the last fifteen years the Forest Service has rapidly expanded its role in managing national forest mineral resources. Indeed, the evolution of Forest Service mineral policy is likely to be one of the most enduring developments within the agency during modern times. The Service has steadily gained a significant measure of control over hardrock mining operations and, despite the considerable amount of authority vested in the BLM, seems to have become the dominant federal agency in the management of both hardrock and leasable minerals in the national forests. As we discuss in this section, the National Forest Management Act (NFMA) planning process appears certain to accelerate these trends.

This section first traces the evolution of Forest Service mineral policy. It then analyzes current Forest Service authority over mineral development. Finally, it discusses the role of mineral resources in land management planning. The subject of mining in wilderness areas is treated separately in the wilderness section.

A. Evolution of Policy

1. Early Minerals Policy (1785-1891)

Congress recognized the special value of minerals as early as the Ordinance of 1785,[1284] when Congress reserved "one-third

---

[1282] *See infra* text accompanying notes 1293-95.

[1283] The BLM has recorded 1.7 million mining claims, of which approximately 1.1 million are still active, since 1976; approximately 140,000 new claims are received each year. BUREAU OF LAND MANAGEMENT, U.S. DEP'T OF THE INTERIOR, MANAGING THE NATION'S PUBLIC LANDS—FISCAL YEAR 1984, 20 (1985). No breakdown was made for claims on national forest lands.

[1284] Ordinance of May 20, 1785, 28 J. CONTINENTAL CONGRESS 375-376, 378 (Fitzpatrick ed. 1933), *quoted in* 1 AMERICAN LAW OF MINING § 408 (2d ed. 1985).

part of all the gold, silver, lead and copper mines to be sold or otherwise disposed of as Congress shall hereafter direct." In the early days of the Republic, some were aware that minerals might prove a source of national revenue.[1285] However, federal mining legislation lagged because miners on the public lands preferred to be governed by their own regulations. When the California Gold Rush ensued in 1848 and the need for order became critical, the miners themselves quickly developed rudimentary mining laws. Their system, initially based on custom, was sanctioned by judicial decision and incorporated into state statutes.[1286] Early federal policy was one of benign neglect.[1287]

In 1866 and 1870 Congress validated the miners' actions on the public land.[1288] The public domain lands were declared "free and open to exploration . . . by all citizens of the United States."[1289] Subsequently, Congress consolidated the provisions of the two existing statutes and passed the General Mining Law of 1872, which remains the basic law governing hardrock mining.[1290]

[1285] 1 C. LINDLEY, LINDLEY ON MINES § 30, at 60-61 (3d ed. 1914).

[1286] *See, e.g.,* Morton v. Solambo Copper Mining Co., 26 Cal. 528 (1864) (laws based on custom); Hicks v. Bell, 3 Cal. 220 (1853) (state regulation of miners). On customs in the mining camps, see R. PAUL, CALIFORNIA GOLD: THE BEGINNING OF MINING IN THE FAR WEST 69-90, 210-39 (1947).

[1287] The miners were technically trespassers on the public land. United States v. Gear, 44 U.S. (3 How.) 120 (1845). At the time of the gold rush there were no statutes authorizing the removal of minerals from the public domain. The miners asserted that right, however, and federal law enforcement authorities could do little to stop them. LINDLEY ON MINES, *supra* note 1285, § 41, at 72. The Department of the Interior, which had been created on March 3, 1849, was responsible for supervising the mining lands through the General Land Office.

[1288] Under the Act of July 26, 1866, ch. 262, 14 Stat. 251-52, lode claims were subject to patent. A lode deposit, often referred to as a "vein", is a zone of mineralized rock embedded in neighboring nonmineralized rock. *See generally* FOREST SERVICE, U.S. DEP'T OF AGRICULTURE, ANATOMY OF A MINE—FROM PROSPECT TO PRODUCTION 5 (1975) [hereinafter cited as ANATOMY OF A MINE]. The 1866 Act has been called the "miner's Magna Carta" because it legalized existing trespass. Placer claims were made patentable under the Act of July 9, 1870, ch. 235, 16 Stat. 217. Placers are superficial deposits not in place, created by ancient rivers or found in alluvial beds of active streams. *See* ANATOMY OF A MINE, *supra,* at 5.

[1289] Act of July 26, 1866, ch. 262, 14 Stat. 251-52 (currently codified as amended at 30 U.S.C. § 22 (1982)).

[1290] Act of May 10, 1872, ch. 152, 17 Stat. 91 (currently codified as amended at 30 U.S.C. §§ 22-54 (1982)). The opening section of the Act states:

Except as otherwise provided, all valuable mineral deposits in lands belonging to the United States, both surveyed and unsurveyed, shall be free and open to exploration and purchase, and the lands in which they are found to occupation and purchase, by citizens of the United States and

The 1872 Act provides that the public lands, unless withdrawn by the President or Congress, are open to prospecting. A prospecting miner is protected in the immediate region of the mine by the doctrine of *pedis possessio*.[1291] If a miner then discovers a valuable mineral deposit,[1292] the miner obtains a vested real property interest in the minerals and overlying twenty acres called an unpatented mining claim.[1293] An unpatented claim gives the miner "the exclusive right of possession and enjoyment of all the surface . . . within the lines of" the location[1294] and the right to proceed

---

those who have declared their intention to become such, under regulations prescribed by law, and according to the local customs or rules of miners in the several mining districts, so far as the same are applicable and not inconsistent with the laws of the United States.

30 U.S.C. § 22 (1982).

This law reenacted the 1866 and 1870 Acts, with several alterations, as a single statute. *See id.* §§ 22-39. *See generally* Reeves, *The Origin and Development of the Rules of Discovery*, 8 LAND & WATER L. REV. 1 (1973); Strauss, *Mining Claims on Public Lands: A Study of Interior Department Procedures*, 1974 UTAH L. REV. 185.

[1291] The Supreme Court in Union Oil Co. v. Smith, 249 U.S. 337 (1919), described the miner's *pedis possessio* interest as:

an express invitation to all qualified persons to explore the lands of the United States for valuable mineral deposits, and this and the following sections hold out to one who succeeds in making discovery the promise of a full reward . . . [They] are not treated as mere trespassers, but as licensees or tenants at will. . . . It is held that upon the public domain a miner may hold the place in which he may be working against all others having no better right, and while he remains in possession, diligently working towards discovery, is entitled—at least for a reasonable time—to be protected against forcible, fraudulent, and clandestine intrusions upon his possession.

Id. at 346-47. *See generally* 2 AMERICAN LAW OF MINING, *supra* note 1284, at §§ 34.01-.06.

[1292] On the definition of "discovery", see United States v. Coleman, 390 U.S. 599 (1968) (construing 30 U.S.C. § 22 (1982)). There are two components to the modern test for discovery. First, "a person of ordinary prudence" must be "justified in the further expenditure of his labor and means, with a reasonable prospect of success, in developing a valuable mine." Second, the mine must meet the so-called "marketability test"—the mineral must be "extracted, removed and marketed at a profit." *Id.* at 602-03. *See generally* 2 AMERICAN LAW OF MINING, *supra* note 1284, at §§ 35.11-.12. After discovery, a miner must locate, or stake, the claim and comply with state recording requirements. 30 U.S.C. §§ 23, 28 (1982).

[1293] On the nature of the vested property right, see, *e.g.*, United States v. Etcheverry, 230 F.2d 193, 195 (10th Cir. 1956); Freese v. United States, 639 F.2d 754 (Ct. Cl.), *cert. denied*, 454 U.S. 827 (1981); Skaw v. United States, 740 F.2d 932 (Ct. Cl. 1984).

[1294] 30 U.S.C. § 26 (1982).

to mine the mineral without any payment to the government.[1295] A miner with a valid discovery of a valuable mineral then has the option of purchasing the land for a nominal price and receiving a patent in fee.[1296] This body of law, so favorable to hardrock miners, traces to the need to develop the young country's mineral potential, the federal policy of opening the West and disposing of public land, and the miners' determination to be left to local, rather than federal, control.[1297]

The General Mining Law, then, is short and unambiguous. Nineteenth century federal agents assumed that they could perform only the most perfunctory ministerial tasks. Indeed, the Interior Department's longstanding position was that there was no authority to regulate mining or miners and that the Department could do little but issue patents.[1298]

2. Early Forest Service Policy (1891-1950)

Initially, mining was not permitted in the forest reserves, which were created by presidential proclamation and withdrawn from mineral and other forms of entry.[1299] From 1891 until 1897, western and eastern lawmakers battled over this locking up of mineral lands.[1300] After six years of heated controversy, the western repre-

---

[1295] *See generally* 2 AMERICAN LAW OF MINING, *supra* note 1284, at §§ 36.01-.05. The holder of an unpatented claim must expend $100 per year in labor or improvements in order to keep the unpatented claim alive. 30 U.S.C. § 28 (1982). The Federal Land Policy and Management Act of 1976 (FLPMA) established requirements for recordation of all mining claims. *See* 43 U.S.C. § 1744 (1982). The recordation provisions were upheld in United States v. Locke, _ U.S. _, 105 S. Ct. 1785 (1985).

[1296] *See* 30 U.S.C. § 29 (1982) ($5 per acre for lode claims); 30 U.S.C. § 37 (1982) ($2.50 per acre for placer claims).

[1297] *See generally* J. LESHY, THE MINING LAW OF 1872: A STUDY IN PERPETUAL MOTION (publication forthcoming 1986); Hochmuth, *Government Administration and Attitudes in Contest and Patent Proceedings*, 10 ROCKY MTN. MIN. L. INST. 467 (1965).

[1298] *See* Clipper Mining Co. v. Eli Mining & Land Co., 194 U.S. 220 (1904); Francis M. Bishop, 5 Pub. Lands Dec. 429 (1887).

[1299] J. ISE, *supra* note 48, at 125; LINDLEY ON MINES, *supra* note 1285, at 413.

[1300] Several bills introduced during the early 1890s dealt with the forest reserves. *See supra* text accompanying notes 226-59. However, since none provided for opening the reserves to mining, western lawmakers opposed them. Representative Hermann of Oregon led the westerners' opposition by offering an amendment to the McRae bill, *infra* note 248, stating that "prospectors and mineral claimants shall have access to such forest reservations for the purpose of prospecting, locating, and developing the mineral resources thereof." 27 CONG. REC. 86 (1894). Hermann explained that "[w]e of the West, particularly the

sentatives prevailed. Eastern conservationists realized that if forest reserves were not opened to mining, they would be abolished altogether. As a result, they did not wage a "very spirited contest" to the compromise bill of 1897.[1301] Thus, the 1897 Organic Act permitted not only mining in the forest reserves, but also gave miners free access to the timber and stone their operations required.[1302]

Congress did not completely relinquish federal control over mining on national forests. The 1897 Act provides "that such . . . [prospectors and locators] must comply with rules and regulations covering such forest reservations."[1303] However, the Forest Service interpreted this regulatory authority narrowly.[1304] For instance, Gifford Pinchot, then Chief Forester, believed that "it was not the intention of government in creating National Forests to antagonize the mining industry."[1305]

When Congress transferred administrative jurisdiction over the national forests from the Department of the Interior to the Department of Agriculture in 1905, minerals management remained with Interior. Thus, Interior held primary authority over

---

Representatives from the mineral land States felt that a gross injustice was perpetrated on the mineral interests by reason of the proposed legislation, and we protested against the discrimination." *Id.* at 110. Representative Thomas R. McRae acceded to the amendment reluctantly: "More concessions have been made to the mining interests than I thought necessary or just, but I was willing, in order to pass the bill, to accept them." *Id.* at 113. Once the mining issue was resolved, the western legislators favored the bill. For example, Representative Pence of Colorado stated, "I favor it especially for the reason that the experience of the last three years has shown us that the forest reservations stand as a dead wall against the progress of prospecting for gold ores." *Id.* at 366. *See also id.* at 367 (remarks of Rep. Coffeen of Wyoming).

[1301] J. ISE, *supra* note 48, at 136, 141.

[1302] Act of June 4, 1897, ch. 2, 30 Stat. 35 (codified at 16 U.S.C. §§ 477, 478 (1982)).

[1303] 16 U.S.C. § 478 (1982).

[1304] As evidence of the Act's effects on agency policy ten years later, the Forest Service 1907 Use Book stated:

[Prospectors] go on just as if there were no National Forests there. The prospector is absolutely free to travel about and explore just as much as he pleases and wherever he pleases without asking anybody's permission. . . . Prospecting and mining are absolutely unchecked. The resources of the National Forests must be used and the country opened up. Therefore, the more mining and prospecting the better.

1907 USE BOOK, *supra* note 1104, at 10-11.

[1305] LINDLEY ON MINES, *supra* note 1285, § 198, at 417-18.

mining in the national forests while the extent of Forest Service authority over minerals was undefined.[1306]

In spite of the general laissez-faire attitude toward mining on the public lands, some restrictions on the miner's right in national forests did evolve. The Department of the Interior developed the "prudent person" test to define a "valuable" mineral discovery.[1307] In response to widespread abuse of the mining laws for nonmining purposes, the Forest Service adopted regulations that restricted use and occupancy of mining claims to those activities necessary for development of the claim.[1308] Further, the Service sometimes limited rights-of-way across national forest lands for mining purposes. In some instances, miners were required to obtain access permits that could be denied if incompatible with the public interest.[1309] The Forest Service made no attempt with these early programs, however, to regulate valid prospecting or mining activity.

National forest mining law and policy underwent major reform in 1920, when Congress placed most energy fuels under a leasing system.[1310] Change began in 1909 when President Taft, fearful that the Navy's fuel supply was diminishing, unilaterally withdrew

---

[1306] The Transfer Act of Feb. 1, 1905, states, "The Secretary of Agriculture . . . shall . . . execute . . . all laws affecting public lands heretofore or hereafter reserved . . . excepting such laws as affect surveying, prospecting, appropriating, entering, . . . or patenting of any such lands." Act of Feb. 1, 1905, ch. 288, 33 Stat. 628 (codified at 16 U.S.C. § 472 (1982)). See infra text accompanying notes 1366-1422.

[1307] Castle v. Womble, 19 Pub. Lands Dec. 455 (1894) (discovery valid only if a person of ordinary prudence would be justified in making further expenditures on claims with a reasonable prospect of success).

[1308] Federal mining regulations were upheld in Teller v. United States, 113 F. 273 (10th Cir. 1901) (unlawful cutting and exporting of timber from mining claim); United States v. Rizzinelli, 182 F. 675 (D. Idaho 1910) (operating of saloon on mining claim held unlawful). For examples of illegal activities, see J. ISE, supra note 48, at 265; COMPTROLLER GENERAL, U.S. GENERAL ACCOUNTING OFFICE, REPORT TO THE CONGRESS: MODERNIZATION OF 1872 MINING LAW NEEDED TO ENCOURAGE DOMESTIC MINERAL PRODUCTION, PROTECT THE ENVIRONMENT, AND IMPROVE PUBLIC LAND MANAGEMENT (July 25, 1974) (hereinafter cited as 1974 GAO REPORT); Miller, Surface Use Rights Under The General Mining Law: Good Faith and Common Sense, 28 ROCKY MTN. MIN. L. INST. 761, 770-76 (1983).

[1309] LINDLEY ON MINES, supra note 1285, § 198, at 425-27. On access to mining claims see generally Biddle, supra note 338; Martz, Love & Kaiser, supra note 342. See also supra notes 338-42.

[1310] See Mineral Leasing Act of 1920, 30 U.S.C. §§ 181-287 (1982).

large amounts of public lands from oil and gas entry.[1311] In 1910, Congress enacted the Pickett Act,[1312] which authorized the President temporarily to withdraw land from mining for nonmetalliferous fuel minerals. Pursuant to this authority, the executive withdrew from mineral location virtually all of the unappropriated public lands.[1313] Between 1910 and 1920, conservationists pressed continuously for a leasing system for fuel and fertilizer minerals and ultimately prevailed. The Mineral Leasing Act of 1920 effectively withdrew all such minerals from location under the General Mining Law.[1314] Congress also authorized the Secretary of the Interior to lease these minerals at his discretion and to attach conditions to the leases in order to protect public resources and the public interest. Thus the Mineral Leasing Act eliminated the miner's unqualified access to an important class of minerals.

Initially the Forest Service had little control over mineral leasing in the national forests because leasable minerals, like hardrock deposits, were managed by the Interior Department. However, the Acquired Lands Act of 1947[1315] established a separate mineral leasing system for all minerals, including hardrock minerals,

---

[1311] President Taft withdrew 3,000,000 acres of valuable oil lands in Wyoming and California to conserve the mineral resources. His action was affirmed in United States v. Midwest Oil Co., 236 U.S. 459 (1915).

[1312] Pickett Act, ch. 421, 36 Stat. 847 (1910) (codified at 43 U.S.C. §§ 141, 142, *repealed by* PUB. L. No. 94-579, § 704(a), 90 Stat. 2792 (1976).

[1313] P. GATES, *supra* note 26, at 736.

[1314] Nonmetalliferous fuel minerals include the fossil fuel minerals (oil, gas, shale oil, coal, native asphalt, and bituminous rock) and the fertilizer and chemical minerals (phosphate, potash, and sodium). Uranium is an energy fuel but it remains open for location under the General Mining Law. *See* 1 THE AMERICAN LAW OF MINING, *supra* note 1284, §§ 4.15-.19.

Coal had long been treated differently from other minerals. Under the first coal act in 1864, Act of July 1, 1864, ch. 205, 13 Stat. §§ 343-344, which preceded the General Mining Law, coal deposits were reserved by the United States and subject to sale. Coal continued to be treated separately under an 1873 act, 17 Stat. 607 (1873). *See* P. GATES, *supra* note 26, at 724-30. Then, in 1920, the Mineral Leasing Act superceded the prior coal acts and included coal as a leasable mineral. 30 U.S.C. § 193 (1982). *See generally* L. MALL, PUBLIC LAND AND MINING LAW 85-86 (3d ed. 1981); Barry, *The Surface Mining Control and Reclamation Act of 1977 and the Office of Surface Mining: Moving Targets or Immovable Objects?*, 27 ROCKY MTN. MIN. L. INST. 169 (1982); Krulitz, *Management of Federal Coal Reserves*, 24 ROCKY MTN. MIN. L. INST. 139 (1978). Geothermal resources are now also subject to leasing under the Geothermal Steam Act of 1970, 30 U.S.C. §§ 1001-1025 (1982).

[1315] 30 U.S.C. §§ 351-359 (1982).

found on acquired public lands.[1316] Under this system the Interior Department can issue leases only with approval by the agency managing the affected surface lands.[1317] The power to deny lease approval therefore allowed the Forest Service to gain control over mineral development on acquired national forest lands. In 1947 Congress also passed the Materials Disposal Act,[1318] which provided for the sale of certain specified common variety minerals. Under this Act, the Forest Service, not Interior, was granted authority over these deposits within national forests.[1319]

In sum, by the end of the 1940s minerals were divided into three major categories: those locatable under the General Mining Law of 1872, those leasable under the Mineral Leasing Act of 1920 and the Acquired Lands Act of 1947, and those salable under the Materials Disposal Act of 1947. The Forest Service exercised very limited authority under the two major acts of 1872 and 1920, held a veto power over Interior's leases of minerals on acquired lands, and had primary responsibility for sales of common variety deposits.

3. *Active Forest Service Involvement in Minerals Management (1950-1969)*

Mineral lease applications on national forest land increased dramatically after World War II.[1320] This led to a greater awareness by the Forest Service of the effects of mineral development on

---

[1316] The Interior Department's leasing authority over acquired-lands minerals not explicitly covered by the 1947 Act (including hardrock minerals) is based on Reorganization Plan No. 3 of 1946, 5 U.S.C. app. § 402 (1982). Thus, all minerals on acquired lands are under a leasing regime.

Acquired lands are found mostly in the East, where the United States purchased private land to create national forests. See MINING IN NATIONAL FORESTS, *supra* note 1279, at 3. About 20.5 million acres, or 11% of all national forest lands, are acquired lands. See G. ROBINSON, *supra* note 2, at 11.

[1317] 30 U.S.C. § 352 (1982).

[1318] 30 U.S.C. §§ 601-602 (1982). The Act covers "mineral materials (including but not limited to common varieties of the following: sand, stone, gravel, pumice, pumicite, cinders, and clay)." The Common Varieties Act of 1955, 30 U.S.C. § 611 (1982), amended the 1947 Act to provide that the definition of "common varieties" shall not include deposits of such minerals possessing "distinct and special values." The 1947 Act also included specified vegetative materials as common varieties subject to sales. 30 U.S.C. § 601 (1982).

[1319] 30 U.S.C. § 601 (1982).

[1320] See 1944 ANNUAL REPORT OF THE CHIEF, *supra* note 710, at 16-17; FOREST SERVICE, U.S. DEP'T OF AGRICULTURE, [1949 ANNUAL] REPORT OF THE CHIEF 50 (1949).

other forest resources.[1321] Previously, the Forest Service did not even consider minerals to be a forest resource.[1322] As the multiple-use concept broadened to include resources other than timber and grazing, the agency began to view minerals as a resource to be managed along with these other forest resources.[1323] The Forest Service was particularly sensitive to fraudulent or destructive mineral practices.[1324] By the early 1950s, various proposals were made for separation of surface and mineral rights or for leasing of all minerals.[1325]

The Forest Service's heightened concern with the mineral resource contributed to expansions of the agency's authority. First, the Secretary of the Interior and the Secretary of Agriculture agreed that the Forest Service would recommend to Interior stipulations that should be incorporated in mineral leases on national forest land to protect other resources.[1326] Second, Congress passed the Surface Resources Act in 1955.[1327]

The Surface Resources Act was an attempt to combat widespread abuses of the General Mining Law.[1328] The attack was

---

[1321] For instance, one annual report stated:
[T]here should be provision for development in such a way that these necessary resources can be obtained without needless damage to watersheds, timber, recreation or other values . . . . Often reasonable restrictions will make possible utilization of a resource without impairment of other values.
1948 ANNUAL REPORT OF THE CHIEF, *supra* note 559, at 18-19.

[1322] Up until 1950, minerals were viewed by the Forest Service only as a category of special land uses. Beginning in 1950 the Chief's annual report included a section on "Mining and Special Land Uses." 1950 ANNUAL REPORT OF THE CHIEF, *supra* note 118, at iii.

[1323] *See* 1951 ANNUAL REPORT OF THE CHIEF, *supra* note 716, at 49.

[1324] The agency's 1953 annual report highlights these statistics: "Of 36,600 mining claims covering 918,000 patented acres, only 15% were ever commercially mined. And of 84,000 unpatented claims on 2,163,000 acres, supporting timber worth more than $1,000,000, only 2% are being commercially mined." 1953 ANNUAL REPORT OF THE CHIEF, *supra* note 553, at 28.

[1325] *See* 1952 ANNUAL REPORT OF THE CHIEF, *supra* note 717, at 29-30.

[1326] 1950 ANNUAL REPORT OF THE CHIEF, *supra* note 118, at 45. *See infra* text accompanying notes 1387-93.

[1327] 30 U.S.C. §§ 612-615 (1982).

[1328] The Act provides: "Any mining claim hereafter located under the mining laws of the United States shall not be used, prior to issuance of patent therefor, for any purposes other than prospecting, mining or processing operations and uses reasonably incident thereto." 30 U.S.C. § 612(a) (1982). The legislative history states:
The effect of nonmining activity under color of existing mining law should be clear to all: a waste of valuable resources of the surface on lands embraced within claims which might satisfy the basic requirement of mineral discovery, but which were, in fact, made for a purpose other than mining;

two-pronged. First, the Surface Resources Act provided for multiple-use of the surface resources of forest land under Forest Service management.[1329] Miners locating claims after the passage of the 1955 Act no longer had the right to exclusive possession of the area within their claims, and the Forest Service received explicit authority to protect the other forest resources.[1330] Second, certain common variety minerals were explicitly declared not valuable and therefore not open or "locatable" under the General Mining Law.[1331] This provision was designed to foreclose a convenient way to gain access to valuable timber stands or recreation lands.[1332] Judicial interpretations of the Surface Resources Act have affirmed the Forest Service's broad regulatory authority to protect other surface resources, including recreation and wildlife,

---

for lands adjacent to such locations, timber, water, forage, fish and wildlife, and recreational values wasted or destroyed because of increased cost of management, difficulty of administration, or inaccessability.

H.R. REP. NO. 730, 84th Cong., 1st Sess. 6, *reprinted in* 1955 U.S. CODE CONG. & AD. NEWS (USCCAN) 2479. *See also* Converse v. Udall, 399 F.2d 616 (9th Cir. 1968) (applied restrictions of Surface Resources Act), *cert. denied*, 393 U.S. 1025 (1969). The legislative history "emphasizes the committee's insistence that this legislation not have the effect of modifying long-standing essential rights springing from location of a mining claim." H.R. REP. NO. 730, 84th Cong., 1st Sess. 10, *reprinted in* 1955 USCCAN at 2483. A prohibition against uses of mining claims except those "reasonably incident" to mining has been applied to pre-1955 locations on the ground that the 1872 Act impliedly prohibited such uses. *See* United States v. Langley, 587 F. Supp. 1258, 1262-63 (E.D. Cal. 1984), and the authorities cited therein.

For comprehensive treatments of reform of the General Mining Law of 1872, *see* J. LESHY, *supra* note 1297; MacDonnell, *Public Policy for Hard-Rock Minerals Access on Federal Lands: A Legal-Economic Analysis*, 71 COLO. SCHOOL OF MINES Q. 1 (1976).

[1329] The Act, which also applies to land administered by the Interior Department, states, "Rights under any mining claim hereafter located under the mining laws of the United States shall be subject, prior to issuance of patent therefor, to the right of the United States to manage and dispose of the vegetative surface resources thereof and to manage other surface resources thereof . . . ." 30 U.S.C. § 612(b) (1982).

[1330] *See, e.g.*, United States v. Curtis-Nevada Mines, Inc., 611 F.2d 1277 (9th Cir. 1980), upholding public access to claims covered by the 1955 Act.

[1331] 30 U.S.C. § 611 (1982). This section is commonly referred to as the Common Varieties Act of 1955. Common variety minerals, such as "sand, stone, gravel, pumice and pumicite are really building materials, and are not the type of material contemplated to be handled under the mining laws." 101 CONG. REC. 8743 (1955) (remarks of Rep. Engle). This provision clarified the coverage of the Materials Act of 1947, 30 U.S.C. §§ 601-602 (1982), *discussed supra* in text accompanying notes 1318-19.

[1332] 101 CONG. REC. 8743 (1955) (remarks of Rep. Engle). Examples of widespread fraud in this regard are catalogued in *Curtis-Nevada Mines*, 611 F.2d at 1282-83.

over all post-1955 locations and some pre-1955 claims.[1333] Thus, the 1955 Act has proved to be a significant step in the evolution of Forest Service mineral policy.

The Multiple-Use Sustained-Yield (MUSY) Act of 1960[1334] subtly influenced Forest Service mineral policy. Congress did not include minerals as one of the national forest resources to be managed by the Forest Service.[1335] In fact, the Act confirmed the separate status of minerals.[1336] The MUSY Act did, however, recognize that multiple-use land management can limit the extent of uses, or require that some uses not be permitted at all, on some land areas.[1337] Planning for the multiple-use of land began to evolve to embrace minerals management.

The development of modern Forest Service mineral policy accelerated during the 1960s. The agency studied the effects of strip and surface mining on the other forest resources and researched various reclamation methods.[1338] In addition, the Forest Service markedly increased its recommendations to Interior for

---

[1333] *See, e.g., Curtis-Nevada Mines*, 611 F.2d 1277; United States v. Richardson, 599 F.2d 290 (9th Cir. 1979); United States v. Springer, 491 F.2d 239 (9th Cir. 1974), *cert. denied*, 419 U.S. 834 (1974). *See generally* Marsh & Sherwood, *Metamorphisis in Mining Law: Federal Legislative and Regulatory Amendment and Supplementation of the General Mining Law Since 1955*, 26 ROCKY MTN. MIN. L. INST. 209, 220-23 (1980).

The Act is prospective, as it applies only to claims "hereafter located." 30 U.S.C. § 612(b) (1982). Holders of existing claims, however, were required to file verified statements setting out basic details concerning their claims. *Id.* § 613(a). If a filing was not made, the claim was not deemed abandoned, but any pre-1955 claim would become subject to the Forest Service's authority to manage other surface resources under § 612. *Id.* § 613(b). Large numbers of pre-1955 claims within national forests were brought under the 1955 Act in this manner, but those that were not continue to be subject to "exclusive" use under the 1872 Act. *See* United States v. Langley, 587 F. Supp. at 1263-64, denying public access to such claims.

[1334] 16 U.S.C. §§ 528-531 (1982), *discussed supra* in text accompanying notes 125-32.

[1335] 16 U.S.C. § 528 (1982).

[1336] The Act states: "Nothing herein shall be construed so as to affect the use or administration of the mineral resources of National Forest lands." *Id.*

[1337] " 'Multiple-use' means: The management of all the various renewable surface resources of the national forests so that they are utilized in the combination that will best meet the needs of the American people . . . that some land will be used for less than all of the resources . . . ." 16 U.S.C. § 531(a) (1982). *See* Marsh & Sherwood, *supra* note 1333, at 244-45.

[1338] *See* 1966 ANNUAL REPORT OF THE CHIEF, *supra* note 397, at 15.

stipulations in mineral leases.[1339] These studies and stipulations were prepared with the cooperation of the mining interests, evidencing a degree of industry acquiescence in the Forest Service's authority over minerals on national forest lands.[1340] Thus, while the Forest Service still had no express legal authority to manage minerals other than the 1897 Act's general grant to regulate "occupancy and use" within the national forests,[1341] the agency's influence over mineral development and reclamation on national forest lands burgeoned during the 1960s.

4. Controversy and Regulation (1969-1980)

The Forest Service's growing involvement in minerals management came to a climax during two conservation battles in 1969 and 1970. The first involved a highly scenic and remote area of the White Cloud Mountains in the Challis National Forest in Idaho.[1342] The American Smelting and Refining Company (ASARCO) applied for a special use permit to build an eight-mile access road into a molybdenum claim.[1343] Conservationists ob-

---

[1339] For example, on an oil exploration permit in the Kaibab National Forest in Arizona, the reconciliation of wildlife habitat and oil development produced 35 stipulations to protect wildlife. *See id.* at 16.

[1340] In the Allegheny National Forest in Pennsylvania, mining began under a cooperative coal recovery study project designed to test and evaluate various techniques to protect resource values of forested lands and to restore productivity during and after mining of coal by open-pit methods. The Forest Service required the mining company to adhere to rigid standards and specifications. *See* 1963 ANNUAL REPORT OF THE CHIEF, *supra* note 162, at 12. The company suspended operations after crews encountered a hard sandstone formation that made the mine uneconomical. The Forest Service found the conservation aspects of the project encouraging: "The operations have had no measurable effects on the quality of water in the streams draining the area." 1965 ANNUAL REPORT OF THE CHIEF, *supra* note 787, at 9.

[1341] 16 U.S.C. § 551 (1982).

[1342] The White Clouds area is about 10 miles long and 8 miles wide, contains 54 pristine lakes, and has been described as one of the most scenic and game-rich areas in the country. It also contains one of the only remaining glaciers in Idaho. Clement, *White Cloud Peaks, A Time For Decision,* AM. FORESTS, Sept. 1969, at 28, 30. One commentator called the White Cloud controversy "an historic conservation battle to force our federal government to consider other values besides minerals before allowing the destruction of another unique wild area." Trueblood, *Time Bomb at White Clouds,* NATIONAL WILDLIFE, June-July 1970, at 5.

[1343] *See* FOREST SERVICE, U.S. DEP'T OF AGRICULTURE, 1969 ANNUAL REPORT OF THE CHIEF 20 (1969) [hereinafter cited as 1969 ANNUAL REPORT OF THE CHIEF]. ASARCO made its application pursuant to the Forest Service's access regulations requiring a special use permit to construct a road. 36 C.F.R. § 251.53(k)(6) (1984).

jected to the proposal and argued that the Forest Service should deny the permit because the threat to wildlife, water quality, and scenic values outweighed the value of mining a relatively abundant mineral. Authors in the popular press questioned the rationale that gave mining first priority on national forest lands and argued that the area be completely closed to mining.[1344] National figures, including former Interior Secretary Stewart Udall, blasted the General Mining Law as an outright giveaway of vital national resources without any requirements for protection and restoration of the environment.[1345] Despite doubts over its authority to deny the permit,[1346] the Forest Service held three public hearings on the White Clouds issue.[1347] ASARCO then withdrew its application for the road and suspended all work on its claim.[1348]

The second incident involved the Stillwater Complex in the Custer and Gallatin National Forests in Montana. Statewide concern over the mineral development in that area led Senate

---

[1344] *See, e.g.*, N.Y. Times, Jan. 26, 1972, at 36; Clement, *supra* note 1342; Jackson, *Whose Wilderness?*, LIFE, Jan. 9, 1970, at 110; Merriam, *Idaho White Clouds: Wilderness in Trouble*, LIVING WILDERNESS, Spring 1970, at 33; Trueblood, *supra* note 1342. The Life magazine article concluded: "Shouldn't someone, somewhere, be weighing these concerns, and making a balanced judgment, rather than hiding behind laws drawn up in the age of the Homestead Act?" Jackson, *supra*, at 112.

[1345] Udall, *The Mining Law of 1872 Must Be Scrapped*, NATIONAL WILDLIFE, June-July 1970, at 9.

[1346] A Forest Service lawyer stated, "The law enables us to regulate the manner and course in which such a road is built but not to deny it." Jackson, *supra* note 1344, at 112. Similarly, Chief Edward Cliff stated:

The Forest Service does not have authority to prohibit ingress and egress to and from a valid mining claim. It does have authority to restrict and control such ingress and egress. . . . The Forest Service has no authority to prohibit or restrict actual mining operations on a valid claim or to regulate or control the type of mining involved, such as 'open pit,' 'strip,' or 'subsurface.' . . . [N]o regulations have been promulgated to enable the Forest Service to control methods by which prospecting is undertaken under the mining laws in order to protect surface areas, water quality, fish, wildlife, timber, and soil resources.

Letter from Edward P. Cliff, Chief, Forest Service, to Sen. Frank Church (June 6, 1969), *quoted in* Burns, *Preservationist Pressure on the Forest Service*, 17 ROCKY MTN. MIN. L. INST. 91, 93-94 (1972).

[1347] *See* 1969 ANNUAL REPORT OF THE CHIEF, *supra* note 1343, at 20.

[1348] Trueblood, *supra* note 1342, at 8. Since 1970, there has been no development on the ASARCO claim because of its political sensitivity and a weakened molybdenum market. Congress eventually included the White Clouds area in the Sawtooth National Recreation area, where mining is allowed only under strict regulation. *See* Sawtooth National Recreation Area Act, 16 U.S.C. §§ 460aa. to 460aa.-14 (1982).

Majority Leader Mike Mansfield of Montana tò intervene directly.[1349] He expressed to the Forest Service his alarm over the resultant environmental destruction in the area and over the Service's asserted powerlessness to control it.[1350] Mansfield suggested that the Forest Service promulgate regulations to control mining activities in the national forests, citing as authority the Surface Resources Act.[1351]

Thus by 1970 the Forest Service was armed with significant political and public support for expanding its control over mining in national forests.[1352] In addition, Congress passed the National Environmental Policy Act of 1969[1353] (NEPA), which directed federal agencies to "promote efforts which will prevent or eliminate damage to the environment" and to administer the public lands in accordance with that policy "to the fullest extent possible."[1354] The Forest Service responded on March 23, 1971, by distributing proposed regulations to the American Mining Congress, state mining associations, and conservation groups.[1355] The flood of comments received by the Forest Service[1356] prompted hearings

---

[1349] Burns, *supra* note 1346, at 95.

[1350] *Id.*

[1351] 30 U.S.C. §§ 612-615 (1982), *discussed supra* in text accompanying notes 1327-33.

[1352] The mining industry acknowledged the effect of those factors. A mining company spokesperson said, "No doubt there will be regulations and that's okay, too. The trend of public opinion is the greatest enforcer of conservation measures." Jackson, *supra* note 1344, at 110.

[1353] 42 U.S.C. §§ 4321-4370 (1982).

[1354] *Id.* § 4332(1).

[1355] Letter from Edward Cliff, Chief, Forest Service, to J. Allen Overton, Pres., Am. Mining Cong. (Apr. 12, 1971), *cited in* Dempsey, *Forest Service Regulations Concerning the Effect of Mining Operations on Surface Resources*, 8 NAT. RESOURCES LAW. 481, 483 (1975).

[1356] *See* 39 Fed. Reg. 31,317 (1974). The mining industry was skeptical of Forest Service authority to adopt such regulations but responded with their concerns and proposed changes. Letter from Stanley Dempsey, Am. Mining Cong., to Edward Cliff, Chief, Forest Service (Apr. 27, 1971), *cited in* Burns, *supra* note 1346, at 103. By this time, industry acknowledged the need to protect the environment from destructive mining practices. Robert Burns, Director of Government Relations of the American Mining Congress, stated, "No longer does anyone contend that environmental controls are unnecessary. The need to revise the mining law is clearly recognized by all responsible elements. . . . In the judgment of most of our members the imposition of reasonable and responsible controls over these lands is both good citizenship and good sense." Burns, *supra* note 1346, at 111-12.

by the House Subcommittee on Public Lands on the proposed regulations.[1357] The subcommittee expressed doubt about the extent of the Forest Service's authority and cautioned the Forest Service to implement the regulations with the greatest discretion in order to avoid conflict with miners' statutory rights under the General Mining Law.[1358]

The Forest Service promulgated its final regulations on August 28, 1974.[1359] The regulations have greatly strengthened local Forest Service officials' control over mining operations.[1360] The Forest Service's authority to adopt the regulations was finally resolved in a landmark case, *United States v. Weiss*,[1361] when the Court of Appeals for the Ninth Circuit found such authority in the 1897 Organic Act's grant of power to regulate "occupancy

---

[1357] *Proposed Forest Service Mining Regulations: Hearings Before the Subcomm. on Public Lands of the House Comm. on Interior and Insular Affairs*, 93d Cong., 2d Sess. (1974).

[1358] Letter from Rep. John Melcher, Chairman, Subcomm. on Public Lands, to John McGuire, Chief, Forest Service (June 20, 1974), *reprinted in* G. COGGINS & C. WILKINSON, *supra* note 345, at 374-77.

[1359] 36 C.F.R. § 228 (1984). As authority for the regulations, the Forest Service cited the 1897 Organic Act, 16 U.S.C. §§ 478, 551 (1982). Initially, the Forest Service had cited the Organic Act; the Surface Resources Act, 30 U.S.C. §§ 612-615 (1982); the Multiple-Use Sustained-Yield Act, 16 U.S.C. 528 (1982); and § 102 of NEPA, 42 U.S.C. § 4332 (1982). In Public Lands Subcommittee Chairman Melcher's letter, however, he strongly suggested that the Forest Service's authority depended exclusively on the Organic Act. *See supra* note 1358. There is further hair-splitting: the regulations technically do not purport to regulate or manage mining, the responsibility for which lies with the Interior Department; rather, the regulations apply to "operations" that "affect surface resources." 36 C.F.R. § 228.1 (1984).

[1360] Before the final regulations were promulgated, the Forest Service district rangers had operated under internal directives and guidelines for restraining the unwarranted surface destruction of the national forests. However, in United States v. Floyd J. Patrin, No. 1-72-135 (D. Idaho, Nov. 7, 1974), the district court found the Forest Service had no authority to halt mining operations due to damage to the surface resources. The Forest Service had relied on its internal management directives in imposing certain conditions on Patrin's use of his claim. The court stated, "The [mining] guidelines . . . do not have the force or effect of law and are not binding on defendant." *Id.* at 5. However, in United States v. Richardson, 599 F.2d 290 (9th Cir. 1979), *cert. denied*, 444 U.S. 1014 (1980), the Court of Appeals for the Ninth Circuit enjoined blasting and bulldozing that the Forest Service found to be unnecessary and unreasonably destructive of surface resources and damaging to the environment. 599 F.2d at 291. While the only sources of Forest Service authority at issue in this case were the same internal directives discussed in *Patrin*, the court stated that under the Surface Resources Act, the Forest Service "may require the locator of an unpatented mining claim on national forest lands to use nondestructive methods of prospecting." *Id.*

[1361] 642 F.2d 296 (9th Cir. 1981).

and use" within the national forests.[1362] Regulation of hardrock mining remains a sensitive and somewhat uncertain area of Forest Service activities; among other things, the Forest Service has recognized the importance of agency cooperation with miners, an attitude that remains an element of its current hardrock mineral policy.[1363]

Since the mid-1970s the Forest Service has also become more deeply involved in managing leasable minerals. The Forest Service now considers the effects of mineral development on other surface resources when deciding whether to condition or grant leases.[1364] The NFMA regulations direct the Forest Service to include an analysis of the mineral resource in its forest planning process.[1365]

A well-developed body of law has given minerals something of a distinct status in the national forests. Nevertheless, the integration of minerals into the planning process suggests equality with, rather than dominance over, other resources. Thus, implementation of the NFMA signals the latest phase in the Forest Service's role in minerals management, that of coordinating mineral development with other surface resources.

[1362] The Ninth Circuit also relied upon 16 U.S.C. § 478 (1982), allowing access to the forests by inholders and miners but providing that "such persons must comply with the rules and regulations covering such national forests." 642 F.2d at 297. *See also* United States v. Goldfield Deep Mines Co. of Nev., 644 F.2d 1307 (9th Cir. 1981), *cert. denied*, 102 S. Ct. 1252 (1982).

[1363] The Forest Service Manual states:

The primary means for obtaining protection of surface resources should be by securing the willing cooperation of prospectors and miners. The willingness of the majority of prospectors and miners to comply with regulations, reasonably administered, is a principal key to the protection of environmental quality in the National Forest System. Face to face dialogue with operators is encouraged.

FOREST SERVICE MANUAL § 2817.03 (1984). "Ours has not been a hardnosed approach. We've walked softly and in most cases the miners have been cooperative." Remarks by Norman Stark, Forest Service geologist, Ogden, Utah, *quoted in* Sheridan, *Hard Rock Mining on the Public Land*, in COUNCIL ON ENVTL. QUALITY BULLETIN 18 (1977). This policy was confirmed in a conversation with Don Schulz, Forest Service staff officer, Minerals and Geology, Intermountain Regional Headquarters, Odgen, Utah (Nov. 18, 1983). *See also infra* note 1374.

[1364] The use of surface protection stipulations is now a matter of course. "[T]he Forest Service has the authority and obligation to ensure that mineral activities on National Forest System lands are conducted so as to minimize conflicts with other uses and damage to surface resources, and that damaged areas are rehabilitated after mineral operations." FOREST SERVICE MANUAL § 2820 (1984). *See also* Burton, *Federal Leasing—Restrictions and Extensions*, 28 ROCKY MTN. MIN. L. INST. 1133 (1983).

[1365] *See infra* text accompanying notes 1424-45.

B. *Forest Service Regulation of Mining*

Minerals on federal lands often are divided into three legal categories: locatable (hardrock minerals subject to the General Mining Law), leasable (energy and fertilizer minerals wherever located and all minerals of acquired lands), and salable (common varieties).[1366] We will use those traditional categories here but will note that several different variations occur among situations involving leasable minerals on national forests. In particular, under the Mineral Leasing Act of 1920, the Forest Service makes recommendations on lease conditions and issuance; but under the Acquired Lands Act of 1947 the Forest Service must consent before Interior may enter into a lease of any minerals from acquired lands. In this section we will first discuss these three basic systems of mineral disposition. We will then analyze other statutes implicating mineral disposition on the national forests.

1. *Systems for Mineral Disposition*

(a) *Hardrock, or Locatable, Minerals*

Under the Forest Service surface use regulations, first adopted in 1974,[1367] all miners must conduct operations, to the extent feasible, so as to minimize adverse environmental effects on the national forest surface resources.[1368] The miner must file a notice of intent with the local district ranger for any operation that might cause surface resource disturbance.[1369] If the district ranger determines that such operations will "likely cause significant disturbance of surface resources," the miner must then submit a plan of operations.[1370] The district ranger reviews and revises the submit-

---

[1366] FOREST SERVICE, U.S. DEP'T OF AGRICULTURE, MINERALS PROGRAM HANDBOOK § 1.33 (1981) [hereinafter cited as MINERALS PROGRAM HANDBOOK]. The descriptions refer to method of disposal.

[1367] *See supra* text accompanying notes 1359-63.

[1368] 36 C.F.R. § 228.8 (1984). The operator is specifically required to comply with federal and state air and water quality and solid waste treatment and disposal standards; to protect scenic values, fisheries and wildlife habitat; to construct and maintain roads with minimal damage; and to reclaim the disturbed surface.

[1369] *Id.* § 228.4(a). "Claim staking, subsurface operations, and work that does not disturb vegetation or use mechanized earth moving equipment are exempt from the notice requirements under the regulations." ANATOMY OF A MINE, *supra* note 1288, at 19.

[1370] 36 C.F.R. § 228.4(a) (1984). "Significant" is further defined in the Forest Service Manual. An "onsite" disturbance is significant if natural recovery would not be expected to occur within a reasonable period of time. An "offsite" disturbance is significant if it would result in unnecessary or unreasonable injury, loss,

ted plan with the operator until both agree upon an acceptable plan.[1371] The final operating plan includes surface environmental protection and reclamation requirements, as well as a bond requirement to cover the costs of damage or unfinished reclamation.[1372] Additionally, the regulations provide for access restrictions, operations in wilderness areas, periodic inspection by the Forest Service, and remedies for noncompliance with the regulations.[1373]

Forest Service implementation of the regulations has been somewhat tentative. Many district rangers are still uncertain about their authority,[1374] partly because the Forest Service Manual does not generally allow rejection of operating plans.[1375] Furthermore, the relatively small number of Forest Service personnel responsible for enforcement of the minerals regulations must cover large tracts of land.[1376] Compliance with the regulations, however, has been high.[1377]

---

or damage to national forest system resources, would cause air or water degradation, or would be a risk to health or safety. FOREST SERVICE MANUAL § 2817.11 (1984).

[1371] Under Forest Service directions, "not approved" actions are not allowed. FOREST SERVICE MANUAL § 2817.23 (1984). Presumably, the miner and the district ranger must come to some sort of compromise. In all cases, the district ranger must do an environmental assessment, as required by NEPA, to determine if an environmental impact statement is necessary. 36 C.F.R. § 228.4(f) (1984).

[1372] 36 C.F.R. § 228.4(c) (1984) (operating plan); *id.* § 228.13 (bond requirement); *id.* § 228.9 (public safety requirements).

[1373] *Id.* § 228.12 (access); *id.* § 228.15 (wilderness); *id.* § 228.7 (inspection and noncompliance). Although not expressed in the regulations, the Forest Service Manual provides that the district ranger may initiate a civil action for damages and an injunction or a criminal action under 36 C.F.R. §§ 261, 262 (1984). FOREST SERVICE MANUAL § 2817.3(5) (1984).

[1374] "When I am sitting down with a mining company and proposing changes in their operating plan or suggesting a $10,000 reclamation bond, there is, in the back of my mind, the worry—'what do I do if they tell me to go to hell.' " A. Clair Baldwin, Forest Service District Ranger, Austin, Nev. (Mar. 5, 1977), *quoted in* Sheridan, *supra* note 1363, at 18. Similar concerns were expressed in our interview with Gordon Reid, Minerals Staff Officer, Challis Nat'l Forest (Oct. 5, 1983). As a legal matter, however, the Court of Appeals for the Ninth Circuit has made it clear that the Forest Service has "the power to prohibit the initiation or continuation of mining in national forests for failure to abide by applicable environmental regulations." Granite Rock Co. v. California Coastal Comm'n, 768 F.2d 1077, 1083 (9th Cir. 1985).

[1375] FOREST SERVICE MANUAL § 2817.23 (1984). Rejection is allowed only when the area is withdrawn from entry. *See also supra* note 1371.

[1376] For example, on the Toiyabe National Forest one district ranger is responsible for overseeing 1.4 million acres of land. Sheridan, *supra* note 1363, at 19.

[1377] *Id.*

In addition to protecting surface resources through the regulations, the Forest Service also can cause the BLM to initiate contests challenging the validity of unpatented mining claims on national forest land. The large number of such claims of dubious validity in western national forests has made them a significant land planning issue.[1378] By interdepartmental agreement with the Department of the Interior, the Forest Service prepares a mineral examination to determine a claim's validity. If the findings so warrant, Interior then brings the contest proceedings.[1379] These procedures have helped produce a general trend toward stricter application of the General Mining Law.[1380]

After valid discovery and improvement work, the miner may apply for a patent.[1381] As with contests regarding unpatented claims, administration of patent applications has been strict.[1382] Once the patent issues, the miner owns the land and normally is no longer subject to the General Mining Law, the Surface Resources Act, or the Forest Service surface use regulations.[1383]

(b) Leasable Minerals

The dominant statute governing leasable minerals occurring on national forest lands that are neither acquired nor withdrawn is the Mineral Leasing Act of 1920.[1384] This Act exempts certain minerals, including oil, gas, oil shale, and coal from operation of the General Mining Law and authorizes prospecting and develop-

---

[1378] *See* United States v. Coleman, 390 U.S. 599 (1968). *See also* Marsh & Sherwood, *supra* note 1333, at 220-23; Hochmuth, *supra* note 1297, at 486, 489; Strauss, *supra* note 1290, at 187.

[1379] FOREST SERVICE MANUAL §§ 2818.31-.33 (1984); MINERALS PROGRAM HANDBOOK, *supra* note 1366, § 1.41.

[1380] *See supra* note 1378.

[1381] Requirements for patent are set out in 30 U.S.C §§ 29 and 37 (1982). If all the requirements are met, issuance is nondiscretionary. South Dakota v. Andrus, 614 F.2d 1190 (8th Cir.), *cert. denied*, 449 U.S. 822 (1980). The miner is entitled to ownership of the land for the price of $5 per acre for a lode claim and $2.50 per acre for a placer claim. 30 U.S.C. §§ 29, 37 (1982).

[1382] *See* Marsh & Sherwood, *supra* note 1333, at 220.

[1383] Patents located in wilderness areas include only the minerals, not the surface estate. 16 U.S.C. § 1133(d)(3) (1982). Wilderness mining law is discussed further *infra* in section IX(C). Federal power to regulate private inholdings does exist, see *supra* note 345, and in a few instances the Forest Service has been granted authority to regulate inholdings. *See, e.g.*, Act of Aug. 22, 1972, § 4(b), 86 Stat. 612, 613 (Sawtooth National Recreation Area).

[1384] 30 U.S.C. §§ 181-287 (1982).

ment of these minerals under permits or leases.[1385] Authority to issue all leases, including those on national forest lands, vests in the Department of the Interior through the BLM. The Forest Service does, however, play a major role in lease issuance and management of minerals subject to the Mineral Leasing Act.[1386]

When the BLM receives an application for a lease on national forest land, the application is forwarded to the Forest Service for review and environmental analysis of the proposed operation.[1387] Upon review, the Forest Service may attach stipulations to the lease to protect the surface resources.[1388] If the mineral is coal or geothermal steam, the Forest Service decision to deny a lease or to lease pursuant to specific stipulations is final,[1389] and Interior must accept the Forest Service decision. Interior will consider the Forest Service analysis for leasables other than coal or steam but is required to make an independent judgment on lease issuance.[1390] In practice, Interior generally accepts Forest Service recommendations.[1391] The Forest Service's use of stipulations increased dra-

---

[1385] The leasing system is summarized in G. COGGINS & C. WILKINSON, *supra* note 345, at 396-400. Geothermal energy is under a separate leasing system that resembles the procedures of the 1920 Act. *See* Geothermal Steam Act of 1970, 30 U.S.C. §§ 1001-1025 (1982).

[1386] *See, e.g.*, 43 C.F.R. § 3111 (1982) (oil and gas); *id.* § 3210 (geothermal); *id.* § 3510 (prospecting permits) of the BLM regulations.

[1387] This review must include: coordination with the appropriate land management plan and existing planned uses; evaluation of the impacts, degree of damage to surface resources, and the difficulty in restoring the areas; assessment of probable damage to watershed, access needs, and special values of the area; analysis of the terms and nature of the operation; and comparison of alternatives. FOREST SERVICE MANUAL § 2822.41 (1984).

[1388] *Id.* § 2822.42; MINERALS PROGRAM HANDBOOK, *supra* note 1366, § 7.11b. *See generally* FOREST SERVICE, U.S. DEP'T OF AGRICULTURE, OIL AND GAS, SURFACE OPERATING STANDARDS FOR OIL AND GAS EXPLORATION AND DEVELOPMENT (2d ed. 1978).

[1389] Coal Leasing Amendments of 1975, 30 U.S.C. § 201 (1982); Geothermal Steam Act of 1970, 30 U.S.C. § 1014 (1984). Coal strip mining is also subject to the Surface Mining Control and Reclamation Act of 1977 (SMCRA), 30 U.S.C. § 1201 (1984), and regulations adopted pursuant to it, 30 C.F.R. §§ 700-707, 730-845 (1984). For articles on coal leasing, *see* Hustace, *The New Federal Coal Leasing System*, 10 NAT. RESOURCES J. 323 (1977); Krulitz, *supra* note 1314. On SMCRA, *see* Kite, *S.M.C.R.A. of 1977: An Overview of Reclamation Requirements and Implementation*, 13 LAND & WATER L. REV. 703 (1978).

[1390] MEMORANDUM OF UNDERSTANDING BETWEEN THE BUREAU OF LAND MANAGEMENT AND THE FOREST SERVICE 3 (1980), *reprinted in* FOREST SERVICE MANUAL. The memorandum and the interagency procedures are discussed in Sierra Club v. Peterson, 12 ENVTL. L. REP. (ENVTL. L. INST.) 20,454 (D.D.C. 1982), *rev'd on other grounds*, 717 F.2d 1409 (D.C. Cir. 1983).

[1391] MEMORANDUM OF UNDERSTANDING, *supra* note 1390, at 4.

matically during the early 1970s, although the trend in recent years has been to reduce stipulations that duplicate restrictions contained in the lease terms.[1392] Leasing issues have been especially controversial in highly sensitive areas or those with wilderness characteristics.[1393]

When development on a lease occurs, the operator must submit to the Forest Service an operating plan describing proposed methods, access routes, waste disposal plans, environmental protection measures, and a reclamation plan.[1394] The Forest Service reviews and revises the plan with the operator and conducts reviews of the plan in operation.[1395] Otherwise, the operations are managed by Interior except in emergency situations "of improper use that are imminently likely to endanger public health or safety, or life or property, or to cause irreparable damage to resources."[1396]

(c) Salable Minerals, or Common Varieties

Salable minerals are governed by the Materials Disposal Act of 1947 as supplemented by the Common Varieties Act of 1955.[1397]

[1392] Telephone conversation with David Friendly, Ass't Director, Mineral Operations, U.S. Forest Service, Washington, D.C. (Oct. 4, 1985).

[1393] Sierra Club v. Peterson, 717 F.2d 1409 (D.C. Cir. 1983); Conner v. Burford, 605 F. Supp. 107 (D. Mont. 1985); Mountain States Legal Found. v. Andrus, 499 F. Supp. 383 (D. Wyo. 1980). For examples of stipulations see GRAND MESA, UNCOMPAHGRE, AND GUNNISON NAT'L FORESTS LAND & RESOURCE MANAGEMENT PLAN, *supra* note 977, at App. H.

[1394] MINERALS PROGRAM HANDBOOK, *supra* note 1366, § 7.13a.

[1395] *Id.* § 1.42.

[1396] FOREST SERVICE MANUAL § 2822.62 (1984). All minerals, including hardrock minerals, occurring on acquired lands are subject to the 1947 Mineral Leasing Act for Acquired Lands. 30 U.S.C. §§ 351-359 (1982). The 1947 Act differs from the Mineral Leasing Act of 1920 in that the Forest Service must consent to all leases issued by the BLM on acquired national forest lands. 30 U.S.C. § 352 (1982), discussed *supra* in text accompanying notes 1316-17. Thus, "leases on [national forest] acquired lands may only be issued with the consent of the Forest Service and are subject to conditions ensuring that the lands are used for the purpose for which they were acquired or are being administered." MINERALS PROGRAM HANDBOOK, *supra* note 1366, § 1.2(5).

[1397] Materials Disposal Act of 1947, 30 U.S.C. §§ 601-602 (1982) as amended by the Common Varieties Act of 1955, 30 U.S.C. § 611 (1982). The 1947 Act made common mineral varieties such as sand and stone subject to sale. *See supra* text accompanying notes 1318-19. However, the 1947 Act did not state whether these minerals continued to be subject to location under the General Mining Law of 1872. The 1955 Act resolved the ambiguity by stating that common varieties were removed from the coverage of the 1872 Act; the 1955 Act also gave common varieties a generic definition as those minerals lacking "distinct and special value." 30 U.S.C. § 611 (1982).

The 1947 Act provides for Forest Service sale of commonly found minerals located on national forest public domain lands.[1398] If found on national forest acquired lands, the Forest Service has authority to sell them by interdepartmental agreement with the Department of the Interior.[1399] In either case, the minerals must be sold at not less than the appraised value,[1400] unless disposal is to a federal or state agency, a municipality, or a nonprofit organization.[1401] In such instances, the Forest Service issues a free-use permit as long as the agency or organization does not use the mineral for commercial purposes or for resale.[1402] As a condition of sale or disposal, the operator must reclaim the extraction site. The Forest Service published proposed regulations governing disposal of these minerals on August 4, 1983.[1403]

2. Other Relevant Considerations

Several additional issues may affect planning and management of a particular mineral interest. First, the Surface Resources Act of 1955 in some circumstances effectively divides mineral land into surface and subsurface estates; for unpatented claims located after 1955, the Forest Service has the right to manage the surface for other uses, such as logging, grazing, or recreation.[1404] Second, the land on which the mineral is discovered may be the subject of

---

[1398] 30 U.S.C. § 601 (1982); 36 C.F.R. § 251.4(a)(1) (1984).

[1399] *See* Act of June 11, 1960, § 1(l), 74 Stat. 205; 36 C.F.R. § 251.4a(a) (1984).

[1400] 36 C.F.R. § 251.4(b)(1) (1984); *id.* § 251.4a(e)(2).

[1401] *Id.* § 251.4(b)(4); *id.* § 251.4a(f)(5)(i)(a)(b).

[1402] *Id.* § 251.4(b)(4)(i); *id.* § 251.4a(f)(5)(i)(b).

[1403] 48 Fed. Reg. 35,580 (1983). The proposed regulations change only the procedures, not the substance, of prior regulations.

[1404] 30 U.S.C. § 612(b) (1982). *See generally* United States v. Curtis-Nevada Mines, Inc., 611 F.2d 1277 (9th Cir. 1980). The 1955 Act is generally prospective only, but pre-1955 claims can be made subject to surface management under certain circumstances. *See supra* note 1333. The surface-subsurface distinction is also important on some national forests in the East where the Forest Service purchased forest land without obtaining ownership of subsurface mineral rights. These privately owned mineral rights are not always subject to surface protection practices. *See, e.g.,* FOREST SERVICE MANUAL § 2832 (1984); FOREST SERVICE, U.S. DEP'T OF AGRICULTURE, LAND MANAGER'S HANDBOOK ON MINERALS MANAGEMENT §§ 163-166. *See generally* Hultin, *Recent Developments in Statutory and Judicial Accommodation Between Surface and Mineral Owners,* 28 ROCKY MTN. MIN. L. INST. 1021 (1983); Lopez, *Upstairs/Downstairs: Conflicts Between Surface and Mineral Owners,* 26 ROCKY MTN. MIN. L. INST. 995 (1980).

an executive or congressional withdrawal.[1405] Such action may entirely exclude the land from operation of the mining laws or allow mining only with certain restrictions or within certain boundaries.[1406] The acts or public land orders themselves must be consulted to determine the status of the land in question.

Third, coal leasing in national forests is subject to the Surface Mining Control and Reclamation Act[1407] (SMCRA), and the Coal Leasing Amendments of 1975.[1408] SMCRA requires that national forest lands deemed unsuitable for surface coal mining be withdrawn from entry.[1409] The Forest Service generally has adopted the "unsuitability criteria" established by the BLM to apply to national forest lands.[1410] The BLM withdraws from mineral entry those lands determined by the Forest Service to be unsuitable.

Fourth, miners are also governed by various state laws, which in some cases are stricter than federal laws.[1411] Finally, miners must

---

[1405] *See generally* Getches, *Managing the Public Lands: The Authority of the Executive to Withdraw Lands*, 22 NAT. RESOURCES J. 279 (1982). Withdrawals made after 1976 are governed by the Federal Land Policy and Management Act of 1976 (FLPMA), 43 U.S.C. § 1714 (1982). The Forest Service has no independent withdrawal power. FOREST SERVICE MANUAL §§ 2760, 2810, 2820 (1984). *See also infra* note 1431. *See generally* 1 AMERICAN LAW OF MINING, *supra* note 1284, at §§ 299-365.

[1406] For example, the Wild and Scenic Rivers Act withdraws from location minerals found on the beds or banks, or within one-quarter mile of the banks, of rivers classified as "wild". 16 U.S.C. § 1280(a)(iii) (1982). Other such instances include the Wilderness Act of 1964, 16 U.S.C. § 1133(d)(3), discussed *supra* in section IX(C); National Conservation Recreation Areas Act, 16 U.S.C. §§ 460k to 1-460k-5; municipal watershed agreements, 16 U.S.C. § 552(a); and some specific national forest reservations, 16 U.S.C. § 539a (portion of Chugach National Forest).

[1407] 30 U.S.C. §§ 1201-1328 (1982).

[1408] 30 U.S.C. §§ 201-209. *See generally* sources cited *supra* in note 1389.

[1409] 30 U.S.C. § 1272(e) (1982). *See* Van Buskirk & Drazoo, *The Designation of Coal Lands as "Unsuitable" For Surface Coal Mining Operations*, 27A ROCKY MTN. MIN. L. INST. 339 (1982).

[1410] Telephone interview with John Hill, Forest Geologist, Gunnison Nat'l Forest, Rocky Mtn. Region, U.S. Forest Service (Oct. 4, 1985). The BLM has developed criteria for unsuitable lands in its land use planning process, as mandated by the FLPMA, 43 U.S.C. § 1712 (1982). *See* 43 Fed. Reg. 57,662 (1978).

[1411] *See generally*, Barnhill, *Role of Local Government in Mineral Development*, 28 ROCKY MTN. MIN. L. INST. 221 (1983); Note, *State and Local Control of Energy Development on Federal Lands*, 32 STAN. L. REV. 373 (1980). *See generally supra* text accompanying notes 343-61.

comply with other protective legislation, such as the Endangered Species Act, the Clean Air Act, and the Clean Water Act.[1412]

Three policy acts also affect the Forest Service's mineral policy. First, and perhaps most influential, is NEPA[1413] and regulations adopted pursuant to it.[1414] With the exception of patent applications, the effect of NEPA on Forest Service mineral policy has been considerable.[1415] However, the Forest Service does not require an environmental impact statement (EIS) for hardrock operating plans except for large or controversial projects.[1416]

In addition to NEPA, the Mining and Minerals Policy Act of 1970[1417] and the National Materials and Mineral Policy, Research and Development Act of 1980[1418] apply to the Forest Service. The 1970 Act reaffirms the policy of the federal government to "foster and encourage private enterprise in (1) the development of economically sound and stable domestic mining [and]

[1412] Endangered Species Act of 1973, 16 U.S.C. §§ 1531-1543 (1982); Clean Air Act, 42 U.S.C. §§ 7401-7642 (1982); Clean Water Act, 33 U.S.C. §§ 1251-1376 (1982). *See generally* Hecox & Desautels, *Federal Environmental Regulations Applicable to Exploration, Mining and Milling*, 25 ROCKY MTN. MIN. L. INST. 9-1 (1979); Miller, *Dump, Heap, and In Site Leaching: Legal Constraints*, 27A ROCKY MTN. MIN. L. INST. 787 (1982).

[1413] 42 U.S.C. §§ 4321-4370 (1982).

[1414] 40 C.F.R. § 1501 (1984). To some, including many in the mining industry, NEPA's impact on mining has been a "regrettable nightmare." Memorandum from Treasury Secretary, William E. Simon (Apr. 1, 1975), *cited in* Haggard, *Regulation of Mining Law Activities on Federal Lands*, 21 ROCKY MTN. MIN. L. INST. 349, 352, 357 (1975). *See also* Marsh & Sherwood, *supra* note 1333, at 250.

[1415] *See* South Dakota v. Andrus, 614 F.2d 1190 (8th Cir. 1980) (issuance of a mining patent is not a "major" federal action and is "probably" a nondiscretionary act, so an EIS is not required on two grounds). As for other mineral activities, the Forest Service presumes that NEPA applies. MINERALS PROGRAM HANDBOOK, *supra* note 1366, § 1.31. These activities include review of operating plans and lease issuance. The Forest Service first prepares an environmental analysis report to determine if an environmental impact statement is necessary. This process was upheld in Friends of the Earth v. Butz, 406 F. Supp. 742 (D. Mont. 1975), *appeal dismissed for mootness*, 576 F.2d 1377 (9th Cir. 1978). Mineral activities not subject to NEPA are listed in 46 Fed. Reg. 7495 (1981).

[1416] *See, e.g.*, FOREST SERVICE, U.S. DEP'T OF AGRICULTURE, DRAFT ENVIRONMENTAL IMPACT STATEMENT, LOMEX CORPORATION'S PROPOSED MINERAL EXPLORATIONS IN THE NAVAJO VICINITY, LOS PADRES NATIONAL FOREST (1980) (EIS prepared because of the "potential for public conflict" and "to provide greater opportunity for public involvement"); FOREST SERVICE, U.S. DEP'T OF AGRICULTURE, DRAFT ENVIRONMENTAL IMPACT STATEMENT, MT. EMMONS MINING PROJECT, GRAND MESA, UNCOMPAHGRE, AND GUNNISON NAT'L FORESTS (1982) (very large operation).

[1417] 30 U.S.C. § 21a (1982).

[1418] 30 U.S.C. §§ 1601-1605 (1982).

mineral[s] . . . industries, [and] (2) the orderly and economic development of domestic mineral resources . . . ."[1419] The Act has
not received the public attention that NEPA has, and the mining
industry has criticized the Interior and Agriculture Departments
for ignoring it.[1420] The National Materials and Mineral Policy
Act of 1980 was enacted to strengthen the 1970 Act. The 1980
Act indirectly encourages mineral planning on national forests by
requiring the Secretary of the Interior to "improve the availability
and analysis of mineral data in Federal land use
decisionmaking."[1421]

C. *Minerals Planning Under the NFMA*

During the last fifteen years, then, the Forest Service has become increasingly vigorous in protecting its surface resources from
damage due to mining. Its efforts have included direct regulation
of hardrock mining under the authority of the Organic Act of
1897, inclusion of stipulations in mineral leases, enforcement of
reclamation and environmental protection requirements, proposals
for withdrawals of areas from mineral activity, and advocacy with
the BLM to force contests by Interior of questionable hardrock
claims. However, the Forest Service's role generally has been a
reactive one, with environmental analysis performed after some
mineral activity has already occurred. As a result, the agency
often has been unable to develop adequate hydrological or wildlife
data in advance of decisionmaking, to assess the cumulative effects of multiple mineral operations, to budget for new enforcement and personnel needs, or to resolve conflicts between mineral
development and other uses in advance. To some extent these circumstances are unavoidable as miners have the right under the
General Mining Law of 1872 to begin exploration on their own
initiative. However, with the NFMA regulations the Forest
Service has the opportunity to take a more ordered and forward-
looking approach toward protecting surface resources and coordinating mineral activity with other planned uses.[1422]

[1419] 30 U.S.C. § 21a (1982).
[1420] *See* Haggard, *supra* note 1414, at 357; Marsh & Sherwood, *supra* note
1333, at 258. The policy of the 1970 Act was reaffirmed in FLPMA, 43 U.S.C. §
1701(a)(12) (1982).
[1421] 30 U.S.C. § 1605(e)(3) (1982).
[1422] FOREST SERVICE, U.S. DEP'T OF AGRICULTURE, MINERALS PLANNING
HANDBOOK § 5.22 [hereinafter cited as MINERALS PLANNING HANDBOOK]. The
Forest Service Manual states, "The Forest Service . . . objectives are to . . .

Neither the NFMA nor the RPA mentions minerals as a resource subject to Forest Service jurisdiction. By addressing only renewable resources, Congress conceivably might have intended to relieve the Forest Service of any statutory obligation to consider minerals in the planning process. Indeed, as the Committee of Scientists observed, "It can therefore be argued that the subject of mineral resources lies outside the jurisdiction of [the NFMA] regulations."[1423] Nevertheless, the Committee concluded that "minerals must be taken into account during the planning process. There is little logic to deciding the allocation of National Forest lands for various purposes without attention to all reasonably foreseeable uses, which in some forests include recovery of minerals."[1424] As a result, the 1979 NFMA regulations instructed the Forest Service to expand significantly its minerals planning program.

In addition to general planning requirements that may affect mineral resources, the Forest Service must include in the forest plan five components relating specifically to minerals. First, the plan must describe the important mineral issues identified through public involvement.[1425] Second, the plan must include various inventories in order to forecast future mineral development and to enforce existing laws and regulations.[1426] Third, the forest plan

---

[i]ntegrate exploration, development, and production of energy and other mineral resources . . . with the use and conservation of other resources to the fullest extent possible." FOREST SERVICE MANUAL § 2802 (1984).

[1423] *Comm. of Scientists Final Report, supra* note 864, at 26,641.

[1424] *Id.* The Committee declined to suggest specific language because of their "limited expertise in the area of minerals." *Id.* The Committee's concern over the Forest Service's jurisdiction has since been resolved. The courts have acknowledged broad agency authority to regulate mineral development on the national forests. *See supra* text accompanying notes 1366-1422.

[1425] The Forest Service directs the minerals planning representative to contact representatives of mineral industries and mineral industry associations, to analyze public comments related to mining, and to contact state and local government agencies and other federal government agencies for input. MINERALS PLANNING HANDBOOK, *supra* note 1422, § 1.22.

[1426] Initially, planners must inventory active mines in the planning area. 36 C.F.R. § 219.22(a) (1984); *id.* § 219.12(d). The forest plan should provide a means to check the validity of unpatented claims, mining law abuses, and compliance with approved operating plans and stipulations. *See, e.g.,* GRAND MESA, UNCOMPAHGRE, AND GUNNISON NAT'L FORESTS LAND & RESOURCE MANAGEMENT PLAN, *supra* note 977, at III-54-55. Next, planners must inventory outstanding and reserved mineral rights. 36 C.F.R. § 219.22(a), (b) (1984). The Forest Service then can anticipate mineral development on these lands. In addition, the inventory must include an estimate of the probable occurrence of various minerals, *id.* § 219.22(c), although it is often difficult to predict exactly where minerals will occur. COMPTROLLER GENERAL, U.S. GENERAL

must include forecasts of the planning area's potential for future mineral development and potential need for withdrawal from development.[1427] Making recommendations for withdrawals,[1428] which can be made only by the Department of the Interior,[1429] is a key aspect of this forecasting.[1430] Withdrawal is a powerful land

---

ACCOUNTING OFFICE, REPORT TO THE CONGRESS: MINING LAW REFORM AND BALANCED RESOURCE MANAGEMENT 30 (1979). Nevertheless, the Forest Service requires planners to seek out the best information available. FOREST SERVICE MANUAL §§ 2807.2-.3 (1984); MINERALS PROGRAM HANDBOOK, *supra* note 1366, §§ 3.3, 3.21; MINERALS PLANNING HANDBOOK, *supra* note 1422, § 1.23(c). The final steps in the inventorying process are to identify existing withdrawn lands and to review the need for existing withdrawals or schedule the reviews during the plan period. 36 C.F.R. § 219.22(d) (1984); MINERALS PLANNING HANDBOOK, *supra* note 1422, § 1.23(d)(2)(a), (b). The FLPMA withdrawal review process, 43 U.S.C. § 1714(1) (1982), should be incorporated into the forest planning process. An example of withdrawal review is described by the Grand Mesa Forest Plan:

> The review process will include a determination of whether continuation, modification, revocation, or partial revocation of each withdrawal is appropriate. The basic steps in the review process are: (1) field examination; (2) preparation of required mineral, threatened and endangered species, and wetlands and floodplain reports; (3) preparation of an Environmental Assessment; and (4) preparation of a Decision Notice and Finding of No Significant Impact.

GRAND MESA, UNCOMPAHGRE, AND GUNNISON NAT'L FORESTS LAND & RESOURCE MANAGEMENT PLAN, *supra* note 977, at J-2.

[1427] 36 C.F.R. § 219.22(d) (1984). Predicting mineral development years in advance is necessarily imprecise. ANATOMY OF A MINE, *supra* note 1288, at 2. *See* MINERALS PROGRAM HANDBOOK, *supra* note 1366, § 4, for further Forest Service direction on forecasting mineral development. Therefore, the forecasting methods and reliability of data must be described in the forest plan. MINERALS PLANNING HANDBOOK, *supra* note 1422, § 1.23(d)(1). The forecast should cover the areas most likely to be developed inside the planning area as well as major developments in areas outside, but in the vicinity of, the planning area. *Id.*

[1428] 36 C.F.R. § 219.22(d) (1984).

[1429] Under FLPMA, the Forest Service only has authority to request withdrawals. *See supra* note 1405. The Forest Service Manual states:

> No authority has been granted to the Secretary of Agriculture to withdraw lands. Executive Order 10355 requires that the consent of the Secretary of Agriculture be obtained to withdraw lands under his jurisdiction. Lands under the jurisdiction of the Secretary of Agriculture can be withdrawn without his consent under the reclamation and power laws or by the President. The Secretary can request the withdrawal, by Executive Order 10355, of certain lands under his jurisdiction and lands under the jurisdiction of other agencies.

FOREST SERVICE MANUAL § 2760.11 (1984).

[1430] Forest Service policy generally considers withdrawal only of forest lands open to entry under the General Mining Law. FOREST SERVICE MANUAL § 2860.2 (1984). The Forest Service directs that withdrawals from mineral leasing will be rare because the land and surface resources can be protected with lease stipulations. *See supra* note 1364. "However, where there are numerous or re-management tool and the regulations require that it be given appropriate consideration in the land management plan. Plans must include criteria for determining what land should be withdrawn and the probable mineral potential of those lands.[1431]

Fourth, the forest plan should assess the impacts of the probable mineral development on the forest resources.[1432] This analysis should include on-site, off-site, and socio-economic impacts from all phases of expected development.[1433] If the projected mineral activities in an area are likely to cause significant disturbance to other surface resources, planners should draft a management prescription that focuses upon the mineral resource for the area.[1434] Otherwise, mineral management will be included as part of surface management prescriptions.[1435] In either case, the plan should specify all management practices associated with such development,[1436] including means of access.[1437]

---

peated offers or applications to lease certain lands where leasing would be incompatible with existing or planned uses, it may be advantageous to request withdrawal." FOREST SERVICE MANUAL § 2822.21 (1984). Such lands may be withdrawn for special purposes such as public recreation areas, riparian zones, scenic and botanical areas, and observation points. For a more detailed explanation, see *id.* § 2860.3.

[1431] MINERALS PLANNING HANDBOOK, *supra* note 1422, § 1.23(d)(2)(b). Existing withdrawals must also be evaluated. *See supra* note 1426.

[1432] 36 C.F.R. § 219.27(a)(7) (1984); MINERALS PLANNING HANDBOOK, *supra* note 1424, § 1.23(f). This assessment would include access requirements of probable mineral development. 36 C.F.R. § 219.22(e) (1984).

[1433] On-site impacts would include those activities having significant impacts on national forest land, such as major surface excavation and major oil and gas exploration. MINERALS PLANNING HANDBOOK, *supra* note 1422, § 1.23f(1)(a). Off-site impacts would include major pipelines, powerlines, access systems, and waste and tailings disposal areas. *Id.* § 1.23f(1)(b). Socio-economic impacts include significant mineral industry repercussions that will change community services and demand for national forest services. *Id.* § 1.23f(1)(c). *See also* MINERALS PROGRAM HANDBOOK, *supra* note 1366, § 4.21-4.

[1434] A prescription is a recipe for use of the land. "In such instances, mineral development can be thought of as an interim land use and warrants a separate prescription to facilitate the modeling process." MINERALS PLANNING HANDBOOK, *supra* note 1422, § 4.26. The Forest Service could also request the Department of the Interior to withdraw the land or to refuse lease issuance. FOREST SERVICE MANUAL § 2761.01 (1984).

[1435] MINERALS PLANNING HANDBOOK, *supra* note 1422, § 4.26.

[1436] Practices should be developed for the important mineral activities expected to occur on the planning unit during the planning period. Practices should include: (1) Expected phase of development, such as prospecting, exploration, development or production. (2) Type of activity, such as road construction, pipelines, or open pit mining. (3) Size of operation - large, medium, or small. (4) Type of access such as road or helicopter. (5) General location of activities. (6) Duration of activity.

Finally, the plan should evaluate the effects of renewable resource allocations and management on mineral development. This requirement provides an overview of the availability of land for mineral development. Under the plan, land initially should be divided into two categories. The first is land already withdrawn from mineral entry and proposed withdrawals.[1438] The second category, land open to mineral entry,[1439] is further divided into four categories: (1) land with specific protective or mitigation measures provided by statute or executive order;[1440] (2) land with mitigation measures and practices required by the regional forester;[1441] (3) land requiring only standard stipulations or "blanket" conditions;[1442] and (4) land with opportunities for coordination of surface and mineral resource development.[1443] Plotted with these land allocations should be the mineral potential of each area.[1444] Evaluation of the effects should be in terms of their economic and socio-economic impacts.[1445] In this manner, planning for other valid land uses can be coordinated with mineral development.

Id. § 4.25.

[1437] The problem of access is especially thorny. *See supra* note 1309. On access to national forest lands for mining and other purposes, see generally *supra* text at notes 338-42. Access routes often cause erosion and create conflicts with wildlife habitat. *Compare* Cabinet Mountains Wilderness v. Peterson, 685 F.2d 678 (D.C. Cir. 1982), *with* Foundation for N. Am. Wild Sheep v. United States Dep't of Agriculture, 681 F.2d 1172 (9th Cir. 1982).

[1438] MINERALS PLANNING HANDBOOK, *supra* note 1422, § 6.22(1).

[1439] *Id.* § 6.22(2).

[1440] These areas would include lands allocated for wilderness areas, protection of threatened and endangered species, or cultural or historic preservation. *Id.* § 6.22(2)(a).

[1441] These areas would include lands allocated to winter game range, visual corridors or exceptionally sensitive biophysical areas. Protective measures can be handled by lease and permit stipulations or conditions in operating plans. *Id.* § 6.22(2)(b).

[1442] These are lands with a minimum biophysical sensitivity and with no specific protection required by statute, executive order, or the regional forester. *Id.* § 6.22(2)(c).

[1443] "[F]or example, areas where timber could become available or manageable if road construction and/or maintenance costs could be shared with mineral development." *Id.* § 6.22(2)(d).

[1444] *See, e.g., id.* § 6, exhibit 1.

[1445] Economic effects include benefits attributable to mineral outputs and costs of minerals management. *Id.* § 6.23(1). Socio-economic effects "include changes in adequacy of schools, roads, and other public facilities and services as well as income and tax levels." *Id.* § 6.23(2).

The planning regulations, if properly implemented, have the potential of providing each national forest with an overall picture of present and anticipated mineral development and of its effects on the other surface resources. Nevertheless, major obstacles inhibit effective, integrated minerals planning. The scope of the endeavor is massive. The planner must confront vast surface areas, numerous mining claims (some valid and some not), incomplete data, inadequate surface reclamation techniques, insufficient funding, and a setting in which it is inherently difficult to make geologic and economic projections. Further, the fragmentation of management authority and the internal uncertainty of Forest Service authority continue to hamper Forest Service efforts to manage its surface resources.

However, it is now settled that the Forest Service holds considerable authority to control mineral development, both for hardrock and leasable resources. The agency possesses a variety of tools to mitigate the effects of fragmented authority, safeguard other resources, and allow development to proceed in an economically and environmentally acceptable manner. The magnitude of the undertaking will not disappear, but the work of the last fifteen years has laid a foundation for integrating mineral development with the co-equal resources that the Forest Service is mandated to manage.

VII

WILDLIFE

National forest habitats support half of the population of big game and cold water fish in the nation.[1446] Some of the animals attract recreational hunters and fishers to the national forests, while others are harvested for commercial purposes: recreational trout fishing and hunting for deer, elk, antelope, and other big game species generate substantial dollar outputs,[1447] and the sport and commercial market value of salmon in the national forests is estimated at over sixty-five million dollars annually.[1448] The Forest Service monitors all species that are federally designated as threatened or endangered. At present, the agency manages habitat for sixty-eight threatened or endangered species.[1449] Most national forest wildlife, however, consists of "nongame" species, a wide variety of animals with diverse life histories and habitat needs.[1450]

Wildlife resource planning is one of the most dynamic and unsettled areas of modern Forest Service responsibility. Wildlife planning in the national forests theoretically could encompass all members of the animal kingdom,[1451] but this is an impossible and perhaps undesirable goal. Instead, forest planners focus on vertebrate species of fish and wildlife and assume that providing a full diversity of vertebrates will also maintain diversity of the invertebrates and plants.[1452]

While concern for wildlife and their habitats is not new to the Forest Service, the agency historically has deferred to state wildlife agencies for planning and management of wildlife populations. Wildlife species conservation on federal lands was generally left to the national parks and wildlife refuges.[1453] The impetus for recent policy changes within the agency traces to activities occurring in the post-World War II period. An increased demand for wood

---

[1446] *1985 Forest Service Budget, supra* note 10, at 1340.
[1447] *Id.*
[1448] *Id.* at 1270.
[1449] *Id.*
[1450] *See* 1981 ASSESSMENT, *supra* note 9, at 119, 127.
[1451] This is the definition of "fish or wildlife" adopted by Congress in the Endangered Species Act of 1973. 16 U.S.C. § 1532(8) (1982). *See generally* Coggins & Ward, *supra* note 345, at 68.
[1452] *See* 36 C.F.R. § 219.19 (1984), discussed *infra* text accompanying notes 1585-1628.
[1453] *See generally* M. BEAN, *supra* note 601; Coggins & Ward, *supra* note 345, at 92-127.

products after the war resulted in the rapid transformation and loss of existing wildlife habitats such as salmon spawning beds, roadless range for grizzly bear, and woodpecker feeding and nesting trees. Public and congressional activism during the 1970s resulted in a broad statutory mandate in the National Forest Management Act (NFMA) to redirect traditional multiple-use policy as applied to wildlife.[1454]

Since enactment of the NFMA, wildlife has assumed a new and expanded role in national forest planning. The Forest Service is now responsible for managing national forests in order to augment the national parks and refuges as part of the nation's federal reserve system for wildlife and fish.[1455] As one recent study aptly stated, the NFMA and its implementing regulations extend "the Leopold Land Ethic to over 3,000 species and about 190 million acres of national forest lands."[1456] At the same time, the Forest Service has continued to maintain its partnership with the states in regard to national forest wildlife. Thus, current Forest Service wildlife policy is a combination of newly emerging concepts and traditional relationships.

A. Evolution of Policy

1. Early Legal Background (1891-1905)

Although by 1885 all states and territories had enacted legislation to protect game against uncontrolled and commercial hunting,[1457] federal wildlife law prior to 1900 has been described as "limited in scope and relatively insignificant in impact"[1458] and, less kindly, as "[not] worth mentioning."[1459] Since the Creative Act of 1891[1460] was silent on the subject of wildlife in the forest reserves, it remained for the public forest administrators to decide

---

[1454] *See infra* text accompanying notes 1553-82.

[1455] *See* H. SALWASSER, S. MEALEY & K. JOHNSON, FOREST SERVICE, U.S. DEP'T OF AGRICULTURE, WILDLIFE POPULATION VIABILITY—A QUESTION OF RISK 1 (1984) (presented at the 49th North American Wildlife and Natural Resources Conference, Boston, Mass.) [hereinafter cited as WILDLIFE POPULATION VIABILITY].

[1456] *Id.* at i. *See infra* note 1504.

[1457] G. ROBINSON, *supra* note 2, at 225.

[1458] M. BEAN, *supra* note 601, at 14.

[1459] Coggins & Ward, *supra* note 345, at 75.

[1460] Act of Mar. 3, 1891, 26 Stat. 1103 § 24, repealed by the Federal Land Policy and Management Act of 1976, 43 U.S.C. §§ 1701-1784.

what role, if any, the federal government would play in managing the wildlife resource.

Opinion in the administration during the 1890s was divided. Chief of the Division of Forestry Bernhard Fernow took a conservative approach, recommending that hunting and fishing be restricted only so far "as to enforce the State game laws, except on smaller reservations nearer settlements, when special regulations should provide checks against waste and wanton extirpation of the game and fish."[1461] Secretary of the Interior John W. Noble suggested a more preservation-oriented policy concerning wildlife on the forest reserves.[1462]

Congress considered several approaches toward the wildlife issue before passing the 1897 Organic Act. A bill introduced in 1892 provided that state or territorial game laws would apply except in limited circumstances: "[If] for special reasons the commissioner of forests deems it desirable, he may provide regulations for hunting and fishing on the reservations, not inconsistent with state or territorial laws."[1463] Representative Thomas R. McRae's competing bill was completely silent on the subject of wildlife.[1464] In 1896 Commissioner of the General Land Office S.W. Lamoreux prepared a substitute bill granting the Secretary power to preserve all resources, including game, from "injury, waste, fire, spoliation, or other destruction."[1465] The House passed this revised

---

[1461] 1891 ANNUAL REPORT OF THE CHIEF, *supra* note 228, at 228.

[1462] Noble stated, "[I]t is to be considered also that these parks will preserve the fauna, fish and flora of our country, and become resorts for the people seeking instruction and recreation, at the same time that they subserve the important agricultural and economic purposes . . . ." ANNUAL REPORT OF THE SECRETARY OF THE INTERIOR, Exec. Doc. No. 1, pt. 5, 52d Cong., 1st Sess. 15 (1891).

[1463] S. 3235, 52d Cong., 1st Sess., (1892).

[1464] H.R. 119 was introduced in 1893. H.R. REP. No. 119, 52d Cong., 1st Sess., 27 CONG. REC. 2779 (1893). The omission evidenced the general lack of concern for federal wildlife regulation in the reserves during the 1890s. There was no reference to wildlife or wild animals in the annual reports of the Secretary of the Interior from 1892 to 1896. Similarly, President Cleveland's annual messages to Congress are devoid of any reference to protection of wildlife in the reserves, yet in every message he requested legislation to protect the reserves themselves.

[1465] H.R. REP. No. 1593, 54th Cong., 1st Sess., 28 CONG. REC. 6410 (1896). Lamoreux felt that the legislation should recognize that forests are valuable for more than simple economic exploitation. He stated: "Inasmuch as, in addition to the timber on these reservations, there is much other valuable property to be cared for I have provided for the protection of the timber and other resources, including the herbage, and such natural wonders and curiosities and game as

bill with little comment on June 10, 1896,[1466] but the Senate failed to take action on the bill.[1467]

The Senate's failure to act on Lamoreux's version might have resulted from the Supreme Court's decision of *Geer v. Connecticut*,[1468] on March 2, 1896. Just three months prior to House passage of the Lamoreux bill, the Court stated that wild game was the property of the state in which it was found.[1469] Even though the *Geer* decision did not actually hold that the federal government was powerless to assert jurisdiction over wildlife on the public lands, many states interpreted it as such.[1470] As a result, Congress seems to have been uncertain of its own power.[1471]

Thus, when Congress passed the Forest Service Organic Act in 1897, it may well have harbored doubts concerning federal authority to manage wildlife. Although the Act authorized the Secretary of the Interior to make "such rules and regulations" as will "insure the objects" of the forest reserves and "to regulate

---

may be therein . . . ." Letter from S.W. Lamoreux to Hoke Smith (Feb. 7, 1896), *reprinted in id.*

[1466] 28 CONG. REC. 6410-11 (1896). The following colloquy took place on the floor of the House immediately preceding House passage:

MR. TERRY. I would like to ask the gentleman from Colorado if this is the bill that was prepared or revised by my colleague, Mr. McRae?

MR. BELL of Colorado. Yes, sir; it is.

MR. LACEY. The bill is the joint work of Mr. McRae, the Forestry Commission, the Land Office, and the Committee on Public Lands. It is a bill that has been prepared with a great deal of labor, and covers the question of the preservation and management of the forest reservations.

MR. ELLIS. And has the approval of all the members of the committee and members from the public-land States.

MR. HERMANN. It embraces the Senate amendments prepared at the last session.

MR. SHAFROTH. It is the same bill that passed the Senate last session, but failed to pass the House.

MR. HERMANN. It meets the approval of all the members from the public-lands States.

Id. at 6410. The statement of Representative Shafroth is curious in that there is no record of a similar bill having been considered by the Senate. The Senate had considered and passed a bill styled after Representative McRae's bill 16 months earlier. *See* 27 CONG. REC. 2779 (1895).

[1467] It has been argued that the intent of the Lamoreux bill survives in the Organic Act of 1897. *See* United States v. New Mexico, 438 U.S. 696, 722 (Powell, J., dissenting in part).

[1468] 161 U.S. 519 (1896).

[1469] *Id.* at 522.

[1470] *See* Hunt v. United States, 278 U.S. 96 (1928).

[1471] *See* M. BEAN, *supra* note 601, at 105, n.5.

their occupancy and use,"[1472] it is not clear whether Congress intended to delegate any power to regulate the taking of wildlife in the reserves.

Whatever the congressional intent when the 1897 Act was passed, subsequent actions by both Congress and President Theodore Roosevelt suggested that the Act was inadequate to protect wildlife in the forest reserves. In 1899 Congress discouraged development of a national forest wildlife policy by enacting a statute that required federal employees to "aid in the enforcement of the laws of the State or Territory in which said forest reservation is situated in relation to the protection of fish and game."[1473] The Act was cited four years later by the Senate Committee on Forest Reservations and the Protection of Game as having recognized "the fact that the States and Territories are in control of the fish and game."[1474] Congress had further bolstered the states' regulatory authority with passage of the Lacey Act of 1900,[1475] which made interstate transportation of wildlife killed in violation of state law a federal crime.

President Roosevelt was an avid champion of wildlife preservation.[1476] At the time, although Roosevelt and other

---

[1472] 16 U.S.C. § 551 (1982), discussed *supra* section II(A)(2).

[1473] Act of Mar. 3, 1899, 30 Stat. 1095. It was not until March 3, 1905 that Forest Service employees were given authority to make warrantless arrests of persons who violated laws, including state fish and game laws, in the forest reserves. *See supra* note 262. The 1899 Act was so ineffectual that three months after its passage Attorney General John Griggs stated, "[T]he statutes for the protection of these forest reserves seem singularly deficient in that they do not provide any efficient means for the arrest of persons violating the laws or the rules and regulations for the protection of these reservations." 1899 GLO REPORT, *supra* note 503, at 102.

[1474] S. REP. NO. 2620, 57th Cong., 2d Sess. 1 (1903). This report accompanied S. 6689, a bill that would have given the President power to designate game preserves within the forest reserves. *See infra* text accompanying notes 1477-91. The report cited the need for legislation to protect wildlife: "[U]nfortunately, there is no provision in the act of 1897 for the protection of game, and consequently the game question is relegated to the jurisdiction of the state authorities." S. REP. NO. 2620, *supra*, at 2.

[1475] Act of May 25, 1900, ch. 553, 31 Stat. 187 (codified as amended at 16 U.S.C. § 701 (1982)).

[1476] Roosevelt, was an active outdoorsman and enthusiastic hunter. After traveling to the Dakota Territory in 1883 for the purpose of killing a buffalo, Roosevelt reportedly shot one of the last buffalo in the Territory, then did a war dance around the carcass. Eliot, *T.R.'s Wilderness Legacy*, 162 NAT'L GEOGRAPHIC 340, 344 (1982). Roosevelt was a founding member of the Boone and Crockett Club, a group formed in 1888 "[t]o work for the preservation of the large game of this country, and, so far as possible, to further legislation for

278 *Land and Resource Planning in the National Forests*

conservationists of the period sought the establishment of "game refuges" in order to prevent wildlife depletion,[1477] wildlife policy was premised almost exclusively on the notion that regulation of killing would suffice to protect against depletion.[1478] On November 13, 1901, less than two months after becoming President, Roosevelt asked Attorney General Philander C. Knox if either the Organic Act of 1897 or the Act of 1899 provided administrative authority to prohibit hunting on the forest reserves.[1479] In an opinion that continues to embody a basic assumption of national forest wildlife policy, Knox replied that Congress had not intended to change "the settled policy and practice of the Government . . . to permit free access to the public lands for hunting, trapping, and fishing."[1480] Furthermore, since the 1897 Act expressly recognized state civil and criminal jurisdiction within the reserves, "if State laws permit hunting or fishing there, the Secretary may not forbid it, or, if unlawful, he can not permit it."[1481]

Four days after receiving Knox's negative response, Roosevelt took his cause to Congress. Roosevelt declared:

> Some at least of the forest reserves should afford perpetual protection to the native fauna and flora, safe havens of refuge to our rapidly diminishing wild animals of the larger kinds, and free camping-grounds for the ever-increasing numbers of men and women who have learned to find rest, health, and recreation in the splendid forests and flower-clad meadows of our mountains. The forest reserves should be set apart forever for the use and benefit of our people as a whole and not sacrificed to the short-sighted greed of a few.[1482]

---

that purpose, and to assist in enforcing the existing laws." Const. of the Boone and Crockett Club, art. 2, § 3 (1888), *reprinted in* J. TREFETHEN, CRUSADE FOR WILDLIFE 356 (1961). Members of the club later included Gifford Pinchot, *id.* at 44; Representative John F. Lacey, *id.* at 40; and Senator George C. Perkins, *id.* at 70. Both Lacey and Perkins introduced legislation to allow Roosevelt to declare game preserves in the forest reserves. *See infra* text accompanying notes 1483-91.

[1477] *See infra* note 1491.

[1478] In spite of the existence of state game laws, there were few effective controls to abate the slaughter of American wildlife during the 19th and early 20th centuries. For an emotional account, *see* W. HORNADAY, OUR VANISHING WILD LIFE (1913).

[1479] 23 OP. ATT'Y GEN. 589 (1901). The question was posed on behalf of Roosevelt by Gifford Pinchot, then Chief of the Bureau of Forestry.

[1480] *Id.* at 592.

[1481] *Id.* at 594. The provision on state jurisdiction is 16 U.S.C. § 480 (1982).

[1482] *First Annual Message* (Dec. 3, 1901), *reprinted in* T. ROOSEVELT, STATE PAPERS AS GOVERNOR AND PRESIDENT 1899-1909, 81, 104 (1926) [hereinafter cited as ROOSEVELT PAPERS].

Two days later Representative John Lacey inquired of Attorney General Knox whether Congress possessed constitutional power to enact legislation prohibiting hunting on the forest reserves.[1483] Knox's affirmative answer[1484] prompted Lacey to introduce legislation that would have given the President authority to create game refuges in the forest reserves upon the request of the governor of the state in which the reserves were located.[1485] While the House generally supported the proposal for game refuges, objections to another section of the bill were strong enough to defeat the proposal.[1486]

[1483] Letter from Rep. John F. Lacey to Hon. P.C. Knox (Dec. 5, 1901), *reprinted in* H.R. REP. NO. 968, 57th Cong., 1st Sess. 6 (1902). Lacey's letter to Knox stated that Congress knew it had the power to prohibit transport of game from one state to another when killed in violation of state laws. But Lacey did not know if the constitutional power existed for Congress to frame statutes which directly prohibited hunting on the public land. "In this borderland of State and national authority . . .," Lacey stated, "care should be exercised to avoid conflict of jurisdiction where so much depends upon having the laws backed up by a friendly local public sentiment." *Id.* at 7.

[1484] Attorney General Knox's reply of January 3, 1902, concluded that the United States, as a proprietor, could limit the purposes for entry on the public lands and could protect game by making illegal the entry on or use of a forest reserve for the purpose of killing or capturing game. *Id.* at 14. Knox reasoned that since any proprietor could prohibit entry for any purpose on private land, the United States could do the same without contravening state wildlife laws. *Id.* at 13, 14. Thus Knox avoided the question of federal preemption of state wildlife law. However, Knox closed his opinion by suggesting that Congress make killing or capturing game evidence of the illegal purpose of entry. *Id.* at 15. He recognized that this was tantamount to direct regulation of the act of hunting but stated, "[T]his may be questionable in case, for example, when one who is properly there, kills game. I would insert it at any rate, and it will . . . operate as a preventive." *Id.*

[1485] H.R. 11,536, 57th Cong., 1st Sess., 35 CONG. REC. 6509-27 (1902). Lacey believed that hunting, not forest management, was the cause of wildlife depletion. During consideration of the bill, Lacey declared:

> Our ancestors were all killers. . . . If these cruel forefathers of ours had owned breech-loaders the . . . horse, the cow, the sheep, and the ox would have disappeared from the earth . . . . The boy of to-day is as bloody-minded as his naked forefather . . . . From the days of the troglodyte the unequal contest has raged. . . . The immensity of man's power to slay imposes great responsibilities. . . . The birdless world would be a dreary place to live in and a birdless air would be unfit to breathe. . . . Mankind must conserve the resources of nature.

35 Cong. Rec. 6512 (1902).

[1486] Lacey's bill, which included a controversial provision that transferred administrative control of the forest reserves from the Department of the Interior to the Department of Agriculture, had been referred to his own Committee on the Public Lands. A minority of the committee submitted a report that objected only to the proposed transfer, stating "[t]he idea embodied in the bill of establishing

On December 2, 1902, Roosevelt again appealed to Congress for legislation to protect wildlife in the forest reserves.[1487] Contemporaneously, Senator George Perkins introduced a bill providing for administratively designated game refuges.[1488] This bill passed the Senate and was referred to the House Committee on Public Lands, of which Lacey was Chairman. Two committee members who had approved the game refuge provision in Lacey's previous bill[1489] issued a blistering condemnation of the Senate bill, calling it "the fad of game preservation run stark raving mad."[1490] The bill died for lack of action as the 57th Congress ended. Undeterred in his determination to establish game refuges, Roosevelt created the Pelican Island Bird Refuge by presidential proclamation on March 14, 1903.[1491]

---

by Executive order game and fish preserves . . . meets with our approval . . . ." H.R. REP. NO. 968, 57th Cong., 1st Sess., pt. 2, at 6 (1902).

[1487] *Second Annual Message* (Dec. 2, 1902), *reprinted in* ROOSEVELT PAPERS, *supra* note 1482, at 139, 161.

[1488] S. 6689, 57th Cong., 2d Sess., 36 CONG. REC. 467 (1902).

[1489] The minority report on the Lacey bill was signed by Representatives Mondell, Jones, Fordney, and Shafroth. H.R. REP. NO. 968, *supra* note 1486, pt. 2, at 6. The House minority report on Perkins' bill, S. 6689, was signed by Mondell and Fordney. H.R. REP. NO. 3862, 57th Cong., 2d Sess., pt. 2, at 4 (1903).

[1490] H.R. REP. NO. 3862, *supra* note 1489, pt. 2, at 3. The reason for this drastic change of position was probably that S. 6689 failed to include a provision for recommendation by the Governor of the state in which the game preserve was established. The minority report declared, "It would be difficult to conceive of a message which more contemptuously ignores and insolently disregards the rights and wishes of the people of the States in which the 'preserves' provided for will be located." *Id.* at 2. There was also the fear that the preserves would become "enormous breeding grounds—larger than States of the Union—for the purpose of breeding, among other animals, bear, mountain lion, wildcats, wolves and coyotes to prey upon the people of the surrounding regions . . . . [T]he Government would be steadily nurturing them in the woods and mountains to become a terror by night and a menace by day . . . ." Further, the minority report argued that those who were honestly interested in game preservation should expend their energy influencing the people of the states, rather than attempting by federal legislation to rob the states of that right and to "transform the forest reserves from regions set apart for timber preservation and water conservation into jungles of wild beasts." *Id.* at 3.

[1491] By one account, after Congress had twice refused to grant Roosevelt authority to create refuges, he simply asked, "Is there any law that will prevent me from declaring Pelican Island a Federal Bird Reservation?" When told that the island was federal property, he delivered a fiat: "Very well, then I so declare it." Eliot, *supra* note 1476, at 350. Within two years of Roosevelt's declaration of Pelican Island as a bird refuge, Congress became directly involved in the creation of wildlife refuges, first by authorizing the President to create them and later by establishing them through direct congressional acts. *See* M. BEAN, *supra* note 601, at 120.

In sum, legal uncertainty[1492] and political resistance severely
hampered the early development of national forest wildlife policy.
As a result, the Forest Service inherited a federal wildlife policy
that was deferential to state authority and limited in management
direction.

2. *Management and Conservation (1905-1960)*

Initially, the Forest Service paid little attention to wildlife,
aside from strictly utilitarian management. During Gifford
Pinchot's tenure as Chief Forester, the emphasis in national forest
wildlife management was on predator control.[1493] Although an incidental benefit of predator eradication was an increase in game
populations, the intended beneficiaries were grazing interests.[1494]
Predator control and other aspects of wildlife management were

---

[1492] *See supra* text accompanying notes 1468-72. Congress's power over wildlife on the public lands was not finally settled until 1976 when the Supreme
Court decided Kleppe v. New Mexico, 426 U.S. 529 (1976). In *Kleppe* the Court
held that Congress had power under the property clause, U.S. Const. art. IV, § 3
cl. 2, to assert regulatory authority over animals found on the public lands and
that such regulation pre-empts state law.

Kleppe was foreshadowed by a series of cases that had whittled away the state
ownership doctrine of Geer v. Connecticut, 161 U.S. 519 (1896), discussed *supra*
at notes 1468-71 and accompanying text. In 1928 the Court held that the Forest
Service could reduce the size of a deer herd, notwithstanding the state hunting
laws of Arizona, for the purpose of protecting federal lands. Hunt v. United
States, 278 U.S. 96 (1928). The "protection of the land" rationale was later
extended in New Mexico State Game Comm'n v. Udall, 410 F.2d 1197 (10th
Cir. 1969), where the Forest Service killed deer without state permission simply
for research purposes. Three years after *Kleppe*, the state ownership doctrine
came to an end when the Court expressly overruled *Geer* in Hughes v.
Oklahoma, 441 U.S. 322 (1979). Together, *Hughes* and *Kleppe* left no doubt as
to Congress' power to assert supreme jurisdiction over wildlife on the public
lands. For accounts of the development of federal wildlife laws, *see* M. BEAN,
supra note 601, at 20; Coggins & Ward, *supra* note 345, at 75. On federal-state
relations see generally *supra* text accompanying notes 343-61.

[1493] *See, e.g.*, 1908 USE BOOK, *supra* note 1114, at 148:
  Whenever it is found that the stock interests are suffering or that the number of game animals or birds is on the decrease on account of wolves, cou-
  gars, coyotes, bobcats, or other predatory animals, a report should be made
  to the Forester, with recommendations for such action as is necessary to
  get rid of them.
Wolves were considered particularly pernicious. A Forest Service bulletin said,
"Their complete extermination on the western range is not, however, to be expected in the near future, and it is only by constant and concerted effort that
their numbers can be kept down sufficiently to prevent serious depredations."
FOREST SERVICE, U.S. DEP'T OF AGRICULTURE, BULLETIN NO. 72 (1907).

[1494] *See* H. STEEN, *supra* note 49, at 87.

the responsibility of local rangers who were trained principally for timber management.[1495] Forest officers were instructed to aid in the enforcement of state game laws, but only "so far as they can without undue interference with their regular Forest work."[1496]

Under Chief Henry Graves, the Forest Service gave more attention to the protection and enhancement of wildlife habitat. To protect game animals and birds from molestation or extinction, the agency closed limited range areas to livestock grazing.[1497] The Forest Service cooperated with states, territories, and the federal Bureau of Fisheries in stocking streams with fish.[1498] In 1921 Chief William Greeley recognized wildlife as having value beyond meat and fur: "The wild life of the forests has various kinds of values—material, esthetic, scientific, educational. All should be recognized."[1499] Additionally, Greeley stated that:

> The use of the National Forests as the habitat of wild game is of considerable public importance. The presence of game adds to their attractiveness not only to hunters but to occupants generally, and anything that contributes to the abundance and variety of game increases the value of the Forests for public purposes. The same thing applies to fish in the Forest streams. The Forest Service has a corresponding duty and obligation.[1500]

Still, Chief Greeley considered wildlife a usable resource: "Under skillful management the quantity produced can be increased, its kind regulated, and its most desirable utilization secured."[1501] The

---

[1495] Early Forest service publications encouraged prospective rangers to study botany, chemistry, physical geography, and other subjects; however, there was no mention of animal sciences. *See*, FOREST SERVICE, U.S. DEP'T OF AGRICULTURE, SUGGESTIONS TO PROSPECTIVE FOREST STUDENTS 3 (3d rev. 1905).

[1496] 1907 USE BOOK, *supra* note 1104, at 116.

[1497] 1915 USE BOOK, *supra* note 700, at 73.

[1498] *Id.* at 28. Congress first appropriated money for fish management in the national forests in 1907. Agriculture Appropriations Act of 1907, 34 Stat. 1269, 1270.

[1499] 1921 ANNUAL REPORT OF THE CHIEF, *supra* note 1121, at 29.

[1500] *Id.* at 27.

[1501] *Id.* at 29. Similarly, in the Copeland Report of 1933, the Forest Service stated:

> Good wild-life management on forest lands in the ultimate analysis is simply one phase of good multiple-purpose forest land management, which seeks for the highest quality and quantity output of products, uses, and services. In general the practices that contribute to the perpetuation and development of other products, services, and uses may be made to contribute to the welfare of wild life.

COPELAND REPORT, *supra* note 112, at 506.

major concern in wildlife management was to provide good hunting and fishing.[1502]

Hunters and fishers, however, were not the only group interested in forest wildlife. The modern conservation movement, with its emphasis on habitats and ecosystems, was in its infancy. There was a young and growing wildlife management profession,[1503] sensitive to wildlife values beyond hunting and fishing. Additionally, there was the voice of Aldo Leopold—a leader in Forest Service wildlife conservation policy.[1504]

During the 1930s tension developed between the traditional forester and the wildlife specialist over the role of wildlife in multiple-use management policy.[1505] For instance, the Game Policy

---

[1502] The Forest Service annual reports typically referred to forest wildlife as "game." Species referred to were big-game animals such as antelope, bear, deer, elk, moose, mountain goats, sheep, and beaver. *E.g.*, 1931 ANNUAL REPORT OF THE CHIEF, *supra* note 1060, at 49-50.

Meeting the demands for game animals, however, was not an easy task. Domestic livestock and wildlife competed for forage, and livestock drove wildlife away. Grazing interests chafed at reductions in allotments that were designed to protect game. *See id.* at 47-48. In some areas predator eradication had been so effective that the game populations exploded, prompting the Forest Service to license hunters to reduce herd size. *See* Hunt v. United States, 278 U.S. 96 (1928). Further problems were caused by non-uniform state game laws, which reflected sometimes inconsistent or uninformed policy. Thus, the Forest Service was faced with shortages of game in some areas and overabundant game in others. For an account of these problems, see generally J. TREFETHEN, *supra* note 1476.

[1503] The first undergraduate program in game management began in 1924. There were three such programs in 1929. *See* Soc'y of Am. Foresters, *Report of the Comm. on Game Management with Reference to Forestry*, 37 J. FORESTRY 130 (1939).

[1504] Leopold described the change in the conservation movement thus:

The recent trend in wild life conservation shows the direction in which ideas are evolving. At the inception of the movement fifty years ago, its underlying thesis was to save species from extermination. The means to this end were a series of restrictive enactments. The duty of the individual was to cherish and extend these enactments, and to see that his neighbor obeyed them. The whole structure was negative and prohibitory. It assumed land to be a constant in the ecological equation. Gun-powder and blood-lust were the variables needing control.

There is now being superimposed on this a positive and affirmatory ideology, the thesis of which is to prevent the deterioration of environment.

Leopold, *The Conservation Ethic*, 31 J. FORESTRY 634, 641 (1933). *See generally* A. LEOPOLD, GAME MANAGEMENT (1933).

[1505] Before the emergence of the wildlife management profession, traditionally trained foresters had been placed in wildlife management positions. By 1939 this practice was brought into question:

The difficulty is in large measure due to the lack of appreciation of the real meaning of wildlife management. In cases where those in charge of a for-

Committee of the Society of American Foresters found that wild-life management and silviculture did not fit together easily, "[n]or can the fitting be accomplished without mutual concessions."[1506] The Committee criticized the foresters' lack of concern for non-game species: "It is hard to find instances in which the new and powerful tools now available have been deliberately employed in the interest of nongame, rare, or threatened species, either by for-esters or by anyone else."[1507]

In 1936 the Forest Service recognized the changing role of wild-life in multiple-use policy by establishing a Division of Wildlife Management, which employed eighty-three specialists.[1508] While game remained the top wildlife priority,[1509] there also was a devel-oping concern within the Forest Service for the preservation of rare, nongame species. For example, the Forest Service closed "to trespass" an area of the Los Padres National Forest to protect a nesting colony of thirty-five California condors.[1510] The agency ex-pected that this type of protection "will be extended to other spe-cies of plants or animals as occasion demands."[1511]

Thus, by the late 1930s it appeared that the Forest Service, with the addition of a division of wildlife specialists, would con-tinue to expand its emphasis on wildlife conservation. World War II, however, presented more pressing national priorities, and the Forest Service discontinued its emerging wildlife conservation pol-icy in favor of strict utilitarianism. The Division of Wildlife was gutted,[1512] production of timber became paramount, and forest

---

est think that the information incidentally picked up while fishing or mark-ing timber in a watershed is all that is needed for the management of its wildife, we cannot hope for much progress.

Soc'y of Am. Foresters, *supra* note 1503, at 131.

[1506] Soc'y of Am. Foresters, *Second Report of Game Policy Comm.*, 35 J. FORESTRY 228 (1937).

[1507] *Id.* The report squared the forester against the wildlife manager: "It should occasion no surprise when the hiring of a game technician to argue wild-life interests with the timber-stand improvement crew raises more questions than it answers." *Id.*

[1508] 1937 ANNUAL REPORT OF THE CHIEF, *supra* note 114, at 22.

[1509] Chief of the Division of Wildlife Management, H.L. Shantz, reported to the Society of American Foresters: "Management regards wildlife as a crop, the product of the land and suitable local environment, produced for both the eco-nomic and social welfare of man." Shantz, *Recent Developments in Wildlife Management*, 36 J. FORESTRY 149 (1938).

[1510] *Id.* at 151.

[1511] *Id.*

[1512] 1946 ANNUAL REPORT OF THE CHIEF, *supra* note 711, at 24-25.

fauna was viewed primarily as providing "a liberal meat diet for 225,000 people."[1513]

After the war ended, several factors combined to foreclose a return to pre-war Forest Service wildlife policy. The Forest Service received no congressional appropriations for fish and wildlife management in the years immediately after the war.[1514] The number of Americans who hunted and fished reached an all-time high and attention was thus deflected away from nongame species.[1515] Timber harvest was increasing rapidly.[1516] The states played a larger role in wildlife planning.[1517] For the Forest Service, wildlife habitat management took the form of "coordination and adjustment of other resource management activities" and cooperative habitat improvement projects with the states.[1518] Appropriations for wildlife habitat management eventually resumed but were miniscule relative to appropriations for timber management.[1519]

3. Multiple Use (1960-1976)

(a) Congressional and Judicial Action

The MUSY Act of 1960[1520] made clear for the first time that wildlife and fish resource management was a valid purpose for es-

---

[1513] 1942 ANNUAL REPORT OF THE CHIEF, *supra* note 706, at 20. The following year the Chief reported that the forests were suffering from a big game surplus and that failure to harvest the surplus "means a loss of some 30 million pounds of meat to the Nation's food supply." FOREST SERVICE, U.S. DEP'T OF AGRICULTURE, [1943 ANNUAL] REPORT OF THE CHIEF 19-20 (1943).

[1514] 1950 ANNUAL REPORT OF THE CHIEF, *supra* note 118, at 46. The report stated that "only a skeleton organization was maintained by the transfer of funds from other activities. Not only did this greatly restrict wildlife-management work but other activities suffered likewise." *Id.*

[1515] Between 1940 and 1965 the number of recreational fishers nearly doubled. U.S. PUBLIC LAND LAW REVIEW COMM'N, FISH AND WILDLIFE RESOURCES ON THE PUBLIC LANDS 199 (rev. 1969) [hereinafter cited as FISH & WILDLIFE RESOURCES]. The number of licensed hunters relative to the population at large was 9.2% in 1955. Since then, this percentage has decreased. *Id.*

[1516] *See supra* text accompanying notes 710-20.

[1517] *See, e.g.,* 1956 ANNUAL REPORT OF THE CHIEF, *supra* note 713, at 6-7.

[1518] *Id.* at 6.

[1519] In 1936 the ratio of expenditures for "timber use" management to "fish and game protection" was about two to one. 1936 ANNUAL REPORT OF THE CHIEF, *supra* note 95, at 57. From 1955 through 1960 the ratio averaged approximately thirteen to one. 106 CONG. REC. 12,079-82 (1960).

[1520] 16 U.S.C. § 528 (1982). *See infra* text accompanying notes 1636-41.

tablishing and administering the national forests.[1521] "Wildlife and fish" were mentioned last in the list of multiple-use resources because the Forest Service desired to underscore state control over fish and wildlife.[1522] Congress, however, stated its intent that the listing order be "merely alphabetical" and not be construed as indicating any priority among resources.[1523]

Congress also set out its intent not to disturb the existing balance of state and federal responsibility for wildlife management. The MUSY Act states, "Nothing herein shall be construed as affecting the jurisdiction or responsibilities of the several states with respect to wildlife and fish on the national forests."[1524] The effect of this provision was to reinforce the Forest Service's historically dominant conception of responsibility for wildlife in the national forests: wildlife policy continued to be governed largely by state priorities, which leaned heavily toward game and sportfish.

While the MUSY Act recognized wildlife and fish as co-equal to other national forest resources, Congress gave no guidance for resolving conflicts and making trade-offs, other than to require sustained yield of "various renewable resources."[1525] The Act also proved an ineffective vehicle for judicial review of Forest Service

---

[1521] The Sustained-Yield Forest Management Act of 1944, 16 U.S.C. § 583 (1982), expressly mentioned wildlife preservation as one of its goals, but it did not apply to the national forests as a system and its application was discretionary with the secretaries of Agriculture and Interior.

[1522] In drafting the bill, the Forest Service reversed the order of the standard term "fish and wildlife" to "wildlife and fish." The reason was to prevent fish and wildlife from coming first in the alphabetical list—outdoor recreation, range, timber, watershed, and wildlife and fish, 16 U.S.C. § 28 (1982). Former Assistant Chief of the Forest Service Edward C. Crafts, who participated in drafting the bill, later explained:

> The only reason we chose "wildlife and fish" was to make that resource group come last in the listing because fish and wildlife are under control of the States on the national forests. This was the real reason. The customary way is to say "fish and wildlife." This would have made those resources come first and we didn't want fish to be listed first in an enumeration of national-forest resources. As a matter of fact, our critics were correct in their suspicion but we never admitted it.

Crafts, *Saga of Law Part I*, AM. FORESTS, June 1970, at 18. In its letter to Congress transmitting the draft bill, the Forest Service listed the resources as "watershed, timber, range, outdoor recreation, and fish and wildlife." H.R. REP. NO. 1551, 86th Cong., 2d Sess., *reprinted in* 1960 U.S. CODE CONG. & AD. NEWS (USCCAN), 2377, 2381.

[1523] H.R. REP. NO. 1551, at 3, *reprinted in* 1960 USCCAN at 2379.

[1524] 16 U.S.C. § 528 (1982). The legislative history of this provision is discussed *infra* note 1638.

[1525] 16 U.S.C. § 531(b) (1982).

decisions that adversely affected wildlife. For example, in *Kisner v. Butz*,[1526] local residents challenged the Forest Service's decision to construct a 4.3 mile segment of road through the Monongahela National Forest in West Virginia. Two state wildlife biologists and the director of West Virginia's Department of Natural Resources believed that the proposed road would constitute a threat to scarce black bear breeding grounds. Further, a "multiple use survey" prepared by the district ranger recommended that the road not be built. However, the forest supervisor concluded that there was "reasonable professional disagreement" concerning the impact of the road on the black bear habitat and decided to proceed with construction.[1527] On the basis of a trial court record containing no administrative record "upon which to base a judicial review,"[1528] the district court dismissed the complaint. The court summarily characterized the MUSY Act as "involved, in a peripheral way."[1529] The controversy was one of several that created national unrest over development in the national forests and led to remedial action by Congress.[1530]

[1526] 350 F. Supp. 310 (N.D.W. Va. 1972).

[1527] *Id.* at 314.

[1528] *Id.* at 315.

[1529] *Id.* at 310.

[1530] *Kisner*, decided in 1972, was "an opening shot in the Monongahela National Forest battle," which damaged the Forest Service's credibility. Coggins & Evans, *supra* note 30, at 426. However, the cold war over Forest Service management of the wildlife resource in West Virginia predated *Kisner* by at least five years. In March 1967 the West Virginia legislature appointed a special committee to investigate forest management practices in the national forests situated in West Virginia, expressing the concern that such practices "may not be conducive to the best utilization of such forests for recreational and other uses." It further found that "[t]he great natural beauty and game habitat of West Virginia is being depleted by such practices in many instances . . . ." W. VA. S. CON. RES. 47, 58th Leg., 1st Sess. (1967).

Criticism of Forest Service wildlife management was by no means universal. For instance, in 1969 the Forest Service was cited as the most active federal agency involved in wildlife habitat improvement programs by the Public Land Law Review Commission. *See* FISH & WILDLIFE RESOURCES, *supra* note 1515, at 267. Beginning in 1960, the Forest Service trained selected timber and wildlife specialists in timber management-wildlife habitat management coordination techniques. 1960 ANNUAL REPORT OF THE CHIEF, *supra* note 128, at 25. The hope was "to improve the integration of wildlife management with other resource management activities and uses on National Forests." *Id.* Subsequently, the Forest Service developed a variety of wildlife management plans and techniques. *See* G. ROBINSON, *supra* note 2, at 230-31.

(b) The Emerging Concept of Diversity

After passage of the MUSY Act, two major systems of wildlife management developed in the Forest Service: species richness and featured species.[1531] Based in part on the ecological principles of Leopold and other conservationists in the 1930s, the management systems both were designed to achieve "habitat diversity."[1532]

The general goal of the species richness system was to ensure that most, if not all, wildlife species within the managed area were maintained in viable numbers.[1533] The system emphasized management techniques to provide or maintain diverse habitats for a wider variety of species. Such methods included clearcutting to create forage, as well as protecting old-growth forests to maintain cover.[1534] While wildlife managers using the species richness system would occasionally focus on a specific species,[1535] they usually did not establish management standards for any particular species.[1536] As a result, the system could not ensure that all native species would be maintained.[1537]

[1531] *See* J. Gill, B. Radtke, & J. Thomas, Forest Wildlife Habitat Management: Ecological and Management Systems, in *Senate NFMA Hearings, supra* note 194, at 820. This paper, authored by three Forest Service wildlife experts, appears to be a significant document in the legislative history of the NFMA's wildlife planning requirements. Chief John McGuire inserted the paper into the record of the Senate hearings on proposed NFMA legislation, after explaining that the paper had been prepared for the Senate committee's use. *See* Senate NFMA Hearings, *supra* note 194, at 289.

[1532] J. Gill, R. Radtke & J. Thomas, *supra* note 1531, at 821.

[1533] *Id.* at 820.

[1534] *Id.* at 822; Salwasser, Siderits & Holbrook, *Applying Species-Habitat Relationships in Managing for National Forest Wildlife Diversity, reprinted in* Natural Diversity in Forest Ecosystems 173, 174 (1984) (proceedings of workshop at the Inst. of Ecology, Univ. of Ga., Athens, Ga.).

[1535] *See* J. Gill, R. Radtke & J. Thomas, *supra* note 1531, at 822.

[1536] *See* Salwasser, Siderits, & Holbrook, *supra* note 1534, at 174.

[1537] *See* J. Gill, R. Radtke & J. Thomas, *supra* note 1531, at 821. One influential report on federal wildlife policies in the early 1970s was especially critical of the lack of effective management standards and prescriptions:

> Forest management plans must include positive action programs designed to create and improve habitat which will maintain and increase diversity of wildlife populations. . . . Simple prescriptions are not acceptable. For example, the dictum—good silviculture is good wildlife management—is not an adequate response.
>   * * *
> [I]t is necessary to develop a specific prescription for each unit of land which will create and maintain habitat conditions for a wide variety of wildlife species, and which will maintain populations at a level where those species will not be threatened with extirpation or extinction.

The featured species wildlife management system, which was primarily applied in the Southeast, focused on individual species whose habitat needs could be defined and then meshed with the needs for production of timber and other resources.[1538] Featured species management expanded the traditional game management emphasis to encompass nongame species. The concept was ideal for dealing with rare, threatened, or endangered species—particularly those whose habitats were jeopardized by other resource management activities.

Featured species management was not a new concept. Before World War II the Forest Service had made various efforts to protect threatened species.[1539] The system, however, was much more difficult for wildlife planners to implement when nonthreatened species were involved. The task of choosing featured species and coordinating their management with other species and resources required "[d]eliberate, well-reasoned trade-offs."[1540] For instance, choosing one particular species might result in management incompatible with the needs of other resident species.[1541] Furthermore, forest managers were often reluctant to reduce timber production to accommodate wildlife habitat needs.[1542] While managers would reduce resource outputs to protect threatened species, little or no reduction was ordinarily allowed for nonthreatened species.[1543]

Webb, *Timber and Wildlife,* REPORT OF THE PRESIDENT'S ADVISORY PANEL ON TIMBER AND THE ENVIRONMENT, app. N (1973), *reprinted in* SENATE NFMA HEARINGS, *supra* note 194, at 664, 682-83. The author of the wildlife report, Dr. William L. Webb, subsequently was appointed to the Committee of Scientists, which assisted the Forest Service in drafting regulations to implement the NFMA.

[1538] *See, e.g.,* Zeedyk & Hazel, *The Southeastern Featured Species Plan,* in proceedings of Timber-Wildlife Mgmt. Symp., Univ. of Mo. 58 (1974).

[1539] *See supra* text accompanying notes 1510-11.

[1540] Zeedyk & Hazel, *supra* note 1538, at 61.

[1541] *Id.*

[1542] One scholar wrote in 1975 that "wildlife management continues to struggle for independent recognition; in most national forests it must still be considered a distinctly secondary, even incidental, function." G. ROBINSON, *supra* note 2, at 229.

[1543] Zeedyk & Hazel, *supra* note 1538, at 62. Secondary featured species can be promoted if done "without negating coordination for the primary species . . . or if done without unduly complicating timber management beyond those practices prescribed in behalf of the featured species." *Id.* at 61-62. Dr. Webb's 1973 report on wildlife proposed that specific objectives be set for a wide variety of featured species, which Webb referred to as "indicator species." The report stated:

While conceptually distinct, species richness and featured species were not mutually exclusive management systems. In fact, most of those national forest planners giving serious attention to wildlife issues used a combination of the two habitat management systems.[1544]

Congress adopted the common objective of the species richness and featured species systems—to achieve habitat diversity—in the NFMA. These systems were translated, respectively, into two key elements of post-NFMA wildlife planning: populations of all vertebrates well distributed over the forests and productive habitat for management indicator species.[1545] The Forest Service has endeavored to combine both elements into a "comprehensive habitat" approach.[1546] These aspects of post-NFMA planning will be discussed fully following an examination of Congress's intent in enacting the "diversity provision" of the NFMA.

B. Wildlife Planning and the NFMA—The Diversity Provision

During the sixteen years following enactment of the MUSY Act, Congress imposed only one major substantive restriction on the Forest Service's discretion in wildlife matters.[1547] The Endangered Species Act of 1973[1548] (ESA) set out mandatory con-

---

Inclusion of wildlife in multiple-use management requires establishment of specific indicator species as management objectives. Highest priority must go to endangered species which often require dedication of land to maintain habitat for that species alone. Rare species often require special management consideration where other management objectives are subordinated. In the majority of areas, diversity of wildlife populations should be the management objective, and the group of indicator species selected must represent a wide variety of habitat requirements.

Webb, *supra* note 1537, at 683.

[1544] *See* J. GILL, R. RADTKE & J. THOMAS, *supra* note 1531, at 822.

[1545] *See infra* text accompanying notes 1583-1617.

[1546] *See* Salwasser, Siderits & Holbrook, *supra* note 1534, at 174.

[1547] The National Environmental Policy Act of 1969 (NEPA), 42 U.S.C. §§ 4321-4370 (1982), and the Sikes Act Extension, 16 U.S.C. §§ 670g-670o (1982), were both enacted during this period. NEPA, however, is mainly a procedural statute and, as such, does not limit substantive agency discretion. *See* Strycker's Bay Neighborhood Council, Inc. v. Karlen, 444 U.S. 223 (1980). The Sikes Act Extension is similarly devoid of substantive standards for wildlife planning. *See* M. BEAN, *supra* note 601, at 154. The Wild, Free-Roaming Horses and Burros Act of 1971, 16 U.S.C. §§ 1331-1340 (1982), applies to the Forest Service but most of the covered animals are found on BLM lands, not in the national forests. *See supra* note 464.

[1548] 16 U.S.C. §§ 1531-1543 (1982). *See generally* M. BEAN, *supra* note 601, at 310-83; Thomas v. Peterson, 753 F.2d 754 (9th Cir. 1985).

straints on all land use decisions that might adversely affect the habitat of any threatened or endangered species.[1549] However, the ESA extended protection only to those species specifically listed by the Secretary of the Interior.[1550] For all other species, the Forest Service possessed virtually unreviewable discretion under the MUSY Act to set wildlife management priorities in relation to other forest resources.[1551] Public controversy over the use of that discretion led Congress to intervene, first by oversight[1552] and later through enactment of the NFMA.

The NFMA addresses wildlife management on several levels. Some of the provisions are general,[1553] while others, such as those dealing with fish habitat,[1554] are far more specific. This section will focus on the NFMA's requirement that national forest planning "provide for diversity of plant and animal communities based on the suitability and capability of the specific land area in order to meet overall multiple-use objectives."[1555] This so-called "diversity provision" was born out of a patchwork of legislation. The drafters cut and spliced until they achieved a suitable compromise.

One of the primary drafters of the diversity provision was Senator Hubert H. Humphrey.[1556] Humphrey, who was dissatisfied with the Forest Service's performance in administering the MUSY Act,[1557] introduced legislation calling for the national forests to be managed on a more balanced and ecologically sound basis.[1558] Humphrey called for a change in existing Forest Service priorities:

[1549] 16 U.S.C. § 1536(a)(2) (1982). "Species" includes plants, *id.* § 1532(16).

[1550] *Id.* § 1533(a).

[1551] *See supra* text accompanying notes 1525-30.

[1552] *See supra* text accompanying notes 721-800.

[1553] *See, e.g.,* 16 U.S.C. § 1604(e)(2) (1982).

[1554] *Id.* § 1604(g)(3)(E)(iii).

[1555] *Id.* § 1604(g)(3)(B). The remainder of the section provides, with qualifications, that steps must be taken to preserve "the diversity of tree species similar to that existing in the region controlled by the plan." *Id.* This provision arose from a desire to prevent timber management resulting in monoculture. *See supra* text accompanying notes 873-95.

[1556] *See supra* text accompanying notes 362-68.

[1557] *Id.*

[1558] Explaining his bill, Humphrey noted that it would require "environmentally approved" forest practices, "ecologically sensible" treatment of all renewable resources, and "ecologically effective" resource management. *See* SENATE NFMA HEARINGS, *supra* note 194, at 260.

The days have ended when the forest may be viewed only as trees and trees viewed only as timber. The soil and water, the grasses and the shrubs, the fish and the wildlife, and the beauty that is the forest must become integral parts of resource managers' thinking and actions.[1559]

Senator Jennings Randolph was also disturbed over the loss of wildlife habitat resulting from timber-oriented management of national forests.[1560] Randolph introduced his own bill, concurrent with Humphrey's proposal, that required timber management to be adapted to preservation of the natural diversity of forest types and species.[1561] Randolph sought to prohibit any action in a national forest that would result in significant loss of fish or wildlife habitat.[1562] Under this bill the Secretary was also required to take affirmative action to preserve habitats and populations of the native species of plants and animals found in the national forests.[1563]

The principal difference between the bills was the degree to which the two Senators sought to control the actions of the Forest Service. Humphrey made a direct reference to wildlife management and compared the bills as follows:

Forest harvest systems are covered by both bills with [Randolph's] S. 2926 writing in prescriptions that would rigorously limit what is called even-aged management and clearcutting and further would prescribe selection cutting and uneven-aged management for eastern hardwoods.

Frankly, this degree of specificity in the law troubles me. Wildlife experts indicate that it presents problems in their field. I am convinced that we could require the Secretary to use the systems of management and silviculture that are adapted to the site in establishing a healthy plant and animal community. We also could re-

---

[1559] *Id.*

[1560] *See id.* at 437-38 (statement of Sen. Randolph).

[1561] S. 2926, 94th Cong., 2d Sess. § 12(a)(1976), *reprinted in* SENATE NFMA HEARINGS, *supra* note 194, at 7. Principal drafter of the bill, James Moorman, explained:

   One big concern to the public, which is dealt with in S.2926, is the protection of nontimber resources impacted by timber management, principally soils, fish and wildlife, and the natural ecosystems of the forests. Section 12 of S. 2926 includes several provisions for the preservation of natural ecosystems. The basic injunction of that section is to preserve the natural diversity of forest types and species.

SENATE NFMA HEARINGS, *supra* note 194, at 517.

[1562] S. 2926, *supra* note 1561 § 14(b), *reprinted in* SENATE NFMA HEARINGS, *supra* note 194, at 8.

[1563] *Id.* § 12(d), *reprinted in* SENATE NFMA HEARINGS, *supra* note 194, at 7.

quire greater use of proven research data in applying any management system.[1564]

While Humphrey and Randolph disagreed on how specific the statutory provisions should be,[1565] they were united in their concern that timber management had taken top priority at the expense of other forest resources.[1566] Despite the Forest Service's strenuous objections to the Randolph bill,[1567] Humphrey suggested that his bill could be amended to bring it and Randolph's "more closely together."[1568]

Before Humphrey's bill reached the Senate joint committee mark-up session, it was amended to include a requirement that planning regulations "provide for plant and animal communities based on the suitability and capability of the specific land area."[1569] The amendment reflected Humphrey's desire for site-specific adaptation of timber management to establish "a healthy plant and animal community."[1570] The Senate committees used Humphrey's language as a basis to forge what became the diversity requirement of the NFMA. The final bill, however, incorporated an amendment, offered by Senators Lee Metcalf and Dale Bumpers, that drew heavily from Senator Randolph's bill.

[1564] SENATE NFMA HEARINGS, *supra* note 194, at 261.

[1565] Humphrey showed some ambivalence on this issue:

In conclusion, I would suggest that the degree to which we write rigid standards into law ought to depend on the extent to which we get unreserved commitments from the Secretary of Agriculture that in developing regulations he will effectively and openly consult with the public. We also can judge from his willingness to follow the multiple use and sustained yield principles rather than turning the national forests into tree production programs which override other values.

Id. at 262.

[1566] *See supra* text accompanying notes 362-74.

[1567] The Forest Service argued that the fish and wildlife standards in S. 2926 prohibiting significant loss of habitat "would be counterproductive to the management of specific plants and animals." U.S. DEP'T OF AGRICULTURE, SUPPLEMENTAL STATEMENT—SUMMARY ANALYSIS OF THE IMPACTS OF S. 2926, *reprinted in* SENATE NFMA HEARINGS, *supra* note 194, at 20. This statement that the forests should be managed for "specific plants and animals" is a holdover from the early days of forest management, when the major wildlife goal was to provide big-game forage. *See infra* section VII(A)(2). The NFMA requires management for diversity of plant and animal communities. 16 U.S.C. § 1604(g)(3)(B)(1982).

[1568] SENATE NFMA HEARINGS, *supra* note 194, at 261.

[1569] COMPARISON OF S. 3091, *supra* note 440, *reprinted in* D. LEMASTER, *supra* note 162, at 198.

[1570] SENATE NFMA HEARINGS, *supra* note 194, at 261.

Metcalf and Bumpers were particularly concerned with the Forest Service practice of converting eastern hardwood forests to "pine tree farms."[1571] Metcalf proposed that the committees add language taken from the Randolph bill that would "insure the use of such systems of silviculture which maintain the diversity of forest types and species found naturally in each national forest."[1572] The committee members could not agree to this amendment, principally because the term "found naturally" was not acceptable to Forest Service Chief John McGuire.[1573] The members did not resolve the issue, but directed the joint committee staff to "draft some language, with the Metcalf amendment, that the committee can accept."[1574] The committee staff incorporated Metcalf's amendment into Humphrey's plant and animal language by adding the words "diversity of" and "in order to meet overall multiple-use objectives."[1575] The committees accepted the change without objection.

The reasons for including the Metcalf language were twofold. First, the words "diversity" and "overall multiple-use objectives" place limits on forest conversions, especially in the East. In addition, the committees apparently intended the amendment to draw the Humphrey and Randolph bills closer together on the wildlife issue, particularly in regard to preserving species whose habitats and populations were diminishing.[1576] The Metcalf-Bumpers contribution strengthens the objectives of the Humphrey bill. The

---

[1571] *April 27, 1976, Transcript of Senate Markup, supra* note 374, at 63. Bumpers's concerns are discussed in detail in *supra* text accompanying notes 879-92.

[1572] COMPARISON OF S. 3091, *supra* note 440, *reprinted in* D. LeMASTER, *supra* note 162, at 201.

[1573] *April 27, 1976, Transcript of Senate Markup, supra* note 374, at 60.

[1574] *Id.* at 64.

[1575] *See supra* text accompanying note 1555.

[1576] During the final day of the Senate mark-up, the committees considered several amendments offered by Senator Randolph. One amendment would have required the Forest Service to "take affirmative action to preserve habitats and populations of the native species of plants and animals found in the National Forests," and to "devote special attention to the preservation of the habitats and populations of native plants and animals whose habitats and populations are diminishing." *May 4, 1976, Transcript of Senate Mark-up, supra* note 374, at 98-99. The language was identical to a section of Randolph's bill. *See* S. 2926, 94th Cong., 2d Sess. § 12(d)(1976), *reprinted in* SENATE NFMA HEARINGS, *supra* note 194, at 7. Staff advisor Robert Wolf explained to the committees that "the plant and animal community language in the existing bill . . . is intended to cover this area." *May 4, 1976, Transcript of Senate Mark-up, supra* note 374, at 99. Randolph did not request a vote on this amendment.

"diversity" and "overall multiple-use" terminology promotes balanced resource management in national forests, which was one of Humphrey's primary goals.[1577]

The Conference Committee, for its part, was satisfied with the Senate's diversity language. The only change made at this point was the addition of a clause from the House bill designed to preserve tree diversity.[1578]

To summarize, the so-called "diversity" provision, section 6(g)(3)(B), contains two components with major implications for national forest wildlife policy.[1579] The first of these is composed of the language from the Humphrey bill—to protect "plant and animal communities based on the suitability and capability of the specific land area"—which was intended to remedy the Forest Service's excessive emphasis on timber production at the expense of healthy forest ecosystems.[1580] Senator Humphrey's statements at the Senate hearings, and the addition made in connection with them, support this interpretation. The language from the Humphrey bill calls for a fundamental reordering of the Forest Service's post-World War II management priorities for timber and wildlife, but, as is the case with all of the provisions of section 6(g) of the NFMA, the specific standards to implement the policy change were left for the agency and the Committee of Scientists to establish through the promulgation of regulations.[1581]

The second important component of section 6(g)(3)(B) is the "diversity" and "overall multiple-use objectives" language added by Bumpers and Metcalf. A principal effect of this provision was to limit forest type conversions in the eastern national forests. In addition, this terminology preserves one of the central features of the Randolph bill by requiring that the diversity of forest species and ecosystems be maintained and by placing particular emphasis on the habitat needs of diminishing species. Again, Congress

---

[1577] This general theme was repeatedly expressed during the floor debates. *See supra* text accompanying notes 369-78.

[1578] *See supra* text accompanying notes 893-95.

[1579] A third component, not related specifically to wildlife, prohibits timber management resulting in monoculture. *See supra* notes 1555 and 1578 and *supra* text accompanying notes 893-95.

[1580] *See supra* text accompanying notes 1565-77.

[1581] *See supra* note 211. The NFMA regulations do, in fact, contain standards designed to "provide for . . . animal communities" by requiring forest plans to insure viable, well distributed populations of all vertebrate species in each national forest. *See infra* text accompanying notes 1583-96.

made no attempt to prescribe precise standards to implement the policies of this component.

The diversity requirement of section 6(g)(3)(B)—that planning "provide for diversity of plant and animal communities based on the suitability and capability of the specific land area in order to meet overall multiple-use objectives"—has broad significance for national forest wildlife policy and planning. To be sure, it is difficult to discern any concrete legal standards on the face of the provision. The term "diversity," while meaningful to professional wildlife managers,[1582] is not defined in the NFMA; likewise, the term "multiple-use" provides little aid in assessing use priorities. On the other hand, when the section is read in light of the historical context and overall purposes of the NFMA, as well as the legislative history of the section, it is evident that section 6(g)(3)(B) requires Forest Service planners to treat the wildlife resource as a controlling, co-equal factor in forest management and, in particular, as a substantive limitation on timber production. This mandate is reflected in the regulations subsequently developed by the Committee of Scientists and the Forest Service.

C.   The NFMA Regulations—Planning for the Wildlife Resource

In developing regulations to implement the wildlife provisions of the NFMA, the Committee of Scientists and the Forest Service were faced with a formidable task. The NFMA called for a fundamental reshaping of national forest wildlife policy. Unfortunately, the statute provided only general guidance concerning the implementation of these new objectives.[1583] Furthermore, there was considerable disagreement among wildlife and forestry ex-

---

[1582] *See, e.g.*, Salwasser, Thomson & Samson, *Applying the Diversity Concept to National Forest Management, reprinted in* Natural Diversity in Forest Ecosystems 59 (1984) (proceedings of workshop at the Inst. of Ecology, Univ. of Ga., Athens, Ga.).

[1583] *See, e.g.*, 16 U.S.C. § 1604(g)(2)(B) (1982) (requiring inventory data on renewable resources); *id.* § 1604(g)(2)(C) (on the identification of hazards to various resources); *id.* § 1604(g)(3)(A) (concerning economic and environmental analysis of resource management systems); *id.* § 1604(g)(3)(B) (mandating the diversity objectives); *id.* § 1604(g)(3)(C) (requiring research on the effects of each management system); *id.* § 1604(g)(3)(E)(iii) (mandating protection of fish habitat during harvesting); and *id.* § 1604(g)(3)(F)(v) (requiring that even-age timber management be used in a manner consistent with fish and wildlife protection).

perts over the effects of timber management on wildlife.[1584] Nevertheless, the NFMA regulations appear to provide both the change in policy sought by Congress and the clear planning standards necessary to resolve conflicts between wildlife and other resources.

The regulations translate the NFMA's requirements into three basic management directives. First, "viable" populations of existing forest vertebrates must be maintained and "well distributed" in each national forest. Second, certain species must be chosen and used as "indicators" of the effects of management on forest ecology.[1585] Third, the regulations constrain timber management and other management practices that result in serious and adverse effects on fish habitat, an issue already discussed in relation to the timber and water resources.[1586] These substantive provisions are implemented by regulations dealing with inventory data and monitoring, the last subject to be dealt with in this subsection.

1. Viable Populations and Distribution

The regulations specify that "fish and wildlife habitat shall be managed to maintain viable populations of existing native and desired non-native vertebrate species in the planning area."[1587] A viable population for planning purposes is defined as "one which has the estimated numbers and distribution of reproductive individuals to insure its continued existence is well distributed in the planning area."[1588] In other words, there are two aspects to the viable population requirement. First, a sufficient number of reproductive individuals of all existing vertebrate species must be maintained in order to ensure viable populations; second, habitat for any particular species must be distributed throughout each national forest.

[1584] *Compare* SENATE NFMA HEARINGS, *supra* note 194, at 65-67 (testimony of Dr. John Grandy) *with id.* at 96-98 (testimony of Dr. David H. Jenkins).

[1585] *See* 36 C.F.R. § 219.19 (1984).

[1586] *See* text accompanying notes 826-29 and 1165-82.

[1587] 36 C.F.R. § 219.19 (1984). The viable populations requirement applies to all vertebrates "in the planning area." *Id.* The regulations define "planning area" as "area of the National Forest System covered by a regional guide or forest plan." *Id.* § 219.3. Therefore, the viable populations requirement apparently applies to regional guides as well as to forest plans.

[1588] *Id.* § 219.19.

The meaning of the term "viable population" is likely to be highly controversial in planning. The regulations state that "in order to insure that viable populations will be maintained, habitat must be provided to support, at least, a minimum number of reproductive individuals . . . ."[1589] The phrase "minimum number" might be interpreted to allow planners to set habitat and population levels at the margin between viability and nonviability as one of the planning alternatives. However, marginally viable populations are not legally supportable.

First, the regulations require the Forest Service to provide sufficient habitat to "insure" the continued existence of existing vertebrate species in each national forest.[1590] Planners must allow for contingencies that threaten a species' viability. Examples of such hazards would include fire, disease, pest infestation, accidental chemical exposure, and natural ecological changes.[1591] These contingencies are often reasonably predictable, and their likelihood and impact on wildlife can be determined through historical and experimental data. Populations that are vulnerable to extirpation by foreseeable contingencies are not ensured of continued existence; they are not viable. Planners therefore do not meet the legal requirements of the regulations by setting minimum viable population levels that assume ideal conditions. A realistic safety factor must be built into the minimum level alternative that accounts for the unknown.

Moreover, forest plans must insure that viable populations of vertebrates are "well distributed in the planning area."[1592] Habitat "must be well distributed so that [reproductive] individuals can interact with others in the planning area."[1593] Thus, while plans can result in habitat conditions that reduce a species' *density*, the plans must allow that species to maintain its existing *dis-*

[1589] *Id.*

[1590] *See supra* text accompanying note 1589.

[1591] *See* WILDLIFE POPULATION VIABILITY, *supra* note 1455, at 6. One biologist has observed: "Ecological processes that are normal and even necessary for the maintenance of species diversity on a regional scale can be fatal on a small scale. Catastrophes such as landslides and fires, for example, can maintain a healthy balance of successional stages in a large forest, but in an isolated patch they can extinguish entire populations." Soule, *What Do We Really Know About Extinction?*, in GENETICS AND CONSERVATION 111, 121 (1983). *See generally* O. FRANKEL & M. SOULE, CONSERVATION AND EVOLUTION (1981).

[1592] 36 C.F.R. § 219.19 (1984).

[1593] *Id.*

tribution.[1594] The practical effect of this requirement, which was added to the 1982 revision of the NFMA regulations, is to make distribution of wildlife habitat a controlling factor in forest planning.

Species isolation, which can result from a sudden decrease in habitat area, has been called "the trigger for an erosion of species diversity."[1595] The distribution requirement will prevent species from becoming isolated on islands of suitable habitat. For instance, planners may not rely on a single wilderness area to furnish habitat for a species dependent on old-growth forests or roadless solitude, if that habitat exists elsewhere in the national forest.[1596] In addition, by distributing habitat, planners will be able to provide greater safety against events that could threaten viability.

2. Management Indicator Species

The requirement that the Forest Service must plan to manage habitats to maintain viable populations of all existing vertebrate species well distributed over every national forest would be virtually impossible to satisfy if each species had to be addressed in detail. Wild vertebrate populations are extremely difficult to measure; merely obtaining an inventory of existing vertebrates

---

[1594] FOREST SERVICE AND PANEL OF CONSULTANTS ON PROPOSED REVISION OF NFMA REGULATIONS, SUMMARY REPORT 4 (June 30-July 2, 1982), (on file at Oregon Law Review) [hereinafter cited as NFMA REGULATIONS REPORT].

[1595] Soule, *supra* note 1591, at 121.

[1596] The requirement of a well-distributed population grew out of the following query to the Forest Service's national headquarters from the Wallowa-Whitman National Forest: "Is an alternative which places all the land proposed for management of old-growth in the Eagle Cap Wilderness and the Hell's Canyon NRA and specifies full timber production on the remainder of the forest a legally acceptable alternative?" Memorandum from J.B. Hilmon to Regional Forester, Region 6 (Feb. 24, 1982) (on file at Oregon Law Review office). Assistant Deputy Chief Hilmon's reply stated:

First, the maintenance of old-growth is ordinarily not a management objective in itself. Instead the question should relate to the requirement to maintain viable populations of all vertebrate species. In this case, your question relates to the continued viability of old-growth associated wildlife populations on the planning area. The alternative which you have described may or may not be legal. A viable population, for planning purposes, is one which has the estimated numbers and *distribution* of reproductive individuals to insure its continued existence throughout its existing range in the planning area.

Id. (emphasis added).

could take decades, and be out of date when finished. Without some method of simplifying the planning task, no forest plan could realistically be expected to comply with the regulations.

The Committee of Scientists dealt with the problem of providing for all vertebrate species by recommending the "management indicator species" (MIS) concept.[1597] The use of MIS in no way diminishes the requirement to maintain well-distributed, viable populations of existing vertebrates; in fact, proper use of MIS should help to ensure them. The MIS concept allows forest planners to select, from among the 200 to 400 vertebrate species typically inhabiting each national forest, a reasonable number of vertebrates and invertebrates to act as proxies for all the others.[1598]

The MIS is a sampling process that planners first applied to featured species management.[1599] The success of this or any sampling process depends on several factors, including the size and diversity of the sample and nature of the bias in selection of the sample. It is evident that the success or failure of wildlife and fish resources planning will depend largely upon the manner in which individual national forests choose their MIS.

The regulations identify five categories to consider in selecting MIS: (1) threatened and endangered species, (2) species sensitive to intended management, (3) game and commercial wildlife and fish, (4) nongame species of special interest, and (5) ecological indicators.[1600] While the regulations' MIS requirements seem straightforward, the Forest Service's choices of MIS may cause confusion for at least two reasons.

First, the choice of some MIS is not made by local planners. Threatened and endangered species are designated by the state

---

[1597] *See Committee of Scientists, Minutes of Jan. 16-18, 1978* at 8-9.

[1598] Salwasser, Siderits, & Holbrook, *supra* note 1534, at 176.

[1599] *See id.* at 174; *see also supra* note 1537 and accompanying text.

[1600] 36 C.F.R. § 219.19(a)(1) (1984). The fifth category, ecological indicators, is defined as "plant or animal species selected because their population changes are believed to indicate the effects of management activities on other species of selected major biological communities or on water quality." *Id.* The Committee of Scientists explained that there are two basic categories of MIS:

Species in one group are included because of particular interest in them. Endangered species are in this group . . . to meet the requirements of the Endangered Species Act. Species in the second group are chosen because they indicate the consequences of management on other species whose populations fluctuate in some measurable manner with the indicator species.

Comm. of Scientists Final Report, supra note 864, at 26,627.

and federal agencies responsible for administering threatened and endangered species laws.[1601] Nationally significant game and commercial animals are chosen by wildlife planners in the Forest Service's national headquarters as part of the RPA planning process.[1602] Sensitive species may be selected either regionally or locally. Currently, sensitive species are designated by some regional offices,[1603] while other regions have left this MIS class to the choice of local forest planners.[1604] Surprisingly, few forest planners have selected MIS solely because they are ecological indicators even though ecological indicators are usually the most reliable category of MIS. Wildlife specialists consider the relationship between individual species and general ecological conditions to be too complex and unreliable for planners to address in the first generation of forest plans.[1605] Thus, local planners will usually confine their MIS choices to locally important game and commercial species, nongame species of special interest, and, in some instances, sensitive species.

The second potential source of confusion is the requirement in the regulations that each of the five MIS classes shall be represented "where appropriate." The "where appropriate" qualifier, which is not defined either in the NFMA or in the regulations,[1606] did not appear in the 1979 regulations in this context[1607] but was added during the 1982 revision. This provision gives the Forest

---

[1601] *See* 36 C.F.R. § 219.19(1) (1984).

[1602] *See, e.g.*, FOREST SERVICE, U.S. DEP'T OF AGRICULTURE, DRAFT ENVIRONMENTAL IMPACT STATEMENT FOR 1985 RESOURCES PLANNING ACT 2-91 (1984).

[1603] *See, e.g.*, B. SHERMAN, LAND AND RESOURCES PLANNING—REGIONAL GUIDELINE FOR INCORPORATION OF MINIMUM MANAGEMENT REQUIREMENTS IN FOREST PLANNING app. II, 23 (Feb. 9, 1983) (available in Office of Regional Forester, Forest Service, Portland, Or.).

[1604] Interview with Kathy Johnson, wildlife planner, Willamette Nat'l Forest, in Eugene, Or., Dec. 18, 1984.

[1605] *Id.*

[1606] Early in the drafting process the Committee of Scientists considered defining the term "where appropriate." The term appears several times in the NFMA, including the diversity provision. 16 U.S.C.] 160]4(g)(3)(B) (1982). A proposed definition defined the term to mean "non-mandatory provision" that provides the Forest Service with "discretion in formulating regulations to apply to situations or circumstances which, in the opinion of the agency, are unique, or require special provisions." *See Definitions of NFMA/Section 6 Procedural Terms*, in *Committee of Scientists, Minutes of May 24-26, 1977*, app. This definition was rejected by the Committee as "Not Acceptable; Redefine." *See Committee of Scientists, Minutes of June 19-21, 1977, supra* note 402. The term was never redefined and is not defined in the regulations.

[1607] 36 C.F.R. § 219.12(g)(2) (1980).

Service only limited discretion. First, the selection of MIS is mandatory; only the choice of species in the five categories is subject to the "where appropriate" language.[1608] Second, the regulations, and the MIS concept generally, suggest a strong presumption for the selection of ecological indicators as MIS.[1609] Third, planners must, consistent with the data on existing vertebrates, choose a sufficient number of MIS to meet the viable populations requirement.[1610] Furthermore, MIS will normally include threatened and endangered species, which must in any event be monitored in connection with the Endangered Species Act, if such species are found in the planning area. Thus, in many cases, the discretion supplied by the "where appropriate" language will be limited to the choice of species of local interest within the game and nongame categories.[1611]

In sum, planners must choose MIS that adequately reflect the impact of management on wildlife habitats. The regulations require that MIS "shall be selected because their population changes are believed to indicate the effects of management activities."[1612] Thus, planners must justify their MIS choices based upon the extent to which those selections will ensure that adequate habitat is maintained for all existing vertebrate species.

[1608] The section provides that "certain vertebrate and/or invertebrate species shall be identified and selected as management indicator species and the reasons for their selection shall be stated." 36 C.F.R. § 219.19(a) (1984).

[1609] The regulations state that MIS "shall be selected because their population changes are believed to indicate the effects of management activities." 36 C.F.R. § 219.19(a)(1) (1984), a description similar to the definition of ecological indicators, *see supra* note 1600.

[1610] *See supra* notes 1587-91.

[1611] Such special interest species might include, for example, certain game species whose populations are of local interest. In addition, such choices would be valuable to the state fish and wildlife agencies who rely on the Forest Service to maintain habitat for fish and game.

[1612] 36 C.F.R. § 219.19(a)(1) (1984). In choosing appropriate MIS planners should consider a broad range of management activities. The term "management activities" is not defined by either the regulations or the NFMA. However, the term "management practice" is defined as "specific activity, measure, course of action, or treatment." *Id.* § 219.3. Neither the regulation nor its history indicates that the meaning of "management activity" should be narrower than that of "management practice." In addition, there is no indication the term is meant to be limited to activities of the Forest Service and its agents, licensees, and contractors. Both the states and other federal agencies may engage in activities that affect wildlife populations. For instance, the Department of the Interior administers mineral leasing in the national forests and the states license hunters and fishers. Such programs, therefore, would seem to be management activities that must be considered in the selection of MIS.

Since the Forest Service is primarily responsible for habitat maintenance, MIS proxy species should represent all major habitat types, including water habitat.[1613]

After forest planners have chosen MIS, they must "establish objectives for the maintenance and improvement of habitat" for each chosen species and for each planning alternative "to the degree consistent with overall multiple-use objectives of the alternative."[1614] The objectives must be stated in terms of quantity and quality of habitat and population trends of the MIS.[1615] Population objectives must ensure a viable and well-distributed population, one that is self-sustaining throughout the national forest.

Species such as the grizzly bear, cougar, and wolverine pose a special problem for the planner. While they have relatively low population densities, these species and others often have a range encompassing more than one national forest. This issue can best be addressed by the use of regional guides. The regulations specify that regional guides shall contain "a description of management direction including programs, goals, and objectives."[1616] Thus, re-

---

[1613] At least one national forest has chosen not to select any fish species as M.I.S. *See* FOREST SERVICE, U.S. DEP'T OF AGRICULTURE, FINAL ENVIRONMENTAL IMPACT STATEMENT FOR THE NEBRASKA NATIONAL FOREST LAND AND RESOURCE MANAGEMENT PLAN III-34 (1984). This omission could constitute a violation of the NFMA and the regulations. The MIS provision expressly refers to water quality. 36 C.F.R. § 219(a)(1) (1984). Stringent protection of riparian areas is mandated elsewhere in the regulations. *Id.* § 219.27(e). In addition, the NFMA expressly limits timber harvesting to those lands where protection is provided for streams, lakes, wetlands, and riparian areas if there is a likely serious and adverse affect on fish habitat. 16 U.S.C. § 1604(g)(3)(E)(iii) (1982). The Act also prohibits even-aged timber management unless carried out "consistent with protection of . . . watershed [and] fish." *Id.* at § 1604(g)(3)(F)(v). Thus, the NFMA clearly contemplates a causal connection between some management activities and degradation of fish habitat. It would seem to follow that any national forest that has substantial fish habitat should choose at least one aquatic fish species as an MIS in order to provide protection for fish and other aquatic animals.

[1614] 36 C.F.R. § 219.19(a) (1984). The qualifying language regarding "overall multiple-use objectives" did not appear in the 1979 regulations. Instead, the 1979 regulations required the Forest Service "to maintain and improve habitat of management indicator species." 36 C.F.R. § 219.12(g) (1980). Concern that the provision could be interpreted to allow no change in the present habitat of a MIS led drafters to include the multiple-use language from the 1982 revised regulations. *See* NFMA REGULATIONS REPORT, *supra* note 1594, at 4. For instance, very little change might have been permitted in the old-growth forest habitat in southeast Alaska if the Sitka black-tailed deer were chosen as an MIS. *Id.*

[1615] 36 C.F.R. § 219.19(a)(2) (1984).

[1616] *Id.* § 219.9(a)(2). Regional guides, for example, apparently should address the viable populations requirement. *See supra* note 1587.

gional guides should direct national forests to include a particular MIS or devote particular attention to certain species or habitats.[1617]

3. *Inventory Data and Monitoring*

Monitoring the wildlife resource is one of the foremost challenges facing Forest Service planners. The NFMA regulations provide that "[p]opulation trends of the management indicator species will be monitored and relationships to habitat changes determined."[1618] Monitoring MIS populations is essential to verify and, if necessary, modify the forest plan's assumptions about the effects of timber harvesting and other management activities on wildlife.[1619] The extent of the monitoring effort should vary according to the degree of risk that the monitored species faces. If there is a danger that the population or distribution of a species might fall below its viability level, then the monitoring effort should be intensified.[1620]

In order to meet the monitoring requirement, planners will need to obtain adequate inventories of wildlife populations and distribution. The NFMA requires that the agency gather inventory data on the various renewable resources[1621] and identify hazards to those resources.[1622] The Committee of Scientists devoted particular attention to the need for adequate wildlife inventories,[1623] and

---

[1617] *See, e.g., infra* text accompanying note 1667; *see also* FOREST SERVICE, U.S. DEP'T OF AGRICULTURE, NORTHERN REGIONAL PLAN 4-15 to -16 (1981).

[1618] 36 C.F.R. § 219.19(a)(6) (1984).

[1619] *See* WILDLIFE POPULATION VIABILITY, *supra* note 1455, at 24.

[1620] *See* FOREST SERVICE MANUAL § 2664-3 (1984).

[1621] 16 U.S.C. § 1604(g)(3)(C) (1982).

[1622] *Id.* § 1604(g)(2)(C).

[1623] While drafting the 1979 regulations the Committee considered a requirement that the Forest Service must inventory "existing vegetation or biotic communities and associated fish and wildlife species." FOREST SERVICE, U.S. DEP'T OF AGRICULTURE, , NATIONAL FOREST SYSTEM RESOURCE PLANNING 14 (1978), *Committee of Scientists, Minutes of Feb. 23-24, 1978, supra* note 402, app. (draft proposed rule § 219.8(f)(1)(iii)). The Committee was concerned that such an inventory requirement would be unduly burdensome on the agency, so the words "associated fish and wildlife species" were deleted. *Committee of Scientists, Minutes of Feb. 23-24, 1978, supra.* The final regulations contain a provision for inventories in connection with the diversity requirement, see *infra* text accompanying note 1624, and generally do require that each forest supervisor "obtain and keep current inventory data appropriate for planning and managing the resources under his or her administrative jurisdiction." 36 C.F.R. § 219.12(d) (1984). The data must be "of a kind, character, and quality and to the detail appropriate for the management decisions to be made." *Id.*

the regulations require that in providing for diversity of plant and animal communities, "inventories shall include quantitative data making possible the evaluation of diversity in terms of its prior and present condition."[1624] The Committee explained, "No plan is better than the resource inventory data that support it. Each forest plan should be based on sound, detailed inventories of soils, vegetation, water resources, wildlife, and the other resources to be managed."[1625]

It is difficult to see how the Forest Service can meet the requirement of maintaining viable populations of all existing vertebrate species in each national forest without compiling a reasonably thorough inventory of the species' habitats. In 1979 the Committee of Scientists felt that current resource inventory data would be inadequate to support judgments made in NFMA plans:

> Unfortunately, it does not follow that truly adequate resource data will be available to support the development of every plan. In many cases, inventory data are too fragmentary or insufficiently detailed to allow firm judgments in developing management programs of the complexity demanded by RPA/NFMA. In other cases, data on certain organisms, resources, or management effects have simply never been gathered.[1626]

The Committee's prognosis for the first round of plans was not hopeful: "In practice, what this means is that the data base for a number of plans is likely to be marginally adequate or even shaky."[1627] Six years later it remains evident that there is not sufficient data to justify all wildlife management decisions. The plans will have to be considered with sensitivity both to the central role of good inventories in resource planning and the scope of the task, as evidenced by the Committee's words in 1979: "Even if a Federal Government-wide crash program of data acquisition and storage were to begin tomorrow, it would not provide adequate data in time to be of much value in developing the first forest plans . . . . [T]he Forest Service cannot remedy decades of national indifference toward basic resource data in 5 years."[1628]

To summarize, the NFMA regulations have significantly broadened and enhanced the role of wildlife planning in the Forest Service. The central goal is to provide sufficient habitat to sustain

[1624] 36 C.F.R. § 219.26 (1984).
[1625] *Comm. of Scientists Final Report, supra* note 864, at 26,608.
[1626] *Id.*
[1627] *Id.*
[1628] *Id.*

viable and well-distributed wildlife populations in each national forest. Realistically, this goal can only be achieved by carefully selecting and monitoring management indicator species and by collecting adequate inventory data.

D. *Authority of the Forest Service to Manage the Wildlife Resource*

1. *Authority to Preempt State Hunting and Fishing Law*

The conventional wisdom regarding Forest Service authority to manage and plan for the wildlife resource is that the states manage the animals and the Forest Service manages habitat. This apparently bifurcated authority is rooted in the legal history of the Forest Service and the evolution of federal wildife policy.[1629] As discussed earlier, the basic source of Forest Service authority—the 1897 Organic Act—is silent on the subject of wildlife. At the time, Congress itself was uncertain of federal power to make hunting and fishing laws.[1630]

The Forest Service generally has chosen not to test the extent of its organic authority to regulate wildlife. There are, however, some notable exceptions. In the mid-1920s the Forest Service disregarded state game law and hired hunters to thin the deer herd in the Kaibab National Forest in Arizona in order to protect the rangeland and young trees from injury due to overgrazing. The agency claimed authority for its actions under the 1897 Act.[1631] This power was upheld by the Supreme Court in *Hunt v. United States*.[1632] The Court ruled that the Forest Service was not constrained by state wildlife law in its efforts to protect federal land.

The *Hunt* court did not construe definitively the Forest Service's power to regulate hunting and fishing. In response to *Hunt*, the Forest Service asserted such authority by issuing a regulation in 1936 that established hunting and fishing seasons, set bag and creel limits, and required fees for hunting and fishing in the forests.[1633] This regulation evoked such a strong negative response from the states that it was replaced in 1941 with regulations that

---

[1629] *See supra* text accompanying notes 1457-92.
[1630] *See supra* text accompanying notes 1468-72. It is now clear that Congress can preempt state laws. *See supra* note 1492. The only question is whether Congress has delegated to the Forest Service the authority to override state law.
[1631] United States v. Hunt, 19 F.2d 634 (D. Ariz. 1927).
[1632] 278 U.S. 96 (1928).
[1633] Regulation G-20-A, 1 Fed. Reg. 1097 (Aug. 15, 1936).

recognized state law as controlling the taking of most fish and game.[1634] Those regulations are still in effect today.[1635]

Arguably, the MUSY Act of 1960 expanded Forest Service authority over wildlife by providing that the national forests "shall be administered for outdoor recreation, range, timber, watershed, and wildlife and fish purposes."[1636] However, the Act contains a proviso that "[n]othing herein shall be construed as affecting the jurisdiction or responsibilities of the several states with respect to wildlife and fish in the national forests."[1637] The proviso was added during the House floor debate in response to the concern of some representatives that the Forest Service might use the MUSY Act to displace state hunting and fishing law.[1638]

The MUSY Act's proviso is problematic. As noted above, the floor debates of the MUSY Act indicate that Congress was uncertain whether the Forest Service did possess the statutory authority to override state fish and game law but feared that the courts might construe the Act to have granted the agency that power.[1639] However, the wording of the proviso leaves open the possibility that a court could find the MUSY Act to be neutral on the issue

---

[1634] M. BEAN, *supra* note 601, at 139.

[1635] 36 C.F.R. §§ 241.1-.2 (1984).

[1636] *See* 16 U.S.C. § 528 (1982).

[1637] *Id.*

[1638] The bill authorized and directed the Secretary of Agriculture to "develop and adminster the renewable surface resources of the national forests." *Id.* § 529. During House debate there was a fear that the Secretary would use this provision to oust the states from their traditional roles as regulators of hunting and fishing. The proviso was added at the insistence of Representative Hoffman of Michigan, who felt that without an express statement to the contrary, the Act would be used to "interfere with States' rights." 106 CONG. REC. 11,719 (1960). Hoffman stated:

> Everyone who reads the recent Supreme Court decisions remembers that the Court said on several occasions that we did not know what we were talking about and did not mean what we said. They took away jurisdiction from the States and gave it to the Federal Government in a number of cases.
>
> What I am trying to do here is to make certain that the States will retain their jurisdiction in this matter.

Id. Earlier, Representative Dixon had tried to assuage this fear by stating, "I believe the committee has the privilege of defining the terms here, and this term 'surface resources' or habitat can be defined as not including the fish, game and wildlife and the committee so defines it." *Id.* at 11,707. The House preferred Hoffman's proviso to Dixon's assurances.

[1639] *See supra* note 1638.

and look to the 1897 Act as the source of such power.[1640] With the exception of *Hunt*,[1641] which upheld agency authority over claims of state law, this issue has not been squarely raised in any court. Thus, the MUSY Act proviso may well have simply left in place the uncertain wildlife jurisdiction of the Forest Service vis-a-vis state law. While the case law under the Organic Act is uniformly supportive of Forest Service authority so that a holding in favor of an expansive power over wildlife would in one sense be unremarkable, the fact remains that the history of federal wildlife law shows a continuing solicitude for state perogatives.

It is possible that the authority granted by the Federal Land Management Policy Act of 1976[1642] (FLPMA), which allows the Forest Service to close areas of the national forests to hunting or fishing, will settle the question and eliminate the need to litigate Forest Service authority under the Organic Act and the MUSY Act. Section 1732(b) of FLPMA states:

> [N]othing in this Act shall be construed as authorizing the Secretary concerned to require Federal permits to hunt and fish on public lands or on lands in the National Forest System and adjacent waters or as enlarging or diminishing the responsibility and authority of the States for management of fish and resident wildlife. However, the Secretary concerned may designate areas of public land and of lands in the National Forest System where, and establish periods when, no hunting or fishing will be permitted for reasons of public safety, administration, or compliance with provisions of applicable law. Except in emergencies, any regulations of the Secretary concerned relating to hunting and fishing pursuant to this section shall be put into effect only after consultation with the appropriate State fish and game department.[1643]

This section has not been definitively construed by any court. The legislative history of the section is ambiguous.[1644] Although the section clearly grants the Forest Service same quantum of power

---

[1640] The Interior Solicitor has construed similar provisos as expressing an intent to leave intact the *status quo* as to federal and state power. *See supra* note 1214. The 1897 Act has regularly been construed to grant broad management authority to the Forest Service. *See supra* section II(A)(2).

[1641] *See supra* text accompanying notes 1631-32. *C.f.* New Mexico State Game Comm'n v. Udall, 410 F.2d 1197 (10th Cir. 1969) (upholding authority of National Park Service to adopt a deer-kill program).

[1642] 43 U.S.C. §§ 1701-1784 (1982).

[1643] *Id.* § 1732(b).

[1644] For a discussion of the ambiguities in the legislative history of § 1732(b), see G. COGGINS & C. WILKINSON, *supra* note 345, at 604-06. *See also* Defenders of Wildlife v. Andrus, 627 F.2d 1238 (D.C. Cir. 1980).

to stop hunting and fishing irrespective of state law, the language suffers from the essential failing of the MUSY Act: it preserves an unknown status quo. Basic questions remain concerning the scope of this power.

2. Cooperation with the States

Both Congress and the Forest Service actively seek a partnership with the states in planning for the wildlife resource. The Forest Service has traditionally aided in enforcement of state fish and game law.[1645] When the major emphasis in forest wildlife management was to aid the proliferation of game, the Forest Service voluntarily cooperated with the states to provide winter range and to stock game fish.[1646] More recently, the Forest Service's cooperative policy has been written into law and incorporated into the agency's NFMA planning process.

The Public Land Law Review Commission recommended in 1970 that formal cooperative agreements be used to coordinate federal and state wildlife programs.[1647] Congress enacted this recommendation into law with the Sikes Act Extension of 1974.[1648] The Act mandates "comprehensive" plans to "plan, develop, maintain, and coordinate programs for the conservation and rehabilitation of wildlife, fish, and game."[1649] These plans must be produced in cooperation with state agencies.[1650] The Act allows the states and the Forest Service to enter into cooperative agreements for planning and implementing wildlife habitat construction and improvement programs.[1651] Agreements must contain certain features, including provisions for range rehabilitation, control of off-road vehicles, protection of species listed as threatened or endangered, and other terms and conditions as the parties may deem "necessary and appropriate."[1652] The Act does not alter jurisdictional authority, and it specifically requires that cooperative plans must be consistent with "any overall land use and management plans for the lands involved."[1653] Further, where hunting and

---

[1645] *See supra* text accompanying note 1496.
[1646] *See supra* text accompanying notes 1497-98.
[1647] PUBLIC LAND LAW REVIEW COMM'N, *supra* note 338, at 159.
[1648] 16 U.S.C. §§ 670g-670o (1982).
[1649] *Id.* § 670g(a).
[1650] *Id.*
[1651] *Id.* § 670h(c)(1).
[1652] *Id.* § 670h(c)(3).
[1653] *Id.* § 670h(b).

fishing are permitted under a plan, state law and regulation control.[1654]

The impact of the Sikes Extension Act on Forest Service authority and policy is difficult to assess. In effect, the Act mandates communication between state and federal agencies regarding wildlife planning and management. The involvement of state wildlife managers in the federal planning process may serve to enhance the status of wildlife in multiple-use decisionmaking.[1655] However, the communication may also serve to reinforce an historical emphasis on hunting and fishing, rather than management of nongame species, on both the state and federal levels. This will be determined by the policy direction of each state agency and on the results of the NFMA planning process.

The NFMA mandates that land management planning be coordinated with the planning processes of state and federal agencies.[1656] The NFMA regulations require consultation with state fish and wildlife biologists to coordinate planning.[1657] The Committee of Scientists recommended that state wildlife biologists be appointed to the Forest Service interdisciplinary planning teams.[1658] Although this recommendation was not incorporated in the regulations, there is no prohibition against including state wildlife biologists on the interdisciplinary teams.

The regulations require that species identified by the states as threatened or endangered be made management indicator species "where appropriate."[1659] Population monitoring of all MIS must be done in cooperation with state agencies to the extent practicable.[1660] Indeed, the Forest Service intends to obtain the inventory data needed to meet its monitoring obligation largely from ongoing state surveys and investigations.[1661] Thus, the Forest Service and the states can plan for coordinated protection of species of local interest concern.

An example of a species-specific cooperative planning effort is the Interagency Spotted Owl Management Plan in the Pacific Northwest. The northern spotted owl (*Strix occidentalis caurina*)

[1654] *Id.*

[1655] *See generally* M. BEAN, *supra* note 601, at 146-47.

[1656] 16 U.S.C. § 1604(a) (1982).

[1657] 36 C.F.R. § 219.19(a)(3) (1984).

[1658] *Comm. of Scientists Final Report, supra* note 864, at 26,627.

[1659] 36 C.F.R. § 219.19(a)(1) (1984).

[1660] *Id.* § 219.19(a)(6).

[1661] Interview with Kathy Johnson, *supra* note 1604.

is not listed under the Endangered Species Act as a threatened or endangered species. It is listed as a migratory bird,[1662] however, and therefore is afforded protection under the Migratory Bird Treaty Act.[1663] The state of Washington has classified the owl as "sensitive", and Oregon has classified the owl as "threatened."[1664] The owl requires old-growth coniferous forests as habitat, and much of the remaining old growth is in national forests and Bureau of Land Management land.[1665] The Oregon Fish and Wildlife Department, working in cooperation with the Forest Service and the BLM, produced a plan to retain sufficient old-growth habitat to preserve existence of the owl throughout Oregon.[1666] Although implementation of the plan has been hampered by inter-agency conflict, the Forest Service has named the owl as an MIS, which will ensure continued monitoring of owl populations.[1667]

[1662] 50 C.F.R. § 10.13 (1984).

[1663] Species listed as migratory birds can receive federal protection from hunting under the Migratory Bird Treaty Act. 16 U.S.C. §§ 703-711 (1982). *See generally* M. BEAN, *supra* note 601, at 68-69.

[1664] The northern spotted owl has caused considerable controversy due to its need for commercially valuable old-growth habitat. *See* Heinrichs, *The Winged Snail Darter*, 81 J. FORESTRY 212 (1983).

[1665] *Id.*

[1666] *Id.*

[1667] *See* FOREST SERVICE, U.S. DEP'T OF AGRICULTURE, REGIONAL GUIDE FOR THE PACIFIC NORTHWEST REGION (1982).

VIII

RECREATION

Recreation encompasses a broad range of activities, including automobile sightseeing, roadside camping, hunting, fishing, hiking, skiing, and snowmobiling.[1668] The national forests provide forty percent of all recreation use of federal lands.[1669] One-quarter of the recreation use of national forests occurs at campgrounds, picnic areas, and similar facilities maintained by the Forest Service.[1670] Ski resorts, summer homes, and other private facilities in national forests operate under special-use permits issued by the Forest Service. These privately operated facilities provide only one-tenth of total recreation user days, yet they contribute over $16 million in receipts.[1671]

Because recreation is a "personal or social phenomenon," rather than a physical commodity like water, timber, or forage,[1672] recreation planning requires different kinds of inventory data and management concepts than does planning for other resources.[1673] The subjective nature of the recreation experience also creates difficulties in comparing the value produced by recreation management with the value created by commodity resource management.[1674] In some cases, Congress has minimized these difficulties by designating specific national forest lands and rivers as recreation areas.[1675] However, for the most part, recreation area management remains a highly discretionary and frequently controversial component of Forest Service planning.

A. Evolution of Policy

1. Early Recreation Policy (1891-1939)

Recreation was viewed as a secondary, incidental use of the national forests until after World War I. As early as 1891 the Chief of the Division of Forestry, Bernhard Fernow, assigned recreation

---

[1668] 1981 ASSESSMENT, *supra* note 9, at 63.

[1669] *1985 Forest Service Budget, supra* note 10, at 1283.

[1670] *Id.* at 1192.

[1671] *Id.* Receipts from ski areas typically constitute 75% of all revenues derived from special-use permits. 1981 ANNUAL REPORT, *supra* note 19, at 18.

[1672] *Comm. of Scientists Final Report, supra* note 864, at 26,628.

[1673] *Id.* at 26,628-29.

[1674] *See generally* K. DAVIS, *supra* note 29, at 130-44.

[1675] *See infra* text accompanying notes 1725-30.

a minor role, subordinate to timber and water.[1676] The omission of recreation from the 1897 Organic Act reflected Fernow's view that the purposes of the forest reserves should be clearly distinguished from those of the national parks.[1677] Gifford Pinchot concurred with Fernow's view on recreation policy and relegated recreation planning to a relatively obscure position.[1678] According to Pinchot, utilization of the forests for timber production, grazing, and water power took precedence over recreation.[1679]

Congress first recognized recreation as a use of the national forests in 1915, when it authorized the Forest Service to grant permits to build summer homes, stores, and hotels in the national forests.[1680] After the National Park Service was created in 1916, the Forest Service began to give serious consideration to recreation in national forest planning. Under the leadership of Steven Mather, the Park Service witnessed a boom in the use of the

---

[1676] 1891 ANNUAL REPORT OF THE CHIEF, *supra* note 228, at 224. Fernow reported in 1891 that timber and water were the primary objects of the newly created forest reserves. *See supra* text accompanying note 229-33. In contrast,

Secondary objects . . . are those of an aesthetic nature, namely, to preserve natural scenery, remarkable objects of interest, and to secure places of retreat for those in quest of health, recreation, and pleasure. Both objects are legitimate, but the first class [i.e., timber and water supply] is infinitely more important, and the second is easily provided for in securing the first.

1891 ANNUAL REPORT OF THE CHIEF, *supra*, at 224.

[1677] *See supra* note 231.

[1678] 1907 USE BOOK, *supra* note 1104, at 24. Pinchot summarized the role of recreation planning on the national forests as follows:

Quite incidentally, also, the National Forests serve a good purpose as great playgrounds for the people. They are used more or less every year by campers, hunters, fishermen, and thousands of pleasure seekers from the near-by towns. They are great recreation grounds for a very large part of the people of the West, and their value in this respect is well worth considering.

Id.

[1679] See *infra* note 1684. *See also* S. HAYS, CONSERVATION AND THE GOSPEL OF EFFICIENCY: THE PROGRESSIVE CONSERVATION MOVEMENT, 1890-1920 (1959); McConnell, *The Multiple-Use Concept in Forest Service Policy*, 44 SIERRA CLUB BULLETIN 14 (1959).

[1680] Act of Mar. 4, 1915, ch. 144, 38 Stat. 1101 (codified as amended at 16 U.S.C. § 497 (1982)) (authority to issue permits for hotels and resorts, not to exceed 80 acres and 30 years, and for summer homes and stores, not to exceed 5 acres and 30 years, provided that "the authority provided by this section shall be exercised in such manner as not to preclude the general public from full enjoyment of the natural, scenic, recreational, and other aspects of the national forests").

national parks by an increasingly mobile population.[1681] Tourists also swarmed into the national forests, tripling the number of recreation visits between 1917 and 1924.[1682] As one historian has observed, "The irresistable force of recreation use was sweeping through the forests and carrying forest policy along with it."[1683]

The arrival of the recreation-seeking motoring public in the national forests caused the Forest Service to revise Pinchot's policy of managing the forests primarily for the benefit of local, commodity-based economies.[1684] Pinchot's successor, Henry Graves, reported in 1919 that "[p]lans for the management of the National Forests . . . would be incomplete if they failed to take into account . . . the recreation resources."[1685] Graves suggested

---

[1681] *See* H. STEEN, *supra* note 49, at 156; D. SWAIN, FEDERAL CONSERVATION POLICY, 1921-1933, at 127 (1963).

[1682] J. Gilligan, The Development of Policy and Administration of Forest Service Primitive and Wilderness Areas in the Western United States 95 (1953) (unpublished Ph.D. thesis, Univ. of Michigan).

[1683] *Id.*

[1684]*Id.* at 80-81:
At the national level, "the greatest good of the greatest number in the long run" was the watchword in formulation of policy concerning use of the national forests. A translation of this somewhat generalized creed for application by regional offices and individual national forests was, that "forests should be managed for the maintenance and improvement of the local economy." . . . Plans for retention of a permanent supply of timber, grass, and water fitted the principle of maintenance of the local economy excellently. . . .
The addition of recreation as a major use of national forests . . . could not fit the pattern of automatic national good derived from locally beneficial management. Recreation opportunity was, of course, available to persons only a few hours away from forest lands, but the provision of facilities and areas for the kind of recreation desired by the national motoring public could not be so readily included in multiple use concepts. To give priority to the needs of outdoor recreationists from all parts of the United States would conflict immediately with local management of natural resources and require subordination, in many instances, of local enterprise.
Id.

[1685] FOREST SERVICE, U.S. DEP'T OF AGRICULTURE [1919 ANNUAL] REPORT OF THE CHIEF 194 (1919). Graves continued:
There is not a single Forest, and there is scarcely a ranger district, which does not have some features of recreation interest. Sometimes it is the mountain scenery, sometimes the beauty of forests, lakes, and streams, sometimes the opportunities for sport in the form of fishing, hunting, or mountain climbing, and sometimes it is still other kinds of attractions which lead yearly increasing number of visitors to the Forests for recreation and health.
Because of this expanding use adequate administration of the recreation resource has become of marked importance. The western National Forests are, by virtue of their location and character, the natural public

modifying timber sales "to protect scenic features, roads, camping places, and the like against loss of attractiveness."[1686]

The shift in recreation policy accelerated during the 1920s under the leadership of Chief William Greeley and Assistant Chief L.F. Kneipp.[1687] In 1921, Greeley declared recreation to be a major use of the national forests.[1688] That same year the Forest Service redrafted its administrative manual to include a statement of policy mandating recognition and conservation of recreation resources.[1689] 1921 was also the year in which Aldo Leopold, a forest assistant in the Forest Service's Southwest District, published his seminal article in which he argued that developed recreation sites and resource exploitation should be excluded from large areas where wilderness recreation was the "highest use."[1690]

---

playgrounds for most of the country west of the Mississippi, and they also draw many thousands of visitors from the East. They must be handled with full recognition of their recreation values, present and future. This requires careful and forward-looking plans providing both for the protection and the development of this important resource.
Id. at 194-95.

[1686] *Id.* at 195. Graves later wrote, "The preservation of the beauty of the forests along our highways is important in the public reservations . . . ." Graves, *A Crisis in National Recreation*, 26 AM. FORESTS 391, 399 (1920). Graves's views on recreation planning may have been influenced by a 1918 study made at Graves's request by Frank A. Waugh, a landscape architect. J. Gilligan, *supra* note 1682, at 74. Waugh recommended that "sightseeing, camping, and hiking be given equal consideration with economic criteria in determining the use of the forests." R. NASH, WILDERNESS AND THE AMERICAN MIND 185 (3d ed. 1982).

[1687] Greeley and Kneipp both assumed their positions in 1920. J. Gilligan, *supra* note 1682, at 92.

[1688] 1921 ANNUAL REPORT OF THE CHIEF, *supra* note 1121, at 26.

[1689] Kneipp, *supra* note 104, at 620. The Manual stated:

It is not the purpose of the Forest Service to duplicate within the national forests the functions, methods, or activities of national, state, or municipal park services, nor to compete with such parks for public patronage or support. Recognition must, however, be given to the occurrence within the national forests of mountains, cliffs, canyons, glaciers, streams, lakes, and other landscape features; natural formations such as caves or bridges; objects of scientific, historic, or archaeological interest; timber, shrubs, and flowers; game animals and fish; and areas preeminently suited as sites for camps, resorts, sanatoria, picnic grounds, and summer homes. These utilities, which singly or in combination afford the bases for outdoor recreation, contributing to the entertainment and instruction of the public or to public health, constitute recreation resources of great extent, economic value, and social importance. No plan of national forest administration would be complete which did not conserve and make them fully available for public use.
Id. (quoting Forest Service Manual).

[1690] Leopold, *The Wilderness and Its Place in Forest Recreational Policy*, 19 J. FORESTRY 718, 719 (1921). For further discussion of Leopold's contribution to Forest Service wilderness policy, see *infra* text accompanying notes 1813-17.

The Forest Service's departure from the orthodox doctrine espoused by Pinchot met with resistance from inside and outside of the agency. Many of the local foresters did not want to adapt their management plans to accommodate noncommodity uses.[1691] Congress refused to appropriate recreation funds for the Forest Service, claiming that the National Park Service was in charge of recreation on federal lands and that Forest Service involvement in recreation amounted to a duplication of services.[1692] As a result, Secretary of Agriculture, W.M. Jardine, urged the Forest Service to "soft pedal" recreation[1693]—a resource that he felt was "a by-product of [the National Forests'] systematic management" and should not impair the primary function of the forests.[1694]

Notwithstanding this opposition, the Forest Service continued to build its recreation policy. Protection of natural scenic features was a major policy consideration. In the late 1920s, Greeley vetoed three major development proposals in the West—a highway across the Sierra Nevadas, a toll road to the top of Mount Whitney in California, and a cable car to the top of Mount Hood

---

[1691] *See* Kneipp, *supra* note 104, at 619-20. In 1930 Assistant Forester Kneipp explained the reasons that foresters initially resisted the new emphasis on recreation:

Generally speaking, the first reaction of the Forest Service, of foresters as a class, to this new phase of social development, was negative. It was in direct conflict with the first phase, that of work, of production and utilization. The swarming hordes were a menace. Their careless camp fires caused widespread forest destruction. Their disregard of sanitary precautions menaced public health. They shot live-stock or ran it off the range or camped alongside of water holes and thus prevented stock from securing needed water. They opposed logging, grazing, reservoir development, or other utilitarian activities, without regard to whether they were or were not indispensable to economic security and growth. More than one old-time forest ranger deliberately concealed the entrances to newly constructed trails, or refrained from posting directional signboards on roads, so as to avert or minimize the invasion of his district by this conflicting host.

Id.

[1692] *See* D. Cate, Recreation and the U.S. Forest Service: A Study of Organizational Response to Changing Demands 63-64 (1963) (unpublished Ph.D. thesis, Stanford Univ.). Congress responded to the Forest Service's first request for recreation funding in 1922 by appropriating $10,000 for sanitation and fire prevention rather than the $50,000 requested for recreation purposes. *Id.*

[1693] *Id.* at 81-82.

[1694] *Recreation Principles for the National Forests*, 31 AM. FORESTS & FOREST LIFE 423 (1925) (quoting letter from Secretary of Agriculture William M. Jardine).

in Oregon.[1695] Greeley's opposition to the Mount Hood cable car was supported by a special committee, appointed by Jardine to undertake a study of the area.[1696] This committee concluded that the project would lead to "the gradual frittering away of the extraordinary potentialities of the area."[1697]

In addition, during the 1920's the Forest Service began to set aside large portions of the national forests as "primitive areas," a policy formalized by Regulation L-20, which was promulgated in 1929.[1698] The primitive area policy gave the Forest Service an

---

[1695] *See* J. Gilligan, *supra* note 1682, at 112. Greeley based his opposition to the projects on the ground that motorized recreation should not be allowed to penetrate so far into the national forests as to completely conquer the wilderness:

These mountain wildernesses may not be used by numbers of people in any wise commensurate with those who will throng the highways, but their individual service will be immeasurably greater . . . . It is not a matter of providing for one type of recreation to the exclusion of the other. We need both and we can have both. It is a matter rather of preventing motorized recreation from sweeping wilderness recreation, dear to the souls of many folk, off the face of the map.

Greeley, *What Shall We Do With Our Mountains?*, 59 Sunset 14, 82-83 (Dec. 1927).

[1696] Public Values of the Mount Hood Area, S. Doc. No. 164, 71st Cong., 2d Sess. III (1930). The special study committee consisted of John C. Merriam, president of the Carnegie Institution of Washington; Professor Frank A. Waugh, author of a 1918 study that helped shape initial Forest Service recreation policy, *see supra* note 1686; and Frederick Law Olmstead, a nationally recognized land planner.

[1697] S. Doc. No. 164, 71st Cong., 2d Sess. III at 33.

[1698] *See* J. Gilligan, *supra* note 1682, at 132-37. For further discussion of primitive areas and other aspects of early Forest Service wilderness policy, see *infra* notes 1816-27 and accompanying text. Assistant Chief Kneipp explained the reasons for setting aside primitive areas in a 1931 memorandum to his staff:

The basic purpose of the Forest Service is to derive from the lands committed to its care the highest attainable social service to the largest number of people and in the most permanent form. If preponderant public sentiment is in favor of preserving bodies of timber for their scenic beauty as against making firewood or lumber out of them, or . . . [regarding] picturesque bodies of water as objects of beauty rather than as sources of hydroelectric energy, can the Forest Service long sustain a contrary policy? There is nothing fixed or irrevocable in a decision to withhold natural values or resources from industrial exploitation since such a policy can be modified whenever the need arises. That, however, cannot be said of a policy of complete industrial utilization, for primitive conditions once destroyed cannot readily be restored, especially if private interests become established.

Id. at 143.

inexpensive foil to use against the Park Service's efforts to obtain control over undeveloped parts of the national forests.[1699]

By the 1930s, the Forest Service had developed a fairly sophisticated land classification system for various forms of recreation use. In 1933, Robert Marshall identified seven "distinct types of recreational forest areas" in a chapter that he wrote for the Forest Service's Copeland Report.[1700] The seven classes generally corresponded to the Forest Service's primitive areas,[1701] research reserves,[1702] scenic roadside areas,[1703] campgrounds, summer

---

[1699] Some historians have characterized federal recreation policy in the 1920s as a race for dominance between the Forest Service and the Park Service. *See, e.g.,* D. SWAIN, *supra* note 1681, at 134-38. One scholar has observed, "There are some firm opinions among prominent scholars of the wilderness preservation movement that a desire to prevent loss of lands to an expanding National Park Service motivated Forest Service action in setting aside wilderness areas rather than any strong belief in the wilderness principle." D. Cate, *supra* note 1692, at 100.

[1700] COPELAND REPORT, *supra* note 112, at 471. For discussion of Marshall's contribution to the development of wilderness policy, see *infra* notes 1828-31 and accompanying text.

[1701] Marshall called the primitive areas "wilderness areas" in the Copeland Report and recommended that 20 million acres be set aside as wilderness. COPELAND REPORT, *supra* note 112, at 475. Marshall recommended that another 3 million acres be preserved as "superlative areas," *id.* at 485, which he described as "localities with unique scenic value, so surpassing and stupendous in their beauty as to affect almost everyone who sees them." *Id.* at 471.

[1702] Research reserves for scientific, research, and educational purposes were created in 1929 pursuant to Regulation L-20. J. Gilligan, *supra* note 1682, at 126. A year later, these research reserves were divided into experimental forests, experimental ranges, and natural areas. *Id.* Marshall called the research reserves "primeval areas" in the Copeland Report and recommended preserving 9.5 million acres. COPELAND REPORT, *supra* note 112, at 485. Marshall argued that preserving these tracts of virgin timber would benefit timber management because "it is of utmost importance to have various unmodified stands with which to compare the results of human modification." *Id.* at 471.

[1703] Marshall stated:

The great majority of people who visit the forests for recreation do so by automobile. While most of these visitors do not penetrate into the forest, they are very much concerned with the part which they can see from the highway. If this were destroyed or seriously damaged, their enjoyment of touring would be immeasurably impaired, and indeed many of them would largely give up their vacation journeys. Consequently, it follows that for these people it is of great importance to preserve from serious scenic damage the timbered strips adjoining the more important roads. These strips will be referred to as "roadside areas."

The width desirable for these strips varies with the density of the forest, the topography, and the danger of windfall. Along roads that are used chiefly in summer, when forest visibility is much less than in winter, the strips can be narrower. In most cases the width of the strips on each side

homes, and other developed sites.[1704] In general, Marshall encouraged developed recreation, but he believed that strict regulation and careful planning were necessary to prevent misuse.[1705] Marshall acknowledged that recreational values were often antithetical to commodity values;[1706] nevertheless, he argued that the two could coexist if forests were managed for sustained yield.[1707] After 1933, Marshall worked fervently to persuade the Forest Service to expand its primitive area system.[1708]

During the mid-1930s, the Forest Service came under renewed pressure from the National Park Service. With the encouragement of Secretary of Interior Harold Ickes, the Park Service

---

of the road should probably range from 125 to 250 feet, which would be sufficient to hide any impairment of the scenery behind them.
COPELAND REPORT, *supra* note 112, at 476-77. Marshall intended the classification to "include also strips of timber left along lakes, rivers, and all other boat and canoe routes." *Id.* at 476.

[1704] In addition, Marshall proposed to designate "outing areas" to serve the segment of the motoring public that desired to find out "what lies beyond the roadside fringe." *Id.* at 478. Marshall saw the outing area as "intermediate between primeval areas and commercially operated timber tracts," and necessary to provide short day hikes. *Id.* He also thought outing areas would have "special value as buffers" between the superlative areas and the developed recreation sites, where "the large number of visitors can reside comfortably and amid pleasant surroundings, and yet not mar by their presence the value of the beauty which they came to enjoy." *Id.* at 479.

[1705] *Id.* at 479-81.

[1706] *Id.* at 468. Marshall stated:
[T]he most important values of forest recreation are not susceptible of measurement in monetary terms. They are concerned with such intangible considerations such as inspiration, esthetic enjoyment, and a gain in understanding . . . . The only common denominator for the recreational and commodity value of the forest is the human happiness which may be derived from each use.
Id.

[1707] *Id.* at 484-85:
[N]o matter how solemnly we may set aside in perpetuity lands on which timber may be neither "sold, removed, nor destroyed," the fact remains that if the need for timber becomes sufficiently acute the protected lands will be opened for exploitation. Men in general have always attended to their physical needs ahead of their aesthetic and recreational ones. Consequently, if our physical forest needs cannot be met on the areas devoted to commodity production, it is almost certain that the aesthetic and inspirational forest values will be sacrificed. But if the commodity forests are managed on a sustained-yield basis there will be no need to call on the recreational forests for wood products, and people may still continue to enjoy the adventure, the beauty, the inspiration, and the opportunity of communion with nature which the forest alone can supply.
Id.

[1708] *See* R. NASH, *supra* note 1686, at 204-06.

recommended that large tracts of national forest land be designated as national parks.[1709] In particular, the Park Service desired
authority over part of the Sierra Nevada Mountains in California
and a large portion of the Olympic Peninsula in Washington.[1710]
The Forest Service's rivalry with the Park Service, coupled with
Marshall's visionary proposals, served as the impetus for additional changes in Forest Service recreation policy.

In 1937, Chief F.A. Silcox appointed Marshall to head the
Division of Recreation and Lands.[1711] On September 20, 1939,
two months before Marshall died, the Forest Service promulgated
the "U Regulations," which formally classified wilderness, wild,
recreation, experimental, and natural areas.[1712] With respect to
recreation areas, Regulation U-3 stated that "suitable areas of national forest land other than wilderness or wild areas which should
be managed principally for recreation use but on which certain
other uses are permitted may be given special classification."[1713]
Marshall's terse U-3 Regulation remains essentially unchanged to
the present and provides the legal basis for a broad range of special, recreation-oriented land classifications.[1714]

Thus, by the 1940s many elements of the Forest Service's current recreation planning system were already in place. They

---

[1709] *See* J. Gilligan, *supra* note 1682, at 158-60.

[1710] *See id.* at 165. The Forest Service countered the park proposal on the
Olympic Peninsula by establishing a primitive area and "by inciting the local
communities and lumbering industries to oppose the park proposal—which did
not require much encouragement." *Id.* Nevertheless, Congress approved the
transfer in 1938 of more than half a million acres to the Olympic National Parks
Id. at 166. Similarly, the Forest Service lost 450,000 acres of the High Sierra
Primitive Area to the Kings Canyon National Park in 1940, over the objection of
the regional forester of California. *Id.*

[1711] R. NASH, *supra* note 1686, at 206.

[1712] 4 Fed. Reg. 3994 (1930). For discussion of wilderness and wild areas, see
infra text accompanying notes 1832-34.

[1713] 4 Fed. Reg. 3994 (1939). The Forest Service promptly amended Regulation U-3 to clarify that other uses "may or may not be permitted," rather than
that they "are permitted." *Id.* at 4156.

[1714] 36 C.F.R. § 294.1 (1984). The current version of Regulation U-3 states:
    Suitable areas of national forest land, other than wilderness or wild ar-
    eas, which should be managed principally for recreation use may be given
    special classification as follows:
    (a) Areas which should be managed principally for recreation use sub-
    stantially in their natural condition and on which, in the discretion of the
    officer making the classification, certain other uses may or may not be per-
    mitted may be approved and classified . . . .
Id. For discussion of agency flexibility in recreational land classification, see also
infra text accompanying notes 1745-54.

included visual management of highway and water corridors, limitations on motorized recreation, and classification of land areas for various types of recreation use. Other than the 1915 law governing permits for summer homes and resorts, the only statutory authority or guidance for these policy decisions was the 1897 Organic Act.

2. *Expansion of the Recreation Program (1940-1976)*

After a temporary decline in use during World War II, use of national forests for recreation increased and diversified at a phenomenal rate.[1715] For the first time, Congress began to appropriate substantial sums of money for campgrounds and other recreational facilities.[1716] The Forest Service leased many high-elevation sites to private entities for downhill ski operations, causing recreation to become a year-round activity.[1717]

The increase in recreational use exacerbated conflicts among different recreation interests, as well as between recreationists and commodity interests. Proposals for ski areas and other developed sites met with resistance from some conservation groups.[1718]

[1715] Recreation use declined from almost 11 million visits in 1941 to approximately 6 million visits during the war. 1946 ANNUAL REPORT OF THE CHIEF, *supra* note 711, at 23. In 1946 use climbed to more than 18 million visits. 1947 ANNUAL REPORT OF THE CHIEF, *supra* note 712, at 29. By 1961 national forests were receiving more than 100 million visits. 1961 ANNUAL REPORT OF THE CHIEF, *supra* note 98, at 13. Recreation use included picnicking, fishing, hunting, camping, skiing, swimming, hiking, and riding. *Id.*

[1716] The Forest Service actively promoted recreation appropriations through national planning. In 1957 the Forest Service launched "Operation Outdoors"—a five-year program designed to improve maintenance of existing recreation facilities and to develop new facilities. *See* 1957 ANNUAL REPORT OF THE CHIEF, *supra* note 1070, at 13. Operation Outdoors was in some respects "a defensive counter-program to the National Park Service's 'Mission 66'." *See* Crafts, *supra* note 1522, at 15. Operation Outdoors and Mission 66 are discussed in S. DANA & S. FAIRFAX, *supra* note 52, at 192, 194.

[1717] The first ski run in the national forests was established in Sun Valley, Idaho, in 1936; by 1973 there were 218 ski areas. *See* G. ROBINSON, *supra* note 2, at 126.

[1718] For example, in the early 1940s the Forest Service considered a proposal to build a ski resort in the San Gorgonio Primitive Area in California. Wilderness advocates opposed the project, and after five years of hearings the Forest Service decided not to permit the development. *See* J. Gilligan, *supra* note 1682, at 328-29. However, in the 1960s the Forest Service decided to proceed with development of a large skiing and resort project at another site in California's Sierra Nevada Mountains, the Mineral King valley. This proposal generated intense controversy and extensive litigation. *See* Sierra Club v. Morton, 405 U.S. 727, 728-31 (1972); G. ROBINSON, *supra* note 2, at 130-36.

Forest Service efforts to develop previously classified primitive areas resulted in demands for statutory wilderness protection.[1719] The increasing pressure for wilderness legislation prompted the agency to set aside large tracts of land as undeveloped Scenic Areas under the authority of Marshall's U-3 Regulation.[1720]

In the 1960s Congress passed several laws pertaining to recreation use of the national forests. First and most important, the Multiple-Use Sustained-Yield (MUSY) Act of 1960[1721] confirmed the Forest Service's authority to regulate recreation use[1722] and gave outdoor recreation first billing on its alphabetical list of multiple uses.[1723] Second, the Land and Water Conservation Fund Act of 1965 gave the Forest Service authority to purchase recreation lands and to charge user fees.[1724] Third, the Wilderness Act of 1964 created a system of lands devoted principally to primitive recreation.[1725] Fourth, the Wild and Scenic Rivers Act of 1968 established a somewhat comparable system for rivers, giving priority to recreation values over water development projects.[1726] Fifth, the National Trail System Act of 1968 forbade motorized vehicle use on certain scenic trails.[1727]

In addition, Congress began to create National Recreation Areas (NRAs) on national forest lands. Typically, an NRA was established by a separate statute that spelled out management direction for the area.[1728] During the 1970s and 1980s NRA statutes

---

[1719] *See infra* text accompanying notes 1836-52.

[1720] *See* 1962 ANNUAL REPORT OF THE CHIEF, *supra* note 718, at 15; 1963 ANNUAL REPORT OF THE CHIEF, *supra* note 162, at 11; D. Cate, *supra* note 1692, at 510.

[1721] 16 U.S.C. § 528 (1982), discussed *supra* at text accompanying notes 125-32.

[1722] *Id. See* United States v. McMichael, 355 F.2d. 283 (9th Cir. 1965).

[1723] 16 U.S.C. § 528 (1982). The Forest Service gave careful thought to the order of the multiple uses. *See supra* note 1522.

[1724] Land and Water Conservation Fund Act of 1965, Pub. L. No. 88-578, 78 Stat. 897 (codified as amended at 16 U.S.C. § 460*l*-4 to 460*l*-11 (1982)). Subsequent amendments allowed the Forest Service to charge fees for use of most campgrounds. *See* G. ROBINSON, *supra* note 2, at 123-25; S. DANA & S. FAIRFAX, *supra* note 52, at 213.

[1725] 16 U.S.C. §§ 1131-1136 (1982). *See infra* section IX(B)(2).

[1726] 16 U.S.C. §§ 1271-1287 (1982). *See generally* Tarlock & Tippy, *supra* note 1263. For a discussion of the Forest Service's treatment of potential W&S rivers in the forest planning process, see *infra* text accompanying notes 1774-96.

[1727] 16 U.S.C. §§ 1241-1249 (1982). *See generally* S. DANA & S. FAIRFAX, *supra* note 52, at 222.

[1728] For example, the Mount Rogers NRA, located in the Jefferson National Forest in Virginia and established in 1966, was generally to be administered to:

commonly required the Forest Service to prepare special management plans for each area.[1729] Some NRAs included land designated as wilderness.[1730]

Passage of the MUSY Act provided the major impetus for the Forest Service to undertake a three-part recreation planning effort in the early 1960s. First, recreation management plans inventoried and classified all suitable recreation lands in each national forest.[1731] Second, recreation composite plans gave management direction for specific areas with outstanding recreational features.[1732] Third, multiple-use plans identified visually sensitive areas on each national forest as Travel and Water Influence Zones.[1733] The Forest Service continued to apply and refine these recreation classifications and visual zoning systems in its unit planning process.[1734]

The clearcutting controversy of the early 1970s resulted in additional direction from Congress.[1735] In response to public criticism of the impact of clearcutting on visual aesthetics,[1736] the congressional guidelines specified that "[c]learcutting should not be used . . . where . . . [a]esthetic values outweigh other considerations."[1737] The Forest Service, in turn, instituted a new landscape management program in 1973 designed to extend consideration of

provide for (1) public outdoor recreation benefits; (2) conservation of scenic, scientific, historic, and other values contributing to public enjoyment; and (3) such management, utilzation, and disposal of natural resources as . . . will promote, or is compatible with, and does not significantly impair the purposes for which the recreation area is established.
16 U.S.C. § 460r-4 (1982). Congress authorized the Forest Service to ban hunting and fishing from portions of the NRA. *Id.* § 460r-5.

[1729] *See, e.g., id.* § 460jj(c) (Arapaho NRA). The area encompassed land on two national forests. *Id.* § 460jj(a).

[1730] *See, e.g., id.* §§ 460*ll*-1 to 460*ll*-2 (Rattlesnake NRA).

[1731] *See* 1961 ANNUAL REPORT OF THE CHIEF, *supra* note 98, at 15. The plans were based on a two-year National Forest Recreation Survey, which inventoried lands suitable and available to meet future recreation needs. *Id.* The survey was initiated in 1959, one year after Congress had established an Outdoor Recreation Resources Review Commission (ORRRC) to study recreation management nationally. *See* 1959 ANNUAL REPORT OF THE CHIEF, *supra* note 119, at 10; S. DANA & S. FAIRFAX, *supra* note 52, at 196.

[1732] *See supra* note 122.

[1733] *See supra* note 136.

[1734] *See supra* note 156.

[1735] *See supra* section IV.

[1736] *See, e.g.,* D. BARNEY, *supra* note 764, at 41-68.

[1737] CHURCH SUBCOMMITTEE REPORT, *supra* note 194, at 9, *reprinted in* SENATE NFMA HEARINGS, *supra* note 194, at 959. For a discussion of the "Church guidelines," see *supra* text accompanying notes 721-83.

visual resources throughout an entire forest, rather than to only the most scenic or heavily travelled areas.[1738]

During the early 1970s controversy over motorized recreation demanded the attention of Forest Service planners. In 1972 President Richard Nixon issued Executive Order 11,644, requiring the agency to designate "specific areas and trails on public lands on which the use of off-road vehicles may be permitted, and areas in which the use of off-road vehicles may not be permitted."[1739] By 1978 the Forest Service had completed off-road vehicle plans on 150 of the 154 national forests.[1740]

In sum, recreation planning prior to the NFMA occurred in an increasingly contentious atmosphere. Congress occasionally acted as an arbitrator in controversies over specific wilderness areas, trails, and rivers. Otherwise the MUSY Act's broad language provided the only statutory direction for recreation management on the vast majority of the national forest land. While possessing ample authority to regulate conflicting uses,[1741] the Forest Service was reluctant to implement comprehensive recreation plans. The result, as one commentator has observed, was a "rather loose and amorphous" recreation planning system.[1742]

B.   *Recreation Planning on General Forest Lands*

Congress made only general reference to recreation in the NFMA.[1743] Nevertheless, the NFMA regulations specifically direct Forest Service planners to address several issues pertaining to recreation on general forest lands, i.e., those lands not dedicated by statute for any particular purpose. The regulations focus on zoning, visual resources, and off-road vehicles. Unlike the water, mineral and wildlife resources—where unresolved legal and policy questions relating to state power and private property rights con-

---

[1738] *See infra* notes 1758, 1760.

[1739] Exec. Order No. 11,644, 3 C.F.R. § 368 (1973), *reprinted in* 42 U.S.C. § 4321, app. at 188-89 (1985).

[1740] 43 Fed. Reg. 20,007 (1978).

[1741] *See, e.g.,* McMichael v. United States, 355 F.2d 283 (9th cir. 1965), discussed *supra* in text accompanying notes 317-21.

[1742] G. ROBINSON, *supra* note 2, at 128.

[1743] *See* 16 U.S.C. § 1604(e)(l) (1982) (requiring that plans shall provide for multiple-use, sustained-yield, and coordination of recreation with other resources); *id.* § (g)(3)(A) (requiring that planning regulations shall provide for outdoor recreation, including wilderness); *id.* § (g)(3)(F)(v) (requiring that planning regulations shall insure that methods of even-aged timber harvesting will be carried out in a manner consistent with recreation and esthetic resources).

tinue to complicate the agency's management practices—the Forest Service's expansive authority over recreation has been cemented by a series of court decisions interpreting the Organic Act and the MUSY Act.[1744]

1. *Administrative Recreation Zoning—The Recreation Opportunity Spectrum*

Zoning of land and water for various recreation uses is a traditional function of national forest planning that has assumed even greater importance in the NFMA planning process. The NFMA regulations require that "a broad spectrum of . . . outdoor recreation opportunities shall be provided" in the forest plans.[1745] The Forest Service has generally implemented this requirement through a planning system called Recreation Opportunity Spectrum (ROS).

The basic objective of ROS planning is to provide a diverse set of recreation opportunities to satisfy the wide range of public tastes and preferences, both now and in the future.[1746] The ROS system divides recreation activities, settings, and experiences into six classes, ranging from Primitive to Urban.[1747] Planners use the

---

[1744] *See, e.g.*, United States v. Hell's Canyon Guide Services, Inc., 660 F.2d 735 (9th Cir. 1981) (regulation of commercial boat operators); Sabin v. Butz, 515 F.2d 1061 (10th Cir. 1975), *aff'd on other grounds sub nom.* Sabin v. Berglund, 585 F.2d 955 (10th Cir. 1978) (regulation of ski instructors); McMichael v. United States, 355 F.2d 283 (9th Cir. 1965) (classification of areas for special recreation use and regulation of motor vehicles within such areas). *See generally supra* section II(A)(2).

[1745] 36 C.F.R. § 219.21 (1984). *See also id.* § 294.1, *quoted in supra* note 1714, authorizing special classifications.

[1746] FOREST SERVICE, U.S. DEP'T OF AGRICULTURE, THE RECREATION OPPORTUNITY SPECTRUM: A FRAMEWORK FOR PLANNING, MANAGEMENT, AND RESEARCH 4 (1979).

[1747] FOREST SERVICE, U.S. DEP'T OF AGRICULTURE, ROS USERS GUIDE 5 (undated) [hereinafter cited as ROS USERS GUIDE]. The other classes are Semi-Primitive Non-Motorized, Semi-Primitive Motorized, Roaded Natural, and Rural. *Id.* Additional classes are often used in different regions of the country. Interview with Bob Longcore, Recreation Planner, Willamette Nat'l Forest, in Eugene, Or. (Nov. 19, 1984). The ROS classes roughly correspond to a 6-class zoning system recommended in 1962 by a federal commission. The commission stated that the 6 classes "constitute a spectrum ranging from areas suitable for high-density use to sparsely used extensive primitive areas." UNITED STATES OUTDOOR RECREATION RESOURCES REVIEW COMM'N, OUTDOOR RECREATION FOR AMERICA 96 (1962).

ROS classifications to inventory and map land and water areas and to identify the recreation opportunities they afford.[1748]

More important, ROS provides a framework to divide land into specific recreation zones, or "management areas," and to establish standards for future management of those zones.[1749] In other words, by zoning an area as a particular ROS class the Forest Service must exclude activities from the area that are inconsistent with providing the features associated with that ROS class.

For example, Forest Service planners in the Willamette National Forest have grouped potential recreation zones into two categories, "Dispersed" and "Developed" Recreation.[1750] The Dispersed category is divided into four of the six ROS classes—Primitive, Semiprimitive Nonmotorized, Semiprimitive Motorized, and Roaded Natural.[1751] Specific standards and "operational considerations" apply to each ROS class. Timber harvesting in the Semiprimitive Nonmotorized class, for instance, is limited to units of land three to five acres in size, and the rate of harvest allowed is less than one-half of the maximum sustained-yield rate.[1752] Thus, when the Willamette's forest plan zones an area of that national forest as Semiprimitive Nonmotorized, the Forest Service will be required to follow the standards for timber harvesting and other activities that apply to that zone.[1753]

[1748] ROS USERS GUIDE, *supra* note 1747, at 14. Areas are grouped into ROS classes based on several criteria, such as remoteness from human sights and sounds, amount of relatively undeveloped land, and evidence of human influence or modification. *Id.* at 14-22.

[1749] *Id.* at 9-10. The NFMA regulations require each forest plan to contain "[m]ultiple-use prescriptions and associated standards and guidelines for each management area." 36 C.F.R. § 219.11(c) (1984). "Prescriptions are closely integrated sets of specific management activities . . . [that] should include consideration for recreation use." ROS USERS GUIDE, *supra* note 1747, at 10.

[1750] FOREST SERVICE, U.S. DEP'T OF AGRICULTURE, MANAGEMENT STRATEGIES FOR THE WILLAMETTE NATIONAL FOREST 1-3, 7-8 (1984).

[1751] *Id.* at 1-3.

[1752] FOREST SERVICE, U.S. DEP'T OF AGRICULTURE, WILLAMETTE NATIONAL FOREST BENCHMARK PRESCRIPTIONS § 2.12 (2d ed. 1984). An example of the "operational considerations" specified for the Semiprimitive Nonmotorized class is the direction to "[f]lush cut stumps in trailside and streamside zones, around lakes and dispersed sites and key interest areas." *Id.* For a discussion of sustained-yield harvest rates, see *supra* text accompanying notes 644-64.

[1753] *See supra* text accompanying note 390. Congress has also established specific recreation areas with unique management requirements. For instance, the Oregon Wilderness Act of 1984 created an Oregon Cascades Recreation Area (OCRA) consisting partly of two wilderness areas. In the nonwilderness portion of the OCRA, motorized recreation is permitted on "specific and appropriate areas and routes" to be identified in a management plan. Pub. L. No. 98-328, §

The ROS system allows for highly individualized land classification for recreation. ROS decisions complement the agency's authority to designate land for research natural areas,[1754] cultural and historic resources,[1755] and other purposes. As a result, the Forest Service has great latitude in creatively classifying and managing land according to the special characteristics of specific parcels.

2. Visual Resource Management

The NFMA regulations provide, as a part of the forest planning process, for consideration of "the landscape's visual attractiveness and the public's visual expectation."[1756] In its Final Report the Committee of Scientists noted the lack of direction concerning visual resources and recommended that "visual and esthetic considerations should be acknowledged in the final regulations."[1757] The Committee did not recommend specific language; instead, they suggested that the regulations provide "brief general guidance," based on the Forest Service's existing visual management program.[1758]

Accordingly, the regulations simply require planners to set "visual quality objectives" (VQOs) for the land-use zones in the forest plan.[1759] The definitions and procedures for setting VQOs are contained in the Forest Service Manual and handbooks.[1760] Planners

---

4(g), 98 Stat. 277 (1984). Timber harvesting is allowed where "necessary to prevent catastrophic mortality from insects, diseases, or fire," *id.* § 4(e)(1), but the area is withdrawn from the allowable harvest base. S. REP. NO. 465, 98th Cong. 2d Sess. (1984).

[1754] 36 C.F.R. § 219.25 (1984).

[1755] *Id.* § 219.24.

[1756] *Id.* § 219.21(f). The regulations require that the "visual resources" be "inventoried and evaluated as an integrated part of evaluating alternatives" in the planning process. *Id.*

[1757] *Comm. of Scientists Final Report, supra* note 864, at 26,641.

[1758] *Id.* The Forest Service Manual was the source of direction for visual management. The Manual states:

The visual resource will be treated as an essential part of, and receive equal consideration with, the other resources of the land. Landscape management principles will be applied not only in especially sensitive areas or unusual circumstances, but routinely in all activities, and by all disciplines throughout the National Forest System.

FOREST SERVICE MANUAL § 2380.3 (1984).

[1759] 36 C.F.R. § 219.21(f) (1984).

[1760] The 1979 regulations referred specifically to the visual management section of the Forest Service Manual. 44 Fed. Reg. 53,996 (1979). The Manual, in turn, relies on the agency's landscape management handbook to define the vari-

generally recognize five VQOs: Preservation, Retention, Partial Retention, Modification, and Maximum Modification.[1761] The two criteria for assigning a VQO to a particular area are (1) public concern for scenic quality and (2) diversity of natural features.[1762]

A VQO provides the Forest Service with a measurable standard for management of an area's visual resource.[1763] For instance, in an area with a Retention VQO the Forest Service will only allow management activities that are "not visually evident."[1764] Thus, timber harvesting in a Retention zone might be limited to selective cutting or small, unobtrusive clearcuts.[1765]

The NFMA requires forest uses to be "consistent with the land management plans."[1766] Since the NFMA regulations require plans to include VQOs, the VQOs impose legal limits on the use of the national forests. VQOs involve complex and subjective judgments; as a result, with the possible exception of some forms

---

ous VQOs. *See* FOREST SERVICE MANUAL § 2382 (1984). The Forest Service distributed the handbook in the early 1970s as a training document to illustrate the principles of the landscape management program. FOREST SERVICE, U.S. DEP'T OF AGRICULTURE, *Foreword, The Visual Management System,* in 2 NATIONAL FOREST LANDSCAPE MANAGEMENT, (1974) [hereinafter cited as LANDSCAPE MANAGEMENT].

[1761] LANDSCAPE MANAGEMENT, *supra* note 1760, at 28.

[1762] *Id.* Planners measure public concern according to various "sensitivity levels." *Id.* at 18. Measuring an area's sensitivity involves two steps. First, planners identify all travel routes, use areas, and water bodies as of either primary or secondary importance within the area. *Id.* Second, they identify the major and minor concern of users for scenic quality For instance,

> Major concern for aesthetics is usually expressed by people who are driving for pleasure, hiking scenic trails, camping at primary use areas, using lakes and streams along with other forms of recreational activities. Minor concern for aesthetics is usually expressed by those people involved with daily commuter driving, hauling forest products, employed in the woods and other commercial uses of the Forest.

Id. The diversity criterion requires evaluation of an area's landform, vegetation, and water resources. Based on this evaluation, planners will place each area into one of three variety classes—distinctive, common, or minimal. *Id.* at 12.

The Forest Service Manual recognizes a third criterion for visual management—Visual Absorption Capability (VAC). VAC analysis estimates a given landscape's ability to withstand management activity without significantly changing its visual character. *See* FOREST SERVICE MANUAL § 2383.21 (1984). Thus, a low VAC rating "would indicate a visually intolerant landscape, one where brightly colored soils, slow growing vegatation, steep slopes or other factors make it difficult to meet any VQO." *Id.* § 2383.3.

[1763] LANDSCAPE MANAGEMENT, *supra* note 1760, at 2.

[1764] *Id.* at 30.

[1765] *Id.* at 30-31.

[1766] 16 U.S.C. § 1604(i)(1982), discussed *supra* in text accompanying note 390.

of timber harvesting,[1767] the Forest Service has broad discretion to set VQOs to control the impact of various uses on visual resources. Once VQOs are established in the plans, however, these limitations will apply to proposals for ski resorts, mining, timber harvesting, and other commercial uses that operate under permit or contract.

3. Off-Road Vehicles

Off-road vehicle (ORV) use has intensified recreation pressures on national forests and has increased air, noise, and visual pollution.[1768] Noise pollution, in particular, can disrupt wildlife and detract from the enjoyment of other recreation users who seek peace and quiet in the forests.[1769] The NFMA regulations require Forest Service planners to address the problems and conflicts resulting from ORV use.

The forest plans must "classify areas and trails . . . as to whether or not off-road vehicle use may be permitted."[1770] The plans must minimize (1) damage to soil, watershed, vegetation, and other resources, (2) harassment of wildlife and disruption of habitat, and (3) conflicts between ORV use and other recreation uses.[1771] The plans must also take into account noise and other

---

[1767] The NFMA provides that clearcutting and other even-aged harvest methods may be used only where "cut blocks, patches, or strips are shaped and blended to the extent practicable with the natural terrain." 16 U.S.C. § 1604(g)(3)(F)(iii) (1982). The report of the Senate Committee on Agriculture and Forestry uses stronger language, stating that "the Committee intends that cuts will be shaped and blended *whenever possible.*" S. Rep. No. 893, 94th Cong., 2d Sess. 40 (1976) *reprinted in* 1976 U.S. Code Cong. & Ad. News 6699, *and in* RPA Compilation, *supra* note 173, at 320 (emphasis added).

The Maximum Modification VQO currently used by the Forest Service allows changes in the landscape that do "not appear to completely borrow from naturally established form, line, color, or texture. Alterations may also be out of scale or contain detail which is incongruent with natural occurrences as seen in foreground or middle ground." Landscape Management, *supra* note 1760, at 36. Since the Maximum Modification VQO apparently does not require Forest Service adherence to the NFMA's standard "to the extent practicable" and "whenever possible," it is questionable whether Maximum Modification is a valid VQO as applied to even-aged timber harvesting.

[1768] 1981 Assessment, *supra* note 9, at 83. Off-road vehicles include motorcycles, mini-bikes, snowmobiles, dune buggies, and all-terrain vehicles. Exec. Order No. 11,644, 3 C.F.R. 368 (1973), *reprinted in* 42 U.S.C.A. § 4321 app. at 188-89 (1985).

[1769] 1981 Assessment, *supra* note 9, at 83.

[1770] 36 C.F.R. § 219.21(g) (1984).

[1771] *Id.* § 295.2(b).

factors to ensure that ORV use is compatible with existing conditions in populated areas.[1772] Areas and trails may be designated as open, restricted, or closed to ORV use.[1773]

C. *Recreation Planning for Additions to the Wild and Scenic River System*

The national forests include many rivers designated as wild, scenic, or recreational rivers by the Wild and Scenic Rivers Act of 1968.[1774] The management of rivers designated by Congress for inclusion within that system has already been discussed.[1775]

One of the most challenging areas of congressionally mandated planning involves the classification of new Wild and Scenic (W&S) Rivers.[1776] W&S rivers can be established only by an act of Congress or upon application by individual states to the Secretary of the Interior.[1777] However, the Act requires federal agencies to study rivers specifically designated by Congress as potential additions to the system.[1778] Furthermore, the Act directs the agencies to consider potential W&S river areas "[i]n all planning for the use and development of water and related land resources" and to "make specific studies and investigations to determine which

---

[1772] *Id.* In related contexts, the courts have been rigorous in scrutinizing ORV planning decisions by the BLM. *See* American Motorists Ass'n v. Watt, 534 F. Supp. 923 (C.D. Cal. 1980), 543 F. Supp. 789 (C.D. Cal. 1982), *aff'd*, 714 F.2d 962 (9th Cir. 1983). Permanent closures of two ORV corridors in the Imperial Sand Dunes were upheld in California Assn. of 4WD Clubs v. Andrus, 672 F.2d 921 (9th Cir. 1982) (text of order at 12 ENVTL. L. REP. (ENVTL. L. INST.) 23,457 (1981)).

[1773] All types of ORVs are allowed to operate without restriction in "open" areas. FOREST SERVICE MANUAL § 2355.11(1) (1984). ORV use in "restricted" areas is limited as to times or season of use, types of vehicles, vehicle equipment, designated areas or trails, or types of activity. *Id.* § 2355.11(2). All ORV use is generally prohibited in "closed" areas, which include wilderness areas, natural areas, and key wildlife areas. *Id.* § 2355 (3).

[1774] 16 U.S.C. §§ 1271-1287 (1982).

[1775] *See supra* text accompanying notes 1263-78.

[1776] One commentator has described the W&S rivers system as being "at once diffuse, vague, and highly complex, and as such [it] is vulnerable to an extraordinary mix of confusions and misconceptions." Palmer, *A Time for Rivers*, WILDERNESS, Fall 1984, at 12, 13.

[1777] *Id.* § 1273. By mid-1984 50 rivers had been classified by Act of Congress and 11 by state application. *See* Stegner, *Inland Passages*, WILDERNESS, Fall 1984, at 4, 9. *See generally* County of Del Norte v. United States, 732 F.2d 1462 (9th Cir. 1984) (W&S classification of five northern California rivers upheld despite procedural objections of several California counties).

[1778] 16 U.S.C. § 1275 (1982). Guidelines for congressionally authorized W&S river studies are published in 47 Fed. Reg. 39,454 (1982).

additional wild, scenic and recreational river areas . . . shall be evaluated in planning reports."[1779] Thus, Congress did not intend to limit consideration of potential W&S rivers to those designated by statute; rather, federal land management agencies were expected to examine "additional" rivers for potential study and classification.

Although the Wild and Scenic Rivers Act was passed in 1968, the federal land agencies have only recently begun to evaluate potential additions to the system, other than congressionally designated study rivers. During the 1970s the Department of the Interior prepared a nationwide inventory of rivers that appeared to have high potential for inclusion in the W&S rivers system.[1780] In 1981 the Forest Service decided to undertake its own comprehensive evaluation of potential W&S rivers through the NFMA planning process.[1781]

Although the NFMA regulations do not mention W&S rivers, the Forest Service Manual directs planners to consider classification of rivers that are included in the Interior Department's inventory or that have received strong local or regional support for classification.[1782] The same guidelines used to evaluate rivers designated for study by Congress apply to determine eligibility for W&S classification through forest planning.[1783] If a river is found to be "eligible", then planners must decide whether it is also

---

[1779] 16 U.S.C. § 1276(d) (1982).

[1780] *See* HERITAGE CONSERVATION RECREATION SERV., U.S. DEP'T OF THE INTERIOR, NATIONWIDE RIVERS INVENTORY: A REPORT ON NATURAL AND FREE-FLOWING RIVERS IN THE NORTHWESTERN UNITED STATES 4-5 (1980). In the Northwest Region, the agency initially examined 700 rivers to determine the amount of development that had occurred either in or along the rivers—85 rivers were selected for further study. *Id.* at 4.

[1781] The agency's decision to incorporate W&S river evaluation into the NFMA plans was apparently derived from directions by President Carter in 1979. *See* Letter from R.M. Housley, Deputy Chief, to Regional Foresters and Area Directors (Mar. 3, 1981) (on file at Oregon Law Review office). President Carter instructed federal land management agencies to assess the suitability for legislative classification of all rivers that were located on their lands and were identified in the inventory prepared by the Heritage Conservation and Recreation Service. Environmental Priorities and Programs, President's Message to the Congress, Aug. 2, 1979, PUB. PAPERS OF THE PRESIDENTS, Jimmy Carter, 1353, 1365 (1980). Since the Heritage Conservation and Recreation Service has been disbanded, the W&S rivers inventory has become the responsibility of the National Park Service.

[1782] FOREST SERVICE MANUAL § 1924 (1984).

[1783] *See id.* The guidelines are set out in 47 Fed. Reg. 39,454 (1982).

"suitable for and needed in" the W&S rivers system.[1784] However, the forest plans are only required to evaluate eligibility; determination of suitability and need may be documented outside the forest planning process.[1785] If the eligibility, suitability, and need standards are met, then the river must be proposed for formal designation in at least one alternative of the forest plan.[1786] If the W&S river proposal is included in the selected alternative, then a legislative EIS will be prepared to support the Forest Service's recommendation to Congress for W&S designation or for formal study of the river.[1787] In the meantime, the values that make the river eligible and suitable must be preserved until Congress takes action on the recommendation.[1788] Presumably, if the W&S river proposal is not in the selected alternative, and the river is not a congressionally mandated study river, the Forest Service will not necessarily continue to preserve the river's W&S values.[1789]

In many respects the Forest Service's W&S river evaluation resembles the evaluation of roadless areas being performed through forest planning in many national forests to determine which roadless areas should be recommended to Congress for designation as wilderness.[1790] Procedurally, the river and roadless area studies are similar. As one deputy chief of the Forest Service has observed, "In essence, the procedures for looking at a potential wild and scenic river in the Forest plan are . . . essentially the same as those followed in looking at a potential wilderness."[1791]

There are also similarities in the substantive laws that created the wilderness and W&S river systems. The first W&S river bill was introduced in 1965, one year after the Wilderness Act was passed.[1792] At that time the sponsor of the W&S river bill, Senator Frank Church of Idaho, stated that the bill "is patterned

---

[1784] *See* 47 Fed. Reg. 39,454 (1982). The criteria for determining suitability and need will be stated in Forest Service Handbook § 1909.12 (forthcoming).

[1785] 47 Fed. Reg. 39,454 (1982).

[1786] *Id.*

[1787] *See* Letter from R.M. Housley, *supra* note 1781.

[1788] FOREST SERVICE MANUAL § 1924 (1984).

[1789] Of course, if a river is not recommended to Congress for inclusion within the W&S system, the Forest Service still has the discretion to classify all or part of the area for some form of recreation use. *See, e.g., supra* text accompanying notes 1745-55.

[1790] For discussion of current roadless area planning, see *infra* text accompanying notes 1863-84.

[1791] Letter from R.M. Housley, *supra* note 1781.

[1792] S. 1446, 89th Cong., 1st Sess., *reprinted in* 111 CONG. REC. 4292-93 (1965).

after, and intended to be, a working partner to the Wilderness Act."[1793] Both acts are dedicated to preservation of natural conditions for the benefit "of present and future generations."[1794]

The similarities between the roadless area and river evaluation processes raise the possibility that courts will choose to apply comparable legal analysis to both processes. Potentially, much of the case law that roadless area litigation has generated could be applied to controversies involving potential W&S rivers.[1795] For example, a decision not to recommend an inventoried W&S river for statutory designation or further study could require the same site-specific analysis of the river's W&S characteristics that courts have required of a roadless area's wilderness characteristics. Therefore, Forest Service planners should give careful attention to inventoried W&S rivers in their forest plan EISs. Likewise, analyses of inventoried rivers undertaken outside of the forest planning process should be supported by reasonably site-specific EISs.

[1793] 111 CONG. REC. 4290 (1965). For discussions of the Act's legislative history, see Stegner, *supra* note 1777, at 8; Tarlock & Tippy, *supra* note 1263, at 707-12.

[1794] *Compare* 16 U.S.C. § 1131(a) (1982) (Wilderness Act) *with* 16 U.S.C. § 1271 (W&S Rivers Act).

[1795] For discussion of judicial review of roadless area planning, see *infra* text accompanying notes 1885-93.

IX

WILDERNESS

The Forest Service can rightfully claim credit for pioneering the concepts and methods of wilderness planning. Thirty-six years before reference to "wilderness" appeared in any federal statute,[1796] the Forest Service began to establish wilderness areas. The management standards of the Wilderness Act of 1964[1797] are nearly identical to Forest Service regulations written twenty-five years earlier. The agency now has more than half of a century of experience in preparing wilderness inventories, studies, and management plans.

In light of the agency's traditional leadership, it is paradoxical that wilderness planning has become "the most difficult problem that the Forest Service has ever had to face."[1798] The issue has engendered conflict with Congress, interference by the Department of Agriculture, paralysis of NFMA planning, low morale among local planners, and erosion of the agency's credibility and public trust. The problem stems from a basic tension between the Forest Service's long-standing, utilitarian policies and relatively recent congressional policies favoring preservation. This conflict appears repeatedly in federal litigation over wilderness dating back to 1970. In virtually every case the courts have resolved the conflict against Forest Service proposals for nonwilderness management.[1799]

The Forest Service currently administers 32.1 million acres of national forest wilderness, including 5.5 million acres in Alaska.[1800] These lands have been designated by Congress for protection under the Wilderness Act of 1964 and subsequent legislation. In addition, there are approximately sixty million acres of

---

[1796] *See* Multiple-Use Sustained-Yield Act of 1960, 16 U.S.C. § 529 (1982).

[1797] 16 U.S.C. §§ 1131-1136 (1982).

[1798] Interview with John White, Land Management Planning Staff, Forest Service, U.S. Dep't of Agriculture, Washington, D.C. (Sept. 10, 1983).

[1799] *See e.g.*, Wyoming Outdoor Coordinating Council v. Butz, 484 F.2d 1244 (10th Cir. 1973); Northwest Indian Cemetery Protective Ass'n v. Peterson, 565 F. Supp. 586 (N.D. Cal. 1983), *aff'd*, 764 F.2d 581 (9th Cir. 1985); Earth First v. Block, 569 F. Supp. 415 (D. Or. 1983); California v. Bergland, 483 F. Supp. 465 (E.D. Cal. 1980), *aff'd sub nom.* California v. Block, 690 F.2d 753 (9th Cir. 1982); Sierra Club v. Butz, 3 ENVTL. L. REP. (ENVTL. L. INST.) 20,071 (N.D. Cal. 1972); Parker v. United States, 309 F. Supp. 593 (D. Colo. 1970), *aff'd*, 448 F.2d 793 (10th Cir. 1971), *cert. denied*, 405 U.S. 989 (1972).

[1800] Telephone interview with Ed Bloedel, Wilderness Management Staff, Forest Service, U.S. Dep't of Agriculture (Dec. 14, 1984).

"roadless areas" on national forests.[1801] These roadless areas meet one basic criterion for wilderness designation: they contain at least 5000 acres of undeveloped federal land.[1802] Thus, although Congress has not formally added the roadless areas to the wilderness system, they are often referred to as "de facto" wilderness. The NFMA requires the Forest Service to include both statutory and de facto wilderness in the forest planning process.[1803]

This section begins by reviewing the evolution of the Forest Service wilderness policy. Next, we examine the two central functions of wilderness planning: classification and management. Classification pertains primarily to the analysis of the suitability of roadless areas for inclusion in the statutory wilderness system, while management applies principally to the use of statutorily-designated wilderness areas. The section concludes with a discussion of the special relevance of mining in wilderness planning.

A. Evolution of Policy

1. Origins of the Wilderness Concept (1905-1939)

Wilderness preservation did not become a part of Forest Service management policy or planning until the 1920s. Pinchot's utilitarian philosophy in the early part of the century was basically antithetical to the views of John Muir and other wilderness advocates.[1804] However, soon after Pinchot left the agency in 1910, interest in preserving the public lands increased significantly.[1805] For example, in 1916 Congress directed the National Park Service to "conserve the scenery and the natural and historic objects and the wildlife . . . unimpaired for the enjoyment of future generations."[1806] At the same time, however, Congress began to appro-

---

[1801] *Id.*

[1802] *See* 16 U.S.C. § 1131(c) (1982).

[1803] *See infra* text accompanying notes 1878-79.

[1804] *See generally* R. NASH, *supra* note 1686, at 135-40. Recent scholarship, however, suggests that Pinchot may have been far more interested in preservation than is commonly assumed. *See* M. FROME, WILDERNESS AND ITS PROPONENTS 115-16, 205 (1984).

[1805] Public concern centered on the proposal to dam Hetch Hetchy Valley in California, a project that Pinchot strongly supported. *See generally* R. NASH, *supra* note 1686, at 161-81. Nash has observed that "[s]cattered sentiment for wilderness preservation had, in truth, become a national movement in the course of the Hetch Hetchy controversy." *Id.* at 180.

[1806] 16 U.S.C. § 1 (1982). Efforts at this time by Park Service Director Stephen T. Mather to expand the National Park System threatened to reduce the size of the national forests. "If the Forest Service did not move to protect its

priate money to expand the road system in the national forests.[1807] Between 1907 and 1927 the national forest road system increased from roughly 5000 miles to 35,000 miles.[1808] As a result, the unpenetrated wilderness regions in the national forests began to disappear rapidly.[1809] Botanists and zoologists spoke out against excessive road development and requested land to be set aside permanently.[1810]

During the 1920s the Forest Service recognized the need to plan for future wilderness preservation. Two Forest Service employees, Arthur Carhart and Aldo Leopold, were among the first to propose national forest wilderness areas.[1811] Leopold disagreed with plans to build a road into a large, undeveloped portion of the Gila National Forest in New Mexico and Arizona.[1812] In 1921, after Congress appropriated nearly $14,000,000 for national forest road development,[1813] Leopold wrote an article advocating preservation of wilderness in the Gila and elsewhere.[1814] He acknowledged that his proposal would "seem a far cry . . . and rank heresy to some minds" but argued that wilderness preservation, as the "highest recreational use" for certain areas, could be reconciled with traditional utilitarian doctrine.[1815]

---

spectacular scenery and develop its recreational resources, there was a good chance that some of its land might be turned over to the National Park Service." Nash, *Historical Roots of Wilderness Management*, in FOREST SERVICE, U.S. DEP'T OF AGRICULTURE, WILDERNESS MANAGEMENT 35 (Misc. Publ. No. 1365) (1978) [hereinafter cited as WILDERNESS MANAGEMENT].

[1807] Between 1917 and 1921 over $33,000,000 was appropriated. *See* J. Gilligan, *supra* note 1682, at 73.

[1808] *See* Greeley, *supra* note 1695, at 15.

[1809] J. Gilligan, *supra* note 1682, at 74.

[1810] *See, e.g.*, Sumner, *The Need for a More Serious Effort to Rescue a Few Fragments of Vanishing Nature*, 10 SCIENTIFIC MONTHLY 236 (1920).

[1811] *See* WILDERNESS MANAGEMENT, *supra* note 1806, at 35: "The efforts of Carhart and Leopold produced the first allocation of public land specifically for wilderness values in American history, and indeed in the world." *Id.* Carhart, a Forest Service landscape architect, is remembered for forestalling lakeshore development at Trapper Lake in Colorado in 1920. *Id.* at 34-35. *See also* Robinson, *Wilderness: The Last Frontier*, 59 MINN. L. REV. 1, 7-8 (1974). For an account of Leopold's early experiences with the Forest Service, see R. NASH, *supra* note 1686, at 182-86.

[1812] *See* J. Gilligan, *supra* note 1682, at 83; Robinson, *supra* note 1811, at 6.

[1813] *See* J. Gilligan, *supra* note 1682, at 83-84.

[1814] *See* Leopold, *supra* note 1690.

[1815] *Id.* at 719. Leopold presaged the decline that Pinchot's strictly utilitarian policy experienced during the late 1920s and 1930s:

Pinchot's promise of development has been made good. The process must, of course, continue indefinitely. But it has already gone far enough to raise

In 1924 the southwest regional forester established the Gila Primitive Area.[1816] It was the first formally protected wilderness in the United States, perhaps in the world. By the end of 1925 five more wilderness areas in other national forests had received similar protection.[1817]

Chief William B. Greeley committed the Forest Service to full-scale wilderness planning in the late 1920s. In 1926 Greeley encouraged regional foresters to follow the example of the Gila Primitive Area and directed Assistant Chief L.F. Kneipp to inventory all national forest roadless areas.[1818] The next year Greeley reported that "the Forest Service believes it to be in the public interest to retain a substantial number of large roadless areas within which some of the most attractive, rugged, and inspiring sections of our mountain country will remain for at least a long time in substantially their natural condition."[1819] Chief Greeley considered wilderness preservation to be an essential element of multiple-use planning. He wrote:

> the question of whether the policy of development (construed in the narrower sense of industrial development) should continue to govern in absolutely every instance, or whether the principle of highest use does not itself demand that representative portions of some forests be preserved as wilderness.

Id. at 718. In 1925 Leopold reiterated these sentiments in three more articles: Leopold, *The Last Stand of the Wilderness*, 31 AM. FORESTS & FOREST LIFE 599 (1925); Leopold, *Wilderness As a Form of Land Use*, 1 J. LAND & PUB. UTIL. ECONOMICS 398 (1925); and Leopold, *Conserving the Covered Wagon*, 54 SUNSET 56 (1925).

[1816] R. NASH, *supra* note 1686, at 187.

[1817] *See* Robinson, *supra* note 1811, at 7. Much of the Boundary Water Canoe Area Wilderness in Minnesota was created in 1926, after sportsmen's groups protested a proposal to build roads into the area. *Id.* at 7-8.

[1818] *See* J. Gilligan, *supra* note 1682, at 101-05. Greeley instructed the regional foresters to review their road plans "to make sure that they do not contemplate a needless invasion of areas adapted to wilderness forms of use." *Id.* at 104, quoting Letter from W.B. Greeley to District Foresters (Dec. 30, 1926). Greeley thought grazing was a permissible use of wilderness; however, demands for timber and water development and for roads to mining claims "should be dealt with at the time in accordance with our best judgment." *Id.* Concerning recreation management, Greeley stated:

> I have no sympathy for the viewpoint that *people* should be kept out of wilderness areas . . . .
>
> It is my idea that having kept out the roads and the buildings, we should encourage public use of wilderness ares just as freely as in any other portion of the National Forests; and should impose only such restrictions as may be necessary for the protection of the National Forests.

Id. at 105.

[1819] 1927 ANNUAL REPORT OF THE CHIEF, *supra* note 1058, at 13.

[T]o my thinking, a good National Forest plan must . . . provide some sizeable areas of real wilderness, unpenetrated by roads . . . . Only by this course can we adequately preserve the great gifts of health and character which our mountains have given us in the past and which they offer without stint for all time to come.[1820]

In 1929 the Forest Service issued Regulation L-20 providing formal guidelines for establishing and managing "primitive" areas.[1821] Assistant Chief Kneipp's inventory recorded 55 million acres of roadless land ranging in size from 230,000 to 7 million acres per area.[1822] By 1933 the agency had established sixty-three primitive areas totalling over 8.4 million acres.[1823] The Forest Service generally regarded these early primitive areas as temporary withdrawals from haphazard development, not as permanent wilderness preserves.[1824]

[1820] Greeley, *supra* note 1695, at 82. Greeley also emphasized the need for wilderness planning in his 1927 annual report:

The national forests are rich in resources of very great value for other than purely material purposes. As our population grows and land use becomes more intensive, there will be an increasingly felt need for wilderness areas where refreshment of body and spirit may be obtained in the surroundings of unspoiled nature, and where the choicest features of our great mountain regions may be enjoyed in all of their native beauty and grandeur. It is not too soon to give thought to future social requirements along these lines and to make definite provisions for them, in due measure, as a part of the planning necessary for the orderly development of forest resources and the realization from them of the maximum public benefits.

1927 ANNUAL REPORT OF THE CHIEF, *supra* note 1058, at 32.

[1821] Regulation L-20 stated:

The Chief of the Forest Service shall determine, define, and permanently record . . . a series of areas to be known as primitive areas, and within which will be maintained primitive conditions of environment, transportation, habitation, and subsistence, with a view to conserving the value of such areas for purposes of public education and recreation. Within any area so designated . . . no occupancy under special-use permit shall be allowed, or the construction of permanent improvements by any public agency be permitted, except as authorized by the Chief of the Forest Service or the Secretary.

McMichael v. United States, 355 F.2d 283, 284 n.3 (9th Cir. 1965).

[1822] J. Gilligan, *supra* note 1682, at 102.

[1823] *Id.* at 103. *See* COPELAND REPORT, *supra* note 112, at 473 (the Report refers to "primeval areas").

[1824] Greeley reported: "What the future may bring forth as to the ultimate needs for timber and water and minerals in the present undeveloped hinterland of many national forests can not be foreseen and must remain a question to be dealt with as such future requirements unfold." 1927 ANNUAL REPORT OF THE CHIEF, *supra* note 1058, at 13.

Regulation L-20 stated broad management guidelines and allowed local managers to provide the details through individual area plans.[1825] Assistant Chief Kneipp encouraged planners to prohibit nonwilderness activity:

> [A] specific and detailed management plan should be developed for each area, which will be clear cut and restrictive and mandatory. To avoid misunderstanding or unintentional departure it should be prohibitive; that is, with reference to each major activity it should tell what should not be done. The urgent need is for a plan of management which clearly will make it impossible, barring intentional departure, for any gradual infiltration of uses or modifications to eventually impair or destroy the value of the area for the purpose for which set aside.[1826]

Nevertheless, the primitive area plans rarely imposed limitations on logging and other commercial uses.[1827]

The Forest Service significantly strengthened its wilderness management policy in the late 1930s under the guidance of one of the most influential figures in United States preservation policy, Robert Marshall.[1828] With the encouragement of Chief F.A.

[1825] The following instructions accompanied Regulation L-20:

> The establishment of a primitive area ordinarily will not operate to withdraw timber, forage or water resources from industrial use, since the utilization of such resources, if properly regulated, will not be incompatible with the purpose for which the area is designated. Where special circumstances warrant a partial or complete restriction of the use of timber, forage or water, that fact will be set forth in the plan of the management for the area.

WILDLAND RESEARCH CENTER, UNIV. OF CAL., BERKELEY, OUTDOOR RECREATION RESOURCES REVIEW COMM'N, WILDERNESS AND RECREATION—A REPORT ON RESOURCES, VALUES, AND PROBLEMS, STUDY REPORT 3, at 20-21 (1962) [hereinafter cited as ORRRC REPORT]. Similarly, Greeley reported that the roadless area designations

> will not prevent the orderly use of timber, forage, and water resources as future needs may dictate. It will, however, prevent the unwise destruction of recreational values which are steadily attaining greater social significance and importance. The Forest Service plans to withhold these areas against unnecessary road building and forms of special use of a commercial character which would impair their wilderness character.

1927 ANNUAL REPORT OF THE CHIEF, *supra* note 1058, at 32.

[1826] J. Gilligan, *supra* note 1682, at 138-39, quoting Letter from L.F. Kneipp to Regional Forester Show (undated).

[1827] *See* Robinson, *supra* note 1811, at 8. Local plans often specified recreational developments such as corrals and shelters. Kneipp reprimanded forest supervisors for exceeding the standard of "primitive simplicity" in managing the areas. *See* WILDERNESS MANAGEMENT, *supra* note 1806, at 36.

[1828] For an account of Marshall's early efforts toward wilderness protection, *see* R. NASH, *supra* note 1686, at 200-05. Marshall's first involvement in Forest Service wilderness policy was his authorship of the recreation chapter of the

Silcox,[1829] Marshall cultivated support for adding both acreage and management safeguards for the primitive area system.[1830] In 1939, the year that Marshall and Silcox both died, primitive areas covered more than fourteen million acres.[1831]

Also in 1939, the Forest Service replaced Regulation L-20 with the more restrictive "U Regulations."[1832] These provided for all primitive areas to be reclassified as "wilderness," "wild," or "recreation."[1833] Roads, logging, and motorized vehicles were prohibited in both wilderness and wild areas.[1834] Twenty-five years later,

---

Copeland Report in 1933. *See supra* notes 1700-10 and accompanying text. For a bibliography of Marshall's writings, see Marshall, *Robert Marshall as a Writer*, 16 LIVING WILDERNESS 14, 20-23 (1951).

[1829] Silcox appointed Marshall to head the agency's Division of Recreation and Lands in 1937. J. Gilligan, *supra* note 1682, at 189. Silcox kept a low profile on wilderness issues. Nevertheless,

[i]t was generally well known throughout the Service that Marshall had the personal support of Chief Forester Silcox and, therefore, his proposals carried more influence than the ordinary recommendations of staff officers to forest and regional administrators. Silcox's transformed support for the wilderness idea has been attributed to his liberal social views and Marshall's persuasions that these areas provided space for the average or little man on par with everyone else.

Id. at 191.

[1830] Marshall and Leopold co-founded The Wilderness Society in 1935. *See* R. NASH, *supra* note 1686, at 207. The same year Marshall (then in his position as Director of Forestry in the Office of Indian Affairs) asked Secretary of the Interior Harold L. Ickes to withhold funds for roads in undeveloped areas of the national forests pending further study. J. Gilligan, *supra* note 1682, at 181. After joining the Forest Service in 1937, Marshall undertook "his remarkable crusade to preserve all remaining large roadless areas in the West. Between 1937 and 1939 there was probably no undeveloped area over 100,000 acres on national forest land that he did not recommend to regional foresters to be considered for primitive classification." *Id.* at 191.

[1831] *See* WILDERNESS MANAGEMENT, *supra* note 1806, at 36.

[1832] 36 C.F.R. §§ 251.20-.21 (1939).

[1833] The U Regulations distinguished wilderness from wild areas simply on the basis of size: areas larger than 100,000 acres were wilderness; areas between 5,000 and 100,000 acres were wild. *Id.*

[1834] Regulation U-1 required that

[T]here shall be no roads or other provision for motorized transportation, no commercial timber cutting, and no occupancy under special use permit for hotels, stores, resorts, summer homes, organization camps, hunting and fishing lodges, or similar uses; provided, however, that where roads are necessary for ingress or egress to private property these may be allowed under appropriate conditions determined by the forest supervisor, and the boundary of the wilderness area shall thereupon be modified to exclude the portion affected by the road.

Grazing of domestic livestock, development of water storage projects which do not involve road construction, and improvements necessary for fire protection may be permitted subject to such restrictions as the Chief

and with the Forest Service's full support, these regulations became the basis for the Wilderness Act of 1964. In the 1940s, however, agency officials reacted coolly and implemented the U Regulations reluctantly.[1835]

2. Evolution from Administrative to Legislative Wilderness (1940-1963)

Forest Service wilderness policy entered a dormant phase following Marshall's death in 1939. The demands of World War II and the post-war housing boom commanded first priority. Demands for commercial use of areas began to result in some reclassifications from protected status during the 1940s and early 1950s.[1836] Typically the agency would delete commercially valua-

---

deems desirable. Within such designated wilderness, the landing of airplanes on national forest land or water and the use of motor boats on national forest waters are prohibited, except where such use has already become well established or for administrative needs and emergencies.
36 C.F.R. § 251.20 (1939). Entry for hardrock mining could not be administratively prohibited since national forests were open for that purpose by statute. *See* 30 U.S.C. § 22 and *supra* text accompanying notes 1288-98. Recreation areas were managed with the flexibility that was characteristic of Regulation L-20 for primitive areas. *See supra* text accompanying notes 1713-14.

[1835] Robinson explained: ,
The Second World War had a somewhat retarding effect, but probably more significant was the antagonism of many, within and outside the Service, to the permanent preservation of wilderness lands. Foresters, unhappy that their fire protection or resource-management programs would be complicated by the reclassification of areas and the proscription of roads from their lands, did not vigorously press forward with the reclassification efforts.
Robinson, *supra* note 1811, at 10. At the end of World War II, only 12 of the original 76 primitive areas had been reclassified according to the U Regulations. *See* WILDERNESS MANAGEMENT, *supra* note 1806, at 63. During the interim, primitive areas were to be managed under the more restrictive U Regulation standards for wilderness areas. *See* ORRRC REPORT, *supra* note 1825, at 22, quoting Forest Service Circular U-164 (Dec. 15, 1947).

[1836] *See* Robinson, *supra* note 1811, at 11. By the 1950s, demand for timber and other resources had increased enough to cause agency managers to question the wisdom of "locking up" those resources in primitive areas. A wilderness advocate and historian made the following analysis:
Many resources which, in the 1920's and 1930's, had been thought "uneconomic" for development were now within the reach of development. Forest Service policy was aimed primarily at reclassification of those areas which had been "protected" prior to 1939, and the process of reclassification increasingly appeared to be a major threat to the quality and variety of wilderness that had been thought to have been protected once already. As reclassification proceeded, conservationists recognized a pattern of serious and steady erosion. That pattern left the distinct impression that the

ble portions of existing primitive areas and add other areas of low economic value.[1837] This practice comported with the agency's increasing efforts to bring the "hinterlands" of the national forests under management.[1838] Illustrative of these deletions are two that aroused particularly strong opposition and produced support for passage of the Wilderness Act of 1964.

First, in 1950 the Forest Service proposed to redesignate about one-fourth of the Gila Primitive Area, including 75,000 acres of commercial timber.[1839] The principal reason was to allow timber harvesting.[1840] A three-year controversy ensued, in which Senator Clinton P. Anderson of New Mexico personally intervened to stop

---

real, working definition of wilderness within the Department and the Eisenhower Administration (if not within the Forest Service itself) was that wilderness was simply a *residue*: the steadily diminishing margin of land not yet sufficient [sic] valuable to exploit for some other, more "practical" use. Those lands had been "cheap" to preserve when they lay well outside the "economic frontier", but the trend of reclassification suggested clearly that once they came within that "economic frontier", the working presumption was that they would be removed from the wilderness boundary and put to use.

D. Scott, History of Wilderness Allocation and Management, *reprinted in Committee of Scientists, Minutes of Dec. 1, 1978, supra* note 402.

[1837] Gilligan's study of the reclassification process found

a national trend of wilderness boundary modification which, since 1940, has eliminated over a half million acres of land from 33 different units. Most of these deletions have been for commonplace reasons such as removing zones for timber harvest, motorized recreation development, intercity road construction, or areas where mining or tourist facilities have already been established on private lands. These deletions have largely been offset by the addition of high, rocky zones to each area where there is little possibility of development demands or timber harvest.

Gilligan, *Wilderness in a Democracy*, Living Wilderness, Spring-Summer 1955, at 26.

[1838] In 1953 Chief Richard McArdle reported:

The national forests are becoming increasingly valuable properties subject to ever greater use. And their administrators are becoming subject to ever greater pressures. We welcome this change as part of the normal development of our economy and the normal increase in our population. The national forests are no longer hinterlands.

1953 Annual Report of the Chief, *supra* note 553, at ii.

[1839] *See* D. Cate, *supra* note 1692, at 414.

[1840] *Id.* at 430. Cate has suggested that:

[S]trong personal desires of field foresters to harvest the prime timber in the primitive area provided the real impetus for the proposal. . . . The undramatic chore of protecting a wilderness area offered less appeal than the more concrete administrative satisfactions of managing the 75,000 acres as part of a sustained-yield, timber harvesting unit.

Id. at 430-31.

the deletion.[1841] Anderson later became chairman of the Senate Interior Committee and a main champion of the Wilderness Act in the Senate.[1842]

Second, in 1953 the Forest Service, with the approval of the Department of Agriculture, removed 53,000 acres of old-growth forest from the Three Sisters Primitive Area in Oregon.[1843] The agency justified the decision on the ground that the area was not "predominantly valuable for wilderness."[1844] Oregon Senators Richard Neuberger and Wayne Morse denounced the Forest Service's action and actively supported wilderness legislation to prevent future deletions.[1845]

In 1956 Senator Hubert H. Humphrey introduced the first wilderness bill.[1846] The management provisions of this bill were

---

[1841] *See id.* at 419-26; *see also* LIVING WILDERNESS, Winter 1952-1953, at 26.

[1842] *See* McCloskey, *The Wilderness Act of 1964: Its Background and Meaning*, 45 OR. L. REV. 288, 299 (1966).

[1843] *See* D. Cate, *supra* note 1692, at 464-94; *see also* LIVING WILDERNESS, Fall-Winter 1956-1957, at 34.

[1844] Assistant Secretary of Agriculture E.L. Peterson explained the "predominately valuable" rationale in a letter to the Sierra Club:

We all realize that wilderness protection and preservation is a complex subject and that it needs careful study and careful administration. We are in full accord with the preservation on the national forests of areas which are predominately valuable for wilderness. We will continue to give all questions involving wilderness areas very careful attention, and will fully appraise all public values when considering the need for wilderness or the suitability of an area for wilderness designation. Our decision will in each case be based on the same principle that was used in the Three Sisters Primitive area—namely, that those portions of the national forests which are predominantly valuable for wilderness will be managed as wilderness and those portions which have greater public value for purposes other than for wilderness will be so managed.

Letter from E.L. Peterson to David R. Brower, Exec. Director, Sierra Club (June 5, 1957), *reprinted in* NATIONAL WILDERNESS PRESERVATION ACT: HEARINGS ON S. 1176 BEFORE THE SENATE COMM. ON INTERIOR AND INSULAR AFFAIRS, 85th Cong., 1st Sess. 90 (Comm. Print 1957) [hereinafter cited as 1957 WILDERNESS HEARINGS].

[1845] Senator Richard Neuberger of Oregon, a member of the Senate Interior and Insular Affairs Committee, cited the Three Sisters deletion as an example of "the urgent need for some form of congressional action to safeguard these scenic realms." 103 CONG. REC. 1903 (1957). Similarly, Oregon Senator Wayne Morse expressed outrage at the deletion: "I would make the same fight for the preservation of a wilderness area in any other State if facts existed in support of its preservation, as they do exist in the case of the Three Sisters Area." *Id.* at 1909.

[1846] S. 4013, 84th Cong., 2d Sess., 102 CONG. REC. 9772-77 (1956). The wilderness bill was originally drafted by Howard Zahniser, then executive director of The Wilderness Society. *See* Roth, *The National Forests and the Campaign for Wilderness Legislation*, J. FOREST HIST., July 1984, at 121. *See generally* R. NASH, *supra* note 1686, at 221-24; McCloskey, *supra* note 1842, at 298.

substantially the same as Regulation U-1.[1847] Nevertheless, Chief McArdle opposed the bill in 1957, finding that it was "excessively restrictive" and "would strike at the heart of the multiple-use policy of national-forest administration."[1848] The Forest Service offered an alternative bill, couched in multiple-use, sustained-yield language,[1849] that provided somewhat less restrictive management requirements[1850] and limited preservation to areas "predominantly valuable for wilderness."[1851] However, by 1961 the Forest Service gave unqualified support to wilderness legislation.[1852]

[1847] Humphrey's bill generally prohibited logging, mining, water developments, structures, and use of motorized vehicles. S. 4013, 84th Cong., 2d Sess. § 3(b), 102 CONG. REC. 9776 (1956). Grazing and use of airplanes and motorboats were permitted, *id.* § 3(c)(2), as were roads for access to private property. *Id.* § 3(c)(1). Thus, the significant difference between S. 4013 and Regulation U-1 was that the bill prohibited mining. *Compare supra* note 1834.

[1848] 1957 WILDERNESS HEARINGS, *supra* note 1844, at 90, 93-94 (statement of Richard E. McArdle). McArdle argued that wilderness legislation would discriminate against other uses:

> It would give a degree of congressional protection to wilderness use of the national forests not now enjoyed by any other use. It would tend to hamper free and effective application of administrative judgment which now determines, and should continue to determine, the use, or combination of uses, to which a particular national-forest area should be devoted. If this special congressional protection is given to wilderness use, it is reasonable to expect that other user groups will subsequently seek congressional protection for their special interests.

Id. See also McCloskey, *supra* note 1842, at 299.

[1849] The Forest Service subsequently proposed a separate multiple-use, sustained-yield bill, which was enacted in 1960. *See supra* text accompanying notes 125-32.

[1850] Only resorts and other permanent facilities were strictly banned. Logging and other nonwilderness uses could be authorized by the President. *See* S. 1176, 85th Cong., 1st Sess. § 7 (1957), *reprinted in* 1957 WILDERNESS HEARINGS, *supra* note 1844, at 13.

[1851] *Id.* § 2, *reprinted in* 1957 WILDERNESS HEARINGS, *supra* note 1844, at 12.

[1852] *See The Wilderness Act: Hearings on S. 174 Before the Senate Comm. on Interior and Insular Affairs*, 87th Cong., 1st Sess. 43 (1961) (statement of Richard E. McArdle). Three factors might account for the Forest Service's change in position. First, the 1961 bill dropped a provision contained in the original bill establishing a National Wilderness Preservation Council to oversee the wilderness system. Second, Congress had passed the Multiple-Use Sustained-Yield Act in 1960, 16 U.S.C. §§ 528-531 (1982), thereby affirming the agency's multiple-use authority. Third, President John F. Kennedy supported wilderness legislation. *See* President's Message to Congress on Natural Resources, PUB. PAPERS OF THE PRESIDENTS, John F. Kennedy, 121 (1961).

3. RARE Planning and the Expansion of the System (1964-Present)

Passage of the Wilderness Act of 1964[1853], which the agency interpreted as an endorsement of its traditional wilderness management policies,[1854] produced something of a renaissance within the Forest Service regarding attention to the wilderness resource. The Act incorporated all of the 9.1 million acres classified as wilderness and wild areas under the U Regulations.[1855] In addition, Congress directed the agency to study and report on the "suitability or nonsuitability for preservation as wilderness" of the remaining 5.4 million acres of primitive areas.[1856]

In 1967 the Forest Service went beyond the requirements of the Act by proposing a study of the wilderness potential of all previously unclassified roadless areas larger than 5000 acres.[1857] This

---

[1853] 16 U.S.C. §§ 1131-1136 (1982). For an analysis of the Act, see McCloskey, *supra* note 1842, at 301-14; WILDERNESS MANAGEMENT, *supra* note 1806, at 66-75.

[1854] In 1965 Chief Edward P. Cliff reported:

The new act made it plain that Congress approved of the areas that had already been set aside administratively as "wilderness" and "wild" areas and the Boundary Waters Canoe Area. It endorsed in principle the wilderness concepts and management practices the Forest Service had been pioneering for four decades. The act made it necessary that those concepts and practices be formalized into policies, regulations, and instructions governing the management of National Forest Wilderness. Future management will differ little as to philosophy, but considerably as to degree.

1965 ANNUAL REPORT OF THE CHIEF, *supra* note 787, at 7. Similarly, Forest Service recreation director Richard J. Costley stated: "[T]here was considerable Forest Service satisfaction and comfort in the knowledge that in its action Congress had . . . fully accepted wilderness management concepts which had evolved as the result of years of Forest Service field testing." Costley, *An Enduring Resource*, AM. FORESTS, June 1972, at 8, 10.

[1855] 16 U.S.C. § 1132(a) (1982).

[1856] *Id.* § 1132(b). The Forest Service completed its primitive area studies and reports on schedule, but court decisions compelled the agency to address the wilderness potential of areas adjacent to the primitive areas. *See* Parker v. United States, 309 F. Supp. 593 (D. Colo. 1970), *aff'd*, 448 F.2d 793 (10th Cir. 1971), *cert. denied*, 405 U.S. 989 (1972). The Act also mandated 10 year wilderness studies by the National Park Service and Fish and Wildlife Service of all roadless areas under their jurisdictions in excess of 5,000 acres. 16 U.S.C. § 1132(c) (1982).

[1857] The roadless area study was originally recommended by a 4-person team appointed to draft policy guidelines to implement the Wilderness Act. *See* WILDERNESS MANAGEMENT, *supra* note 1806, at 94. In late 1964 the team had advised forest supervisors to "review each National Forest and identify, but not formally designate in any way, all potential new wilderness." *Id.* at 99, quoting E. SLUSHER, A. SNYDER, G. WILLIAMS & W. WORF, FOREST SERVICE, U.S. DEP'T

was the agency's first comprehensive review of its remaining roadless land since the inventory ordered by Chief Greeley in 1926. Chief Edward P. Cliff's decision to undertake the new inventory recognized that Congress was likely to include more than the primitive areas in the wilderness system.[1858] Thus, the inventory would provide a factual basis for agency recommendations on future wilderness legislation.[1859]

In the mid-1960s the Forest Service adopted a "purist" approach toward both management and classification of wilderness.[1860] The purist policy prohibited local managers from practices such as using chain saws to clear trails or helicopters to monitor snow gauges in statutory wilderness areas.[1861] In addition, purity of wilderness qualities became an important factor in selecting roadless areas for wilderness study. The effect of assessing the wilderness qualities of the roadless areas by purity criteria was to disqualify many areas from serious consideration. Areas with

---

OF AGRICULTURE, A DISCUSSION DRAFT OF SUGGESTED OBJECTIVES, POLICIES, PROCEDURES, AND REGULATIONS (1964).

[1858] In 1965 Chief Cliff observed that, in addition to the primitive areas, "other suitable lands administered by the . . . Forest Service . . . may be added to the system by act of Congress." 1965 ANNUAL REPORT OF THE CHIEF, *supra* note 787, at 7.

[1859] *See* Robinson, *supra* note 1811, at 19:

In order to facilitate resource planning, and in particular planning for timber and recreation, it was essential to know what lands might become wilderness—the "maximum universe" of lands suitable for wilderness classification. The problem [to determine the amount of land suitable for wilderness classification] was made more acute by virtue of the fact that, as the primitive area review program progressed, numerous demands were being made to Congress to preserve individual areas outside existing primitive areas. Since the lands lay outside the primitive areas being studied, the Forest Service was hard pressed to respond to these demands in the absence of some systematic inventory. The continued addition of such individual areas not only impeded its management planning, but also threatened to take initiative and control over wilderness classification away from the Service and subject it to the "caprice" of local interests and pressures.

[1860] *See generally* D. ROTH, THE WILDERNESS MOVEMENT AND THE NATIONAL FORESTS: 1964-1980 (1984).

[1861] Costley, *supra* note 1854, at 10. As director of the Forest Service's Division of Recreation, Costley was a principal architect of the purism policy. Costley cited the Wilderness Act's purpose of securing an "enduring" wilderness resource as authority for the purism approach. Costley explained that as specific questions concerning use of motorized equipment and permanent structures arose, "[t]he constraining language of the Wilderness Act began to take on an on-the-ground meaning; a Forest Service wilderness management posture began to evolve and take shape. And slowly, but surely, that posture emerged as an increasingly 'pure' one." *Id.*

"nonconforming features" such as cabins and jeep trails, or the "sights and sounds of civilization" in an otherwise pristine area, were unsuitable.[1862]

The Forest Service completed its Roadless Area Review and Evaluation (RARE I) in 1972.[1863] The agency identified fifty-six million acres of roadless areas and designated 12.3 million acres for detailed study to determine wilderness suitability. However, by this time the Forest Service was engulfed in controversy over its purist policy,[1864] and its timber management practices.[1865] In *Sierra Club v. Butz*,[1866] the Sierra Club brought suit under the National Environmental Policy Act[1867] (NEPA) to enjoin all timber sales and other development in the California RARE I roadless areas.[1868] In an out-of-court settlement, Chief John McGuire directed all local managers to prepare EISs before authorizing future developments in roadless areas.[1869]

The result of RARE I and the ensuing litigation was a new, two-part wilderness review during the mid-1970s, conducted in

---

[1862] *See* Robinson, *supra* note 1811, at 21-22; WILDERNESS MANAGEMENT, *supra* note 1806, at 100-02. Costley explained the rationale for applying purity criteria to classification, as well as to management: "The Forest Service simply cannot afford to bless by recommending the incorporation into the Wilderness System (as part of areas being added) the kind of nonconforming developments or established practices which it must resist in its management of that System." Costley, *supra* note 1854, at 11. The alternative, Costley believed, would "make a diluted, watered-down, and specious 'wilderness' out of almost any scenic area in the country." *Id.* at 55.

[1863] *See* FOREST SERVICE, U.S. DEP'T OF AGRICULTURE, NEW WILDERNESS STUDY AREAS (Current Information Rep. No. 11) (1973).

[1864] *See, e.g.,* Foote, *Wilderness—A Question of Purity*, 3 ENVTL. L. 255, 265 (1973).

[1865] *See supra* text accompanying notes 721-803.

[1866] 3 ENVTL. L. REP. (ENVTL. L. INST.) 20,071 (N.D. Cal. 1972).

[1867] 42 U.S.C. §§ 4321-4370 (1982).

[1868] The Forest Service argued that the Wilderness Act did not mandate any study of the roadless areas and that developing the roadless areas was a "nondecision" and, therefore, not an action covered by NEPA. The court rejected this argument, stating: "Sometimes a non-decision or a non-action can be a breach of an affirmative duty to act. . . . [W]here the Forest Service [is] not acting upon this land in an affirmative manner . . ., in effect you are classifying it . . . as timber that is available for harvesting." *Id.* at 20,072. The Court of Appeals for the Tenth Circuit adopted the reasoning from *Sierra Club v. Butz* to reach the same result in Wyoming Outdoor Coordinating Council v. Butz, 484 F.2d 1244 (10th Cir. 1973). In that decision the court enjoined two timber sales that were already under contract pending preparation of an EIS. The court found that "there is an overriding public interest in preservation of the undeveloped character of the area." *Id.* at 1250.

[1869] WILDERNESS MANAGEMENT, *supra* note 1806, at 105.

conjunction with the unit planning process.[1870] Of the fifty-six million acres inventoried in RARE I, the 12.3 million acres selected for wilderness study underwent "detailed and in-depth" review for addition to the wilderness system.[1871] The remaining forty-four million acres of roadless areas were to receive sufficient "consideration" to satisfy NEPA requirements.[1872] This new planning system proceeded slowly, partly because the agency realized that RARE I provided an inadequate basis for the review.[1873]

In the meantime, Congress and the Department of Agriculture were directing the Forest Service to make fundamental changes in its wilderness policy. First, Congress passed the Eastern Wilderness Act of 1975,[1874] designating thirty-two wilderness and wilderness study areas in eastern national forests. Congress rejected Forest Service objections that many of the areas did not meet the criteria of the Wilderness Act.[1875] In the Endangered American Wilderness Act of 1978,[1876] Congress extended its liberal policy on wilderness eligibility to the western national forests.[1877] Second, the NFMA explicitly directed that wilderness be considered in forest planning on an equal footing with the other

---

[1870] For an explanation of unit planning, *see supra* text accompanying notes 149-56.

[1871] FOREST SERVICE MANUAL § 8260 (1974).

[1872] *Id.* § 8262.2.

[1873] In 1977 Chief McGuire stated:

[F]or some time we have realized there were significant weaknesses in RARE. Contiguous area was subdivided and considered as individual parts rather than as a whole. The boundaries for some inventoried roadless areas stopped short of the actual state of roadlessness and undevelopedness. Some areas were entirely missed. Some regions used their own modifications of Servicewide criteria, causing inconsistency. RARE dealt essentially with the West, with National Forests in the East and the National Grasslands being given little attention.

RARE II Briefing Paper from John R. McGuire to Regional Foresters and Directors (July 13, 1977) at 2, *reprinted in Committee of Scientists, Minutes of Dec. 1-2, 1977, supra* note 402.

[1874] Pub. L. No. 93-622, 88 Stat. 2096 (1975).

[1875] Few areas in the East were sufficiently undisturbed to qualify as wilderness under the agency's purist policy. The Forest Service proposed protection of the unsuitable areas through using a different designation. Instead, the Act directed the Forest Service to manage all of the areas "in accordance with the provisions of the Wilderness Act." Pub. L. No. 93-622, § 6(a), 88 Stat. 2096, 2100 (1975).

[1876] Pub. L. No. 95-200, 91 Stat. 1425 (1978).

[1877] *See* H.R. REP. NO. 540, 95th Cong., 2d Sess. (1978).

multiple-use resources.[1878] The NFMA's wilderness planning requirements applied to all roadless areas and wilderness values in general, as well as to areas already placed in the wilderness system.[1879]

In addition to continued congressional action on wilderness, the Department of Agriculture began to assert its rarely exercised authority over national forest policy. In 1977 the Assistant Secretary of Agriculture, M. Rupert Cutler, initiated two unprecedented intrusions into Forest Service decision-making. First, he directed the agency to liberalize its purist policy,[1880] including the "sights and sounds" criterion.[1881] Second, Cutler decided to accelerate

---

[1878] The NFMA requires the agency to assure that forest plans "include coordination of outdoor recreation, range, timber, watershed, wildlife and fish, and wilderness." 16 U.S.C. § 1604(e)(1) (1982). The language first appeared in Representative Litton's bill. H.R. 13,236, 94th Cong., 2d Sess. § 2(e)(1), *reprinted in* TRANSCRIPT OF HOUSE MARK-UP, *supra* note 448, at 456.

[1879] *See* California v. Bergland, 483 F. Supp. 465, 478-79 (E.D. Cal. 1980), *aff'd sub nom.* California v. Block, 690 F.2d 753 (9th Cir. 1982). *But cf.* 690 F.2d at 775-76 (discussing whether the NFMA requires site-specific local planning process rather than a national review process).

[1880] Cutler formally stated this policy change in a detailed memorandum to Chief McGuire. McGuire fully endorsed the change and passed it along to the regional foresters. Memorandum from John R. McGuire, Chief, Forest Service, to Regional Foresters (Nov. 4, 1977), *reprinted in Committee of Scientists, Minutes of Dec. 1-2, 1977, supra* note 402. The preface to Cutler's memorandum stated:

> A critical reading of the Wilderness Act of 1964 confirms that its framers intended that lands which bear some indications of man may be wilderness. The Act contains a philosophical definition of wilderness followed by a pragmatic one. The latter contains qualifiers, such as "generally," "primarily," "substantially unnoticeable," and "practicable."

Cutler then advised the Forest Service that roadless areas may be suitable for wilderness recommendation in RARE II despite the presence of administrative facilities, visitor use facilities, extensive management developments, water impoundments and underground utility lines. Additionally, roadless area suitability would not be affected by conditions outside of the area. Finally, "the effects of any single or any combination of several marks of man's activity must be judged in context of the large area." Memorandum from M. Rupert Cutler, Asst. Sec. for Conservation, Research, and Educ., U.S. Dep't of Agriculture to Chief, Forest Service (Nov. 2, 1977), *reprinted in Committee of Scientists, Minutes of Dec. 1-2, 1977,* supra note 402.

[1881] Cutler first expressed the administration's views on wilderness purity in congressional testimony early in 1977. The following exchange is illustrative:

> MR. RONCALIO. Does the Wilderness Act require that this so-called sight and sounds doctrine be a guiding principle in evaluating wilderness potential, or is this merely a Forest Service policy which is not required by the law?
> DR. CUTLER. That is neither a guiding principle nor is it Forest Service policy as far as I am concerned. The intrinsic nature of the landscape as to

roadless area planning by ordering the Forest Service to conduct a nationwide study, later called RARE II.[1882]

The RARE II inventory identified sixty-two million acres of roadless land[1883]—nearly one-third of the National Forest System. In early 1979 the Forest Service announced the results of its evaluation of the RARE II inventory: 15 million acres were designated for wilderness designation, 36 million acres were allocated to nonwilderness management, and 10.8 million acres were designated for further planning under the NFMA.[1884]

The Forest Service had prepared an EIS for RARE II. However, in 1980 a federal district judge in *California v. Bergland*[1885] held that the EIS was inadequate under NEPA and granted an injunction to halt any further development of forty-eight roadless areas in California allocated to nonwilderness. The court faulted the agency for inadequate site-specific analysis of the areas and for an anti-wilderness bias in the range of alternatives. The Forest Service appealed the decision and continued to sell timber in the nonwilderness roadless areas outside of California, which were not covered by the injunction.[1886] Meanwhile, some members of Congress introduced legislation declaring the RARE II EIS to be legally "sufficient" and "releasing" the nonwilderness areas from further wilderness consideration.[1887]

---

whether or not it qualifies because of its undeveloped nature is the criterion.
Endangered American Wilderness Act: Hearings on H.R. 3454 Before the Subcomm. on Indian Affairs and Public Lands of the House Comm. on Interior and Insular Affairs, 95th Cong., 1st Sess. 100 (1977).

[1882] Cutler announced the decision while testifying at a congressional hearing. He stated:
[W]e are going to take another complete look at the roadless and undeveloped lands in the entire National Forest System. . . .
The need to determine which of these lands will be wilderness and which will not be wilderness need not wait for the years needed to complete the land management planning process on all national forests.
Id. at 97-98.

[1883] FOREST SERVICE, U.S. DEP'T OF AGRICULTURE, FINAL ENVIRONMENTAL STATEMENT, ROADLESS AREA REVIEW AND EVALUATION 7 (1979) [hereinafter cited as RARE II EIS].

[1884] *Id.*

[1885] 483 F. Supp. 465 (E.D. Cal. 1980), *aff'd sub nom.* California v. Block, 690 F.2d 753 (9th Cir. 1982).

[1886] The decision to appeal was contrary to a recommendation by the Department of Agriculture's Office of General Counsel. Interview with Clarence Brizee, *supra* note 409.

[1887] *See* H.R. 6070, 96th Cong., 1st Sess. (1979) (introduced by Rep. Foley); S. 842, 97th Cong., 1st Sess. (1981) (introduced by Sen. Hayakawa). Congress

In 1982 the Forest Service's appeal from the RARE II injunction was denied by the Court of Appeals for the Ninth Circuit, in *California v. Block*,[1888] and the injunction was continued. Assistant Secretary of Agriculture John B. Crowell responded by directing the Forest Service to reevaluate all roadless areas through forest plans[1889] and to continue with development plans for nonwilderness areas outside of California.[1890] Subsequently, Chief R. Max Peterson advised regional foresters to incorporate the reevaluation process into forest plans.[1891]

In 1984 Congress resolved much of the controversy over national forest roadless areas. Statutes were enacted designating 6.8 million acres of national forest lands as wilderness in twenty states.[1892] The remaining roadless areas in those states covered by the legislation were exempted by "release" language from further wilderness review during the first generation of NFMA

---

rejected national release legislation, but several single-state wilderness bills were enacted with "sufficiency" language. *See* Pub. L. No. 96-550, 94 Stat. 3221 (1980) (New Mexico); Pub. L. No. 96-560, 94 Stat. 3265 (1980) (Colorado). *See also infra* note 1895.

[1888] 690 F.2d 753 (9th Cir. 1982), *aff'g* California v. Bergland, 483 F. Supp. 465 (E.D. Cal. 1980).

[1889] The reevaluation included the areas allocated both to wilderness and to nonwilderness. Although Crowell justified the reevaluation of the wilderness allocations by relying on *California v. Block*, the Ninth Circuit's opinion did not require reevaluating wilderness designations. *See id.* at 776 (holding the RARE II EIS legally sufficient to support wilderness designations). The reevaluation did not apply to Colorado, New Mexico, and four other states for which Congress had passed "sufficiency" legislation. *See* U.S. DEP'T OF AGRICULTURE, NATIONAL FOREST ROADLESS AREAS SUBJECT TO REEVALUATION (press release, Feb. 1, 1983) (on file at Oregon Law Review office).

[1890] Crowell acknowledged that his decision to develop the roadless areas was based on practical considerations:

When I announced my Feb. 1 decision, I candidly admitted one element of it was vulnerable to legal attack. That element was the decision to carry out already planned and on-going timber sale and road construction activities on a very small number of acres in the roadless areas that had not been recommended for wilderness by RARE II. . . . [O]n-going activities in the roadless areas could be stopped by legal action instituted by almost anyone who so desired simply by asserting the appeals court's decision as precedent.

Why did I decide to let such activities proceed? It was on the chance that the Forest Service could continue those activities with only small disruption from occasional, carefully targeted lawsuits.

Portland Oregonian, Mar. 22, 1983, at B-7.

[1891] Memorandum from R. Max Peterson to Regional Foresters 2, (Mar. 9, 1983) (on file at Oregon Law Review office).

[1892] *See* SIERRA CLUB, NATIONAL NEWS REPORT 1 (Oct. 17, 1984).

planning.[1893] The controversy remained unresolved in several states not covered by 1984 statutes, including Idaho, Utah, and Montana. Nevertheless, by 1985 most national forests were no longer faced with the immediate task of reevaluating their roadless areas.

B. *Planning for Preservation*

Wilderness planning occurs in both forest plans and individual wilderness resource management plans. Forest plans evaluate roadless areas for potential wilderness recommendations to Congress and establish general management direction for congressionally designated wilderness areas. The management plans provide detailed direction to preserve the undisturbed character of individual wilderness areas.

1. *Roadless Areas*

Roadless areas included in the RARE II inventory must be evaluated for their wilderness potential in each forest plan unless Congress has enacted "release" legislation.[1894] In states covered by release legislation, the Forest Service is generally not required to evaluate the roadless areas through forest plans until at least the next planning cycle.[1895] Therefore, the following discussion is currently applicable only to national forests in states not covered by release legislation.

[1893] *See infra* note 1895.

[1894] The 1982 NFMA regulations exempted all nonwilderness RARE II areas from wilderness consideration until the forest plans were revised. 36 C.F.R. § 219.17(a) (1983). The regulations were modified in 1983, following California v. Block, 690 F.2d 753 (9th Cir. 1982) and the decision by the Department of Agriculture to require consideration of all roadless areas for wilderness designation, unless excused by statutory release legislation. 48 Fed. Reg. 40,381-83 (1983). *See also supra* note 1889.

[1895] Typically, release legislation states that "the Department of Agriculture shall not be required to review the wilderness option prior to the revisions of the plans" Pub. L. No. 98-328, 98 Stat. 272 (1984) (Oregon Wilderness Act). Thus, a national forest that completes its forest plan in 1985 will not evaluate its roadless areas until at least 1995. However, a plan may be revised prior to that time. *See* 36 C.F.R. § 219.10(g) (1984). For the full text and legislative interpretation of release language, see H.R. REP. NO. 643, 98th Cong., 2d Sess. (1984) (Arizona Wilderness Act). Release language does not apply to wilderness study areas nor to further planning areas that are not specifically released in the wilderness legislation.

California v. Block[1896] and similar litigation[1897] indicate that the courts will closely scrutinize the forest plan's EIS for roadless areas allocated to nonwilderness management. Courts have repeatedly enjoined nonwilderness activities in roadless areas, finding that the Forest Service failed to comply with the EIS requirements of NEPA.[1898] As the Ninth Circuit stated in *California v. Block*, "The foreclosing of the wilderness management option requires a careful assessment of how this new management strategy will affect each area's [wilderness] characteristics."[1899]

Perhaps the single most important feature of the forest plan's EIS for a roadless area is a detailed, site-specific analysis of the environmental consequences of nonwilderness management.[1900] First, the plan must identify the roadless area's wilderness characteristics and values, such as wildlife types and existence of rare and endangered wildlife species.[1901] Second, the plan must assess the area's wilderness value and the impact of nonwilderness allocation upon the "intrinsic worth of the wilderness features" of the area under various development alternatives.[1902] Third, the forest plan must consider the effect of nonwilderness management upon future opportunities for wilderness classification.[1903] Finally, the economic benefit of developing the area must be weighed against the adverse environmental consequences.[1904]

Another important requirement of roadless area planning is presentation of a reasonable range of alternatives. For example, the *California v. Block* court directed the Forest Service to consider increasing resource production on federal land that is currently open to development rather than commencing production in roadless areas.[1905] The range of alternatives a plan presents cannot

---

[1896] 690 F.2d 753 (9th Cir. 1982).

[1897] *See supra* note 1799.

[1898] *Id.* All of the cases cited in this section, with the exception of Parker v. United States, 448 F.2d 793 (10th Cir. 1971), *cert. denied*, 405 U.S. 989 (1972), were decided at least partly on the basis of NEPA.

[1899] 690 F.2d 753, 764 (9th Cir. 1982).

[1900] *Id.* at 765.

[1901] *Id.* at 763-64.

[1902] *Id.* at 764.

[1903] *Id.*

[1904] *Id.*

[1905] The policy at hand demands a trade-off between wilderness use and development. This trade-off, however, cannot be intelligently made without examining whether it can be softened or eliminated by increasing resource extraction and use from already developed areas. The economic value of nonwilderness use is a function of its scarcity. Benefits accrue from

be heavily skewed to one result,[1906] and the agency has the burden of justifying any failure to present a reasonable range of alternatives.[1907]

The NFMA regulations require planners to consider several criteria in evaluating each roadless area, including wilderness values, effects on adjacent lands, feasibility of management, and proximity to other wilderness areas.[1908] Furthermore, planners must evaluate roadless areas in terms of their contribution to the diversity of natural plant and animal communities in the national forest.[1909] This latter requirement, proposed by the Committee of Scientists,[1910] echoes the policy of the Wilderness Act to preserve areas "where the earth and its community of life are untrammeled by man."[1911]

2. *Wilderness Areas*

Whereas roadless area planning is governed largely by NEPA and the Forest Service regulations, the Wilderness Act is the primary source of planning direction for congressionally designated wilderness areas. Subsequent legislation and congressional committee reports have provided additional mangement direction, most notably for grazing.

As discussed, wilderness area planning occurs at two levels. The forest plan sets general standards for managing all wilderness areas within the national forest. Individual wilderness resource plans provide site-specific management direction for each wilderness area. Both planning phases often require analysis of complex

---

opening virgin land to nonwilderness use, but the benefits' worth depend upon their relative availability elsewhere, and the comparative environmental costs of focusing development in these other areas.

Id. at 767.

[1906] California v. Bergland, 483 F. Supp. 465, 489 (E.D. Cal. 1980), *aff'd sub nom.* California v. Block, 690 F.2d 753 (9th Cir. 1982).

[1907] *Id.* at 488.

[1908] 36 C.F.R. § 219.17(b)(2)(i)-(iv) (1984).

[1909] *Id.* § 219.17(b)(2)(v). On the diversity requirement, see *supra* section VII(B).

[1910] *See Comm. of Scientists Final Report, supra* note 864, at 26,640.

[1911] 16 U.S.C. § 1131(c) (1982). The Act defines wilderness as an area that may contain "ecological" features of value. *Id.*

problems involving adjacent lands,[1912] overlapping jurisdiction,[1913] and access to private inholdings.[1914]

The following discussion of wilderness area planning will focus on issues concerning specific resources. The mining resource will be examined separately because of the "fundamental inconsistencies"[1915] of mining in wilderness areas and because of the high level of controversy that has surrounded this aspect of wilderness planning.

(a) Range

Section 4(d)(4) of the Wilderness Act states that "the grazing of livestock, where established prior to [1964] shall be permitted to continue subject to such reasonable regulations as are deemed

---

[1912] Wilderness may also abut proposed wilderness, a National Park, and State and private lands. Such cases really do exist. Millions of largely inaccessible acres are involved. If it all sounds complicated, it is. The boundaries may signify different restrictions governing such variables as allowable party size, types of fires permitted, and whether dogs, firearms, or fires are even allowed. WILDERNESS MANAGEMENT, *supra* note 1806, at 224.

[1913] "Wilderness management on the National Forests is also complicated by geographic and administative dispersal. For example, a designated Forest Service Wilderness may encompass multiple planning units; ranger districts and regions in two or more National Forests." *Id.*

[1914] Section 5(a) of the Wilderness Act requires the Forest Service either to grant a right of access to any non-federal land that is "completely surrounded by national forest lands within areas designated . . . as wilderness," or to exchange the inholding for other federal land in the state. 16 U.S.C. § 1134(a) (1982). Furthermore, § 1323(a) of the Alaska National Interest Lands Conservation Act states that "the Secretary shall provide such access to nonfederally owned land within the boundaries of the National Forest System as the Secretary deems adequate to secure to the owner the reasonable use and enjoyment thereof." 16 U.S.C. § 3210(a) (1982).

The latter, subsequently enacted provision raises the question whether the Forest Service still has the option to exchange lands in lieu of providing access to inholdings in wilderness areas. In Montana Wilderness Ass'n v. United States Forest Service, 655 F.2d 951 (9th Cir. 1981), *cert. denied*, 455 U.S. 989 (1982), the court "recognize[d] a facial problem or tension" between these two provisions. *Id.* at 957 n.12. The court stated:

We need not decide in this case whether there is repeal by implication. In passing, we note only that it is arguable that the two can stand together . . . . Thus, [16 U.S.C.] § 1134(a) could be construed to apply in the specific case of a wilderness area, and [16 U.S.C. § 3210(a)] could be construed to apply in all other cases.

Id. For a discussion of access to private inholdings, see Note, *Public Access to Federal Lands: Dilemma*, 3 PUB. LAND L. REV. 194 (1982).

[1915] Izaak Walton League of Am. v. St. Clair, 353 F. Supp. 698, 714 (D. Minn. 1973), *rev'd* 497 F.2d 849 (8th Cir. 1974).

necessary by the Secretary of Agriculture."[1916] In the Colorado Wilderness Act of 1980,[1917] Congress elaborated on the meaning of this language. Section 108 of the Colorado Act provides that the grazing provision of the Wilderness Act "shall be interpreted in accordance with the guidelines contained . . . in the House Committee Report . . . accompanying this Act."[1918] Thus, section 108 mandates that the guidelines in the committee report apply to all national forest wilderness areas, not just those in Colorado.[1919]

First, there may not be reductions in livestock grazing solely because the area covered by the grazing allotment is designated as wilderness.[1920] However, grazing may be reduced through "normal" planning processes to improve poor range conditions or to prevent deterioration of the range resources.[1921] While grazing use should normally remain at the level established prior to wilderness designation, grazing use can be increased only if the normal planning process reveals conclusively that no adverse impacts on wilderness values will occur.[1922]

Second, existing range structures may be maintained with motorized equipment.[1923] The amount of maintenance is limited by a "rule of practical necessity and reasonableness."[1924] Motorized equipment for maintenance will ordinarily be permitted only if used prior to wilderness designation, or for a "true" emergency to rescue or feed animals.[1925]

Finally, replacement and new construction of grazing-related structures may be justified for resource protection and "more effective management."[1926] The structures may be constructed with non-natural materials to avoid "unreasonable" costs.[1927]

In sum, the Colorado Wilderness Act established guidelines designed to preserve the status quo for grazing use of national

---

[1916] 16 U.S.C. § 1133(d)(4) (1982). This language does not confer statutory rights on existing grazers; instead, grazing can continue so long as it is consistent with wilderness values and soil protection. McCloskey, *supra* note 1842, at 311.

[1917] Pub. L. No. 96-560, 94 Stat. 3266 (1980).

[1918] 94 Stat. 3271.

[1919] FOREST SERVICE MANUAL § 2320.3a(3) (1984).

[1920] H.R. REP. No. 617, 96th Cong., 1st Sess. 11 (1980).

[1921] *Id.* On grazing redutions see *supra* section III(B).

[1922] *Id.* at 11-12.

[1923] The structure may include fences, cabins, water wells and lines, and stock tanks. *Id.* at 12.

[1924] *Id.*

[1925] *Id.*

[1926] *Id.*

[1927] *Id.*

forest wilderness areas. Existing use ordinarily will be allowed to continue, but the Forest Service may also pursue its traditional policy of reducing livestock use to prevent resource degradation.

(b) Control of Forest Fire, Insects, and Disease

Section 4(d)(1) of the Wilderness Act allows the Forest Service to take "such measures . . . as may be necessary in the control of fire, insects, and diseases, subject to such conditions as the Secretary deems desirable."[1928] The House Committee report on the Endangered American Wilderness Act of 1978 construed this language to mean that "anything necessary for the protection of public health or safety is clearly permissible."[1929] However, control measures that drastically alter the wilderness resource must be adequately justified and documented.[1930]

The NFMA regulations require planners to consider measures to control forest fires, insect infestations, and outbreaks of disease in wilderness areas.[1931] The central issue for planners is to determine the extent to which the agency should exercise its authority. Biologists acknowledge that fire has numerous beneficial effects on wilderness ecosystems. For instance, periodic fires prevent excessive build-up of fuel material, allow certain species of trees and other plants to regenerate, control insects and disease, recycle nutrients, and maintain ecological diversity.[1932] Therefore, planners may choose to restore fire to its natural role in the wilderness.[1933] The plan may institute a "let burn" policy, where natural, lightning-caused fires are simply monitored and allowed to burn

---

[1928] 16 U.S.C. § 1133(d)(1) (1982).

[1929] H.R. REP. No. 540, 95th Cong., 1st Sess. 6 (1977). "This includes the use of mechanized equipment, the building of fire roads, fire towers, fire breaks or fire pre-suppression facilities where necessary, and other techniques for fire control." *Id.*

[1930] *See* Sierra Club v. Block, 614 F.Supp. 488 (D.C. D.C. 1985).

[1931] 36 C.F.R. § 219.18(b) (1984).

[1932] WILDERNESS MANAGEMENT, *supra* note 1806, at 250-54.

[1933] *See* FOREST SERVICE MANUAL § 2324.02 (1985).

[T]he objective is to restore the naturalness of the environment and let natural processes take over. This will help to produce an ecosystem "where the earth and its community of life are untrammelled by man." Such an objective is in keeping with a biocentric focus for wilderness management, which places strong emphasis on preservation of the natural physical and biotic wilderness resources.

WILDERNESS MANAGEMENT, *supra* note 1806, at 267.

themselves out, or even use prescribed, i.e., intentionally set fire.[1934]

(c) Wildlife

National forest wilderness areas provide a substantial amount of the undisturbed habitat that numerous species of wildlife require for survival.[1935] Controlling human activity that threatens wilderness-dependent species is an important element of wilderness area planning.[1936]

The House Committee Report on the California Wilderness Act of 1984 recognized that "certain wildlife management activities were compatible, and sometimes essential, elements in the management of certain wildlife populations in many wilderness areas."[1937] Specifically, water supplies may be maintained and developed with mechanical equipment when essential to wildlife survival.[1938] Temporary use of motor vehicles, boats, and aircraft is permitted for wildlife studies; however, no roads may be built for wildlife purposes.[1939]

The Wilderness Act's only explicit reference to wildlife is a disclaimer of any federal interference with the states' traditional jurisdiction over wildlife management.[1940] While generally deferring to the states' regulation of hunting, trapping, and fishing, the Forest Service also exercises some control over these activities in wilderness areas. For instance, local planners may "[c]lose or restrict access or indirectly discourage use to decrease fishing pres-

---

[1934] *See* FOREST SERVICE MANUAL § 2324.03 (1984). *See generally* Johnson, *Prescribed Burning: Requiem or Renaissance?*, 82 J. FORESTRY 82, 85 (1984).

[1935] *See* WILDERNESS MANAGEMENT, *supra* note 1806, at 216-19.

[1936] *Id.* at 229-32.

[1937] H.R. REP. No. 40, 98th Cong., 1st Sess. 42 (1983).

[1938] *Id.* at 45.

[1939] *Id.* at 46.

[1940] Section 4(d)(7) states, "Nothing in this Chapter shall be construed as affecting the jurisdiction or responsibilities of the several States with respect to wildlife and fish in the national forests." 16 U.S.C. § 1133(d)(7) (1982). The Multiple-Use Sustained-Yield Act of 1960 is to the same effect. 16 U.S.C. § 528 (1982). A similar disclaimer in the Federal Land Policy and Management Act of 1976 also applies to the national forests, as well as to BLM lands. 43 U.S.C. § 1732(b) (1982). It is unclear from these provisions whether, and to what extent, the Forest Service can override state law pursuant to its general authority to manage the wildlife resource. *See supra* section VII(D). The strong preservationist policies of the Wilderness Act probably make wilderness the strongest setting for an assertion of Forest Service authority as against state wildlife law.

sure on over utilized fishing waters."[1941] Similarly, the Forest Service Manual specifies that "[t]he proper balance of game animals with their habitat may be achieved by managing public hunting."[1942] Commercial trapping of furbearers is categorically forbidden in wilderness areas.[1943]

Ideally, the restrictive measures authorized by the Manual should be implemented through cooperative agreements with state wildlife agencies or through FLPMA closures.[1944] However, Forest Service regulatory authority is probably broad enough to support the Manual restrictions if there is an adequate record to justify the action.[1945]

(d) Recreation

Recreational use of national forest wilderness has increased dramatically since World War II, growing at a faster rate than overall national forest recreational use.[1946] Most recreation occurs on access trails and campsites located near fragile shorelines of lakes and streams.[1947] Thus, managing wilderness campsites both to minimize the impacts of people and pack animals and to provide a high-quality wilderness experience often requires "a tightrope walker's sense of balance."[1948]

[1941] FOREST SERVICE MANUAL § 2323.35-3 (1984).

[1942] *Id.* § 2323.31.

[1943] *Id.* § 2323.34.

[1944] *See supra* notes 1642-44. Wilderness areas are potential sites of jurisdictional overlap between the Forest Service and state wildlife agencies. *See* WILDERNESS MANAGEMENT, *supra* note 1806, at 224. For this reason,
> [i]t is extremely important that a statesmanlike communication prevail among the wilderness managing agencies, State fish and wildlife agencies, and wildlife conservation groups, so that everybody concerned can at least acknowledge where they disagree on wilderness-wildlife management issues, interpretations of the law, and advisable policy. This is a major, current challenge, particularly critical as it relates to different purposes, philosophies, and perspectives of State Fish and Game departments as compared to those of the Federal Wilderness management Agencies.

Id. at 236.

[1945] The House Committee Report on the Endangered American Wilderness Act states that hunting and fishing in wilderness areas are "subject to applicable state and federal laws and regulations (Wilderness Act, section 4(d)(8)), and such other reasonable restrictions as may be necessary under principles of sound land management." H.R. REP. No. 540, 95th Cong., 1st Sess. (1977).

[1946] WILDERNESS MANAGEMENT, *supra* note 1806, at 307.

[1947] A study of two representative wilderness areas found that one-half of the most frequently used campsites were located within 50 feet of a lake or stream and 85% were within 200 feet. *Id.* at 304.

[1948] *Id.* at 359.

A central purpose of the Wilderness Act is to provide "opportunities for solitude or a primitive and unconfined type of recreation."[1949] The Act generally prohibits structures, installations, and motorized equipment.[1950] Thus, recreational shelters are prohibited but fire rings and some temporary structures may be permitted.[1951] Trail signs, bridges, and chain saws to construct and maintain trails are also allowed.[1952]

Excessive recreational use of wilderness areas concerned the Committee of Scientists.[1953] Accordingly, the NFMA regulations require planners to set maximum use levels, or carrying capacities, for specific wilderness areas.[1954] Recreational use must be sufficiently limited and distributed to "allow natural processes to operate freely and . . . not impair the values for which wilderness areas were created."[1955]

The Forest Service has several methods to limit and control recreational use in wilderness areas. First, the Forest Service can directly control use by closing campgrounds, trails, and entire areas

---

[1949] 16 U.S.C. § 1131(c) (1982).

[1950] *Id.* § 1133(c).

[1951] H.R. REP. No. 540, 95th Cong., 1st Sess., 7 (1977).

[1952] *Id.*

[1953] Maintenance of the unique opportunities for research, education, and human enjoyment of wilderness plainly depends on minimal evidence of man an[d] his works, and minimal damage by users. Yet already the wild quality of some portions of some designated Wilderness Areas is being degraded by excessive human activities. Managerial options available to prevent or repair such over-use are essentially only two: (1) Diversion of visitors to less heavily used portions or corridors of an area; or (2) restrictions on number of visitors, or the duration and condition of their visit. The first option deserves continuous study but physical features of the area will often limit its applicability. Both this and the second option, limitations on visitors, should be applied before damage is generally evident or before "wilderness experience" attributes for visitors are impaired.
Comm. of Scientists Final Report, supra note 864, at 26,640.

[1954] 36 C.F.R. § 219.18(a) (1984). The Committee of Scientists wanted planners
to estimate tolerable limits of use, or "carrying capacity," in advance and to regulate visitor numbers accordingly. This approach obviously parallels the use of carrying capacity for range and wildlife resources, and the "allowable cut" in timber management. Although methods for determining "carrying capacity" of wilderness are not well advanced at this time, we believe reasonable and objective estimates can be made and frequently updated as experience grows. Such estimates would facilitate planning in advance to avoid or mitigate impairment of the paramount values for which Wilderness Areas were designed by Congress.
Comm. of Scientists Final Report, supra note 864, at 26,640-41.

[1955] 36 C.F.R. § 219.18(a) (1984).

to horses and humans.[1956] Second, it may issue permits to limit the number of campers, their location, and their length of stay.[1957] In addition, it can limit or prohibit specific activites, such as building campfires or fishing.[1958] In short, the Forest Service has broad authority to regulate recreation "to preserve wilderness character."[1959]

C. Wilderness Mining

1. Extent of Resource and Evolution of Policy

The unique geologic features that characterize national forest wildernesses have led some to believe that these areas are probable sources of valuable mineral deposits.[1960] However, while hardrock mineral resources have been discovered in isolated wilderness areas,[1961] mineral surveys generally have not uncovered major deposits.[1962] Similarly, recent studies have concluded that only four percent of the congressionally designated wilderness lands have a high potential for oil and gas production.[1963] In roadless areas being considered for wilderness designation the potential for oil and gas production is largely unknown.[1964] Yet, even where oil, gas, or locatable minerals are discovered, the prohibitive costs of mining in remote and rugged wilderness or roadless areas frequently preclude development.[1965] In spite of these factors, mining is likely to remain an important and difficult issue in wilderness law and pol-

---

[1956] WILDERNESS MANAGEMENT, *supra* note 1806, at 327.

[1957] *Id.* at 327-32. *See also* FOREST SERVICE, U.S. DEP'T OF AGRICULTURE, RATIONING WILDERNESS USE: METHODS, PROBLEMS, AND GUIDELINES (Research Paper INT-192) (1977).

[1958] WILDERNESS MANAGEMENT, *supra* note 1806, at 333.

[1959] 16 U.S.C. § 1133(b) (1982).

[1960] *See* Ferguson, *Forest Service and BLM Wilderness Review Programs and Their Effect on Mining Law Activities*, 24 ROCKY MTN. MIN. L. INST. 717, 718 (1978); Comment, *Closing the Mining Loophole in the 1964 Wilderness Act*, 6 ENVTL. L. 469 (1975).

[1961] *See, e.g.*, FOREST SERVICE, U.S. DEP'T OF AGRICULTURE, ELKHORN WILDERNESS STUDY 64-70 (1981).

[1962] *See* WILDERNESS MANAGEMENT, *supra* note 1806, at 285.

[1963] U.S. GEOLOGICAL SURVEY, DEP'T OF THE INTERIOR, PETROLEUM POTENTIAL OF WILDERNESS LANDS IN THE WESTERN UNITED STATES (1983).

[1964] As late as 1979, the Forest Service characterized current knowledge of oil and gas potential in roadless areas as "fragmentary and far from conclusive. In most areas, virtually no exploration for oil and gas has occurred." RARE II EIS, *supra* note 1883, at 97.

[1965] Interview with John Collier and John Lowe, Div. of Lands & Minerals, Forest Service, Region 6, in Portland, Or. (Feb. 2, 1984).

icy. There are, for example, at least 10,000 hardrock mining claims in national forest wilderness areas[1966] and, while the great majority of these claims are almost certainly invalid, the existence of such a large number of potential private property interests poses a formidable challenge to Forest Service wilderness planning.

Forest Service wilderness regulations did not directly refer to mineral activities until 1963.[1967] While the early L-20 and U Regulations generally prohibited road building and motor vehicle use and restricted surface occupancy,[1968] wilderness areas, like the rest of the national forest system, remained subject to the hardrock mining laws.[1969] As a matter of policy, local Forest Service officials prohibited road and vehicle access for mineral exploration, but, upon discovery of a valuable mineral deposit, a miner would be granted permission to construct an access road.[1970] Thus, before 1963 the agency informally attempted to minimize environmental damage caused by mineral development.[1971]

In 1963 the Forest Service amended its U Regulations to exempt prospecting, locating, and developing mineral resources from the general restrictions on activities within wilderness areas.[1972] However, mineral activities continued to be subject to "appropriate conditions determined by the Chief."[1973] The amended regulations foreshadowed the competing policies of the Wilderness Act that would pass the next year and place the Forest Service in the unenviable position of "serving two masters which may tend to be mutually exclusive."[1974]

[1966] Toffenetti, Valid Mining Rights and Wilderness Areas, 20 LAND & WATER L. REV. 31, n.1 (1985).

[1967] *See* 4 Fed. Reg. 3994 (1939); 19 Fed. Reg. 8140 (1954); 20 Fed. Reg. 8422-23 (1955).

[1968] *See supra* text accompanying notes 1824-34.

[1969] *See supra* note 1834; Roth, *The National Forests and the Campaign for Wilderness Legislation*, 28 J. FOREST HIST. 112, 116 (1984).

[1970] Schroeder, *Wilderness: An Example of Agency Technique in the Creation of Social Policy*, 16 IDAHO L. REV. 511, 529-30 (1980), citing unpublished paper by B. Rasmussen, Mining and Prospecting in the National Forest (Dec. 1, 1961).

[1971] On the right of access across national forest lands to mining claims during this era, see generally Biddle, *supra* note 338.

[1972] 28 Fed. Reg. 5617 (1963).

[1973] *Id.*

[1974] FOREST SERVICE MANUAL § 2323.7 (1984).

2. The Wilderness Act of 1964

The Wilderness Act is important to the Forest Service's mineral management policy in three ways. First, the Act withdrew from entry under the mining laws all lands within wilderness areas as of January 1, 1984, subject only to development of valid claims existing before that date.[1975] This general withdrawal of lands from the effect of the mining laws is subject to the miners' right to prospect "in a manner consistent with the wilderness environment."[1976] The incentive to prospect, however, is minimal. Because of the general withdrawal, a miner making a strike would be required to obtain a waiver from Congress before proceeding to develop the deposit.

Second, the Act required the Forest Service to regulate mineral activities so as to preserve and protect wilderness values.[1977] Specifically, the Forest Service can condition access to valid claims in wilderness areas, regulate mineral exploration and development, and require restoration of surface areas.[1978] Use of motorized air or ground equipment will be approved only "where essential."[1979] The Act also requires protective measures concerning mineral leases, permits, and licenses, which must contain "reasonable stipulations as may be prescribed by the Secretary of Agriculture for the protection of the wilderness character of the land."[1980] As the

---

[1975] 16 U.S.C. § 1133(d)(3) (1982). In a very few instances, special provisions were made for individual wilderness areas. Several areas were withdrawn from mining as of the date of their establishment and thus mining was prohibited in advance of the general closure on January 1, 1984. In at least one instance, the Gospel Hump Wilderness in Idaho, withdrawal will not occur until 1988. Endangered American Wilderness Act of 1978 § 5, 92 Stat. 46 (1978). The River of No Return Wilderness, also in Idaho, has a "Special Management Zone," within which mining for cobalt is allowed. Central Idaho Wilderness Act of 1980 § 4(d)(1), 94 Stat. 949 (1980).

[1976] *Id.* § 1133(d)(2).

[1977] *Id.* § 1133(b). The Forest Service's authority to regulate mining generally on national forest lands was not resolved until 1981. In United States v. Weiss, 642 F.2d 296 (9th Cir. 1981), the court held that the Forest Service, by virtue of the Organic Act of 1897, possessed authority to regulate mining on all national forest lands. *See supra* notes 1359-63, 1367-83, and accompanying text. The Wilderness Act, however, contains express authority and special provisions to guide the regulation of mining operations in wilderness. *See* 16 U.S.C. § 1133(d)(3) (1982).

[1978] 16 U.S.C. § 1133(d)(3) (1982). The Forest Service must grant access to valid mining claims "consistent with the preservation of the area as wilderness." *Id.* § 1134(b).

[1979] *Id.* § 1133(d)(3).

[1980] *Id.*

Forest Service Manual provides, "where alternatives exist, wilderness values shall be dominant over all other considerations in reaching management decisions."[1981]

Third, although the mining exception in the 1964 Act does allow mining in spite of the conflict with wilderness preservation, the Act diminishes some of the privileges traditionally enjoyed by hardrock miners. Patents issued after September 3, 1964, for claims in wilderness areas convey title only to the subsurface mineral estate.[1982] Title to the surface estate and surface resources remains in the United States, although the patentee may use standing timber for mining purposes if none is otherwise available. Occupancy and use of patented mining claims are strictly limited to activities necessary for mining purposes.[1983] Since title to the surface estate remains in the United States, the Forest Service may regulate surface activity on claims patented after 1964.[1984]

3. Regulation of Wilderness Mining

(a) Hardrock Mining

The Forest Service issued its first regulations governing prospecting, exploration, and development of hardrock minerals in wilderness areas in June 1966.[1985] Current mining regulations and supplemental directives in the Forest Service Manual cover access, operations on claims, reclamation, harvesting timber for mining purposes, and prospecting and gathering information about minerals.[1986] Regulation of these activities in wilderness areas is consid-

---

[1981] FOREST SERVICE MANUAL § 2320.3-8 (1984).

[1982] 16 U.S.C. § 1133(d)(3) (1982). The provision will raise takings objections since miners with pre-1964 discoveries possessed the right to apply for patents to the surface until the passage of the Wilderness Act. This opportunity to apply for a patent, however, apparently falls short of being a compensable property right. *See* Freese v. United States, 639 F.2d 754 (Ct. Cl.), *cert. denied*, 454 U.S. 827 (1981).

[1983] 16 U.S.C. § 1133(d)(3) (1982).

[1984] *Id.* Traditionally, only unpatented mining claims were subject to any surface regulation. When a claim "went to patent" the patentee gained a full and unrestricted property right, not subject to any regulation. *See supra* text accompanying notes 1381-83.

[1985] 36 C.F.R. § 251.15 (1966).

[1986] General Forest Service mining regulations are set out at 36 C.F.R. pt. 228 (1984), discussed *supra* in text accompanying notes 1367-77. Additional requirements for wilderness areas are found at *id.* § 228.15. *See also* FOREST SERVICE MANUAL § 2323.7 (1984). The regulations assume that the mining exception in 16 U.S.C. § 1133(d)(3) (1982), which allows limited mining activity in spite of its conflict with wilderness values, applies in all national forest wilderness areas.

erably stricter than for other national forest lands.[1987] The focal point for management is the operating plans that miners must submit.[1988]

Perhaps the most difficult problems arise when miners must transport equipment into wilderness areas. Access to claims in wilderness must occur in a manner consistent with preserving wilderness values.[1989] To ensure this, miners must submit an operating plan if they anticipate any potential surface disturbance or use of motorized transport.[1990] The Service has specified that access by foot or horseback is the preferred mode;[1991] motorized transport may be approved only when there is no reasonable alternative.[1992]

Decisions about allowable access are most critical during exploration. Abandoned exploration routes may create long-lasting scars in the wilderness.[1993] Consequently, operating plans may require helicopter transport of drills and other equipment into wilderness-surrounded claims.[1994] While the Forest Service can place strict conditions upon access,[1995] once a valid claim has been

---

Professor Leshy, on the other hand, has concluded that the wilderness exception, which is limited to wilderness areas designated by this chapter, applies only in areas originally designated in the 1964 Act. Additions to the wilderness system are not subject to the wilderness exception unless § 1133(d)(3) is made applicable to subsequently-designated areas in the legislation creating them. *See* Leshy, *Wilderness and Its Discontents: Wilderness Review Comes to the Public Lands*, 1981 ARIZ. ST. L.J. 361, 385-90. No court has ruled on the issue and, as noted, the administrative practice is to treat all wilderness areas as subject to the mining exception.

[1987] Interview with John Collier and John Lowe, *supra* note 1965. *See also* Toffenetti, *supra* note 1966, at 61-64.

[1988] *See generally supra* text accompanying notes 1367-77.

[1989] 16 U.S.C. § 1134(b) (1982); 36 C.F.R. § 228.15(c) (1984).

[1990] 36 C.F.R. § 228.15(c) (1984).

[1991] FOREST SERVICE MANUAL § 2323.71a-2 (1984).

[1992] *Id.*

[1993] A Sierra Club representative describes the "thousands of miles of roads built by miners [and] the diggings and drill sites of prospectors [as] the most conspicuous man-made scars on millions of acres of western landscape." John McComb, Southwest Representative, Sierra Club, in interview with David Seridan (Apr. 1977), *quoted in* COUNCIL ON ENVIRONMENTAL QUALITY, HARDROCK MINING ON THE PUBLIC LANDS 12 (1977).

[1994] Interview with John Collier and John Lowe, *supra* note 1965.

[1995] The Forest Service's authority to restrict exploration and access was clarified by Senator Anderson in his remarks on the conference committee's decision to accept the House amendment on mining:

I feared that the language of the amendment might be misinterpreted to mean that mechanized equipment could be used in prospecting—that bulldozers might be used to prospect or even cut long roads to the prospect areas.

established within a wilderness area, access will not be denied altogether.[1996]

The Forest Service will scrutinize other aspects of miners' operating plans for wilderness claims. The agency must "ensure that provisions approved in operating plans are the minimum necessary to accomplish the rights of the claimant while creating the least impact on the wilderness resource."[1997] In addition, the agency must prepare an environmental analysis to determine whether an environmental impact statement will be required.[1998] The plan must contain information on all aspects of planned use, including proposed environmental restoration and pollution prevention.[1999] Finally, the operating plan must include an objective that site reclamation will "minimize remaining evidence of man's activities"[2000] and will "return [the surface] to a contour which might appear to be natural."[2001]

The Forest Service also regulates hardrock mining in roadless areas under study for wilderness designation.[2002] Unless specific legislation provides otherwise,[2003] the roadless areas are not subject to the restrictive mining management provisions of the Wilderness Act. Although these areas remain open to exploration and development under the general mining laws beyond December

---

We were assured by the House conferees that the House language has no such meaning.
110 Cong. Rec. 20,601 (1964).

[1996] Interview with John Collier and John Lowe, *supra* note 1965. 16 U.S.C. § 1134(b) (1982). *Cf.* Montana Wilderness Ass'n v. United States Forest Service, 655 F.2d 951 (9th Cir. 1981), *cert. denied*, 455 U.S. 989 (1982)(§ 1323(a) of Alaska National Interest Lands Conservation Act, 16 U.S.C. 3210 (1982), provides independent basis for grant of access to certain inholdings and is applicable nationwide), discussed *supra* at note 1914. Although access cannot be generally denied, mining can be prohibited as to any miner who fails to comply with the valid requirements of a Forest Service operation plan. *See, e.g.,* Granite Rock Co. v. California Coastal Comm'n, 763 F.2d 1077, 1083 (9th Cir. 1985).

[1997] FOREST SERVICE MANUAL § 2323.7 (1984).

[1998] For a list of items that must be analyzed, see *id.* § 2323.71.

[1999] *Id.* § 2323.71b.

[2000] *Id.* § 2323.71a-5.

[2001] *Id.* Strict enforcement requires not only high standards of reclamation but also some type of insurance that the reclamation work will be performed. This is accomplished by requiring that performance bonds, commensurate with the anticipated cost of doing restoration work, be posted. *Id.* § 2323.71a-9.

[2002] *See supra* text accompanying notes 1801-03.

[2003] *See, e.g.,* Montana Wilderness Study Act of 1977, Pub. L. No. 95-150, 91 Stat. 1243 (1977); Indian Peaks Area Wilderness Study Act, Pub. L. No. 92-528, 86 Stat. 1050 (1972).

31, 1983,[2004] the Forest Service can reasonably regulate mineral activities affecting surface resources under the same regulatory authority that the agency has over all national forest lands.[2005] In general, the Forest Service has exercised special care in evaluating operating plans covering claims in roadless areas.[2006] The agency has attempted to ensure that surface-disturbing activities occur only if there are strong indications that a valuable deposit has been discovered.[2007]

As of January 1, 1984, the effective date of the Wilderness Act's withdrawal provision, mining in wilderness areas is prohibited unless the miner has established a valid unpatented claim.[2008] To be valid, a discovery of a valuable mineral deposit within the wilderness area boundaries must have been made before January 1, 1984. The standard for determining the deposit's value requires that the mineral must be able to be "extracted, removed and marketed at a profit."[2009] In practical terms, the requirement of marketability for profit will be especially difficult to establish in wilderness areas because of the costs of mining in remote areas and of complying with the heightened regulatory requirements.[2010] Forest Service employees, especially mining engineers, have initial responsibility for examining the claim and reporting its value. If the Forest Service determines that the claim is not valid, the BLM will usually initiate a contest proceeding.[2011] Since the

---

[2004] *See supra* text accompanying note 1975.

[2005] *See supra* text accompanying notes 1367-77.

[2006] Interview with Mike Burnside, Div. of Lands & Minerals, Forest Service, Region 1, Missoula, Mont. (Feb. 10, 1984).

[2007] *Id.* On mining in BLM roadless areas being studied for their wilderness potential pursuant to FLPMA, see Leshy, *supra* note 1986, at 377-425.

[2008] *See supra* text accompanying note 1975. As noted, although development is prohibited, prospecting may proceed under restrictive conditions. *See supra* note 1976.

[2009] *See* United States v. Coleman, 390 U.S. 599 (1968), discussed *supra* in note 1292.

[2010] The Interior Board of Land Appeals has ruled that the legal test for discovery is the same in important recreation areas as in other public land areas. In Re Pacific Coast Molybdenum, 90 I.D. 352, 363, 75 IBLA 16, 34 (1983). Nevertheless, although the legal burden of proof may be the same, weather, terrain, and regulatory demands make the proof more difficult. *See generally* Toffenetti, *supra* note 1966.

[2011] Interview with John Collier and John Lowe, *supra* note 1965. Jurisdiction for administrative contests to mining claims on all public lands is vested in the BLM. *See supra* notes 1378-80 and accompanying text. Pursuant to a 1957 Forest Service-BLM Memorandum of Understanding, however, the Forest Service investigates the claim; if the Service recommends a contest, the BLM will

government's primary witness in a contest proceeding is usually the Forest Service mining engineer who examined the claim, the agency remains involved throughout the adjudication process.[2012]

In the past, the Forest Service was criticized both for its reluctance to challenge the validity of wilderness claims and for its failure to argue that proof of a profitable, valuable deposit must justify the increased costs associated with mining in wilderness. For example, in the early 1970s wilderness preservationists in Oregon challenged the Forest Service's examination validating a block pumice claim located in the Three Sisters Wilderness as a valuable discovery.[2013] The Forest Service's actions led one commentator to complain that "the responsibility of protecting . . . [wilderness areas] has shifted from the Forest Service to the environmental and public interest groups."[2014] Recently, however, the Forest Service seems to have taken a more rigorous stance in enforcing validity requirements, and now requires the verification of claims in wilderness areas prior to any surface-disturbing activity.[2015]

(b) Mineral Leasing

The Forest Service possesses substantial control over mineral leasing in wilderness areas.[2016] The Wilderness Act provides that mineral leases in wilderness areas shall contain such reasonable stipulations as the Secretary of Agriculture may require to protect the wilderness character of the land.[2017] In addition, while the Department of the Interior retains final leasing authority, pursuant to a memorandum of understanding with the BLM the Forest

---

initiate the contest, which will be tried by a Department of Agriculture attorney. *See* FOREST SERVICE MANUAL § 1531.12a-1 (1984).

[2012] Interview with John Collier and John Lowe, *supra* note 1965.

[2013] *See* Comment, *supra* note 1960, at 473.

[2014] *Id.*

[2015] Interview with Mike Burnside, *supra* note 2006; *see* Toffenetti, *supra* note 1966, at 62-65.

[2016] *See generally* WILDERNESS MANAGEMENT, *supra* note 1806, at 71; Hubbard, *Ah Wilderness! (But What About Access and Prospecting?)*, 15 ROCKY MTN. MIN. L. INST. 585, 591-92 (1969).

[2017] 16 U.S.C. § 1133(d)(3) (1982). For a discussion of lease stipulations used by the Forest Service, see Edelson, *The Management of Oil and Gas Leasing on Federal Wilderness Lands*, 10 B.C. ENVTL. AFF. L. REV. 905 (1983); Comment, *The Interrelationships of the Mineral Lands Leasing Act, the Wilderness Act and the Endangered Species Act: A Conflict In Search of Resolution*, 12 ENVTL. L. 363, 408-10 (1982).

Service recommends to Interior whether a lease should be granted and Interior normally follows Forest Service recommendations.[2018]

The Forest Service's stated policy has been "not normally [to] recommend or approve mineral leases or permits in wildernesses or primitive areas unless directional drilling or other methods can be used which will avoid any invasion of the surface."[2019] Leases issued after the areas are designated for wilderness almost always contain "no surface occupancy" stipulations.[2020] Consequently, for these areas directional drilling from outside the wilderness is virtually mandatory.

As of the early 1980s, there were thirty-eight oil and gas leases in designated wildernesses.[2021] This was not due to a dearth of applicants. There was a backlog of 1400 unprocessed lease applications in wildernesses,[2022] due to the practice of the Forest Service and the Interior Department in previous years to withhold action on lease applications in wildernesses.

However, in May, 1981, the Forest Service announced that it was studying pending lease applications in the Bob Marshall, Great Bear, and Scapegoat Wilderness areas.[2023] In response, the House Committee on Interior and Insular Affairs directed Interior Secretary James Watt to make an emergency withdrawal of those areas pursuant to FLPMA and Secretary Watt complied.[2024] After Secretary Watt revoked the withdrawal, Congress passed an appropriations act providing that no money could be spent in the fiscal year ending September 30, 1983, to process mineral lease applications in wilderness areas, wilderness study areas, and areas recommended by RARE II for further planning or for wilderness designation.[2025] This left a three-month period before January 1,

---

[2018] Interview with John Collier and John Lowe, *supra* note 1965. The 1980 Memorandum of Understanding discussed *supra* in text accompanying notes 1390-91.

[2019] FOREST SERVICE MANUAL § 2323.73 (1984).

[2020] Interview with Mark Weber, Div. of Lands & Minerals, Forest Service, Region 1, Missoula, Mont. (Feb. 16, 1984).

[2021] *Id.*

[2022] FOREST SERVICE, U.S. DEP'T OF AGRICULTURE, REPORT OF THE FOREST SERVICE, FISCAL YEAR 1982, at 5 (1983) [hereinafter 1982 ANNUAL REPORT OF THE CHIEF].

[2023] 46 Fed. Reg. 22,735 (1981).

[2024] These events are detailed in Pacific Legal Found. v. Watt, 529 F. Supp. 982, 986 (D. Mont. 1981).

[2025] Pub. L. No. 276, § 126, 96 Stat. 1196 (1982).

1984, when wilderness areas were withdrawn from mining.[2026] Secretary Watt resolved the controversy by announcing that Interior would issue no new leases in wilderness areas.[2027]

As a result, no more leases were issued in wilderness areas prior to the effective date of withdrawal from mining under the Wilderness Act, January 1, 1984. In addition, it appears that development will not proceed on lease applications pending on December 31, 1983, because the withdrawal provision is subject only to "valid rights then existing."[2028] The courts uniformly have held that filing an application does not confer the right to a lease.[2029] Thus, barring amendment of the Wilderness Act, the number of leases in existing wildernesses should never exceed the thirty-eight that were held in November 1982.

[2026] 16 U.S.C. § 1133(d)(3) (1982), discussed *supra* text accompanying notes 1975-76.

[2027] *See generally* Public Land News No. 1, at 1-2 (Jan. 6, 1983). Although few leases have been issued in congressionally designated wilderness areas, *supra* note 2021, at the end of fiscal year 1982 there were 500 unprocessed lease applications in wilderness study areas, 1000 in RARE II recommended wilderness areas, and 400 in RARE II further planning areas. 1982 ANNUAL REPORT OF THE CHIEF, *supra* note 2025, at 5.

[2028] 16 U.S.C. § 1137(d)(3) (1982).

[2029] Burglin v. Morton, 527 F.2d 486 (9th Cir. 1976); Schraier v. Hickel, 419 F.2d 663 (D.C. Cir. 1969); Duesing v. Udall, 350 F.2d 748, 750-51 (D.C. Cir. 1965), *cert. denied*, 383 U.S. 912 (1966). *Cf.* Freese v. United States, 639 F.2d 754 (Ct. Cl.), *cert. denied*, 454 U.S. 827 (1984), discussed *supra* note 1982.

CONCLUSION

From its inception, the Forest Service has been a study in excellence. A truly great man—Gifford Pinchot was nothing less than a visionary—drew outstanding talent around him. Today the agency, coupling progressive working conditions with a mystique bred of tradition and the outdoors, continues to attract able young people and to groom exceptional, often charismatic, line officers. The Forest Service began, and has remained, at the frontiers of administrative creativity and efficiency. It has made trailblazing contributions by establishing research programs in private and public forestry, acquiring watershed lands in the eastern states, bringing management to the neglected public grazing lands, instituting the world's first wilderness program, and imposing regulatory controls on hardrock mining. No one can much criticize the agency for failing to achieve the goals it has set out to accomplish.

The upswelling of the mid-1970s, by any mark one of the signal events in public lands history, was not a response to a lack of quality within the Forest Service; it was a reaction to timber-domination. The agency always had been run by foresters trained to produce wood products, but the demand for those products had remained low for the first two-thirds of the agency's life. As a result, the level of timber harvesting never seriously disrupted the backwoods loved by so many segments of American society. When the disruption occurred, the NFMA was not far behind.

The NFMA was a revolutionary law. The long swing of congressional and judicial action had included few inroads into on-the-ground management in the national forests. In retrospect, the sway historically given to the Forest Service is evidenced by the considerable attention given to the Multiple-Use Sustained-Yield Act of 1960 and the Resources Planning Act of 1974, laws that barely nudged even the outer reaches of agency discretion.

The NFMA, however, pushed deep into the Forest Service's established autonomy. This is seen in the various substantive restrictions, almost all of which revolve around timber harvesting because Congress accurately perceived that most Forest Service actions radiate from its timber program. But the fundamentals of the NFMA played out in two other ways—the requirements that the Forest Service bring in the public and reach out to disciplines other than forestry and road engineering. Viewed in that light, the character of the NFMA is perhaps best demonstrated by the creation of the Committee of Scientists, imbued with such great authority in the process of drafting the NFMA regulations. Congress's enlistment of outside experts in this manner, to our knowledge a unique statutory device in public policy, highlights the dogged legislative determination to open the Forest Service to public, interdisciplinary participation.

Nine years later, as all who deal with the agency know, the Forest Service still is timber-dominated. The agency's budget is heavily tilted toward timber, half of all professional Forest Service employees are foresters, and many of the draft NFMA plans are plainly oriented toward timber production. At the same time, there is movement on most fronts. Good resource planning must be built upon good inventories. During the last several years most national forest staffs have vastly expanded their knowledge about the resources within their land areas. Based on that knowledge, it becomes easier to make reasoned projections about how much intensive development the animals, water, and recreational opportunities can absorb. There are signs, too, that the agency is increasingly aware that integrated planning must breed integrated management, or the planning will have been for naught. The long-time engine of national forest policy has been wood products policy. Ranger districts, for example, classically have been organized along lines described as "timber" and "other resources." If that changes—if the Forest Service really does create thorough inventories, make objective projections from the inventories, and craft a management direction that balances the stress on all the resources—then the central charge of the NFMA will be met.

As we recognize in our introduction, there are proper concerns about the complexity and expense of this far-flung planning venture. This Article amply demonstrates the mélange of statutes, regulations, manual provisions, draft plans, interdisciplinary committees, administrative reviews, and judicial interpretations that the NFMA has called into play. But national forest planning is, after all, dealing with 191 million acres in absolute ownership, an area nearly the size of Wyoming, Colorado, and New Mexico combined. The Pacific Northwest Region of the Forest Service alone easily meets the requirements for inclusion in the Fortune 500. In looking to the future and resolving the tough questions that must be asked about the first, second, and third generations of plans, it surely is not enough to say that this first round of planning has been expensive and that it has drawn needed staff away from day-to-day management—all of which plainly is the case. Rather, we must ask: How does the Forest Service commitment to the planning process compare with that of a large, excellent corporation? Is the investment in line with the full spectrum of the commodity and noncommodity values found within the national forests?

The NFMA is one of the most ambitious programs ever undertaken with respect to the one-third of the nation's land mass owned by the federal government. The 1976 Act seeks to preserve the best of traditional Forest Service policies and procedures that so effectively met the needs of fewer people in simpler times. But the NFMA also charts a modified formula. The result is an uneasy marriage of science, economics, history, public administration, abstract values, and the rule of law. Whether this modified formula can work will play a powerful role in determining whether the national forests will continue to make the cardinal contributions, both tangible and intangible, that these remarkable lands have made for so long to the quality of life in the United States.

Since the original publication of the foregoing account in late 1985, the forest planning process has proceeded amid growing controversy. By early 1987 the Forest Service had completed draft plans for virtually all national forests, except for several in Washington, Oregon, and California. Final plans were in place for a slim majority of national forests. No lawsuits had been filed seeking judicial review of forest plans under the NFMA. However, many administrative appeals of forest plans resembled lawsuits: lawyers filed lengthy briefs, the Forest Service granted or denied stays of planned activities, and parties entered into negotiations and settlements. Since the Forest Service chief can remand plans to correct deficiencies, some potential court challenges may be delayed or averted. Indeed, one former congressional staff member has observed that the NFMA "succeeded because we have traded lawsuits for the much less costly administrative appeals process."[1]

While forest planning and appeals have occupied the center of debate over the NFMA, several important developments have occurred in Congress, in the courts, and in national and regional planning. The following discussion highlights the half dozen most significant of these developments.

A. Below-Cost Timber Sales and Roads

Forest Service timber sales and road development policies have come under increased scrutiny by Congress. During 1984 several studies of national forest timber sale receipts and expenditures aroused congressional ire over below-cost timber sales. One commentator stated that "timber sale economics have replaced clear-cutting and wilderness as the major source of indigestion for the Forest Service."[2]

To date, Congress has addressed the below-cost sales issue primarily through the appropriations process rather than through amendments to the NFMA or other substantive legislation. The House Appropriations Committee proposed to halt increases in

---

[1] REVIEW OF THE NATION'S FOREST MANAGEMENT AND RESEARCH NEEDS AND THE 1985 RENEWABLE RESOURCES PLANNING ACT PROGRAM: HEARINGS BEFORE THE SUBCOMM. ON FORESTS, FAMILY FARMS, AND ENERGY OF THE HOUSE COMM. ON AGRICULTURE, 99th Cong., 2d Sess. 474 (Comm. Print 1987) [hereinafter cited as RPA HEARINGS] (statement of James W. Giltmier).

[2] Popovich, *How Do You Account for Deficit Sales?* J. FORESTRY 594, 595 (1984). *See generally* BELOW-COST SALES: A CONFERENCE ON THE ECONOMICS OF NATIONAL FOREST TIMBER SALES (D. LeMaster, & Master, B. Flamm & J. Hendel eds. 1986).

timber sale volumes on national forests where sale costs exceeded revenues in three of the last five years.[3] This directive was removed during House floor consideration of the Fiscal Year 1985 appropriations bill to give the Agriculture Committee an opportunity to review the issue. To provide further information, Congress appropriated funds to develop a timber sale cost accounting system to compare actual costs and receipts for the timber sales program.[4]

In 1985 the House Agriculture Committee conducted several oversight hearings on the below-cost sales issue. The Forest Service insisted that timber harvesting provides many benefits—such as improved wildlife habitat, reduced insect and disease problems, and enhanced future timber productivity—in addition to timber sale receipts.[5] The agency argued that timber access roads are essential for multiple-use management and that road costs should be amortized over several decades. The Forest Service also stated that it was considering a policy of establishing a minimum selling price for timber sufficient to recover the direct cost of sale preparation and administration.[6] Subsequently, the agency decided not to adopt such a minimum price policy.

Opponents of below-cost sales accused the Forest Service of "stonewalling" the problem.[7] They challenged the side benefits of timber harvesting claimed by the Forest Service and took particular aim at logging road construction, calling it the most expensive and environmentally damaging aspect of the agency's timber program. Timber industry representatives, on the other hand, attacked the validity of existing studies of the issue and urged Congress to postpone action until better information became available.

During the 99th Congress the focus of the debate shifted somewhat from below-cost sales to logging road construction. To a large extent, however, the effort to reduce appropriations of roads served as a proxy for opposition to below-cost timber sales. Frequently the advocates of fewer logging roads cited savings to the National Treasury as one of their prime objectives. For example, Senator William Proxmire of Wisconsin declared that

---

[3] H.R. REP. No. 886, 98th Cong., 2d Sess. 70–71 (1984).

[4] S. REP. No. 578, 98th Cong., 2d Sess. 85 (1984); H. J. RES. 648, 98 Stat. 1837 (1984).

[5] ECONOMICS OF FEDERAL TIMBER SALES: HEARINGS BEFORE THE SUBCOMM. ON FORESTS, FAMILY FARMS, AND ENERGY OF THE HOUSE COMM. ON AGRICULTURE, 99th Cong., 1st Sess. 18 (1985) (statement of R. Max Peterson).

[6] *Id.* at 156.

[7] *Id.* at 199 (statement of Peter C. Kirby).

"timber sales served by these roads are often big, big money losers for the taxpayer" and asked, "Does it make sense for Congress to lavish excessive sums on forest roads which provide access to money-losing sales?"[8]

The House of Representatives voted to reduce Forest Service road appropriations in both 1985 and 1986. The Senate succeeded in restoring the road funds in 1985[9] with relatively little controversy, but in 1986 the roads/below-cost sales issue heated to a full boil in the Senate. A proposal by Senator James McClure of Idaho to increase the administration's request for road funding by $75 million was narrowly defeated by the Senate Interior Appropriations Subcommittee, which McClure chaired. Subsequently, however, McClure's proposal was approved by the full committee. A similar seesaw debate ensued on the Senate floor, with opponents of forest roads prevailing on the first vote and Senator McClure's proposal succeeding on the second. The conference committee generally accepted the higher funding level approved by the Senate.[10]

Clearly, the debate over forest road appropriations will continue at least into the 100th Congress. What is less clear is whether the underlying issue of below-cost timber sales will surface and, if so, what sort of remedial action Congress will pursue. For example, Congress may consider substantive legislation to phase out below-cost sales by requiring timber sale prices to recover all or a portion of sale costs, as the Forest Service considered doing administratively in 1985. Congress may also take action to reduce appropriations for timber sales in those Forest Service regions that are below cost.

B.   Water Quality Standards

One of the most important recent court decisions involving the Forest Service emphasizes the role of state water quality standards in national forest planning and management. In *Northwest Indian Cemetery Protective Association v. Peterson,*[11] the Court of Appeals for the Ninth Circuit upheld an injunction against timber harvesting and road construction in the Blue Creek drainage of the

---

[8]132 CONG. REC. S12160 (daily ed. Sept. 9, 1986).

[9]S REP. NO. 141, 99th Cong., 1st Sess. (1985); H. J. RES. 465, 99 Stat. 1185 (1985).

[10]*See* PUBLIC LANDS NEWS, Oct. 16, 1986.

[11]764 F.2d 581 (9th Cir. 1985), *aff'g* 565 F. Supp. 586 (N.D. Cal. 1983), *aff'd on rehearing,* 795 F.2d 688 (9th Cir. 1986).

Six Rivers National Forest in northern California. The court ruled that the proposed logging and road building would violate NEPA, the Clean Water Act, and Indian rights to free exercise of religion under the First Amendment. With respect to the Clean Water Act, the court held that the Act requires the Forest Service to comply with applicable state water quality standards.[12] California state standards allow no more than a 20 percent increase in turbidity above natural levels. Based on evidence that the proposed logging would likely increase turbidity in Blue Creek by up to 500 percent, the district court enjoined any logging in the drainage until the Forest Service completed studies demonstrating that the activities would not violate state standards.[13]

The Forest Service objected strenuously to the circuit court's interpretation of the Clean Water Act. In a petition for rehearing of the court's decision, the government maintained that state water quality standards do not apply to timber harvesting and other nonpoint sources of pollution.[14] Rather, the government argued, nonpoint source activities on national forest lands need only comply with "best management practices" (BMPs) approved by the state and the U.S. Environmental Protection Agency (EPA). The court rejected these arguments and reiterated its earlier conclusion that BMPs "are merely a means to achieve the appropriate state . . . water quality standards. . . . Adherence to BMPs does not automatically ensure that the applicable state standards are being met."[15] The Forest Service then attempted to convince the EPA to issue guidance to the states specifying that BMPs are the only enforceable requirements for nonpoint source activities. The EPA responded that it could not agree because the Forest Service proposal would contravene the circuit court's interpretation of the Clean Water Act.[16]

The Blue Creek case may have significant implications for national forest planning. The Forest Service currently attempts to reduce adverse effects on water quality and fisheries through BMPs, streamside buffer areas, and other mitigation techniques. Experience has shown, however, that even state-of-the-art road

---

[12]*Id.* at 588.

[13]565 F. Supp. at 606-607.

[14]*See* PETITION OF THE FEDERAL APPELLANTS FOR REHEARING WITH SUGGESTION FOR REHEARING EN BANC (Aug. 1985).

[15]797 F. 2d at 697.

[16]*See* Anderson, *Water Quality Planning for the National Forests,* 17 ENVT'L LAW 591 (1987).

construction can greatly heighten environmental degradation in geologically unstable areas. In order to comply with Clean Water Act requirements, some of these areas, such as the Blue Creek drainage, will need to remain essentially undisturbed. Moreover, the Forest Service faces the task of complying with different standards in each state. In any event, the effect of the Blue Creek case should be to move the Forest Service in the same direction as Congress intended in the NFMA—toward greater protection of clean water and fisheries in the national forests.

C. Old-Growth Forests, Biological Diversity, and Spotted Owls

The future of the old-growth forests in the Pacific Northwest is one of the weightiest and most difficult issues in forest planning. Estimated to cover up to seven million acres in Washington, Oregon, and northern California, these forests hold some of the world's most valuable timber, wildlife, water, and recreational resources. The large majority of the old growth is located on national forest lands and is neither specifically withdrawn from, nor designated for, timber harvesting by statute. Therefore, the Forest Service exercises considerable authority to decide how to manage the remaining old growth—and all of its associated economic, aesthetic, and ecological values—through the forest plans.

The Forest Service, in order to implement the diversity provisions of the NFMA and the implementing regulations, selected the northern spotted owl as a management indicator species for old-growth habitat in its forest plans for Oregon and Washington. Pursuant to direction by the Department of Agriculture, the Forest Service prepared a draft Supplemental Environmental Impact Statement (SEIS) to reconsider its regional spotted owl habitat management guidelines.[17] The draft SEIS focused on two issues: how many acres of old-growth forest are needed to support a pair of spotted owls and how many pairs of owls constitute a viable population. The Forest Service's preferred alternative proposed to set aside as many as 2200 acres of old growth per pair of owls and to provide enough habitat to support 550 pairs. Under this alternative, approximately 25 percent of existing spotted owl

---

[17]FOREST SERVICE, U.S. DEP'T OF AGRICULTURE, DRAFT SUPPLEMENT TO THE ENVIRONMENTAL IMPACT STATEMENT FOR AN AMENDMENT TO PACIFIC NORTHWEST REGIONAL GUIDE (1986).

habitat would be logged after 15 years, and 60 percent of existing habitat would be logged after 50 years.[18]

The Spotted Owl SEIS aroused great controversy in the Pacific Northwest. The draft SEIS generated over 40,000 public comments —more than any other Forest Service proposal except the nationwide RARE II recommendations. The timber industry strongly opposed setting aside additional old-growth forest for the spotted owl, arguing that more research was needed to justify such action. Environmentalists, on the other hand, recommended calling a moratorium on logging in spotted owl habitat and shifting timber sales to mature second-growth forest. Meanwhile, the U.S. Fish and Wildlife Service was considering a petition to list the northern spotted owl under the Endangered Species Act, and the Bureau of Land Management was reconsidering the impact on the owl of its timber harvest plans in western Oregon.

D.   The RPA Program

The Forest Service and the administration presented the 1985 RPA program amid continuing confusion over the program's relationship to local forest planning. Release of the program was delayed by more than a year and a half due to dissatisfaction by the Department of Agriculture and the Office of Management and Budget. Former Assistant Secretary of Agriculture John Crowell had called the RPA process "unduly complicated, . . . unnecessarily expensive, and . . . leading to a product which would be virtually useless."[19] Crowell directed the Forest Service to increase the timber sale level in the program to 20 billion board feet per year by 2030—almost double the current sale level. This direction prompted charges by Representative James Weaver that the program was "a political document [that] threatens our forests terribly."[20] Other members of Congress criticized the administration for presenting a range of potential activities and outputs rather than a single specific course of action.

By early 1987 Congress had taken no formal action to approve, amend, or disapprove the program. However, Congress expressed

---

[18]*Id.* at 4–15. On the rapidly increasing attention being given to the issue of biological diversity, *see generally* OFFICE OF TECHNOLOGY ASSESSMENT, TECHNOLOGIES TO MAINTAIN BIOLOGICAL DIVERSITY (1987).

[19]Memorandum from John B. Crowell to R. Max Peterson (Jan. 7, 1985), *reprinted in* RPA HEARINGS, *supra* note 1, at 463.

[20]RPA HEARINGS, *supra* note 1, at 452.

frustration with the RPA process by limiting appropriations for costs of developing the 1990 program.[21] In addition, Congress directed the Forest Service to explain why local forest plans differed from RPA goals and what action the agency would take if plans did not agree with those goals. The Forest Service responded that it was unrealistic to expect forest plans and RPA goals to be identical and that adjustments could be made in regular updates of plans and the RPA program to correct major disparities.

A further noteworthy development relating to the RPA was a directive by outgoing Forest Service chief Max Peterson on the timber resource in forest planning. Among other things, Peterson instructed that forest plans should achieve the "high bound" goals of the 1985 RPA program, which included the 20-billion-board-foot timber goal ordered by Assistant Secretary Crowell, "tempered by local issues, concerns, and conditions."[22] Conservationists cited Peterson's directive as evidence of "timber-first bias" in the Forest Service.[23]

E. State and Federal Regulatory Authority

The Supreme Court in 1987 handed down a landmark decision that strengthens the authority of states to apply environmental regulations on national forest lands. In *California Coastal Commission v. Granite Rock Co.,*[24] the Court decided that California could require a company to obtain a state permit for open-pit limestone mining in a national forest even though the Forest Service had already approved the mining project. The Court rejected arguments that the federal government had preempted state authority through Forest Service mining regulations, the 1872 Mining Act, the NFMA, and other laws. The Court characterized the California permitting system as regulatory rather than prohibitory in nature and concluded that the state system therefore was not in conflict with federal laws governing the use of national forest land.

---

[21]*Id.* at 732.

[22]Memorandum from R. Max Peterson to Regional Foresters (Jan. 12, 1987), *reprinted in* STATEMENT OF BARRY R. FLAMM, THE WILDERNESS SOCIETY, ON THE FISCAL YEAR 1988 BUDGET REQUEST FOR THE FOREST SERVICE, USDA, BEFORE THE INTERIOR SUBCOMMITTEE OF THE APPROPRIATIONS COMMITTEE, UNITED STATES HOUSE OF REPRESENTATIVES, February 26, 1987 [hereinafter cited as WILDERNESS SOCIETY TESTIMONY].

[23]WILDERNESS SOCIETY TESTIMONY, *supra* note 22.

[24]107 S.Ct. 1419 (1987).

The ruling substantially enhances the ability of states to impose environmental controls on the national forests.

On the other hand, the courts continued to reaffirm broad Forest Service authority to regulate the use and occupancy of the national forests under the 1897 Organic Act. For example, in *Great American Houseboat Company v. United States,*[25] the Ninth Circuit Court of Appeals upheld the Forest Service's decision to ban time-share houseboats on Shasta Lake in northern California because the time-share device would lead to overcrowding of the lake.

F. Mineral Leasing

Controversy over oil and gas development in the northern Rockies has resulted in several recent court decisions and legislative proposals in Congress. The courts have held that the issuance of oil and gas leases on national forest lands constitutes a major federal action requiring the preparation of an environmental impact statement.[26] Additional oil and gas leases were suspended in at least one Forest Service region pending a decision by the Ninth Circuit Court of Appeals. In Congress, legislation was introduced that would require national forest plans or other federal land use plans to include the thoroughgoing evaluations of all potential oil and gas lands to be certain that leasing "will not result in unacceptable environmental damage."[27]

---

[25]780 F.2d 741 (9th Cir. 1986).
[26]*See, e.g.,* Conner v. Burford, 605 F. Supp. 107 (D. Mont. 1985), *appeal pending.*
[27]*See* H.R. 4741, 99th Cong., 2d Sess. sec. 4 (1986).

Index

Also Available from Island Press

Last Stand of the Red Spruce
By Robert A. Mello; sponsored by National Resources Defense Council

Acid rain—the debates rage between those who believe that the cause of the problem is clear and identifiable and those who believe that the evidence is inconclusive. In *Last Stand of the Red Spruce,* Robert A. Mello has written an ecological detective story that unravels this confusion and explains how air pollution is killing our nation's forests. Writing for a lay audience, the author traces the efforts of scientists trying to solve the mystery of the dying red spruce trees on Camels Hump in Vermont. Mello clearly and succinctly presents both sides of an issue on which even the scientific community is split and concludes that the scientific evidence uncovered on Camels Hump elevates the issues of air pollution and acid rain to new levels of national significance.

1987. xx, 156 pp., illus., references, bibliography.
Paper, ISBN 0-933280-37-8. **$14.95**

High Country News: Western Water Made Simple
Edited by Ed Marston

Winner of the 1986 George Polk Award for environmental reporting, these four special issues of *High Country News* are here available for the first time in book form. Much has been written about the water crisis in the West, yet the issue remains confusing and difficult to understand. *High Country News: Western Water Made Simple* lays out in clear language the complex issues of Western water. A survey of the West's three great rivers—the Colorado, the Columbia, and the Missouri—this work includes material that reaches to the heart of the West—its ways of life, its politics, and its aspirations. *Western Water Made Simple* approaches these three river basins in terms of overarching themes combined with case studies—the Columbia in an age of reform, the Colorado in the midst of a fight for control, and the Missouri in search of its destiny.

1987. 224 pp., maps, photographs, bibliography, index.
Paper, ISBN 0-933280-39-4. **$15.95**

The Report of the President's Commission on Americans Outdoors: The Legacy, The Challenge
With Case Studies
Preface by William K. Reilly

"If there is an example of pulling victory from the jaws of disaster, this report is it. The Commission did more than anyone expected, especially the administration. It gave Americans something serious to think about if we are to begin saving our natural resources."—Paul C. Pritchard, President, National Parks and Conservation Association.

This report is the first comprehensive attempt to examine the impact of a changing American society and its recreation habits since the work of the Outdoor Recreation Resource Review Commission, chaired by Laurence Rockefeller in 1962. The President's Commission took more than two years to complete its study; the Report contains over sixty recommendations, such as the preservation of a nationwide network of "greenways" for recreational purposes and the establishment of an annual $1 billion trust fund to finance the protection and preservation of our recreational resources. The Island Press edition provides the full text of the report, much of the additional material compiled by the Commission, and twelve selected case studies.

1987. xvi, 426 pp., illus., appendixes, case studies.
Paper, ISBN 0-933280-36-X. **$24.95**

Public Opinion Polling: A Handbook for Public Interest and Citizen Advocacy Groups
By Celinda C. Lake, with Pat Callbeck Harper

"Lake has taken the complex science of polling and written a very usable 'how-to' book. I would recommend this book to both candidates and organizations interested in professional, low-budget, in-house polling." —Stephanie Solien, Executive Director, Women's Campaign Fund.

Public Opinion Polling is the first book to provide practical information on planning, conducting, and analyzing public opinion polls as well as guidelines for interpreting polls conducted by others. It is a book for anyone—candidates, state and local officials, community organizations, church groups, labor organizations, public policy research centers, and coalitions focusing on specific economic issues—interested in measuring public opinion.

1987. x, 166 pp., tables, bibliography, appendix, index.
Paper, ISBN 0-933280-32-7. **$19.95**
Companion software soon to become available.

Green Fields Forever: The Conservation Tillage Revolution in America
By Charles E. Little

"*Green Fields Forever* is a fascinating and lively account of one of the most important technological developments in American agriculture. . . . Be prepared to enjoy an exceptionally well-told tale, full of stubborn inventors, forgotten pioneers, enterprising farmers—and no small amount of controversy."—Ken Cook, World Wildlife Fund and The Conservation Foundation.

Here is the book that will change the way Americans think about agriculture. It is the story of "conservation tillage"—a new way to grow food that, for the first time, works *with,* rather than against, the soil. Farmers who are revolutionizing the course of American agriculture explain here how conservation tillage works. Some environmentalists think there are problems with the methods, however; author Charles E. Little demonstrates that on this issue both sides have a case, and the jury is still out.

1987. 189 pp., illus., appendixes, index, bibliography.
Cloth, ISBN 0-933280-35-1. **$24.95**
Paper, ISBN 0-933280-34-3. **$14.95**

Federal Lands: A Guide to Planning, Management, and State Revenues
By Sally K. Fairfax and Carolyn E. Yale

"An invaluable tool for state land managers. Here, in summary, is everything that one needs to know about federal resource management policies."—Rowena Rogers, President, Colorado State Board of Land Commissioners.

Federal Lands is the first book to introduce and analyze in one accessible volume the diverse programs for developing resources on federal lands. Offshore and onshore oil and gas leasing, coal and geothermal leasing, timber sales, grazing permits, and all other programs that share receipts and revenues with states and localities are considered in the context of their common historical evolution as well as in the specific context of current issues and policy debates.

1987. xx, 252 pp., charts, maps, bibliography, index.
Paper, ISBN 0-933280-33-5. **$24.95**

Hazardous Waste Management: Reducing the Risk
By Benjamin A. Goldman, James A. Hulme, and Cameron Johnson for the Council on Economic Priorities

Hazardous Waste Management: Reducing the Risk is a comprehensive sourcebook of facts and strategies that provides the analytic tools needed by policy makers, regulating agencies, hazardous waste generators, and host communities to compare facilities on the basis of site, management, and technology. The Council on Economic Priorities' innovative ranking system applies to real-world, site-specific evaluations, establishes a consistent protocol for multiple applications, assesses relative benefits and risks, and evaluates and ranks ten active facilities and eight leading commercial management corporations.

1986. xx, 316 pp., notes, tables, glossary, index.
Cloth, ISBN 0-933280-30-0. **$64.95**
Paper, ISBN 0-933280-31-9. **$34.95**

An Environmental Agenda for the Future
By Leaders of America's Foremost Environmental Organizations

". . . a substantive book addressing the most serious questions about the future of our resources."—John Chaffee, U.S. Senator, Environmental and Public Works Committee. "While I am not in agreement with many of the positions the authors take, I believe this book can be the basis for constructive dialogue with industry representatives seeking solutions to environmental problems."—Louis Fernandez, Chairman of the Board, Monsanto Corporation.

The chief executive officers of the ten major environmental and conservation organizations launched a joint venture to examine goals that the environmental movement should pursue now and into the twenty-first century. This book presents policy recommendations for implementing changes needed to bring about a healthier, safer world. Topics discussed include nuclear issues, human population growth, energy strategies, toxic waste and pollution control, and urban environments.

1985. viii, 155 pp., bibliography.
Paper, ISBN 0-933280-29-7. **$7.95**

Water in the West
By Western Network

Water in the West is an essential reference tool for water managers, public officials, farmers, attorneys, industry officials, and students and professors attempting to understand the competing pressures on our most important natural resource: water. Here is an in-depth analysis of the effects of energy development, Indian rights, and urban growth on other water users.

1985. *Vol. III: Western Water Flows to the Cities*
v, 217 pp., maps, table of cases, documents, bibliography, index.
Paper, ISBN 0-933280-28-9. **$25.00**

Community Open Spaces
By Mark Francis, Lisa Cashdan, and Lynn Paxson

Over the past decade, thousands of community gardens and parks have been developed on vacant neighborhood land in America's major cities. *Community Open Spaces* documents this movement in the United States and Europe, explaining how planners, public officials, and local residents can work in their own communities to successfully develop open space.

1984. xiv, 250 pp., key contacts: resource organizations, appendixes, bibliography, index.
Cloth, ISBN 0-933280-27-0.   **$24.95**

Land-Saving Action
Edited by Russell L. Brenneman and Sarah M. Bates

Land-Saving Action is the definitive guide for conservation practitioners. It is a written symposium by the twenty-nine leading experts in land conservation. This book presents, in detail, land-saving tools and techniques that have been perfected by individuals and organizations across the nation. This is the first time such information has been available in one volume.

1984. xvi, 249 pp., tables, notes, author
bibliographies, selected readings, index.
Cloth, ISBN 0-933280-23-8.   **$39.95**
Paper, ISBN 0-933280-22-X.   **$24.95**

The Conservation Easement in California
By Thomas S. Barrett and Putnam Livermore for The Trust for Public Land

This is the authoritative legal handbook on conservation easements. *The Conservation Easement in California* examines the California law as a model for the nation, emphasizing the effectiveness and flexibility of the California code. Also covered are the historical and legal backgrounds of easement technology, state and federal tax implications, and solutions to the most difficult drafting problems.

1983. xiv, 173 pp., appendixes, notes, selected bibliography, index.
Cloth, ISBN 0-933280-20-3.   **$34.95**

Private Options: Tools and Concepts for Land Conservation
By Montana Land Reliance and Land Trust Exchange

Techniques and strategies for saving the family farm are presented by thirty experts. *Private Options* details the proceedings of a national conference and brings together, for the first time, the experience and advice of land conservation experts from all over the nation.

1982. xiv, 292 pp., key contacts: resources for local conservation organizations, conference participants, bibliography, index.
Paper, ISBN 0-933280-15-7. **$25.00**

These titles are available directly from Island Press, Box 7, Covelo, CA 95428. Please enclose $2.75 shipping and handling for the first book and $1.25 for each additional book. California and Washington, DC residents add 6% sales tax. A catalogue of current and forthcoming titles is available free of charge.